We will miss you
& all the best in your new
journey!

Henrichs Family
Dianne, Myles, Devon
& Melissa 2002

Reader's Digest

CANADA
Coast to Coast

CANADA
Coast to Coast

A guide to over 2,000 places to visit along the Trans-Canada and other great highways

The Reader's Digest Association (Canada) Ltd., Montreal

CANADA COAST TO COAST

Project Editor
Andrew R. Byers

Associate Editor
Enza Micheletti

Designer
Andrée Payette

Picture Editor
Rachel Irwin

Copy Editor
Gilles Humbert

Production
Holger Lorenzen

Coordinator
Susan Wong

CONTRIBUTORS

Highway Writers Karen Evoy, Alan Hustak, Dane Lanken

Feature Writers Vivien Bowers, Ron Brown, Chery Coull, Orland French, Don Gillmor, Jurgen Gothe, Louise Bernice Halfe, Lawrence Jackson, Barb and Ron Kroll, Jake MacDonald, Mary MacPherson, Rosemary Neering, Jean O'Neil, Larry Pynn, André Robitaille, Dan Schneider, James Smedley, Charles Wilkins

Research Editor Karen Evoy

Copy Editor Joseph Marchetti

Indexer Judy Yelon

Illustrator Normand Cousineau (Fairs and Festivals)

Strip maps researcher Geneviève Beullac

Cartographers
Schwerdt Graphic Arts Ltd. (Map Art) (Atlas section)
Dimension DPR

READER'S DIGEST BOOKS AND HOME ENTERTAINMENT

Editorial Director Deirdre Gilbert

Managing Editor Philomena Rutherford

Art Director John McGuffie

Director of Publishing Loraine Taylor

Acknowledgments

The publisher gratefully acknowledges the assistance of the following:

Tourism British Columbia and regional tourism associations
BC Parks
Vancouver Travel InfoCentre
Victoria Travel InfoCentre
Travel Alberta
Calgary Convention and Visitors Bureau
Edmonton Tourism
Tourism Saskatchewan
Tourism Regina
Travel Manitoba
Tourism Winnipeg
Tourism Ontario and regional tourism associations
Ontario Ministry of Natural Resources
Ottawa Tourism and Convention Authority
Metropolitan Toronto Convention & Visitors Association
Tourisme Québec and regional tourism associations
Greater Montreal Convention and Tourism Bureau
Quebec City Region Tourism and Convention Centre
Tourism New Brunswick
Fredericton Tourism
Prince Edward Island Tourism
City of Charlottetown
Tourism Nova Scotia and regional tourism associations
Tourism Halifax
Tourism Newfoundland and Labrador
City of St. John's
Tourism Yukon
Northwest Territories Tourism

Thanks are also expressed to the following:

Canadian Geographic Magazine, Ottawa
Canadian Heritage Parks Canada
Quebec Ministry of Transport
Transportation Association of Canada, Ottawa
Transport Canada
Yellowhead Highway Association, Edmonton

The credits and acknowledgments that appear on page 400 are hereby made a part of this copyright page.

Copyright © 1998 The Reader's Digest Association (Canada) Ltd.

All rights reserved. Unauthorized reproduction, in any manner, is prohibited. Reader's Digest and the Pegasus logo are registered trademarks of The Reader's Digest Association, Inc.

Canadian Cataloguing in Publication Data
Main entry under title:
Canada coast to coast: a guide to over 2,000 places to visit along the Trans-Canada and other great highways
Includes index.
ISBN 0-88850-575-2
1. Canada—Guidebooks. 2. Trans-Canada Highway—Guidebooks.
FC38.C233 1998   917.104'648   C97-901282-1
F1009.C35 1998

Printed in Canada
98 99 00/3 2 1

To order additional copies of *Canada Coast to Coast*, or to request a catalogue of other Reader's Digest products, call our 24-hour Customer Service hotline at 1-800-465-0780.

You can also visit us on the World Wide Web at http://www.readersdigest.ca
Canada Coast to Coast is also available on CD-ROM.

About the Book

Canada Coast to Coast maps virtually every stretch of our major highways and describes places to visit on or near these routes. This book highlights the world's longest national road, the 7,800 km Trans-Canada Highway, covering all the attractions along this ribbon of road across 10 provinces from Victoria, British Columbia, to St. John's, Newfoundland. Similar treatment is given to other major routes— the Trans-Canada Yellowhead and the Crowsnest in western Canada, and the combined highways 401, 20 and 40, which run from Windsor to Quebec City through our country's most populous region. For adventurous travelers, *Canada Coast to Coast* also contains a section on our northern highways—John Hart, Alaska, Klondike, Dempster, Mackenzie, and Yellowknife. Other highlights include walking tours in 14 major cities, 21 specially commissioned features about intriguing roadside sites and activities, and a directory to some of the important fairs and festivals that take place in communities along our major highways.

Contents

Drives, Walks & Features

TRANS-CANADA HIGHWAY—PAGES 26-229

USING THE MAPS

Canada Coast to Coast contains 134 highway spreads and 14 city walking tours.
The strip map—a central feature of each
highway spread—shows a specific stretch
of road, the main roadside attractions, and
point-to-point and cumulative distances.

(Cumulative distances vary from spread
to spread.) The strip maps—linked one to
another—move generally west to east or
south to north and cover virtually every
stretch of the Trans-Canada and other
highways. An atlas section on the immedi-

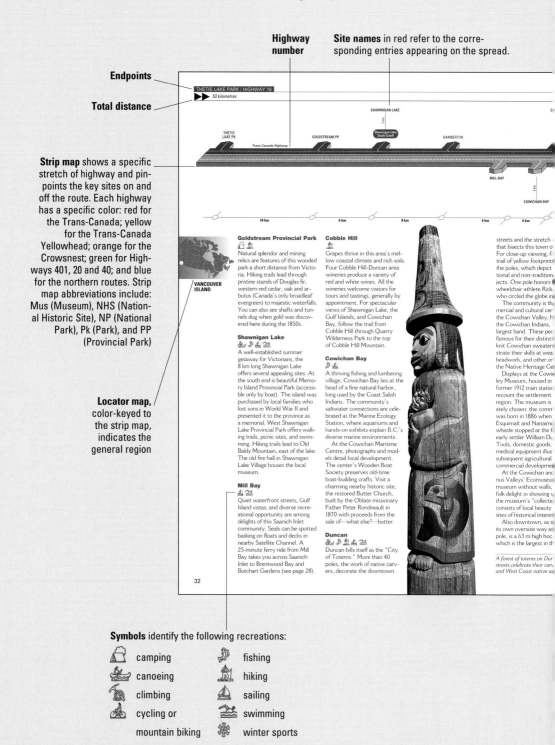

Highway number

Site names in red refer to the corre-
sponding entries appearing on the spread.

Endpoints

Total distance

THETIS LAKE PARK / HIGHWAY 18
▶▶ 53 *kilometres*

SHAWNIGAN LAKE

THETIS
LAKE PK

Trans-Canada Highway 1

GOLDSTREAM PP

Shawnigan Lake
South Cutoff

BAMBERTON

MILL BAY

COWICHAN BAY

Strip map shows a specific
stretch of highway and pin-
points the key sites on and
off the route. Each highway
has a specific color: red for
the Trans-Canada; yellow
for the Trans-Canada
Yellowhead; orange for the
Crowsnest; green for Highways 401, 20 and 40; and blue
for the northern routes. Strip
map abbreviations include:
Mus (Museum), NHS (National Historic Site), NP (National
Park), Pk (Park), and PP
(Provincial Park)

Locator map,
color-keyed to
the strip map,
indicates the
general region

VANCOUVER
ISLAND

10 km   6 km   8 km   6 km   4 km

Goldstream Provincial Park

Natural splendor and mining
relics are features of this wooded
park a short distance from Victoria. Hiking trails lead through
pristine stands of Douglas fir,
western red cedar, oak and arbutus (Canada's only broadleaf
evergreen) to majestic waterfalls.
You can also see shafts and tunnels dug when gold was discovered here during the 1850s.

Shawnigan Lake

A well-established summer
getaway for Victorians, the
8 km long Shawnigan Lake
offers several appealing sites. At
the south end is beautiful Memory Island Provincial Park (accessible only by boat). The island was
purchased by local families who
lost sons in World War II and
presented it to the province as
a memorial. West Shawnigan
Lake Provincial Park offers walking trails, picnic sites, and swimming. Hiking trails lead to Old
Baldy Mountain, east of the lake.
The old fire hall in Shawnigan
Lake Village houses the local
museum.

Mill Bay

Quiet waterfront streets, Gulf
Island vistas, and diverse recreational opportunity are among
delights of this Saanich Inlet
community. Seals can be spotted
basking on floats and decks in
nearby Satellite Channel. A
25-minute ferry ride from Mill
Bay takes you across Saanich
Inlet to Brentwood Bay and
Butchart Gardens (see page 28).

32

Cobble Hill

Grapes thrive in this area's mellow coastal climate and rich soils.
Four Cobble Hill-Duncan area
wineries produce a variety of
red and white wines. All the
wineries welcome visitors for
tours and tastings, generally by
appointment. For spectacular
views of Shawnigan Lake, the
Gulf Islands, and Cowichan
Bay, follow the trail from
Cobble Hill through Quarry
Wilderness Park to the top
of Cobble Hill Mountain.

Cowichan Bay

A thriving fishing and lumbering
village, Cowichan Bay lies at the
head of a fine natural harbor,
long used by the Coast Salish
Indians. The community's
saltwater connections are celebrated at the Marine Ecology
Station, where aquariums and
hands-on exhibits explain B.C.'s
diverse marine environments.
At the Cowichan Maritime
Centre, photographs and models detail local development.
The center's Wooden Boat
Society preserves old-time
boat-building crafts. Visit a
charming nearby historic site,
the restored Butter Church,
built by the Oblate missionary
Father Peter Rondreault in
1870 with proceeds from the
sale of—what else?—butter.

Duncan

Duncan bills itself as the "City
of Totems." More than 40
poles, the work of native carvers, decorate the downtown

streets and the stretch o
that bisects this town o
For close-up viewing, f
trail of yellow footprints
the poles, which depict
tional and non-tradition
jects. One pole honors
wheelchair athlete Rick
who circled the globe in
The community is the
mercial and cultural cer
the Cowichan Valley, h
the Cowichan Indians,
largest band. These peo
famous for their distinc
knit Cowichan sweaters
strate their skills at wea
beadwork, and other cr
the Native Heritage Cer
Displays at the Cowie
ley Museum, housed in
former 1912 train statio
recount the settlement
region. The museum is
ately chosen: the comm
was born in 1886 when
Esquimalt and Nanaimo
whistle stopped at the f
early settler William Du
Tools, domestic goods,
medical equipment illus
subsequent agricultural
commercial developmen
At the Cowichan and
nus Valleys' Ecomuseu
museum without walls,
folk delight in showing v
the museum's "collectic
consists of local beauty
sites of historical interes
Also downtown, as si
its own oversize way as
pole, is a 63 m high hoc
which is the largest in th

*A forest of totems on Dur
streets celebrate their carv
and West Coast native ar*

Symbols identify the following recreations:

- camping
- canoeing
- climbing
- cycling or
  mountain biking
- fishing
- hiking
- sailing
- swimming
- winter sports

8

ately following pages identifies the general location and gives the page numbers of each highway spread discussed in this travel guide. Interspersed at appropriate points throughout the highway spreads are the special features and the city

walking tours. City walk spreads describe a route through the downtown core of 14 major cities. A colored line shows how you can make your way through each city's streets to that community's outstanding points of interest.

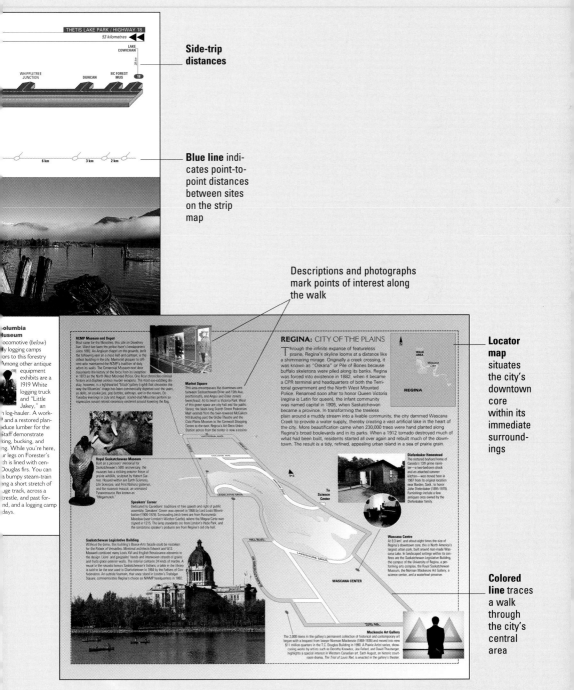

Side-trip distances

Blue line indicates point-to-point distances between sites on the strip map

Descriptions and photographs mark points of interest along the walk

Locator map situates the city's downtown core within its immediate surroundings

Colored line traces a walk through the city's central area

ALASKA
U.S.A. / États-Unis

NUNAVUT
(APRIL 1, 1999)
(1er AVRIL 1999)

YUKON TERRITORY

TERRITOIRE DU YUKON

NORTHWEST TERRITORIES

TERRIT

Inuvik

Fort McPherson

Dawson City

Carmacks

Haines Junction

Whitehorse

Teslin

Watson Lake

Rae-Edzo

Fort Providence

Yellowknife

Fort Nelson

Hay River

BRITISH COLUMBIA

Queen Charlotte Islands
Archipel de la Reine-Charlotte

Prince Rupert

Fort St. James

COLOMBIE-

Fort St. John

Dawson Creek

Peace River

Prince George

Grande Prairie

ALBERTA

SASKATCHEWAN

MANITOBA

BRITANNIQUE

Hinton

Jasper

Edmonton

Lloydminster

PACIFIC OCEAN

OCÉAN

Nanaimo

Victoria

Vancouver

Kamloops

Revelstoke

Banff

Calgary

North Battleford

Saskatoon

Chilliwack

Kimberley

Nelson

Lethbridge

Brooks

Trail

Cranbrook

Medicine Hat

Swift Current

Moose Jaw

Regina

Yorkton

Neepawa

Portage la Prairie

Brandon

Winnipeg

Kenora

Dryden

Atikoka

Fort Frances

OCÉAN

PACIFIQUE

UNITED   STATES   OF   AMERICA

ÉTATS-UNIS   D'AM

10

HIGHWAY ATLAS
—

By referring to this 16-page atlas, you can identify the pages where specific stretches of the various highways are described in *Canada Coast to Coast*. All of the Trans-Canada strip maps are in red. Yellow indicates the Trans-Canada Yellowhead; orange, the Crowsnest; green, Hwys. 401, 20 and 40; and blue, the northern routes. Generally, the routes follow west-to-east or south-to-north directions. One exception is the Kamloops-to-Tete Jaune Cache stretch of the Yellowhead Highway (pages 242-243), which runs north to south.

In Ontario, the Trans-Canada Highway follows several interconnecting routes. Hwy. 17 (Kenora to North Bay) is outlined on pages 98-101 and 106-139; Hwys. 71 and 11 (via Fort Frances), on pages 102-105; Hwy. 11 (via Kapuskasing), on pages 140-147; and Hwys. 69 and 7 (via Parry Sound), on pages 152-169. Hwy. 117, a branch of the Trans-Canada in Quebec, is described on pages 148-151.

ICELAND
ISLANDE

RES DU NORD-OUEST

ATLANTIC
OCÉAN

ATLANTIQUE

Hudson
Bay

Baie
Hudson

NEWFOUNDLAND AND LABRADOR
TERRE-NEUVE ET LABRADOR

Grand Falls-
Windsor
Gander
St. John's

Corner
Brook

Channel-Port
aux Basques

QUÉBEC

PRINCE EDWARD
ISLAND
ÎLE-DU-PRINCE-
ÉDOUARD
Charlottetown
Sydney

NEW
BRUNSWICK
NOUVEAU-
BRUNSWICK

Moncton
New
Glasgow

NOVA SCOTIA

Truro

Halifax
NOUVELLE-ÉCOSSE

Rivière-
du-Loup
Edmundston

TARIO

Hearst

eraldton

Kapuskasing

Rouyn-
Noranda

Val-d'Or

Québec
Montmagny
Fredericton

jon

Iroquois
Falls
Kirkland
Lake

Mont-
Laurier

Trois-
Rivières

Drummondville

Thunder
Bay

Wawa

North
Bay

St-Jérôme
Montréal

Elliot
Lake
Sudbury

Pembroke
Ottawa
Cornwall

Sault
Ste. Marie

Parry
Sound
Orillia

Brockville
Kingston

QUE

Belleville

Toronto
Oshawa

Kitchener

London
Woodstock

Windsor
Chatham

11

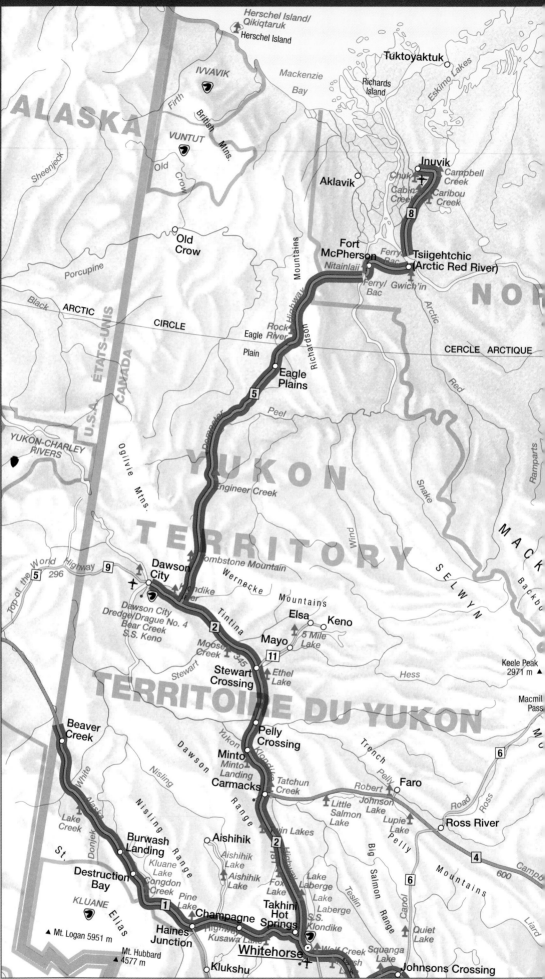

ALASKA

Herschel Island/
Qikiqtaruk
Herschel Island

Tuktoyaktuk

Mackenzie
Bay

Richards
Island

Eskimo Lakes

IVVAVIK

Firth

British Mts.

VUNTUT

Inuvik

Campbell
Creek

Chuk
Cabin
Creek

Caribou
Creek

Aklavik

8

Old
Crow

Old Crow

Porcupine

Sheenjeck

Mountains

Fort
McPherson

Ferry/
Bac

Tsiigehtchic
(Arctic Red River)

N O

Nitainlaii

Gwich'in

Ferry/
Bac

Black

ARCTIC

CIRCLE

Rock
River

Arctic

Red

CERCLE ARCTIQUE

Eagle
Plain

Ramparts

YUKON-CHARLEY
RIVERS

Ogilvie Mtns.

Dempster

Y U K O N

Eagle
Plains

5

Peel

Snake

Engineer Creek

T E R R I T O R Y

Wind

M A C
K

Backbu

5

296

Top of the World Highway

9

Dawson
City

Tombstone Mountain

Wernecke

Mountains

S E L W Y N

Keele Peak
2971 m ▲

Dawson City
Dredge/Drague No. 4
Bear Creek
S.S. Keno

Klondike
River

Tintina

Elsa

Keno

Mayo

5 Mile
Lake

Hess

Macmil
Pass

Moose
Creek

345

2

11

Stewart
Crossing

Ethel
Lake

T E R R I T O I R E   D U   Y U K O N

Stewart

Beaver
Creek

Dawson

Yukon

Pelly
Crossing

Klondike

Trench

Pelly

6

Minto

Minto
Landing

Tatchun
Creek

Robert

Johnson
Lake

Faro

White

Alaska

Nisling

Carmacks

Little
Salmon
Lake

Lupie
Lake

Ross River

Lake
Creek

Nisling Range

Range

Dawson

Twin Lakes

Pelly

Road

Ross

Burwash
Landing

Aishihik

2

Big
Salmon

4

600

St.

Donjek

Kluane
Lake

Aishihik
Lake

Aishihik
Lake

Fox
Lake

Lake
Laberge

Range

Teslin

Campb

Destruction
Bay

Congdon
Creek

Pine
Lake

Lake
Laberge

6

KLUANE

Ellas

1

Takhini
Hot
Springs

S.S.
Klondike

Canol

Quiet
Lake

Liard

▲ Mt. Logan 5951 m

Champagne

Haines
Junction

Highway

Kusawa Lake

Wolf Creek

Squanga
Lake

Mt. Hubbard
▲ 4577 m

Whitehorse

Klukshu

Johnsons Crossing

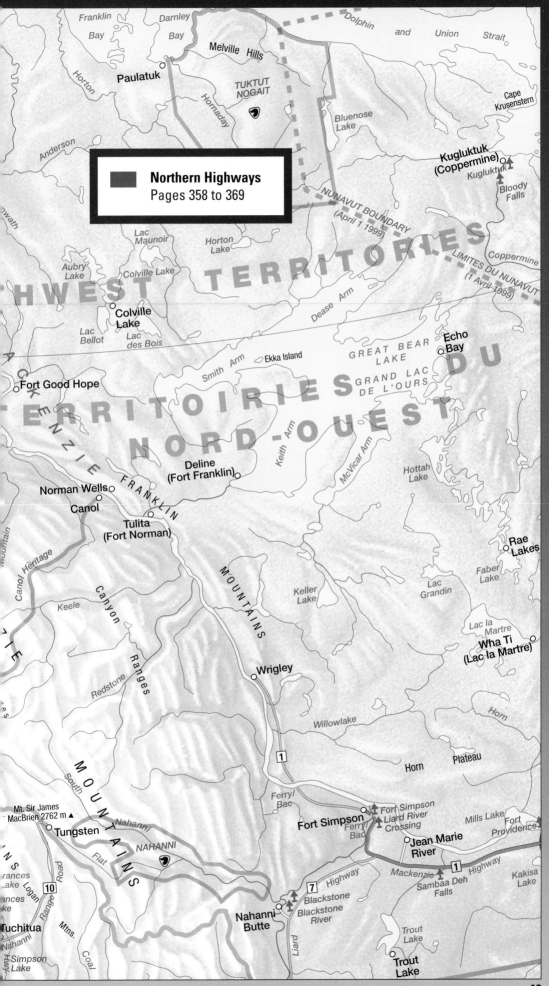

Northern Highways
Pages 358 to 369

Franklin Bay
Darnley Bay
Dolphin and Union Strait
Melville Hills
Paulatuk
TUKTUT NOGAIT
Bluenose Lake
Cape Krusenstern
Horton
Hornaday
Anderson
Kugluktuk (Coppermine)
Kugluktuk
Bloody Falls
NUNAVUT BOUNDARY (April 1 1999)
Lac Maunoir
Horton Lake
T E R R I T O R I E S
LIMITES DU NUNAVUT (1 Avril 1999)
Aubry Lake
Colville Lake
H W E S T
Dease Arm
Coppermine
Colville Lake
GREAT BEAR LAKE
Echo Bay
Lac Bellot
Lac des Bois
Smith Arm
Ekka Island
GRAND LAC DE L'OURS
Fort Good Hope
T E R R I T O R I E S   D U
Keith Arm
McVicar Arm
Hottah Lake
Deline (Fort Franklin)
N O R D - O U E S T
Norman Wells
Canol
FRANKLIN
Rae Lakes
Tulita (Fort Norman)
Faber Lake
Lac Grandin
Canol Heritage
Keele
Canyon Ranges
M O U N T A I N S
Keller Lake
Lac la Martre
Wha Ti (Lac la Martre)
Redstone
Wrigley
Horn
Willowlake
Horn Plateau
Mt. Sir James MacBrien 2762 m ▲
Tungsten
M O U N T A I N S
South
Nahanni
Flat
NAHANNI
Ferry/Bac
Fort Simpson
Fort Simpson Liard River Crossing
Mills Lake
Fort Providence
Ferry/Bac
Jean Marie River
1
Range Road
Logan
10
ances Lake
ances ke
Tuchitua
Nahanni
Simpson Lake
Coal
Mtns.
7
Highway
Blackstone
Blackstone River
Nahanni Butte
Liard
Mackenzie
Sambaa Deh Falls
1
Highway
Kakisa Lake
Trout Lake
Trout Lake

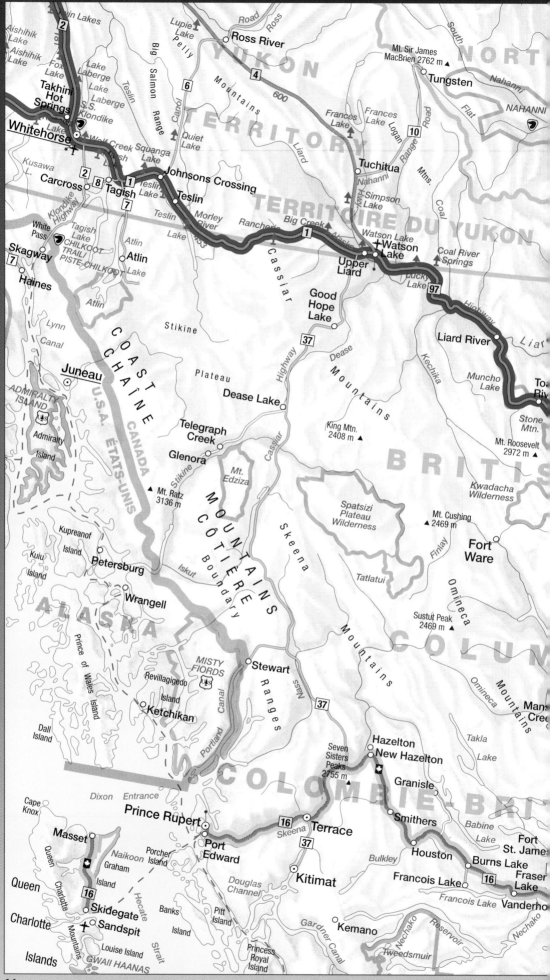

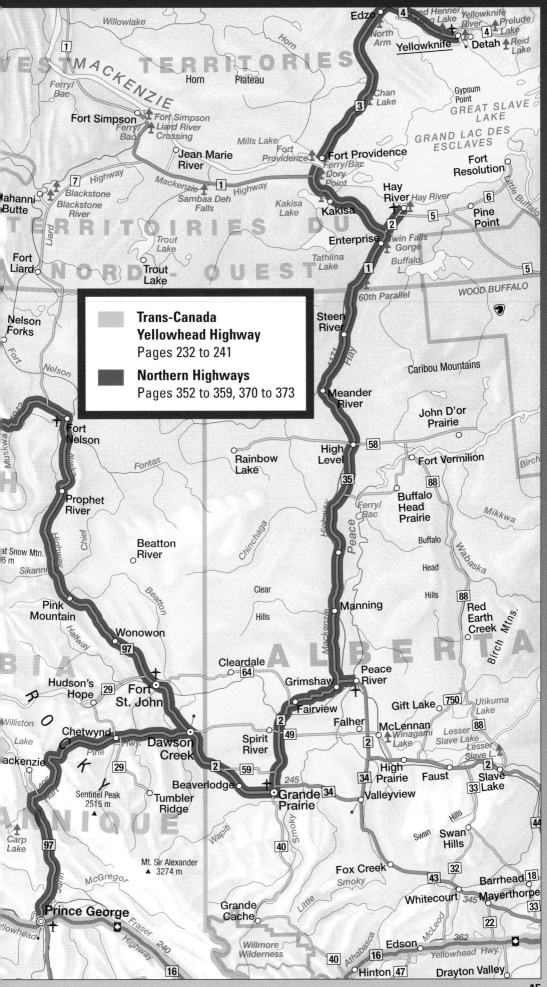

WEST MACKENZIE TERRITORIES

Willowlake

Horn Plateau

Horn

1

Ferry/ Bac

Fort Simpson

Fort Simpson Liard River Crossing

Ferry/ Bac

Jean Marie River

Mills Lake

Fort Providence

Edzo

Red Hennel Long Lake

4

Yellowknife River

4

Prelude Lake

North Arm

Yellowknife

Detah

Reid Lake

Chan Lake

Gypsum Point

GREAT SLAVE LAKE

3

GRAND LAC DES ESCLAVES

Fort Providence Ferry/Bac Dory Point

Fort Resolution

Little Buffalo

6

7

Highway

Mackenzie

1

Highway

Blackstone

Blackstone River

Sambaa Deh Falls

Kakisa Lake

Kakisa

Hay River Hay River

5

Pine Point

ahanni Butte

Enterprise

Twin Falls Gorge

2

TERRITOIRES

Fort Liard

DU

Trout Lake

Trout Lake

Tathlina Lake

Buffalo L.

1

5

NORD- OUEST

60th Parallel

WOOD BUFFALO

Nelson Forks

Steen River

Caribou Mountains

Hay

Hay

Fort Nelson

Alaska

Fontas

Meander River

John D'or Prairie

58

High Level

Fort Vermilion

Birch

Rainbow Lake

35

88

Prophet River

Chief

Beatton River

Chinchaga

Ferry/ Bac

Buffalo Head Prairie

Mikkwa

Wabaska

Clear Hills

Buffalo Head Hills

88

at Snow Mtn. 6 m

Sikanni

Beatton

Peace

Manning

88

Red Earth Creek

Birch Mtns.

Pink Mountain

Halfway

Wonowon

97

Cleardale

64

ALBERTA

Mackenzie

Peace River

Grimshaw

Gift Lake

750

Utikuma Lake

Hudson's Hope

29

Fort St. John

Williston Lake

Fairview

2

Falher

McLennan

Winagami Lake

Lesser

88

ackenzie

Chetwynd

Hwy.

Pine

Dawson Creek

2

59

49

Spirit River

245

2

High Prairie

34

Lesser Slave Lake

Faust

Lesser Slave L.

2

Slave Lake

33

Beaverlodge

Grande Prairie

34

Valleyview

44

Carp Lake

97

Sentinel Peak 2515 m

Tumbler Ridge

Wapiti

40

Swan

Swan Hills

Hills

McGregor

Mt. Sir Alexander 3274 m

Smoky

Fox Creek

Smoky

43

32

Barrhead

18

Whitecourt

345

Mayerthorpe

ANNIQUE

Prince George

Fraser

Grande Cache

Little

McLeod

22

33

ellowhead

Yellowhead

Highway

240

Willmore Wilderness

40

Athabasca

16

Edson

Yellowhead Hwy.

362

Drayton Valley

Hinton

47

16

Trans-Canada Yellowhead Highway
Pages 232 to 241

Northern Highways
Pages 352 to 359, 370 to 373

15

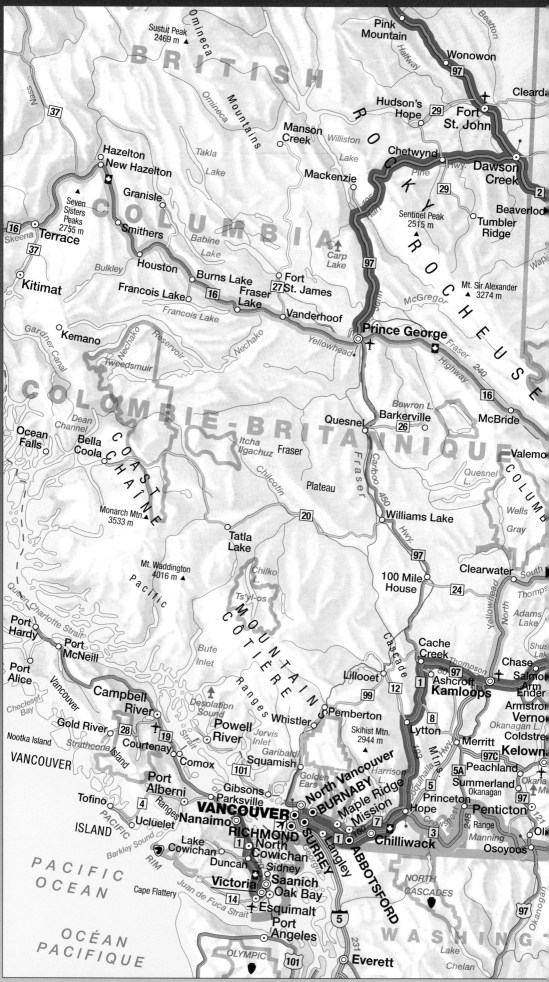

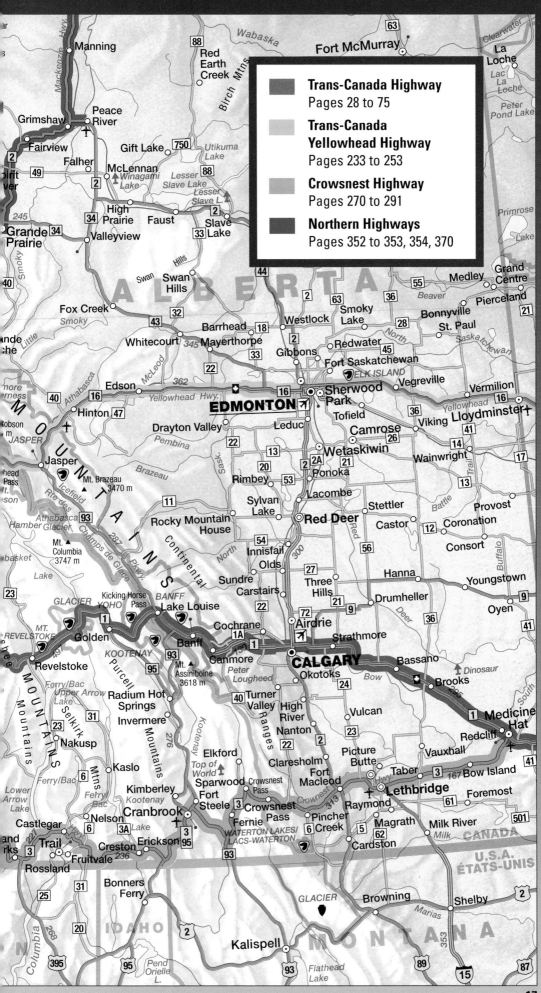

Trans-Canada Highway
Pages 28 to 75

Trans-Canada
Yellowhead Highway
Pages 233 to 253

Crowsnest Highway
Pages 270 to 291

Northern Highways
Pages 352 to 353, 354, 370

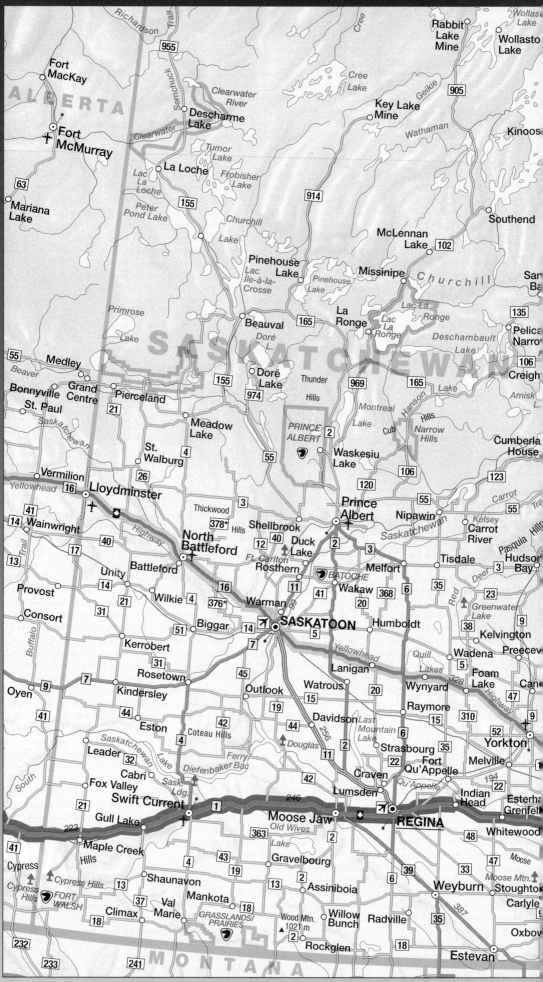

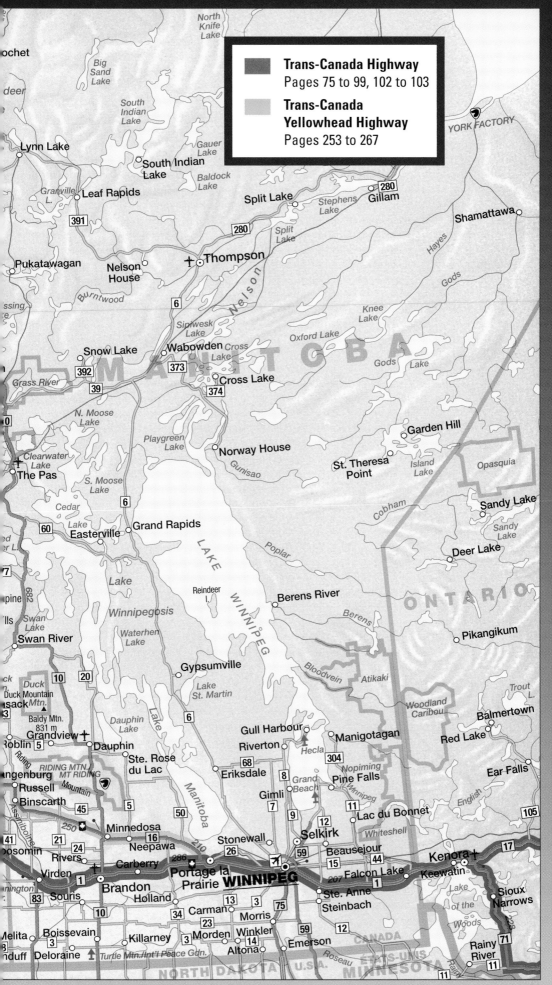

Trans-Canada Highway
Pages 75 to 99, 102 to 103

Trans-Canada
Yellowhead Highway
Pages 253 to 267

YORK FACTORY

North Knife Lake

ochet

Big Sand Lake

deer

South Indian Lake

Lynn Lake

Gauer Lake

Baldock Lake

Granville L.   Leaf Rapids

Split Lake   Gillam

Stephens Lake   280

Shamattawa

391

280

Split Lake

Pukatawagan

Nelson House

Thompson

Hayes

Gods

Burntwood

ssing

6

Nelson

Knee Lake

Sipiwesk Lake

Oxford Lake

MANITOBA

Snow Lake

Wabowden   Cross Lake

373

Gods Lake

392

39

Cross Lake

Grass River

374

Garden Hill

Opasquia

N. Moose Lake

Clearwater Lake

Playgreen Lake

Norway House

St. Theresa Point

Island Lake

The Pas

S. Moose Lake

Gunisao

Cedar Lake

6

Cobham

Sandy Lake

60

Easterville   Grand Rapids

Poplar

Sandy Lake

Deer Lake

7

Lake

Reindeer I.

Berens River

ONTARIO

pine

682

Winnipegosis

LAKE WINNIPEG

Berens

Pikangikum

lls

Swan Lake

Waterhen Lake

Bloodvein   Atikaki

Trout L.

Swan River

Gypsumville

Lake St. Martin

Woodland Caribou

Balmertown

ck

Duck

10   20

Baldy Mtn. 831 m

Dauphin Lake

6

Gull Harbour

Red Lake

sack Mtn.

Manigotagan

43

Grandview

Riverton   Hecla

Nopiming

Ear Falls

Roblin   5

Dauphin

304

Pine Falls

Riding

Ste. Rose du Lac

68

English

ngenburg   RIDING MTN. MT RIDING

Eriksdale   8

Grand Beach

11

105

Russell   Mountain

Gimli   Lac du Bonnet

Binscarth

5

7   9

45   50

12

41   21   24

Minnedosa

16

Stonewall

Selkirk

Whiteshell

Kenora

17

osomin   Rivers

Neepawa

26   59

Beausejour

44

Keewatin

Virden   1

Carberry   286

210

15   Falcon Lake   1   Lake

Sioux Narrows

Brandon   Portage la Prairie   WINNIPEG

207

of the   Woods

83   Souis

Hølland   250

Ste. Anne

Steinbach

12

Melita   Boissevain

10

13   3

Carman   Morris

59   71

nduff   Deloraine   Turtle Mtn./Int'l Peace Gdn.

34   23

Killarney   3   Morden   Winkler   Altona   Emerson

14

Roseau

Rainy River

NORTH DAKOTA U.S.A.   MINNESOTA   CANADA ÉTATS-UNIS

11   11

19

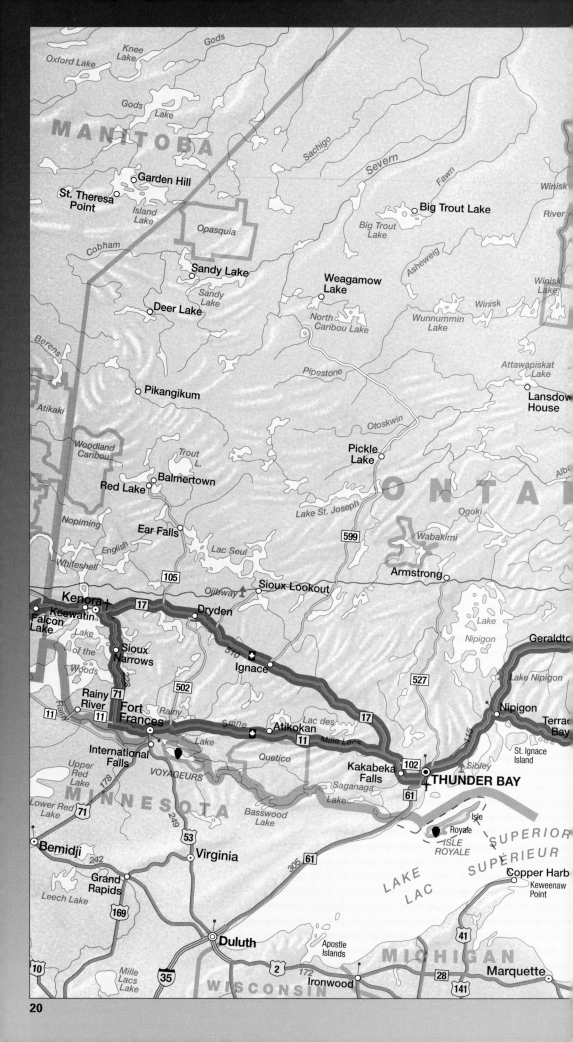

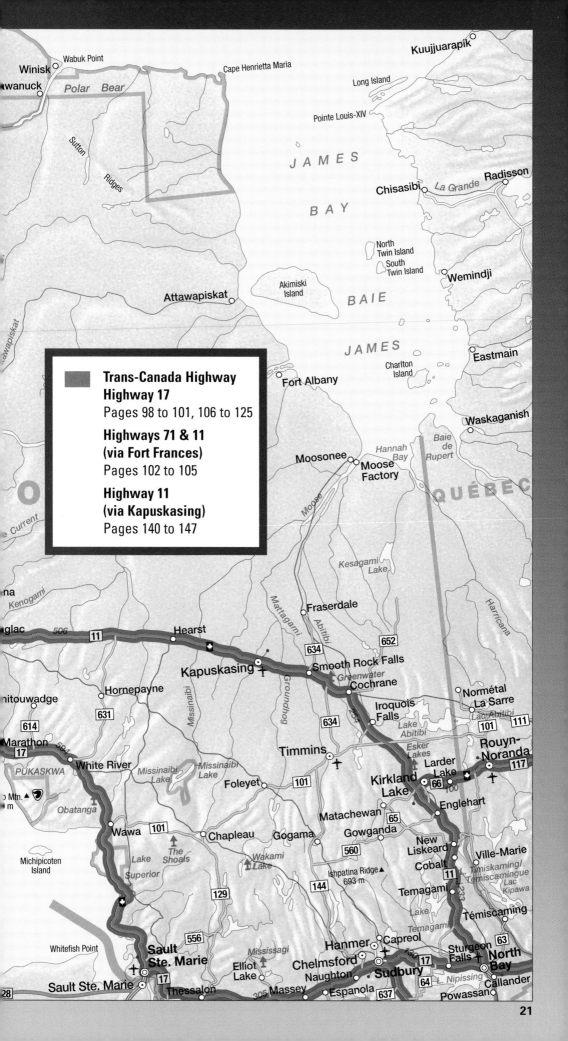

Trans-Canada Highway
Highway 17
Pages 98 to 101, 106 to 125

Highways 71 & 11
(via Fort Frances)
Pages 102 to 105

Highway 11
(via Kapuskasing)
Pages 140 to 147

Winisk
Wabuk Point
wanuck
Polar Bear
Sutton
Ridges

Cape Henrietta Maria

Kuujjuarapik

Long Island

J A M E S

B A Y

Chisasibi
La Grande
Radisson

Pointe Louis-XIV

North
Twin Island
South
Twin Island

Wemindji

Akimiski
Island

Attawapiskat

B A I E

J A M E S

Charlton
Island

Eastmain

Fort Albany

Waskaganish

*Baie
de
Rupert*

Moosonee
Moose
Factory

*Hannah
Bay*

Q U É B E C

Moose

na
Kenogami

*Kesagami
Lake*

Harricana

Fraserdale

glac   *506*   **11**   Hearst

Mattagami

Abitibi

652

634

Kapuskasing

Missinaibi

Smooth Rock Falls

Groundhog

Greenwater
Cochrane

Normétal
La Sarre

Hornepayne

631

Lac Abitibi

nitouwadge

614

634

Iroquois
Falls

*Lake
Abitibi*

101   111

Marathon
17

PUKASKWA

White River

*Missinaibi
Lake*

*Missinaibi
Lake*

Timmins

*Esker
Lakes*

Rouyn-
Noranda

Mtn.▲
m

Foleyet

101

Kirkland
Lake

Larder
Lake

117

Obatanga

Wawa   101

Chapleau

Gogama

101

Matachewan

65

Gowganda

66

Englehart

*Lake
Shoals*

The
Shoals

*Wakami
Lake*

560

New
Liskeard

Ville-Marie

Michipicoten
Island

*Lake
Superior*

Ishpatina Ridge ▲
693 m

144

Cobalt

11

*Timiskaming/
Témiscamingue
Lac
Kipawa*

129

Temagami

*Lake
Temagami*

Témiscaming

556

Whitefish Point

Mississagi

Hanmer

Capreol

Sturgeon
Falls

63

North
Bay

Sault
Ste. Marie

Elliot
Lake

Chelmsford

17

64

Sault Ste. Marie   17

Thessalon

Naughton

305   Massey

Sudbury

L. Nipissing

Espanola

637

Callander

Powassan

28

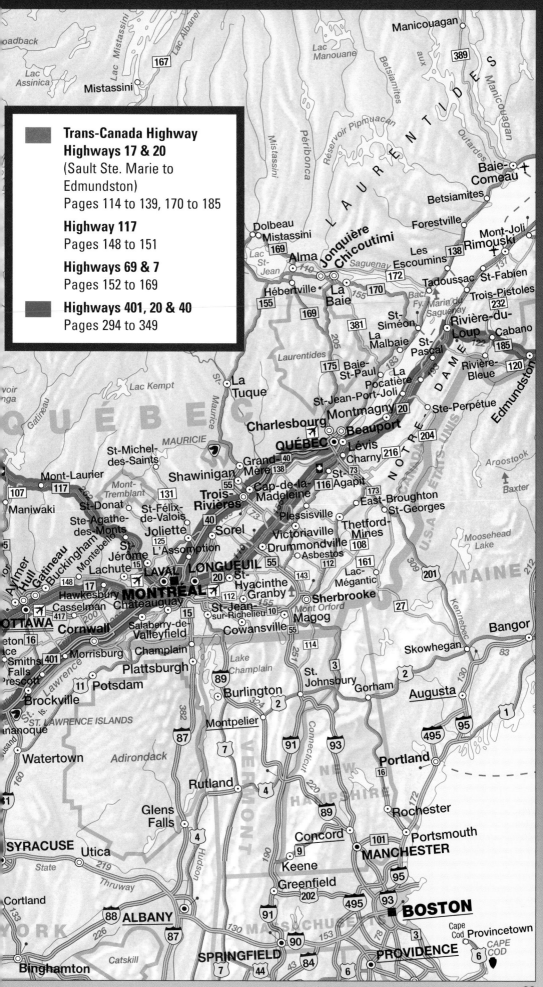

**Trans-Canada Highway
Highways 17 & 20**
(Sault Ste. Marie to
Edmundston)
Pages 114 to 139, 170 to 185

Highway 117
Pages 148 to 151

Highways 69 & 7
Pages 152 to 169

Highways 401, 20 & 40
Pages 294 to 349

23

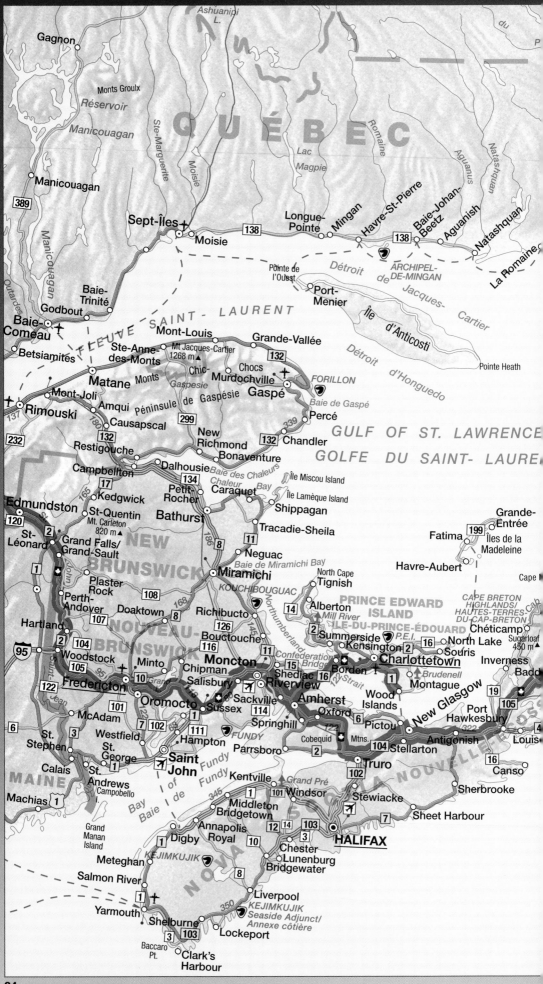

Gagnon

Manicouagan

389

Monts Groulx
Réservoir
Manicouagan
Ste-Marguerite

QUÉBEC

Ashuanipi
L.

Romaine

du
P

Lac
Magpie

Aguanus

Natashquan

Sept-Îles
Moisie

138

Longue-
Pointe

Mingan

Havre-St-Pierre

138

Baie-Johan-
Beetz

Aguanish

Natashquan

La Romaine

Baie-
Trinité

Godbout

Baie-
Comeau

Betsiamites

FLEUVE SAINT- LAURENT

Pointe de
l'Ouest

Port-
Menier

ARCHIPEL-
DE-MINGAN

Détroit
de
Jacques-
Cartier

Île d'Anticosti

Détroit d'Honguedo

Pointe Heath

Mont-Louis

Ste-Anne-
des-Monts

Grande-Vallée

Mt Jacques-Cartier
1268 m ▲

132

Chocs

Monts
Gaspésie

Chic-

Murdochville

FORILLON

Matane

Mont-Joli

Rimouski

137

Amqui

Causapscal

péninsule de Gaspésie

Gaspé

Baie de Gaspé

Percé

232

132

Restigouche

New
Richmond
Bonaventure

299

132

Chandler

339

GULF OF ST. LAWRENCE
GOLFE DU SAINT- LAUREN

Campbellton

Dalhousie

Baie des Chaleurs
Chaleur Bay

Île Miscou Island

Kedgwick

134

Petit-
Rocher

Caraquet

Île Lamèque Island

Edmundston

St-Quentin

Mt. Carleton
820 m ▲

Bathurst

Shippagan

Grande-
Entrée

Fatima

199

Îles de la
Madeleine

120

St-
Léonard

17

Grand Falls/
Grand-Sault

2

NEW
BRUNSWICK

186

8

11

Tracadie-Sheila

Havre-Aubert

Cape

1

Plaster
Rock

Neguac

Baie de Miramichi Bay

Perth-
Andover

108

Miramichi

KOUCHIBOUGUAC

North Cape
Tignish

PRINCE EDWARD
ISLAND
ÎLE-DU-PRINCE-ÉDOUARD

CAPE BRETON
HIGHLANDS/
HAUTES-TERRES-
DU-CAP-BRETON

Hartland

107

Doaktown

168

8

Richibucto

14

Alberton

Mill River

Chéticamp

Sugarloaf
450 m ▲

NOUVEAU-
BRUNSWICK

126

Bouctouche

145

Summerside

Kensington

P.E.I.

2

16

North Lake

Souris

Inverness

95

2

104

Woodstock

105

Minto

116

Moncton

Chipman

Salisbury

11

Shediac

Confederation
Bridge

Borden

16

Charlottetown

Brudenell

2

1

Montague

Badd

McAdam

122

Fredericton

10

Oromocto

Sackville

Riverview

101

Sussex

7

102

Amherst

Oxford

Wood
Islands

6

Pictou

New Glasgow

19

105

St.
Stephen

6

3

111

Westfield
St.
George

Hampton

FUNDY

Springhill

Cobequid

Mtns.

122

2

Parrsboro

104

Stellarton

Antigonish

Loui

16

Calais

St.
Andrews

Campobello

Saint
John

Kentville

Grand Pré

Truro

102

Canso

MAINE

Machias

1

Bay of Fundy
Baie de Fundy

101

Windsor

Stewiacke

Sherbrooke

345

Middleton
Bridgetown

12

14

103

Sheet Harbour

7

Grand
Manan
Island

Digby

Annapolis
Royal

1

10

Chester

3

HALIFAX

Meteghan

KEJIMKUJIK

8

Lunenburg
Bridgewater

Salmon River

NOVA
NOUVELLE

1

Yarmouth

Shelburne

350

Liverpool

KEJIMKUJIK
Seaside Adjunct/
Annexe côtière

3

103

Lockeport

Baccaro
Pt.

Clark's
Harbour

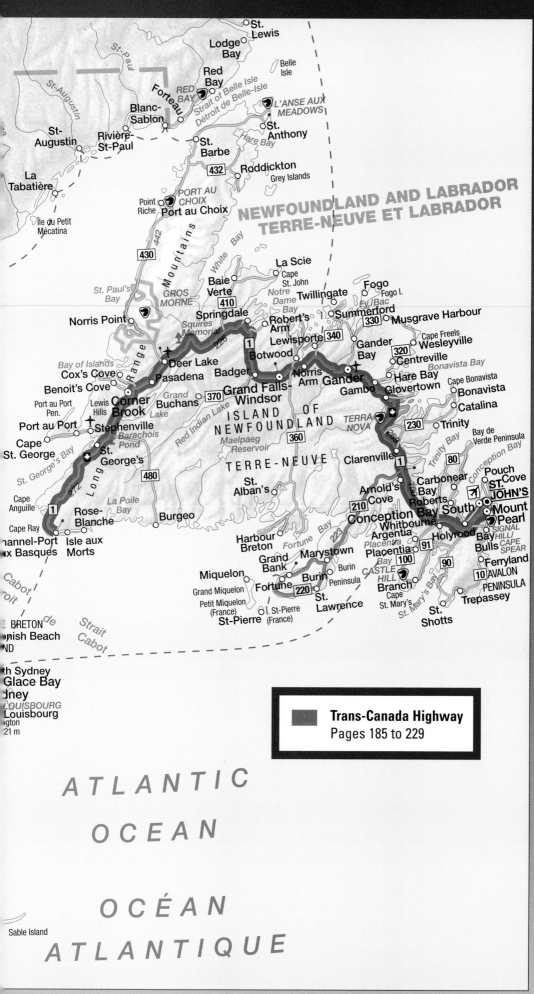

St. Lewis

Lodge Bay

Belle Isle

Red Bay

RED BAY

Forteau

Strait of Belle Isle
Détroit de Belle-Isle

L'ANSE AUX MEADOWS

Blanc-Sablon

St. Anthony

St-Augustin

Rivière-St-Paul

St. Barbe

Hare Bay

La Tabatière

Roddickton

432

Grey Islands

Point Riche

PORT AU CHOIX
Port au Choix

Île du Petit Mécatina

NEWFOUNDLAND AND LABRADOR
TERRE-NEUVE ET LABRADOR

White Bay

430

La Scie

Baie Verte

Cape St. John

Fogo

Notre Dame Bay

Twillingate

Fogo I.

Fv./Bac

GROS MORNE

410

Springdale

Robert's Arm

Summerford

Musgrave Harbour

Norris Point

Squires Memorial

1

Lewisporte

340

Cape Freels

Wesleyville

Botwood

330

Gander Bay

320

Deer Lake

Pasadena

Badger

Norris Arm

Gander

Centreville

Bonavista Bay

Cox's Cove

Grand

Buchans

Grand Falls-Windsor

Hare Bay

Glovertown

Cape Bonavista

Benoit's Cove

370

Gambo

Bonavista

Port au Port Pen.

Lewis Hills

Corner Brook

Red Indian Lake

Grand Lake

ISLAND OF NEWFOUNDLAND

TERRA NOVA

Catalina

Port au Port

Stephenville

Barachois Pond

Maelpaeg Reservoir

360

230

Trinity

Cape St. George

St. George's

TERRE-NEUVE

Clarenville

Bay de Verde Peninsula

St. George's Bay

480

St. Alban's

1

Trinity Bay

80

Conception Bay

Cape Anguille

La Poile Bay

Burgeo

Arnold's Cove

Pouch Cove

Cape Ray

Rose-Blanche

Carbonear

ST. JOHN'S

Channel-Port aux Basques

Isle aux Morts

Harbour Breton

Fortune Bay

Conception Bay South

Whitbourne

Roberts

Mount Pearl

Grand Bank

Marystown

Burin

210

Argentia

Holyrood

SIGNAL HILL
CAPE SPEAR

Cabot roit

Miquelon

Fortune

Burin Peninsula

Placentia Bay

Placentia

91

Bay Bulls

Ferryland

Grand Miquelon

220

St. Lawrence

100

CASTLE HILL

90

10

AVALON PENINSULA

Petit Miquelon (France)

Î. St-Pierre

Branch

Trepassey

St-Pierre (France)

Cape St. Mary's

St. Mary's Bay

St. Shotts

BRETON

nish Beach

ND

th Sydney

Glace Bay

ney

LOUISBOURG

Louisbourg

gton

21 m

Strait Cabot

ATLANTIC

OCEAN

OCÉAN

Sable Island

ATLANTIQUE

	Trans-Canada Highway
	Pages 185 to 229

TRANS-CANADA HIGHWAY

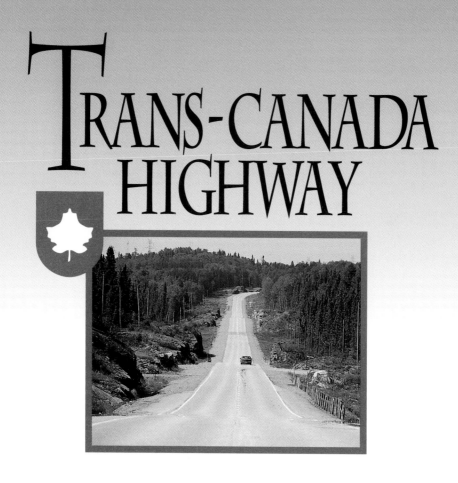

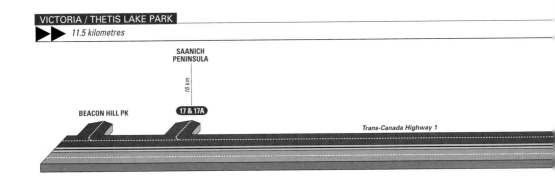

▶▶ *11.5 kilometres*

SAANICH
PENINSULA

16 km

BEACON HILL PK

17 & 17A

Trans-Canada Highway 1

1 km   6 km

**IN AND
AROUND
VICTORIA**

Beacon Hill Park, Victoria

This centrally located park is Victoria's preeminent garden and playground. Spring daffodils and blue camas, and some 30,000 other flowers planted twice each year, enliven the grounds. Landmarks are a 38 m high totem pole (said to be the world's second tallest) and the Mile 0 signpost (*above*), the beginning (or end, depending on your direction) of the Trans-Canada, the world's longest national highway.

Carr House, Victoria

You will find the childhood home of painter and writer Emily Carr (1871-1945) at Simcoe and Government streets in the residential neighborhood of the city just a short walk west of Beacon Hill Park. The picturesque cottage (*left*), restored and furnished in the Victorian style, displays school books, easels, and other early mementos of the artist whose bold paintings were profoundly influenced by Northwest Coast native art. The Art Gallery of Greater Victoria (1040 Moss St.) showcases examples of her work.

Saanich Peninsula

"Saanich" (meaning "good" or "fertile" soil) was how the Coast Salish Indians described this peninsula to the north of Victoria. The prosperous farmland of the region is an exception to Vancouver Island's overall ruggedness. Despite an encroaching suburban sprawl, a pastoral gentleness survives along Hwy. 17A (accessible from downtown Victoria via Blanshard St. and Hwy. 1).

The Dominion Astrophysical Observatory, at the end of a winding road just off Hwy. 17A, welcomes stargazing enthusiasts. The Butchart Gardens, at Benvenuto Rd. and Hwy. 17A, are a lush landscape of flowers and foliages, created in 1904 from a limestone quarry. Just beyond the turnoff to the gardens, Butterfly Gardens shelter some 150 species in a semitropical setting.

Craigflower Manor and Schoolhouse, Victoria

You can sample oven-baked scones at the Craigflower Farmhouse, built in 1856 as the main house of Vancouver Island's first farming community. It was built by settler Kenneth McKenzie, and the style of the dwelling is reminiscent of McKenzie's native Scotland. Next door is the Craigflower Schoolhouse (1855), one of the oldest in Western Canada.

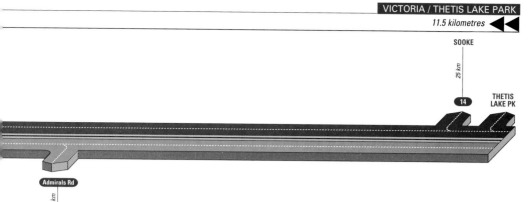

SOOKE

25 km

14   THETIS
LAKE PK

Admirals Rd

2 km

CRAIGFLOWER
MANOR & SCHOOLHOUSE

4 km   0.5 km

The beacon atop the Fisgard Light-house (above) has guided vessels through Juan de Fuca Strait since the 1860s. In clear weather, its beam can be seen 16 km away.

The Italian Garden (below) is only one of many distinctive sections of the world-renowned Butchart Gardens, which encompass thousands of flowering plants, trees, and shrubs.

Sooke

Take Hwy. 14 (the Sooke Rd.) to the Fisgard Lighthouse and Fort Rodd Hill (more below). If time permits, continue along the densely forested, often fog-bound, southwest coast of Van-couver Island to Sooke. The huge East Sooke Regional Park enroute is ideal for hiking or strolling along the seashore.

At Sooke, you can take boat and heritage tours, cruises to sea caves, and helicopter flights over mountains and ancient forests. In late afternoon, the fishing boats sail into Sooke's snug har-bor, bringing seafood (including two dozens kinds of crab), which local restaurants serve with style.

In July, All Sooke Day cele-brates West Coast lumbering traditions. Join the 10,000 who come here for ax-throwing, logrolling, and other contests.

Fort Rodd Hill and Fisgard Lighthouse, Victoria

These two national historic sites, almost side by side, honor Victo-ria's military and maritime links. Fort Rodd's three bat-teries, still intact, never saw action. Military prepared-ness led to the fort's construction, and although it was used from 1878 to 1956 it was never called on to defend Victoria. Guarding Esquimalt Har-bour, the Fisgard Lighthouse is the oldest structure of

its kind on Canada's West Coast. Built in 1860, the white tower, with the adjacent red keeper's cottage, was a welcome sight to sailors. Climb the iron staircase to the oil lantern; the wick once was trimmed every four hours.

Royal Roads University, Victoria

In 1908, James Dunsmuir, B.C. premier (1900-1902) and lieu-tenant-governor (1906-1909), built Hatley Castle, once the heart of his vast waterfront estate. Today, this grand pile is the imposing centerpiece of Royal Roads University. (Duns-muir shared his father's taste for architectural flamboyance. In 1888, Robert Dunsmuir, "the coal king of Vancouver Island," put up the equally ornate Craig-darroch Castle, at 1050 Joan Cres., in Victoria.)

The federal government bought Hatley Castle in 1940, when the estate became Royal Roads Military College. The col-lege was granted university status in 1995. Its grounds rival the bet-ter-known Butchart Gardens in floral grandeur. Visitors may stroll among pathways and flowerbeds, exquisitely arranged in the Eng-lish, Italian, and Japanese styles.

Thetis Lake Park

This nature sanctuary on the outskirts of Victoria contains dense groves of Douglas firs, soaring to heights of 70 m and dating back more than 500 years. Follow the Clark and Seymour Hill trails to inspect these endur-ing ancient specimens.

Fan Tan Alley

A ramble down Fan Tan Alley, said to be the narrowest street in North America, will take you into Canada's oldest Chinatown. The community dates back to 1858, when Chinese immigrants arrived to build the railway. Gone are the opium and gambling dens, and the brothels that flourished briefly in the late 19th century. Instead, you will find fine restaurants serving great Cantonese food.

Gate of Harmonious Interest

The red gateway to Victoria's Chinatown is marked by hand-carved stone lions imported in 1981 from Suzhou, China, Victoria's "twin" city.

Centennial Square

English daisies and primroses bloom here alongside other dwarf flowers in what may be Canada's only Elizabethan Knot Garden, a replica of one at London's Hampton Court. Knot gardens are named for their intricately designed lavender- and boxwood-edged floral beds (knots). Flanking the square are the baroque McPherson Playhouse and the refurbished City Hall.

MacPherson Playhouse

Market Square

City Hall

N

Bastion Square

In 1843 the Hudson's Bay Company constructed Fort Victoria on what is now Bastion Square, and around it grew the historic heart of the city. No traces of the fort remain today, but you can still glimpses the old "downtown" bustle in Bastion Square's restored 19-century buildings.

Government Street

As you stroll along Government St., note the British flavor of shops selling tea cups, tartans, and imported preserves.

FISGARD ST.
PANDORA AVE.
JOHNSON ST.
YATES ST.
GOVERNMENT ST.
Inner Harbour
WHARF ST.
FORT ST.
BROUGHTON ST.
COURTNEY ST.

Empress Hotel

The opulent past lives on within the thick, ivy-covered brick walls of the Empress Hotel. Built in 1908, the six-story turreted chateau boasts a restored Crystal Ballroom, antique chandeliers, mahogany doors, and the Palm Court's stained glass dome. Indulge in the curry buffet of the Bengal Room or take afternoon tea—as Rudyard Kipling and Queen Elizabeth II once did—in the Tea Lobby, where silver platters of fruit compotes, finger sandwiches, and pastries are served daily on crisp, white linen.

Undersea Gardens

MENZIES ST.

British Columbia's Parliament Buildings

Designed by British architect Francis Rattenbury, who also created the nearby Empress Hotel, the legislature has been the city's reigning landmark since its completion in 1897. Spot the gilded statue of Capt. George Vancouver atop the highest copper dome. Queen Victoria was 60 years on the throne in 1897 and a stained glass window in the Lower Rotunda—one of hundreds in the building—honored her diamond jubilee. Exterior lighting, originally mounted to celebrate the jubilee, is now a nighttime spectacle of 3,330 twinkling light bulbs.

Netherlands Centennial Carillon

Check out the 62 bells in Heritage Court. The tall white tower houses the largest carillon in Canada. It was a Centennial Year gift to the city by British Columbians of Dutch heritage.

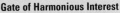

VICTORIA—A MILD, WELL-MANNERED CAPITAL

Tucked into the southern tip of Vancouver Island, British Columbia's capital radiates from the crescent-shaped, stonewalled Inner Harbour. Sheltered from the open Pacific by the Juan de Fuca Strait, and warmed by the California Current, the city enjoys year-round mild weather and about 2,200 hours of sunshine a year. Victorians are passionate gardeners, who tally the blossoms in their miniature Edens at an Annual Flower Count each February. Though this gardening love affair is fostered by the gentle climate and large numbers of retirees, it is rooted in Victoria's British heritage. Victorians rejoice in their Britishness, reveling in English customs. It imparts a certain reserve, an unhurried pace, an overall civility. The ambience is evident even along the waterfront, where you stroll past streets lined with tea shops, heritage buildings, and flower-festooned lampposts.

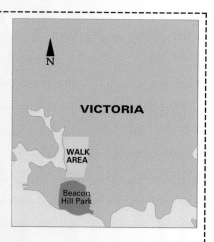

VICTORIA

WALK AREA

Beacon Hill Park

To Craig darroch Castle

JMBOLDT ST.

Convention Centre

Crystal Garden

DOUGLAS ST.

BELLEVILLE ST.

GOVERNMENT ST.

SUPERIOR ST.

To Beacon Hill Park

Maritime Museum of British Columbia
Housed in an 1889 Romanesque towered building that once served as the provincial courthouse, the Maritime Museum dominates Bastion Square. Inside, you can ride the grille-caged elevator—said to be the oldest working elevator in North America, or marvel at some of the 30,000 models, tools, uniforms and other nautical treasures on display, items such as a hands-on engine room, Canada's largest model ship collection, and the 1860 *Tilikum*—an 11 m dugout canoe, which was converted into a three-masted schooner and sailed from Victoria to London in 1901-04.

Royal British Columbia Museum
A collection of some 10 million objects contribute to stunning displays in this world-class museum, renowned for its aboriginal art and history exhibits. You can board a replica of Capt. Vancouver's ship, *Discovery*, wander along a seashore, or through a frontier town or old-growth forest; explore huge recreations of various natural habitats; and get an up-close look at a soft-bodied vampire squid on a simulated journey to the Pacific Ocean floor.

Helmcken House
Built in 1852, the Dr. John Helmcken residence is British Columbia's oldest house still standing on its original site. The home of Fort Victoria's pioneer doctor, it houses one of Canada's most extensive collections of 19th-century medical instruments. However, the fainthearted may cringe at some surgical tool exhibits. One such oddity is the trepanning saw the HBC doctor used to treat "swelling of the brain."

Thunderbird Park
You will find an open-air display of West Coast totem poles and the replica of a traditional Haida house, created by world-famous native carver Mungo Martin, if you stroll through the Royal British Columbia Museum grounds, past the Native Plant Gardens, into Thunderbird Park. In summer, carvers often work in the park.

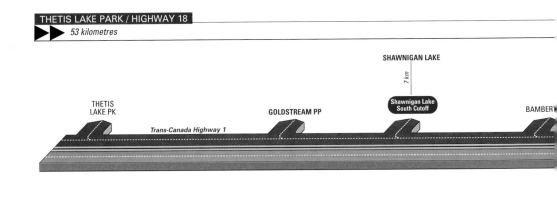

SHAWNIGAN LAKE

7 km

THETIS
LAKE PK

GOLDSTREAM PP

Shawnigan Lake
South Cutoff

BAMBER

Trans-Canada Highway 1

10 km   6 km   8 km

**VANCOUVER
ISLAND**

Goldstream Provincial Park

Natural splendor and mining relics are features of this wooded park a short distance from Victoria. Hiking trails lead through pristine stands of Douglas fir, western red cedar, oak and arbutus (Canada's only broadleaf evergreen) to majestic waterfalls. You can also see shafts and tunnels dug when gold was discovered here during the 1850s.

Shawnigan Lake

A well-established summer getaway for Victorians, the 8 km long Shawnigan Lake offers several appealing sites. At the south end is beautiful Memory Island Provincial Park (accessible only by boat). The island was purchased by local families who lost sons in World War II and presented it to the province as a memorial. West Shawnigan Lake Provincial Park offers walking trails, picnic sites, and swimming. Hiking trails lead to Old Baldy Mountain, east of the lake. The old fire hall in Shawnigan Lake Village houses the local museum.

Mill Bay

Quiet waterfront streets, Gulf Island vistas, and diverse recreational opportunity are among delights of this Saanich Inlet community. Seals can be spotted basking on floats and decks in nearby Satellite Channel. A 25-minute ferry ride from Mill Bay takes you across Saanich Inlet to Brentwood Bay and Butchart Gardens (see page 28).

Cobble Hill

Grapes thrive in this area's mellow coastal climate and rich soils. Four Cobble Hill-Duncan area wineries produce a variety of red and white wines. All the wineries welcome visitors for tours and tastings, generally by appointment. For spectacular views of Shawnigan Lake, the Gulf Islands, and Cowichan Bay, follow the trail from Cobble Hill through Quarry Wilderness Park to the top of Cobble Hill Mountain.

Cowichan Bay

A thriving fishing and lumbering village, Cowichan Bay lies at the head of a fine natural harbor, long used by the Coast Salish Indians. The community's saltwater connections are celebrated at the Marine Ecology Station, where aquariums and hands-on exhibits explain B.C.'s diverse marine environments.

At the Cowichan Maritime Centre, photographs and models detail local development. The center's Wooden Boat Society preserves old-time boat-building crafts. Visit a charming nearby historic site, the restored Butter Church, built by the Oblate missionary Father Peter Rondreault in 1870 with proceeds from the sale of—what else?—butter.

Duncan

Duncan bills itself as the "City of Totems." More than 40 poles, the work of native carvers, decorate the downtown

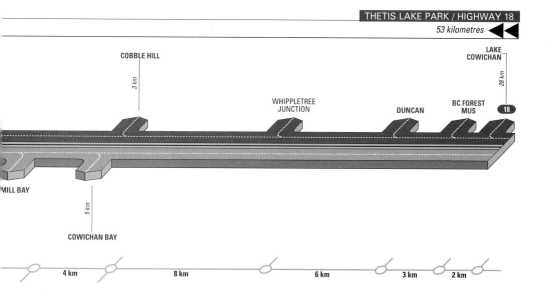

LAKE COWICHAN
28 km

COBBLE HILL
3 km

WHIPPLETREE JUNCTION

DUNCAN

BC FOREST MUS

18

MILL BAY
5 km

COWICHAN BAY

4 km   8 km   6 km   3 km   2 km

streets and the stretch of Hwy. I that bisects this town of 4,300. For close-up viewing, follow the trail of yellow footprints linking the poles, which depict traditional and non-traditional subjects. One pole honors B.C.'s wheelchair athlete Rick Hansen, who circled the globe in 1985-87.

The community is the commercial and cultural center for the Cowichan Valley, home of the Cowichan Indians, B.C.'s largest band. These people, famous for their distinctive handknit Cowichan sweaters, demonstrate their skills at weaving, beadwork, and other crafts at the Native Heritage Centre.

Displays at the Cowichan Valley Museum, housed in Duncan's former 1912 train station, recount the settlement of the region. The museum is appropriately chosen: the community was born in 1886 when the Esquimalt and Nanaimo Railway whistle stopped at the farm of early settler William Duncan. Tools, domestic goods, and medical equipment illustrate subsequent agricultural and commercial developments.

At the Cowichan and Chemainus Valleys' Ecomuseum, "a museum without walls," local folk delight in showing visitors the museum's "collection." It consists of local beauty spots and sites of historical interest.

Also downtown, as striking in its own oversize way as a totem pole, is a 63 m high hockey stick, which is the largest in the world.

A forest of totems on Duncan streets celebrate their carvers' skill and West Coast native art.

British Columbia Forest Museum

A vintage locomotive (*below*) used in early logging camps greets visitors to this forestry museum. Among other antique

equipment exhibits are a 1919 White logging truck and "Little Jakey," an 1890 steam log-hauler. A working sawmill and a restored planing mill produce lumber for the museum. Staff demonstrate shake-splitting, bucking, and papermaking. While you're here, stretch your legs on Forester's Walk, which is lined with centuries-old Douglas firs. You can also enjoy a bumpy steam-train journey along a short stretch of narrow-gauge track, across a 92 m high trestle, and past forest, farmland, and a logging camp of bygone days.

At daybreak, a canopy of mist hovers lightly above placid Lake Cowichan. A fisherman's paradise, the lake is a prime source of giant cutthroat and rainbow trout.

Lake Cowichan

If you want diversion, take a pleasant side trip west on Hwy. 18 to this sparkling lake set amid dense forests, and the village of the same name. The village was born as a lumbering community in the 1880s. Its Kaatza Station Museum (in the former 1913 railway station) offers exhibits on pioneer life. You can tour the local research station which is seeking to improve growth in B.C.'s coastal forests. From the village, take the 75 km route around the lake, past old-growth and demonstration forests, campsites, and parks. Drive with care: logging trucks use this road, too.

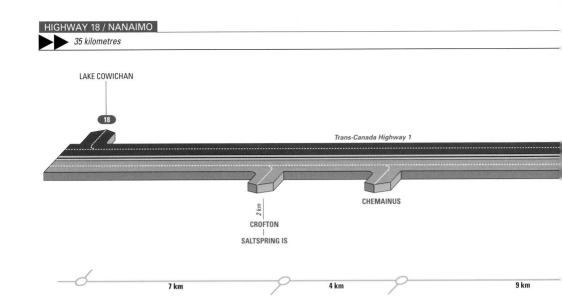

LAKE COWICHAN

18

Trans-Canada Highway 1

CHEMAINUS

2 km
CROFTON
SALTSPRING IS

7 km   4 km   9 km

**VANCOUVER
ISLAND**

Crofton

Crofton once smelted copper ore from mines on nearby Mount Sicker; today, its mainstay is a pulp-mill. Exhibits at the local museum celebrate its mining and smelting past. A 20-minute ferry ride from Crofton takes you to Vesuvius on Saltspring Island, largest of the lovely Gulf Islands.

Saltspring Island

Once the island was known for its orchards and delectable lamb, now it is renowned for leisure pursuits, from arts and crafts to yachting. Its 10,000 permanent residents enjoy a mild climate, seaside vistas, and sweet seclusion for much of the year. But the population skyrockets and seclusion is less assured with the arrival of summer visitors. Accommodations, including 70 bed-and-breakfast spots, are plentiful. With shops, galleries, and museums to visit, your days will be full. For views of the other Gulf Islands, drive to the top of Mount Maxwell.

In Chemainus, larger-than-life murals depict scenes ranging from the life of native peoples and early pioneers to the heyday of the logging industry.

Chemainus

"The world's largest outdoor art gallery" is how Chemainus bills itself. Economic uncertainty engulfed the town in the early 1980s when its sawmill, the world's largest at that time, closed. That was when Chemainus transformed itself into the mural capital of Canada by painting huge historically themed pictures on some three dozen outdoor walls. Today, the town's 3,900 residents receive as many as a quarter-million admiring visitors annually. Follow the yellow footprints for a self-guided tour of the murals.

Ladysmith

Welcome to Vancouver Island's prize-winning town! Perched prettily on high slopes above the sea, Ladysmith has been honored provincially as the island's most beautiful community and received a national award for its attractively restored main street.

Once known as Oyster Bay, the town was renamed in 1900 to mark the relief of Ladysmith in South Africa, a British Boer War victory. Street names still honor British leaders of that day—Baden-Powell, Kitchener, and Roberts—and the Black Nugget Museum recalls Ladysmith's past.

The Railway Museum has rolling stock from mines and forests that enriched the town, and Transfer Beach claims the warmest saltwater swimming in Canada. You may want to stop here and test the waters for yourself.

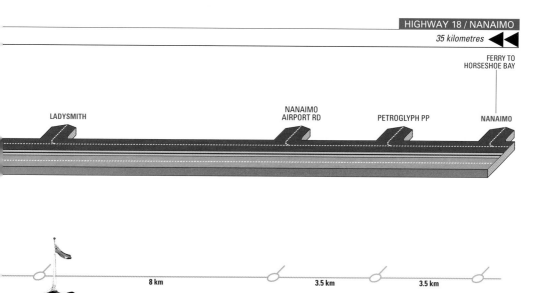

FERRY TO
HORSESHOE BAY

LADYSMITH   NANAIMO
AIRPORT RD   PETROGLYPH PP   NANAIMO

8 km   3.5 km   3.5 km

The Bastion (1853) recalls Nanaimo's beginnings as an HBC trading post. Exhibits include coin and rifle collections, military records and property deeds.

Newcastle Island Provincial Marine Park

Tranquil and vehicle-free, Newcastle Island is just a short ferry ride from Nanaimo. The park's steep sandstone cliffs, gravel beaches, and lush forest provide an ideal setting for picnicking and camping. Hikers and cyclists can enjoy some 20 km of trails. The island was a CPR cruise ship pleasure resort in the 1930s, a past echoed in a restored dance pavilion.

Nanaimo

Vancouver Island's fastest-growing city is famed for a delicious confection (the Nanaimo bar) and a popular July event (the Nanaimo-to-Vancouver bathtub race). But this forestry and fishing center also rejoices in its beautiful setting, and a mild, sunny climate. With the ongoing harbor front renewal, Nanaimo has become a popular travel destination. This is a great spot for arranging sightseeing cruises to observe sea lions, killer whales, and other creatures that flourish in the offshore waters.

In 1849, the Hudson's Bay Company opened a post on the site of present-day Nanaimo. The Bastion (*above*), built some years later, survives as the oldest HBC fort in Canada. Other architectural legacies include landmarks such as the 1889 Palace Hotel and the 1911 Dakin Building. Nanaimo's coal-mining past is a theme of the Centennial Museum, which contains a replica mine and a restored miner's cottage.

Gabriola Island

This northernmost "Queen" of the Gulf Islands was a well-kept secret for years. From 400 residents in the 1960s, the population has increased tenfold. Natural beauty and a mild climate, as well as easy access (just 20 minutes by ferry from Nanaimo), all contribute to its appeal. You can tour this island paradise by car or bicycle. A 60 km/h speed limit on the narrow roads protects peripatetic humans and wildlife. Popular spots include the sandstone beaches and galleries at Gabriola Sands Provincial Park, the petroglyphs at Degenen Bay, and the high cliffs where eagles and seabirds nest.

Erosion and ice have shaped giant waves of sandstone, known as the Galiano Galleries (above), which stretch along Malaspina Point on Gabriola Island.

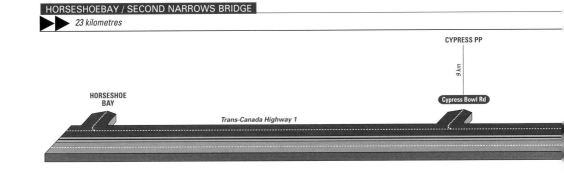

CYPRESS PP

9 km

HORSESHOE
BAY

Cypress Bowl Rd

Trans-Canada Highway 1

8 km

5 km

**NORTH SHORE,
VANCOUVER**

Horseshoe Bay

Situated on a sheltered inlet on the sheer shoreline of Howe Sound, Horseshoe Bay provides ferry services to Nanaimo on Vancouver Island, Bowen Island, and the Sunshine Coast. A great place to watch ferries and pleasure craft on Howe Sound is the viewpoint some 2 km north of town on Hwy. 99 (also known as the Squamish Highway).

Cypress Provincial Park

Atop a peak overlooking Vancouver, Cypress Provincial Park offers a stunning vista of the city skyline, Mount Baker in Washington State and, on clear days, the Gulf Islands in Georgia Strait. Hiking and skiing are serious pastimes here. But if you're just passing through, the easy Yew Lake Interpretive Trail is a pleasant introduction to Cypress Park's mix of mountain meadows, lakes, and forests.

Grouse Mountain's Skyride (below), North America's largest aerial tramway system, offers a panoramic view of spectacular scenery.

Stanley Park

This forest oasis on Vancouver's doorstep is one of North America's largest city parks. Established in 1886, it remains a bosky haven of beauty and recreation only minutes from the city's hubbub. To reach the park from West Vancouver, take Taylor Way (Hwy. 99) and the Lions Gate Bridge. On the south side of the bridge, the route bisects the park, before entering Vancouver's core at Georgia St.

A 10 km circle drive (starting at Georgia St.) links the park's points of interest: the Pauline Johnson Memorial at Ferguson Point, the SS *Empress of Japan* figurehead, and the totems near Brockton Point. For those who prefer to explore on foot, a 10 km seawall promenade provides close-up views, particularly at Prospect Point, where ocean-going vessels glide beneath the arch of Lions Gate Bridge. For kids, there is a children's zoo and a miniature railway. Stanley Park also has Canada's largest aquarium, which shelters 9,000 marine creatures. The bronze sculpture of a killer whale gracing the entrance was fashioned by famed Haida artist Bill Reid.

Capilano River Regional Park

Swaying 70 m over the Capilano River, a 137 m suspension bridge, reputedly the world's longest, thrills visitors as it has since 1899. The first wood-and-hemp span, called the "Laughing Bridge" by natives, was replaced in 1956 by the present sturdy structure of

At night, Lions Gate Bridge becomes a mighty span of twinkling lights over Burrard Inlet. Completed in 1938, the bridge links Vancouver's North Shore suburbs with downtown Vancouver.

▶

GROUSE MOUNTAIN

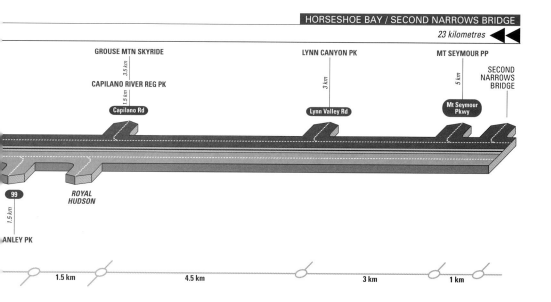

GROUSE MTN SKYRIDE

3.5 km

CAPILANO RIVER REG PK

1.5 km

Capilano Rd

LYNN CANYON PK

3 km

Lynn Valley Rd

MT SEYMOUR PP

5 km

SECOND
NARROWS
BRIDGE

Mt Seymour
Pkwy

99

ROYAL
HUDSON

1.5 km

ANLEY PK

1.5 km   4.5 km   3 km   1 km

wire rope and wooden decking. The bridge is just outside Capilano River Regional Park, where footpaths cut through woods of Douglas fir and cedar. In the park's northern sector, Capilano Salmon Hatchery, set up in 1977 as B.C.'s first fish farm, welcomes visitors. The nearby Cleveland Dam holds back the Capilano Lake, the source of water for more than half Vancouver's households.

Grouse Mountain Skyride

Sports-minded Vancouverites have long favored this year-round recreational getaway, accessible via Capilano Rd. and Nancy Greene Way. An 8-minute trip on the Grouse Mountain Skyride brings you to the 1,250 m level of this North Shore peak. There, at the Grouse Nest Restaurant, you can feast on fine food and views. In winter, skiers glide and swerve on 16 runs; in summer, hang gliders float down the cliff face on gentle breezes. The mountain trails challenge hikers. But the easy shoreline loop beside Blue Grouse Lake is just right for a woodsy walk.

Royal Hudson

For a refreshing change, highway-lagged travelers will enjoy riding the *Royal Hudson* steam train. The train-and-boat 6½-hour return trip from North Vancouver to Squamish skirts Howe Sound's sheer

shoreline. *Royal Hudson* departs from the station at Pemberton and First Avenue; MV *Britannia* returns to Harbour Cruises Marina, at Denman St. in downtown Vancouver.

Lynn Canyon Park

The heart-stopping highlight of this park is a 68 m long suspension bridge. Hanging more than 80 m over a mountain gorge cut by Lynn Creek, the span is higher and shorter than the Capilano Bridge. At the park's entrance, the Centennial Ecology Centre explains the interaction of plants, animals, and man in West Coast forests.

Mount Seymour Provincial Park

North Vancouver's largest park, Mount Seymour Provincial Park can be reached via a scenic parkway.

Stretch your legs on the Goldie Lake Trail, which loops through a forest of mountain hemlock. Hikers may prefer the steeper trail to the top of 1,453 m Mount Seymour. If backpacking is your bag, try the Baden-Powell Centennial Trail, which links Mount Seymour and Cypress parks. A rustic gateway (*above*) marks this challenging wilderness trek.

37

VANCOUVER—IN THE HEART OF A PACIFIC METROPOLIS

The snow-capped Coast Mountains provide a breathtaking backdrop for Vancouver's mushrooming skyline. With its front door on the booming Pacific Rim, the city now sprawls across British Columbia's Lower Mainland from Burrard Inlet to the Fraser River Delta. The expanding suburbs, burgeoning Burnaby and Richmond among them, account for almost a third of Greater Vancouver's 1.7 million residents. The city has become one of the fastest growing metropolises in North America. This walk through its varied, vigorous downtown core passes some of the city's latest architectural *chefs d'oeuvre*, such as the impressive new library, and winds beside Gastown's handsomely restored turn-of-the-century buildings, and along the colorful streets of Chinatown.

Robson Square
The courthouse, with its sloping glass roof, is the most striking feature in this downtown square designed by Vancouver's internationally acclaimed architect Arthur Erickson.

Canadian Craft Museum/Christ Church Cathedral
An elegant courtyard in Cathedral Place leads into the Canadian Craft Museum, where wooden cuckoo clocks, cutlery, and furniture are part of the craft collection. Christ Church Cathedral, the oldest standing church in Vancouver, is next door. Completed in 1895, and enlarged in 1909, this Anglican cathedral church boasts a hammer beam roof in the English Gothic tradition. A tablet on the interior east wall honors Captain Cook for revealing British Columbia's beauty to the world. Like most visitors, you will marvel at the building's Douglas fir beams and historic stained glass windows. The cathedral, which is open daily, hosts a summer music festival with jazz, rock, and sacred music performers.

Marine Building
Vancouver's finest example of Art Deco style, the Marine Building, completed in 1930, was the city's largest building that time. Mayan and Egyptian motifs and marine flora and fauna ornamentation add to its charm. Among interesting architectural details are terra-cotta panels depicting European discovery of the Pacific Coast.

Hotel Vancouver
This château-style hotel, completed in 1939, is a visual delight with its green copper roof, dormer windows, and grimacing gargoyles.

To Stanley Park

To Granville Island

BURRARD ST.
HORNBY ST.
HOWE ST.
W. PENDER
DUNSMUIR ST.
GRANVILLE ST.
SEYMOUR
THURLOW ST.
HARO ST.
ROBSON ST.
W. GEORGIA ST.
RICHARDS ST.
BARCLAY ST.
BURRARD ST.
HORNBY ST.
SMITHE ST.
ROBSON ST.
NELSON ST.
HOWE ST.
GRANVILLE ST.

Ford Centre

Vancouver Art Gallery
Housed in a neoclassical 1907 former courthouse, the gallery features contemporary shows and a permanent collection of paintings by Emily Carr (1871-1945), one of British Columbia's best-known artists. On weekends, visitors gather on the steps facing Robson St., to relax or watch chess-for-hire matches played out in the bustling courtyard below.

Vancouver Library Square
Designed by Moshie Safdie, the new Library Square resembles a postmodern colosseum of rust sandstone. Home to more than one million books, the library is seen by many as the future heart of the city. Across the street, the 1,824-seat **Ford Centre for the Performing Arts,** another Safdie structure, presents long-running shows.

Queen Elizabeth Theatre and Playhouse
The 2,800-seat theater, nicknamed the "Queen E," offers a wide range of attractions and also serves as the home for Ballet British Columbia, which was formed in 1986.

Canada Place
The landmark site of Vancouver's Expo 86, Canada Place juts into Burrard Inlet, its roof resembling white sails billowing in the wind. The complex houses the Vancouver Trade and Convention Centre, the Vancouver Board of Trade, and the CN Imax Theatre. It is also a terminal for cruise ships bound for Alaska. You can stroll along the promenade and watch the ships dock.

Gastown Steam Clock
This Water St. timepiece, which whistles every quarter hour, is the world's first clock run by the steam which heats local buildings. Visitors can peer at the inner workings through side glass panels.

Gastown
A saloon that John "Gassy Jack" Deighton opened here in 1867 started commerce bustling in what eventually became Vancouver. As the city grew westward, Gastown declined for a time. Today, however, the area's cobblestone streets have been restored and **Gassy Jack's Statue** marks Maple Tree Square where his tavern stood. The statue faces **Hotel Europe,** completed in 1908, and still ranked as one of the world's finest examples of a flatiron building.

Sun Tower
Built in 1912, the 17-story, 83 m high Sun Tower stood the tallest in Canada for two years, when it was surpassed by a 20-story bank building in Toronto. Note the tall copper roof, the mounted tower, and the ornately sculpted columns, known as the "nine maidens," which grace the upper cornice.

Harbour Centre
A glass elevator whisks visitors 167 m to the top of the Harbour Centre Tower, where an observation deck offers a fine view of the North Shore Mountains, Burrard Inlet, and the Lower Mainland.

Chinatown
Vancouver's Chinatown is the world's third-largest after San Francisco and New York. Wander along busy streets, where store signs are mostly in Chinese, and crimson-hued chickens, coils of sausage, and bok choy crowd window displays. Stop at the **Dr. Sun Yat-sen Classical Chinese Gardens,** the only full-sized authentic Ming Dynasty garden ever built outside China. Stroll through the Jade and Water pavilions, where covered walkways and carvings create a serene environment. Nearby, the 1.8 m wide **Sam Kee Building** holds the Guinness record as the world's thinnest building.

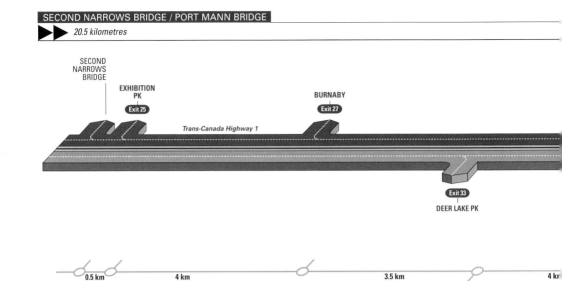

SECOND
NARROWS
BRIDGE

EXHIBITION
PK
Exit 25

BURNABY
Exit 27

Trans-Canada Highway 1

Exit 33
DEER LAKE PK

0.5 km   4 km   3.5 km   4 kr

**GREATER
VANCOUVER**

Exhibition Park

Just across the Second Narrows Bridge, the Trans-Canada passes Exhibition Park, which occupies a great chunk of prime Vancouver waterfront property. This is the site of the Pacific National Exhibition, held from late August to early September. The exhibition (second largest of its kind in Canada and seventh largest in North America) hosts demolition derbies, bronco rides, and rock concerts, as well as agricultural and livestock exhibits. Amusement rides, including Canada's largest wooden roller coaster, operate year-round in the park's "Playland." Nearby, between Renfrew and Cassiar streets, the B.C. Pavilion displays a relief map of British Columbia made from some 960,000 bits of plywood. This lilliputian view of the province's mountainous surface intrigues just about everybody.

Burnaby

🏛 ⛵ ❄

The Trans-Canada Highway curves through this heavily populated city, which is named for Robert Burnaby, an 1860s merchant and legislator. Once a bedroom community for Vancouver, Burnaby and its more than 160,000 residents have outgrown peripheral status. Second to Vancouver proper in economic clout, Burnaby has its own noteworthy points of interest. In the center of town, just north of the Trans-Canada, Burnaby Lake Regional Park has a sport complex and skating rinks, and offers nature walks and hikes through this great expanse of forest and marsh.

Deer Lake Park, Burnaby

🎵 ⛱ ⛵

Art, history, and recreation can all be enjoyed at this Burnaby park, on Sperling Ave., just south of the Trans-Canada. The north section of the park is the site of an art gallery (in a magnificent 1909 Tudor-style house), a theater and the Burnaby Historic Village. The park is popular with roller bladers as well as leisurely strollers who like to enjoy the rhododendron and rose gardens. You can kayak or row to the center of the lake for a close-up look at mallards, geese, and the occasional, elegantly posed blue heron. On Sundays, local artists and artisans display and sell their wares on Summer Set Lane. A big hit with kids is a model train, which operates on weekends and holidays.

Burnaby Village Museum (above) is the perfect place for local folk to celebrate the suburb's past and present on Burnaby's Birthday in September.

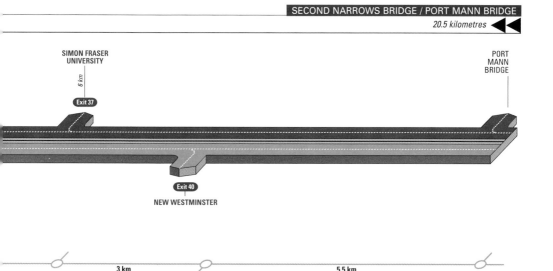

SIMON FRASER
UNIVERSITY

6 km

Exit 37

PORT
MANN
BRIDGE

Exit 40

NEW WESTMINSTER

3 km   5.5 km

Burnaby Village Museum

This museum has been wonderfully successful in bringing to life the good old days (1890-1925) in the Lower Fraser Valley. The handsomely restored exhibits include a general store, a one-classroom school, a Victorian pharmacy (complete with glass-fronted cabinets and antique medicine vials). Pride of place belongs to the 1861 log cabin of Burnaby's first settler, William Holmes, whose dwelling was moved here from its original site on the nearby Brunette River. To reach the museum, take the Kensington turnoff from Hwy. 1.

Simon Fraser University, Burnaby

A complex of low, interconnected buildings, Simon Fraser University hugs the heights of Burnaby Mountain. The bold design by Vancouver architects Arthur Erikson and Geoffrey Massey still stirs controversy as it did when the university opened in 1965. Make up your own mind by touring the campus. Pick up a walking tour at the Transportation Centre. The must-see sites are the spacious and monumental Academic Quadrangle and the Museum of Archaeology and Ethnology, with its collection of West Coast Indian art. Visit nearby Burnaby Centennial Park, where the view across Burrard Inlet to the North Shore peaks will lift even the lowliest spirit.

New Westminster

Recent efforts to put "new" back into New Westminster have revived the fortunes of this Fraser River port. In the 1860s, the city was B.C.'s colonial capital and gold rush boomtown. But, before that decade was out, decline began with the transfer of capital status to Victoria and the collapse of the Cariboo gold rush. This story of brief glory is told at Irving House and New Westminster Museum, fittingly housed in an 1864 mansion.

Today, this city of 45,000 glories in new heritage-style dwellings and a picturesque waterfront. Riverside pleasures can include a boardwalk ramble along Westminster Quay, or shopping at the cheerful two-story public market, opened in 1892, when Fraser Valley farmers first started to bring produce here to sell. You can also venture out onto the Fraser aboard *The Native*. This replica of an oldtime paddle wheeler sails to nearby Poplar and Douglas islands and makes a return trip to Fort Langley upstream.

Flocks of trumpeter swans (above) rise from habitats along the Fraser River near Burnaby, where Simon Fraser University sits astride Burnaby Mountain. The heart of the university is the Academic Quadrangle with its reflecting pool (right) and lush garden.

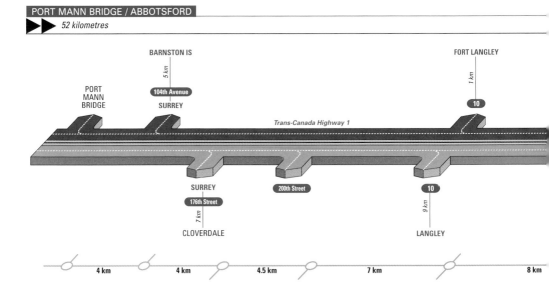

BARNSTON IS

5 km

104th Avenue
SURREY

PORT
MANN
BRIDGE

FORT LANGLEY

1 km

10

Trans-Canada Highway 1

SURREY

176th Street

7 km

CLOVERDALE

200th Street

10
LANGLEY

9 km

4 km   4 km   4.5 km   7 km   8 km

**LOWER FRASER
RIVER VALLEY**

Surrey

Just across the Port Mann Bridge lies Surrey. Vancouver's rapid growth in recent years has left Surrey and other outlying districts a blend of urban and rural influences. High rises routinely overlook dairy farms and berry fields. The changing scene is a theme of the Surrey Museum and Archives, located at Cloverdale. With one of B.C.'s biggest community historical collections, the museum displays relics from prehistoric to pioneer times.

Barnston Island

A 5-minute ferry ride (*below*) brings you to Barnston Island. The departure point is located 5 minutes from the Trans-Canada. Farming and fishing are occupational mainstays for the 150 or so local people. Try a bike or car tour of the 10 km road encircling the island, just 30 minutes from downtown Vancouver. Rusticity rarely gets better than this.

Langley

About 50 airplanes dating from the 1920s to the present, some restored and ready to fly, can be seen at the Canadian Museum of Flight and Transportation at Langley Airport. The museum also has collections of aircraft artifacts and a large aviation library. There are two Langleys, the city and the adjacent farming district, mostly horse country, with pastures, stables, trails, and equestrian events.

Fort Langley

Check out the steam tractors, stump-pullers, and other mechanical marvels of the past at the B.C. Farm Machinery and Agricultural Museum. Located in the historic Village of Fort Langley, the museum also boasts a working century-old sawmill. The Centennial Museum next door has a homestead, a Victorian parlor, and a general store.

Albion Ferry, with 15-minute departures, links the Trans-Canada Highway with Hwy. 7, which runs along the north shore of the Fraser River.

Fort Langley
National Historic Site

Once a Hudson's Bay Company post, Fort Langley, known as British Columbia's birthplace, flourished from 1840 to 1886. Inside a wooden palisade, you will find a whitewashed storehouse, the only surviving remnant of the original fort and one of the province's oldest buildings. There are also reconstructions of six other buildings, notably the "big house," where, on November 19, 1858, British Columbia was proclaimed a Crown colony. Guides in period garb demonstrate pioneer skills and will gladly stop to talk about their roles, and the important part this fort played in B.C.'s history.

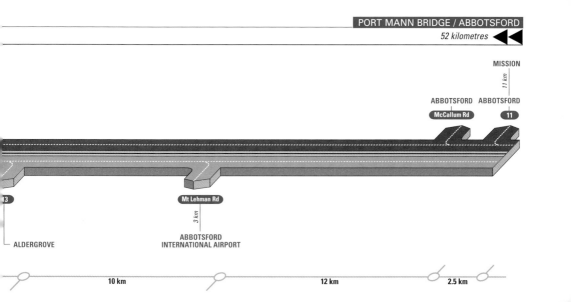

MISSION
11 km

ABBOTSFORD   ABBOTSFORD
McCallum Rd   11

3

Mt Lehman Rd
3 km

ALDERGROVE

ABBOTSFORD
INTERNATIONAL AIRPORT

10 km   12 km   2.5 km

Aldergrove

Elephants, giraffes, and hippos—beasts you'd hardly expect to find in the Fraser Valley—thrive here at the Greater Vancouver Zoological Centre. The site shelters more than 115 species, including endangered creatures such as Siberian tigers and white rhinos. You can tour the zoo by foot, bike, or mini-train. A petting zoo will appeal to kids.

The Aldergrove Lake Regional Park, near the U.S. border, is a popular spot for swimming, hiking, and horseback riding—and mountain viewing. A commanding peak, the potentially volcanic Mount Baker, looms largely just across the border.

Abbotsford International Airport

During the second weekend in August, more than 300,000 flying fans flock to the Abbotsford International Air Show, the largest event of its kind in North America. Featured performers include the world's top stunt pilots and aerobatic teams. Participants in the week-long festival preceding the main show can enjoy skydiving, hot-air balloon rides, and kite flying.

Abbotsford

Abbotsford—"the raspberry capital of Canada"—is situated in one of the nation's most productive agricultural areas. Its setting is also picturesque: snowy peaks form a backdrop for rolling pastures and berry fields. Apart from the International Air Show, Abbotsford celebrates two other popular events: the Bradner Flower Show in April showcases daffodils, tulips, and other floral output from nearby fields and nurseries, and the Abbotsford Berry Festival in July celebrates the region's abundant crops.

Abbotsford's past lives on at Trethewey House, built in the 1920s and now a museum. Exhibits at the Fraser River Trout Hatchery trace the development of rainbow, cutthroat, and steelhead trout.

Mission

Pointing with pride to some 10 mills producing cedar products, Mission can support its claim as "the world's shakes and shingles capital." At nearby Hatzic Rock, archaeologists have uncovered evidence of human habitation dating back 9,000 years, a find which makes this region one of B.C.'s oldest-known dwelling places. The first European settlement at Mission itself was a Roman Catholic mission founded by Oblate Fathers in 1861. The remnants survive at Fraser River Heritage Regional Park. Westminster Abbey, a Benedictine monastery built in 1952-84, is open on weekdays and Sunday afternoons. The 51 m high Pfitzer Tower dominates the monastery's site on Mount Mary Ann, overlooking the Fraser River.

At the Abbotsford International Air Show, teams from all over the world perform amazing aerobatic feats. Among the star performers are Canada's Snow Birds.

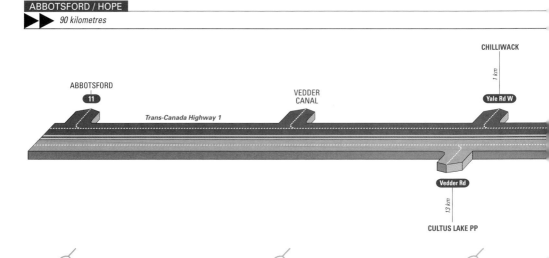

CHILLIWACK

1 km

ABBOTSFORD
11

VEDDER
CANAL

Yale Rd W

Trans-Canada Highway 1

Vedder Rd

13 km

CULTUS LAKE PP

19 km   17 km   16 km

LOWER FRASER
RIVER VALLEY

Chilliwack

This Fraser Valley community of 62,000 calls itself the "city of festivals." The year-round lineup of happenings embraces the performing arts as well as agricultural and community events. In May, the three-week Country Living Days offer horse racing, parades, and the sweet sounds of Dixieland jazz. Those who prefer physical challenges can try whitewater rafting on the Chilliwack River rapids.

Situated amid prosperous farms and forests, Chilliwack has earned another epithet—"the green heart of B.C." Agricultural history is one of the themes of the Chilliwack Museum, housed in a restored turn-of-the-century former city hall. Old-fashioned farm gear also illustrates this theme at Antique Powerland.

Cultus Lake Provincial Park

Despite an unpromising name—"cultus" means "worthless" in Chinook—Cultus Lake is one of B.C.'s leading recreational havens. Cultus Lake Provincial Park offers lakeside and wilderness campsites, plus kayaking, windsurfing, and horseback riding. One of the park's best hiking trails is the "Seven Sisters," named for seven mighty Douglas firs on the route. Nearby Cultus Lake Waterpark offers a heart-stopping 22 m free-fall "Fear Zone" slide. In June, the Cultus Lake Indian Festival highlights war-canoe races with teams of up to 11 native paddlers.

Minter Gardens

In 1972 Brian and Fay Minter set up this show garden as an offshoot of their nursery and greenhouse business. Today, Minter Gardens, with a variety of magnificent theme gardens, have become a popular tourist attraction. Aviaries, fountains, mazes, topiary, a petting zoo for kids, and a fragrance garden for the blind are among elements the Minters have added to enhance their charming creation.

Bridal Veil Falls Provincial Park

Located as it is just off the Trans-Canada Highway, this delightful provincial park about 1 km east of Minter Gardens is a spot that you might pass unawares. A short walk in the woods leads to Bridal Veil Falls, a cascade as delicate and lovely as its

The Minter Gardens boast 11 differently themed sections. This picturesque walkway passes through a section devoted to the art of topiary.

On the beach at Harrison Lake, artists, who are expert in fashioning fabulous forms by mixing grains of sand with water, compete in the World's Sand Sculpture Competition in early September.

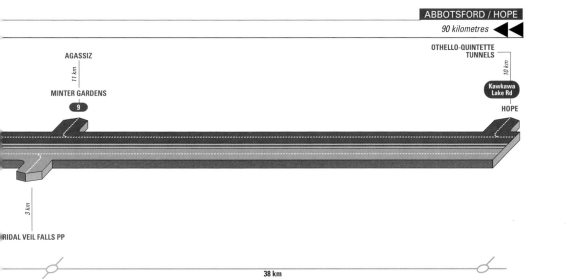

name suggests. A viewing platform, at the foot of mighty Mount Cheam, is also a perfect venue for picnics.

Agassiz

Worth a detour, Agassiz on the north shore of the Fraser River is an ideal base for exploring sites in the Harrison Lake region. (Head north on Hwy. 9 Interchange.) Stop to visit Agassiz's railway museum, located in one of B.C.'s oldest surviving train stations.

Just north of Agassiz, turn west on Hwy. 7 to Harrison Mills. The Kilby Historic Store and Farm there offers a nostalgic look at small-town commerce in the Fraser Valley River during the 1920s and 1930s.

At Harrison Hot Springs (north on Hwy. 9), soak in the steamy, salubrious sulfur- and potash-rich waters, cooled to bearable temperatures at the public baths or the Harrison Hot Springs Hotel. If you visit in the fall, bring your pail and shovel (and your kids) for The World Sand Sculpture Championship at Harrison Lake (see below left).

Hope

If you've seen the action thriller *First Blood*, with Sylvester Stallone as the raging Rambo, you may recognize Hope. Hollywood moviemakers used the rugged forests, gorges, and peaks near town as locations for this and several other movies. Unswayed by

fleeting film fame, Hope is keeping its day jobs in logging, mining, and tourism. Exhibits at the Hope Museum illustrate the region's mining heritage. Other displays recount the stories of native people, explorers, fur traders, and prospectors who have enriched Hope's past.

At Memorial Park downtown, local artist Peter Ryan used a chainsaw to carve root-rot-infected trees into a dozen impressive sculptures of bears, eagles, and other wild creatures.

Next to Memorial Park, the Friendship Gardens commemorate a dark chapter of Canada's history: the internment of more than 2,000 Japanese-Canadians at Tashme Camp near Hope during World War II.

Othello-Quintette Tunnels

One of the must-see sights in southern B.C. is this man-made marvel of five tunnels and two bridges at the edge of a 90 m high gorge on the Coquihalla River. Andrew McCulloch, the chief CPR engineer for this section of railway, considered several routes before cutting straight through solid rock. To map the tunnel sites, he was lowered into the gorge in a wicker basket.

The railway opened in 1916 and the tunnels were used intermittently from then to 1959. Now they are the star attraction of Coquihalla Canyon Provincial Park, some 10 km from Hope on the Kakawa Lake Rd. McCulloch, whose love of Shakespearean drama inspired the tunnel names, may well have appreciated their use as a movie location.

If heights don't bother you, and you're up to a long walk (close to 3 km), follow the Othello-Quintette Tunnels, which skirt a 90 m high gorge at Coquihalla Canyon Provincial Park. The spectacular gorge scenery has attracted many Hollywood filmmakers.

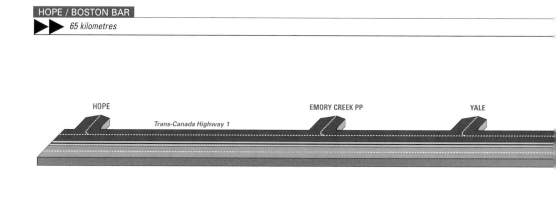

HOPE   EMORY CREEK PP   YALE

Trans-Canada Highway 1

15 km   9 km

FRASER RIVER CANYON

Emory Creek Provincial Park

This quiet park was once a prospecting hot spot. In 1858 gold discoveries on the Fraser River sandbars spawned a sizable settlement (13 streets, nine saloons, a brewery, a newspaper, and a sawmill). It faded quickly, only to rise again in the 1880s as a Chinese settlement, and in the 1930s as a mining training center.

A provincial park since 1956, Emory Creek has campsites, picnic spots, hiking trails—and maybe some ghosts left over from its gold rush past.

Yale

Gold rush memories linger on at Yale. If you dream of striking it lucky, stop here and ask the old-timers for gold-panning lessons.

Originally a raffish, ramshackle river port, Yale served a throng of 20,000 prospectors and other roughnecks during the 1858 gold rush. This city of shacks struck it lucky a second time in the early 1860s, when it became the starting point of the 640 km Cariboo Wagon Road to the Barkerville goldfields. From 1871 to 1886, it served as the CPR's western construction headquarters. In all these hurly-burly years, Yale knew one shining hour: it was here that B.C.'s entry into Canada was proclaimed in 1871.

All this is told at the Yale museum, housed in a restored 1868 dwelling. A walking tour identifies key sites, notably the 1861 Church of St. John the Divine, the oldest church on the B.C. mainland. The cemetery offers many poignant reminders of lives lost during the gold rush and railway booms.

Spirit Cave Trail, 1 km south of town, rewards hikers with grand views of the Cascade Mountains. Yale also offers the adventurous first-class white-water rafting on the Fraser.

Alexandra Bridge

This is the one spot where road builders have been able to span the steep, narrow walls of the Fraser Canyon. Two of three bridges built here survive.

The 1926 suspension bridge (*left*) replaced the original 1863 span created for the Cariboo Wagon Road. (The nearby Alexandra Lodge, built in 1862, was once a popular hostelry on the Cariboo Wagon Road.) In 1962, a fixed arch, linking Chapman (on the Fraser's east bank) with Spuzzum (on the west), was built for the Trans-Canada. At 500 m, this is the world's second longest bridge of its type.

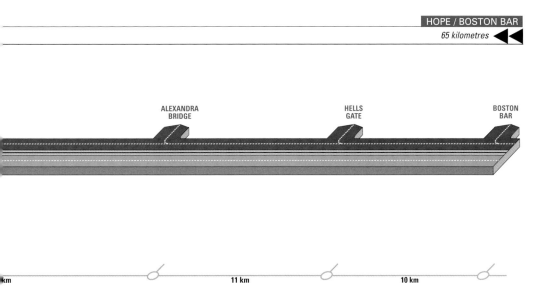

ALEXANDRA BRIDGE   HELLS GATE   BOSTON BAR

km   11 km   10 km

Hell's Gate

At Hell's Gate, the Fraser River, pinched by sheer walls only 36 m wide, is at the narrowest point of its 1,368 km long course. The river surges by at more than 7 m per second. In 1808, Simon Fraser, the first European to explore the entire river, survived his perilous passage through Hell's Gate, and observed: "We had to pass where no human being should venture."

Today, Hell's Gate Airtram affords travelers a thrilling close-up of the river's fury. A 25-passenger cable car (*left*), starting from the Trans-Canada side, descends some 152 m into the gorge on a thrilling journey to the terminal on the west shore. Here are gardens, a restaurant, and displays about salmon. A set of "fishways," built in the mid-1940s and visible from the cable car, help 2 million sockeye a year pass by enroute to spawning grounds upriver.

Boston Bar

Altogether there are seven tunnels between Hope and Boston Bar. The 610 m China Bar Tunnel here is one of the longest in North America. Be sure to drive with care: for a few seconds, a twist in the tunnel hides the light at the end.

The name Boston Bar dates from the 1858 gold rush when the local aboriginal population referred to the numerous American prospectors in the area as "Boston men." The "Bar," a term commonly used locally, refers to sandbars in the Fraser, where gold was first found.

47

Rope-Tethered Rafters Defy the Roiling Fraser Rapids

HIGHWAY 1 / LYTTON

LARRY PYNN, *environment reporter for* The Vancouver Sun, *is a correspondent for* Equinox *and frequent contributor to* Canadian Geographic. *His books include* The Forgotten Trail: One Man's Adventure on the Canadian Route to the Klondike, *published by Doubleday Canada.*

THERE'S NO TURNING BACK NOW. Like locked steel gates, sheer granite cliffs rise vertically on each side of the Fraser Canyon as a gush of water propels our 8.5 m long inflated pontoon forward. Sailor Bar rapids, one of the wildest stretches of white water in British Columbia, lie straight ahead. When the raft hits, a wall of foaming river cascades over the bow, tugging hard at life jackets and soaking everyone in its path.

Screams of terror and excitement rise like a blast of hot steam. Tethered to the twisting, bucking craft by only a hand-held rope, passengers are experiencing the ride of their lives. When, after what seems like an eternity, the Fraser finally spits everyone out the bottom end of the rapids, the sense of euphoria kicks in like a narcotic. With enthusiastic approval of the 20 people aboard, the rafting guide revs up the 40-hp motor, turns the raft around, and heads back up the eddies to do it all over again.

Sailor Bar is just one of many heart-stopping spots on a raft excursion down the Fraser River. How eagerly explorer Simon Fraser would have tackled them on one of today's rafts. These well-engineered craft are built of neoprene, a resilient synthetic rubber that absorbs shocks well when inflated. Fraser, for whom the river is named, had only birch-bark canoes to navigate British Columbia's longest, mightiest river. Indeed, the roiling waters of the Fraser Canyon—a 600 m deep geologic formation carved into the Interior Plateau over millions of years—were fierce enough to snap canoes in half during the 1808 North West Company expedition downriver. Even portaging proved life-threatening, forcing Fraser's men to scale the steep canyon walls on spindly wooden ladders fashioned by Interior Salish Natives.

Today, the small Fraser Canyon communities of Lytton, Boston Bar, and Yale cater to adventure-seekers wishing to experience the tumultous thrills of early exploration. Guided rafting excursions range from easy half-day trips to challenging five-day journeys. Only motorized rafting is allowed through the canyon.

Many rafting excursions begin at Lytton, which holds a strategic position at the confluence of the silty brown Fraser and the deep-blue Thompson, an equally popular rafting river flowing in from the northeast. Once launched, the raft follows the current, passing through a semiarid landscape dominated by ponderosa pine and bunch-grass, where California bighorn sheep munch and rattlesnakes lurk. Summer temperatures here occasionally soar to 40°C.

Out of Lytton, the Fraser proceeds calmly at first, allowing glimpses of ranch land snaking up the hillsides. This is no pristine wilderness. That disappeared when the railway arrived. The Canadian Pacific and Canadian National railway lines now occupy opposite riverbanks. High above the south bank, motorists speed along the Trans-Canada. And nearby, there are reminders of the Cariboo Wagon Road—a trail pushed through to the Interior during the 1858 gold rush.

Clear-cuts on the hillsides are noticeable as you approach Boston Bar. Now the Fraser begins to flex its muscles, picking up speed as the terrain gradually changes to a wet coastal forest. Rafters sense the canyon whizzing by as they hurtle through a series of rapids—Scuzzy Rock, China Bar and, ultimately, Hells Gate—the narrowest part of the canyon.

Huge whirlpools and waves often hit the raft at this infamous, churning gorge—a 36 m wide, 180 m deep squeeze. Water has been clocked rushing through here at more than 7 m per second. Because of the extreme danger, expedition companies are forbidden to raft Hells Gate during a six-week period of high runoff in spring. The danger was highlighted in 1979, when a guide and two passengers drowned. It was but one tragedy in a series of rafting mishaps, in which 1987 was the blackest year. The deaths of 12 people across British Columbia over a seven-week period that year led to greater provincial regulation of commercial rafting.

A provincial Registrar of Commercial River Rafting now works with the industry to set standards for commercial operators—licensing guides, setting minimum raft sizes, even closing certain stretches of water such as Bridge River Rapids on the Fraser above Lillooet. Today, rafts flip rarely, and rafting fatalities are rarer still.

> *Huge whirlpools and waves often hit the raft ...*

As you bounce your way through Hells Gate, you are conscious of the aerial tram dropping 150 m to a restaurant and viewing station. And in salmon-migration season, you will thrill to the sight of millions of salmon surging upriver through a man-made fishway.

Some 30 km downstream, the biggest rapids await on the lower canyon—at Sailor Bar and Saddle Rock, just below Spuzzum. Along this stretch in late summer, you will see Natives at their traditional salmon fishing spots, perched precariously on rock outcrops.

A short, calming drift downriver leads to the tiny community of Yale. A bustling city of 20,000 during the gold rush, it marked the southern terminus of the Cariboo Road. Yale has also served as navigation headquarters for ships headed up the Fraser, so it is a fitting place to end a wild, wet raft ride on the river.

Larry Pynn

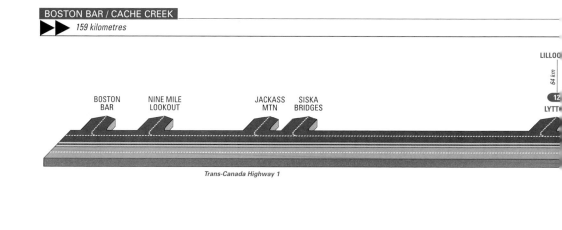

LILLOO

64 km

12

LYTT

BOSTON BAR NINE MILE LOOKOUT JACKASS MTN SISKA BRIDGES LYTT

Trans-Canada Highway 1

9 km   16.5 km   6 km   42.5 km

ALONG THE THOMPSON RIVER

Lytton

The name honors Sir Edward Bulwer-Lytton (1803-1873), who was British colonial secretary when this spot became a gold rush hotbed in 1858. The village, at the junction of the Fraser and Thompson rivers, is one of Canada's warmest and driest places. Known as "The Rafting Capital of Canada," Lytton offers trips—ranging from three hours to five days—on local rivers (see pages 48-49). A hiking trail leads to nearby Stein Valley and Nlaka'pamux Heritage Park, the last major, biologically complete, unlogged valley in southwestern B.C.

Lillooet

Lillooet's past is bound up with the Cariboo Wagon Road: the Mile 0 cairn marks the original southern departure point. The extra-wide main street was built to ensure that wagons, pulled by teams of up to 20 oxen, could make U-turns. The Bridge of 23 Camels recalls the use of these animals for carrying miner's supplies. Gold rush relics are among the displays at the Lillooet Museum, housed in a converted Anglican church. The Miyazaki Heritage House, built in 1890, has an art gallery and the office of Dr. Masajiro Miyazaki, who gave the house to the community.

Ashcroft Manor

The Cornwall brothers, Clement and Henry, settled here in 1862, establishing a ranch they called Ashcroft Manor after their family home in England. Even in the wilderness, the brothers kept up English country life rituals, such as afternoon tea and riding to hounds—albeit across scrubland in pursuit of coyote. When the Cariboo Wagon Road came by in 1863, the Cornwalls built a road-house for miners heading north to the goldfields. Reincarnated as an arts-and-crafts store, art gallery, and tea room, the road-house still welcomes visitors.

Ashcroft

Deep in British Columbia's hot, dry, and high interior, Ashcroft nestles in the greenery beside the Thompson River. With a huge open-pit copper mine nearby (tours are available), the community bills itself as the "copper capital of Canada." Ashcroft Museum exhibits recall the village's role in the late 1800s as a key transshipment point between the CPR and the Cariboo Wagon Road. A heritage B.C. Express depot, built in 1911, now houses a bookstore and an arts-and-crafts shop.

Cache Creek

Vast cattle ranches, wide-open grass-lands, and working cowboys perpetu-ate the aura of the "old west" in the Cache Creek area. Originally a hiding place for trappers' furs, Cache Creek became a stopover on the Cariboo Wagon Road in the 1860s. Cariboo Highway 97 improvements in the 1950s, and the opening of the Trans-Canada

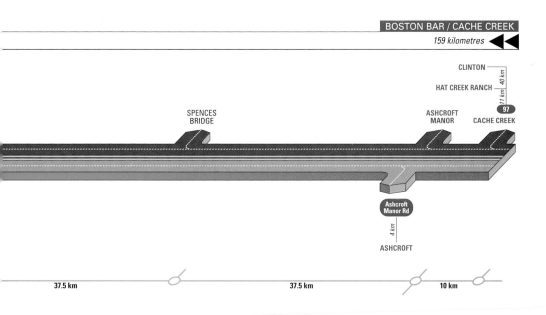

CLINTON
HAT CREEK RANCH — *40 km*
11 km
97
SPENCES BRIDGE
ASHCROFT MANOR
CACHE CREEK

Ashcroft Manor Rd
4 km
ASHCROFT

37.5 km   37.5 km   10 km

Ashcroft Manor (left) was renowned for its hospitality to miners passing through on the Cariboo Wagon Road. Present-day guests at the Historic Hat Creek Ranch, also a stopping place on the old road, still take wagon rides, but now strictly for fun.

Highway in the 1960s, revived the community. The area, rich in jade, attracts rock hounds, and local enthusiasm for vintage automobiles is reflected in the '50s cars seen in town and at the "Graffiti Days" each June. The Nl'ak'apxm Eagle Motorplex is a popular regional drag strip. Whitewater rafting and trail riding are also available.

The board-covered 1894 log church in the village of Bonaparte, some 3 km north of town, merits a visit.

Cariboo Highway 97

Stretching from Cache Creek to Prince George, Hwy. 97 retraces portions of the original Cariboo Wagon Road. Built in the early 1860s to handle the flow of gold seekers heading north, the road ran from Lillooet to Soda Creek. Stopping places, every 15 miles or so on the route, were named for their distance from Mile 0 at Lillooet. When the road was extended south from Clinton to Yale and north to the Barkerville goldfields, some of these rest-stop names were changed—Mile 47, for example, became Clinton. Today's Hwy. 97 remains a vital route for transport and travel.

Historic Hat Creek Ranch

Many stopping houses once lined the Cariboo Wagon Road. Now, only one remains in its original condition, Historic Hat Creek Ranch, which is just off Hwy. 99, some 11 km north of Cache Creek. Built in 1863,

the ranch, now run by the B.C. Heritage Trust, comprises 24 buildings, including the Hat Creek House Hotel and an 1893 B.C. Express horse barn. An original stagecoach, farm machinery, a blacksmith shop, and a saddlemaker are at the site. Trail rides and wagon tours are available.

Clinton

Originally called 47 Mile House, this town was renamed for Lord Henry Clinton (1811-1864), the British colonial secretary after Sir Edward Bulwer-Lytton. With something of a frontier atmosphere still, present-day Clinton is a base for resorts, guest ranches, and fishing camps. It also offers year-round recreational opportunities, ranging from trail riding in the summer to alpine and cross-country skiing in the winter.

In May, Clinton hosts its annual ball, possibly the oldest social event of its kind in the province. First held in 1868, the ball drew people from all over the region to dance, drink, and gamble at the Clinton Hotel. The hotel was destroyed by fire in 1958, but wine decanters from the bar and other mementos can be seen at the South Cariboo Historical Museum.

A must-see site north of Clinton is The Chasm, a 1.5 km long and 120 m deep gash in the earth dating back some 10,000 years. When sunlight streams in, the mineral layers of the sheer walls blaze brilliantly with color. The park at the site has picnic sites and hiking trails.

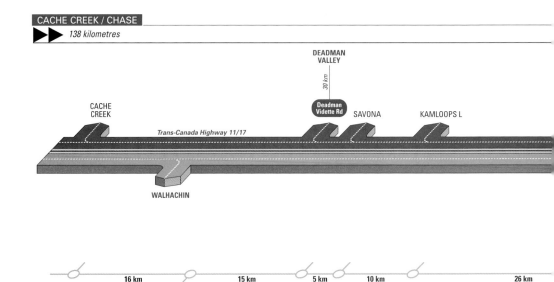

DEADMAN
VALLEY

30 km

CACHE
CREEK

Deadman
Vidette Rd   SAVONA   KAMLOOPS L

Trans-Canada Highway 11/17

WALHACHIN

16 km   15 km   5 km   10 km   26 km

**ALONG
THE THOMPSON
RIVER**

Walhachin

Just north of Hwy. 1, about 15 km west of Cache Creek, you can spot remnants—withered fruit trees, an abandoned irrigation system—of a dream to make the desert bloom. In 1908, a group of 70 English settlers arrived at Walhachin hoping to transform an 18 km² tract of arid land into orchards. The planned community contained houses set on substantial lots, a hotel, a golf course, and a polo field. The settlers successfully constructed an elaborate system of ditches and conduits to irrigate some 16,000 fruit trees. But their inexperience, compounded by the hard climate and poor soil, brought setbacks. When World War I broke out, nearly every man in Walhachin volunteered, possibly to escape the hardship of their pioneer existence. In their absence, storms and flooding destroyed the irrigation system. After the war, few settlers returned, and their dream became a memory.

Deadman Valley

Take a day to explore the secrets of this intriguing valley by following the 30 km gravel road running north from Hwy. 1. Its natural features include a chain of fishing lakes, a 60 m waterfall, and hoodoos (rock pillars). Rock hounds can unearth agates and petrified wood in this valley. (You can get

Mantled in pine forests, eroded reddish cliffs of volcanic origin rise up along the road running through Deadman Valley, one of the hottest and driest spots in B.C.'s interior.

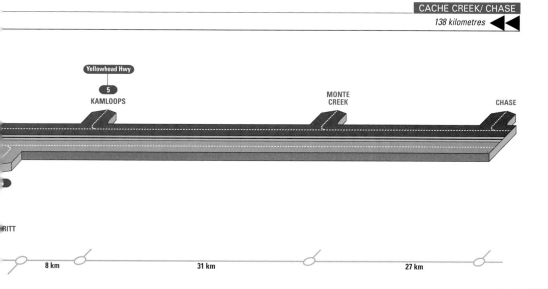

8 km   31 km   27 km

rockhounding permission from Deadman Creek Ranch.) If you decide to stay a while, area resorts offer comfortable chalets. Trail rides can be arranged (by the hour, day, or week) to gold mines and abandoned homesteads. The valley's beauty is somewhat belied by the name, which recalls the 1815 murder of a North-West Company employee.

Merritt

The Coldwater Hotel, this city's major landmark, features a shrimp-pink exterior, tiered balconies, and a four-story tower topped by a copper dome. Built in 1908, two years after Merritt was founded, the hotel has been the center of the community's social life ever since. Other notable landmarks are the 1876 Murray Church and the two-story log tourism office. Built at the junction of the Coldwater and Nicola rivers, Merritt is encircled by ranching country. Canada's largest ranch, the 2,200 km² Douglas Lake Ranch (tours available) is within easy reach. Merritt promises "A lake a day as long as you stay." With 15 lakes and abundant water sports in the Nicola Valley, it can easily make good on the promise.

Kamloops

This city of 75,000 enjoys more than 2,000 hours of sunshine per year. Such toasty weather makes Kamloops a golfers' paradise, and there are five 18-hole courses within easy reach of downtown. The region is renowned for some of British Columbia's best fishing. A 2,786 m double-chair lift at nearby Tod Mountain is the longest in North America. Situated at the junction of the North and South Thompson rivers, Kamloops has been a destination for travelers since its establishment as a fur-trading post in 1812. Today, the city is a trade and distribution crossroads and the administrative center for a

Between Savona and the city of Kamloops, the Trans-Canada Highway skirts Kamloops Lake, whose blue-green waters are framed by a hilly, bone-dry terrain.

vast area of B.C.'s interior. Its mainstays are farming, mining, and forestry. With some 1,100 ranches in the area, Kamloops is also the center of B.C.'s cattle industry. The area's history is recounted at Kamloops Museum, the Firehall Museum, and the

Rocky Mountain Rangers Military Museum. Popular activities include a two-hour cruise on the paddle wheeler *Wanda Sue* or a walk through the city's turn-of-the-century core. (For more information about Kamloops, see page 243.)

Monte Creek

An infamous American outlaw's last robbery on Canadian soil occurred at Monte Creek. On May 8, 1906, Bill Miner (the "Gentleman Bandit") held up a train, but made away with a measly $15. After an 80 km chase, Miner was captured and sentenced to 25 years in New Westminster Penitentiary. Within a year, he escaped to the United States, where he resumed robbing banks and trains until he was locked up in a Georgia Jail. Miner's story—he was a folk hero in the West, where many disliked the CPR—was told in a much-praised 1982 Canadian film, *The Grey Fox*.

Chase

A popular spot with houseboat enthusiasts, Chase is the westernmost launching point for exploring Shuswap Lake. A road from here leads to Niskonlith Lake Provincial Park, which offers hiking, bird-watching, boating, and swimming. Chase is named for its first settler, Whitfield Chase (1820-1896), who came west from New York State, prospected unsuccessfully for gold on the Fraser and Thompson rivers, then stayed on to become a prosperous rancher.

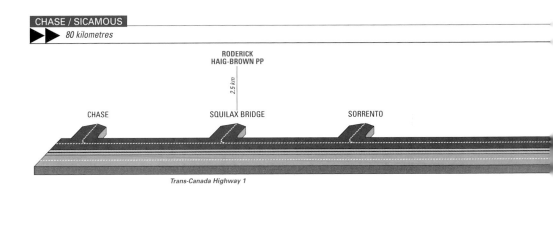

Trans-Canada Highway 1

11 km   10 km   32 km

SHUSWAP LAKE

Roderick Haig-Brown Provincial Park

One of North America's largest sockeye salmon runs occurs on a stretch of the Adams River, which flows through Roderick Haig-Brown Provincial Park. Every four years (1998 and 2002, for example), the run peaks, and as many as 2 million sockeye return here to the river of their birth. (In the intervening years, the numbers, although significant, are fewer.) In early October, the salmon begin their journey from the Pacific, traveling inland along the Fraser, Thompson, and South Thompson rivers, through Little Shuswap and Shuswap lakes, to the Adams River. The arduous upstream journey takes 17 days and cover 485 km. Although the fish die after spawning, their eggs hatch in the gravel, which protects them from scavengers and the winter cold. In February, the offspring set off from the Adams River for the Pacific—and the sockeye's life cycle begins again.

The park is named for a B.C. magistrate, angler, and writer, who campaigned to have the

Silvery sockeye salmon turn crimson first, then green, on their arduous journey from the Pacific to their spawning grounds in the Adams River shallows.

spawning grounds protected. Outside the spawning season, the river is used by kayakers, canoeists, and rafters eager to try its white waters. On the river's banks, archaeologists have unearthed evidence of prehistoric native settlements.

Shuswap Lake

Situated amid the Monashee Mountains and the Shuswap Highlands, Shuswap Lake's four large arms (Main, Salmon, Anstey, and Seymour) give it the appearance of a crooked H. With 1,000 km of shoreline, this aquatic playground offers beaches, picnic areas, nature walks, and camp sites. These amenities can be enjoyed at more than 20 provincial parks,

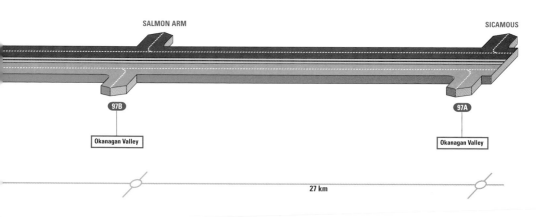

SALMON ARM · SICAMOUS · 97B · Okanagan Valley · 97A · Okanagan Valley · 27 km

some accessible by car or ferry, others only by boat. Houseboats are a popular way of exploring the lake, and several parks provide day and overnight mooring facilities. Hiking trails on Copper Island lead to superb vistas of the lake, which is named after the Shuswap Indians, the largest tribe in the B.C. interior.

Salmon Arm

With a view to creating "a face on the lake," Salmon Arm is renewing its waterfront. This city of 15,000 already claims North America's largest fresh-water pier, a 300 m structure that juts into the shimmering blue waters of Shuswap Lake.

Bird-watchers will delight in the Salmon Arm Bay Nature Enhancement Area near downtown. It offers glimpses of the rare Clark's and western grebes, as well as 230 other bird species. R.J. Haney Heritage Park includes a 1918 schoolhouse and the turn-of-the-century Mount Ida Church, where marriages are still performed.

Sicamous

In Shuswap, Sicamous means "squeezed in the middle," an apt name for the "narrows," or slim channel, between Mara and Shuswap lakes, which Sicamous overlooks. Known as the "houseboat capital of Canada," Sicamous has the largest fleet of rental houseboats in the country. Anyone planning a cruising holiday can choose from hundreds of such vessels offered for rent at a dozen or so firms at Sicamous

With passengers crowded on the decks, the paddle-driven MV Phoebe Ann leaves the Sicamous waterfront on one of its daily excursions to other Shuswap Lake destinations.

marinas. The pleasure craft are easy to run according to the houseboat operators, who will provide instructions before you set sail.

A cruising holiday is the best way to see some of the region's hidden beauty spots and water-falls, but especially such treasures as the native pictographs painted with ocher on rock faces centuries ago. Sicamous is also the home port of the stern-wheeler *Phoebe Ann*, which sails from here carrying mail, supplies, and passengers. Visitors will enjoy the popular day-long run to Seymour Arm.

Okanagan Valley

Hwys. 97A and 97B lead south to the 20 km wide Okanagan Valley, which stretches from Salmon Arm to the U.S. border. The valley lies between the Cascade and Columbia mountains, its heart the Okanagan Lake, and its mild climate making it an ever-more-popular recreational and residential area.

The valley's northern section favors market and dairy farming; the desertlike southern section grows fruit by irrigation. Apples were first planted here in 1859 by Oblate Father Charles-Marie Pandosy. Viticulture began in the 1920s and now 22 of B.C.'s 25 major wineries are found here. Grapes ripening on the vine (*above*) are a common sight. Local people celebrate the bountiful crop at wine festivals, held in May and September.

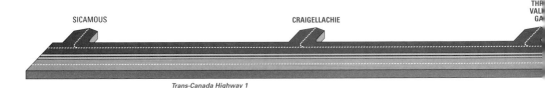

SICAMOUS   CRAIGELLACHIE   THR
                                                            VAL
                                                            GA

Trans-Canada Highway 1

25.5 km   22 km

MOUNT REVELSTOKE NATIONAL PARK

Against a picturesque mountain backdrop, historic buildings from all over B.C. have been reassembled at Three Valley Gap, where the life and spirit of the old mining towns have been re-created.

Craigellachie

Here, on Nov. 7, 1885, the last spike in the Canadian Pacific Railway was driven by Donald Smith (later Lord Strathcona). A cairn, erected in 1927, marks the site. There is a picnic area alongside. The spot is named for a rocky landscape in Morayshire, Scotland, where Smith grew up.

Craigellachie is also the site of Beardale Castle Miniatureland. There, in startling contrast to their mountainous surroundings, one finds an English Tudor village, a prairie town, a Swiss mountain community and other re-creations in perfect 1/25 scale.

Three Valley Gap

A town called Three Valley flourished briefly in the 1880s, where Eagle Pass cuts through the rugged Monashee Mountains. In the 1950s, the Bell

At Craigellachie, a cairn marks the spot where the "last spike" to complete the CPR was driven in 1885.

family decided to bring it back and, over the years, family members have assembled a collection of historic buildings from around the province. Among the structures are the Hotel Bellevue from Sicamous, St. Stephen's Church (now a popular site for weddings), and the Golden Wheel Saloon. The Walter Moberly Theatre honors the government surveyor who, in 1865, found the route through the Monashees by watching the path of the eagles.

Revelstoke

A railway town for a century, Revelstoke has been renewing its image as a travel destination in recent years. It is a natural move for a city blessed with extraordinary natural attractions—the Monashee and Selkirk mountains, two national parks just minutes away, location on the Columbia River—and a strong tourism history—the community was originally known as "The Capital of Canada's Alps" and later as "The Mountain Paradise." Revitalization has involved restoring its Victorian downtown and opening Grizzly Plaza, where a band shell provides free summer entertainment. Visitors can explore the community on a self-guided heritage walking/driving tour, or visit any of several museums. The Revelstoke Museum, housed in the old post office, features local rail, logging, mining, business,

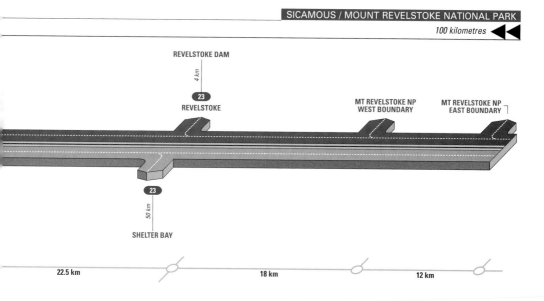

REVELSTOKE DAM

4 km

23
REVELSTOKE

MT REVELSTOKE NP
WEST BOUNDARY

MT REVELSTOKE NP
EAST BOUNDARY

23

50 km

SHELTER BAY

22.5 km   18 km   12 km

Meadow in the Sky Parkway ascends from Mount Revelstoke's forested base to its meadowed summit, which offers hiking trails and superb vistas of the Columbia River valley, the city of Revelstoke, and various peaks of the Monashee and Selkirk ranges.

and social history. Displays at the Revelstoke Railway Museum recall the age of steam. One impressive specimen is the Mikado P-2k 2-8-2 engine that pulled CPR freight trains through the mountains in the 1940s and 1950s. A 1923 Bickle fire engine has pride of place at The Firemen's Museum, and if you are interested in pianos, you will find all sorts of squares, uprights, and baby grands at the piano museum. The Enchanted Forest features 250 fairy-folk figurines and a boardwalk through an old-growth forest.

Shelter Bay

Hwy. 23 south of Revelstoke is a pleasant drive along the shores of Upper Arrow Lake. At Shelter Bay, there is camping, swimming, boating and fishing in Arrow Lakes Provincial Park.

Revelstoke Dam

At 175 m, this dam on the Columbia River just north of Revelstoke is Canada's highest concrete dam. On a self-guiding tour, you take an elevator to the crest of the dam, which offers spectacular views of mountains, forests, water, and the big dam itself. There are picnic sites at Columbia View Provincial Park at the park entrance, and recreational facilities upriver.

Meadows in the Sky Parkway

Open from about mid-July to mid-October, this 26 km road from the heart of Revelstoke to

the top of Mount Revelstoke begins in a dense rain forest and zigzags upward to alpine meadows. From the summit lookout, the short Meadows in the Sky Trail leads to The Icebox—a shaded rock cleft enclosing a permanent patch of ice. This trail leads to others going to Eva and Miller lakes, and Upper and Lower Jades lakes. One of the summit's most breathtaking sights, Eva Lake, is situated on a ledge that plummets more than 100 m into a valley below.

Mount Revelstoke National Park

This region's beauty and splendor led local folk to push for the creation of the national park in 1914. It encompasses mountain meadows and lakes, and the jagged peaks of the Selkirk Range. From Revelstoke, you can take Meadows in the Sky Parkway to the park's western sector, or follow the Trans-Canada, which parallels the Illecillewaet River for about 16 km before entering the park, where it skirts the southeastern boundary.

Some 60 km of hiking trails traverse the park. Two of the shortest are accessible just off the Trans-Canada: the Skunk Cabbage Boardwalk follows a valley teeming with bird life, and the Giant Cedars Boardwalk lets you stroll through an ancient rain forest.

Although the park has no campgrounds (some backcountry camping is permitted), there are private campgrounds in the city of Revelstoke.

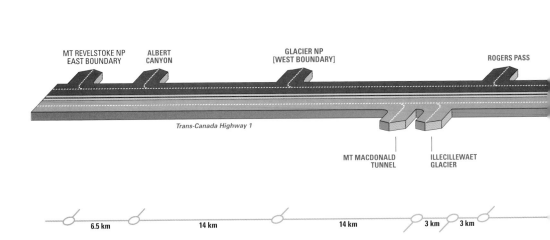

MT REVELSTOKE NP
EAST BOUNDARY ALBERT CANYON GLACIER NP [WEST BOUNDARY] ROGERS PASS

MT MACDONALD TUNNEL ILLECILLEWAET GLACIER

Trans-Canada Highway 1

6.5 km 14 km 14 km 3 km 3 km

GLACIER NATIONAL PARK

Albert Canyon

Naturally heated mineral waters are piped to hot baths and a slightly cooler swimming pool at the Canyon Hot Springs resort here. There are campgrounds, hiking and riding trails, and rafting sites along the Trans-Canada between Mount Revelstoke and Glacier national parks. Look for a roadside ghost town, where old cabins and a school stand forlornly in a field of wild flowers.

Glacier National Park

Until the CPR put the Rogers Pass line through the Selkirk Mountains in the 1880s, few people had ventured into this region of massive glaciers, heavy snows, and frequent avalanches. Within months of the rail line's opening, the beauty of this forbidding land became widely known, and by 1886 the area was declared a national park.

Its most remarkable feature is extensive glaciation: more than 400 glaciers cover 12 percent of this vast park. Heavy snowfalls, up to 23 m in some years, combined with steep mountainsides, make it one of the world's most active avalanche areas. To protect its rail lines, the CPR built snowsheds, which can still be seen. The Trans-Canada passes by the park's main inter-

Construction of the Trans-Canada Highway through Rogers Pass began in 1956 and was completed in 1962. Visible from the highway are several of the lofty, icy peaks that dominate Glacier National Park.

58

GLACIER NP
[EAST BOUNDARY]

DONALD
STATION

36 km

Mount Macdonald Tunnel

Some 15 km in length, this is the longest tunnel in North America, and the longest railway tunnel in the Western Hemisphere. Completed by the CPR in 1986, it cuts through Mount Macdonald and Cheops Mountain, some 390 m below Rogers Pass. It was constructed by two companies working from opposite ends of the mountains: one used a boring machine; the other, the traditional drill-and-blast method. Satellite and laser technology ensured the teams met in the middle. The tunnel's west portal is visible to eastbound Trans-Canada traffic.

Illecillewaet Glacier

Known as "the great glacier," the magnificent Illecillewaet is the product of this region's enormous annual snowfall. You can see it from the Trans-Canada, and from hiking trails that begin at Illecillewaet Campground. For about 75 of the last 100 or so years, the Illecillewaet retreated steadily each year. Then, in 1972, it began advancing, and has continued to do so since at the rate of about 6 m a year.

Nearby is the ruin of a former CPR grand hotel, Glacier House, where once railway passengers detrained to dine. It was built in 1886 so that trains would not have to haul heavy dining cars over Rogers Pass. The 90-room hotel was popular with tourists, especially mountaineering expeditions. But business declined after 1916, when construction of the Connaught Tunnel changed the rail route, and Glacier House closed in 1925.

Rogers Pass

The spectacular road through Rogers Pass has its origins in 1881, when the CPR commissioned Maj. A.B. Rogers to find a route through the Selkirk Mountains. Rogers found that route, through the 1,325 m pass that now bears his name.

But building the line here was a challenge. Ravines east of the pass had to be bridged, and steep grades on the west side required endless loops—and 13 bridges across the Illecillewaet River between the pass and Revelstoke. Snow closed the line during its first winter in 1885, requiring the construction of 31 snowsheds the following year. (The sheds of the original line may still be seen. See also feature, pages 60-61.) In 1916, the opening of the Connaught Tunnel overcame many of these hazards.

The Trans-Canada Highway parallels the railway line through Rogers Pass. A memorial arch at the summit commemorates the highway's completion in 1962. The adjacent Rogers Pass interpretation center, built of massive logs, opened in 1983. Exhibits, including a model of the original CPR railway line, tell the history of the area, the pass, and Glacier and Mount Revelstoke national parks.

Donald Station

A CPR stop grew up at this spot, where the transcontinental line first crossed the Columbia River. The name honors CPR president Donald Smith (later Lord Strathcona).

pretive center, which is at the Rogers Pass summit. Camping is available amid towering cedars at the Loop Brook Campground, or beside a fast-flowing glacier-fed river in the Illecillewaet Campground, both near the highway.

Hikers can explore a variety of wilderness trails, such as the Sir Donald to the Vaux Glacier, and the Flat Creek, which winds through giant hemlock forests. The Loop Brook Trail follows an abandoned rail line, from where you see the glaciers on Mount Bonney and the stone pillars of a bridge that once carried tracks across Loop Brook. (The trail's name recalls the switchbacks on the original line.)

Artillery Fire Keeps Rogers Pass Traffic on the Move

HIGHWAY 1 / ROGERS PASS

VIVIEN BOWERS *writes for several national magazines, including* Canadian Geographic, Beautiful British Columbia, *and* Equinox. *She is a frequent contributor to CBC-Radio's* Almanac.

HEADS UP! Imagine thousands of tonnes of snow thundering down toward you at 320 km/hr. There may be a quiet hissing, or the avalanche may descend with the roar of a freight train, snapping trees, uprooting buildings, tearing up railway lines, and generally wreaking havoc. Between November and April, such terror is a constant threat in the Rogers Pass stretch of the Trans-Canada. At this tight squeeze through the Selkirk Mountains, more than 140 avalanche paths spill downward.

Avalanches in the area have terrorized people since the Pass was discovered by Canadian Pacific Railway (CPR) surveyor Albert Rogers in 1881. The Pass saved the railway a 240 km detour, but its human cost was exorbitant—more than 200 people killed between 1885 and 1911 alone. On one single night in 1910, 62 crewmen, clearing snow and trees from one slide, were fatally buried when a second avalanche swept down from the other side of the Pass. Shortly after, the CPR conceded defeat: by 1916, trains were being routed *under* the treacherous Pass via the 8 km Connaught Tunnel.

Avalanches in the Pass flowed unimpeded until the Trans-Canada was constructed on the old rail bed. The section was completed in 1962, and although two equipment operators were killed in a 1960s slide, no motorist deaths have occurred at the Pass since. Avalanches are as much a threat as ever, but the highway is guarded by a sophisticated, effective defense system. You can see some of the elements as you drive along.

All along the route, slopes above the road have been gouged with earth dams and rubble barriers to block slides from reaching the road. Metal gun emplacements on both sides hold 106 mm recoilless rifles for firing into snow slopes to "control" the avalanches. In effect, slides are triggered while they are small, rather than letting them build up into highway-gobbling monsters. Other safeguards are in place at the highway's eastern end, where the road threads its way through five concrete snowsheds.

A team of guardian angels—nine snow technicians—use their expertise and intuition, backed by sophisticated data from weather stations high in the mountains, to "read" the snowpack and predict when it is likely to slide. They ski into the mountains to dig snow pits, where they look for signs of poor bonding between snow layers—where one layer of snow rests uneasily on another.

Technicians also keep an eye on "indicator" slopes—avalanche paths that do not threaten the road, but where loose layers and slides warn that the snow is becoming unstable. As the hazard mounts, they drop explosives onto test slopes to see if the snow can be persuaded to slide.

Deciding just when the weight of accumulated snow, combined with the pull of gravity, is about to unleash its destructive force is tricky. The technicians do not want to leave it too late, but if they trigger a slide before meteorological conditions are just right, it will not release. There is another factor to consider. Closing the Trans-Canada for too long or too often results in significant economic losses, not to mention a convoy of fuming truckers. Of course public safety is the number one consideration. So when the snow is ready to let loose, the decision is made to clear all traffic from the Pass, and call in the troops.

During the high-risk months, a 10-man artillery crew based at the Pass operates a mobile 105 mm howitzer that fires shells into the snow slopes to send out shock waves that trigger the avalanches. (Technicians must fire the 106 mm rifles if avalanches become a threat in the "shoulder" seasons, when the army is not stationed at the Pass.)

Slides are set off one by one, with the technicians directing the army where to aim the howitzer. Visibility is often awful. In blizzards, targeted areas may not become visible for weeks. To tell whether an avalanche has released adequately, technicians often drive their trucks underneath the slide path to listen to the snow come down. Occasionally, the slide is bigger than anticipated, which calls for a quick getaway.

During the staged slides, the Pass is closed to traffic. Most closures—there are about 60 per winter—last two to four hours. In extreme storms, the highway may be shut for days. But even when the snow is cleared and traffic is moving again, motorists must watch out for dangerous "dusters." Avalanches that are caught by the earth dams above the highway often release clouds of airborne snow that travel great distances. Drive into one of these dusters at your peril: you cannot see a thing. Better get off the road and wait for the snow to settle.

Can the public watch a controlled avalanche coming down? Not a chance. However, there is a good view of the avalanche zone from Avalanche Defence Viewpoint, about 5 km east of the Pass summit. At the summit itself, the visitors' center has several exhibits, describing various aspects of the ongoing battle between men and mountains.

"They drop explosives onto test slopes to see if the snow can be persuaded to slide"

Vivien Bowers

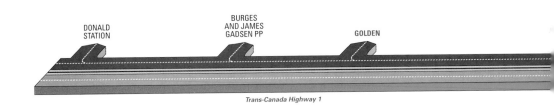

DONALD
STATION

BURGES
AND JAMES
GADSEN PP

GOLDEN

Trans-Canada Highway 1

14 km   11.5 km   26 km

**YOHO
NATIONAL
PARK**

Golden

Situated where
the turbulent
Kicking Horse
and Columbia
rivers meet,
Golden is a railway town,
a lumbering center, and
a recreational paradise. To pro-
mote its mountaineering potential in the early 1900s, the CPR
imported Swiss guides, whose
chalets can still be seen at Edel-
weiss Village, northeast of town.
Today, this community of 4,000
attracts all sorts of outdoor
enthusiasts, ranging from rafters
(*above*) on the Kicking Horse
River to the hang glider wafted
by breezes from nearby peaks.

Yoho National Park

"Yoho," a Cree word expressing
awe, is an apt name for a park
that encompasses belts of rain
forest, great glaciers, and 28
peaks more than 3,000 m high.
Among its best-known sights are

the natural rock bridge
cut by Kicking Horse
River, towering
hoodoos (boulders bal-
anced on pillars of
glacial till), Wapta and
Takakkaw falls, and
beautiful Lake O'Hara (accessible by foot or shuttle bus).
Established in 1886, shortly after
the CPR cut through the Rocky
Mountains at Kicking Horse
Pass, the park had been enlarged
to its present 1,313 km² by 1930.
The Trans-Canada follows the
twisting, Kicking Horse River
through the park. Campers have
a choice of six campgrounds,
including one suitable for winter
camping. Trails, ranging from
short saunters to extended backcountry treks, invite exploration.

Wapta Falls, Yoho National Park

At Wapta Falls, the Kicking
Horse River drops over a ledge
forming a cascade 60 m wide and
nearly 30 m high. You can reach

*Emerald Lake Lodge gives guests
an exhilarating view of blue-green
Emerald Lake, nestling among
Yoho's imposing peaks. A lakeshore
walk leads through the evergreen
woods encircling this beauty spot.*

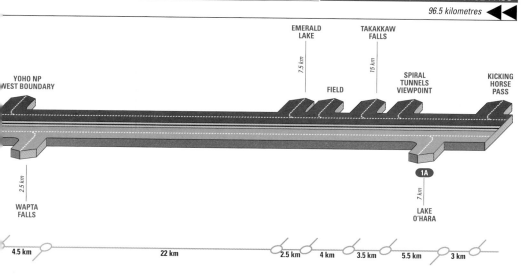

EMERALD LAKE — 7.5 km

TAKAKKAW FALLS — 15 km

YOHO NP WEST BOUNDARY

FIELD

SPIRAL TUNNELS VIEWPOINT

KICKING HORSE PASS

2.5 km

WAPTA FALLS

1A

7 km

LAKE O'HARA

4.5 km | 22 km | 2.5 km | 4 km | 3.5 km | 5.5 km | 3 km

the falls by following a gravel road from the Trans-Canada. It will take you past the Leanchoil March, a natural wildlife viewing area, to a parking lot, where a trail leads to the falls.

Emerald Lake

Fine glacial silt, or rock flour, is the ingredient responsible for the brilliant color that gives this lake its name. Just beside the lake is Emerald Lake Lodge, built in 1902 of hand-hewn timbers. Hiking trails, canoe rentals, and horseback riding are all available nearby. The Natural Bridge, carved from solid rock by the Kicking Horse River, is along the road to the lake.

Field

Situated in the heart of Yoho National Park, Field is both a service center for park visitors and a base for outdoor adventurers, especially mountain climbers. The town lies in the shadow of Mount Stephen. As you look up, you will see a hanging glacier on the side of the mountain and, to its right, an old-mine entrance.

Takakkaw Falls

Takakkaw is Cree for "It is magnificent." Most people who see this 254 m cascade on the glacier-fed Yoho River agree. It is Canada's second-highest waterfall after B.C.'s Della Falls. You can see the falls from a parking lot (accessible by sideroad off the Trans-Canada) or, once there, you can hike to the base for an even more superb view.

Spiral Tunnel Viewpoint

The most treacherous stretch on the original CPR line was the Big Hill between Kicking Horse Pass and Field. For 25 years its 4.5 percent incline (about 45 m to the kilometre) was the cause of wrecks and fatalities. In 1909 two spiral tunnels, located in Mount Ogden and Cathedral Crags, replaced the Big Hill. (The Trans-Canada is built on the Big Hill roadbed.) Though still steep, the Spiral Tunnels provide a more manageable 2.2 percent grade. At the viewpoint, you can watch trains execute their figure-eight maneuver through the tunnels. Displays explain the tunnels' operation.

Lake O'Hara

Another gorgeous green lake in a magnificent mountain setting. And you can get there via a 13 km hike, by shuttle bus or, in winter, by skis. Trails from a lakeshore campground lead to six remote valleys and 16 clear mountain lakes.

Kicking Horse Pass

This 1,625 m high pass straddles several boundaries: the B.C.-Alberta border, the Continental Divide, and Yoho and Banff national parks. The name commemorates an incident near Wapta Lake, where an ornery horse kicked the chest of James Hector, leader of an 1858 survey team. With luck, railway buffs may be rewarded by the sight of freight trains with eight locomotives—equivalent to 24,000 hp—pulling boxcars of lumber over Kicking Horse Pass.

One of the must-see sights in Yoho National Park, Takakkaw Falls is fed by melted snow and ice from Daly Glacier in the Rockies.

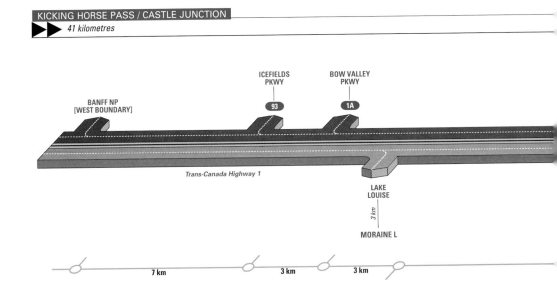

ICEFIELDS PKWY

BOW VALLEY PKWY

BANFF NP [WEST BOUNDARY]

93

1A

Trans-Canada Highway 1

LAKE LOUISE

3 km

MORAINE L

7 km   3 km   3 km

BANFF NATIONAL PARK

Banff National Park

What began in 1885 as a small reserve set up around the hot springs at the base of Sulphur Mountain is now an international mecca. Banff, established in 1887 as Canada's first national park, attracts more than 4 million visitors from around the world annually. Popularity exacts its price: the park is now Canada's most crowded. But that is understandable when you consider that Banff's scenic wonders include 25 mountains—all more than 3,000 m high—and the world's most photographed lakes, Louise and Moraine. It also offers 1,300 km of hiking trails,

14 campgrounds. museums, a lively summer arts festival, and the world-famous Château Lake Louise and Banff Springs hotels.

Icefields Parkway

Hwy. 93, known as the Icefields Parkway, qualifies as one of the most scenic drives in the world. Stretching 229 km from Lake Louise to Jasper, it traverses an unspoiled wilderness of more than 100 glaciers, pristine lakes, and some of the highest Rockies. Within a 50 km of the junction with Hwy. 1 are lakes (Herbert, Hector, Bow, and Peyto) and splendid scenery worth a detour. Some 3 km north of the junction, Herbert Lake warms sufficiently for swimming (rare in this area). Crowfoot Glacier is some 30 km farther on.

Bow Valley Parkway

The 55 km Bow Valley Parkway, or Hwy. 1A, the original route between Banff and Lake Louise, is a leisurely alternative to the Trans-Canada. It offers possible sightings of elk, moose, wolf or bear; and breathtaking views of the Sawback Range and magnificent Castle Mountain. There are lookouts, picnic sites, interpretive displays, and campgrounds along the way.

The parkway provides access to Johnston Canyon (see entry, opposite page) as well as to the ruins of Silver City, a mining town that sprang up in 1883 and was abandoned the following year when prospectors found less silver in the ground than they had hoped.

Banff visitors can stroll across the heights of Sulphur Mountain. It was at the base of this mountain in 1883 that CPR workers found the hot springs that led to the creation of the park. Elk (right) are a common sight at lower levels.

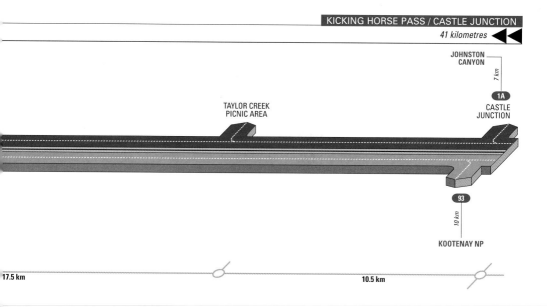

JOHNSTON
CANYON

7 km

1A
CASTLE
JUNCTION

TAYLOR CREEK
PICNIC AREA

93

10 km

KOOTENAY NP

17.5 km   10.5 km

From its birthplace in the icefields of the Rockies, the Bow River flows east to the prairies through Banff National Park. Within the park, the Trans-Canada Highway and Bow Valley Parkway parallel the river's scenic course.

Lake Louise

Canada's most famous lake is known for its turquoise waters, an exquisite setting in an amphitheater of snowcapped peaks, and an imposing waterfront hotel. The lake is named for Princess Louise Caroline Alberta, a daughter of Queen Victoria: the monarch's own name is enshrined in glacier-mantled Mount Victoria that rises majestically from the lake's western shore. Built in 1928 to replace the original 1890 CPR resort hotel, the majestic Château Lake Louise was recently expanded and adds its own imposing style to this mountain grandeur.

Swimming, however tempting, is not possible in Lake Louise, where icy meltwaters keep the water frigid year-round. You can skim its emerald surface by canoe, however, or explore its shoreline on the Lake Louise Stroll, a popular walk by day and delightful on moonlit evenings.

From Lake Louise, you can also head out (with or without park guides) on a network of trails. One popular but demanding trail makes a steep ascent to Lake Agnes. Another challenging, day-long outing leads to the Plain of Six Glaciers, a glorious assemblage of peaks and ice.

For a stirring but effortless view of the area, you can ride the gondola up the side of Mount Whitehorn.

Moraine Lake

If Moraine Lake looks familiar, it may be because you've seen it on one of the older $20 bills.

Encircled by a mountainous palisade, it forms the emerald heart of the Valley of Ten Peaks. You can hike to the top of a moraine at the lake's west side, or follow a trail to Larch Valley, especially lovely when the larches turn golden in the fall. You can also take a 6-hour hike (with park guides) to Eiffel Lake. Accommodation is available at Moraine Lake Lodge, which was designed by internationally acclaimed architect Arthur Erickson.

Johnston Canyon

One of the most traveled trails in the Rockies leads through the grandeur of Johnston Canyon to mountain meadows and a series of cascades and waterfalls. The first section is an easy 45-minute walk through the canyon to the first falls. The next section is a steeper, 3-hour hike to the upper falls. After that, it is another 3 km to the Ink Pots, so called because cold mineral springs bubble into blue- and jade-colored pools in a scenic meadow.

Kootenay National Park

From Banff, take the Kootenay Parkway (Hwy. 93) to some of the intriguing sights in the northern sector of neighboring Kootenay National Park. At Vermilion Pass is the Fireweed Trail, which was burned over in 1968 and has become an area of surprising beauty. Other nearby highlights include Marble Canyon's deep, narrow gorge, and the Paint Pots, cold mineral springs filled with pools of red clay, a traditional source of ocher.

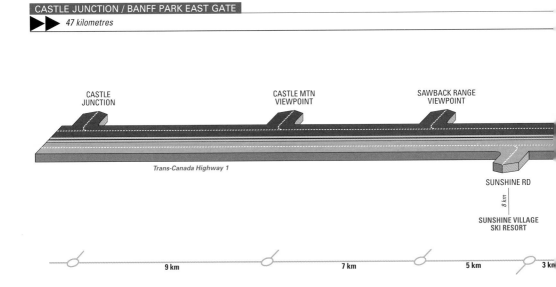

CASTLE
JUNCTION

CASTLE MTN
VIEWPOINT

SAWBACK RANGE
VIEWPOINT

Trans-Canada Highway 1

SUNSHINE RD

8 km

SUNSHINE VILLAGE
SKI RESORT

9 km   7 km   5 km   3 km

**BANFF
NATIONAL
PARK**

Sunshine Village Ski Resort

A ski destination of superlatives,
Sunshine Village (at 2,215 m) is
North America's highest resort.
It has 80 ski runs spread over
three mountains and served by
12 lifts (including eight chair lifts
and a gondola). It also has the
only on-mountain accommodation in the Canadian Rockies, the
longest season, and, not least,
the most snow—a minimum
10 m a year. Sunshine Village is a
major reason why many skiers
consider Banff National Park an
unparalleled ski destination.

Town of Banff

Winter or summer, this town at
the center of Canada's busiest
park bustles with activity. With a
permanent population of about
8,000 it hosts as many as 5 million tourists annually. Hotels and
shopping malls have sprouted in
recent years, creating an up-
tempo, urban atmosphere that
contrasts sharply with the surrounding grandeur, and the ease
with which elk and other wildlife
roam residential areas.

High on the list of attractions
is the Banff Springs Hotel, the

*In addition to
its splendid set-
ting, the town
of Banff is rich
in recreational
and cultural
choices. This
view of Banff
Ave. looks east
to Cascade
Mountain.*

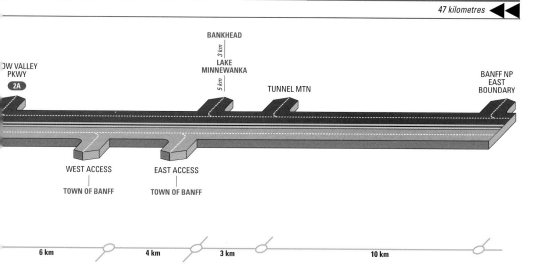

BANKHEAD

3 km

OW VALLEY
PKWY

2A

LAKE
MINNEWANKA

5 km

TUNNEL MTN

BANFF NP
EAST
BOUNDARY

WEST ACCESS

TOWN OF BANFF

EAST ACCESS

TOWN OF BANFF

6 km 4 km 3 km 10 km

first resort in the Canadian Rockies when built in 1888. Enlarged over the years, its 829 rooms are among 3,500 hotel and motel rooms in town, all of them booked all summer.

See the Cave and Basin Hot Springs—the original sulphur springs whose chance discovery led to the park's creation. If you prefer soaking to viewing, try the Banff Upper Hot Springs: this outdoor spring is the only one where swimming is permitted.

Museums and the arts figure prominently among attractions and activities. The Whyte Museum of the Canadian Rockies has art and photographic exhibits and historical displays. You will find local wildlife specimens dating back to the 1860s in the Banff Park Museum. Prehistoric native life on the northern plains and Canadian Rockies is the special focus of the Luxton Museum.

The Banff Arts Festival offers chamber and choral music, opera, jazz, dance and theater. The Bard is here, too, thanks to the Rocky Mountain Shakespeare Company. The Banff Centre for Continuing Education, established in 1933, remains Canada's premier continuing education facility for accomplished musicians, performing and visual artists.

For an over view of the area take one of the Mount Norquay or Sulphur Mountain gondolas. For an up close look, there are horseback tours and covered-wagon trips. Remember, too, that the town is the starting point for canoeing, rafting, hiking trails, and guided sailplane and helicopter outings.

Lake Minnewanka

A 2-hour cruise in a glass-enclosed launch takes visitors across the length of Lake Minnewanka, and through some of the grandest scenery in Banff National Park. Snowcapped peaks rise from the edge of emerald waters. Bighorn sheep, deer, and even bears, routinely appear at water's edge.

Man-made Lake Minnewanka, the largest of Banff's lakes, was created during hydroelectric development in 1941. The old, drowned tourist center of Minnewanka Landing, once the haunt of summer vacationers, is now visited by scuba divers. There are hiking trails along the lake—including a 2-hour tour with park interpreters—plus picnic sites, and boat rentals. This is the only lake in the park where powerboats are permitted. It is especially popular with trout fishermen.

Bankhead

Now a ghost town, Bankhead—at the base of Cascade Mountain, 8 km northeast of Banff on the road to Lake Minnewanka—was a thriving coal-mining center in the early 1900s. With 1,200 residents, tennis courts, a skating rink, and a library, it was the largest town in the region. From 1904 to 1922, it supplied 180,000 tonnes of coal a year to the CPR. But the quality of coal was poor and eventually the mines were shut and the community abandoned. Today the coal mine and the town site are the destinations of an easy walking tour.

The Banff Springs Hotel, a mix of French and Scottish baronial styles, was completed in 1928. Its picturesque locale between the mountains and the Bow River has ensured its enduring popularity with travelers.

67

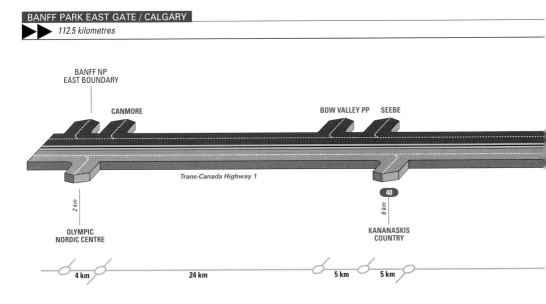

BANFF NP
EAST BOUNDARY

CANMORE

BOW VALLEY PP   SEEBE

Trans-Canada Highway 1

40

2 km

OLYMPIC
NORDIC CENTRE

6 km

KANANASKIS
COUNTRY

4 km   24 km   5 km   5 km

**ALBERTA
FOOTHILLS
COUNTRY**

Canmore

Nestling in the shadow of the Rockies on the Bow River, Canmore, now an outdoor sports center, was born in the 1880s as a railway and coal-mining town. Coal remained king here until the late 1970s, and its role in local development is celebrated at the Canmore Centennial Museum. Exhibits at the restored Northwest Mounted Police barracks, the oldest structure of its kind in Western Canada still on its original site, also recall the early days.

Ralph Connor fans will want to visit the local United Church that bears his name. Under the Connor pen name, the Reverend Charles Gordon (1860-1937) who ministered here in the 1890s was the best-selling author of red-blooded Christian novels such as *The Prospector* and *The Man from Glengarry*.

Olympic Nordic Centre, Canmore

Beginners or experts can explore this center's 70 km of groomed cross-country ski trails, including a lighted 2.5 km trail, especially designed for night skiing. At the 1988 Winter Olympics, this complex was host to competitors in cross-country skiing, biathlon, and other events.

Bow Valley Provincial Park

If you're traveling west, this park on the Bow River is the gateway to the High Rockies. Towering peaks ring its aspen and evergreen forests and its flower-filled meadows create the perfect setting for a summer stroll. You may even glimpse a hummingbird or some of the park's wild orchids.

Internationally renowned for its superb cross-country ski and biathlon trails, the Olympic Nordic Centre near Canmore is a year-round recreational paradise. Here, a mountain biker takes a bumpy spin along one of the forest trails used by Olympian competitors during the 1988 Winter Games.

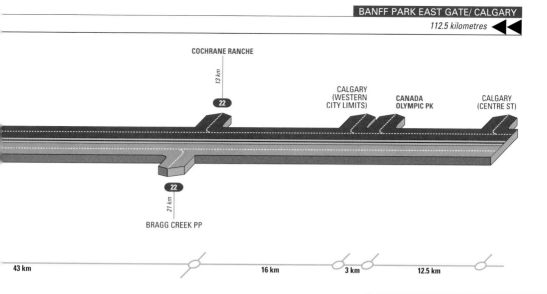

COCHRANE RANCHE

13 km

22

CALGARY
(WESTERN
CITY LIMITS)

CANADA
OLYMPIC PK

CALGARY
(CENTRE ST)

22

21 km

BRAGG CREEK PP

43 km   16 km   3 km   12.5 km

Flags of all nations welcome visitors to Calgary's Olympic Park (below). The Hall of Fame and Museum salutes winter event winners, such as skater Barbara Ann Scott, a 1948 gold medalist, and skier Karen Percy, winner of two bronze medals in 1988.

Seebe

The Passing of the Legends Museum is part of the Rafter Six Ranch, a Western-style resort here that has been the setting for several movies. The museum focuses on Indian themes and hosts native dancing and craft shows during the annual Buffalo Nations Tribal Days in August.

Kananaskis Country

With an abundance of ski hills, hiking trails, and campgrounds, Kananaskis Country—4,250 km² of prairie and mountain southwest of Calgary—is a year-round playground. Its main street is the Kananaskis Trail (Hwy. 40), which runs south from the Trans-Canada and links all major attractions. Accommodations range from high-class hotels to hostels and about 3,000 campsites, some car-accessible, others backcountry, and some suited for recreational vehicles and equestrian groups.

Kananaskis Country has extensive hiking trails, bike paths, and cross-country skiing and snowmobile routes. Ski centers include Nakiska, site of the 1988 Winter Olympic alpine events, with 28 ski runs, a 735 m vertical rise, four chair lifts and no lift lines, and similarly outfitted Fortress Mountain. "Mountain golf at its best" is promised at two 18-hole courses.

And if you are still full of pep and rarin' to go, there are covered-wagon trips, helitours, boating that ranges from calm sailing to whitewater rafting, sleigh rides, and more.

Cochrane Ranche

In 1881, Senator M. H. Cochrane (1824-1903), a Quebec businessman, stocked a 750 km² ranch with thousands of head of cattle imported from the United States. It was the first large scale ranching venture in the region, and even though it collapsed after a few hard winters, it led the way for Alberta's cattle industry. The ranch site is now a provincial historic site with a park offering Western-theme interpretive programs and events. Alberta's ranching and rodeo history is described in the Western Heritage Centre. A *Men of Vision* statue (*above*), honors the pioneering spirit of early ranchers.

Canada Olympic Park, Calgary

On Calgary's outskirts, this site of ski-jumping and luge and bobsled competitions during the 1988 Winter Olympics is now a year-round sports center. Olympic achievers down the years are the subject of exhibits and interactive displays in a three-story Olympic Hall of Fame and Museum. Sport enthusiasts can test their prowess on computerized simulators of the Olympic bobsled/luge track. Summer visitors can hurtle down the last five turns of the real thing. Summer activities also include camps on luge, speed skating, roller jumping, biking, and in-line skating.

69

CALGARY: CITY ON THE MOVE

Wealth from ranching, farming, and oil and natural gas has put Calgary on the fast track to a dynamic future. Dominated by a cluster of jostling skyscrapers, the downtown consists of a compact grid of streets, with attractions ranging from the prestigious Glenbow Museum to the bustling Eau Claire Market, all within easy walking distance. Suburbia begins close to the core, with outskirts proliferating across a landscape of river bluffs and rolling hills. The nearby Rockies hold out the promise of year-round recreation and scenery beyond compare.

Stampede Park and Saddledome
Soaring skyscrapers rise majestically behind the curved roof of the Canadian Airlines Saddledome, home of the Calgary Flames hockey team. A local landmark since 1980, the Saddledome is the centerpiece of Stampede Park, site of the celebrated Calgary Stampede: the 10-day jamboree has been held every July since 1923. The park also hosts trade shows, sports events, concerts, and horseracing. The quickest way to reach the park from downtown is via the rapid transit C-Train.

To The Energeum
This small, intriguing museum, on the main floor of the Energy Resources Building at 640 5th Ave. SW, takes a close-up look at Alberta's oil industry.

To Calgary Science Centre
Just west of downtown at 701 11 St. SW, the centre houses a planetarium and hands-on displays, and presents changing exhibitions.

Eau Claire Market
Adjacent to the Bow River and Prince's Island Park, this busy downtown marketplace has speciality retail stores, restaurants, and a food market.

N

DAQING AVE.

3 AVE.

4 AVE.

5 AVE.

6 AVE.

7 AVE.

8 AVE.

9 AVE.

3 ST. SW

2 ST. SW

1 ST. SW

CENTRE ST.

Petro Canada Centre

Centre for the Performing Arts

Banker's Hall

Devonian Gardens
Alberta's largest indoor garden, the Devonian Gardens are located 15 m above street level on the fourth floor of the Toronto Dominion Square. Visitors can admire more than 20,000 plants, or wander along pathways leading past a creekbed, a forest grove, and fish-filled pools.

Grain Exchange Building
Calgary's first skyscraper, the Grain Exchange (1910) boasts an elegant yellow sandstone exterior. This locally quarried material was widely used in an early 1900s building boom when many of the city's public buildings were erected. Much of the work was reconstruction: the original, mainly wooden structures were destroyed in an 1886 fire. The widespread use of sandstone earned Calgary its Sandstone City nickname.

Calgary Tower
After it opened in 1968, the Calgary Tower's 191 m spire stood tallest in the city—until surpassed by the 210 m **Petro Canada Centre** in 1985, and the 196 m **Banker's Hall** in 1989. In just 62 seconds, the tower's elevator whisks visitors to a revolving observation terrace offering the best views of downtown Calgary and the snow-mantled Rockies rimming the western horizon. The **Visitor Information Centre** is located on the ground floor of the tower.

Chinese Cultural Center

In 1993, artisans renowned for classical architectural workmanship were flown in from China to help build this center, where a museum and ongoing exhibitions provide an overview of Chinese culture and history. Beijing's Temple of Heaven inspired the six-story Great Cultural Hall, which is surmounted by a spectacular, intricately designed, blue, glazed-tile dome with a golden dragon glistening at its center.

CALGARY

Bow River WALK AREA

Calgary Zoo, Botanical Garden, and Prehistoric Park

A footbridge across the Bow River leads to the south entrance of Calgary Zoo, part of which is on St. George's Island. Giraffes and polar bears (*right*) are among the more than 1,200 zoo denizens, as are endangered species such as western lowland gorillas, Siberian tigers, and Sri Lankan elephants. The **Botanical Garden** (consisting of the **Conservatory and Dorothy Harvie Gardens**), also on St. George's Island, contains samples of arid, rain forest, and tropical environments, as well as butterfly gardens. Another footbridge across the Bow leads to the zoo's north shore sites and to **Prehistoric Park,** which displays life-size dinosaur replicas.

Olympic Plaza

Specially created for the 1988 Olympic Winter Games, this spacious open-air space was where the champions received their medals. Now the plaza is used year-round for concerts, festivals, and other events.

Bow River

RIVERFRONT AVE.

MACLEOD TRAIL

Footbridge to St. George's Island

ST. GEORGE'S ISLAND

To Stampede Park and Saddledome (see *above left*)

Calgary Civic Complex

The spiky tower and gables of Calgary's 1911 sandstone City Hall contrast dramatically with the sleek blue glass walls of the adjacent 1985 Municipal Building. This assembly of past and present architectural styles can be best appreciated when viewed from the Olympic Plaza, located just across the street from the civic complex.

Fort Calgary

Volunteers using wooden nails, old-style saws, picks, square-ended shovels, and other 1800s tools and techniques have rebuilt Fort Calgary on its original site at the junction of the Bow and Elbow rivers. Seven years after its 1875 construction by the North West Mounted Police, the original log palisade was torn down and replaced with a barracks. Settlement began around the fort, but when the CPR arrived in 1883, the population shifted from the fort to the area around the railway station. A year later, the city of Calgary was born. An interpretive center describes the fort's history and the NWMP's role in the opening of western Canada.

Glenbow Museum

The epic story of Canada's West comes alive at the Glenbow. The museum's diverse and impressive collection ranges from a native dancer's outfit (*right*) to the personal possessions of families who came west between 1880 and 1950. Western Canada's largest museum, the Glenbow also has a military and arms collection, and offers ongoing art exhibitions. Just across the street from the museum is the city's **Centre for the Performing Arts.**

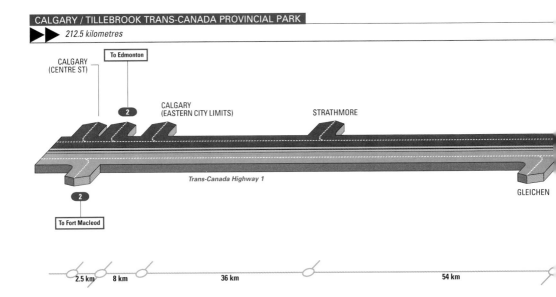

To Edmonton

CALGARY
(CENTRE ST)

CALGARY
(EASTERN CITY LIMITS)

STRATHMORE

2

Trans-Canada Highway 1

GLEICHEN

2

To Fort Macleod

2.5 km   8 km   36 km   54 km

**SOUTH
CENTRAL
ALBERTA**

Now sparsely covered with dry earth plants such as sage and cacti, the distorted, multicolored Badlands were once lush ferny marshlands where prehistoric beasts stomped and lunged through sycamore, magnolia, fig, and chestnut forests. Their skeletons have made Dinosaur Provincial Park a paleontologist's heaven.

Drumheller

If Canada has a dinosaur capital, Drumheller is it. The city lies in the heart of the parched, eroded Alberta Badlands that may be the world's greatest repository of dinosaur fossils. Until the 1950s, Drumheller was a coal-mining area. Now there are oil and gas wells and a lively dinosaur-based tourist industry.

You can tour the Badlands and Red Deer River valley on foot, horseback or hovercraft. Displays at the Drumheller Dinosaur and Fossil Museum explain prehistoric life and such geological processes as coal formation and fossilization. Native and pioneer artifacts are the focus of the Homestead Antique Museum. The Historic Atlas Coal Mine offers guided tours that recount the region's coal-mining history.

Royal Tyrrell Museum of Palaeontology, Drumheller

Canada's only museum devoted exclusively to paleontology (the study of ancient life) is 6 km northwest of Drumheller in Midland Provincial Park. Its 800-fossil collection includes the world's largest displays of complete dinosaur skeletons, including *Tyrannosaurus rex* and *Stegosaurus* (*right*). Exhibits describe 4.5 billion years of the earth's history, and explain Alberta's fossil heritage. There are hands-on displays, computer simulations, and a prehistoric garden. The museum honors the man who, in 1884, discovered the skull of *Albertosaurus*, explorer-geologist Joseph Burr Tyrrell (1858-1957).

Bassano

"The best in the West by a dam-site," boasts Bassano, where Bow River dams provide irrigation for 800 km^2 of agricultural and recreational areas. An 80-site campground at Crawling Valley Reservoir offers swimming, boating, and fishing. Local farmers, blessed with Alberta's longest growing season, grow wheat, oats, canola, and raise beef cattle.

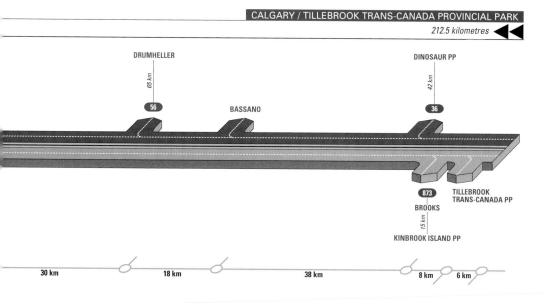

DRUMHELLER
65 km
56

BASSANO

DINOSAUR PP
42 km
36

873 TILLEBROOK
TRANS-CANADA PP

BROOKS
15 km

KINBROOK ISLAND PP

30 km   18 km   38 km   8 km   6 km

Dinosaur Provincial Park

New species of dinosaur are discovered virtually every year in this 90 km² patch of the Alberta Badlands, making it one of the world's richest fossil beds. The region was a prime dinosaur habitat 65 million years ago and ongoing erosion of the sandstone and mudstone landscape regularly exposes remains of the ancient creatures. The park has been declared a UNESCO World Heritage Site.

Dinosaur displays and explanations of the area's geological past are featured at the Royal Tyrrell Museum of Palaeontology field station in the park. (The museum itself is about two hours to the west; *see facing page*.) Museum and park personnel cooperate to provide a variety of displays, interpretive programs, slide and video presentations, and lectures. You can watch laboratory staff prepare specimens for preservation and display, or take guided bus tours and hiking trips to the fossil fields, areas where public access is usually restricted.

Brooks

An engineering marvel that was the longest steel-reinforced concrete structure of its kind in its heyday, the Brooks Aqueduct now hangs high and dry above a shallow, 3 km wide valley just off the Trans-Canada about 8 km southeast of Brooks. Completed in 1915, it was part of a CPR scheme to irrigate local farms and ranches, a job it did admirably until replaced by the present canal and pipeline network in 1980. Now a provincial and national historic site, it remains a striking sculpture on the prairie landscape, and a reminder of the scarcity of water in this region, otherwise blessed with good soil and a long growing season.

Brooks is home to the Alberta Crop Diversification Centre, a research center for the commercial horticultural industry. Visitors may take self-guided walking tours of the spectacularly landscaped grounds.

Kinbrook Island Provincial Park

This park is on an island in Lake Newell, an irrigation reservoir and one of Alberta's largest man-made lakes. It includes the Kinbrook Marsh and Sven Bayer bird sanctuaries, vital waterfowl nesting and staging areas, and meccas for nature lovers. The park features sandy beaches, a boat launch, good fishing, and a 167-site campground.

Tillebrook Trans-Canada Provincial Park

This park's manicured, well-watered lawns and trees stand out from the surrounding prairie. Right on the highway, it offers convenient camping and picnic sites, and facilities such as a laundry, showers, and an enclosed picnic shelter with gas stove.

SUFFIELD

Trans-Canada Highway 1

TILLEBROOK
TRANS-CANADA PP

55 km   32 km

**SOUTHEASTERN
ALBERTA**

Redcliff

This is the "greenhouse capital of the Prairies." Some 50 area firms are involved in horticulture, and millions of locally grown cucumbers, tomatoes, peppers, and flowers are exported annually to every corner of the country. Redcliff Greenhouses, the leading rose and cut-flower producer, welcomes visitors, as do many other local high-tech greenhouse operators.

The 18-hole Redcliff Riverview Golf Course offers fine golf and views of the South Saskatchewan River, whose steep red banks give the city its name.

Medicine Hat

On a summer's day, this tree- and park-endowed city of 45,000 on the South Saskatchewan River looks like a green oasis amid the surrounding grainfields. Take time to enjoy an historic walking tour: a guidebook, available locally, leads past grand turn-of-the-century dwellings, and elegant public buildings such as the 1905 CPR station and the twin-towered, 1912 St. Patrick's Church. Many buildings are made of brick, which the city produced at one time.

North America's top cowboys compete at the Medicine Hat Exhibiton and Stampede. Begun in 1887, and held every August since, it is Alberta's second biggest pro rodeo and Hatters' (what local residents call themselves) premier family fun event.

You can swim, boat, or fish in man-made lakes at Echo Dale Regional Park on Hwy. 3, some

8 km from the city center. Other attractions include farm buildings, including a pioneer log house restored and decorated to the early 1900s, and the partially restored Ajax Coal Mine, which operated from 1884 to 1967.

Saamis Tepee, Medicine Hat

Aboriginal craft making and interpretive displays are featured alongside the world's tallest tepee, a 20-story-high steel monument to native people, at the junction of the Trans-Canada and South Ridge Drive. Moved here from Calgary, where it was built for the 1986 Winter Olympics, it overlooks the Saamis Archaeological Site—an ancient buffalo meat-processing camp—in Seven Persons Coulee. Storyboards by noted aboriginal artists reflect native culture.

Clay Products Interpretive Centre, Medicine Hat

Rich clay and plenty of kiln-firing natural gas fueled pottery and china manufacture locally in the late 1800s. Pioneer prairie industries such as Medalta Potteries, Medicine Hat Potteries (later Hycroft China), and Alberta Potteries were the first Alberta companies to send manufactured products to eastern Canada. Although no longer in commercial production, several turn-of-the-century kilns survive. The old Hycroft China plant has become the Clay Products Interpretive Centre. It has an extensive collection of local pottery and offers plant tours and demonstrations of clay-product manufacturing.

REDCLIFF   MEDICINE HAT   IRVINE   WALSH

3
Crowsnest Highway

41
34 km

CYPRESS HILLS
INTERPROVINCIAL PK

8 km   32 km   5 km   17 km

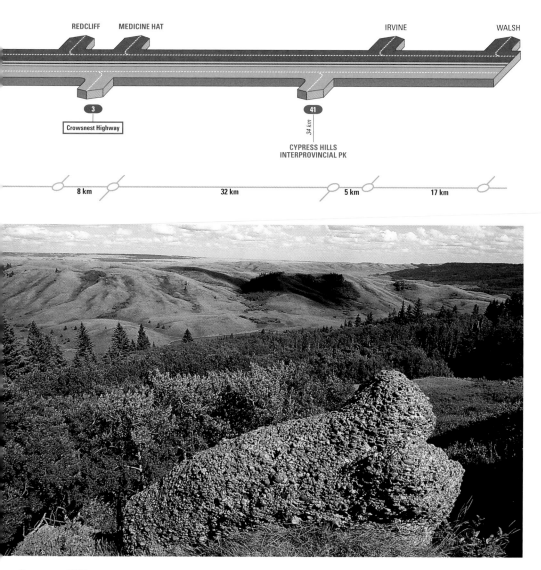

Cypress Hills Interprovincial Park

"A perfect oasis in the desert," wrote 19th-century explorer John Palliser of the lodgepole pine forested highlands that rise up from the flat, semiarid prairie. Formed by sea and river sediments millions of years ago, the hilltops escaped untouched during subsequent glaciation and are now the highest point of land between the Rockies and Labrador. Portions of the terrain are preserved in an interprovincial park that straddles the Alberta–Saskatchewan boundary.

Eighteen species of orchid grow along park roads and trails and more than 200 species of birds, including wild turkeys, have been sighted in the 208 km² Alberta section of the park. Great elk and moose share park groves and meadows with beaver, coyote and red squirrel. Without charge, you can borrow bird and flower guides and binoculars from the visitor center.

Family units are available at a motel in Elkwater, the park's only town, and there are more than 500 campsites, from full hookups to walk-ins, throughout the park. Elkwater's rodeo takes place on the July 1 weekend; its winter festival, in January. The town is on the shore of Elkwater Lake, which has sandy beaches and a marina for 70 boats. There is downhill skiing at Hidden Valley south of town. One must-visit spot is the Horseshoe Canyon Viewpoint, which offers a 100 km prairie vista.

In the Cypress Hills, flat-topped uplands trimmed in spruce and lodgepole pine give way to rolling meadows dotted with harebells, crocus, daisies, and other wildflowers. A wealth of wildlife and an exceptionally rich and varied plant life make the interprovincial park a naturalist's heaven. Fossils of early mammals found in the hills date back 40 million years.

75

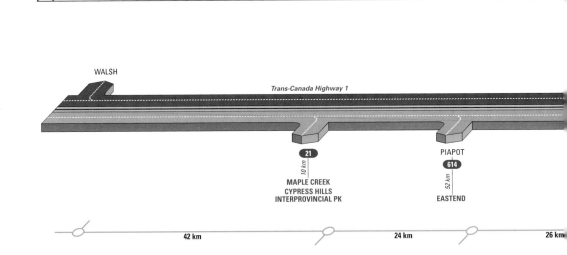

WALSH

Trans-Canada Highway 1

21
10 km
MAPLE CREEK
CYPRESS HILLS
INTERPROVINCIAL PK

PIAPOT
614
52 km
EASTEND

42 km   24 km   26 km

**SOUTHEASTERN
SASKATCHEWAN**

Fort Walsh's palisade, horse barn, and board buildings have been restored to the 1880s, when Mounties here patrolled the border, administered criminal law, helped make treaties, and generally shaped the character of the Northwest.

Maple Creek

No shortage of museums in this "Old Cow Town." Twelve rooms in the Jasper Cultural and Historical Centre, housed in a two-story, brick former school-house, are arranged as living

quarters of a pioneer ranch house (*left*), a general store, a classroom, a railway station and so on. Saskatch-ewan's oldest museum, The Old Timer's Museum has one of the best North West Mounted Police, native and pioneer ranch-ing collections in the region. Steam- and gas-powered trac-tors have pride of place in the Antique Tractor Museum and Frontier Village.

Cypress Hills
Interprovincial Park

Saskatchewan's portion of this park consists of two separate sections, both accessible from Maple Creek. The western sec-tion and Fort Walsh are accessi-ble by Hwy. 271; the smaller eastern section, by Hwy. 21. Both sectors offer beaches, trails, and campsites, with one west block campground catering to equestrians. Conglomerate cliffs formed 40 million years ago offer panoramic views of the prairies.

Fort Walsh
National Historic Site

A North West Mounted Police fort has been reconstructed on the site of the original post built

in 1875 by NWMP Maj. James Walsh. During its eight-year life, the post—and the Mounties it housed—played a major role in bringing law and order to the West. First, Walsh and his men suppressed the illegal whisky trade to the region's Assiniboine, Blackfoot, and Cree Indians. Then, after the 1876 Battle of the Little Big Horn, Walsh greet-ed Chief Sitting Bull and some 5,000 refugee Sioux from the U.S. The last of the Sioux went home in 1881, and the fort was abandoned two years later. From 1942 to 1968, it found new life as an RCMP horse-breeding ranch. Parks Canada has also restored the nearby Farwell's and Solomon's trading posts.

Eastend

This town lies in the Valley of Hidden Secrets, so called for its wealth of paleontological and historical sites. In the 1950s, a triceratops shield was found there; in 1994, a 13 m long *Tyrannosaurus rex* was excavat-ed. So it's no surprise that the Eastend Museum and Cultural Centre, housed in the former 1914 Pastime Theatre, features dinosaur fossils as well as native and pioneer artifacts. You will also find paleontological displays and an on-site interpreter at the Eastend Fossil Research Station.

Eastend was the boyhood home of Pulitzer Prize-winning U.S. writer Wallace Stegner (1909-1993), whose Saskatch-ewan-set books include the 1955 novel *Wolf Willow*. The author's home has been restored as a writer's residence.

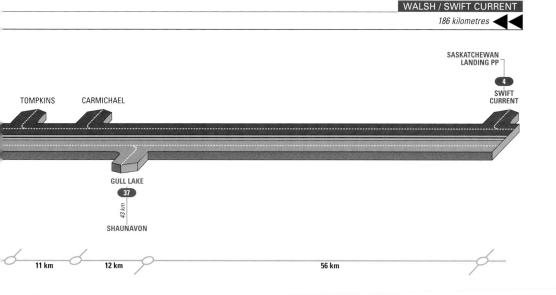

SASKATCHEWAN
LANDING PP

4

SWIFT
CURRENT

TOMPKINS CARMICHAEL

GULL LAKE

37

43 km

SHAUNAVON

11 km   12 km   56 km

Gull Lake

Named for a lake that has long since disappeared, this community was part of the vast '76 Ranch established here in the late 1800s. (The 1888 ranch house is now a school district office.) When the ranch failed, the land was sold in lots, and the town founded. In the early 1900s, it set records for grain production; in the 1950s, oil and gas discoveries brought another boom. The nearby Carmichael Hutterite Colony welcomes afternoon visitors.

Shaunavon

This community is known for its sparkling spring water. In 1939, the Royal Train carrying King George VI and Queen Elizabeth stopped to take on a supply. Fossils, mounted birds and animals, native artifacts and tools are displayed at the Grand Coteau Heritage and Cultural Centre. The surrounding Bone Creek Basin economy is based on ranching, grain crops, and oil and gas wells.

Swift Current

Settlement began with the CPR but the town evolved into a livestock and grain center. Displays in the Swift Current Museum recount the area's history. Doc's Town in Kinetic Park re-creates an early-20th-century prairie village. Also in the park is a Mennonite Heritage Site, with an authentically furnished 1900s Mennonite homestead and barn. (The restaurant here serves a traditional German lunch.)

Lake Diefenbaker

This 220 km long man-made lake was created in the 1960s, when the Gardiner Dam was built on

the South Saskatchewan River. It is named for Prime Minister John Diefenbaker (1895-1979). Creation of the lake also produced three provincial parks, Danielson, Douglas and Saskatchewan Landing.

Saskatchewan Landing Provincial Park

Roughly 50 km north of Swift Current, this park straddles the South Saskatchewan at an ancient river crossing and site of an earlier ferry and bridge. Goodwin House, a restored 1900 stone dwelling built by an NWMP officer, serves as a visitor center. There is a marina and 255-site campground.

Digs in the Frenchman River valley near Eastend have yielded skeletal remains ranging from a near-complete Tyrannosaurus rex skeleton to fossil remains of other prehistoric reptiles, mammals, plants, and birds. Paleontologists carefully wrap a 23 cm long tooth (inset) for later examination in the laboratory.

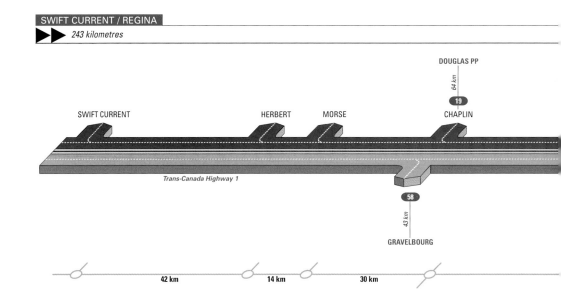

DOUGLAS PP
64 km
19
SWIFT CURRENT   HERBERT   MORSE   CHAPLIN

Trans-Canada Highway 1

58
43 km
GRAVELBOURG

42 km   14 km   30 km

**SOUTH
CENTRAL
SASKATCHEWAN**

This 5 x 15 m mural by Moose Jaw artist Gus Froese recalls when a brass band, the fire department, city officials, and every automobile in town led the Moose Jaw Robin Hoods and their competitors up Main Street to the baseball diamond for the season's opener.

Douglas Provincial Park

Long stretches of beach, a variety of water sports, and a well-shaded campground have made this park at the southeast end of Lake Diefenbaker a favorite with families. Short nature trails let you explore sand dunes (some up to 25 m high), windswept grasslands, and aspen forests. The park was named for Tommy Douglas (1904-1986), premier of Saskatchewan for 17 years.

Gravelbourg

The spirit of its 1906 founders—Père Louis-Joseph-Pierre Gravel, his five brothers and sister, together with other Quebec and New England settlers—still pervades Gravelbourg, the cultural, educational, and religious center of Saskatchewan's Francophones. Murals by Père Charles Maillard and stained glass windows from France adorn the architecturally outstanding

Romanesque Cathédrale Notre-Dame-de-l'Assomption, built in 1918. Reproductions of Renaissance masters hang in the Elementary School Art Gallery, housed in the former chapel of the Couvent Jésus-Marie. Pioneer memorabilia in the Musée de Gravelbourg, in the Centre culturel Charles-Maillard, recount local history.

Moose Jaw

An air force base is the biggest employer in this city at the heart of wheat country. Most Moose Javians work for CFB Moose Jaw, Canada's largest jet training base, the country's busiest airport (in terms of takeoffs and landings), and home of the celebrated aerobatic team, the Snowbirds. "Fly With the Snowbirds," a film presentation at the Snowbird Gallery in the local branch of the Western Development Museum, shows some of the team's amazing maneuvers.

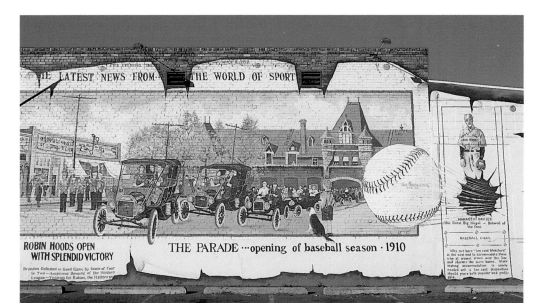

ROBIN HOODS OPEN
WITH SPLENDID VICTORY

THE PARADE ···opening of baseball season · 1910

BUFFALO POUND PP
23 km
[2]
MOOSE JAW
REGINA

[2]
13 km
SUKANEN SHIP,
PIONEER VILLAGE AND MUS

86 km   71 km

In keeping with its transportation theme, the museum also has a collection of antique automobiles and snowmobiles, vintage aircraft, and train engines (*left*).

Naturally heated mineral water from 1,400 m down is piped hot into indoor and outdoor pools, and into 25 deluxe suites at the Temple Gardens Mineral Spa, a four-story geothermal spa-hotel-convention center downtown.

Moose Jaw also boasts a classic collection of giant historical murals, 26 in all, painted on the exterior walls of downtown buildings. Painted by Canadian and American artists, the murals depict different aspects of the city's development, such as the early years, homesteading, the coming of the railway, a Sioux warrior, early agriculture, an old-fashioned baseball game, rum-running exploits, and much else. Guided tours begin at the Murals Centre on 445 Main Street North.

Another downtown attraction is the Tunnels of Little Chicago, a network of underground passages. They are thought to have been built in the late 1800s by Chinese railway workers to hide family members from a head tax. The tunnels were used by liquor smugglers in the 1920s, when Moose Jaw was known as the rum-running capital of Canada.

Sukanen Ship Pioneer Village and Museum

This is the final port of the *Dontianen*, an oceangoing vessel built on the prairies in the early 1900s by Tom Sukanen, a Finnish immigrant. Sukanen planned to sail his ship to Finland (via the South Saskatchewan River and Hudson Bay), but he died in 1943 before completing the work. The ship languished for years before being restored for permanent display here.

Other exhibits include some 25 buildings gathered from around Saskatchewan. Among them are homesteads built in 1886 and 1906 (the latter with its original stove, bed, and a trunkful of cards, letters, and legal papers), a 1904 one-room school, a 1907 church with working organ, a 1911 CNR station, and a 1914 general store.

Buffalo Pound Provincial Park

This park draws its name from a natural corral once used by Plains Indians to trap buffalo. Today, free-roaming herds can be seen from a tower on the Bison Trail, one of several hiking trails here. The park sits on 60 km long, man-made Buffalo Pound Lake. Abundant wildlife is found at the lake's southern end in what is known as the Nicolle Flats Interpretive Area. In this section, you can follow the Nicolle Flats Marsh Boardwalk, past American white pelican haunts, or the Nicolle Flats Trail, which winds through grassy hills and wooded coulees to the 1903 Nicolle family stone homestead and barn.

79

RCMP Museum and Depot

Boot camp for the Mounties, this site on Dewdney Ave. West has been the police force's headquarters since 1882. An Anglican chapel on the grounds, built the following year as a mess hall and canteen, is the oldest building in the city. Memorial plaques to officers who maintained the RCMP's tradition of duty adorn its walls. The Centennial Museum next door documents the history of the force from its inception in 1873 as the North West Mounted Police. One floor chronicles criminal history and displays various murder weapons. The most eye-catching display, however, is a lighthearted "kitsch"gallery (*right*) that chronicles the way the Mounties' image has been commercially depicted over the years, as dolls, on cookie jars, pop bottles, ashtrays, and in the movies. On Tuesday evenings in July and August, scarlet-clad Mounties perform an impressive sunset retreat ceremony centered around lowering the flag.

Market Square

This area encompasses the downtown core between Saskatchewan Drive and 13th Ave. (north/south), and Angus and Osler streets (west/east). At its heart is Victoria Park. West of this green space are city hall and the public library; the block-long Scarth Street Pedestrian Mall extends from the twin-towered McCallum Hill Building past the Globe Theatre and the Civic Plains Museum to the Cornwall Shopping Centre to the east. Regina's Art-Deco Union Station across from the center is now a casino.

Royal Saskatchewan Museum

Built as a pioneers' memorial for Saskatchewan's 50th anniversary, the museum has a striking exterior frieze of prairie wildlife, sculpted by Hubert Garnier. Housed within are Earth Sciences, Life Sciences, and First Nations galleries, and the museum mascot, an animated Tyrannosaurus Rex known as "Megamunch."

Speakers' Corner

Dedicated to Canadians' traditions of free speech and right of public assembly, Speakers' Corner was opened in 1966 by Lord Louis Mountbatten (1900-1979). Surrounding birch trees are from Runnymede Meadow (near London's Windsor Castle), where the Magna Carta was signed in 1215. The lamp standards are from London's Hyde Park, and the sandstone speaker's podiums are from Regina's old city hall.

Saskatchewan Legislative Building

Without the dome, this building's Beaux-Arts facade could be mistaken for the Palace of Versailles. Montreal architects Edward and W.S. Maxwell combined many Louis XVI and English Renaissance elements in the design. Lions' and gargoyles' heads and interwoven strands of grains and fruits grace exterior walls. The interior contains 34 kinds of marble. A mural in the rotunda honors Saskatchewan's Indians; a table in the library is said to be the one used in Charlottetown in 1864 by the Fathers of Confederation. An outside fountain, that once stood in London's Trafalgar Square, commemorates Regina's choice as NWMP headquarters in 1882.

VICTORIA AVE.

ALBERT ST.

BROAD ST.

COLLEGE AVE.

Wascana L

LEGISLATIVE DRIVE

HILL

TCHEWAN RD.

REGINA: CITY OF THE PLAINS

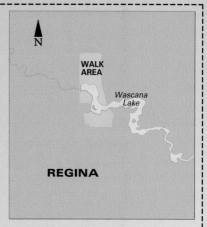

WALK AREA

Wascana Lake

REGINA

Through the infinite expanse of featureless prairie, Regina's skyline looms at a distance like a shimmering mirage. Originally a creek crossing, it was known as "Oskana" or Pile of Bones because buffalo skeletons were piled along its banks. Regina was forced into existence in 1882, when it became a CPR terminal and headquarters of both the Territorial government and the North West Mounted Police. Renamed soon after to honor Queen Victoria (*regina* is Latin for queen), the infant community was named capital in 1905, when Saskatchewan became a province. In transforming the treeless plain around a muddy stream into a livable community, the city dammed Wascana Creek to provide a water supply, thereby creating a vast artificial lake in the heart of the city. More beautification came when 230,000 trees were hand planted along Regina's broad boulevards and in its parks. When a 1912 tornado destroyed much of what had been built, residents started all over again and rebuilt much of the downtown. The result is a tidy, refined, appealing urban island in a sea of prairie grain.

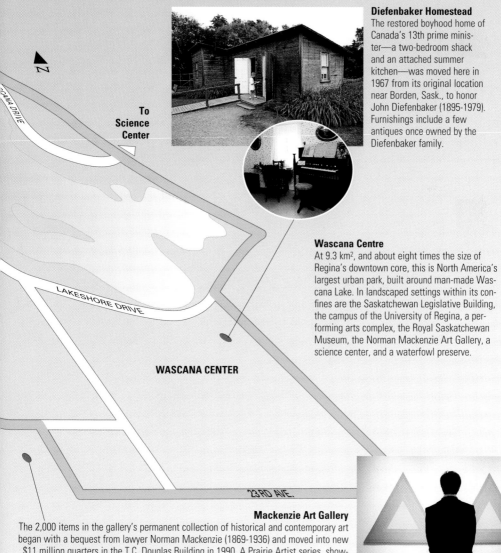

To Science Center

WASCANA DRIVE

LAKESHORE DRIVE

WASCANA CENTER

23RD AVE.

Diefenbaker Homestead
The restored boyhood home of Canada's 13th prime minister—a two-bedroom shack and an attached summer kitchen—was moved here in 1967 from its original location near Borden, Sask., to honor John Diefenbaker (1895-1979). Furnishings include a few antiques once owned by the Diefenbaker family.

Wascana Centre
At 9.3 km², and about eight times the size of Regina's downtown core, this is North America's largest urban park, built around man-made Wascana Lake. In landscaped settings within its confines are the Saskatchewan Legislative Building, the campus of the University of Regina, a performing arts complex, the Royal Saskatchewan Museum, the Norman Mackenzie Art Gallery, a science center, and a waterfowl preserve.

Mackenzie Art Gallery
The 2,000 items in the gallery's permanent collection of historical and contemporary art began with a bequest from lawyer Norman Mackenzie (1869-1936) and moved into new $11 million quarters in the T.C. Douglas Building in 1990. A Prairie Artist series, showcasing works by artists such as Dorothy Knowles, Joe Fafard, and David Thauberger, highlights a special interest in Western Canadian art. Each August, an historic courtroom drama, *The Trial of Louis Riel*, is enacted in the gallery's theater.

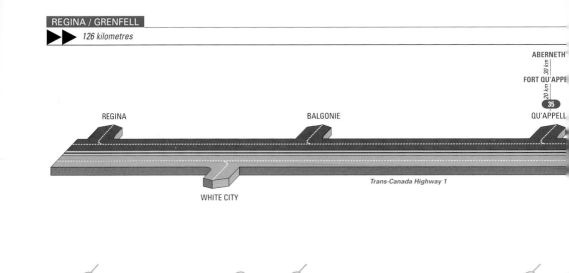

ABERNETH
30 km
FORT QU'APPE
20 km
35
QU'APPELL

REGINA   BALGONIE   QU'APPELL

Trans-Canada Highway 1

WHITE CITY

19 km   7 km   29 km   14 k

**EAST CENTRAL
SASKATCHEWAN**

From dawn to dusk, seven days a week, horticultural experts at Indian Head's Shelterbelt Centre are happy to see visitors and discuss the merits of various trees and shrubs.

Fort Qu'Appelle

Saskatchewan's richest farmland lies in the valley of the Qu'Appelle River, which flows eastward from Lake Diefenbaker to Manitoba. *Kah-tep-was* ("the river that calls") was how the Cree characterized this waterway, where a warrior was said to have heard his dead love call his name. Early French explorers perpetuated the legend with the name *Qu'appelle*? ("Who calls?")

At Fort Qu'Appelle, the river widens into a string of sparkling lakes—the Fishing Lakes, Pasqua, Echo, Mission, and Katepwa. This lakeland paradise in the verdant floor of the valley offers great catches, pleasant camping, and ample opportunities for golfing, hiking, swimming, and water-skiing.

Stately brick buildings and inviting craft and pottery outlets grace the community of Fort Qu'Appelle. It grew around an HBC fort built in 1864 at the hub of several historic trails. The local museum, built on the original fort site, has doors and window frames from the fort, and exhibits about the area's native peoples and first settlers.

Motherwell Homestead National Historic Site, Abernethy

Some 30 km east of Fort Qu'Appelle on Hwy. 22, a gracious stone farmhouse, an L-shaped barn, and beautifully landscaped grounds mark the Motherwell Homestead National Historic Site. Drawn by the promise of free land, and with an Ontario College of Agriculture degree in

hand, W. R. Motherwell (1860-1943) settled here in 1882, introducing dryland farming techniques that achieved remarkable results from the arid prairie. The tree lines he planted provided shade from sun and wind, and helped reduce erosion. Letting land lie fallow in summer helped conserve soil moisture. Motherwell eventually become leader of prairie grain growers, Saskatchewan's first minister of agriculture, and federal minister of agriculture in the 1920s.

Guides in period costume welcome visitors to the restored cut-fieldstone, Italianate-style homestead, which contains original furnishings such as Spanish leather armchairs and a Mason and Riesch piano. Farm animals and vintage equipment occupy the double-pitched, gambrel-roofed barn, also restored to the 1910-1914 era.

Nearby Abernethy has several turn-of-the-century stone dwellings and the 1886 Christ Anglican Church. More than 300 stuffed birds and animals are displayed in the Abernethy Nature Heritage Museum.

Indian Head

At the center of a prime wheat-growing district, Indian Head has become famous for the millions of trees it exports each year. The Prairie Farm Rehabilitation Administration Shelterbelt Centre, established here in 1902, is Canada's only federal tree nursery and the biggest shelterbelt nursery in North America. It grows and distributes up to 10 million shrubs and deciduous

KATEPWA
POINT PP

26 km

56

INDIAN HEAD

SINTALUTA

WOLSELEY

CROOKED
LAKE PP

31 km

47

GRENFELL

18 km   12 km   27 km

Picturesque surroundings and a variety of activities—camping, fishing, hiking, cycling, picnicking, boating, nearby golfing—have made Crooked Lake Provincial Park popular with families.

Pioneer furnishings and clothing are elegantly displayed in the Grenfell Museum, which also contains an impressive military collection.

and evergreen trees annually for use as windbreaks around farm fields, something shown to improve crop yields. The arboretum, horticultural displays, picnic sites and 1 km Sunbeam Creek Nature Trail are open to visitors.

Also in Indian Head, the Dominion Experimental Farm is known for its magnificent barns and fine flower gardens.

Grenfell

Watch for the town's tourist booth, a miniature grain elevator. The surrounding district, settled by English emigrants in 1882, remains a prosperous agricultural area. Grenfell was the hometown of Salteaux Indian long-distance runner and Olympic medalist Paul Acoose (1884-1978), and W. J. Patterson

(1886-1976), Saskatchewan's first native-born premier. The library, established in 1882, has provided the province's longest continuous library service.

The Grenfell Museum is in a large, turreted Victorian home, built in 1904, and restored and refurbished in turn-of-the-century style. It displays clothing, furniture, musical instruments, appliances, military artifacts, and other pioneer memorabilia.

Crooked Lake
Provincial Park

In the Qu'Appelle Valley, northeast of Crooked Lake, this pleasant park encompasses valley slopes and plains, and a sheltered lakeside campground. Visitors enjoy swimming, hiking, and fishing.

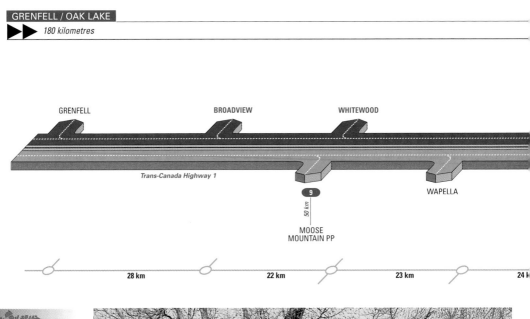

GRENFELL   BROADVIEW   WHITEWOOD

Trans-Canada Highway 1

9

50 km

MOOSE
MOUNTAIN PP

WAPELLA

28 km   22 km   23 km   24 k

**EAST CENTRAL
SASKATCHEWAN
AND WESTERN
MANITOBA**

Broadview

A railway worker looking to the open prairie is credited with naming Broadview. In the Broadview Museum, you will find native beaded clothing, pioneer saddles and military items, farm equipment, a train station, and caboose and other railway mementos such as the poster

(*left*). Other displays include a native log house and pioneer sod house, a blacksmith shop, and windmills.

Summer events include the Jackpot Rodeo, when riders from across North America compete for big money, and several area powwows. Winter attractions include excellent downhill skiing.

Whitewood

Originally called Siding No. 9, Whitehead was later renamed for a nearby bluff of white poplars. Whitewood Historical Museum's three buildings feature pioneer artifacts of the diverse ethnic communities —Hungarian, Finnish, Swedish and French —that settled in the area.

Chopping's Museum, housed in a 20-room, century-old brick dwelling, contains an amazing array of collectibles, some 30,000 in all—coal oil lamps, tin cans, bottles, dolls, tools, toys, and other largely local items gathered by antique collector and author George Chopping.

On a forested plateau, some 50 km south of Whitewood on Hwy. 5, Moose Mountain Provincial Park is ideal for camping, hiking, and other fresh-air activities.

Sod houses such as this one at Broadview Museum were built of "prairie shingles," slabs of sod-piled grass side down to form walls, and laid over a framework of boards for the roof. Many prairie settlers' first homes were made in this fashion, since sod was the most abundant material available.

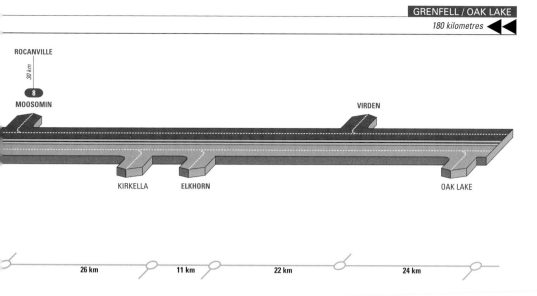

ROCANVILLE
30 km

8
MOOSOMIN

VIRDEN

KIRKELLA   ELKHORN

OAK LAKE

26 km   11 km   22 km   24 km

Moosomin

If you have time to browse, the family-owned Jamieson Museum is a great place to learn about local history. Much of its fine collection is in a turn-of-the-century dwelling and includes a military collection ranging from the Boer to the Korean wars. There is also a one-room schoolhouse, an old church, and a pioneer log home.

In July, the community celebrates the Saskatoon Berry Festival and Rodeo. Camping is available just minutes north on Hwy. 8, or in Moosomin Regional Park, 20 minutes southwest of town. There is a beach here on man-made Moosomin Lake.

Rocanville

This is where you'll find the world's largest oil can, a 9 m high metal replica of the Symons Pump Oiler invented in the 1920s by Ernie Symons. Rocanville and District Museum displays lots of farm equipment, including antique gas- and diesel-powered tractors and steam engines. The museum hosts steam shows on summer Sundays. Antique threshing machine demonstrations are a highlight of Museum Day in September. Just west of Rocanville, the CTM Country Store has a collections of toys, dolls, crafts, buckles, and antiques, and hosts a Farm Toy and Collectibles Show in August.

Elkhorn

Local farmer Isaac Clarkson had restored some 60 vintage automobiles in 1967, when he and Marguerite Ablett built a structure to house them. Thus was born the Manitoba Antique Automobile Museum. Today, its collection ranges from a 1908 Reo to a 1958 Studebaker.

Virden

This small city has great architectural interest. The 1911 Auditorium Theatre (*right*), western Manitoba's first opera house, features an ornate interior, full-sized stage and seating for 500. (The seating capacity is particularly impressive when you consider it was built when the population was 1,500.) The building was painstakingly restored by the community in 1983. St. Mary's Anglican Church (1892), the fieldstone CPR station (1906), and the brick post office (1914) are also notable. The Virden Pioneer Home Museum, in a large 1888 brick house, depicts life in Victorian times. Its 8,000 items include a complete 1894 kitchen. Northeast of Virden, River Valley School, a stone school in use from 1896 to the 1950s, is now a museum and picnic spot.

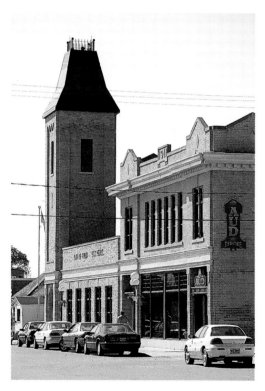

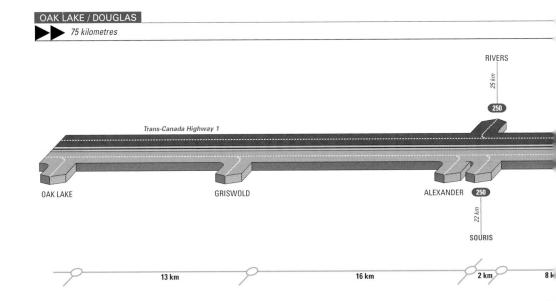

RIVERS
25 km
250

Trans-Canada Highway 1

OAK LAKE   GRISWOLD   ALEXANDER **250**

22 km

SOURIS

13 km   16 km   2 km   8 k

**WESTERN
MANITOBA**

Souris

Many agree that Souris is the
"prettiest of all prairie towns."
Rock hounds prize the local agate
pit for its variety of agate and
multicolored jasper, petrified
wood (ruby-red to brown and
black), and epidote. Fees to
explore the open gravel pit, said
to have North America's largest
variety of semiprecious stones,
can be paid at the local Rock
Shop. Visitors to Hillcrest Museum, formerly Squire Hall, a residence of one of the founding
families, can admire the original
pressed-tin ceiling, oak floors,
etched foyer glass, and winding
staircase, as well as pioneer
household items, tools, and toys.
Nearby are an agricultural museum and the Heritage Church,
which dates from 1883. Downtown Victoria Park has picnic
and camping sites, hiking trails,
and swimming in river or pool.

Brandon

Two-thirds of Manitoba's farmland is within 130 km of Brandon.
And it is agriculture—wheat,
sunflowers, cattle—that has
made Brandon the hub of western Manitoba and the province's
second largest city. Settlement,
begun in 1881 when the CPR
established a major divisional
point at a site it named for the
nearby Brandon Hills, was

*Souris' first swinging bridge, built
in 1903 by a local landowner to
connect his riverside properties,
was destroyed in a 1976 flood. It
was replaced by the bridge (right),
at 177 m Canada's longest free-
suspension footbridge.*

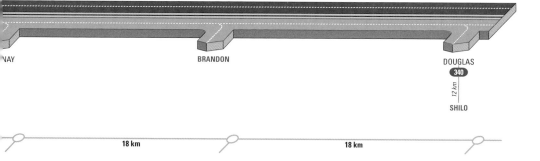

NAY

BRANDON

DOUGLAS
340
12 km
SHILO

18 km   18 km

almost instantaneous. Growth was so fast that the community was never a village or a town; it became a city within a year.

You can browse through four floors of artifacts and archival material in the Daly House Museum, former home of Thomas Mayne Daly (1852-1911), the city's first mayor and Manitoba's first federal cabinet minister. Period furniture, wallpaper, rugs, and ornaments, even the apparel displayed, make this a fine example of an upper middle-class prairie home of the late 1800s. The museum also includes the old Mutter Brothers grocery store, city council chambers, a century-old log house, and relics of early Assiniboine River steamboats.

You can take a drive-through or a guided tour of the Agriculture and Agri-Food Canada Research Station. It was founded in 1886 as one of the first federal experimental farms.

Brandon College, founded in 1899, became Brandon University in 1967. Interactive exhibits, geological and archaeological displays, and more than 500 bird and animal specimens are among the university's B.J. Hales Museum of Natural History collection.

The 26th Field Artillery Regiment Museum Inc. showcases military artifacts, photographs, and memorabilia.

Brandon is host to Dakota Ojibwa Tribal Days in January; the Royal Manitoba Winter Fair in March; the Summer Fair and Pro Rodeo in June; the Brandon Folk, Music and Arts Festival in August, and the International Pickle Festival in September.

Commonwealth Air Training Plan Museum, Brandon

This is the only museum in Canada commemorating the British Commonwealth Air Training Plan—"Canada's greatest single contribution to Allied victory in World War II." Under the plan, thousands of men and women from Britain and the Commonwealth learned to become wartime fliers. Located at Brandon's municipal airport, the museum displays some 5,000 items, everything from working aircraft such as Harvard, Tiger Moth, Cornell, and Stinson planes, to photographs, uniforms, personal papers, and logbooks.

At the site are a memorial book containing short biographies of the 18,000 RCAF airmen and women who died in World War II, and the "barber book," which contains 22,000 signatures of airmen who received haircuts while in training at Brandon.

Shilo

Military activity drives this area's economy. More than 150 major artillery pieces, from the 18th century to the present day, are among the 10,000 items in the Royal Regiment of Canadian Artillery Museum at Canadian Forces Base Shilo. Also on display are small arms, ammunition, technical instruments and World War II vehicles, plus uniforms, and regimental history. The museum was opened in 1962 at CFB Shilo, considered the home station of Canadian artillery.

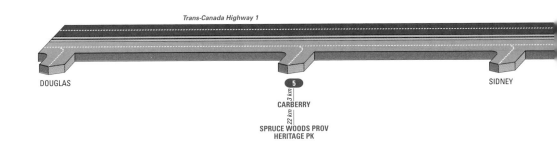

Trans-Canada Highway 1

DOUGLAS

5
3 km

CARBERRY

22 km

SPRUCE WOODS PROV
HERITAGE PK

SIDNEY

24 km | 21 km | 11 k

**CENTRAL
MANITOBA**

Carberry

An important wheat and canola district, Carberry is also the center of Manitoba potato production and processing. Exhibits in the Carberry Plains Museum reflect life locally from pioneer days to the present. Included are Orange Lodge memorabilia, World Wars I and II uniforms, photographs, and artifacts, and artworks by the local pioneer Criddle family. Displays honor World War I flying ace, bush pilot, and native son "Wop" May (1896-1952), and Tommy Douglas (1904-1986), a premier of Saskatchewan and first leader of the New Democratic Party who lived in Manitoba through the 1920s; and author, artist, and naturalist Ernest Thompson Seton (1860-1946). The Seton Centre, also in Carberry, is devoted entirely to works by Seton, who homesteaded here in the 1890s.

Spruce Woods Provincial Heritage Park

🏕️ 🎣 🛶 🎏 🏊 ❄️ 🐾

Named for its spruce-covered rolling hills, this 248 km² park also encompasses grassy plains, aspen parkland, hardwood forest, and the desertlike Spirit Sands—the largest stretch of open sand in Manitoba. Horse-drawn wagon tours offer close-up views of this fascinating world of creeping dunes, remnants of meltwater sediment set down 12,000 years ago where the Assiniboine River, now a mere shadow of its once powerful self, flowed into ancient Lake Agassiz. (See also pages 90-91.) A park museum tells the region's history. Clovis

Self-guiding trails lead through the tract of blowing sand dunes known as the Spirit Sands. Stairs help you navigate the steeper stretches and protect the fragile environment.

peoples hunted the now extinct mammoth and giant bison here 11,000 years ago. Assiniboine, Cree, and Ojibwa Indians hunted buffalo here before European explorers and traders arrived in the mid-18th century. In the 1890s, Ernest Thompson Seton, a naturalist with the Manitoba government, blazed trails through what is now parkland. It was the locale of his 1899 book, *The Trail of a Sandhill Stag.* The park has a 260-site campground, a beach and swimming pool, great fishing, golfing, hiking trails, and canoeing on the Assiniboine River, which meanders through the park.

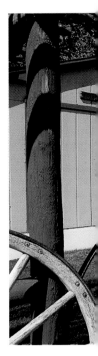

Manitoba Agricultural Museum and Homesteaders Village

Just south of Austin on Hwy. 23, this museum has one of Canada's largest and finest collections of vintage farm machinery. Horse-drawn equipment and dozens of steam-, gas-, and diesel-powered tractors are among exhibits dating from the 1880s to the 1970s. The collection is the work of Austin farmer Don Carrothers.

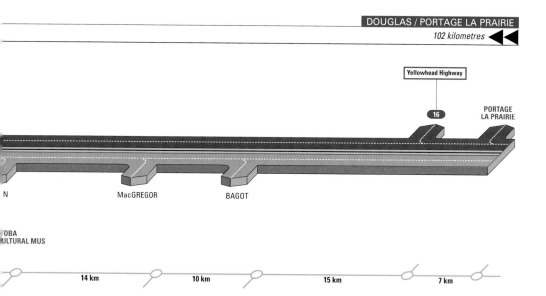

Yellowhead Highway

16

PORTAGE
LA PRAIRIE

N   MacGREGOR   BAGOT

'OBA
ULTURAL MUS

14 km   10 km   15 km   7 km

The adjoining Homesteaders Village was founded in 1960, when the pioneer-era Centreville School was moved to the museum. Twenty buildings now on the site include log dwellings, an old post office, a law office, a mansion with ballroom, a print shop, a smithy, a pioneer telephone building, and St. Saviour's Church—in all, an authentic recreation of a turn-of-the-century rural Manitoba town.

In late July, the museum hosts the four-day Manitoba Threshermen's Reunion and Stampede. It features Canada's largest display of operating antique threshers and other farm equipment. The event also includes a parade, a home craft show, the Manitoba Clydesdale Classic horse show, a rodeo, and fiddling festival.

Portage La Prairie

One of Manitoba's most prosperous communities, Portage La Prairie sits on the Assiniboine River in the heart of the fertile Portage Prairies, the richest farming belts in Manitoba. (The "portage" is a reminder of the voyageur portage between the Assiniboine and Lake Manitoba.)

Fort La Reine Museum and Pioneer Village has a replica of the palisaded post built here in 1738 by Pierre de La Vérendrye (1685-1749). The first fort on the prairies, it was the base from which the explorer and his sons set out on their discoveries.

Life locally in the 19th century is reflected in the pioneer village (*left*), which has an 1879 log cabin, an 1883 church, a print shop, and a doctor's office. Two notable structures are a fire hall with 1930s engines and the railway car used by CPR president William Van Horne during the building of the railway.

In the heart of the city, Island Park on Crescent Lake has a playground and facilities for picnicking, golfing, and tennis. The park has a monument to Arthur Meighen (1874-1960), local MP and prime minister in the 1920s.

A heritage walking tour downtown passes the 1898 city hall, designed by Thomas Fuller, architect of Canada's first Parliament Buildings.

Portage La Prairie hosts the National Strawberry Festival in July. Portagex, another July event, dates from 1872, and is the oldest continuously running agricultural fair in Western Canada.

89

Wagon Wheels Across a Prairie Desert

HIGHWAY 1 / SPRUCE WOODS
PROVINCIAL HERITAGE PARK

JAKE MACDONALD *is a Manitoba novelist who spends summers in a floating cabin, where he writes about wild things and nature for magazines. His latest book is* Juliana and the Medicine Fish.

CROSSING THE PRAIRIES, you can become so mesmerized by the vast landscape and big skies that you cruise right past some of the country's most enthralling curiosities. One such oddity is the Manitoba Desert or Spirit Sands, Canada's only desert. Towering 30 m above the surrounding Prairie near Carberry, Spirit Sands' 5 km^2 of blowing dunes were born 10,000 years ago when glacial Lake Agassiz covered southern Manitoba. The rolling sand-hills are remnants of billions of tonnes of sand and gravel dumped by a powerful river at the edge of the ancient lake.

The dunes at Spirit Sands were virtually inaccessible until the 1960s, when the provincial government enshrined them in Spruce Woods Provincial Heritage Park, some 30 km south of the Trans-Canada Highway. The park is a great place for a roadside break, a place to stretch your legs, have a swim, or take a walk along the Assiniboine River. If you just want to visit the desert area, a horse-drawn covered wagon is a delightful way to explore this delicate ecosystem. Look for the Spirit Sands Wagon Registration Office on Hwy. 5 near the Assiniboine River bridge. Ninety-minute tours depart at 10 a.m., noon, and 2 p.m. daily between the May 24 weekend and Labor Day.

Large, mild-mannered draught horses draw the wagons, which are equipped with padded seats and safety rails. Wagoneers give informative talks on the region's flora and fauna. Elk, deer, coyotes, and timber wolves roam the hills, along with many animals and plants that cannot be found anywhere else in Manitoba. If you are extraordinarily lucky, you may glimpse a scuttling lizard, known as the northern prairie skink, or a spadefoot toad, although the closest most people get to these rare species is to see their tracks in the sand. Should you encounter the homely-looking hognose snake, it may hiss, lunge, or even roll over and play dead, all tactics it employs whenever it feels threatned. Cold-blooded that they are, the reptiles can only survive Manitoba winters by burrowing deep into the sand.

Your wagon ride includes two 15-minute stops, the first at an eerie sunken pit where the action of underground streams has created the Devil's Punch Bowl. A sloping canyonlike pond rimmed by white spruce, the "bowl" is flooded with soupy, blue-green water. Painted turtles sun on surrounding rocks, but quickly slip into the water if approached.

Passengers dismount again at the Spirit Sands, a sea of pinkish dunes shifting and migrating according to the whims of the wind. As you progress into this mini-Sahara, you will notice that the sand in each dune becomes progressively finer toward the top. The heavier sand particles tend to settle at the base on the windward side of the dune, while finer particles blow up the slope and eventually trickle down the other side. In this way, a dune progressively "walks" downwind, only to be pushed the other way, when the wind changes. (In Manitoba, prevailing winds alternate between the south and the northwest.) Each dune is covered in tiny ripples, which are themselves mini-dunes.

These sandhills are not "dry" in the sense that they receive little rainfall. In fact they receive about 500 mm of rain per year, as do other parts of Manitoba. But the dunes are relatively "young" (about 5,000 years old), and the sandy soil is bare because grasses, plants, and trees have not yet successfully colonized the dunes.

On the fringes, the Spirit Sands are populated by small trees such as juniper and spruce, and by grasses, and wildflower. With small leaves that reduce moisture loss and long roots that plunge deep into the soil, these assorted so-called "pioneer plants" are uniquely equipped for surviving in a sandy, dry environment. Among the fighters are pretty pincushion cacti with purple blossoms. Naturalists say that these stubborn, scrubby plants are forebears of a forest that may one day thrive here.

As you and your pioneer-style transportation head back to base, you may see other visitors following your tracks on foot or bike or on horseback. Your guide will likely tell you that NATO troops train in a remote corner of the sandhills at Shilo. Some observers claim that wild animals such as elk are so trusting of the soldiers that they sometimes graze casually right in the middle of a military exercise.

A visit to the Spirit Sands also reveals why author, artist, and renowned naturalist Ernest Thompson Seton (1860-1946) was so entranced by this region. Seton, who delivered some 3,000 lectures around the globe, often described this area as his favorite place. Here he spent his "golden years," rambling the hills and forests and sketching the birds and animals he saw. He wrote stirring tales in which deer, foxes, rabbits, and grouse were the heroes, and which helped popularize animal-centered fiction. His first collection, *Wild Animals I Have Known* (1898), has become a classic. Seton's animal stories were morality tales, in which the basic virtues of duty, honor, and fair play always prevailed. He sought to perpetuate those same values in the Boy Scouts of America—an organization he cofounded and which might not exist if not for his boyhood rambles in these sandhills.

> "*Among the fighters are pretty pincushion cacti with purple flowers.*"

John MacDonald

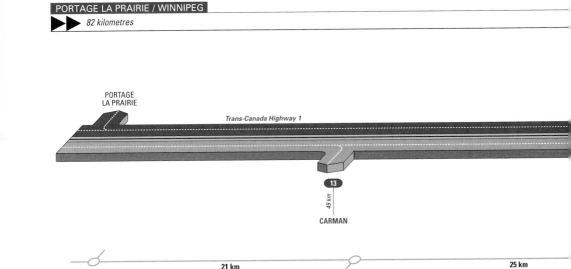

PORTAGE
LA PRAIRIE

Trans-Canada Highway 1

13

49 km

CARMAN

21 km   25 km

**WEST OF
WINNIPEG**

Carman

Pretty, prosperous, and lush, Carman lies on the meandering, tree-lined Boyne River in the rich agricultural district of the Pembina Triangle. Kings Park in the heart of town has a camp-ground, playground, outdoor swimming pool, foot and bike paths, and arenas. It is also the site of the Dufferin Historical Museum, which has a collection of early 1900s toys, dolls, textiles and furnishings, native artifacts, and uniforms.

Self-guided walking or driving tours pass the former Canadian Northern Railway station, the 1903 Ryall Hotel, and several turn-of-the-century houses and churches. Especially notable is the 1913 Boyne Library (originally a post office), built of Medicine Hat brick and Tyndall limestone.

You can tour Friendship Field, a private airfield near town. It contains restored World War II and other vintage aircraft.

St. François Xavier

Just north of the Trans-Canada on Hwy. 26, you will find the town of St. François Xavier. The community dates from 1824 when the famous buffalo hunter Cuthbert Grant (c. 1793-1854) led about 100 Métis families to a settlement modeled on a Quebec seigneury. It is Manitoba's oldest permanent Métis settlement.

Church services were held in Grant's home until a mission chapel was built; then, in 1834, St. François Xavier became a parish (Western Canada's sec-ond after St. Boniface), where births, deaths, and marriages

were registered. Cuthbert Grant is buried inside the present Roman Catholic church.

Just off the Trans-Canada, in an area known as the White Horse Plain, a statue of a white horse perpetuates a tragic love story. According to legend, a Cree warrior got permission to marry an Assiniboine princess, when he presented her father with a snow-white stallion. But the match proved unpopular with the Assiniboines' allies, the Sioux, one of whom had been the bride's suitor. When the father learned the Sioux planned to kill the bridal couple, he gave the young lovers the stallion to speed their getaway. Alas, they were caught and killed.

Historical Museum of St. James-Assiniboia, Winnipeg

Housed in a 1912 former munici-pal hall on Portage Avenue, this museum displays pioneer arti-facts from the settlement of the St. James-Assiniboia region on Winnipeg's western outskirts. After inspecting the exhibits, visitors can take a guided tour of the neighboring William Brown House—an 1850 Red River log home.

Grant's Old Mill, Winnipeg

At Grant's Old Mill on Portage Ave., you can watch grain being ground as in bygone days. This water-powered mill is a replica of one built on this spot in 1829 by Métis leader Cuthbert Grant. To drive the huge wheel, Grant dammed Sturgeon Creek: this was the first use of water power in Western Canada.

A statue of a white horse near St. François Xavier recalls an Indian legend: how a Cree warrior and his Assiniboine bride were pursued and killed by her rejected suitor. The horse escaped and roamed the surrounding plains for years.

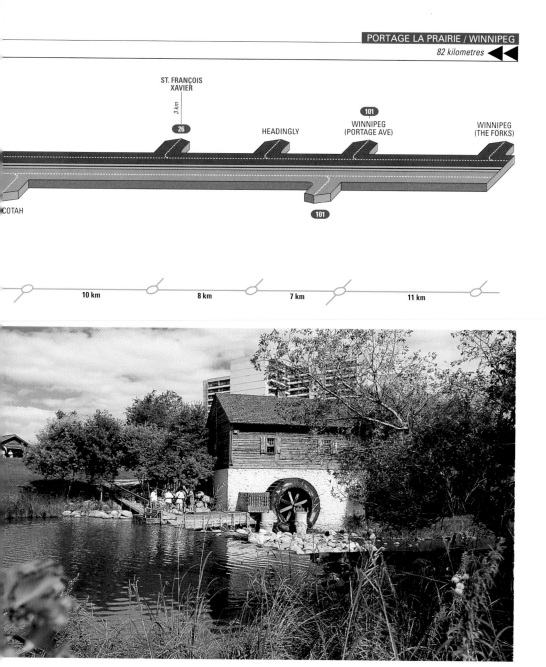

ST. FRANÇOIS
XAVIER

3 km

26

HEADINGLY

101
WINNIPEG
(PORTAGE AVE)

WINNIPEG
(THE FORKS)

COTAH

101

10 km   8 km   7 km   11 km

You can tour this working replica of a mill operated by Cuthbert Grant in 1829 and buy freshly ground buckwheat flour.

Living Prairie Museum, Winnipeg

Wildflowers blend with some 200 native prairie plants within this sheltered tall-grass reserve, the largest surviving tract of unplowed tall-grass prairie in Manitoba. In late April, the purple prairie crocus, the provincial flower, is in full bloom. Displays at the indoor nature center explain the delicate prairie environment, and the sweeping view of grasses from an observation deck gives a sense of how much of North America once looked. A self-guided trail leads through the preserve, but visitors may also choose a guided walk. Along the way, a naturalist will point out milkweed, wild licorice, blue-eyed grass, and other species of wild vegetation.

Western Canada Aviation Museum, Winnipeg

A collection of Canadian airplanes—from early bush planes to modern jets—is preserved in this museum, located near Winnipeg International Airport. Here at Canada's largest hands-on aviation exhibit for children, would-be pilots can sit in the cockpit of a flight simulator, and listen to commentaries by museum staff pointing out the features of vintage aircraft, such as the Junkers JU542-1M, one of the largest aircraft flown in North America in the 1930s. One display recounts the history of Canadian women aviators.

Prairie Dog Central Steam Train, Winnipeg

To board this train is to travel back to the early 1900s. Sunday mornings and afternoons, from June to September, the train and its 1882 locomotive leave St. James Station on the 58 km return trip to Grosse Ile. As well as the passing scenery, passengers can also enjoy the stained glass windows, cast-iron luggage racks, gas ceiling lights, and other fixtures in the mahogany- and oak-paneled coaches.

WINNIPEG: CITY BY THE FORKS

Portage and Main—where Portage Avenue joins Main Street—has long been the heart of Manitoba's largest city. But this bustling intersection saw its share of traffic long before surveyors drew up their urban plans. Following the railway's arrival in the early 1880s, Winnipeg developed rapidly around a natural focal point—the crossroads of two fur-trading trails. More recently, the city has rediscovered and restored another, earlier crossroads—the junction of the Red and Assiniboine rivers. Known as The Forks, it was the traditional meeting place of Native peoples, traders, and settlers. This walk through Winnipeg's downtown core takes in these and other sites that have played a part in the growth of this diverse, exciting city.

Winnipeg Art Gallery
An eye-catching triangular structure sheathed in Tyndall limestone, the Winnipeg Art Gallery has been a distinctive city landmark since 1971. Its nine galleries and rooftop sculpture court contain outstanding examples of European and Canadian art, and one of the world's largest and most comprehensive collections of Inuit art.

Manitoba Legislative Assembly
Tyndall limestone (from the quarries at Garson, northwest of Winnipeg) created this splendid neoclassical building that is the seat of Manitoba's legislative assembly. At the top of the dome is the *Golden Boy*, a 5-tonne bronze statue of a running youth gilded in 23.5 karat gold. A wheat sheaf in the runner's left arm symbolizes Manitoba's agriculture; an upraised torch in his right hand points to the province's rich resources to the north. This beloved city landmark (by French sculptor Charles Gardet) was hoisted into place for the inauguration of the building in 1920. Before skyscrapers changed Winnipeg's skyline in the 1980s, the statue was the highest point in the city. (The tip of the torch is 77 m above ground.) In the southeastern corner of the legislature's grounds is **Government House,** the official residence of the provincial lieutenant governor. Built in 1883, this handsome Victorian dwelling has period features such as the wrought-iron gingerbread on its mansard roof. A striking monument to Louis Riel is located on the grounds near the Assiniboine River. From there, stairs lead to **The Riverwalk,** which runs along the river to The Forks.

Dalnavert
Built for Manitoba's first premier, Sir Hugh John Macdonald (a son of Sir John A. Macdonald, Canada's first prime minister), this restored dwelling is an outstanding example of Queen Anne Revival architecture. When built in 1895, it was one of only four homes in Winnipeg to have hot-water heating, electric lighting, and indoor plumbing. Today, costumed guides escort visitors through Dalnavert, which has been furnished in the Victorian manner.

Winnipeg Commodity Exchange Tower

Established in 1887, the Winnipeg Commodity Exchange occupied several venues before moving to its present location at Portage and Main in 1980. The Exchange—one of the oldest exchanges in the world and the only commodity and futures market in Canada—deals in agricultural products, gold, silver, and interest rates. A visitors' gallery provides an excellent view of the sometimes hectic buying and selling on the trading floor. Prebooked tours are also available.

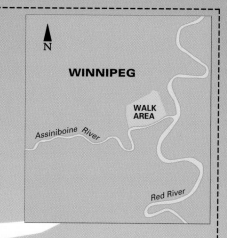

Exchange District

The heart of Winnipeg's thriving commercial life from the arrival of the CPR in 1881 until the early 1920s, the Exchange District developed near the Red River, north of present-day Portage and Main. Nowadays, Winnipeggers and visitors alike are drawn to this downtown district by an array of restaurants, boutiques, and flea markets. The legacy of the boom years—ornate tower blocks, imposing banks, and massive warehouses—will delight architectural buffs. One must-see attraction here is **Centennial Centre,** which includes the **Museum of Man and Nature** and the **Concert Hall,** home to the world-famous Royal Winnipeg Ballet and the Winnipeg Symphony Orchestra. This cluster of cultural institutions also includes the **Manitoba Theatre Centre,** one of Canada's best regional theater companies.

Union Station

Built in 1907, this station was designed in a Beaux Arts style by Warren and Wetmore, the architectural firm that designed Grand Central Station in New York. Ancient fossils can be seen in the locally quarried Tyndall limestone of its walls. Now the VIA Rail Depot, the station has a train gallery on tracks 1 and 2. A prized exhibit is Western Canada's first locomotive, *The Countess of Dufferin,* which was brought to Winnipeg in 1877 and used during the construction of the CPR in the 1880s.

The Forks

A decade of restoration work has transformed a one-time district of bleak, century-old railway yards at the junction of the Red and Assiniboine rivers into one of the city's most popular gathering places. The Forks is also the departure point for daytime and evening river cruises. At **The Forks National Historic Site,** you can follow a riverside trail (with interpretive historic panels) and visit an amphiteater with views across the Red River to St. Boniface Cathedral. Plaques on **The Wall Through Time** recount 10,000 years of local history. A renovated stable houses **The Forks Market,** which offers jewelry, crafts, and an array of fresh, speciality, and ethnic foods. At The Forks, you will also find the **Manitoba Children's Museum,** the largest museum of its kind in Canada, and the **Manitoba Sports Hall of Fame** (located in the Johnson Terminal).

Hotel Fort Garry and Fort Garry Gate

The 1913 Hotel Fort Garry on Broadway is a example of the chateau-style once favored for railway hotels. Just across Fort Street, a small park preserves the gateway to Upper Fort Garry *(above),* the Hudson's Bay Company fort that was a center of social and commercial activity in the Winnipeg area from the mid-1830s to the 1880s.

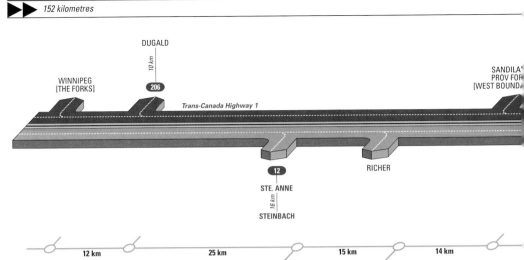

DUGALD

10 km

206

WINNIPEG
[THE FORKS]

SANDILA
PROV FOR
[WEST BOUND

Trans-Canada Highway 1

12

STE. ANNE

16 km

STEINBACH

RICHER

| 12 km | | 25 km | | 15 km | | 14 km | |

**SOUTHEASTERN
MANITOBA**

Ste. Anne

One of Manitoba's earliest settlements, Ste. Anne (some 3 km south of the Trans-Canada on Hwy. 12) began in 1852 when families from St. Boniface fled a Red River flood to new homes at Pointe-des-Chênes (Oak Point) on the Seine River. More settlers arrived from Quebec, and today's community of some 1,500 is the biggest incorporated bilingual village in the province. The original oaks sustained the first arrivals, who went to work producing lumber to build St. Boniface Cathedral. Between 1868 and 1871, local people also helped build the Dawson Trail, the first all-Canadian land and water route linking the East with the Prairies. It ran 850 km from present-day Thunder Bay, Ont., to Winnipeg, and its completion is celebrated during Dawson Trail Days each Labor Day weekend. Local history is also preserved in Le Musée Pointe-des-Chênes.

Giroux

Between Ste. Anne and Steinback, an 8 km trip toward Giroux on 311 takes you to Philip's Magical Paradise, the only museum of its kind in Western Canada. Magicians around the world have donated books, posters, and apparatus to the museum, to complement what 15-year-old Philip Hornan had collected before his

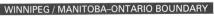

A windmill with 20 m sails dominates the Mennonite Heritage Village, illustrating a way of life that has all but disappeared. Mennonite roots, family farms, and a commitment to hard work have shaped this area.

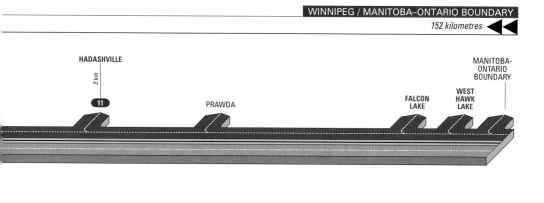

HADASHVILLE

3 km

11

PRAWDA

FALCON LAKE

WEST HAWK LAKE

MANITOBA-ONTARIO BOUNDARY

26 km   18 km   29 km   7 km   6 km

Boating, fishing, swimming, horseback riding, and skiing and snowmobiling in season, are within easy distance of West Hawk townsite.

a scaled down fire tower, and an old railway car filled with local flora and fauna specimens.

Hadashville was named for its first postmaster and store owner Charles Hadash, whose willingness to extend credit to hard-up settlers eventually cost him his business. The town is on the Whitemouth River, a canoeist's delight. Forest center visitors who explore the Beaver Dam Trail cross the Whitemouth on the suspension Beaven Bridge.

untimely death in 1986. Items include a coin owned by Houdini and the Water Torture Cell used by Doug Henning. The museum is located in the former Giroux United Church (built 1904).

Steinbach

An exact replica of an 1877 windmill, several dwellings, churches, schools, a house barn, general store, and various outbuildings in the Mennonite Heritage Village are reminiscent of scores of turn-of-the-century Manitoba villages. Descendants of the 18 Russian immigrant families who founded Steinbach in 1874 organized the local reconstruction. A museum relates Mennonite history from 16th-century Holland and the teachings of Dutch reformer Menno Simons (1496-1561), through migrations to Prussia, Russia, and finally Canada. In the Livery Barn Restaurant, visitors can sample traditional Mennonite

fare in a pioneer setting. Locally crafted items, and products such as stone-ground flour and old-fashioned candy can be purchased in the general store.

Hadashville

Trees are the lifeblood of Hadashville (just north of the Trans-Canada on Hwy. 11). Countless windbreaks, Christmas trees, and reforestation programs get their start at the Pineland Forest Nursery, which produces up to 20 million conifer seedlings annually. All visitors get a free tiny tree to take home. Interpretive programs at Sandilands Forest Centre, an interpretive center adjoining the provincial forest, use self-guiding nature trails and museum displays to teach forest ecology and the province's logging history. Exhibits include dioramas of mounted birds and animals, scale models of forestry operations,

Falcon Lake

Resort facilities in this townsite at Whiteshell Provincial Park's west entrance include overnight accommodations, restaurants, shops, a marina, a first-rate 18-hole golf course, miniature golf, tennis, and riding stables. Long, narrow Falcon Lake is famous for its herons. It was named for Métis poet and troubadour Pierre Falcon (1793-1876).

West Hawk Lake

Because of its depth (115 m) and round shape, geologists believe this lake was created by meteoric impact. Manitoba's deepest lake, West Hawk has a nice beach and is popular with scuba divers and lake trout anglers. Gold mining was carried out in the area early in the 1900s. Both the lake and the West Hawk townsite are in the eastern sector of Whiteshell Provincial Park.

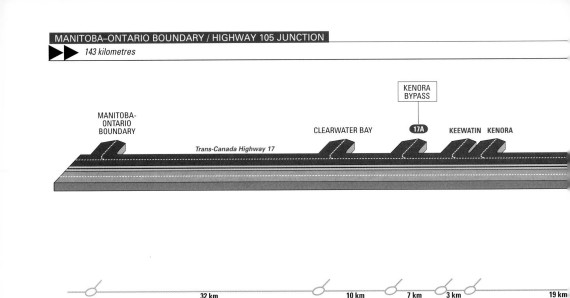

KENORA
BYPASS

MANITOBA-
ONTARIO
BOUNDARY

CLEARWATER BAY

17A

KEEWATIN   KENORA

Trans-Canada Highway 17

32 km   10 km   7 km   3 km   19 km

**NORTHWESTERN
ONTARIO**

Built of wood in 1889, in a Queen Anne style popular in Eastern Canada at that time, the Mather-Walls House has been restored and furnished to its turn-of-the-century grandeur, and is open for guided tours. Light repasts are served in a Victorian Tea Room during opening hours.

Keewatin

Being the western gateway to Lake of the Woods has made this lumber town a tourist mecca. At the boat lift, on the north side of Portage Bay Bridge, you can see watercraft move up or down the 8 m between Lake of the Woods and the lower Winnipeg River system in a matter of minutes. The origin of another local attraction, the Keewatin Potholes, is uncertain. One theory is that the holes, some of which go 2 m into local bedrock, were formed by postglacial whirlpools.

This community began in 1879 when John Mather began lumbering and sawmilling just as railway construction was creating a huge demand for wood. Mather imported workers from his native Scotland to meet the need. He built a boardinghouse and semidetached houses for his workers, a Presbyterian church, three fine houses for his sons and his mill manager (David Mather owned the house at left), and a flour mill that found markets worldwide.

Lake of the Woods

"Lake of the Islands" might be more apt since this 4,350 km^2 of water is dotted with 14,632 islands. A remnant of postglacial Lake Agassiz, Lake of the Woods is fed by the Rainy River and drained by the Winnipeg. Pictographs on lakeside rocks tell of aboriginal habitation dating back

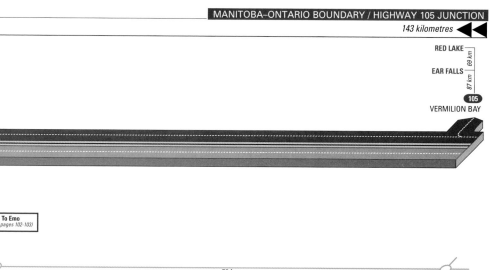

RED LAKE
EAR FALLS
69 km
87 km
105
VERMILION BAY

To Emo
(See pages 102-103)

72 km

Huskie the Muskie stands transfixed in a 12 m leap in McLeod Park on Kenora's waterfront. Built of steel, plywood, fiberglass and other assorted materials, the monster is a worthy symbol for this sport fishing paradise, where outsize muskellunge are commonplace.

thousands of years. In 1688, Jacques de Noyon explored the lake, which later became a crucial link in the main fur trade route. Today's flourishing tourism began when resort lodges were built here in the 1920s. Sailors from all over North America and Britain take part in a midsummer, seven-day regatta, where the main event is a circuit of the lake.

Kenora

The largest town on Lake of the Woods, Kenora is the starting point for scenic tours on the 190-passenger, restaurant-equipped M.S. *Kenora*. Have a look at the rebuilt harborfront and the Heritage Townscapes, a series of outdoor murals downtown, or try some of the local beaches. Turn-of-the-century pioneer memorabilia and examples of the excellent local Ojibwa beadwork are featured in the Lake of the Woods Museum. Fur trading posts were established locally by the De La Vérendrye family (1732) and the Hudson's Bay Company (1836). The arrival of the CPR in 1879 opened up the area to lumbering and mining.

Blue Lake Provincial Park

Bunchberry and blueberry patches dot the boreal forest between Blue and Langton lakes, both remnants of glacial Lake Agassiz. Blue Lake, some 27 m deep, is a favorite with scuba divers. There are natural sand beaches, boating, and tent and trailer sites. Spruce Bog, Boulder Ridge, and

Rock Point trails let you explore different park settings. The park, 8 km northwest of Vermilion Bay, is accessible by Hwy. 647.

Ear Falls

With hundreds of bald eagle nesting in the area and a major bald eagle study in its fifth decade, this town calls itself the "bald eagle capital of North America." The area has numerous resorts, ranging from rustic to deluxe, and recreational facilities from golf to snowmobiling. Ear Falls boasts the "world's longest snowmobile bridge," a 160 m span 12 m above the English River. Gold and iron have been mined locally in the past, but much of today's community is centered on hydroelectricity.

Red Lake

Bush planes are king in this "Norseman capital of the world," a town that 60 years ago was said to have the world's busiest airport. The slogan honors the pug-nosed Noorduyn Norseman, the first plane designed specifically for Canada's North, and vital in opening up mining towns like Red Lake. Several Norseman still operate locally, and aviation buffs come here in July for the annual Norseman Festival.

Red Lake is the jump-off for wilderness canoeing and fly-in lodges. Anishinabee (Ojibwa) artifacts and displays on local gold mining (the area has been in continuous gold production since 1930) and bush flying are featured at the Red Lake Museum.

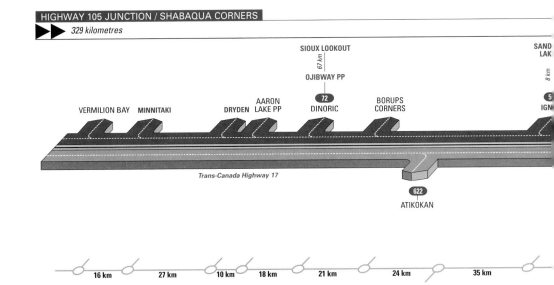

SIOUX LOOKOUT
67 km
OJIBWAY PP

SAND
LAK

8 km

AARON
LAKE PP

VERMILION BAY   MINNITAKI   DRYDEN   **72**   BORUPS   **5**
                                                      DINORIC   CORNERS   IGN

Trans-Canada Highway 17

622
ATIKOKAN

16 km   27 km   10 km   18 km   21 km   24 km   35 km

**NORTHWESTERN
ONTARIO**

Minnitaki

You can see sheepshearing and sheepdog exercises every week morning during July and August at Egli's Sheep Farm, Canada's largest specialty shop for wool and sheepskin products. Year-round, you can see artisans at work on mitts, vests, slippers, teddy bears, and assorted items sold by catalogue and at a store on site, or stroll through fields and barns stocked with Suffolk, Dorset and Corriedale flocks.

Dryden

Gold miners and prospectors were this area's first residents, but the community got its real start in 1894 when Ontario's Agriculture Minister John Dryden set up an experimental farm named New Prospect. On an earlier train stopover, Dryden had noticed lush clover near the rail line and deduced that the land had farming potential. When the farm was later subdivided, the settlers named their community for the sharp-eyed minister. Lumbering and gold mining remain the region's mainstays. In winter, Dryden is a major snowmobiling center. You can tour the Avenor mill, which produces pulp, paper, and lumber, and the Regional Fire Management Centre, which coordinates fire fight-

At 5.5 m high, Dryden mascot Maximillian (Max to his friends) Moose is twice as big as the real moose nibbling leaves in the wildlife-rich forests nearby.

ing operations over much of northwestern Ontario. Aboriginal and pioneer artifacts, trapping equipment, and mineral collections are displayed in the Dryden and District Museum.

Ojibway Provincial Park

Tranquil scenes of natural beauty await visitors to Ojibway Provincial Park. It's unspoiled Canadian Shield country, peaceful stretches of boreal forest and lakes covered with lily pads and wild rice. There are sandy beaches, a boat launch on Little Vermilion Lake (which joins the larger Vermilion Lake), a 50-site campground, and hiking trails.

Sioux Lookout

Music, crafts, picnics, sports and, of course, blueberry bake-offs are among events at Sioux Lookout's Blueberry Festival in early August. Blueberries, which are plentiful in the area, are said to be at their very best at this time. Sioux Lookout is on Pelican Lake, one of countless sparkling lakes that have made the region a popular recreational center. Golf, riding, and fishing are among summer pursuits; snowmobiling is big in winter.

Ignace

Ignace is at the intersection of the Trans-Canada Highway and Hwy. 599, Ontario's northernmost road, which extends 300 km to Pickle Lake, the province's most northerly road-accessible town. Lumbering, mining, and tourism are the main

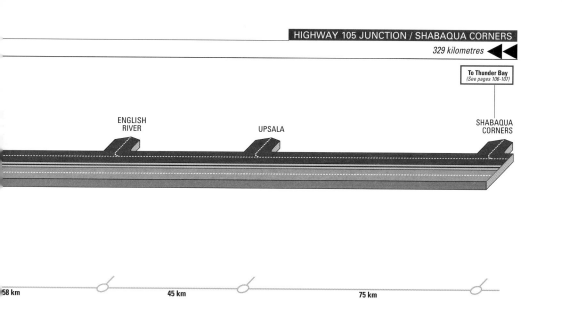

ENGLISH
RIVER

UPSALA

SHABAQUA
CORNERS

58 km

45 km

75 km

industries locally. The community is surrounded by easily accessible lakes, and tourists enjoy some of Ontario's finest fishing and hunting. Hiking trails begin at the Ignace Regional Travel Centre, where you can see the 20 m Bonheur Fire Tower, an arboretum, and displays on forest fires and mining.

McQuat's Castle, White Otter Lake

It is accessible only by plane, boat or snowmobile. Even so, consider making a trip from Ignace to McQuat's Castle on White Otter Lake. An extraordinary four-story log structure in any circumstance, this castle is all the more remarkable because it stands in the wilderness and was built by one man. Jimmy

McQuat (1855-1918), a native of Argenteuil County, Québec, built the castle between about 1904 and 1912. Alone, he cut the trees, squared the logs, dovetailed their corners, and winched them into place. The building has 26 windows, which McQuat portaged in himself, and a 13 m tower. Alas, McQuat drowned nearby within a few years of completing his handmade castle. Some repairs were carried out in the 1950s but the major restoration work began in the 1980s.

Sandbar Lake Provincial Park

If you are seeking a pleasant stopover, this park offers fine sandy beaches, campsites, boating facilities, and hiking trails through rugged Canadian Shield landscapes. The sandy beaches and a long winding esker southwest of the park date from the last ice age, when the region was a glacial outwash area where receding glaciers dumped silt and sand. As well as the lake for which it is named, this heavily forested park is dotted with nine smaller lakes.

Jimmy McQuat was proud of the castle he fashioned from green pine logs on White Otter Lake south of Ignace. But because McQuat built on Crown land, a common practice at the time, the goverrnment denied him title, so he never owned his castle. The building is now part of the Turtle River–White Otter Lakeway Provincial Park.

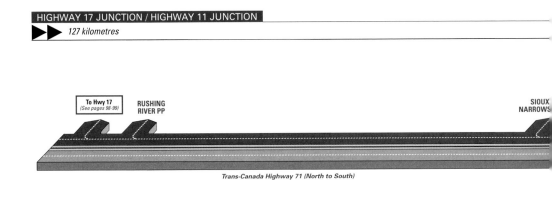

To Hwy 17
(See pages 98-99)

RUSHING
RIVER PP

SIOUX
NARROWS

Trans-Canada Highway 71 (North to South)

6 km   52 km

**NORTHWESTERN
ONTARIO**

Rushing River Provincial Park

This picturesque park at the confluence of Rushing River and Dogtooth Lake is a favorite of canoeists. Boat rentals available nearby make it easy for beginners to test the waters, and the park's three wilderness canoe routes challenge more experienced canoeists. For swimmers, there are four sandy beaches; for hikers, a selection of trails; for campers, 192 campsites. Jack pines in the park's forest are all the same height, a sign that their growth began at the same time, most likely after a great 1910 fire razed the previous forest. The park's log cabin museum dates from road construction in the region in the 1930s.

Sioux Narrows Provincial Park

All the pleasures of Lake of the Woods are available to visitors to this island park—excellent swimming and fishing, boating among the lake's endless islands (look for ancient Indian pictographs along the shoreline), a 71-site campground set amid old-pine forests, and a chance to spot bald eagles, ospreys, cormorants, and mergansers. The 64 m bridge over the Narrows is the longest single span wooden bridge in North America. The Narrows is the site of a legendary ambush of a Sioux raiding party by Cree and Ojibwa Indians. The Whitefish Bay First Nation operates the park.

Nestor Falls

At the heart of the Lake of the Woods tourist district, Nestor Falls has a variety of parks, campgrounds, resorts, guiding operations, fly-in lodges, and magnificent northern lights displays. Local businesses offer canoe and houseboat rentals in summer and snowmobile outings in winter.

Lake of the Woods Provincial Park

Deer are frequently seen in this park set on a peninsula in Lake of the Woods. There is warm water bathing on a sandy beach (the sand is a remnant of glacial Lake Agassiz), a boat launch, and a 100-site campground. The park is noted for its blend of environments—northern jack pine, spruce forests, and southern hardwoods—and the presence of prairie birds such as the yellow-headed blackbird and western meadowlark. White pelicans nest on offshore islands.

Rainy River

A wee bit of the Prairies edges into Ontario between Rainy River and Fort Frances. Farms flourish in this pleasant countryside, where many towns have the wide main streets, grid patterns, and architectural styles of

Scenes such as this waterfall from Kakabikitchiwan Lake and Lake of the Woods are among photographic delights in the Nestor Falls area.

NESTOR FALLS	CALIPER LAKE PP				EMO **11**

600 *50 km* — LAKE OF THE WOODS PP

11 *53 km* — RAINY RIVER

7 km	25 km	19 km

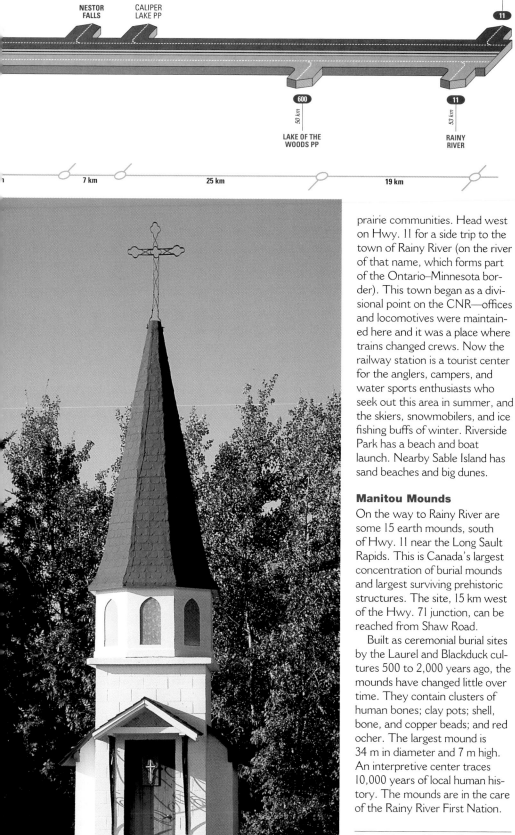

prairie communities. Head west on Hwy. 11 for a side trip to the town of Rainy River (on the river of that name, which forms part of the Ontario–Minnesota border). This town began as a divisional point on the CNR—offices and locomotives were maintained here and it was a place where trains changed crews. Now the railway station is a tourist center for the anglers, campers, and water sports enthusiasts who seek out this area in summer, and the skiers, snowmobilers, and ice fishing buffs of winter. Riverside Park has a beach and boat launch. Nearby Sable Island has sand beaches and big dunes.

Manitou Mounds

On the way to Rainy River are some 15 earth mounds, south of Hwy. 11 near the Long Sault Rapids. This is Canada's largest concentration of burial mounds and largest surviving prehistoric structures. The site, 15 km west of the Hwy. 71 junction, can be reached from Shaw Road.

Built as ceremonial burial sites by the Laurel and Blackduck cultures 500 to 2,000 years ago, the mounds have changed little over time. They contain clusters of human bones; clay pots; shell, bone, and copper beads; and red ocher. The largest mound is 34 m in diameter and 7 m high. An interpretive center traces 10,000 years of local human history. The mounds are in the care of the Rainy River First Nation.

One of the world's smallest churches, the Norlund Chapel at Emo holds eight people. See Emo entry next page.

103

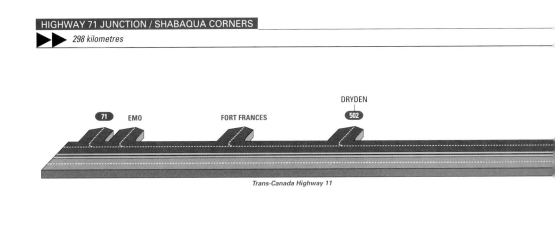

DRYDEN

71 EMO   FORT FRANCES   **502**

Trans-Canada Highway 11

6 km   35 km   32 km   116 km

**NORTHWESTERN
ONTARIO**

Emo

This farming village sits on the Rainy River on the U.S. boundary. From many downtown stores you can look across the river at Indus, Minn. Redevelopment of the riverfront has created terraces overlooking the water, walking and bike trails, and a boat launch. Clothes of the 1900s and household items of early settlers, logging and farm equipment, musical instruments and war memorabilia are among items in the Rainy River District Women's Institute Museum. The Norlund Chapel, built in 1973, holds just eight people (see photo, page 103). Arts, crafts, baking, and livestock exhibits plus stock car races are highlights of Emo's four-day agricultural fall fair. There is weekly stock car racing at the Emo Speedway, and you can golf at the 18-hole Kitchen Creek Golf Course.

Fort Frances

The Fort Frances Museum and Cultural Centre, in a former 1898 school, displays Native and pioneer artifacts alongside modern crafts. It also operates three other sites: the Lookout Tower Museum (climb to its 33 m peak for fine views); the logging tug *Hallett* (from 1941 to 1974 the largest and most powerful tug pulling log booms to paper mills on the Rainy River); and the replica of Fort Saint-Pierre, the wintering post built in 1731 by the explorer La Jemerais (a nephew of De La Vérendrye). The fort is in Pither's Point Park, which has swimming, boating,

and camping facilities. Fort Frances is located where Rainy Lake drains into the Rainy River, and it is connected by bridge to its sister city, International Falls, Minn. Family activities are also scheduled when Canada's largest cash bass derby is held in Fort Frances in July. On summer weekdays, you can tour the Stone-Consolidated paper mill to learn about modern papermaking techniques. (Tours are limited to those 12 years and older and you must wear close-toed footwear.) The island-hopping Noden Causeway (Hwy. 11) just east of town offers spectacular views of Rainy Lake.

Rainy Lake

This lake's 932 km^2 surface lies in rough woodlands astride the Ontario–Minnesota border; 80 percent of the lake is in Canada. In fur trade days, the Rainy Lake–Rainy River–Lake of the Woods waterway was a well-traveled route. In more modern times, forest industries and outdoor recreation have become mainstays. Fort Frances is the lake's largest community.

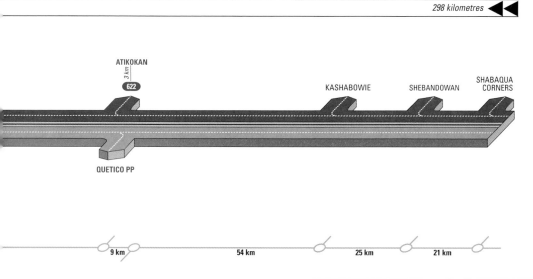

ATIKOKAN

622

QUETICO PP

KASHABOWIE   SHEBANDOWAN   SHABAQUA CORNERS

9 km   54 km   25 km   21 km

log Atikokan Centennial Museum. Two major mines, Steep Rock Iron Mines and Caland Ore Company, brought boom times to the town from about 1940 to 1980. There are lookouts today at the old open pits, and murals in downtown Atikokan commemorating the mines. Atikokan celebrates Native Pow Wow Days in June.

Quetico Provincial Park

This is Ontario's largest and wildest provincial park. Since logging was banned there in 1971, efforts have centered on keeping the park untamed. Although open for canoeing and back-country camping, there are no roads, and motorboats and snowmobiles are banned. The only developed spot is at Dawson Trail, where there are beaches, a boat launch, and a 133-site campground. Otherwise, Quetico's 4,757 km² remain a wilderness, where hundreds of lakes, rivers, and short portages add up to a canoeist's 5,000 km dream. This, combined with the park's great natural beauty—old-growth pine and spruce, majestic cliffs, spectacular waterfalls, ancient pictographs—and varied wildlife, has earned it a reputation as North America's best site for wilderness canoeing.

Five short interpretive trails, a playground, picnic spots, and excellent beaches are all within easy reach of Quetico's Dawson Trail Campground. On French Lake, the campground is the only place in the park accessible by car. Some sites have electrical hookups.

Over 30 years, millions of tonnes of iron ore were extracted from underneath Steep Rock Lake in what is now Atikokan Historic Park Open Mines. The mine site, idle since 1980, is returning to its natural state. The water now in the pits is expected to overflow the pit walls early in the next century.

Atikokan

With 9,000 km² of lakes and backcountry—Quetico Provincial Park included—at its doorstep, Atikokan has strong grounds for claiming to be the "canoeing capital of Canada." It is a major stop for anyone interested in fishing, camping, visiting McQuat's Castle on White Otter Lake (see page 100), hiking, biking, skiing, snowmobiling, and, of course, canoeing. The golf at Little Falls Golf Course has been described as the toughest in northwestern Ontario. An old logging locomotive, as well as photographs and displays from Atikokan's busy days as an iron-mining center, is among collections on local social and logging history in the

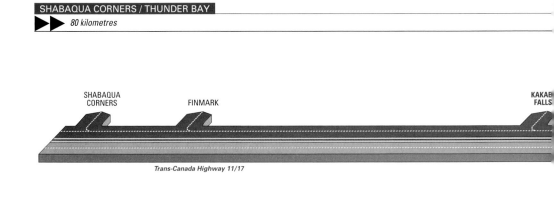

SHABAQUA
CORNERS

FINMARK

KAKAB[ll]
FALLS

Trans-Canada Highway 11/17

8 km   28 km   5 k

**NORTH SHORE
LAKE SUPERIOR**

Kakabeka Falls Provincial Park

"Niagara of the north" is a common name for the awesome Kakabeka Falls, where the waters of the Kaministiquia River plunge 40 m into a sheer-walled gorge. Layered in sedimentary rock at the foot of the falls are fossils 1.6 billion years old. The Mountain Portage hiking trail follows an old voyageur portage around the falls. You can enjoy the park's fine boreal forest scenery by car, bike or on foot. There is a roped-off beach upriver, and a 166-site campground.

Paipoonge Museum

This museum uses displays of Native copper spearheads, fur trade artifacts, pioneer farm machinery, furniture, quilts, and lumbering and mining equipment, to tell the story of the Thunder Bay area. To get there, go south 2 km on Hwy. 130 to Rosslyn Road.

Old Fort William Historic Park

The largest reconstructed fur trade post in the world, Old Fort William is a re-creation of the North West Company's inland headquarters, the most important settlement in interior North America between 1803 and 1821. Sprawled beside the Kaministiquia River are 42 buildings—fur stores, residences, kitchens and shops, a massive wharf and canoe landing, a working farm, and a Native encampment. You can chat with fur trade-era characters, such as company partners, Native trappers, traditional

tradesmen, and voyageurs. In July, hundreds of other costumed characters gather at the park for the Great Rendezvous Festival, 10 days of revelry reminiscent of the music and partying that marked the arrival of the fur brigades of old. Traditional Native foods and crafts are featured at the Ojibwa Keeshigun celebration in August.

Thunder Bay

A great natural harbor, and its location between western rail lines and the Great Lakes–St. Lawrence Seaway, has made Thunder Bay one of the largest grain handling ports in the world. Tour one of the great grain elevators lining the Lake Superior waterfront. Some pulp and paper mills, now the city's largest employer, can be toured as well. You can see the region's most famous natural landmark, the unusual rock formation called the Sleeping Giant (*Nanibijou* in Ojibwa), from Hillcrest Park, which is also renowned for its floral displays. Flower lovers will also revel in the Centennial Botanical Conservatory's three greenhouses, one tropical, anoth-

The sound of bagpipes often fills the air at Fort William, as it did when the shrewd Scottish North West Company partners held trade strategy sessions here. Blueberries are among crops harvested from the fort's farm. Its produce once fed hordes of voyageurs who passed through Fort William each year.

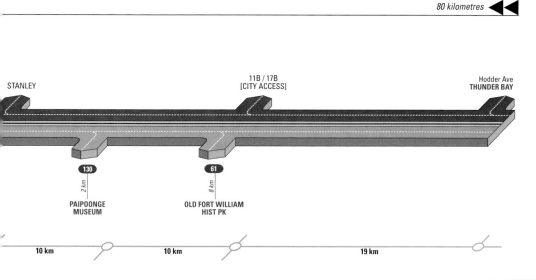

STANLEY

11B / 17B
[CITY ACCESS]

Hodder Ave
THUNDER BAY

130

2 km

PAIPOONGE
MUSEUM

61

8 km

OLD FORT WILLIAM
HIST PK

10 km   10 km   19 km

er containing 280 cacti species, and one with changing floral shows. Another favorite with visitors is the International Friendship Gardens, where shrubbery and raised flower beds celebrate numerous ethnic groups. Centennial Park on the Current River has a reconstructed 1910 logging camp, a logging museum, and a model farm. Mount McKay, which towers 300 m over the city, has a scenic lookout halfway up with picnic areas and campsites.

Aboriginal peoples have lived here for 10,000 years. The first European—explorer Daniel Greysolon DuLhut—arrived in 1679. Thunder Bay itself did not exist until 1970, when it was created through the amalgamation of Fort William and Port Arthur. It claims the largest Finnish community outside Finland.

Thunder Bay has ample facilities for downhill and cross-country skiing, snowmobiling, and ice-climbing. The Canada Games Complex has an Olympic-class pool, water slide, and jogging tracks, and there are myriad recreational possibilities at Hazelwood Lake Conservation Area and Trowbridge Falls, Chippewa, Kakabeka, and Sleeping Giant parks.

Thunder Bay Museum

Here's a museum with a truly eclectic collection: a 65-million-year-old Albertosaurus skeleton and a re-created early-20th-century jail, an iron lung and a World War I airplane engine, fur trade relics, model ships, Thunder Bay's first fire engine, and a 1908 pump organ. There are also local Native artifacts including 10,000-year-old tools, and more recent Ojibwa heritage items, such as beadwork, embroidery, and a wigwam.

Thunder Bay Art Gallery

This gallery on Confederation College campus has an impressive permanent collection of contemporary First Nations art, including early works by Norval Morrisseau. Works by local artists and touring exhibits from other galleries and museums are shown regularly. Exquisite handcrafted jewelry is a specialty of the gallery's gift shop.

Hillcrest Park, on an escarpment overlooking the southern section of Thunder Bay, offers spectacular views of the harbor area of the city and the Sleeping Giant beyond.

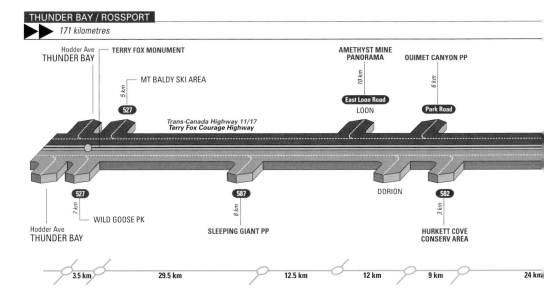

Hodder Ave
THUNDER BAY — TERRY FOX MONUMENT

MT BALDY SKI AREA

527

AMETHYST MINE
PANORAMA   OUIMET CANYON PP

10 km   6 km

East Loon Road
LOON   Park Road

Trans-Canada Highway 11/17
Terry Fox Courage Highway

527   587   DORION   582

7 km   8 km   3 km

WILD GOOSE PK

Hodder Ave
THUNDER BAY   SLEEPING GIANT PP   HURKETT COVE
CONSERV AREA

3.5 km   29.5 km   12.5 km   12 km   9 km   24 km

NORTH SHORE,
LAKE SUPERIOR

*Natural heat
and the earth's
radiation
created this
amethyst,
mined near
Thunder Bay,
Ont. The semi-
precious gem-
stone is said to
bring good luck
to petitioners:
wear one when
asking the boss
for a raise.*

Terry Fox Monument

A larger-than-life bronze statue of Terry Fox (1958–1981) stands on the Trans-Canada near the spot where the one-legged runner was forced to end his "Marathon of Hope" on Sept. 1, 1980. Stone tablets on the monument recount the story of Fox's 5,432 km run for cancer research. The 100 km Thunder Bay-to-Nipigon stretch of the Trans-Canada is called The Terry Fox Courage Highway.

are found in a vein, roughly a metre thick and 300 m long, that runs deep underground and beneath a nearby lake, where the best gems are thought to be. You can dig for your own amethysts at the extensive open pit site: the mine company provides the pails, digging tools, and running water. Many gift shops in the area carry gifts and jewelry crafted from the local gemstone.

Ontario, one of the world's major sources of amethysts, has made the gem its official provincial mineral.

Sleeping Giant Provincial Park

Pass Lake, some 8 km from the Trans-Canada, is the gateway to this park, which occupies the 243 km² Sibley Peninsula on Lake Superior. It is named for an 11 km long rocky tableland—a chain of four 240 m high mesas: when seen from Thunder Bay, the tableland resembles a huge prone giant. Six nature trails wind through the park, whose rugged terrain contains diverse plant and animal life including rare wild orchids and bald eagles. Plantain Lane Trail leads to the Sea Lion, an arch of stone rearing up from Lake Superior's depths, and the ghostly remains of Silver Islet, once one of the world's richest silver mines.

Amethyst Mine Panorama

Precious gemstones in hues from pale lavender to deep blue purple abound here at North America's largest amethyst mine. The gems

Ouimet Canyon Provincial Park

At the heart of this park is Ouimet Canyon, a spectacular gorge sometimes called Canada's Grand Canyon. From the Trans-Canada, you drive through lush, flat farmland before winding up to a rocky plateau. A wide kilometre-long path extends from the parking lot through thick pine woods to a lookout at the western rim of the canyon, which opens up with unexpected splendor. Panoramic views there and at another lookout farther on encompass distant Lake Superior. Walk only on designated trails: there are no barriers or signs marking the canyon's rim.

Hurkett Cove Conservation Area

A 3 km unpaved road leads to the head of Black Bay, site of this marshy haven for a multitude of songbirds, waterfowl, beavers,

108

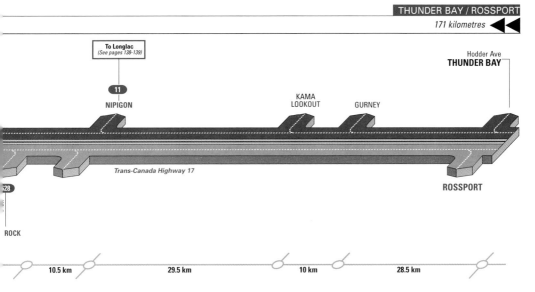

To Longlac
(See pages 138-139)

11
NIPIGON

KAMA
LOOKOUT   GURNEY

Hodder Ave
THUNDER BAY

Trans-Canada Highway 17

ROSSPORT

628

ROCK

10.5 km   29.5 km   10 km   28.5 km

deer, moose, and muskrats. A secluded sandy beach is ideal for a family picnic. A hook of land shielding the placid cove provides a sheltered harbor for canoes and sailboats that venture into rougher waters on nearby Cranberry Bay.

Red Rock

A 300 m long boardwalk, a park, and a marina enhance Red Rock's picturesque waterfront on Nipigon Bay. The region is known for steep-sided ridges called cuestas, which are characterized by rusty red layers of limestone and shale. Red Rock is named for the 120 m high, 3 km long Red Rock Cuesta, which looms over the Trans-Canada, near Hwy. 628. Just off 628, a three-hour hiking trail to Nipigon cuts through woods of black spruce, tamarack, moss and peat, where moose nibble, and Nashville warblers and Lincoln's sparrows sing in summer. Trail maps are available at the local municipal office.

Nipigon

This resort town is situated on the Nipigon River, Lake Superior's largest tributary. In the late 17th century, fur traders set up a

Ouimet Canyon, an impressive tree-lined gorge, some 3 km long, 150 m wide, and 107 m deep, was created when glacial ice cut through ancient volcanic rock a million years ago. Today, winter ice lingers on the canyon floor well into the summer, creating chilly conditions in which a profusion of sub-arctic plants thrive.

fort at Nipigon. This was the first European settlement on Lake Superior's north shore, which has long been home to the Ojibwa Indians. Aboriginal pictographs, possibly 400 to 1,000 years old, are found downstream. Evoking feats of gods and spirits, the pictographs consist of lines and symbols painted in red on cliff faces high above water level at the river mouth. The site is accessible by boat from Nipigon marina. Just east of town, Kama Lookout offers one of the best vistas of Lake Superior's rocky headlands plunging sheerly into clear, cold waters. In recent years, Kama Station has become a center for ice-climbing (see pages 110-111).

Rossport

Just off the Trans-Canada, this village on a big bay sheltered by islands is known for the rustic 1884 Rossport Inn—the oldest operating hotel on Lake Superior's north shore—and a local freshwater fish derby, the longest running event of its kind in North America. (It has been held every year since 1937.) An abundance of lake trout locally attracts sports fishermen from around the world. From the marina, you can make fishing and boating expeditions to Simpson and other islands, which form a tenuous barrier against the 9 m waves of Lake Superior's ferocious storms. The tip of the yacht *Gunilda*, the casualty of one such storm, rises from Rossport harbor. All efforts to salvage the millionaire's pleasure boat, which sank in 1911, have failed.

How to Climb a Waterfall? Wait Until It Freezes!

HIGHWAY 11 / NIPIGON

CHARLES WILKINS, *a frequent contributor to magazines, has written for CBC radio and television. His books include* Breakfast at the Hoito, *a collection of travel essays on the Canadian North.*

ABOUT HALFWAY UP the 90 m cliffs at Kama Lookout, I sink my ice axes and plant my feet atop a nub of solidified snow. My heart is doing a bravura percussion; my inner clothes are drenched; and I am increasingly regretting the months of push-ups neglected, the kilometres I haven't jogged. I have also developed a low-grade case of what ice climbers call "sewing machine leg"—the thigh and calf muscles are so exhausted that the entire leg trembles involuntarily, as if working the treadle on an old-fashioned sewing machine.

What's more, I am fiercely thirsty. But lacking a free hand, I can only gnaw into a bit of loose powder on the ice wall in front of my face. I wolf back a mouthful and go for more, breathing harder than I have in years. Then I reset my axes and take another tentative step against gravity.

Behind me is a vast expanse of Lake Superior. To my left and right stretch headlands of 3-billion-year-old rock and endless tracts of boreal forest. Above me rises a sculpted ice face.

Like most Canadians, I am on familiar terms with ice. Every autumn for decades, I have watched it crystalize on lakes and rivers. I have pushed pucks and curling stones across it, and skated its surface. But until today, it never occurred to me to scramble up an icy cliff in sub-zero weather—and thereby join the growing ranks of Canadians engaged in ice climbing.

The sport begins with a waterfall. You wait until it freezes. Then you climb it with the aid of a range of implements—ice screws, ice axes, ice hooks, and crampons.

Ice axes are high-tech hatchets on which the cutting edge has been reduced to a single clawlike pick about 12 cm long. You hold one in each hand and drive them into the ice to serve as handholds. The equally menacing crampons are rigid steel devices that fasten like a child's bob skates to a climber's boots. Each bears a double row of downward spikes, plus two or more front spikes that point straight forward and can be kicked into the ice as a toehold. All climbers—at least those who wish to remain climbers—wear safety harness. In my case, an emergency rope (or "belay") extends from my harness to an anchored pulley at the top of the icefall and back down to where my partner holds it ready to take up slack as I climb.

Although ice climbing is practiced elsewhere—notably the Rockies, the Laurentians, and the Muskoka region—many regard the Nipigon area as the sport's hot spot. Sites in the Rockies offer longer climbs, but those near Nipigon are more accessible and numerous: you can take in as many as half a dozen climbs in one day. The area is perfect for the sport because of the long line of basalt cliffs or "palisades" along the Lake Superior shoreline and on Highway 11 just north of Nipigon. In summer, hundreds of waterfalls pour over and out of these palisades. By December, each is a glistening cascade of ice. And so they remain until April or early May, when the ice falls away in multi-tonne slabs.

Kama Bay, 22 km east of Nipigon on Lake Superior, has 25 climbing sites on Domtar 81 Road, all within 300 m of the Trans-Canada Hwy. Ice Station Superior, 61 km east of Nipigon, offers 12 climbs, each with a spectacular view of the lake and St. Ignace Island. But the greatest concentration of climbs is at Orient Bay, some 35 km north of Nipigon on Hwy 11. There, more than a hundred icefalls, ranging in height from 40 to 90 m, are within sight and walking distance of the Trans-Canada. Spectators often park their vehicles on the roadside and watch the spectacle.

Ice climbing developed in the area largely because of geologist Shaun Parent, a veteran of climbs in the Rockies, the Andes, and in Oman, Nepal, and Thailand.

> "*A bag of adrenaline seems to burst in my chest . . .*"

With a number of colleagues, he opened up and mapped dozens of Nipigon sites during the 1980s, when the sport was in its infancy. In 1988 Parent started North of Superior Climbing Company, a Thunder Bay-based guiding service and, a year later, founded North America's only annual ice-climbing festival, Ice Fest. Held in Orient Bay in mid-March, it attracts climbers from across Canada and the United States.

Because of the dangers of the sport and the need for highly specialized equipment, those wishing to climb in the area would be wise to contact Parent's company—the only ice-climbing service in northwestern Ontario. It rents equipment and provides group and individual lessons, and guided climbs for beginners to advanced folk. For novices, the prerequisites are overall fitness and a solid training session.

My own amateurish moves eventually get me to within metres of the Kama Lookout summit, but not without price. I am half dead. But, as I take my last tortuous steps upward, I undergo a transformation. Realizing I have all but reached the top, a bag of adrenaline seems to burst in my chest, and I virtually spring up the last few steps onto the little shelf of ice where the belay anchor is planted. Washed by the euphoria that comes of reaching the pinnacle, I stretch out flat and stare at the sky, attempting to catch my breath. As I bask in my achievement, a raven soars out above me, circles ceremoniously, and drifts into the woods. I raise myself on an elbow and gaze out at Lake Superior. Then I dig my ice axes in, ease myself over the edge, and begin my descent.

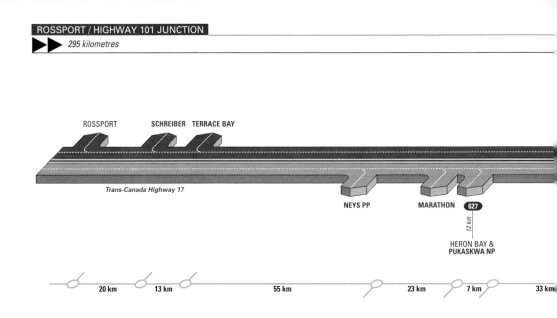

ROSSPORT   SCHREIBER TERRACE BAY

Trans-Canada Highway 17

NEYS PP   MARATHON   627

12 km

HERON BAY &
PUKASKWA NP

20 km   13 km   55 km   23 km   7 km   33 km

**EAST SHORE,
LAKE SUPERIOR**

Schreiber

Half of Schreiber's population is of Italian descent, most tracing their ancestry to Siderno Marina, a town in southern Italy. Italians first came here in 1883 to work for the CPR. Schreiber offers fishing, cross-country skiing, snowmobiling, and hikes on the 48 km Casques Isles Hiking Trail which links Rossport, Terrace Bay, and Schreiber. There are numerous entry points for those wishing to make shorter walks.

Terrace Bay

This model town, built by Kimberly-Clarke paper products in the 1940s, is named for the terraces of sand—relics of melting glaciers—surrounding Lake Superior. Terrace Bay's picturesque appearance and setting have made it the "gem of the North Shore." Aguasabon Falls drop into a deep gorge at the west end of town.

Neys Provincial Park

Pic Island, immortalized by Group of Seven artist Lawren Harris, is visible from the tip of the Coldwell Peninsula. It is among many fine views you can enjoy if you stroll along white, sandy Neys Beach. Swimming is invigorating if you can stand the cold. However, swimmers should be wary of strong undercurrents in the Little Pic River.

Marathon

In 1944, Marathon Paper of Wisconsin established a town and a pulp mill here. Four decades later, Marathon boomed when gold was discovered at nearby Hemlo—the present-day site of Canada's three largest gold mines. The mines and processing plants are open for tours in summer. Rock hounds may want to visit the local spectralite mine, North America's only source of this semiprecious gem. Winter visitors can enjoy excellent alpine and cross-country ski facilities and hundreds of kilometres of groomed snowmobile trails.

Pukaskwa National Park

The "wild shore of an inland sea" is one description of Pukaskwa—that's "puck-a-saw"—National Park. Most of its Lake Superior

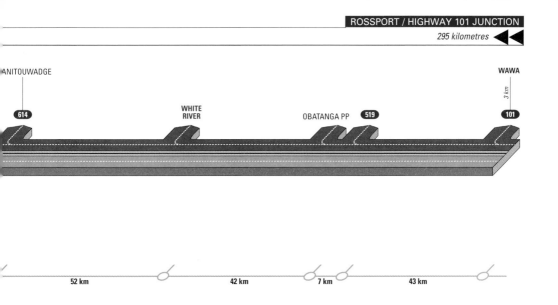

ANITOUWADGE   WAWA

614   WHITE   OBATANGA PP   519   101
             RIVER

52 km   42 km   7 km   43 km

coastline consists of rocky out-crops; just about all its interior is pure Canadian Shield, containing the characteristic rocky terrain, forests, and wildlife. Hattie Cove in the northwest corner has picnic spots, a 67-site campground, beaches, and hiking trails, but this 1,878 km² rugged preserve, Ontario's largest national park, is mostly for the wilderness back-packer or canoeist.

White River

Winnie-the-Pooh's statue at the town entrance recalls the day in 1914 when a black bear cub walked out of the bush and into fame, all because a train carrying World War I soldiers was stopped in White River. One of the troops, Capt. Harry Cole-bourn, bought the bear from a trapper. He named the bear Winnipeg after his hometown, and took it with him to London. When he was leaving for battle, he gave the bear to the London Zoo. A.A. Milne visited the zoo with his son Christopher Robin, saw the bear, and began making up stories about Winnie and some little friends. First published in 1926, the stories have remained enduring favorites. Winnie's Hometown Festival in August features heritage displays, a trade show, drama presentations, and a talent show.

Wawa

The 9 m steel Canada Goose at the entrance to Wawa is one of the most famous pieces of "high-way art" in North America. Wawa, which means wild goose in Ojibwa, is named for the Canada geese that congregate on Lake Wawa. Although gold was discovered locally in 1897, and other gold booms occurred in the 1920s and the 1980s, iron mines have been the town's mainstay since the 1890s. Ore from the George M. MacLeod Mine, Canada's only under-ground iron mine and the only iron mine in Ontario, is shipped to Algoma Steel in Sault Ste. Marie. Wawa Lake Beachfront and Mr. Vallée Park on Ander-son Lake are pleasant places to stroll or picnic. The beachfront is also the site of the annual Prospector's Party in summer and the starting point of the Gold Quest Sled Dog Race in spring.

Summer or winter, scenic High Falls, a 23 m high, 38 m wide drop on the Magpie River just south of Wawa, is well worth a visit. Short walking trails from a park at the base of the falls take you to a lookout at the top.

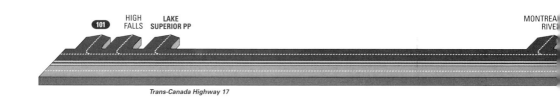

HIGH
FALLS
LAKE
SUPERIOR PP
101
MONTREAL
RIVER

Trans-Canada Highway 17

5 km   10 km   90 km

**EAST SHORE,
LAKE SUPERIOR**

*At Sault
Canal National
Historic Site,
you can stroll
along a board-
walk beside the
historic engi-
neering works,
or explore a
delightful
wilderness trail.*

Lake Superior
Provincial Park

A remarkable feature of this park
is the Ojibwa pictographs at
Agawa Bay. Guides at the nearby campground will show them
to you. The campground also has
an exhibit center describing the
park's geology and wildlife.
Moose are plentiful in the park,
and wood caribou, once common, have been reintroduced.
There are beaches, picnic spaces,
three campgrounds, and access
to unrivaled outdoor adventure.
Trails ranging from 90-minute
outings to arduous treks attract
hikers, especially in fall when the
sugar maples and yellow birches
are at their most brilliant. Seven

canoe routes crisscross dozens of
waterways, beckoning wilderness canoeists on trips ranging
from two hours to five days.

Batchawana Bay
Provincial Park

A roadside pull-off south of this
park marks the midpoint of the
Trans-Canada—it is about
3,925 km either to Victoria,
B.C., or St. John's, Nfld.

Sault Ste. Marie

This city prides itself on offering
"city excitement with wilderness
just minutes away." The Roberta
Bondar Pavilion and Marina, the
centerpiece of the renovated
waterfront, honors Canada's

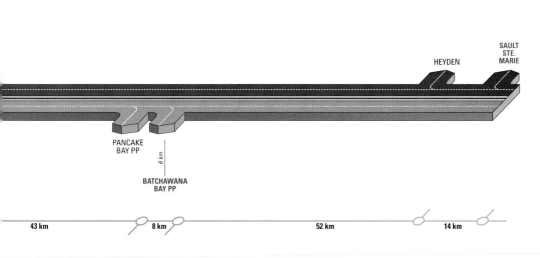

SAULT STE. MARIE

HEYDEN

PANCAKE BAY PP

6 km

BATCHAWANA BAY PP

43 km   8 km   52 km   14 km

first female astronaut, who was born and grew up in Sault Ste. Marie. It hosts conventions, meetings, concerts, and many events of the 10-day Bon Soo winter carnival. Algoma Steel and pulp and paper plants are the city's biggest employers.

Locks that allow ships to overcome the 6 m shift in height from Lake Superior to Lake Huron are the Soo's best known attraction. Visitors can tour them aboard *Chief Shingwauk*. Native artifacts including a birchbark wigwam, fur trade items, and shipping and sports displays are featured in the Sault Ste. Marie Museum. The Art Gallery of Algoma exhibits contemporary and historic Canadian art. Bellevue Park has botanical gardens and greenhouses, a zoo, paddleboats, and outdoor concerts. There are cross-country ski trails in local conservation areas and four downhill skiing resorts nearby. The Algoma Central Railway's tour train runs from the Soo to Hearst. (See pages 116-117.)

Sault Ste. Marie Canal National Historic Site

Between 1887 and 1895, this canal was cut through the red sandstone of St. Mary's Island as part of an all-Canadian route from the Atlantic to Lake Superior. It was an engineering marvel at the time; at 274 m, the longest lock in the world. It was also the first canal to use electricity to power its lock gates and valves, electricity produced by the hydro power of the canal itself. Although the canal was taken out of commercial use in the 1970s, its five sets of lock

gates, vintage machinery, buildings, and collections of engineering drawings are all still in place.

Museum Ship *Norgoma*, Sault Ste. Marie

Now permanently berthed at the Roberta Bondar Marina, this museum ship offers a nostalgic look at the glory days of steamship travel on the Great Lakes. The diesel-powered *Norgoma* was the last overnight cruise vessel built on the lakes. It ran from 1950 until retired from service in 1974.

Canadian Bushplane Heritage Centre Sault Ste. Marie

Located on the waterfront, this museum is a window on the history and drama of bush flying and forest fire fighting in Canada. "Fly-in" visitors are not uncommon. Among exhibits are the world's oldest flying de Havilland DHC2 Beaver, a restored Fairchild KR-34 biplane, and a bush fire fighting pioneer de Havilland DHC3 Otter. There is also an operational 1920s-style waterfront hangar, and exhibits of fire fighting technology.

Ermatinger Old Stone House, Sault Ste. Marie

Built in 1814-1823 by fur trader Charles Oakes Ermatinger, this red fieldstone house with metre-thick walls is the oldest surviving stone house in Canada west of Toronto. Restored and open to the public as a national historic site, it has period furnishings, a fur trade museum, and a garden with plants of the kind that were grown in the early 1800s.

The elegant Ermatinger House was the social center of the community and the site of numerous voyageur rendez-vous when the Ermatinger family was in residence in the early 1800s. Before its restoration in the 1960s, it had been an Anglican missionary's home, a hotel, a courthouse, a sheriff's residence, a YWCA, a social club, and an apartment building.

Riding a Wilderness Railway

HIGHWAY 17 / SAULT STE. MARIE

JAMES SMEDLEY *writes the* Backroads *column for* Ontario Out Of Doors *magazine. He has won awards of merit from the Outdoor Writers of Canada (OWC) for his newspaper articles.*

THE SMELL OF DIESEL hangs in the early morning, waterfront air as you board the train. A blast of the whistle and the long line of passenger cars lurch forward, momentum building creak by groan. You pass a steel plant and a paper mill, then a public address system welcomes you aboard the Algoma Central Railway. Set on its 8-hour, 370 km round-trip excursion to the Agawa River Canyon, your tour train has just pulled out of the Sault Ste. Marie depot.

Briefly, you catch sight of the International Bridge and the St. Mary's River locks, the shipping link between Lakes Superior and Huron. Then, whisked along to the rhythmic clacking of steel wheels on rails, you head north from the steel-producing city into Ontario's vast Algoma wilderness. Around you the Canadian Shield flexes its granitic muscle under a canopy of thick forest, North America's last great stand of hardwood. The swaying of the cars is hypnotic and the speeding locomotive seems to bisect the uneven terrain. Massive blunt-topped hills rise above cottage-lined lakes. White pine, maple, and birch cling to steep hillsides. Thick trunks of northern white cedar twist out of the swampy black earth in river valleys carpeted with spruce and balsam fir.

Mileage boards on trackside telephone poles gauge your progress through this rolling sea of tree-studded granite. Occasionally, you glimpse rustic log cabins and sagging railway buildings. Often, moose and black bear are seen at trackside clearings. Overhead, birds of prey work the updrafts with an eye for mice, grouse, and hare.

Work on this railway line began in 1899 and by 1914, track linked Sault Ste. Marie to Hearst, 476 km to the north. Freight trains, used then as now for shipping mineral and forest products, became popular with sightseers in the sixties. As a result, a separate "tour train" was introduced in 1974. A popular attraction ever since, the train departs daily from early June to mid-October.

Decades earlier, Group of Seven members used the railway to explore the landscape that would become the subject of their paintings. Between 1918 and 1923, Lawren Harris, A.Y. Jackson, Frank Johnston, J.E.H. MacDonald, and Arthur Lismer rented a boxcar for living quarters and had it shunted to choice wilderness sidings. Then they traveled the surrounding country on foot and by canoe, painting a vast and wild land unknown to most Canadians.

As you retrace their journeys, your train takes you over three trestle bridges. The most spectacular is the 472 m long curved trestle at Mile 92, which towers 91 m over the Montreal River. Shortly afterward, the Agawa River appears in the panoramic windows, cradled in a deep valley below.

> **"A blast of the whistle and the long line of passenger cars lurch forward."**

The next 19 km of the ride is a steep, 152 m descent to Agawa Canyon's floor. Sheer cliffs seem to engulf the railcars as the train follows the river's path, funneling through a narrow pass between canyon walls composed of some of the world's oldest rock. More than 1.5 billion years ago, movement beneath the earth's crust cracked open the granite bedrock that had lain in the area for a billion years. Then ice sheets, 1 to 2 km thick, began wearing away at the chasm. When the glaciers retreated some 10,000 years ago, they left a debris-filled spillway in their wake.

Today granite walls rise almost 183 m from the floor of the canyon, the centerpiece of a wilderness park. Cascading waterfalls on both sides of the train mark your arrival. You can enjoy a two-hour stopover in this awesome setting. Passengers can eat in the dining car or buy a box lunch and picnic alongside the tea-colored waters of the Agawa River. A stone picnic shelter provides shelter during foul weather. Riverside benches, a playground, and a food concession are linked by pathways along the canyon floor. A network of hiking trails let you stretch your limbs and explore farther afield.

A steep, graveled path and 372 stairs lead to a lookout 76 m above the tracks. Closer to the canyon floor, the Ed Foote and Talus trails wind past lichen-covered rocks at the base of the west wall. You can feel the spray from the 53 m Black Beaver Falls, and gaze across the Agawa River at 69 m Bridal Veil Falls before returning on the Beaver Trail. Another trail follows Otter Creek to the base of a 14 m waterfall—the smallest in the canyon. Fed from beaver ponds above the canyon walls, its fertile waters flow over spawning beds and nurseries for native brook trout. These speckled creatures are visible in trout-feeding pools along the trail.

During the stopover, seats are turned and the engine is switched from one end of the train to the other. Be sure to switch sides for a different view on the return trip. For a completely new perspective, consider riding the train in winter, when the entire landscape is hunkered down under a thick shroud of snow. The Snow Train makes weekend runs, but with no stopover at the canyon.

James Smedley

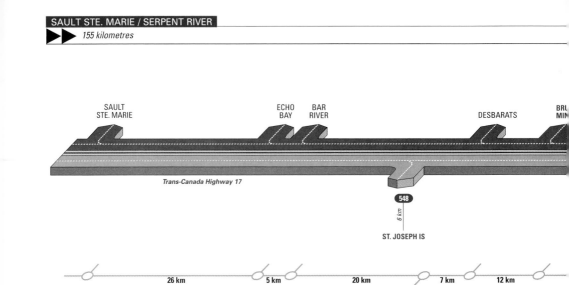

SAULT STE. MARIE   ECHO BAY   BAR RIVER   DESBARATS   BRU MIN

Trans-Canada Highway 17

548
6 km
ST. JOSEPH IS

26 km   5 km   20 km   7 km   12 km

NORTHEASTERN ONTARIO/ LAKE HURON NORTH SHORE

Local history can be relived at St. Joseph Island Museum Village, where some 5,000 artifacts from aboriginal times and early settlement days are housed in a church, two schools, and a two-story barn, as well as in the 1912 general store and 1890s log house shown below.

St. Joseph Island

🏠 🎣 🚶 ⛵ 🚤 🏊 ❄️

A bridge links the mainland to this tranquil island of farms and hardwood forests in the North Channel between Lakes Huron and Superior. Called *Anipich* (the place of hardwood trees) by the Ojibwas, St. Joseph Island is the northern tip of the Niagara Escarpment. Hwy. 548 circles the island linking attractions such as the St. Joseph Island Museum Village; Sailors Encampment, once a place where ships' crews wintered when vessels became icebound in the channel and now a place for up-close views of the busy interlake traffic; Fort St. Joseph National Historic Site; and Hilton Beach.

Rock hounds prize the local "pudding stones," jasper-flecked white quartzite that settlers likened to boiled suet dotted with cherries and currants. Anglers delight in fine catches in the island's protected bays and narrows.

Fort St. Joseph National Historic Site, St. Joseph Island

Built in 1796 on the southeastern tip of St. Joseph Island, the fort was meant to provide a British military presence on a key fur trade route and retain the local Native population's loyalty. Only the ruins remain: the fort was burned by American forces during the War of 1812. Archaeological digs began in the 1960s, and tools, furs, and military uniforms unearthed can be seen in the visitors' center. A large wilderness bird sanctuary, a picnic area, and nature trails are other attractions at the site.

Bruce Mines

🏠 🎣 🚶 ⛵ 🚤 🏊 ❄️

You can take an underground or surface tour of Simpson's Shaft, Canada's first successful copper mine, which operated in 1846-1873. Cornish miners established this community, one of the oldest in northern Ontario. One manager at Bruce Mines was John Sholto Douglas, 9th Marquess of Queensberry. Among the treasured exhibits at the Bruce Mines Museum, housed in an 1894 former Presbyterian church across from the mine, is a large Victorian dollhouse that once belonged to Douglas' granddaughter. Today, Bruce Mines is a popular year-round

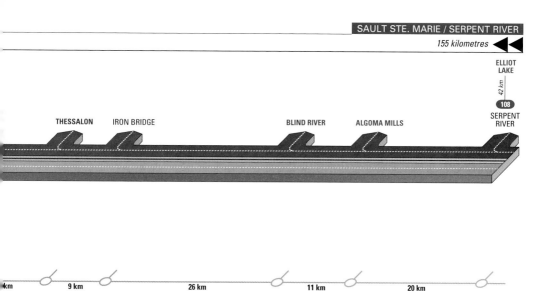

ELLIOT
LAKE

42 km

108
SERPENT
RIVER

THESSALON   IRON BRIDGE   BLIND RIVER   ALGOMA MILLS

km | 9 km | 26 km | 11 km | 20 km

tourist center, with attractions ranging from a full-service marina and parks, to snowmobile and cross-country ski trails and ice fishing.

Thessalon

A popular base for North Channel sailors, Thessalon sits on a point of land jutting into Lake Huron. Exhibits in the Thessalon Township Heritage Park and Museum in nearby Little Rapids recount the region's logging, farming, and commercial fishing history. To explore the scenic hinterland, take the 21 km drive from the museum to The Great White Pine, a 50 m high, 350-year-old tree said to be the tallest east of the Rockies.

Blind River

Early voyageurs, unable to find this river's outlet on Lake Huron, gave it the name that has stuck to this day. When the fur trade declined in 1850, Blind River turned to lumbering, its mainstay into the 1960s. A uranium refinery and tourism are major industries today. A marine park offers a full-service marina, barbecue and horseshoe pits, a volleyball court, weekly events, and a shuttle service to local businesses. Displays of bush-camp utensils and contraptions for braking logs in the Timber Valley Museum evoke winter lumber camps of the past. Other exhibits reflect the culture of the the area's original inhabitants, the Mississagi First Nation, and feature works of art by local artists and artisans.

Algoma Mills

A marina, campgrounds, backwoods trails, and sandy beaches on Lake Lauzon are among this community's attractions.

Elliot Lake

Demand for uranium, discovered here in the 1950s, fueled the ups and downs of this community into the 1980s. Exhibits at the Elliott Lake Nuclear and Mining Museum recall the glory days and mining personalities. When mining declined, the town set about making itself an attractive, affordable center for retirees.

Its name notwithstanding, Elliot Lake's Mining and Nuclear Museum also contains memorabilia on fur trade and logging days, and displays this heritage quilt as well as other works by local artists in a mini-art gallery.

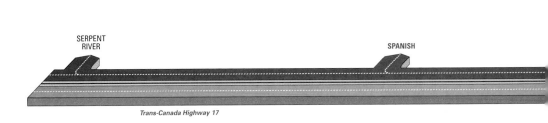

SERPENT
RIVER

SPANISH

Trans-Canada Highway 17

20 km

20 km

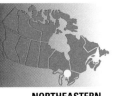

**NORTHEASTERN
ONTARIO/
MANITOULIN
ISLAND**

The Aux Sables River was once part of the network of waterways that carried logs from northern forests to the Great Lakes. Reminders of this logging past live on in Chutes Provincial Park, which is named for a long-ago chute built to steer logs around the river's rapids and this picturesque falls.

Spanish

An all-season outdoor recreation stop, Spanish is especially popular with Lake Huron's North Channel boaters. Two marinas and government dock accommodate all sorts of vessels, from kayaks to yachts. Winter fun enthusiasts will find endless groomed snowmobile trails, plus scenic cross-country ski and snowshoe trails.

Massey

At the junction of the Aux Sables and Spanish rivers, Massey calls itself the "heart of the white pine tourist area" (the recreation district west of Sudbury). Chutes Provincial Park offers camping, a sandy beach, and easy hiking trails. Massey Area Museum focuses on the lumbering boom of the 1870s to the 1920s, and also displays fluorescent minerals and the family trees of 55 Massey-area pioneer families.

Espanola

In July and August, visitors can take a 3-hour or a full-day tour of E.B. Eddy Forest Products Ltd., Espanola's largest employer. The vast Eddy forest is three times the size of Prince Edward Island. You can also tour the Eddy pulp and paper plant and the Nairn Centre sawmill, which produces enough sawn timber annually to build 18,000 houses.

Manitoulin Island

Hwy. 6 takes travelers south across a swing bridge to Manitoulin Island, at 2,766 km², the

world's largest freshwater island. The highway crosses the island, linking Little Current, Sheguiandah, Manitowaning, and South Baymouth, where there is a ferry service to Tobermory on the Bruce Peninsula.

Once a center of logging and commercial fishing, Manitoulin now relies on agriculture and tourism. About a third of the 12,000 population are aboriginal peoples (Odawa, Ojibwa, and Potawotami), who live on seven reserves.

Little Current, Manitoulin Island

The island's largest community, Little Current sits at the North Channel's narrowest gap. Once a Great Lakes lumber port, this "port o' the north" now attracts some 3,000 pleasure boats every summer. Four days of concerts, craft shows, parades, and fireworks mark Haweater Weekend in August. (People born on the island are affectionately known as Haweaters, a reference to the tart, scarlet haws, or hawberries, that flourish on the island's hawthorn trees.)

Sheguiandah, Manitoulin Island

Some 10 km south of Little Current, Sheguiandah includes a First Nation community, site of a colorful annual August pow-wow, and a village established in the 1870s when settlers first took up land here. Two-story log houses and other pioneer-style buildings and 10,000-year-old artifacts discovered in a local

120

MASSEY   WEBBWOOD

ESPANOLA
6

53 km

MANITOULIN IS

17 km   9 km

Boaters in the North Channel off Manitoulin Island's wave scalloped coastline feast on wondrous scenes of forested rocky headlands jutting into shimmering waters.

quarry can be seen in the Little Current–Howland Centennial Museum and Park. Ten Mile Point lookout, between Little Current and Manitowaning, offers breathtaking views of the North Channel and Manitoulin's indented shoreline.

Manitowaning, Manitoulin Island

This community some 25 km south of Sheguiandah is the first permanent European settlement on the island. Begun in 1836 as a center for aboriginal settlement and agricultural training (Manitowaning means "the den of the spirit"), it failed to attract large numbers of Native people, but thrived as a commercial center serving settlers and the boatloads of tourists who began arriving in the 1880s. St. Paul's Church

(1849) is the oldest Anglican parish church in northern Ontario. The lighthouse behind the church dates from 1885. Exhibits in the limestone Assigi-nack Museum, housed in a for-mer jail, depict early life in the area. The grounds contain a blacksmith shop, barn, pioneer home, and early school. Docked in the harbor and open for tours and dining is SS *Norisle*, the last steam-powered passenger ship on the Great Lakes. Nearby, the 1883 Roller Mills grist and flour mill exhibits old-time agricultural equipment. Northeast of Mani-towaning, the Wikwemikong First Nation community, home of the De-ba-jeh-mu-jig Native theater troupe, hosts the Three Fires Festival of contemporary North American Native music (early July) and a competitive powwow (early August).

121

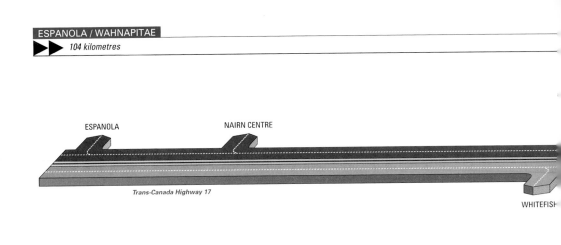

ESPANOLA   NAIRN CENTRE

Trans-Canada Highway 17

WHITEFISH

15 km   38 km

NORTHEASTERN ONTARIO

Seven restored and reconstructed buildings at Anderson Farm Museum in Lively, Ont., paint a portrait of early farming and mining operations and the lives of Finnish and other immigrants.

Onaping Falls

The best view of Onaping Falls is from the A.Y. Jackson Lookout, named for the Group of Seven artist who depicted the cascade on canvas. Nearby Windy Lake Provincial Park features sandy beaches, boating, and a wooded campground with large and secluded sites. Fairbank Provincial Park, also in this area, has the same facilities, and a one-hour hiking trail with lakeside views.

Lively

In 1916, Finnish settlers Frank and Gretta Anderson started a farm at Lively that became a major dairy supplier to Sudbury. Although their operation closed in 1958, the Anderson Farm Museum recalls Frank and Gretta's pioneering efforts.

Copper Cliff

Inco built this planned community, with an orderly street layout and trim houses. Beside it is the creation of Italian miners who came to work here, a picturesque huddle of dwellings clustered together at odd angles, reminiscent of an Italian hillside village.

The log Copper Cliff Museum displays early furnishings, tools, and utensils.

The world's largest coin, Sudbury's landmark Big Nickel is 9 m high and 61 cm thick.

Big Nickel Mine, Sudbury

After Copper Cliff, the 9 m nickel (actually made of stainless steel) comes into view north of the highway. From the hill where the landmark sits, you have a splendid view of the Sudbury area. Science North (see facing page) operates guided tours of nearby Big Nickel Mine, taking visitors down a 20 m shaft for a 30-minute tour of exhibits about mining history and techniques, and such unexpected features as an underground garden and Canada's only underground post office. For those who have more time, Path of Discovery tours offer 2½-hour bus-cum-walking tours of the Sudbury basin and Inco's iron smelter and refinery. Highlights include a visit to Canada's deepest open-pit mine, and a close-up view of Inco's 381 m Superstack, the world's tallest chimney.

Sudbury

On the edge of a huge craterlike basin, Sudbury is the world's nickel capital and Canada's biggest copper producer. Many scientists believe a meteor hit the area eons ago, creating the basin and depositing the minerals first discovered during construction of the CPR. Mining on a big scale began in 1888, and by the mid-1900s, decades of smelting and smoke pollution had blackened and desolated the landscape. The "greening" of Sudbury began in the 1950s, when Inco planted 1.5 million trees on sites stripped of

ONAPING
FALLS

30 km

144

COPPER
CLIFF

SUDBURY

WAHNAPITAE

CONISTON

LIVELY 69

To Parry Sound
(See pages 152-153)

| 15 km | 3 km | 2 km | 7 km | 5 km | 14 km | 5 km |

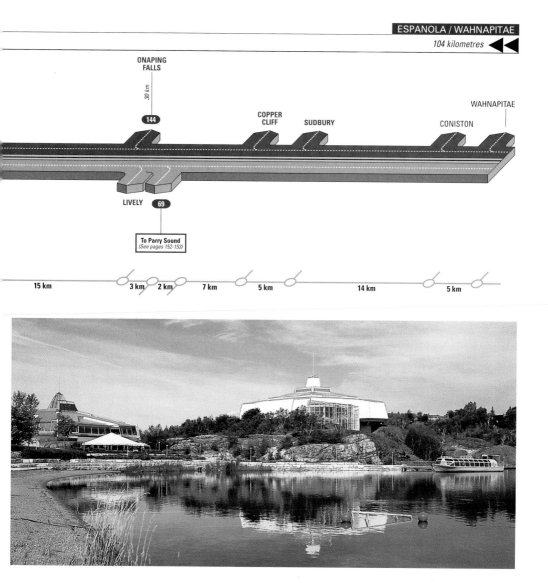

vegetation, and built Superstack, which releases smoke into the upper atmosphere.

The mines still produce a fiery nighttime spectacle, when red-hot slag from the smelters is dumped onto waste heaps (Copper Cliff provides the best viewpoint), but Sudbury has now diversified into health care, telecommunications, and education. Outstanding cultural attractions include Science North (see right), Laurentian University Museum and Arts Centre, in the former estate of a lumber tycoon; the Galerie du Nouvel-Ontario, which houses a fine collection of Franco-Ontarian art; and the Flour Mill Heritage Museum, which honors French Canadians who settled here in the early 1900s. The Northern Lights Festival Boréal in July bills itself as the longest running bilingual multicultural outdoor music event in Canada. Sudbury also holds festivals celebrating blueberries (July) and garlic (August).

Science North, Sudbury

Perched on the rocky shoreline of Lake Ramsey, this stainless steel, hexagonal science center encourages visitors to pet small animals, predict the weather, make electricity, float in space, and perform other simple experiments using computers and special equipment. You enter the center through a rock tunnel, then descend to an underground theater to view gripping, three-dimensional films on a five-story IMAX screen , or you climb a spiral ramp to the exhibition floors. Films, demonstrations, and displays explain animal and insect life, the universe and solar system, communications, fitness, and geology, and other science-related subjects. Staff, many associated with Laurentian University, explain exhibits and answer questions. At Science North, you can board the cruise boat *Cortina* for a one-hour lake cruise that will take you past bilingual Laurentian University.

A rock crater, symbolic of Sudbury basin (source of the nickel and copper that built this area), forms the foundation of Science North, which is topped by hexagons, suggesting snowflakes (and so the glaciation that sculpted Northern Ontario). The project, conceived as a mining museum but broadened to a world-class science center, opened in 1984. Work began three years earlier with an INCO Ltd. donation of $5 million, the largest single corporate donation to a community project in Canadian history. Success was assured when Falconbridge Limited added another million, and Ontario, which operates the center, contributed $10 million.

123

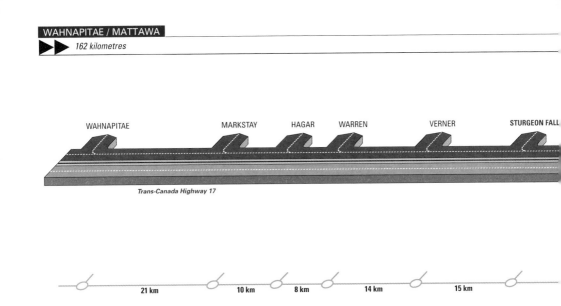

WAHNAPITAE MARKSTAY HAGAR WARREN VERNER STURGEON FALL

Trans-Canada Highway 17

21 km   10 km   8 km   14 km   15 km

**NORTHEASTERN
ONTARIO**

*Spectacular views of Lake Nipissing
and the North Bay area are bonuses
along a wooded path connecting
North Bay's downtown Education
Centre to Duchesnay Falls (below).
The falls, in full spate a gurgling
cascade of rugged splendor, are at
Hwy. 17 West just at the city limits.*

Sturgeon Falls

On the Sturgeon River, 5 km
from Lake Nipissing, this ancient
aboriginal meeting place became
a lumbering center after the CPR
went through in 1881. The Sturgeon River House Museum has a
replica of a Hudson's Bay Company post here from 1848 to
1879, Native artifacts, early logging and farming equipment, a
pioneer home built of squared
white pine logs in 1898, a blacksmith shop, an art gallery, picnic
sites, and a boat launch.

North Bay

Trans-Canada highways 11 and
17 meet at North Bay, which
calls itself the "Gateway to the
North." (An arch marking the
separation of the Near and Far
norths is in Lee Park.) But this
community on Lake Nipissing
has been a crossroads as far back
as fur-trading days. With the
arrival of the CPR in 1882, it
became a transportation and
forest products center.

Tourist information is dispensed beside the Dionne Quintuplets Home Museum, the 1934
birthplace of the community's
star natives. The house, moved
here from nearby Corbeil, is filled
with mementos of the girls' birth
and early years. Railway buffs
will revel in a model rail exhibit in
two boxcars alongside the museum. Model trains speed around
90 m of track through a miniature Canadian landscape.

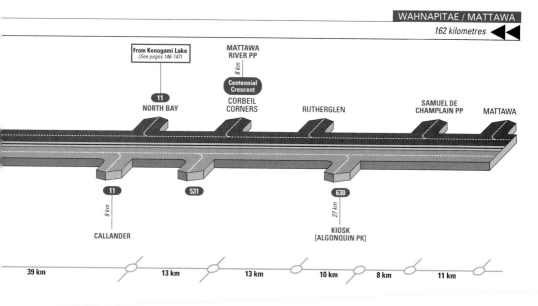

From Kenogami Lake
(See pages 146-147)

MATTAWA
RIVER PP

8 km

Centennial
Crescent

11
NORTH BAY

CORBEIL
CORNERS

RUTHERGLEN

SAMUEL DE
CHAMPLAIN PP

MATTAWA

11

9 km

CALLANDER

531

630

27 km

KIOSK
[ALGONQUIN PK]

39 km   13 km   13 km   10 km   8 km   11 km

North Bay's waterfront has a beach, walkway, bike path, marina, and mini-train, and is the departure point for 90-minute-to-5-hour lake cruises aboard *Chief Commanda II*. In the North Bay Area Museum, 20,000 exhibits recall rail, lumber, steamboat and pioneer history.

Callander

The North Himsworth Museum contains the office of Dr. A. R. Dafoe who practised here from 1914 to 1943. Dr. Dafoe delivered the Dionne quintuplets and was their guardian for many years, so quints' clothing, photographs, and other memorabilia are prominently displayed. Also at the museum is the Old Tyme Barber Shop, operated in Callander by Alex Dufresne and family for 60 years. Exhibits include razors, straps, and other barbering paraphernalia from the turn of the century on.

A scenic lookout just south of town offers choice views of Lake Nipissing.

Mattawa River Provincial Park

Ontario's first waterway park, this nonoperating preserve (though protected and open to the public, it is not actively managed) consists of the historic Mattawa River, the lakes along its course, and a slim scenic strip along the riverbanks. It stretches some 37 km, from the edge of Trout Lake to Samuel de Champlain Park. Etienne Brulé in 1610 and Samuel de Champlain in 1615 were among early explorers and

fur traders to travel the Mattawa River, an ancient Indian trade route. Today's visitors can relive the voyageur adventures by canoeing the historic river and crossing its portages. Centennial Crescent, which runs north from the Trans-Canada, provides an entry point into the park.

The Mattawa and Ottawa rivers meet in the town of Mattawa, which is set amid the grand scenery of the upper Laurentians. Exhibits on Native peoples and early farming and industries are displayed in the Mattawa and District Museum.

Kiosk, Algonquin Park

Hwy. 630 is the only paved road into the northern part of Algonquin Park. At Eau Claire Gorge, near the junction with the Trans-Canada, Amable du Fond River cascades through steep rock outcrops. You can camp beside lovely Kioshkokwi Lake at Kiosk some 25 km south.

Samuel de Champlain Provincial Park

Pictorial displays in the Voyageur Heritage Centre tell how explorers and fur traders influenced Canadian history. The park is on the Mattawa River, an important voyageur canoe route. Some 60 km of canoe routes on the Mattawa and connecting waterways are mapped for exploration by visitors. Campgrounds are set amid towering red and white pines. Trails in the northern section of the park lead through old-growth hemlock and yellow birch forests.

The Dionne quintuplets captured the world's imagination, generating a tourist business that averaged 3,000 visitors a day in the 1930s. Even though the numbers are considerably fewer, fans of the quints still flock to the North Himsworth Museum in Callander, Ont. (top photo), the former residence-office of Dr. A. R. Dafoe, and the house where he delivered the infants, the Dionne Quintuplets Home Museum in North Bay (below).

Flying the Northern Skies

HIGHWAY 11 / NORTH BAY

YOU CLIMB INTO the riveted aluminum fuselage to the hollow gurgle of water lapping against the floats. While you speculate on the function of the cockpit's gauges, knobs, and levers, the pilot describes the plane's safety features. Then the engine bursts to life, the propeller draws the craft into the wind, and with a deafening roar, the plane hunkers down and surges forward. Below, the water slips under the floats with increasing speed until the weight of flight is transferred to the wings. As you gain altitude, objects become smaller, but the landscape looms large. Your flight-seeing adventure has begun.

Flight-seeing—aerial sight-seeing—is far removed from a soporific flight on an airliner. Most flight-seeing is from single-engine bush planes—possibly at 400 m above ground or barely skimming the treetops. And takeoffs and landings are on water.

Easily the most practical means of accessing remote areas, the floatplane is a northern Ontario fixture. Wildlife surveys, law enforcement, aerial searches, and tourism are just some of the jobs that maintain the bush plane as the workhorse of the North. Private air charters provide flights to luxury wilderness lodges and rustic outpost camps, and most offer flight-seeing excursions over scenic areas of the "Near North."

What and how much you see depends on the flight plan and how long you are airborne. A 15-minute flight from North Bay, for example, can take in a long stretch of Lake Nipissing's coastline. You will see the lake's blue-green depths lighten over sandy shallows before breaking into an icy silver at the rocky shore and you may catch sight of long, sand, tree-shaded beaches. Dipping low over wave-washed promontories, you may almost feel gnarled pine reaching up to polish the belly of the plane.

Trails snaking out of North Bay over the granite-ridged Height of Land between Lake Nipissing and Trout Lake—the prehistoric La Vase Portage—come into view.

JAMES SMEDLEY *is also the author of "Riding a Wilderness Railway" (pp. 116-117).*

Traffic over this portage reached its height during the fur trade, when voyageurs paddled up the Ottawa and Mattawa rivers to Trout Lake, portaged to Lake Nipissing and, once across the lake, floated down the French River to Georgian Bay en route to Lake Superior and the North American interior. This was the original Trans-Canada highway, the only route across the country until the railway in the 1880s.

Longer flight-seeing trips trace this historic course. Skirting the Mattawa, the plane's banks and turns mirror the chutes and rapids squeezed between sheer rock walls below. As you buzz over the pine-topped pink granite of Georgian Bay, you see how capillaries of the French River divide the land into long fingers of polished stone.

Flights southeast of North Bay cross Algonquin Provincial Park. Like some giant rolling carpet, this enormous tract of intermingling greens dappled with steely gray lakes unfolds below. Meandering creeks appear like dark squiggling lines over the light green grasses and wetlands. Through the headphones, the pilot points out grazing moose or a black bear lumbering through the trees. For from the sky, little is hidden. Evidence of northern Ontario's resource-based economy is dispersed across the landscape: forests checked with clear-cuts; secluded mining camps; once-wild rivers contained behind hydroelectric dams.

Floatplanes shaped this region, originally opening it up to exploration and development after World War I with ex-military craft. Three decades later, Ontario purchased a fleet of DeHavilland Beavers—one of the first aircraft designed specifically for bush flying. The Beaver combined short takeoff and landing ability with a capacity of more than half a tonne. In the mid 1950s, DeHavilland produced the Otter—a larger floatplane combining the performance of the Beaver with almost twice its capacity. As the newer models were manufactured, the Provincial Air Service sold its older planes to private air charter services. Around the same time, the four-passenger Cessna became popular with fly-in operators. Although some of these aircraft have been in service for nearly 50 years, DeHavilland Beavers, Otters, and Cessna 180/185s still dominate the northern skies of Ontario.

Scanning the perimeter of remote lakes from such venerable craft, you will see the sprawling log structures of fly-in wilderness resorts. These lodges offer gourmet meals and luxury accommodation in a pristine setting. You start to unwind the minute you step onto the dock with only your clothing and fishing gear. For the self-reliant, outpost camps offer small cabins equipped with propane refrigerator, stove, and lights. Most fly-in lodges and outpost camps are built on lakes or rivers accessible only by air. This means great fishing (for walleye, pike, and lake trout) and hunting (for moose, black bear, and waterfowl). Guides are available to ensure success.

For a full dose of the bush, an air service will drop you off at a wilderness campsite. The operator will help you plan the trip and may even provide camping gear. Then as the plane lifts off the lake, you watch your only link with civilization disappear into the sky—its steel wings barely visible through the smoke of a freshly lit campfire.

> "You start to unwind the minute you step onto the dock with only your clothing and fishing gear."

James Smedley

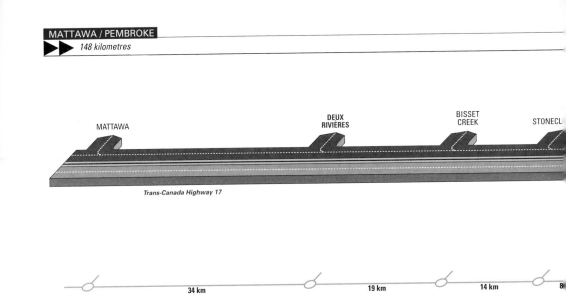

MATTAWA
DEUX
RIVIÈRES
BISSET
CREEK
STONECL

Trans-Canada Highway 17

34 km   19 km   14 km   8

**OTTAWA
RIVER
VALLEY**

Deux Rivières

Just west of here, a gravel road leads to Algonquin Park and the 3 km wide Brent Crater, the second largest meteorite crater in Canada. The site of this much-studied feature may be viewed from an observation tower, or from a 2 km trail that descends to the crater's floor.

Driftwood Provincial Park

On the sheltered shores of Drift-wood Bay, this park offers camp-sites (many by the Ottawa River), sandy beaches, hiking trails, boating, and fishing. Natural features include ancient rock outcrops of the Canadian Shield (visible along the shoreline in the northeast corner of the park) and geological curiosities known as eskers (gravel ridges left by glaciers thousands of years ago). Beachcombers will delight in the sculpted pieces of wood (hence, the park name) that wash ashore in this park, which was set up after the Des Joachims hydro-electric dam was built downriver in 1950. By raising the water level 30 m, the dam created Driftwood Bay.

Chalk River

A backwoods lumbering settle-ment, Chalk River was thrust into the 20th century in 1944, when it became the site of the first nuclear reactor built outside the United States. Now there are five reactors at Chalk River Nuclear Laboratories, an Atomic Energy of Canada operation. A visitors' center offers superb views of the facility and the Ottawa River valley and houses films, exhibits, and models giving background information on nuclear power. Anyone visiting between June and Labor Day can take a 90-minute bus tour of a reactor station.

Some 4 km east of Chalk River, the Petawawa Research Forest, established in 1918, is Canada's oldest continuously monitored research forest. Covering 100 km², it has a long multiple-use history, regularly attracting bird-watchers, canoeists, anglers, and skiers. A vistiors' center with displays on forest management and products is the starting point for two self-guided interpretive trails through towering pines and along the peaceful Chalk River.

Petawawa

Since 1905, Canadian Forces Base Petawawa has been a key training and staging base for military personnel. Visitors can tour the base and use its marina, campgrounds, golf course, and beach. One museum contains artifacts, images, and memorabilia relating to the development of Camp Petawawa; others focus on Canada's post-war airborne forces and The Royal Canadian Dragoons (one of the oldest regiments in Canada).

Pembroke

From its 1828 beginnings as a lumber town, this Ottawa River community has thrived on the bounty of surrounding forests. This heritage and local mile-

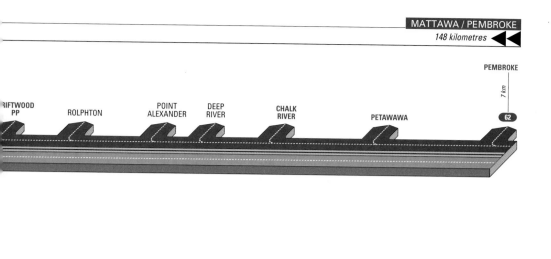

PEMBROKE

7 km

RIFTWOOD
PP

ROLPHTON

POINT
ALEXANDER

DEEP
RIVER

CHALK
RIVER

PETAWAWA

62

10 km   12 km   7 km   10 km   15 km   19 km

stones are depicted in the Heritage Murals—an ongoing series of large-scale downtown paintings. One mural of loggers at work, the 23 by 34 m, multilevel, multiangle *Spring Harvest: An Artist's Sketchbook*, is the largest work of its kind in Canada. A mapped walking tour of local historic buildings is available in most shops. The past is also evoked at the Champlain Trail Museum, which has an authentic smokehouse and bake oven, and a one-room schoolhouse. Pembroke became Canada's first city to use commercial electric street lighting (in 1885), a fact highlighted in one of the street murals and recalled by exhibits at the Hydro-Electric Commission Museum.

Houseboat rentals, family float trips, and whitewater rafting expeditions are among the services available at the Pembroke Marina. Located there is a 10 m steel replica of the Cockburn Pointer boat, designed and built by John Cockburn of Pembroke in the 1850s and widely used throughout Canada into the early 1900s. The 42-passenger *Island Cruise* leaves the marina daily on guided historic tours of the Ottawa River. Beside the marina is one of Pembroke's best-known sites, the Swallow's Roost. In late July and early August, some 100,000 migrating swallows converge there—and attract what sometimes seems like as many bird-watchers.

Visible for miles, and wound every two days, Pembroke's massive, four-sided City Hall clock sits under a copper dome that is topped by a wrought-iron weather vane.

129

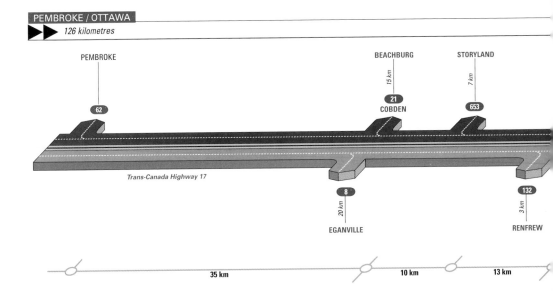

Trans-Canada Highway 17

PEMBROKE — 62
BEACHBURG — 15 km
STORYLAND — 7 km
21 — COBDEN
653
8
20 km
EGANVILLE
132
3 km
RENFREW

35 km   10 km   13 km

**OTTAWA
RIVER
VALLEY**

*The youngsters
(right), two of
thousands who
visit the Bon-
nechere Caves
near Eganville
each year, take
time out to
absorb the fact
that their sur-
roundings were
once the bottom
of a tropical sea
peopled by
aquatic crea-
tures whose fos-
sils are embed-
ded in the cave
walls.*

Cobden

Probably the most remarkable occurrence here was the discovery of Champlain's astrolabe. In 1867, in a nearby farm field, a 14-year-old boy found a navigational device lost by the explorer 254 years earlier. The memory of the event lingers in the name of the Cobden's Astrolabe Arena. (The object itself is now in the Canadian Museum of Civilization, Hull.)

Every Saturday, from spring through fall, the Cobden Farmers' Market sells fresh produce, baking, honey, and flowers and plants. The Cobden Fair, begun in 1854, is held in late August.

Logos Land, a family resort on Muskrat Lake, has five water-slides (three giant ones, two just for tots), plus pedal-boats, mini-golf, camping, riding, hiking trails, and picnic sites.

Beachburg

Wilderness Tours and RiverRun at Beachburg organize whitewater rafting expeditions on the churning channels of the Ottawa River. Each outfit has its own resort offering accommodations and a wide range of water and beach activities. At nearby Foresters Falls, Owl Rafting organizes whitewater expeditions on the thrilling 12 km Rocher Fendu Rapids of the Ottawa River. Options include a return trip and family float trips.

Eganville

Situated on the Bonnechere River, Eganville is a summer cottage town, with a beach and arts and

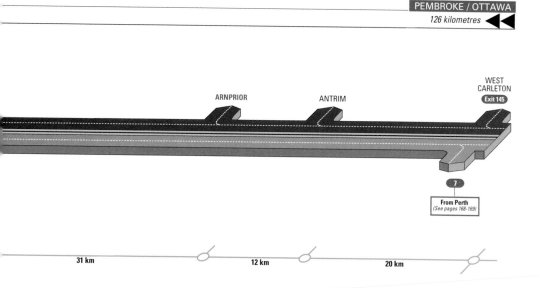

ARNPRIOR   ANTRIM   WEST CARLETON **Exit 145**

7

From Perth
(See pages 168-169)

31 km   12 km   20 km

crafts shops. Its best-known attraction is the Bonnechere Caves, some 8 km southeast of town. Eons of water erosion carved out the limestone cavern and twisting passages, which are open for exploration. Guides will explain the geological formations and point out fossils of creatures that lived here more than 500 million years ago.

Storyland

One for the kids! Storyland is a wooded park with paths where children will encounter some of their favorite storybook characters—who may wave, wink, or even sing to them. Puppet shows, pedal-boats, and an 18-hole mini-golf course are part of the fun. You can reach the park via Hwy. 653 or by Storyland Road from Renfrew.

Renfrew

🚣 🎣 🏛 ⛵ 🏖 ❄

"The pride of the Ottawa Valley," Renfrew began to expand in the 1850s when it became the starting point of the Opeongo Line—a colonization road built to encourage settlement and stretching 150 km west to Barry Bay. You can get a sense of the community's farming and lumbering past at the McDougall Mill Museum. Housed in a three-story stone grist mill, built in 1855 on the Bonnechere River, its collection ranges from pioneer tools and machinery to Victorian dolls and toys. Exhibits include personal items belonging to Renfrew-born Charlotte Whitton (1896-1975), Ottawa mayor for many years and Canada's first female mayor.

Renfrew has a full calendar of events, which include the Lumber Baron Summer Festival (July); the Renfrew Fair—the longest-running event of its kind in the Ottawa Valley (early September), and the Renfrew Winter Carnival (February). A recreation highlight is the downhilll skiing at nearby Calabogie on the biggest slope in eastern Ontario.

Arnprior

🎣 ⛵

The largest town upriver from Ottawa, this "gateway to the Ottawa Valley" is at the junction of the Madawaska and Ottawa rivers. Displays in the red sandstone Arnprior and District Museum recount the area's lumbering history from the time the McLachlin and Gillies families set up the first sawmills. Exhibits also highlight the legendary Archibald McNab, who initiated an ambitious settlement scheme here in the 1820s. McNab's double-dealings with settlers led to years of feuds that ended with his ouster in 1840. Arnprior Fair, begun in 1831, is held in August.

The highest point on the Ottawa River, Champlain Lookout in Storyland offers stunning views of the river and the surrounding landscape.

Period clothing, wartime souvenirs, military uniforms, and local historical items are among exhibits in this renovated, three-story stone McDougall Mill Museum in Renfrew.

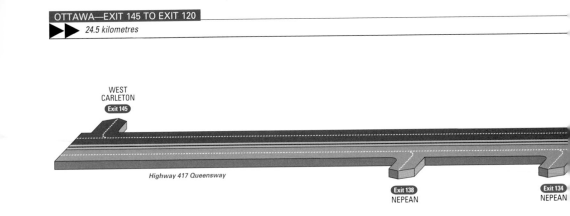

WEST CARLETON
Exit 145

Highway 417 Queensway

Exit 138
NEPEAN

Exit 134
NEPEAN

8 km   4 km

AROUND OTTAWA

Canada's history from prehistoric to modern times is showcased in the Canadian Museum of Civilization, a striking architectural masterpiece magnificently situated in Hull, Que., across the Ottawa River from Parliament Hill.

Central Experimental Farm

On any given summer day, you will find wagons drawn by huge Clydesdales rumbling past hay and grain fields within Ottawa's city boundaries. This "farm in a city" is of course the Central Experimental Farm, which is south of Hwy. 417 and accessible by Exit 121A [Bronson St.]. Visitors are welcome at this Agriculture Canada operation, which carries out research into various aspects of agriculture and horticulture. In summer, wagon rides pass ornamental gardens, bountiful fields, and Canada's largest arboretum. (Sleigh rides through the grounds are a winter treat.) Children can touch lambs, hold freshly laid eggs, and learn about farming basics such as shearing sheep and churning butter.

Billings Estate Museum

Heirlooms and personal possessions of one of Ottawa's founding families are displayed inside this picturesque house, the family home of five generations of Billings'. Bradish and Lamira Billings built the house overlooking the Rideau River in 1827-1828. Now the centerpiece of the Billings Estate Museum, the house and its exhibits reflect changes in family life-styles and interests over the two centuries in which Ottawa evolved from backwoods settlement to city. The grounds include a flower garden, an icehouse, barn, and other outbuildings. In summer, teas are served on the lawn.

Canadian Museum of Nature

You will find everything from glittering gems to dinosaur bones in the castlelike Canadian Museum of Nature. Thousands of specimens—animals, birds, insects, plants, minerals, and fossils from various parts of Canada and the world—are displayed in six galleries, two of which focus on earth's geological and evolutionary development. Life-size dioramas show birds and animals in their native habitats. Other presentations include audiovisual displays and hands-on exhibits. Located at Metcalfe and MacLeod Sts., the museum can be reached from Hwy. 417 via Exit 120 [Kent St.].

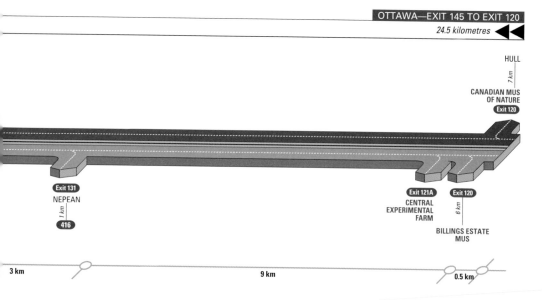

HULL
7 km

CANADIAN MUS
OF NATURE
Exit 120

Exit 131
NEPEAN
1 km
416

Exit 121A
CENTRAL
EXPERIMENTAL
FARM

Exit 120
6 km

BILLINGS ESTATE
MUS

3 km   9 km   0.5 km

Overlooking the Rideau River, this handsome, neoclassical house, once known as Park Hill and now the Billings Estate Museum, is one of Ottawa's oldest homes. Its furnishings and other exhibits trace the lives of five generations of the Billings family who lived here.

Hull

Situated on the north shore of the Ottawa River, Hull developed a lively, fun-loving identity far removed from Ottawa's staid political and administrative activities. Born in 1800 as a small agricultural settlement, Hull grew into one of North America's largest lumber, pulp and paper centers. In recent decades, the construction of federal government complexes, such as the Place du Portage and the Canadian Museum of Civilization, has drawn Hull closer to the national capital region. To get there from Hwy. 417, take Exit 120 [Kent St.] to downtown Ottawa and cross to Hull by the Alexandra Bridge.

Canadian Museum of Civilization, Hull

A dominant feature of Hull's waterfront is the sinuous silhouette of the Canadian Museum of Civilization at the foot of the Alexandra Bridge. Designed by architect Douglas Cardinal, the building itself generates as much discussion and admiration as the 4 million artifacts chronicling Canada's human history stored inside. One vast glass wall of the Grand Hall frames a panoramic view of Parliament Hill. (The hall—the museum's spacious centerpiece—served as the venue for the state dinner that Prime Minister Jean Chrétien hosted during U.S. President Bill Clinton's 1995 visit to Canada.) Displays include the rich cultural artifacts of Canada's West Coast aboriginal peoples. Among the exhibits are six Native houses and the world's largest indoor collection of totem poles.

A thousand years of Canadian history—from the days of Viking explorers to the present—come to life in Canada Hall. Reconstructions range from a 16th-century Basque ship to a turn-of-the-century main street in a small Ontario town. By the time you have finished this part of your tour, you will feel you have supped in a voyageur's camp, strolled about a cobbled square in New France, and ridden a Conestoga wagon across rough terrain.

In the Children's Museum, youngsters can make mini-excursions to destinations such as the Kids' Café, the World Exchange, and the International Village.

OTTAWA—OUR CAPITAL BY A CANAL

Cutting through this city of sober Victorian government buildings and elegant modern architectural gems is the storied Rideau Canal, the city's oldest landmark. As such, it is fitting to make it the midpoint of the walk described on these pages. Wellington Street—site of the Gothic parliamentary buildings—has been Ottawa's principal thoroughfare since the city became our national capital in 1857. In recent times, Sussex Drive (now known as the "Mile of History") has added to Ottawa's rich store of sights. With new museums and restored 19th-century buildings, there is no shortage of fascinating buildings to admire and explore.

Ottawa River

Parliament Hill
On the bluffs overlooking the Ottawa River stand three Gothic-style buildings that house Canada's Parliament. The House of Parliament and the Senate occupy handsome chambers in the **Centre Block.** The great central **Peace Tower** contains a 53-bell carillon, a huge clock, and the Memorial Chamber, which honors Canada's war dead. At the rear is the **Library of Parliament,** the only remnant of the original 19th-century structure to survive a devastating 1916 fire. The **East Block,** completed in 1865, contains a re-creation of Sir John A. Macdonald's office. The West Block, closed to the public, contains MPs' offices. On summer mornings, the military spectacle of the **Changing of the Guard** takes places on the grounds of Parliament Hill.

Currency Museum
Located within the **Bank of Canada,** this museum traces the development of coins and bank notes. It has the world's most complete collection of Canadian notes, coins, and tokens.

KENT ST.

BANK ST.

SPARKS ST.

Supreme Court of Canada
This imposing art deco structure, built during World War II, houses Canada's highest court of appeal. Visitors are welcome to stroll about the grounds or to visit the impressive entrance hall and the courtroom. Guided tours are available in summer.

To National Arts Centre
Just beside Confederation Square, the National Arts Centre offers year-round entertainment. The center has a 2,300-seat Opera House, an 800-seat theater, and a hall for receptions and recitals.

Royal Canadian Mint
Housed in a turreted stone structure, the mint strikes special coins and commemorative pieces. Visitors can tour the building and watch the coin manufacturing process.

N ↑

Ottawa River

WALK AREA

OTTAWA

Canadian War Museum
Weapons, uniforms, vehicles, and artwork here trace the nation's military history. Exhibits range from Native arrowheads and Sir Isaac Broc's tunic (complete with bullet hole) to a 1916 gas mask worn during World War I.

N ↑

Cathedral Basilica of Notre-Dame

▷ **To Nepean Point**

National Gallery of Canada
The most striking aspect of architect Moshe Safdie's design is the polygonal, glass-paneled tower that acts as the gallery's main foyer. Built in 1988, the gallery houses such masterpieces as Rembrandt's *Heroine from the Old Testament*, Van Gogh's *Iris*, and Matisse's *Nude on a Yellow Sofa*. The Canadian Galleries contain the world's largest collection of Canadian art— most notably, *The Jack Pine* by Tom Thomson.

Centennial Flame
On Dec. 31, 1966, Prime Minister Lester B. Pearson lit this flame at a ceremony marking Canada's 100th birthday.

Bytown Museum
Ottawa's oldest stone building (1827), this museum can be seen by the locks on the Parliament Hill side of the Rideau Canal. Exhibits evoke the time it served as offices and storehouse for Rideau Canal builders, Lt.-Col. John By and the Royal Engineers.

Major's Hill Park

Peacekeeping Monument

MACKENZIE AVE.

SUSSEX DR.

Canal Rideau Canal

▷ **To Byward Market**
Established in 1840 for the sale of local produce, this market has been transformed into one of the city's liveliest districts. Some restored original buildings house restaurants, boutiques, and artisans' premises.

Canadian Museum of Contemporary Photography

TON ST.

Château Laurier

▷

Confederation Square

Rideau Canal and Locks
Built between 1826 and 1832 for military purposes, the canal is a chain of lakes, rivers, and canal cuts extending 202 km from Kingston to Ottawa. Pleasure craft use the picturesque canal all summer, when you can stroll—or bike or jog—along pathways through landscaped gardens hugging its northernmost stretch through downtown Ottawa. Frozen, this section of canal becomes the world's longest skating rink in winter. The Ottawa locks, where the canal meets the Ottawa River, lie between Parliament Hill and the majestic **Château Laurier** *(right)*. Completed in 1912, the hotel became an instant mecca for politicians, and was first dubbed the "third chamber of Parliament." Also near the locks, housed in a restored railway tunnel, you will find the **Canadian Museum of Contemporary Photography.** Canada's only museum dedicated to the art of photography, it has a collection of some 157,500 works by the country's most dynamic photographers.

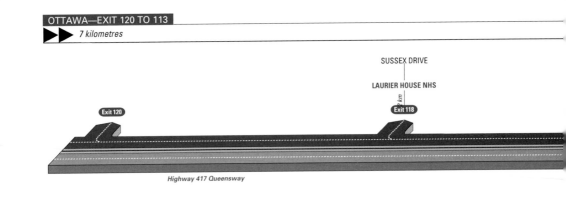

SUSSEX DRIVE

LAURIER HOUSE NHS

Exit 120

Exit 118

Highway 417 Queensway

2 km

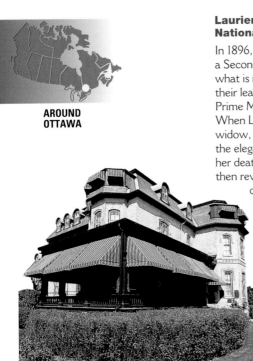

AROUND OTTAWA

This mansion on what is now Laurier Avenue was 17 years old when it was presented to Wilfrid Laurier by political supporters in 1896. Some Laurier memorabilia remain, and there is a replica of Lester B. Pearson's study, but most furnishings and exhibits reflect the interests of Canada's longest serving Prime Minister, Mackenzie King.

Laurier House National Historic Site

In 1896, the Liberal Party bought a Second Empire style house on what is now Laurier Avenue for their leader, then newly elected Prime Minister Wilfrid Laurier. When Laurier died in 1919, his widow, Zoe, continued to live in the elegant stone mansion until her death in 1921. The mansion then reverted to Laurier's successor, Mackenzie King, who was prime minister for 21 years. King took possession of the house in 1923 and it is mostly his furniture and possessions that are displayed throughout. Unusual mementos such as a childhood piano and some of Sir Winston Churchill cigars fill the rooms. A real curiosity is a crystal ball—said to have been used at seances where King sought advice from spirits of departed political figures including Laurier.

Open to the public, Laurier House is accessible from Hwy. 417 via Exit 118 [Nicholas St.].

Sussex Drive

Called the "Mile of History," this grand Ottawa thoroughfare runs from downtown Parliament Hill to Rideau Hall. It passes many of Ottawa's (and the nation's) must-see sites: among them the National Gallery of Art, the Canadian War Museum, and the Royal Canadian Mint. (For detailed descriptions, see pages 132-133.) Beyond the Alexandra Bridge, the drive skirts the Otta-wa River, passing the imposing External Affairs Canada building, the new Ottawa City Hall (see below), and 24 Sussex Drive, the prime minister's residence. Built in 1868 for wealthy mill owner Joseph Merrill Currier, Number 24 is perched high above the Ottawa River. Although closed to the public, the stone house is visible through the trees that encircle the property. Just across the way is Rideau Hall, the residence of the governor general.

Ottawa City Hall

This civic complex is attractively situated on Green Island, where the Rideau River flows into the Ottawa. Originally built in 1958, the town hall was renovated by internationally renowned architect Moshie Safdie, who also designed Ottawa's National Gallery of Art. The island, framed by cataracts on the Rideau River, inspired Safdie to create a "little village on water." Completed in 1993, the city hall is a lively addition to the string of sights along Sussex Drive.

Safdie incorporated the original city hall into what is known as the Sussex Pavilion, and added two others—the Rideau and the Bytown. The postmodern Sussex Drive "ceremonial" entrance is in a pyramid tower enclosed in a huge cube.

You may tour the City Hall on your own, or you can take advantage of one of the guided tours. On the tour, visitors can admire the works of art permanently integrated into the architecture of the pavilions. The well-tended Lamira Dow Gardens are perfect for a stroll.

OTTAWA—EXIT 120 TO 113

7 kilometres ◄◄

NATIONAL
AVIATION
MUS

4 km

Exit 113

Exit 115

4 km

NATIONAL MUS
OF SCIENCE
AND TECHNOLOGY

m | 2 km

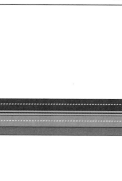

Rideau Hall

Since Confederation this stately house has been home to Canada's governors general. The original dwelling was built in 1838 by Thomas MacKay, a Rideau Canal contractor, who gave it the name by which it is generally known. (Government House is the official name.) Purchased in 1868 by the federal government, Rideau Hall has been enlarged through the years by its distinguished residents. In the 1870s, Lord Dufferin added two wings to each side of the entrance hall. Just before World War I, the Duke of Connaught made many changes, including the addition of the Royal Arms on the front facade. Lord Monck, the first governor general, laid out the grounds, which now contain ornamental gardens, greenhouses, woods, tennis courts, and even a cricket pitch.

Both the house and grounds are open to the public. In summer, you can watch the changing of the guard. This occurs at the main gate every hour on the hour from 10 am to 6 pm. As you explore the grounds, see if there is a blue flag with a lion holding a red maple leaf flying from Rideau Hall. If there is, the governor general is in residence.

National Museum of Science and Technology

A lighthouse that once operated at Cape North, N.S., marks the site of this museum and its technology park on St. Laurent Blvd., south of Hwy. 417. Exhibits chronicle Canadian achievements from agriculture to astronomy and space transportation. Hands-on exhibits inside the museum show how science and technology affect Canadians' everyday life. A 38-cm refracting telescope in the park, originally installed for the Dominion Observatory in 1905, is still used for public viewing of the sky.

National Museum of Science and Technology visitors can enjoy displays ranging from space and communications equipment to old printing presses, antique cars, and farm tools.

National Aviation Museum

Forty-nine aircraft treasures in this museum beside Rockcliffe Airport tell the story of Canadian aviation history. One exhibit is a replica of the *Silver Dart*, which made the first powered flight in Canada (1909). You will also see the Sopwith Snipe (a trusty World War I plane flown by famed ace Billy Bishop), and the nose section of the ill-fated Avro Arrow (the supersonic interceptor jet canceled by the Diefenbaker government in 1959). Various presentations let you learn the principles of flight and relive the adventures of Canada's first bush pilots.

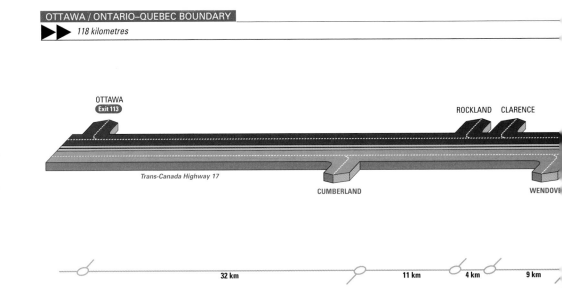

OTTAWA
Exit 113

ROCKLAND   CLARENCE

Trans-Canada Highway 17

CUMBERLAND

WENDOVE

32 km   11 km   4 km   9 km

**OTTAWA
RIVER
VALLEY**

Cumberland

Just east of Ottawa, the Trans-Canada skirts the Ottawa River along a road built in the mid-1800s to link settlements once served by steamship. Many fine dwellings from that era survive in the villages along this stretch of road. A visit to the Cumberland Township Museum will take you back to more leisurely days. A 1908 Grand Trunk Railway station, a 1904 band shell, drive sheds and barns with old-time farming and transportation equipment, an 1870s sawmill (still operating), and Watson's Garage, the oldest surviving example of an original Imperial Oil garage, are among some 20 buildings assembled here from various sites in the Lower Ottawa Valley. The historic village illustrates the period from 1880 to 1935, a period when the pace of life quickened under the impact of rapid industrialization.

Wendover

Star performers from Québec and Ontario converge here for the Wendover Country Music Festival in July. Events include a fiddling jamboree, an amateur talent contest, a horse parade, a casino, bingo, and sea plane and hot-air balloon rides. A special Western mass on Sunday completes the roundup of events.

Alfred

From a boardwalk here, you can view the Alfred Bog, the largest area of marshy ground in eastern Ontario. The marsh contains a variety of rare plants, insects,

and small animals. Alfred is near Caledonia Springs, a major spa and site of a water-bottling plant from the mid-19th century until World War I. Fancy hotels with health clubs and gardens catered to the rich and famous of the day who came "to take the waters." But newer spas such as Banff, Alta., and popular St. Lawrence River resorts such as Cacouna, Metis, and Murray Bay drew the fashionable clientele away from Caledonia Springs. The CPR, owner of several hotels there, closed its Grand Hotel in 1915 and the bottling operation four years later. The sulfurous springs and a wooden shack are all that remain of past glories

L'Orignal

Part of a seigneury granted by the French Crown in 1674, L'Orignal is probably the oldest settlement in the Lower Ottawa River valley. (Cataracoui, present-day Kingston, was the only other seigneurial grant in what is now Ontario.) Its stone District Courthouse and Jail, built in the 1820s and still in use, is Ontario's oldest courthouse. Nearby St. Andrew's Church of Scotland (now a United Church) dates from the 1830s. There are several fine stone homes in the area: Rivercrest, built in 1833, is considered the finest example of Regency architecture in Ontario.

Hawkesbury

Thomas Mears, Hawkesbury's most prominent early resident, arrived here in 1798, built grist and saw mills and the steamboat

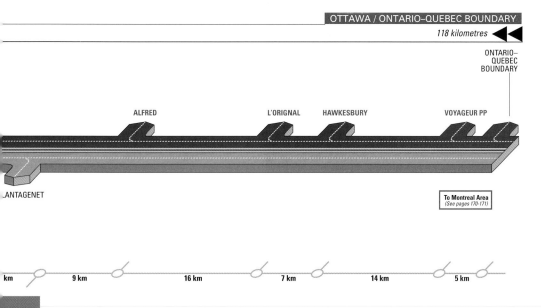

ONTARIO–
QUEBEC
BOUNDARY

ALFRED   L'ORIGNAL   HAWKESBURY   VOYAGEUR PP

_ANTAGENET

To Montreal Area
(See pages 170-171)

km   9 km   16 km   7 km   14 km   5 km

Magnificent, Georgian and neoclassic style buildings, silver steepled church spires, sweeping galleries, and roofs, often colorful, topped by magnificent domes and flag towers, are typical of the mid-1800s architecture gracing villages along the Lower Ottawa River. All the buildings here are in L'Orignal, Ont.

Union, the first steamboat on the Ottawa River. Today, the community prides itself on being the most bilingual town in Canada, with 90 percent of the population fluent in French and English. The Perley Bridge, linking Hawkesbury to Grenville, Qué., is the only bridge across the Ottawa River between Ottawa and Montreal. Île de Chenail, at the foot of the bridge, is the site of the Maison de l'Île, a remnant of an old sawmill. Also offshore, the well-wooded Richelieu and Hamilton islands have pleasant hiking trails. The Hawkesbury Western Festival brings riding competitions to town in spring. Another popular event, The Festival of Colours occurs in late September. The Montreal Soaring Club has its gliding port here. Gliders may be seen soaring through the sky on warm, bright, summer days.

Voyageur Provincial Park

A hiking trail in this park retraces the voyageur portage around the Long Sault Rapids, once located on the opposite side of the Ottawa River. The rapids disappeared when the Carillon hydroelectric dam, built downriver in 1964, raised the water level 20 m. The park has three campgrounds, plus hiking and riding trails. There are rentals for horses, boats, canoes, and pedalboats. Sailing and fishing opportunities are excellent. In summer, the park presents nature programs on wildlife, birds (herons abound here), plants, and stars; in winter, it offers some 10 km of cross-country ski trails.

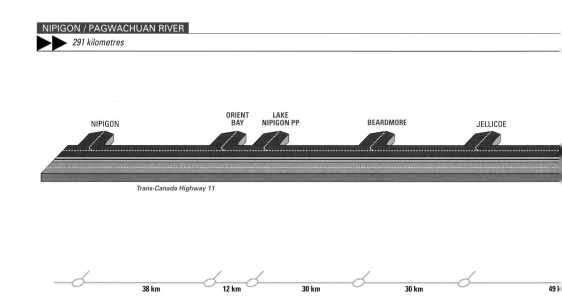

NIPIGON   ORIENT BAY   LAKE NIPIGON PP   BEARDMORE   JELLICOE

Trans-Canada Highway 11

38 km   12 km   30 km   30 km   49 k

**NORTH-
CENTRAL
ONTARIO**

In the rugged wilderness of Lake Nipigon Provincial Park (below), you can camp in a variety of landscapes, stroll along wildflower-rimmed woodland trails crisscrossed by small forest creatures, explore the lake's legendary fishing or some of its 500 islands, or retrace the history of those who preceded you—aboriginal peoples, coureurs de bois, HBC traders, miners, and loggers. All were sustained by the area's fish, furs, gold, and lumber.

Orient Bay

Some 25 km north of Nipigon, Hwy. 11 (the northern Ontario route of the Trans-Canada Highway) skirts the 200 m high Pijitawabik Palisades, a chain of cliffs edging Orient Bay Canyon to your right. In summer, more than 100 falls cascade over the cliff faces; in winter, the frozen falls attract ice-climbers from around the world.

Orient Bay some 20 km farther on, the center of an annual ice-climbing festival (see pages 110-111), has long been a popular destination. In 1919, the Prince of Wales (later Edward VIII) set off on a Lake Nipigon fishing trip and cruise from a railway hostelry south of town. The place where he stayed is now known as the Royal Windsor Lodge.

Lake Nipigon Provincial Park

At 4,848 km², fish-rich Lake Nipigon (sometimes called the sixth Great Lake) is the largest body of water entirely in Ontario. In 1916, a Thunder Bay physician pulled a 7 kg speckled trout from the lake, a world-record catch unsurpassed to this day. Diabase rock weathered into granules by interaction with ice and water over thousands of years produced the park's unusual black sandy beaches. Boaters should remember that lake waters are very cold and often rough: canoeists should stay close to shore.

Two short trails encapsulate the rugged variety of this region. After a fairly demanding climb, the Thunderbird Lookout Trail

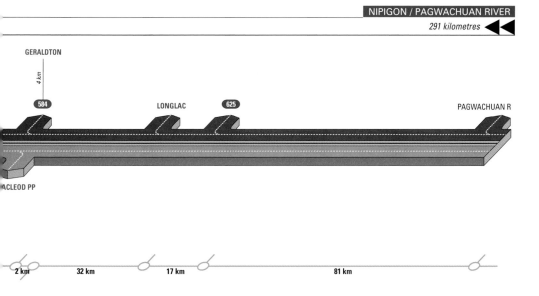

GERALDTON

4 km

584   LONGLAC   625   PAGWACHUAN R

ACLEOD PP

2 km   32 km   17 km   81 km

leads to a clifftop lookout with views of Pijitawabik Bay: the Historic Site Trail passes the former site of a Hudson's Bay Company post and the Sand Point Indian settlement.

Beardmore

A giant snowman—local folk say it is the biggest statue of its kind in the world— welcomes visitors to Beardmore. Originally an isolated railway flag stop, the village first came into its own during the Sturgeon River gold rush of 1934-35. When the gold ran out in the 1960s, Beardmore still had forest industries and tourism as economic mainstays.

Known as "the gateway to Lake Nipigon," Beardmore hosts a fishing derby in June and serves as a jumping-off point for family resorts and fly-in camp. Its best-known son, Ojibwa painter Norval Morrisseau, was born on the nearby Sand Point reserve in 1932.

Geraldton

With some justification, Geraldton bills itself "the friendly town with a heart of gold." The opening of Little Long Lac Mine in 1932 started a gold rush that spurred the community's growth. By the 1940s, with 10 gold-producing mines within a 15 km radius, Geraldton was dubbed "the muskeg metropolis." (The community is named for two mining promoters, J. S. Fitzgerald and Joseph Errington.)

Forest industries are now the economic mainstay, but the headframe of the old MacLeod-

Cockshutt mine is an enduring symbol of the glory days. Visitors can tour some mine sites.

MacLeod Provincial Park

From this park on Kenogamsis Lake, boaters can explore secluded bays, inlets, and islands. The immediate vicinity was the scene of an early 1930s gold rush and the park name recalls the nearby MacLeod-Cockshutt mine. A major forest fire swept through the region about 60 years ago, and much of the surrounding forest is composed of trembling aspen, often the first tree to grow back after such a blaze.

Longlac

Situated where the Kenogami River joins Long Lake, Longlac was a fur-trading center up to the railway's arrival in the early 1900s. In those days, Long Lake flowed north to James Bay. In 1939, however, engineers built a dam at the lake's north end and a concrete canal at its southern tip to divert the lake toward Lake Superior, thus increasing water in the Great Lakes and improving flow to hydroelectric generating dams supplying power to eastern Canada. (The flow is reversed when local hydro generating stations need more water.)

Local prosperity is based on Kimberly-Clark pulp and paper plant and sawmill, and a Weldwood plywood plant. Local recreation facilities include golf courses, beaches, and opportunities for fishing, canoeing, hiking (along the Kenogami River), and cross-country skiing.

A gigantic canoe at the west entrance to Longlac recalls the community's fur-trading past. The first coureurs de bois arrived in the mid-1700s and the rival Hudson's Bay and North West companies later operated posts there.

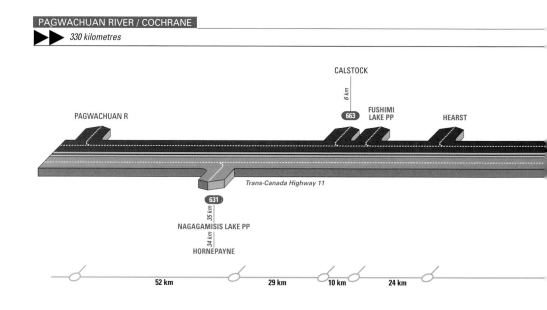

CALSTOCK

↕ 6 km

PAGWACHUAN R

663 FUSHIMI
LAKE PP

HEARST

Trans-Canada Highway 11

631
↕ 35 km
NAGAGAMISIS LAKE PP
↕ 34 km
HORNEPAYNE

52 km   29 km   10 km   24 km

**NORTHEASTERN
ONTARIO**

Nagagamisis Lake Provincial Park

Hwy. 631 cuts through this rugged park, which has facilities for canoeing, boating, and fishing. One of this park's delights is the stretch of sandy beach along Nagagamisis Lake. (*Nagagamisis* is derived from the Cree word for "lake with fine sand shore.") Forests here are mainly composed of tall balsam firs (in the wild, rocky uplands), tamarack, and alder (in the lowlands). A stroll along the Time Trail gives a wonderful overview of the park's natural features. Potsherds unearthed in the park show that Algonkian Indians have lived in this area for at least 1,000 years.

Hornepayne

This railway and lumbering community is at the heart of a region abounding in lakes, rivers, wildlife, resorts, and fly-in fishing lodges. It developed after the CNR pushed through here in 1916. (Originally known as Fitzback, it was renamed for Robert Horne-Payne, the CNR's representative in Britain.) The railway is still a major employer, and the CNR engine house (1921) is a must-see site for railway enthusiasts.

Fushimi Lake Provincial Park

A welcome haven on a lonely stretch of Hwy. 11, this park commemorates a 1907 visit to northern Ontario by His Imperial Majesty Prince Fushimi, a brother of then Emperor Hirohito of

Japan. The lake's cool, clear waters lend themselves to waterskiing and windsurfing. A 3.5 km trail along the north lakeshore passes an abandoned 1930s fire tower and cabin.

Hearst

French is the first language of more than 85 percent of the townspeople here in *"le petit Québec de l'Ontario."* Hearst's other nickname—"The Moose Capital of Ontario"—acknowledges its wilderness location in Ontario's rugged northland. Forest industries employ many locals, but farming is also important. Hearst sits at the western tip of the Great Clay Belt, a stone-free agricultural strip stretching west to Cochrane. Hearst is also the northern terminal of the Algoma Railway (see pages 118-119).

Kapuskasing

Tudor-style buildings are an outstanding feature of this "model town of the North," a planned community where streets radiate from a bend in the Kapuskasing River. Beginning in 1910 as a stop

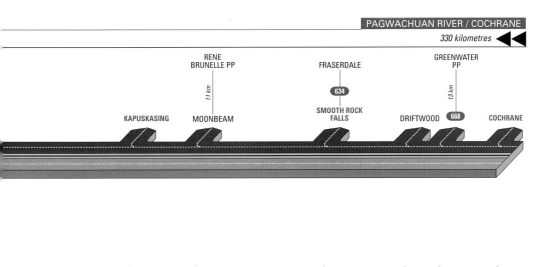

RENE
BRUNELLE PP

FRASERDALE

GREENWATER
PP

11 km

634

13 km

KAPUSKASING   MOONBEAM

SMOOTH ROCK
FALLS

DRIFTWOOD   668

COCHRANE

97 km   21 km   41 km   26 km   11 km   19 km

Stately Tudor architecture, such as the grand gabled inn (above), land-scaped gardens, and curving streets characterize Kapuskasing, planned and built by Ontario in the 1920s as a model for future northern towns.

The Polar Bear Express departs Cochrane on a 4 ½-hour excursion trip to Moosonee and the Arctic tidewaters of James Bay. The railway is the only ground route through the roadless wilds.

on the National Transcontinental Railway, development flagged when many early settlers, disillusioned with the harsh climate and surroundings, returned south. All that changed in the early 1920s, when a pulp and paper company built a mill at the nearby falls and Ontario built a model town to encourage settlement. Visitors can tour the mill—now an employee- and community-owned enterprise—and a nearby demonstration forest. Railway memorabilia and a model railway are housed in boxcars and a CNR 5107 locomotive in the Ron Morel Memorial Museum. Telephones, switchboards, and other communications equipment are displayed in a Telephone Museum in the Chamber of Commerce building.

René Brunelle Provincial Park, some 20 km west of Kapuskasing, is accessible by Hwy. 581. Storyboards along La Vigilance Trail tell the story of bush pilots who fought forest fires and rescued people in distress from their base here at Remi Lake.

Smooth Rock Falls

"The North's biggest little town," Smooth Rock Falls is the gateway to the spectacular Abitibi Canyon and offers year-round recreational opportunities. From this point, it is 76 km on Hwy. 634 to Fraserdale, as far north as you can drive in northeastern Ontario.

Some 37 km west of Smooth Rock Falls, headed toward Cochrane, Hwy. 668 leads to Greenwater Provincial Park. With two dozen lakes and three beaches, the park is ideal for swimming, fishing, and relaxing.

Cochrane

Railways have played a dominant role in developing Cochrane, which is also an agricultural, forestry, and tourism center. Born in 1908 as a major rail junction, the town is the southern terminal of the Polar Bear Express. From late June to Labor Day, this train makes daily 300 km runs north to Moosonee. A museum across from the railway station has a vintage locomotive and rolling stock, and a memorial to Tim Horton (1930-74), Cochrane-born star hockey player and donut shop franchiser, who died in an automobile accident.

143

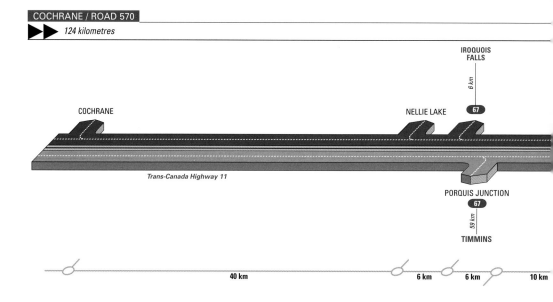

IROQUOIS
FALLS

6 km

COCHRANE

NELLIE LAKE   **67**

Trans-Canada Highway 11

PORQUIS JUNCTION
67

59 km

TIMMINS

40 km   6 km   6 km   10 km

**NORTHEASTERN
ONTARIO**

Iroquois Falls

After Abitibi-Price acquired timber rights here in 1912, it built
Iroquois Falls, the first company
town in Northern Ontario. In the
1920s, a beautification program
by the company enhanced the
community's reputation as the
"garden town of the North."

Exhibits in the Iroquois Falls
Pioneer Museum describe pioneer life and the rise of the local
forest industry. A special feature
is an old-fashioned ice cream parlor and café, which dispenses
refreshments to museum visitors.

You can tour the Abitibi-Price
newsprint mill, which produces
60 km of newsprint daily. In the
Iroquois Falls Model Forest, you
can see a trapper's museum,
reforestation techniques, and
tree-cutting operations, and you
can even plant your own tree.

Matheson

This community once mined gold
and asbestos; it now depends on
farming, tree nurseries, forest
industries, and visitors who come
here to enjoy the great outdoors.
The 1916 fire that destroyed
2,000 km² of forest and claimed
some 300 lives is among events
described at the Thelma Miles
Museum, where farm, store, and
room settings give a sense of
pioneer life.

Kettle Lakes
Provincial Park

This park's name refers to natural feature found here: some 20
small kettles or lakes without surface drainage. Rain or under-

ground streams fill up the lakes,
which began as depressions hol-
lowed out by blocks of ice left in
the wake of retreating glaciers.
Some are as deep as 30 m, and
all have steep, sandy banks. The
great boulders or erratic blocks
throughout the park also date
from the last ice age.

Accessible from both Hwy. 67
and 101 on the way to Timmins,
this park has an interesting environment: it lies in the transition
area between the boreal forest
and subarctic zone.

Timmins

At 3,212 km², an area larger than
Toronto, Montreal, and New
York combined, Timmins is the
largest municipality in Canada. A
1909 gold strike gave birth to this
"city with a heart of gold"
(neighboring Geraldton claims a
town-sized heart of gold) when
Noah Timmins, wealthy from
Cobalt silver, set up the community for his Hollinger mine
employees. (Hollinger was then
the richest gold mine in the
Western Hemisphere.) Timmins
remained a major gold producer
into the 1960s, but in the last 30
years, forest industries and the
Falconbridge Kidd Creek copper
and zinc mine and smelter north
of Timmins have been the main
economic generators.

Timmins got to its present size
—and gained city status—in 1973
by amalgamating with neighboring Schumacher, Mountjoy,
Whitney, Porcupine, and South
Porcupine. The city is home to
Timmins Square, the largest mall
in northeastern Ontario, two golf
courses (one at the old Hollinger

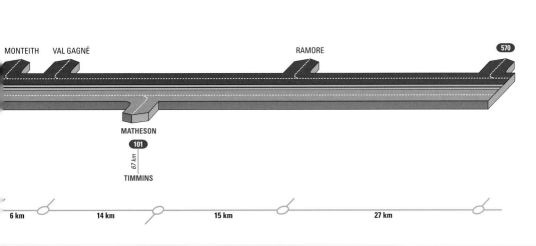

MONTEITH VAL GAGNÉ   RAMORE   570

MATHESON
101

67 km

TIMMINS

6 km   14 km   15 km   27 km

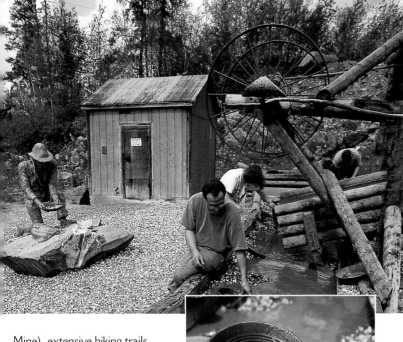

On the Golden Circle
Heritage Tour at Tim-
mins, seasoned hard
rock miners take visitors
to underground and
surface attractions
connected to one of
history's greatest gold
rushes. You can also
visit a prospector's
cabin (left), pan for
gold—and keep any
riches you find—and
explore exhibits at the
Jupiter Headframe
(below), where you
have a panoramic view
of several open pits and
the city of Timmins.

Mine), extensive hiking trails,
marinas (there are 500 lakes and
rivers within city limits), snowmobile trails, and downhill and
cross-country skiing facilities.

**Timmins Museum and
National Exhibition Centre**
This museum, located in South
Porcupine, presents the history
of Timmins from Precambrian
times to the present. Local mining and prospecting are described
with old-time equipment, a reconstructed prospector's cabin,
and high-grade gold ore samples.

**Underground Gold Mine
Tours, Timmins**
You can put on a hard hat and
spend 90 minutes as a hard rock
miner at the old Hollinger Gold
Mine. Retired miners will take
you underground to see drilling,

mucking, and blasting operations. Back on top, you can
explore the old Jupiter Mine
headframe. Its observation deck
offers views of open pit mines
and the city of Timmins. You
can also visit the restored Hollinger house. A gift shop sells
Native crafts and works by local
artists and artisans.

The gold mine tour begins on
Hwy. 101 between Timmins and
Schumacher. The latter cele-
brates its mining heritage with
murals, restored buildings, and a
Revitalization Festival in August.

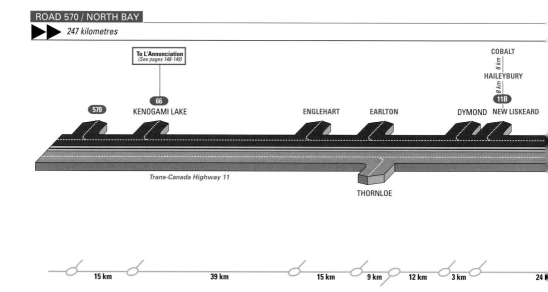

To L'Annonciation
(See pages 148-149)

66
KENOGAMI LAKE

570

ENGLEHART   EARLTON   DYMOND   NEW LISKEARD

COBALT
6 km
HAILEYBURY
8 km
11B

Trans-Canada Highway 11

THORNLOE

15 km   39 km   15 km   9 km   12 km   3 km   24 ▶

NORTHEASTERN ONTARIO

Englehart

In the Englehart and Area Museum, replicas of a settler's home, schoolroom, country store, bank, post office, and other pioneer structures re-create local history from 1908 to the 1940s. An old No. 701 locomotive is a reminder that Englehart began as a divisional point on the railway.

Earlton

This "dairy center of the North" lies in the Little Clay Belt, a fertile strip stretching along an ancient glacial lake bed to New Liskeard. Siberian tigers, yaks, a Bactrian camel, zebras, and monkeys are among some 250 creatures at Earlton Zoo. Manitou, a 5-tonne giant steel buffalo, stands beside the zoo gate.

Morgan mules, dwarf rabbits, Polish hens, pygmy goats, and Sicilian donkeys can be seen at the nearby Mini Farm.

New Liskeard

A new waterfront, with beach, boardwalk, hotel, and marina, is a big draw for visitors to this Lake Timiskaming community. Good farming land drew the first settlers and by the 1900s, New Liskeard was a thriving town. Its fortunes were assured when the railway arrived in 1905.

That past is explored at the Little Clay Belt Homesteaders Museum. (Look for the giant dairy cow, Ms. Claybelt, beside the museum.) From New Liskeard, take Hwy. 11B to Haileybury (8 km south), and Cobalt (another 6 km).

New Liskeard (right) sits at the northwest tip of Lake Temiskaming (Lac Témiscamingue in Québec), a long narrow lake stretching 128 km along the Québec–Ontario border. The great expanse of water beckons swimmers, water-skiers, and boating, sailing, and fishing enthusiasts, and provides delightful panoramas from the rocky, tree-lined shore.

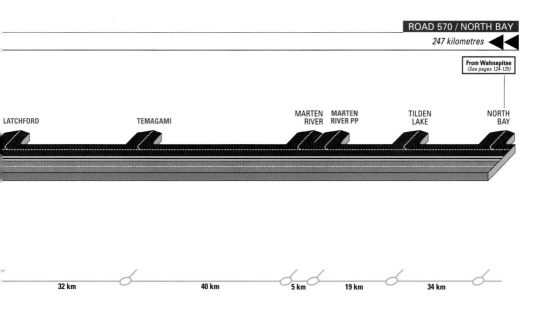

From Wahnapitae
(See pages 124-125)

LATCHFORD   TEMAGAMI   MARTEN RIVER   MARTEN RIVER PP   TILDEN LAKE   NORTH BAY

32 km   40 km   5 km   19 km   34 km

Haileybury

A leading exhibit at Haileybury Fire Museum is a 1904 Toronto streetcar. It is one of 60 sent for housing after a 1922 fire gutted the town and left 3,000 homeless. Haileybury's waterfront has a marina, beach, and water-slide. Devil's Rock offers superb views over Lake Timiskaming.

Cobalt

According to legend, blacksmith Fred LaRose threw a hammer at what he thought was a fox's eyes—and struck a vein of silver. The time was September 1903. Within years, Canada's "silver capital" had 12,000 residents (today's population is 1,500), a streetcar system, and an opera house. After yielding half a billion ounces of silver, the silver mines ran out in the 1930s, but cobalt mining rekindled activity into the 1950s and 1960s.

The Northern Ontario Mining Museum displays mining equipment and silver ores. You can tour the old Colonial Mine (hard hats provided) or follow the Heritage Silver Trail of local mines and mine buildings. Disastrous fires that swept the region are described at the Cobalt-Coleman Fire Fighters Museum in Conigas No. 4 shaft headframe. Uniforms and weapons from the 1880s are displayed in The Bunker Military Museum.

Latchford

At Latchford, you can cross the world's smallest covered bridge here, or ply the Montreal River by freighter canoe, passing mines, steamboats, sawmills, the site of a HBC post, and even a floating café. Latchford's House of Memories Museum recounts local history. Carved, white pine portraits of Ontario's forest industry leaders and a 1940s logging camp are at the Heritage Logging Attraction and Ontario Loggers Hall of Fame.

Temagami

Drawn by the natural beauty of the Temagami area, vacationers began arriving here in the 1890s. The numbers swelled with the opening of the Timiskaming and Northern Ontario Railway in 1903. The first hotel, the Ronnoco, still greets visitors.

Canoeing on Lake Temagami and surrounding waterways is the region's foremost recreation. Sightseeing flights by floatplane are also available here. A plaque at nearby Findlayson Point Park honors naturalist and writer Grey Owl, who lived in this region from 1906 to 1910. The park, popular with boaters and canoeists, contains old-growth pine forests for which this region is renowned.

Marten River Provincial Park

Just off Hwy. 11, the park offers attractions such as a restored early 1900s logging camp and a hiking trail through lowland black spruces and ancient white pines, some 300 years old. A birders' paradise, the region's mixed boreal and deciduous forest fosters high bird populations.

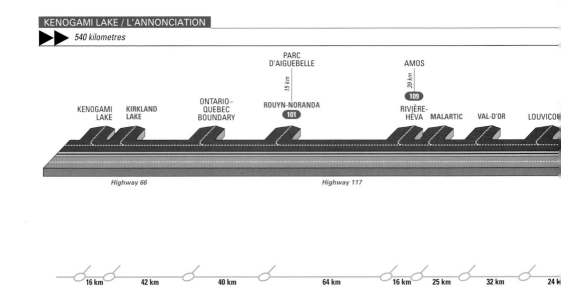

PARC
D'AIGUEBELLE

15 km

AMOS

39 km

109

KENOGAMI
LAKE

KIRKLAND
LAKE

ONTARIO–
QUEBEC
BOUNDARY

ROUYN-NORANDA

101

RIVIÈRE-
HÉVA   MALARTIC   VAL-D'OR   LOUVICO

Highway 66   Highway 117

| 16 km | 42 km | 40 km | 64 km | 16 km | 25 km | 32 km | 24 k |

**NORTHEASTERN
ONTARIO/
NORTHWESTERN
QUEBEC**

Kirkland Lake

Rock hounds haunt old mines and quarries in this town where Harry Oakes discovered the fabled Lake Shore Mine in 1912. His find fueled Kirkland Lake's growth. By the 1930s, some 5,000 miners were at work in seven gold mines. Only one of the seven is still active. (An iron mine is operating, however, and offers tours in August.) A 10 m Miners' Monument at the town entrance recalls the boom years.

Oakes (later Sir Harry), a rags-to-riches character, died in an unsolved murder in the Bahamas in 1943. His mansion houses a museum, where exhibits salute early prospectors and local hockey stars Bill Durnan, Ted Lindsay, and Dick Duff.

Rouyn-Noranda

"Canada's copper capital" was founded by prospector Edmond Horne at the time of gold and copper finds in the 1920s. Eight mines still operate here. Interpretive panels on mining are set out along a walking tour from Parc Trémoy to the Noranda smelter.

The city was created in 1986 by amalgamating two towns. Each retains its original character: Rouyn remains commercial and industrial, with Noranda, originally a company town, being residential and institutional. The Maison Dumulon, a store-cum-post office, has been restored to the 1920s. The Musée religieux occupies a 1955 former Russian Orthodox church.

Malartic

This town was established by Quebec in the 1930s to end the proliferation of squatter camps springing up in the then active

The Museum of Northern Ontario in the Sir Harry Oakes Chateau (above) showcases the history of Kirkland Lake and its colorful cast of pioneers, prospectors, miners, and millionaires. Homegrown hockey heroes figure prominently in the Sports Room (right).

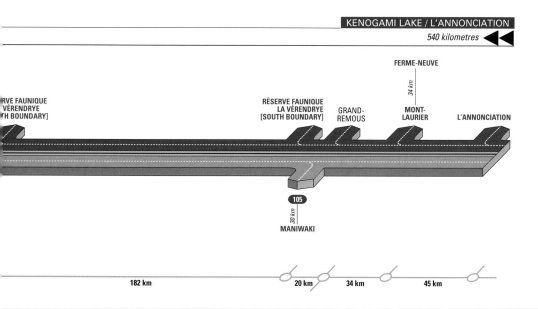

Malartic goldfields. Although the gold rush is over, the town retains an Old West look. The Musée régional des mines, founded by ex-miners, has exhibits on mines and mineralogy, and a simulated mine shaft descent.

Val-d'Or

The name is accurate—"valley of gold." Gold is still being extracted in this place, whose original boom was second only to the Klondike. In the 1930s, Val-d'Or was the biggest gold-mining town in the world. The Village minier de Bourlamaque has been restored to its 1935 appearance. Miners still inhabit most of its 80 log buildings. Exhibits describe the work of prospectors and geologists. Visitors can descend 80 m down a mine shaft. The 18 m Rotary Observation Tower offers panoramic views.

Réserve Faunique La Vérendrye

Hwy. 117 cuts through this vast preserve of lakes and rivers, forests and wildlife. Visitors can choose from dozens of campgrounds, canoe routes, backroads, bike paths, and trails.

Maniwaki

A Donald Doiron sculpture in Parc Le Draveur commemorates the great log drives on the Gatineau River. Trucks move logs and lumber now, but forest industries remain the major employer. Château Logue, a stone house built in 1887 by Irish-born merchant Charles Logue, has been restored and houses a library, art gallery, and exhibits on the forest fire prevention from fire towers to satellite surveillance.

Mont-Laurier

The leading center in the Upper Laurentian region, Mont-Laurier was founded in 1886 on the site of a Rivière du Lièvre lumber camp. Surviving from that year is the Maison Alix-Bail, once a general store. First known as Rapide-de-l'Orignal, this spot was renamed in 1909 to honor Prime Minister Sir Wilfrid Laurier (1841-1919). Timber processing is Mont-Laurier's mainstay.

Ferme-Neuve

Some 34 km north of Hwy. 117, on Hwy. 309, Ferme-Neuve provides access to 783 m high Mont Wilfrid-Laurier, the second highest peak in the Laurentians. Ferme-Neuve (the name means "New Farm") sits on the Rivière du Lièvre, surrounded by farms and forests. The area abounds in cross-country ski trails and groomed snowmobile routes. The Ferme apicole Desrochers has exhibits on beekeeping and sells its own honey wine.

L'Annonciation

Exhibits at the Ecomusée de la Vallée de la Rouge at L'Annonciation include L'Annonciation's original 1903 train station, and the old P'tit Train du Nord that once connected Montreal and the communities in the Upper Laurentians.

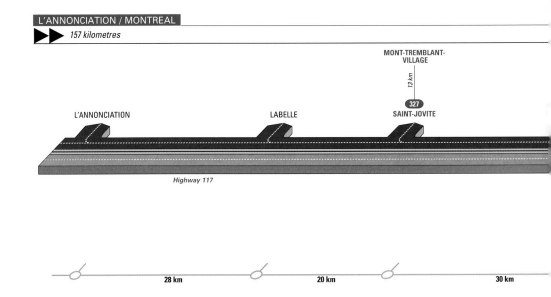

MONT-TREMBLANT-VILLAGE

13 km

327
SAINT-JOVITE

L'ANNONCIATION

LABELLE

Highway 117

28 km   20 km   30 km

THE LAURENTIANS/ NORTH OF MONTREAL

Saint-Jovite

In a beautiful mountain setting, Saint-Jovite is handy for Mont-Tremblant, Gray Rocks, Mont-Blanc, and other major ski centers. Also nearby are some 70 km of cross-country ski trails including 50 km of double track.

Strollers will enjoy Rue Ouimet, with its terraced restaurants, tearooms, antique shops and boutiques, and a Victorian-style shopping center. Even the former railway station has been converted into a restaurant.

Mont-Tremblant-Village

In 1938 Philadelphia millionaire Joe Ryan decided to build a lodge at the base of 960 m Mont-Tremblant, the highest skiable summit in the Laurentians. Expanded and renovated in the 1990s, the world-class Station de Ski Mont-Tremblant now offers accesss to 74 downhill ski runs, six high-speed lifts, cross-country ski trails, and an outdoor skating rink. In summer, there is swimming and sailing on Lac Tremblant, as well as golf, mountain biking, cycling, tennis, and hiking.

The resort's Village Saint-Bernard is accessible by foot, snowshoe, and ski only. Traditional Quebec architectural styles mark its shops, restaurants, and bars. Its Chapelle Saint-Bernard is a replica of an old Île d'Orléans church.

Parc du Mont-Tremblant

Some 5 km from Mont-Tremblant-Village, the Parc de récréation du Mont-Tremblant is the oldest and most frequented park in Quebec. With seven rivers and some 400 lakes, it offers breathtaking mountain, forest, and lake scenery. Facilities include 500 campsites, 100 km of hiking trails, canoe routes, riding trails and horse rentals, paved cycling routes and mountain-bike paths, beaches, sailing and wind-surfing (with boat rentals near park entrances), plus cross-country ski and snowshoeing trails.

Sainte-Agathe-des-Monts

On Lac des Sables in the heart of the Laurentians, Sainte-Agathe-des-Monts was the first of the resorts developed in the mountains north of Montreal. This community has been welcoming visitors since the railway arrived in 1892. Today's accommodations range from overnight to seasonal. The town has several gourmet restaurants. In summer visitors can enjoy the local beaches, sail—or take a cruise boat—around the lake, and drive or bike the popular Chemin du Lac. Winter brings the Hiver en Nord Carnival, and the opening of myriad snowmobile trails and 15 downhill ski centers, all within 30 minutes of town.

Saint-Sauveur-des-Monts

With wall-to-wall restaurants, art galleries, and boutiques, Saint-Sauveur's Rue Principale is the busiest, most crowded street in the Laurentians. Situated in a picturesque valley, the village has long been a tourist and skiing haven. Tourist facilities have grown tremendously in the last

Autumn splashes brilliant red, yellow, orange, and gold splotches across stands of maple and groves of birch and beech intermingling with balsam fir in Parc du Mont-Tremblant. Nourishing the parade of forested hills and valleys are scores of streams, waterfalls, rivers, and smooth lakes such as Lac Monreau (right).

To Montreal Area
(See pages 170-173, 334-335)

SAINTE-AGATHE-DES-MONTS | SAINTE-ADÈLE **Exit 69** | SAINT-SAUVEUR-DES-MONTS **Exit 60** | SAINT-JÉRÔME **Exit 45** | SAINTE-THÉRÈSE **Exit 23** | LAVAL | MONTRÉAL [JCT. HWY. 40]

Highway 15

344

9 km

SAINT-EUSTACHE

15 km | 8 km | 13 km | 18 km | 4 km | 10 km | 11 km

two decades. There are five area ski centers with 84 trails and 32 lifts. A lighting system makes Saint-Sauveur the world's largest night-skiing center. In summertime, there is summer theater, and the Parc aquatique du Mont-Saint-Sauveur offers its wave pool and six water-slides, four of which are spiral.

Saint-Jérôme

Situated on the Rivière du Nord, Saint-Jérôme has long been a farming and papermaking center. The major landmark is the triple-spired Roman Byzantine style Cathédrale de Saint-Jérôme. Opposite the cathedral is a statue of Curé Antoine Labelle, a former parish priest, who created dozens of Laurentian settlements and parishes in the 1870s and 1880s.

Saint-Eustache

The center of an agricultural region that nurtured many of Quebec's intellectual and political elite of the past, this city's residential sections have been expanding rapidly of late. Several apple orchards in the area produce their own cider and welcome visitors. At Moulin Légaré (1762), Canada's oldest still-operating water-powered mill, you can buy the mill's own wheat and buckwheat flours. Shrapnel marks from the Patriotes Rebellion of 1837 are visible on the cut-stone outer walls of the two-towered Palladian Roman Catholic church. Because of its superb acoustics, the Montreal Symphony records there.

Laval

Québec's second largest city, Laval is on Île Jésus, north of Montreal Island. It is the site of the Cosmodome, a museum about space science and technology. Exhibits include a mock-up of the *Apollo* mission control center, the space shuttle *Endeavour,* and the Canadarm.

151

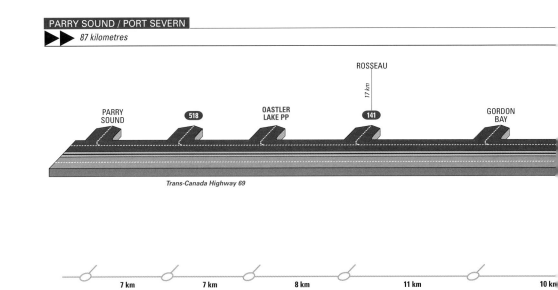

ROSSEAU

17 km

PARRY SOUND · 518 · OASTLER LAKE PP · 141 · GORDON BAY

Trans-Canada Highway 69

7 km · 7 km · 8 km · 11 km · 10 km

CENTRAL ONTARIO/ GEORGIAN BAY

Windswept pines clinging to glacier-scraped rocks typify the 30,000 islands, renowned for their flora and fauna, especially their diversity of amphibians and reptiles. Beausoleil (below), the largest, has all that and more. Southern hardwoods cover half the island, northern evergreens the rest. Nowhere else can you so readily see where the Canadian Shield begins.

Oastler Lake
Provincial Park

Named for a family of early settlers, this tiny park on the shore of Oastler Lake has a hilly, rocky landscape, stands of hemlock and hardwood trees. Inviting walks lead visitors along the lakeshore and through the forests. A large sandy beach has shallow water stretching out for some distance from the shore—where small children can safely swim.

Muskoka Lakes

Just east of Georgian Bay, three major lakes, Rosseau, Joseph and Muskoka, lie at the heart of a dazzling summer destination— the Muskoka Lakes. Intercon-

nected here and there by canals, the lakes have long attracted boaters. This region is also Ontario's fabled "cottage country." Many of the 20,000 summer cottages in the area are owned by affluent Torontonians. But Muskoka also has hundreds of hotels, lodges, resorts, and bed-and-breakfasts for vacationers seeking to sample the area's natural beauty and recreations.

Bala

Hwy. 169 leads to Bala and Port Carling, two popular spots in the Muskoka Lakes region. At the junction of Lake Muskoka and the Moon River, Bala offers lodges, hotels and bed-and-breakfasts. A major attraction with young vacationers is the KEE music center: bands from all over Canada play there in summer. Cranberries are a big local

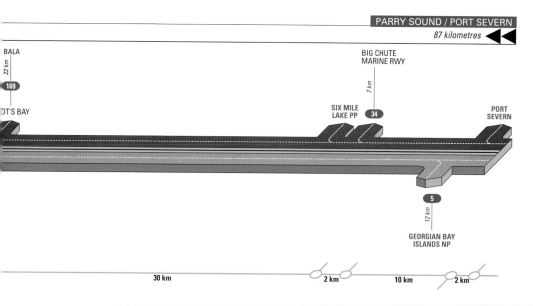

BALA
22 km
169

'T'S BAY

BIG CHUTE
MARINE RWY
7 km

SIX MILE
LAKE PP **34**

PORT
SEVERN

5
12 km

GEORGIAN BAY
ISLANDS NP

30 km 2 km 10 km 2 km

One of Ontario's most photographed attractions, the winch-operated Big Chute Marine Railway near Six Mile Lake Provincial Park enables boats to bypass the Severn River's Big Chute Falls. First built in 1917 and replaced by a larger modernized system in 1977, Big Chute takes boats up and over a 17.7 m height of land.

crop, several farms are open for tours, and the town holds a cranberry festival in October.

Bala Museum honors *Anne of Green Gables*. Author Lucy Maud Montgomery summered here in 1922 and used Muskoka as setting for *The Blue Castle*.

Port Carling

Some 8 km from Bala on Hwy. 118 lies Port Carling. Canal locks linking lakes Muskoka and Rosseau made this spot an early center of transportation and commerce. Today, the village is the hub of a lively tourist area.

Displays in the Muskoka Lakes Museum in Island Park describe the wooden pleasure boat for which this region was once famous.

Six Mile Lake Provincial Park

Attractions here include three sandy beaches, wooded campsites, and first-rate fishing, boating, and hiking. Canoeists can paddle on Six Mile Lake, a reservoir for the Trent-Severn Waterway. (Canoes can be rented in the park.) The lake is at the southern edge of the Canadian

Shield. Travelers, particularly those heading north, will notice the first rugged outcrops of granite and gneiss.

Georgian Bay Islands National Park

The best jumping-off point for any of this park's 59 islands is Honey Harbour (12 km from Hwy. 69 on Road 5). It is the site of the park headquarters, and boat rentals and water taxis are available there. Beausoleil, the largest island, is only a 10-minute boat ride from shore. The big draws are sandy beaches, endless boating opportunities, lush forests and wetlands, rare flora and fauna such as the eastern massasauga rattler, and the glacier-scraped rocks edging the Canadian Shield.

Port Severn

This is the western outlet of the Trent-Severn Waterway that links Lake Ontario with Georgian Bay. Once a commercial artery, the waterway is now used by pleasure craft in summer. (See pages 164-165.) A pleasant diversion here is a cruise to the Big Chute Marine Railway.

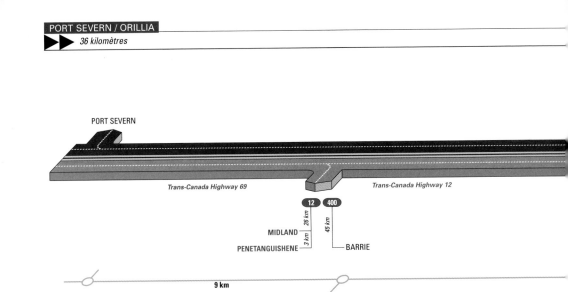

PORT SEVERN

Trans-Canada Highway 69

12   400

MIDLAND | 26 km | 45 km
PENETANGUISHENE | 3 km

Trans-Canada Highway 12

BARRIE

9 km

**CENTRAL
ONTARIO/
GEORGIAN BAY
TO LAKE SIMCOE**

Rebuilt on its original site by the Wye River, Sainte-Marie among the Hurons (below) is a replica of the mission where Jesuit priests lived and worked with the Hurons during the mid-1600s. An interpretive program and museum exhibits enrich visitors' appreciation of how much the missionaries accomplished in their brief time in the Canadian wilderness.

Midland

This community's natural heritage is preserved at the Wye Marsh Wildlife Centre just as its historic heritage is kept alive at Sainte-Marie among the Hurons, The Martyrs' Shrine, and the Huronia Museum and Huron Indian Village.

Wye Marsh Wildlife Centre, Midland

Blinds and an observation tower, self-guided trails, a floating boardwalk, canoe routes and guided canoe excursions introduce you to the wonders of the wetlands and uplands at this major environmental attraction. Wye Marsh encompasses forest, streams, and marshlands, where visitors can hand-feed birds and learn about bees and other insects, birds of prey, and trumpeter swans.

Sainte-Marie among the Hurons, Midland

This is a detailed reconstruction of the fortified mission to the Hurons that French Jesuits founded here in 1639. At its height, more than 60 French priests and workers lived in this first European settlement in what is now Ontario. In 1649, fearing attack by the Iroquois, the Jesuits burned the mission before fleeing with their Huron allies to what is now Christian Island in Georgian Bay. The mission remained only a memory until excavations began in the 1940s. Reconstruction followed, and today costumed staff will guide visitors through residences, church, bastion, hospital, gardens, and shops.

Just opposite Sainte-Marie among the Hurons, the twin-towered Martyrs' Shrine contains relics of Jean de Brébeuf and four other Jesuits who worked from the mission. All five were martyred by the Iroquois, and all were canonized in 1930.

Huronia Museum and Huron Indian Village, Midland

At Little Lake Park, the palisaded Huron village longhouses re-create the kind of community the Jesuits encountered when they arrived here in the early 17th century. The adjacent museum explores Huron history and houses an extensive collection of Native artifacts. Exhibits also focus on local pioneer and military history and photography. An art gallery features works by important Canadian artists.

Penetanguishene

French and English immigrants settled around the military and naval establishments here during the War of 1812, a dual heritage celebrated in the town's restau-

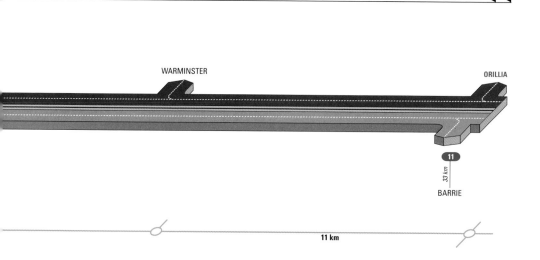

WARMINSTER

ORILLIA

11

33 km

BARRIE

11 km

Leacock memorabilia fill this 19-room mansion on Lake Couchiching's Old Brewery Bay, once the humorist's summer home. Champlain's statue (below) recalls the explorer's visit to the Orillia area.

rants, galleries, and historic attractions. Discovery Harbour is a re-creation of the British naval base that operated from 1817 to 1856. You can visit workshops, dwellings, and officers' quarters, explore replicas of the historic fleet's vessels, and cruise Penetanguishene Bay on HMS *Tecumseth* or HMS *Bee*. You can also cruise Georgian Bay on *Georgian Queen*, which departs from the town dock.

Displays at Penetanguishene Centennial Museum recount the area's pioneer and logging past.

Orillia

This year-round resort town offers myriad recreations and attractions. A calendar of nonstop events range from the Winter Carnival (January) to the Jazz Festival (October).

For 12 weeks each summer, the Orillia Opera House hosts plays and musicals by the local Sunshine Festival Theatre Company. Lake cruises are available aboard the Mississippi-style riverboat, *Island Princess*. The Orillia Farmers' Market opens every Saturday morning as it has since 1875. An historic walking tour (brochure available) highlights Victorian dwellings and other sites, such as the imposing 1896 fire hall. A much admired landmark is the 12 m bronze statue (*left*), erected in 1925 to mark the 300th anniversary of Champlain's visit.

Stephen Leacock Museum, Orillia

This museum honors the professor of political science (at McGill University, Montreal) who is widely regarded as Canada's greatest humorist. Stephen Leacock (1869-1944) summered in Orillia for 36 years, penning much of his vast output—34 volumes of humor, plus 27 books on history, biography, economics and political science— in his boathouse on Lake Couchiching. Orillia is said to be the model for Mariposa, the setting of his 1911 classic, *Sunshine Sketches of a Little Town*. The museum, in the house Leacock built in 1925, offers tours and exhibits and hosts an annual midsummer Leacock Heritage Festival.

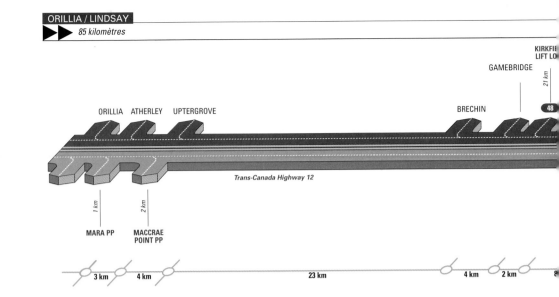

KIRKFIE
LIFT LO

GAMEBRIDGE

21 km

ORILLIA ATHERLEY UPTERGROVE

BRECHIN

48

Trans-Canada Highway 12

1 km

2 km

MARA PP

MACCRAE
POINT PP

3 km 4 km 23 km 4 km 2 km 8

**CENTRAL
ONTARIO/
KAWARTHA
LAKES**

Mara and MacRae Point Provincial Park

Just beyond the Narrows (linking lakes Simcoe and Couchiching), Mara Provincial Park offers a wide sandy beach, one of the finest on Lake Simcoe. Bird-watching is popular in this park which consists of forested areas, open fields, and marshland. Red-backed salamanders can often be seen at the swamp edges.

A few kilometres farther along Hwy. 12, MacRae Point Provincial Park is another tiny retreat, with campsites, sheltered beaches, and a ball field. Along the Pathless Woods Trail, you will see maidenhair, rattlesnake fern, and other vascular plants for which the park is renowned.

Kirkfield

This hamlet is notable for having one of only two hydraulic lift locks in North America. (The other is the better-known lock at Peterborough—see page 162.) Built between 1896 and 1907 as part of the Trent-Severn Waterway, Kirkfield lock has two watertight chambers, large enough to holding sizable vessels, which can raised or lowered 15 m. Thousands of pleasure craft make their way through the locks each year. From an adjoining picnic area, you can watch the vessels being eased from one level to another.

Beaverton

This lakeshore community straddles the Beaver River where it flows into Lake Simcoe. At the Beaver River Museum, you can see an 1848 settler's log dwelling and a 1890s brick house, both with period furnishings, and an old stone jail. The Emporium, a gift shop in the basement of the log house, sells local crafts. Beaverton Town Hall Players present a summer theater season in the local town hall.

Kawartha Lakes

Hwy. 7 skirts the southern fringe of the fingerlike Kawartha Lakes. Linked by canals and locks, these bodies of water form part of the Trent-Severn Waterway (see pages 164-165).

Lindsay

This town's impressive landmarks include the Gothic-style St. Mary's Roman Catholic Church (1858), the County Courthouse (1861), Lindsay Armoury (1913), many fine Victorian dwellings, and the restored Academy Theatre (1892). Built as an opera house, the theater is still Lindsay's cultural center offering summer theater and other presentations year-round.

Located on the Scugog River that links Scugog and Sturgeon lakes, Lindsay is the site of one of more than 40 locks on the Trent-Severn Waterway. Boaters will find ample dock space off Riviera Park.

Victoria County Historical Museum has a re-created 1890s main street, with stores (including a toy shop), doctor's office, railway depot, and blacksmith's shop, and a collection of 19th-century Canadian glassware.

BOBCAYGEON

FENELON
FALLS

20 km

37 km

MANILLA   OAKWOOD

121   **36** LINDSAY

TON

7/12

Trans-Canada Highway 7

15 km   10 km   5 km   10 km   1 km

This pretty waterfall for which Fenelon Falls is named is beside Lock 34 of the Trent-Severn Waterway. (The Fenelon part of the name honors a Sulpician missionary, François de Salignac de Fénelon.) The falls, which mark a 7 m drop from Cameron to Sturgeon lakes, can be viewed from an island between the lakes. The island is also great for picnics and for watching boats make their way through the nearby locks.

Fenelon Falls

"The Jewel of the Kawarthas," Fenelon Falls lies between Cameron and Sturgeon lakes. *Carvelle II* starts a two-hour scenic cruise to Sturgeon Lake from a point just above the local falls.

Maryoro Lodge (1837), the town's oldest building and home of Fenelon Falls founder James Wallis, is now a museum. Visitors can swim and picnic in an adjoining park.

Popular local events include the Old Fashioned Winter Games in February, Fenelon Fair in August, and the Kawartha Arts Festival, a highlight of the Labor Day weekend.

Bobcaygeon

Straddling three bridge-linked islands between Sturgeon and Pigeon lakes, Bobcaygeon (the name is from an Indian word for shallow rapids) is known as the "hub of the Kawarthas." Lock 32, the oldest lock on the Trent-Severn Waterway, is found here. Built originally in 1833, it was later reconstructed. Nine buildings in the Kawartha Settlers' Village reflect turn-of-the-century life. A walking tour passes churches built in the 1800s, an osprey nest-topped feed mill that was once the True Blue Orange Hall, and Bobcaygeon Inn, built in 1924 as Locust Lodge.

161

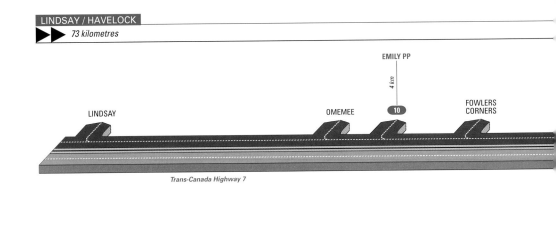

EMILY PP

4 km

LINDSAY   OMEMEE   **10**   FOWLERS
                                                                    CORNERS

Trans-Canada Highway 7

17 km   4 km   6 km   12 km

**CENTRAL
ONTARIO/
KAWARTHA
LAKES**

Emily Provincial Park

Some 4 km north of Hwy. 7, this getaway of rolling hills, forests, and diverse wildlife provides boat launching ramps on the Pigeon River, which links up with the Kawartha Lakes. Boats can be rented at nearby marinas and resorts. A boardwalk runs through a cattail meadow marshland to a sphagnum moss island. From a lookout tower, visitors can survey the park's scenery and watch ospreys diving for fish.

Peterborough

"The Queen of the Kawarthas," Peterborough is the largest city on the Trent-Severn Waterway. (See feature on pages 164-165.) Although its famous lift lock is its best-known landmark, the city's fine 19th-century houses, churches, and commercial buildings are also worth discovering. Heritage site walking tours have been mapped by the local tourism bureau. These walks will take you past the Hutchison House (see next entry) and the Grover-Nicholls House (1847), a superb example of the Greek Revival style. In striking contrast to these historic buildings is the modernity of Trent University in a woodland setting on the Otonabee River.

Photographs in the Centennial Museum and Archives cover a century of local history. Other featured exhibits include military armor, medals, and uniforms. Making boats and canoes is a traditional craft in this area, and the Canadian Canoe Museum holds the world's largest collection of canoes. Hockey and lacrosse luminaries are honored at the Peterborough and District Sports Hall of Fame.

Hutchison House Museum, Peterborough

In 1837 friends and patients of Dr. John Hutchison built this house where he lived and practiced until his death from typhus in 1847. Catharine Parr Traill, author of the classic *Backwoods of Canada,* and her family were among his patients. One room in the museum, which is restored and furnished to the 1840s, con-

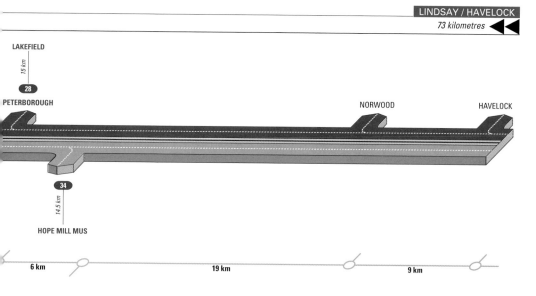

LAKEFIELD
15 km
28
PETERBOROUGH
NORWOOD
HAVELOCK

34
14.5 km
HOPE MILL MUS

6 km | 19 km | 9 km

tains books and medical instruments typical of a doctor's study of that time. Another room has surveying equipment of Hutchison's cousin, Sandford Fleming, CPR engineer and originator of standard time. Fleming spent his late teens here after his arrival from Scotland in the mid-1840s.

Each summer, thousands of pleasure craft pass through the Peterborough lift lock, which consists of two boat chambers connected to a closed hydraulic system. As one chamber takes in water, it sinks, and the other rises.

Peterborough Lift Lock

This lock, which can raise vessels some 20 m—about the height of a seven-story building—is said to be the highest fully operational lift lock in the world. (The nearby, smaller Kirkfield Lift Lock—the only other lock of this kind in North America—falls 5 m short of this mark.) On completion in 1904, the Peterborough lock was one of the largest concrete structures in the world. (The concrete was poured without the use of steel reinforcing—now the standard method.) You can see a working model of the lock at the visitor center, where exhibits and a film describe the history and construction of this national historic site.

Mark S. Burnham Provincial Park, Peterborough

A short trail in this park, west of Peterborough on Hwy. 7, winds through a mature forest containing some of the oldest hemlocks and maples in Ontario. Geological features include several drumlins—teardrop-shaped gravel hills deposited 10,000 years ago by retreating glaciers.

Lakefield

This picturesque village has both literary and royal connections. Col. Samuel Strickland and his sisters Susanna Moodie and Catharine Parr Traill were among 1830s settlers here. All three wrote classics about their experiences. Three decades later, Colonel Strickland's son, Walter, designed Christ Church,

now Christ Church Museum. Its collection includes exhibits about local history and the Strickland family. Novelist Margaret Laurence (1926-1987) spent her later life here. HRH Prince Andrew attended the prestigious Lakefield School.

The town marina can accommodate all sizes of boats. Trent-Severn Waterway boaters who tie up there are within walking distance of restaurants and shops. The marina is also the home port of *Chippewa II*, which offers cruises to Stoney Lake, northeast of town.

Hope Mill Museum

A fine collection of antique carpentry and blacksmithing tools is displayed at this restored, water-powered 1836 sawmill. To reach it, turn south on Rd. 38. Nearby Hope Mill Conservation Area has picnic tables, swimming areas, and camping, and provides access to Indian River canoe routes.

You can glimpse 1800s life in the Kawarthas at Lang Pioneer Village, a collection of restored buildings some 4 km farther south. One building is the 1820s Fife cabin, home of David Fife (1805-77), the man who developed Red Fife wheat.

Another 4 km south, in Serpent Mounds Provincial Park, nine burial mounds dominate a bluff overlooking Rice Lake. The largest, almost 60 m long and zigzag in shape, is the only mound of its kind in Canada. Experts believe the mounds were built over a 200-year period about 2,000 years ago.

Cruising the Trent-Severn Waterway

HIGHWAY 7 / PETERBOROUGH

A BIRD'S-EYE VIEW of the Trent-Severn Waterway reveals a complex chain of lakes and rivers linking Lakes Huron and Ontario. Aboriginal peoples determined the best passageways years before explorer Samuel de Champlain paddled and portaged through in 1615. Pioneer farmers and loggers built canals and locks in 1833-1920 to facilitate trade and commerce. But by the 1930s, rail and road transportation had rendered the system obsolete for all but leisure pursuits.

Now a national historic site, the waterway has become a choice destination for boaters and water-sports enthusiasts. A world-class navigation system, it boasts 36 conventional locks, two flight locks, two hydraulic lift locks, and a marine railway. With a seaworthy craft, you can travel to any port in the world from the towns and villages on its shorelines.

Even a short excursion is memorable. You could begin in Peterborough, gateway to the Kawartha Lakes, for example, and journey the 100-odd kilometres to Balsam Lake, where the Trent River (bound east to Lake Ontario) and the Severn River (bound west to Lake Huron) meet. You can rent a sea-doo by the hour, take a dinner cruise or book a cabin on a cruise boat, captain a rented houseboat, canoe, kayak, or sail boat, or trailer in your own vessel.

There are plenty of campgrounds, hotels, efficiency cabins, and bed-and-breakfast inns enroute. An information center (1-800-663-BOAT) provides lock operating hours, fee schedules, and navigational maps, and will make docking reservations for larger yachts and cruisers.

Lock 21 is the official name of the Peterborough Lift Lock, a 19th-century engineering marvel and still the world's highest hydraulic lift. A cement monolith, it was constructed in 1896-1904 into the embankment below Peterborough's largest drumlin, Armour Hill. The "lift" operates differently from conventional locks in that it raises and lowers boats at the same time in two separate, water-filled chambers.

Mary MacPherson, *a columnist for* Thompson News, *has written many books, including* The Best of Ontario *and* Bird Watch: A Young Person's Introduction to Birding.

Cruising north toward Lock 22, Trent University rises up on both sides of the Otonabee River. Trent's stone facade was built to complement the river's limestone banks. Students sculling racing shells and cyclists pedaling along the scenic banks are a common sight. You will pass Lakefield, onetime home of pioneer sister-writers Catharine Parr Trail and Susanna Moodie and more recently of renowned author Margaret Laurence. Entering Clear Lake, you lock through Youngs Point (Lock 27), where you can moor your boat and visit the local Lockside Trading Company—a country store that sells everything from Tilley hats and telescopes to paddles and rustic furniture.

Back in your boat, note the change in topography as you drift by Clear and Stoney lakes. Rugged pink-granite outcroppings and tall white pines—typical of Stoney Lake's 1,100 islands and the Kawartha Lakes' northern shores—mark where Canadian Shield granite meets southerly limestone. Some of Canada's oldest cottages were built on Stoney Lake during the logging boom years. Today's cottages range from quaint, log-hewn cabins to the distinctive "glass houses" on Lower Stoney's north shore.

Buckhorn is known for its August Wildlife Art Festival. You can dock at Gallery On The Lake on Lower Buckhorn and view the wildlife and nature art of Michael Dumas, Robert Bateman, and other Canadian artists. You may also want to stop off at the Curve Lake First Nation, an aboriginal community occupying the peninsula between Buckhorn and Chemong lakes that is home to internationally renowned artists David Johnson, Norman Knott, and Randy Knott. Whetung's Ojibwa Crafts and Art Gallery

Anglers in the know often seek out the weedy edges of Chemong Lake.

there features authentic Ojibwa clothing, beaded jewelry, quill work, and sculpture. You can sample Native foods in the Summer Tea Room.

Fishing, good to excellent in the Kawarthas, begins in May with the pickerel (walleye) season. You can catch largemouth and smallmouth bass, muskellunge, northern pike, sucker, carp, trout, and panfish. Anglers in the know favor the weedy edges of Chemong Lake. Fishing licenses are available at most bait and tackle shops.

Beach lovers will enjoy a stopover at Emily Provincial Park at the south end of Pigeon Lake. Between Pigeon and Sturgeon lakes you will pass through the oldest lock on the system—Lock 32, built in 1833—right in the heart of Bobcaygeon. Historic buildings, century homes, and shops are all within walking distance.

Many waterfront communities sponsor annual canoe and boat races. Picturesque Sturgeon Lake, veteran of more than 100 annual sailboat regattas, is synonymous with sailing. There you can stay at a luxury inn, a lakeside cottage, or Dunsford House (1832), one of the finest examples of log-house architecture in North America. At a local resort, you can enjoy one of the best pay-as-you-play nine-hole golf courses in the Kawarthas.

Between Sturgeon and Cameron lakes, a 7 m drop marks Fenelon Falls. Then on to Balsam Lake, summit of the waterway. With a 256 m surface elevation, it is North America's highest navigable point above sea level. To reach this point, you will have spent a week or, depending on your stopovers, longer cruising the waterway.

Mary MacPherson

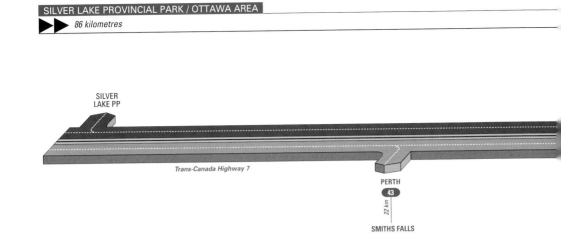

SILVER
LAKE PP

Trans-Canada Highway 7

PERTH
43

22 km

SMITHS FALLS

28 km   22 km

**EASTERN
ONTARIO**

An administrative, judicial, and social center in the early 1800s, Perth attracted a large number of educated, monied settlers whose fine homes still adorn the downtown. Built by stonemasons who came to work on the nearby Rideau Canal, these houses demonstrate architectural features of the day—galleries and trellises typical of Regency styles; gracefully proportioned, rectangular designs, low-pitched roofs, pediments and other geometric Neoclassic details; and the symmetrical designs and classic proportions of the Georgian era.

Perth

Many consider Perth, which is attractively situated on the Tay River, to be Ontario's most picturesque town. Handsome, beautifully preserved, mid-19th century sandstone buildings grace the downtown. At the town hall—built in 1863 of locally quarried stone—you can pick up a brochure that outlines three town walks. Highlights of one tour include Inge-Va (1824), a courthouse built in 1843 but a seat of judgment long before then, the 1848 St. John the Baptist Church, and the 1850 Hotel Imperial, which is still operating. The Matheson House (1830), now the Perth Museum, features period rooms reflecting 19th century life of a well-to-do family, plus an 1840s Scottish garden.

Perth bills itself as Ontario's maple syrup capital, and sugar-bush outings are popular in March. The town hosts the Central Canadian Fiddling and Step Dancing Association competition on the Victoria Day weekend.

Smiths Falls

At the midpoint of the 200 km Rideau Canal, Smiths Falls grew with the waterway. Its dams and falls powered early mills; its steamers opened up the marketplace. In the late 1800s, railways lessened the canal's commercial importance, but its proximity—and that of some 60 lakes—has kept Smiths Falls popular with boaters. Displays in the downtown Rideau Canal Museum illustrate local history and the canal's design and operation.

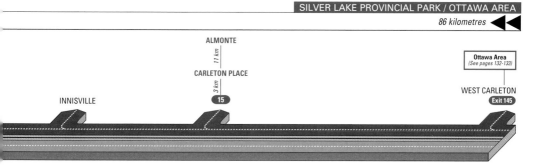

ALMONTE

11 km

CARLETON PLACE

3 km

15

INNISVILLE

Ottawa Area
(See pages 132-133)

WEST CARLETON
Exit 145

12 km   24 km

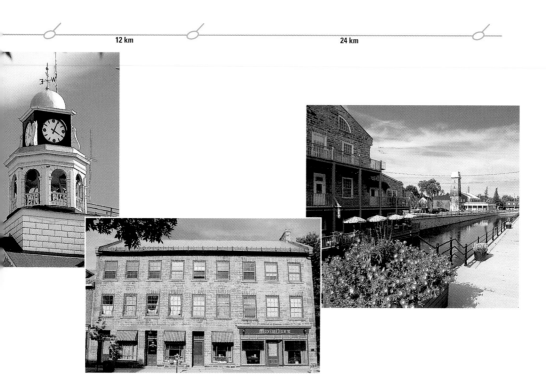

A window into the lifestyle of well-to-do mill owners opens up at the Heritage House Museum, where visitors can explore several rooms furnished as in 1867-75. During July and August, the museum serves Victorian teas.

A mapped walking tour passes the Russell (1885) and Rideau (1901) hotels, the 1894 post office, and other attractive heritage buildings. A railway museum is housed in a 1914 brick-and-stone former CNR station.

A must-do for chocoholics, Hershey Canada offers free self-guiding plant tours and a shop that sells the firm's products.

Carleton Place

On the Mississippi River (a tributary of the Ottawa River), Carleton Place was the site of one of Canada's first woolen mills (established in 1830). The wool connection came to life again in 1918, when the Canadian Co-operative Wool Growers Limited, marketer of Canada's annual 90,000 kg wool clip, set up shop in Carleton Place. Visitors can tour the co-op, which is in a converted 1887 railway locomotive repair shop. Local history is the subject of 10,000 exhibits in the Victoria School Museum. A walking tour introduces visitors to a number of limestone and brick buildings typical of Canadian streetscapes of the late 1800s.

Almonte

This town was known by various names before its citizens settled on Almonte in 1856, their way of honoring Mexican General Juan Almonte's stand against the Americans. (Locals say the name in the anglicized way—*Al-Mont*.) Audiovisual presentations in the Mississippi Valley Textile Museum (in the old Rosamund Textile Mill) recall the glory days when eight woolen mills operated locally on the Mississippi River. The Mill of Kintail Museum, some 8 km north of town, showcases 70 sculptures by native son, Dr. Robert Tait McKenzie (1867-1938), who also designed Almonte's war memorial. The surgeon won fame both for his rehabilitative work with World War I victims and as a sculptor. A plaque at the Robert Young House, some 3 km northwest of town, marks the boyhood home of Dr. James Naismith (1861-1939), the inventor of basketball.

169

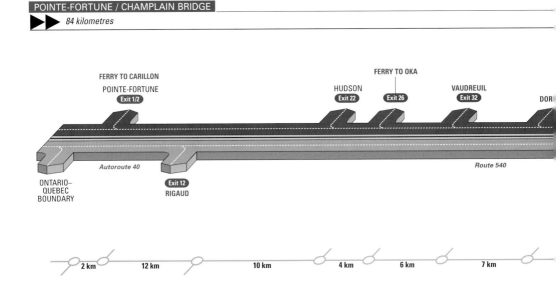

FERRY TO CARILLON
POINTE-FORTUNE
Exit 1/2

FERRY TO OKA

HUDSON
Exit 22

Exit 26

VAUDREUIL
Exit 32

DOR

Autoroute 40

Route 540

ONTARIO–
QUEBEC
BOUNDARY

Exit 12
RIGAUD

2 km   12 km   10 km   4 km   6 km   7 km

**AROUND
MONTREAL**

Carillon

A ferry from Pointe-Fortune will take you across the Ottawa River to Carillon. Monuments there and in Parc Carillon recall the 1660 Battle of Long Sault, where folk hero Adam Dollard des Ormeaux and 16 companions died. Pleasure craft flow through a local canal lock where vessels can be lowered or raised 20 m in 20 minutes. The Argenteuil Historic Museum exhibits scores of settler artifacts.

Mont Rigaud offers a panoramic view of the picturesque village of Rigaud at its feet and the Ottawa River beyond. Inspired by accounts of the Virgin Mary's appearance in Lourdes, a brother from a local religious order placed a statue on a rock shelf on this mountain in 1874. Now thousands of pilgrims come each year to pray at Rigaud's Shrine of Our Lady of Lourdes.

Rigaud

This community began in 1852 when the Clerics de Saint Viateur established the classical Collège Bourget. A field of smooth round stones near Mont Rigaud's summit is known as the Devil's Garden. According to legend, God punished a farmer for planting potatoes on a Sunday by turning the crop to stone. Maple syrup and maple sugar products are available year-round at the Sucrerie de la Montagne.

Oka

A ferry links Hudson to Oka on the east side of Lac des Deux-Montagnes. At nearby Kanesa-take, Mohawk warriors confronted Quebec provincial police and Canadian soldiers in the 1990 Oka crisis. Begun as an Indian mission and named for an Algonkian word for "golden fish"—the once plentiful lake *doré* (walleye)—Oka has been a pilgrimage site from the 1740s. Before the annual hunt, local Mohawks visited seven stone chapels built in the hills along a *Calvaire* (Road of the Cross). Three oratories remain and are the focus of a pilgrimage each September 14, the Feast of the Holy Cross. Trappists, who settled here in 1881, originated the famous Oka cheese. It is still made locally though not by the monks. You can visit the monastery chapel and gardens.

Vaudreuil-Dorion

This community was created in the 1990s by amalgamating two towns at

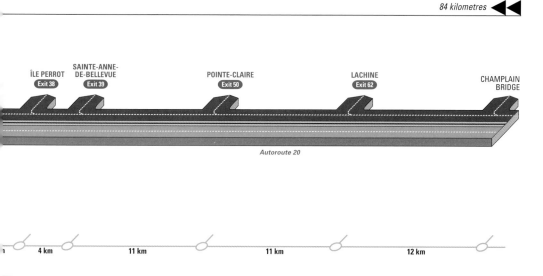

ÎLE PERROT **Exit 38** · SAINTE-ANNE-DE-BELLEVUE **Exit 39** · POINTE-CLAIRE **Exit 50** · LACHINE **Exit 62** · CHAMPLAIN BRIDGE

Autoroute 20

4 km · 11 km · 11 km · 12 km

the confluence of the St. Lawrence and Ottawa rivers. Manoir Trestler (1806) in Vaudreuil, a popular concert and conference site, can be toured by appointment. The pulpit, high altar, candelabra, and statues in the nearby St. Michel church (1783) are by renowned 18th-century sculptor Philippe Liébert. Religious art and antique carvings are among exhibits in the Musée Régional de Vaudreuil-Soulanges, also in Vaudreuil.

Works of local artists are displayed in the Maison Valois Génus, built in Dorion in 1796 of squared timbers set on a high stone foundation.

Île-Perrot

A 1703 windmill, the focal point of a small park, is all that remains of the manor house built here by Joseph Trottier de Desruisseaux. Ste. Jeanne de Chantal Church has an interesting interior.

Sainte-Anne-de-Bellevue

Early settlers called the area "belle vue" for its fine lake views. In the 1700s, this was the departure point for fur brigades heading west. Before launching their canoes, voyageurs prayed for safety and success in a lakeside chapel dedicated to Saint Anne.

Boutiques and restaurants now line the waterfront, and from a terraced promenade, you can watch boats passing through a canal lock linking St. Louis and Deux Montagnes lakes. The Macdonald Agricultural College and Experimental Farm and the Morgan Arboretum, with 20 km of nature trails, are nearby.

Pointe-Claire

A lakeshore retreat in the early 1900s, Pointe-Claire is now a bedroom community for commuters to Montreal. St. Joachim Church and a windmill on the point that gives the town its name date from 1710.

Lachine

Because René Robert Cavelier de La Salle (1643-1687) was obsessed with finding a route across North America to the Orient, his followers jokingly dubbed land he was given here "La Chine" (China). England and France were at war in 1689, when Britain's Iroquois allies massacred most of Lachine's first 77 families. A cairn marks the site. The 14 km Lachine Canal, built in 1821 to bypass local rapids and later made obsolete by the St. Lawrence Seaway, is now a recreational waterway. A stone warehouse (1803) by the canal is a museum of the fur trade. Another museum is in a fieldstone house built in 1669 by Charles Le Moyne, Baron de Longueuil.

Montreal

East of Lachine, Autoroute 20 connects with the 720 leading to central Montreal. For a walking tour of the downtown area, see pages 172-173.

Inside this old stone warehouse at the Fur Trade in Lachine National Historic Site, guides costumed as trappers, voyageurs, and merchants go about their business amid bundles of furs, barrels of provisions, and chests of trade goods. Demonstrations on matters ranging from beaver hat manufacture to handling birchbark canoes are featured on weekend summer afternoons.

MONTREAL—CAREFREE AND COSMOPOLITAN

Although Montreal wears a French face, it is a cosmopolitan place, embracing peoples of culturally diverse origins. A compact core—public and commercial buildings follow a tight midtown grid—makes it easy to explore. A rich array of museums and galleries enliven the heart of the city. Mount Royal is an inescapable landmark most of the time. When not obscured by skyscraper palisades, it can be useful for orienting your walk. One of North America's gastronomic capitals, Montreal is also blessed with a pervasive *joie de vivre*. Visitors often express amazement at Montrealers' friendliness, and how safe and uncongested the city is. The city core shown here sits on a terrace of land that slopes down to Old Montreal and the St. Lawrence River.

Mount Royal Park
An oasis for all-season leisure, this city park at the summit of a so-called 250 m "mountain" was laid out by Frederick Law Olmsted (1822-1903), the landscape architect who designed New York's Central Park. You have a panoramic view of Montreal from the chalet lookout. Behind the chalet is a 30 m high illuminated cross built in 1924 where De Maisonneuve, one of Montreal's founders, planted a cross in 1643.

Montreal Museum of Fine Arts
Dating from 1860, and containing a prestigious collection of Canadian art, the museum is on either side of Sherbrooke Street. Underground galleries lead from the main building, a beaux arts style structure with white marble facade, to a Moshe Safdie-designed pavilion across the street. Behind the Safdie wing, the **Montreal Museum of Decorative Arts** has a fine collection of contemporary furniture, ceramics, textiles, and graphic designs.

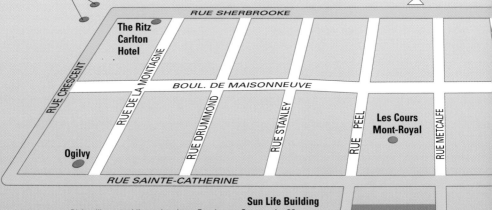

RUE SHERBROOKE

The Ritz Carlton Hotel

BOUL. DE MAISONNEUVE

RUE CRESCENT

RUE DE LA MONTAGNE

RUE DRUMMOND

RUE STANLEY

RUE PEEL

Les Cours Mont-Royal

RUE METCALFE

Ogilvy

RUE SAINTE-CATHERINE

Sun Life Building
Rising like a wedding cake above Dorchester Square, the 26-story, beaux arts style, granite Sun Life Assurance Building took 19 years to build. Completed in 1933, it could accommodate 2,500 employees, and was said to be the largest building in the British Empire. Bank of England reserves were stored in its basement during World War II.

Dorchester Square

BOUL. RENÉ-LÉVESQUE

Place du Canada

Canadian Centre for Architecture
A Victorian mansion once owned by Lord Shaughnessy is the focal point of this $25 million, Peter Rose-designed

museum, a project of Seagram liquor heiress Phyllis (Bronfman) Lambert. Original drawings by Michelangelo and Leonardo da Vinci are among its vast library and archival holdings, one of North America's most important architectural collections. The center hosts concerts, lectures, special tours for children, and up to 10 special exhibitions annually.

Mary Queen of the World Cathedral
Built in 1895 to resemble St. Peter's Basilica in Rome, and originally named St. James the Great, this Roman Catholic church was the first building in Montreal to cost more than $1 million. Its high altar is made of ivory, marble, and onyx. Thirteen wooden figures on the portico are patron saints of city parishes. A statue of Bishop Ignace Bourget, the cathedral's founder, stands to the right of the main door.

McGill University

One of Canada's leading English-language universities, McGill's downtown campus contains several historic mansions. Its Greek Revival Roddick Gates entrance honors a former dean of medicine, Sir Thomas Roddick. A bronze statue of its founder, fur-trade baron James McGill (1744-1813), stands just inside the gates. McGill's grave is nearby, in front of the Arts Building. **The Redpath Museum of Natural History** houses an eclectic collection of dinosaur bones, Egyptian mummies, and medieval armor. According to a 1926 plaque, a boulder on campus marks the site of Hochelaga, the Indian village Cartier found here in 1535, but several archaeologists dispute this location.

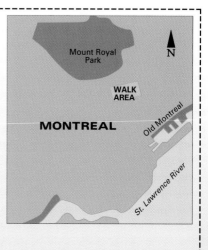

McCord Museum of Canadian History

Often called "Canada's attic," the McCord boasts one of North America's great collections of aboriginal art, period costumes, original newspaper cartoons, and the renowned Notman photo archives of more than 70,000 prints from the late 19th and early 20th centuries.

Place des Arts

Montreal's $9 million performing arts complex, opened in 1963, is home to the Montreal Symphony Orchestra. A 3,000-seat opera house and two smaller theaters are linked to the **Montreal Museum of Contemporary Art,** the country's only gallery dedicated exclusively to modern artworks.

Eaton Center

AV. DU PRÉSIDENT-KENNEDY
RUE VICTORIA
AV. McGILL COLLEGE
RUE UNIVERSITY
AV. UNION
RUE AYLMER
RUE SAINTE-CATHERINE

Birks

Philips Square

Place Ville Marie

When this 41-story, aluminum and glass cruciform landmark opened in 1962, it introduced the concept of underground pedestrian shopping malls to North America. PVM is gateway to an "underground city," a 29 km maze that links downtown office towers and more than 1,600 retail stores.

Old Montreal

North America's greatest concentration of 17th to 19th century buildings has been preserved along a waterfront park here in Montreal's historic quarter. Most surround four public squares: Place Jacques-Cartier, Place d'Armes, Place Royale, and Place d'Youville. Place Jacques-Cartier is bordered by the Second Empire style **City Hall** (1872), **Château de Ramezay** (1705), a one-time residence of colonial governors, **Notre-Dame de Bonsecours Chapel** (1771), also known as the Sailors' Chapel, and the grey-stone 1844 **Bonsecours Market** (*below left*). British Admiral Lord Nelson's statue at the top of the square predates the one in London's Trafalgar Square by 20 years. Place d'Armes, a felicitous mix of old and new, is surrounded by buildings that span four centuries. At its center is a monument to Paul de Chomedey, Sieur de Maisonneuve, who, in 1642, cofounded Ville Marie, the religious colony that became Montreal. Nearby are the **Sulpician Seminary** (1685), the twin-towered, neo-Gothic **Notre-Dame Basilica** (1829), which has a breathtakingly beautiful interior, the classic revival **Bank of Montreal** (1847), the eight-story **New York Life Insurance Building** (1886), the city's first "skyscraper," and the art deco **Aldred Building** (1929). An obelisk in Place Royale—the oldest public square in Montreal—honors the city's 53 original settlers. The actual Pointe-à-Callière settlement site can be seen in the crypt of the nearby **Montreal Museum of Archaeology and History.** A turn-of-the-century, red-brick fire hall in Place d'Youville is now a civic museum.

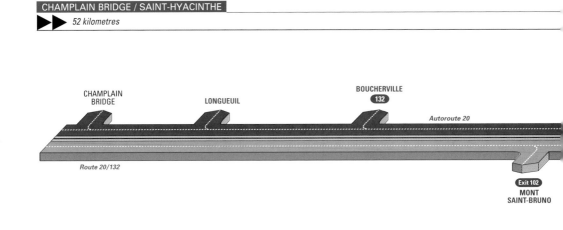

CHAMPLAIN BRIDGE   LONGUEUIL   BOUCHERVILLE **132**   *Autoroute 20*

Route 20/132

Exit 102 MONT SAINT-BRUNO

6 km   8 km   10 km

EAST OF MONTREAL

Longueuil

A dormitory community for Montreal, Longueuil's notable landmarks include the Maison Rollin-Brais (1798) and churches such as the neo-Romanesque St. Mark's (1842), and the imposing St. Antoine de Padoue (1887). Rue Saint-Charles in old Longueuil is the place to look for restaurants and sidewalk cafés.

Boucherville

Stretching for 7 km along the St. Lawrence River, Boucherville is one of Québec's oldest municipalities. Heritage structures include the Manoir François-Pierre-Boucher (1741) and the Ste. Famille Church (1801), which is noted for its paintings. Its 1896 presbytery is now a cultural center. Maison Louis-Hippolyte-Lafontaine was the childhood home of Lower Canada's great reform leader of the 1800s. The Îles de Boucherville, offshore in the St. Lawrence, are ideal for bird-watching, cycling, golfing, and picnicking.

Mont Saint-Bruno

This is one of six hills that rise up from the flat lowlands around Montreal. Composed of meta-

morphic rock, they remained when the land above and around them eroded. Once a summer getaway for wealthy Montrealers, Mont Saint-Bruno is now a park. Hiking trails follow lake shorelines and pass by a charming 19th-century watermill. In winter, the park attracts cross-country skiers.

Mont Saint-Hilaire

This was the birthplace of two important painters: Ozias Leduc (1864-1955) and Paul-Émile Borduas (1905-60). One of Leduc's works can be seen at St. Hilaire Church. The Manoir Rouville-Campbell, built in the 1850s and now an inn, was once the studio of well-known artist Jordi Bonet (1932-79).

With Old Boucherville— "the village"—as a backdrop (this dynamic city of 36,000 dates from 1667), you can hike, bike, picnic, or simply enjoy the great variety of birds in Parc des Îles-de-Boucherville, a cluster of small islands in the St. Lawrence River. You can canoe from one island to the next, and cyclists and pedestrians can island-hop by cable ferry. Some of the islands are still farmed.

SAINT-DENIS

22 km

133
MONT SAINT-HILAIRE

133

19 km

CHAMBLY

Exit 130
SAINT-
HYACINTHE

11 km   17 km

Lac Hertel is the highlight of a nature reserve atop Mont Saint-Hilaire, just east of town. The area is crisscrossed by trails, one of which leads to a lookout with a view of the Richelieu Valley.

Saint-Denis

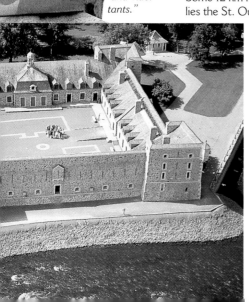

In a Saint-Denis park, a stone Patriote in fighting stance honors 12 rebels killed in the 1837 Battle of St. Denis. Exhibits at restored Fort Chambly (below) recall great moments in the history of New France. Children take special delight in a museum where life-size mannequins depict the lives of 18th-century soldiers and "habitants."

A "footpath of history" here traces events on Nov. 23, 1837 (during the 1837-38 Rebellion), when 200 *Patriotes,* 109 of them armed only with stakes and pitchforks, routed 500 British soldiers. A larger-than-life statue pays tribute to the 12 *Patriotes* killed in the fierce five-hour battle. A bell tower of the 200-year-old, richly ornamented St. Denis Church has the "Cloche de la liberté" that called the *Patriotes* to arms. The Maison nationale des Patriotes, in the 1810 Maison Jean-Baptiste-Mâsse, describes the history of the rebellion.

St. Ours Canal National Historic Site

Some 12 km north of St. Denis lies the St. Ours Canal. Nearby Île Davard, an island in the Richelieu River, is an ideal place to picnic and watch the boats go by. An adjacent dam regulates the height of the Richelieu River. The lock superintendents's house is now a regional art gallery. There are many fine old stone houses in the region, includ-

ing the Manoir de Saint-Ours (1792), which stands amid woods near Saint-Ours.

Chambly

Situated on the Bassin de Chambly—a widening of the Richelieu River—Chambly grew up around forts that have existed here in one form or another since 1665. The present Fort Chambly saw action during the American Revolution and the War of 1812. (It fell to American invaders in 1775-76, but was recaptured in 1777 and remained in British hands until 1851.) In summer, costumed guides re-create its days as a New France stronghold. Nearby, you will find the oldest locks on the Chambly Canal. Built in 1843 to bypass the Richelieu rapids, the canal is now a boaters' paradise. Cyclists ply the towpath between the locks and Saint-Jean-sur-Richelieu (south of Chambly).

Saint-Hyacinthe

Straddling the Yamaska River, the city of Saint-Hyacinthe developed into a textile and industrial center in the mid-1800s: the local Casavant organ factory dates from 1879. An 1885 Casavant organ is still producing glorious sounds at the Cathedral of St. Hyacinthe the Confessor. Famed church architect Victor Bourgeau designed the 1858 Notre-Dame du Rosaire Church. The town has the oldest public market still operating in Quebec. Visitors to the Jardin Daniel-A.-Séguin can explore nine thematic gardens.

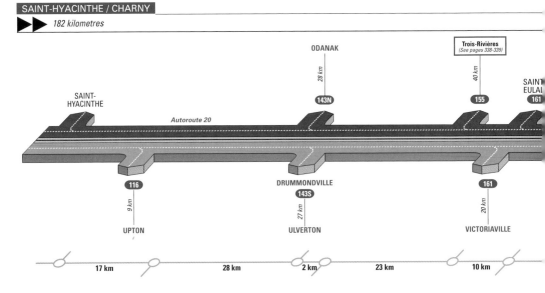

ODANAK

28 km

143N

SAINT-
HYACINTHE

Autoroute 20

Trois-Rivières
(See pages 338-339)

40 km

155

SAINT
EULAL

161

116

9 km

UPTON

DRUMMONDVILLE

143S

27 km

ULVERTON

161

20 km

VICTORIAVILLE

17 km   28 km   2 km   23 km   10 km

SOUTHERN
QUEBEC

*You can sample
19th-century
French cuisine,
and experience a
century of history
just by strolling
the streets and
visiting heritage
buildings in the
Village québécois
d'antan in
Drummondville.*

Upton

In summer, the Théâtre de la Dame-de-Cœur—the Queen of Hearts Theatre—presents a large-scale spectacle, combining live action, giant marionettes, circus acrobatics, a light show, and music. The theater is covered by a gigantic roof, but is open at the sides. Audiences can swivel the seats to take in all the action.

help re-create the era from 1810 to 1910. Costumed staff demonstrate old-time skills, such as wool carding, vegetable dyeing, candle making, and weaving *ceintures fléchées*, colorful French-Canadian sashes.

Drummondville also boasts the Musée de la Cuisine, which recounts the evolution of cooking styles and food preparation in Québec. The Musée de l'Auto presents three shows: antique cars, in late June; custom cars, in early August; and old-time farm machinery on the Labor Day weekend. Another popular event is the annual Festival mondial de folklore, which presents 1,000 performers from 20 countries.

Odanak

A museum on the Odanak reserve displays a model of 17th-century Abenaki fort, a traditional skin tent, and Abenaki translations of biblical scriptures. The Abenaki Indians, originally from New England, allied themselves with the French and settled here in the 1660s.

Ulverton

You can learn all about wool processing at the restored wooden Ulverton Wool Mill. It was built in the mid-1800s, when many Scottish weavers settled in Quebec. You will enjoy strolling or picnicking in its picturesque wooded grounds, where attractions include a covered bridge.

Drummondville

Settled in 1815 by British veterans of the War of 1812, this city was named for colonial governor Sir Gordon Drummond. In the early 1900s, hydroelectric dams on the St. François River sparked industrial development, particularly textile manufacture, which is still an economic mainstay.

Seventy heritage buildings in the Village québécois d'antan

Victoriaville

In 1993, Victoriaville, Arthabaska (traditionally known as the "hardwood capital of Quebec"),

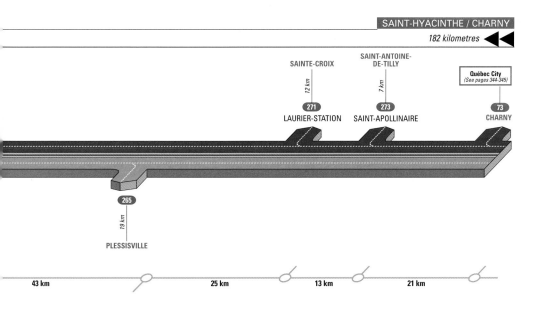

```
                                    SAINT-ANTOINE-
                SAINTE-CROIX        DE-TILLY              ┌─────────────────┐
                                                         │   Québec City   │
                                                         │ (See pages 344-345)│
                   12 km              7 km               └─────────────────┘
                    271               273                        73
               LAURIER-STATION   SAINT-APOLLINAIRE            CHARNY

        265
        19 km

     PLESSISVILLE

   43 km            25 km            13 km            21 km
```

and Sainte-Victoire d'Arthabaska joined to form Victoriaville. The brick Musée Laurier honors Wilfrid Laurier (1841-1919), our first French-Canadian prime minister, who built this house in 1876, and practiced law there.

The nearby Second Empire style, former post office mounts various exhibitions on art, ethnology, and history, and on artists with local connections: Marc-Aurèle de Foy Suzor-Côté (1869-1937), Louis-Philippe Hébert (1850-1917), and Alfred Laliberté (1878-1953). One of Suzor-Côté's works hangs in St. Christophe Church.

Victoriaville hosts an annual avant-garde Festival international de musique actuelle in May. Over five days of jam-packed concerts, scores of international performers play cutting edge, improvised music to fans from around the world.

Local restorations worth a visit include the water-powered Moulin La Pierre (1845), and the Maison d'école du rang Cinq-Chicots, a turn-of-the-century schoolhouse.

Plessisville

This community claims to be the maple syrup and maple sugar capital of the world. Plessisville celebrates a Festival de l'érable in April; Citadelle, a co-operative maple syrup producers' plant, is open for group tours; and visitors to the Carrefour culturel et touristique can explore the Musée de l'Érable and the Institut québécois de l'érable. The peaceful Parc de la Rivière-Bourbon offers picnic areas and pedal boats.

Sainte-Croix

A popular vacation spot, Sainte-Croix is a thriving service and furniture-making center. Reservations are needed for tours of the Domaine Joly de Lotbinière, a balconied villa built in 1851.

Saint-Antoine-de-Tilly

St. Antoine Church, built here in the late 1700s, contains paintings brought here from Paris churches during the French Revolution. The Manoir de Tilly, which dates from the late 1700s, is now an inn.

Charny

At Charny, the 121 m wide Chaudière Falls tumble 35 m into a *chaudière*, a pot-shaped basin. You can view the thundering waters from any of five lookouts. A 113 m suspension bridge over the river gives even more close-up views. The north-flowing Rivière Chaudière originates in Lac Megantic and enters the St. Lawrence just beyond the falls.

Sainte-Croix's imposing Domaine Joly de Lotbinière, together with its superb setting on the St. Lawrence River, evokes the days of seigneurial glory. On the grounds, designated one of Quebec's great gardens, footpaths lead through parkland adorned with flowerbeds, pavilions, and pathways shaded by rare, century-old trees.

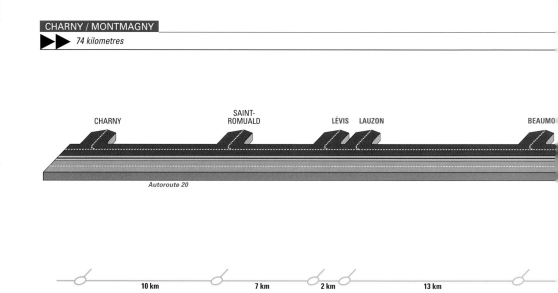

CHARNY   SAINT-ROMUALD   LÉVIS   LAUZON   BEAUMO

Autoroute 20

10 km   7 km   2 km   13 km

SOUTH SHORE, ST. LAWRENCE RIVER

Tens of thousands of ducks and snow geese stop off at Montmagny during spring and fall migrations. Ferries from Montmagny take bird-watchers to Île-aux-Grues and Île-aux-Oies, island bird sanctuaries in the St. Lawrence River.

Lévis

Steep streets and picturesque houses charm visitors to Lévis, on the south shore of the St. Lawrence. The riverside Terrasse de Lévis looks across the river at Quebec City and offers a superb view of Île d'Orléans.

At Pointe-de-Lévy, you can explore stone masonry structures, earthen works, tunnels, and trenches at Fort No. I, the lone survivor of three forts built by the British in 1865-72 to protect Quebec City against an American attack. Fort No. I was abandoned after World War II. During both world wars, soldiers assigned to watch shipping on the St. Lawrence occupied Lévis' other military post, the Fort de la Martinière, built in 1907.

You can visit the restored, Victorian-style Maison Alphonse-Desjardins (1884), birthplace of Quebec's great credit union. Exhibits recount how Desjardins (1854-1920) pioneered the Caisse Populaire Desjardins, now Quebec's largest financial institution.

Lauzon

Davie Shipbuilding, founded here in 1828, is Canada's oldest and largest shipbuilder. A statue in Old Lauzon honors its first settler, Guillaume Couture, who is reckoned to have some 60,000 direct descendants.

Beaumont

This area is noted for superb examples of old Quebec architecture. Look for steep-roofed Norman-style dwellings, dating from

the 18th century, and bell-roofed dwellings of 19th-century origin. The Moulin de Beaumont (1821) still produces and sells stone-ground flour and bread baked in clay ovens. A painting of Saint Stephen by famous artist Antoine Plamondon (1804-1895) hangs in the Church of St. Etienne (1733), one of Quebec's oldest churches still standing.

Montmagny

The accordian's enduring popularity with Quebec's traditional musicians is celebrated at the Manoir de l'Accordéon, which showcases the instrument's manufacture and various forms. Accordionists (and enthusiatic fans) from all over the world gather at an annual August festival to press the bellows and play the keys that produce the instrument's wheezy melodies.

Montmagny's fall Festival de l'Oie Blanche coincides with the passage of some 600,000 snow geese heading south. Exhibits about wildfowl and the immigrants once quarantined on nearby Grosse-Île are found at the Centre éducatif des migrations, which explores the journeyings of animals and people.

Île-aux-Grues

Île-aux-Grues (the island of the cranes) is a chain of 21 islands in the St. Lawrence, which includes Île-aux-Oies (the island of the geese) and Grosse-Île. Its largest and only inhabited island (also called Île-aux-Grues) has about 250 year-round residents, homey visitor accommodations,

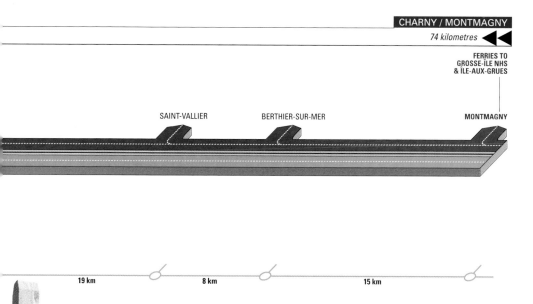

SAINT-VALLIER   BERTHIER-SUR-MER   MONTMAGNY

19 km   8 km   15 km

"In this secluded spot lie the mortal remains of 5,424 persons who, fleeing from pestilence and famine in Ireland in the year 1847, found in America but a grave," reads the English inscription on this Celtic cross at Grosse-Île. The cross also carries epitaphs in French and Gaelic.

campsites, and restaurants that serve a celebrated local cheese. A 30-minute ferry from Montmagny docks about a kilometre from the village of Saint-Antoine-de-l'Isle-aux-Grues. Water taxis to the island—a stopover for flocks of migrating snow geese—are also available from Berthier-sur-Mer and other ports. Bike rentals are available for visitors wanting to explore this peaceful getaway.

Grosse-Île and the Irish Memorial National Historic Site

A Celtic cross and row after row of mass graves recall thousands of Irish immigrants who died on this remote island more than one and a half-centuries ago. In 1832, a quarantine station was set up here to stem the spread of cholera and typhus among immigrants, mainly Irish escaping tyranny and famine in their homeland. Doctors detained the sick: those who died were buried on the island. In 1847 alone, 9,000 Irish men, women, and children died of typhus here; some 8,000 had already been buried at sea, and another 4,500 victims were removed when the ships docked. Today's visitors can explore chapels, hostels, hospitals, and "the lazaret" where the dying were cared for. Half- or full-day excursions to Grosse-Île are available from Montmagny and Berthier-sur-Mer.

Whale-watching on a Mighty River

This feature has been translated and adapted from an article in French by JEAN O'NEIL, *author of 16 books, mainly about the St. Lawrence River.*

AT RIVIÈRE-DU-LOUP, the Trans-Canada Highway leaves the south shore of the St. Lawrence River and veers abruptly southward toward New Brunswick through the backwoods of the Témiscouata region of Quebec. Here, we decide to leave the highway to take a 3½-hour whale-watching excursion on the river in the hope of spotting the largest marine mammal on earth, the blue whale.

Our boat is the fully equipped, 275-seat *Le Cavalier des Mers*, built especially for whale-watching, with a crew recruited from the Institut maritime du Québec. This organization, headquartered at Rimouski, is the heir to Quebec's maritime traditions, specializing in marine studies, coastal surveillance, and salt and freshwater navigation.

Our captain, Réjean Carré, heads directly toward Cape Bon-Désir, just a little below the mouth of the Saguenay River. The first mate, Nathalie Tobak, asks the passengers to buckle up their life jackets, and biologist Jean-David Viel tells us the story of these magnificent creatures that live in an underwater world, virtually unseen by most of us.

Viel was trained at GREMM (le Groupe de recherche et d'éducation sur le milieu marin), which is located at Tadoussac near the spot where we are going. This marine research body is dedicated to learning about the hidden powers of the sea. It has chosen Tadoussac as its base from which to observe the whales in the nearby offshore waters.

We are on a stretch of the St. Lawrence River that whales like to frequent, starting in early spring and continuing into summer. Here, the river changes color and character four times a day according to the ebb and flow of the tide that washes its shores. The St. Lawrence is a restless river, always looking for an equilibrium that it never finds. Watching the river as it flows is always an engaging experience, and always a satisfying one.

At the start of our excursion, Île aux Lièvres appears on the horizon directly in front of us. We catch a glimpse of the island as *Le Cavalier des Mers* heads toward the north shore of the St. Lawrence. This is the point where the mighty river broadens. But the sight of the river presents us with more than just a scenic panorama. It also offers an invitation to adventure and discovery. Here, the fresh continental waters of the St. Lawrence and Saguenay rivers meet and blend with the saltwater brine from the vast oceans. And the most tangible proof of this meeting is the presence of the whales, which gather at the mouth of the Saguenay, the river that lies ahead of us.

These great beasts of the ocean come from the Gulf of St. Lawrence or from the Arctic by way of the Strait of Belle Isle, and follow the coast as far as the mouth of the Saguenay, where krill are plentiful. Krill are plankton, a small, shrimp-like crustacean that abounds in these waters. Whales feed on krill by the ton. With their jaws open and their eyes closed, they scoop up vast quantities of krill by the mouthful.

Here, too, are the belugas, frolicking on the waves. Adult belugas are white; juveniles are gray; and the newborn are brown or dark colored. Unlike other whales, the belugas are year-round residents of these waters. They follow the tides on the St. Lawrence in search of fish. Experienced mariners gauge the tides and the direction of the currents by the movements of the belugas.

Now *Le Cavalier des Mers* approaches our destination—the bay at the tip of Cape Bon-Désir. The wind is favorable, and the waters are almost calm.

> 66 *...the river changes color and character four times a day according to the ebb and flow of the tide that washes its shores.* 99

But even if the surface is calm, what are those ripples surging underneath?

A great jet of water sprays in the air with a powerful blast, a resounding salute from the sea. That's how the mighty blue whale says hello.

Now, this magnificent creature glides to the surface amid squeals of admiration from the passengers on *Le Cavalier des Mers*. The creature is huge. Placid. Blue-gray, just as it is depicted in story books. Its belly is yellow, sulfur-colored by an accumulation of diatoms—tiny water plants. Because of this coloration, these whales were once known as sulfur bottoms.

Depending on its mood, the blue whale may choose to entertain spectators. If it chooses not to do so, other aquatic performers, such as the minke, may oblige us. Overcome by curiosity, the minke may swim toward a vessel, possibly leaping from the surface as it approaches. Another denizen on this stretch of the St. Lawrence is the killer whale, that scavenger of the deep, which comes here to terrorize the herds of seals. The sperm whale—Moby Dick's relative—may also sometimes make an appearance here. But a more frequently observed visitor in these waters is the finback, the fastest whale of all.

At the end of our excursion on *Le Cavalier des Mers*, we've learned that whales are here for all of us to see. The lesson these mighty creatures teach us is that our planet is the sea as well as the land, and together the pleasures they offer us are endless.

Jean O'Neil

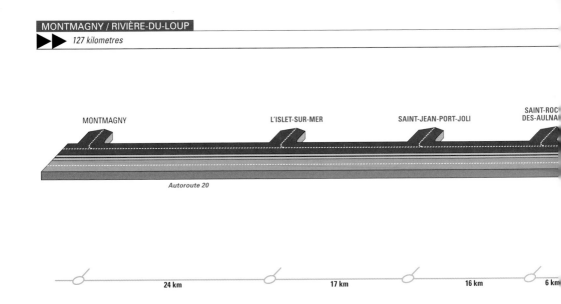

MONTMAGNY   L'ISLET-SUR-MER   SAINT-JEAN-PORT-JOLI   SAINT-ROC DES-AULNA

Autoroute 20

24 km   17 km   16 km   6 km

**SOUTH SHORE,
ST. LAWRENCE
RIVER**

L'Islet-sur-Mer

Canada's largest maritime museum, the Musée maritime Bernier, has a sea interpretation park and vessels such as the icebreaker *Ernest-Lapointe* and the hydrofoil *Bras d'Or 400*. The museum honors L'Islet-sur-Mer-born Capt. Joseph-Elzéar Bernier (1852-1934), who spent $21,000 persuading Ottawa to exert Canadian sovereignty over the Arctic archipelago. At the time, the territory was in danger of claims by Norway and the United States. When the government finally responded, Bernier made four voyages. Between 1904 and 1911, he visited most of the Arctic islands, where he built cairns confirming Canada's claim to the territory.

Notre-Dame de Bonsecours Church (1768) has an interior by the famous artist François Baillairgé (1759-1830).

Saint-Jean-Port-Joli

An international festival, in late June, draws North American and European carvers to Saint-Jean-Port-Joli. Regarded as Quebec's wood-carving center, the town abounds with museums, shops, and galleries devoted to this art. You can see works by great local wood-carvers and learn about the area's rich wood-sculpting history at the Musée des Anciens Canadiens. Many fine carvings can also be seen in St. Jean Baptiste Church, and in

the Maison Médard-Bourgault, home of the famous 1920s wood-carver. An octagonal barn houses the Centre d'art animalier Faunart, which has animal sculptures, paintings, and photographs, and taxidermy exhibits.

Saint-Roch-des-Aulnaies

Aulnaies refers to the alder-covered banks of the Rivière Ferrée. Quebec's seigneurial system, which lasted from the beginning of the French Regime until 1854, is re-created on the grounds and in the verandaed manor house and three-story stone mill of the riverside Seigneurie des Aulnaies.

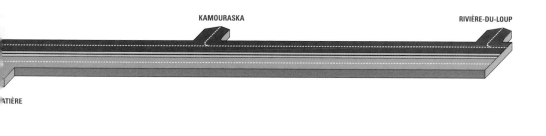

KAMOURASKA

RIVIÈRE-DU-LOUP

ATIÈRE

29 km

35 km

Restored and furnished to the 1850s, the manoir of the Seigneurie des Aulnaies reflects the gracious seigneurial life-style. The house was designed by Charles Baillairgé (1826-1906), one of a famed family of architects and artists.

Interactive displays throughout the manor house describe how seigneurs received land grants, then redistributed portions of their vast properties to farmers (known as *habitants*), thus shaping the face of rural Quebec. Pancakes and muffins from flour ground at the seigneury mill are served at a café in what was once the miller's house.

La Pocatière

Subway cars for New York and Montreal roll off assembly lines at the mighty Bombardier factory in this small town. Canada's first agricultural college was established here in 1859. Its founder's name is commemorated in the Musée François-Pilote, which occupies a former convent and re-creates local rural life in the early 1900s. Energetic travelers in search of a good view can climb the 250-step stairs that leads to a lookout atop Montagne du Collège.

Kamouraska

This village, with narrow streets descending to the St. Lawrence, boasts architectural gems, such as the 1804 Paradis Mill and the 1886 Taché Manor, which have attracted cinematographers down the years. The 1751 Maison L'Anglais was used in exterior scenes of *Kamouraska*, the 1973 film based on Anne Hébert's novel about a local tragedy.

In this region, the eel fishery is an economic mainstay. Weir traps—rows of stakes where eels are caught—can be seen along

the river. Exhibits of local folklore and history can be seen at the Musée Kamouraska.

At the Maison de la Prune, an "economuseum" in Saint-André-de-Kamouraska just west of Kamouraska, visitors can pick apples, berries, plums and other fruit and buy preserves made on site.

Rivière-du-Loup

The best spot for an overview of Rivière-du-Loup and its environs is a lookout by the 30 m waterfall on the river from which the city takes its name. The largest community on the Lower St. Lawrence, Rivière-du-Loup is the region's commercial and administrative headquarters, and a transportation hub. Visitor facilities include golfing, marinas, beaches, and summer theater. There are also whale-watching excursions (see pages 180-181) and boat trips to nearby St. Lawrence islands.

A heritage tour (available from the tourist bureau) passes the Manoir Fraser, built in 1830 and modified in 1888, and other Victorian houses and churches. Local history and art exhibits are featured at the Musée du Bas-Saint-Laurent. The Carillons Touristiques have an extensive collection of bells of varying sizes, weights, and tones, dating from 1718.

Rivière-du-Loup is the northern point on the Petit Témis Linear Park. This interprovincial project stretching south to Cabano, Que., and on to Edmundston, N.B., features extensive hiking and biking trails.

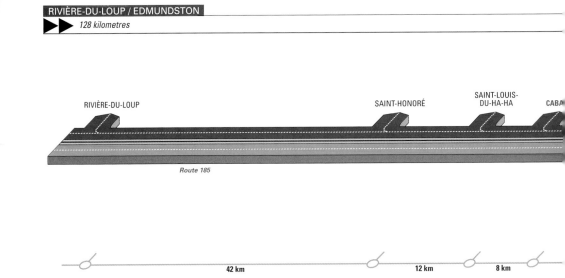

RIVIÈRE-DU-LOUP   SAINT-HONORÉ   SAINT-LOUIS-DU-HA-HA   CABA

Route 185

42 km   12 km   8 km

**SOUTHEASTERN
QUEBEC/
NORTHEASTERN
NEW BRUNSWICK**

Cabano

From Rivière-du-Loup, the Trans-Canada passes south through a hilly region into New Brunswick. Along the western shore of Lac Témiscouata, you will find Cabano and Notre-Dame-du-Lac. Cabano has camping and picnic sites, and a beach. But the main attraction is the restored Fort Ingall, one of several local outposts built in 1839-42 during a British-American dispute over the Quebec–Maine border.

Notre-Dame-du-Lac

In its days as a relay point on the Grand-Portage trail, Notre-Dame-du-Lac was known as "le Détour." The memory of those days lives on at the local museum—the Musée de Détour. A campground, beach, and marina are located on 50 km long Lac Témiscouata. A short ferry ride links the town to Saint-Juste-du-Lac on the opposite shore. Traffic crosses on an ice bridge in winter. Auberge Marie-Blanc, built in 1905 as a hunting lodge, is said to have been designed by Frank Lloyd Wright.

Saint-Jacques

This Madawaska River community is the gateway to north-western New Brunswick and the Upper St. John River valley. At the village entrance, a World War II Lancaster bomber sits across the highway from the visitors' bureau. Visitors to the New Brunswick Botanical Garden—the only garden of its kind in the Maritimes—can enjoy the sight and aroma of well over a 100,000 plants and flowers. You can camp, swim, play tennis, or enjoy a boat ride in the nearby Jardins de la République Provincial Park. ("République" refers to the Republic of Madawaska: see next entry.)

An antique car museum near the park's entrance showcases vintage vehicles from 1905 to 1930. A treasured exhibit is a made-in-New Brunswick Bricklin sports car. Trout-fishing ponds and a collection of wild animals are among attractions at the Ferme Aqua-Zoo.

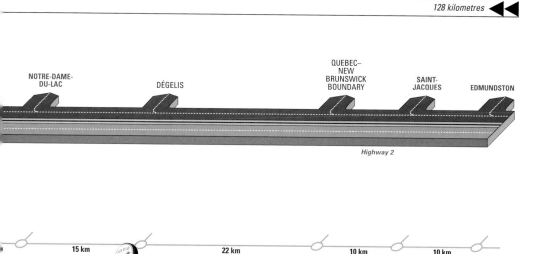

NOTRE-DAME-DU-LAC   DÉGELIS   QUEBEC–NEW BRUNSWICK BOUNDARY   SAINT-JACQUES   EDMUNDSTON

Highway 2

15 km   22 km   10 km   10 km

At Saint-Jacques, N.B., this 1937 Diamond "T" fire truck rubs shoulders with a Bricklin, a 1964 Vauxhall, a 1928 Model "A" Ford, a 1905 Russell and dozens of other treasures in the Antique Automobile Museum located at the entrance to Les Jardins de la République Provincial Park (below). Other park attractions include hiking and biking trails, picnic sites and shelter, volleyball and tennis courts, a boat ramp, a heated swimming pool, a horseshoe pitch, and outdoor and indoor play areas.

Edmundston

Situated at the junction of the Madawaska and the Saint John rivers, Edmundston is the heart of timber-rich northwestern New Brunswick. A handsome boardwalk along the Madawaska River, attractive shrubbery and lampposts, and historical landmark interpretation panels make for pleasant exploration of the downtown. You can also golf on an 18-hole course at the heart of the city and, between January and May, with reservations, you can enjoy a superb meal prepared by students of the provincial hospitality school in Edmundston.

Most people here and in other nearby communities are French-speaking, but consider themselves neither Acadian-French nor Quebec-French, but Brayon. In late July, this distinctive culture finds joyous expression in street parties and other revels at a fair, the Foire Brayonne, said to be the biggest francophone festival outside Québec.

You can discover the colorful history of the region at the Madawaska Historical Museum. Caught up in a prolonged early-19th-century British-American dispute over the international border, local people refused to take sides. Instead, they declared themselves the neutral inhabitants of a mythical state—the Republic of Madawaska. Local tourism boosters later revived the term, now a popular designation for this region. Today, Edmundston proudly calls itself the capital of the republic, of which its mayors automatically become president. Madawaska's flag features a bald eagle (symbol of the region's independent spirit) and six stars representing each of the mythical republic's cultural groups: Indian, Acadian, Canadian, English, American, and Irish.

You can tour Fraser Inc., a tree nursery 14 km from town. It produces 7 million spruce, pine, and cedar seedlings annually, and offers a 5 km hiking trail.

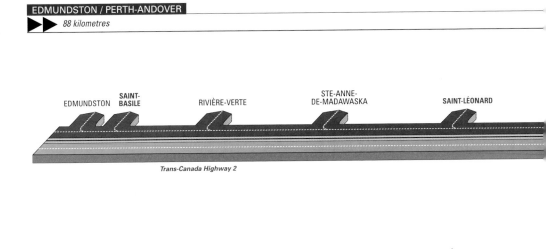

EDMUNDSTON | SAINT-BASILE | RIVIÈRE-VERTE | STE-ANNE-DE-MADAWASKA | SAINT-LÉONARD

Trans-Canada Highway 2

3 km | 8 km | 10 km | 11 km | 15 km

UPPER SAINT JOHN RIVER VALLEY

Saint-Basile

Founded in 1792, Saint-Basile is the oldest community in Madawaska, a region characterized by a chain of picturesque villages along the Saint John River. Its most famous native son is pop singer Roch Voisine.

For nine days of a July *Neuvaine* (novena) leading up to Saint Anne's feast day, hundreds of the faithful attend open-air services in a shrine at Ste-Anne-de-Madawaska, some 18 km farther down the Trans-Canada. The town has a small covered bridge and bird observation site.

les tisserands
MADAWASKA *weavers*

Saint-Léonard

Though they are in different countries, Saint-Léonard and Van Buren, its U.S. sister city directly across the Saint John River, share the same municipal flag. During the Grande Rivière festival each July, the international bridge that links them is blocked to traffic so that residents can party in the middle. Settled by Acadians in 1789, the area was originally called Grande-Rivière. This is the home of Madawaska Weavers (*left*), a family-operated producer of distinctive handwoven fabrics.

Drummond

This pastoral village was settled by Irish fleeing the potato famine in 1847. Retired jockey Ron Turcotte, who rode Secretariat to the Triple Crown in 1973 and winner of more than 3,000 races during his career, is the town's most famous resident.

186

NEW DENMARK
8 km

DRUMMOND
6 km
108   GRAND
         FALLS

PERTH-
ANDOVER

AROOSTOOK

3 km   36 km   2 km

As the spring-time vista (left) shows, potato is king in the rolling country-side around New Denmark, N.B. A succession of rich potato harvests have brought prosperity to this farming community, where Danish can sometimes be heard and mailboxes bear names such as Jensen and Pedersen.

At Grand Falls Gorge Park, N.B. (right), you can see— and hear the deafening roar—where the Saint John River suddenly plunges to a lower level 23 m below. Once known as Chicanekapeag, or "the giant destroyer," the falls have carved a spectacular gorge that encircles half the town.

New Denmark

A touch of Scandinavia flourishes in this community, settled in 1872 by 29 Danish immigrants. The land the government had reserved for them was too sandy to grow grain, so they planted potatoes left over from their long voyage. Seed from that first crop continues to yield the renowned New Denmark potato. From Klokkedal Hill, you have a panoramic view of the country-side, a scene that is especially breathtaking in autumn. A community museum houses antique dolls and Danish porcelain.

If you want to try your luck on one of New Brunswick's great salmon rivers, press on 25 km to Plaster Rock (named for the local red gypsum soil), an angler's paradise on the Tobique River. A downtown park boasts 2 m tall hand-carved statues of fiddle-head greens, a local delicacy.

Grand Falls

Legend has it that a Maliseet maiden sacrificed her own life for her people by luring a war party of 300 enemy Iroquois to its death over the waterfall here.

Although the British built a fort near the falls in 1791, settlement did not begin in earnest until the early 1800s when a round-the-clock sawmilling operation helped clear the land. By the 1870s, Grand Falls was promoting itself as a second Niagara and had become a popular tourist destination. A dam and hydro-electric station have since tamed the falls. Townfolk often stop to chat at a gazebo, smack in the middle of Main Street, a 38 m wide thoroughfare said to be the widest street of any Canadian town. An annual Potato Festival is celebrated in early July.

Perth-Andover

Once separate towns on oppo-site sides of the river, these communities amalgamated in 1966. Perth's Scots settlers named it for a city in Scotland. The skirl of bagpipes at all community celebrations shows the Scottish presence is still strong. Andover, originally known as Tobique, was once a port for stern-wheelers plying the Saint John River between Fredericton and Grand Falls. The town's oldest building, the 1837 Methodist Church, is now a pioneer museum.

187

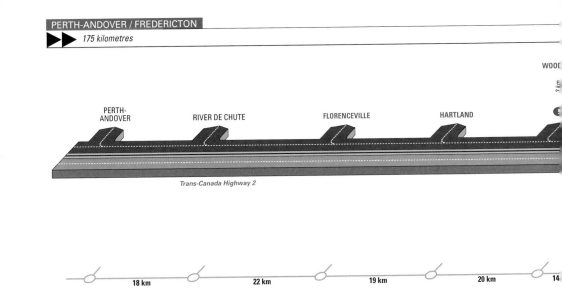

WOOI

PERTH-ANDOVER   RIVER DE CHUTE   FLORENCEVILLE   HARTLAND

Trans-Canada Highway 2

18 km   22 km   19 km   20 km   14

**UPPER
SAINT JOHN
RIVER VALLEY**

Florenceville

As corporate headquarters of McCain Foods, this village is the world's frozen french fry capital. In 1957, brothers Harrison and Wallace McCain founded the local frozen fast-food company that now does more than $4 billion worth of business around the world annually. Originally known as Buttermilk Creek, the village took its present name in 1855 to honor the Crimean War heroine, Florence Nightingale.

Hartland

Covered bridges are known as kissing bridges because in horse-and-buggy days they were an ideal place for young lovers to steal kisses. Hartland boasts the world's longest covered bridge, a 391 m span built for $30,000 in 1901 by townsfolk tired of broken government promises to build one for them. Five years of tolls financed the construction. The bridge was enclosed in 1920 to protect its wooden superstructure. Small Fry Snack Foods, makers of Humpty Dumpty Potato Chips, is located in Hartland. Skeddadle Ridge outside town is named for the Union Army deserters who "skeddadled" into Canada during the U.S. Civil War.

Woodstock

Woodstock, some 3 km off the Trans-Canada on the banks of the Saint John River, used to be known as The Creek, and the adjoining community of Upper Woodstock was once called Hardscrabble. Founded in 1784

by an Empire Loyalist from New Jersey, the towns are distinguished by fine Victorian Gothic houses and two historic sites: Connell House, an imposing Greek Revival mansion built by lumber magnate and politician Charles Connell (1810-1873), and the Carleton County Courthouse, built in Upper Woodstock in 1833. Connell is remembered as the postmaster who had his portrait instead of the Queen's engraved on postage stamps issued in 1860. The stamps were quickly withdrawn and are now a collector's item worth about $8,500 each.

Kings Landing Historical Settlement

Walking into Kings Landing Historical Settlement is like stepping back in time. More than 60 heritage buildings from surrounding York County have been assembled here to create a fully operational Loyalist farming community. Women in calico and men in homespun trousers tend to chores that were commonplace 150 years ago: churning butter, spinning flax, and working the fields. Meals reflective of Loyalist palates and local game are served at the Kings Head Inn, a hostelry meticulously restored to 1855. You can shop at a museum store described as the largest gift shop of its kind in the province. Kings Landing is open from June to October but also showcases special events such as a Sugar Bush Weekend in March and a Victorian Christmas. A five-day Visiting Cousins summer camp lets youngsters, ages 9 to 14, experience life in the pre- radio, televi-

A young visitor to Woolastook Provincial Park at Longs Creek gets to bottle-feed some white-tailed fawns. Visitors can also feed waterfowl, raccoons, porcupines, squirrels, even moose, as well as enjoy miniature golf, four giant waterslides, and a splash poolhouse.

MACTAQUAC
PP

4 km

MEDUCTIC   KINGS LANDING   LONGS   FREDERICTON
            HIST SETTLEMENT   CREEK   Exit 274   Exit 292

46 km   6 km   12.5 km   17.5 km

sion, and video game days of a century ago.

At Longs Creek, some 6 km from Kings Landing, Woolastook Provincial Park has 33 species of Atlantic Canada animals (see facing page). Nature trails lead past enclosures of caribou, lynx, moose, and other creatures.

Mactaquac Provincial Park

From the Trans-Canada, take the road over the Mactaquac Dam to the north shore of the

Saint John River. A five-minute drive will bring you to Macta-quac Provincial Park, which has camping, hiking trails, a beach, excellent fishing for smallmouth bass, and a first-rate 18-hole golf course. Mactaquac is a Maliseet word for "where two rivers (the Nashwaak and the Saint John) meet." The popular provincial park was created in 1968, when the Saint John River was dammed to create a headpond for a hydro-electric generating station.

At Kings Landing Historical Settlement, sturdy rail fences, lush fields, and scores of buildings, including the snug homestead and barns (above), re-create the prosperous communities carved along the Saint John River by industrious Loyalists. From the waterwheel-driven sawmill to the blacksmith's forge, and from the C.B. Ross sash and door factory to the old-fashioned general store, every corner of the settlement is an open air museum.

189

FREDERICTON:
A CITY OF LOYALIST ROOTS

Settled by United Empire Loyalists in 1783, Fredericton developed around a two-block British military compound established the following year. In 1785, Governor Thomas Carleton (1735-1817) named the settlement Frederick's town (after King George III's second son), and decreed it the capital of New Brunswick. Present-day Fredericton falls somewhere between a large town and a small city with the advantages of both. One of its claims to fame is the University of New Brunswick, the country's oldest (1785) post-secondary institution. The city also owes much to its principal benefactor, British newspaper magnate Max Aitken, Lord Beaverbook (1879-1964), who grew up in New Brunswick. His bequests to the city include the Beaverbrook Art Gallery. With a fine collection of British and Canadian paintings, the Beaverbrook occupies an attractive riverside site opposite the Legislative Assembly.

Saint John River

New Brunswick School Days Museum
A school built in the Justice Building Annex in 1914 displays old textbooks, school furniture, and teaching aids. The Justice Building itself housed one of the first schools established under public education legislation of the 1870s.

Guard House

ST. ANNE POINT

Soldiers Barracks

National Exhibition Centre

QUEEN

YORK

CARLETON

REGENT

KING

City Hall
Maritime Canada's oldest city hall still in use, this Romanesque Revival-style landmark was built in 1876 to provide municipal offices and an opera house. (Its opera house role ended in the 1940s.) Local artists created the council chamber wall hangings depicting 200 years of city history. A cherub out front— known as the "Freddy, the Little Nude Dude"—is a replica of one that formed part of a fountain built on the site in 1885.

Wilmot United Church
Built in 1852 for a Methodist congregation, this church is one of last of the great wooden "carpenter gothic" Maritimes' churches still in use. It boasts seating for 1,200, exquisite hand-carvings, one of the few stained glass windows in Canada created by famed British artist William Morris (1834-1896), and stencil decoration by renowned Canadian artist Alex Colville. When the congregation joined the United Church of Canada in 1925, the church was renamed for Lemuel Allen Wilmot, the province's first native-born lieutenant governor.

BRUNSWICK

St. Dunstan's Church
The first house of worship here was a small Roman Catholic wooden chapel built in 1824. The present church, erected in 1965, replaced a cathedral church dating from the 1840s. (St. Dunstan's ceased being a cathedral in 1855, when Saint John became the diocesan see.) Among noteworthy features are its 33 m high, stone and copper spire and its hand-carved, linden wood Stations of the Cross. The episcopal chair of Irish missionary William Dollard, first bishop of the diocese of New Brunswick, is in the sanctuary.

Fredericton's wide ranging roster of festivals and special events focuses on family recreation and children's activities.

Old York County Gaol
One of Canada's oldest jails still in use, this present-day, minimum-security prison opened in 1842 as an ill-lit, ill-heated bread-and-water prison. Its outer walls are 1 m thick.

Officers' Square

A center of military activity from 1785 to 1914, this green area in the old Military Compound—a national historic site—is a summer staging area for musical and theatrical events and changing of the guard ceremonies. The adjoining thick-walled stone buildings replaced the original wooden accommodations on this site. **Officers' Quarters,** built in 1839, house the York-Sunbury Historical Society Museum. A collection of Native-people, pioneer, and Acadian artifacts and world-war memorabilia—including a World War I trench—fills three floors. One remarkable exhibit is a gigantic bullfrog. When the amphibian died in the 1880s, it weighed 19 kilos—possibly because of the tidbits fed it by the local hotelier who had it stuffed. Opposite the museum is the **Soldiers' Barracks,** built in the 1820s. One room and the **Guard House** have been restored to the 1860s, and furnished with muskets, uniforms, soldiers' beds, and other barracks' furnishings of the day.

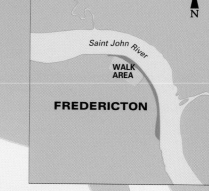

Saint John River

WALK AREA

FREDERICTON

N

New Brunswick Legislature

New Brunswick's legislative assembly meets in a modest sandstone building built in 1882. The main entrance opens onto a hallway hung with portraits of former provincial governors general. An elegant freestanding spiral staircase of walnut, cherry, ash, and pine connects the building's three stories. Waterford Crystal chandeliers and copies of Joshua Reynolds' portraits of George III and his consort Queen Charlotte dominate the assembly chamber.

Crocket House

A circular conical tower, bay windows, and decorative shingles, all typical of Queen Anne Revival architecture, distinguish this three-story frame house. Built in 1900, its design also incorporates motifs of other styles, a trend of the day. Named "Dunrobin" by early owners, its present name derives from a prominent doctor who lived there in the 1930s. Its present occupant, Gallery 78, a commercial gallery, displays paintings, sculptures, and fine crafts.

The Playhouse

ST. JOHN

CHURCH

BRUNSWICK

Joyce Farmer's Market

Christ Church Cathedral

Opened in 1853, this Gothic Revival Anglican cathedral is an almost exact replica of St. Mary's Church in Snettisham, Norfolk, England. Although the roofline and choir deviate from the Norfolkshire church plans, elements such as the Galilee porch (its three arches symbolize the Trinity), window tracery, and turrets are identical. The east window was a gift from New York's Trinity Church. Little Ben, the prototype for London's famous Big Ben, sits in the arch above the nave. A marble effigy of John Medley, the bishop who built the church, is below the east chancel window. The cathedral is said to be haunted by Bishop Medley's first wife, Christiana.

The Green

Limpert Lane, the walkway through this 5 km riverfront park, honors local swimmer and 1996 Olympic Silver medalist Marianne Limpert. A statue of Robert Burns stands near the **Beaverbrook Art Gallery.** A nearby marble fountain from Stowe House in Buckinghamshire, England, is Beaverbrook's memorial to his friend, Sir James Dunn. A lighthouse museum offers a magnificent panorama of the city.

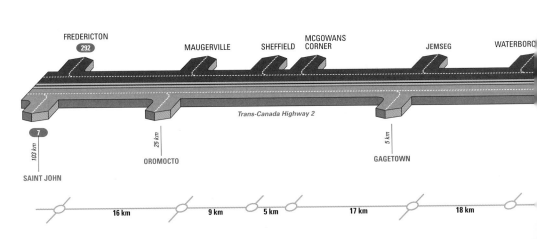

FREDERICTON
292

MAUGERVILLE   SHEFFIELD   MCGOWANS CORNER   JEMSEG   WATERBORO

Trans-Canada Highway 2

7

103 km   25 km   5 km

SAINT JOHN   OROMOCTO   GAGETOWN

16 km   9 km   5 km   17 km   18 km

**SOUTHERN
NEW
BRUNSWICK**

Saint John

Canada's oldest incorporated city (1785) is not to be missed and well worth a 90-minute detour. The city was founded in 1783 by Loyalists, who patterned King's Square after the old Union Jack. Two hundred years before the Loyalists arrived, however, a Mi'kmaq village called Ouigoudi stood on the riverbank. Samuel de Champlain who arrived on June 24, 1604, christened the river for Saint John the Baptist, whose feast day that was. A French fort on the site was destroyed in 1645.

Present-day Saint John (the "Saint" is never abbreviated) has all the allure of an historic seafaring town enriched with a $250 million urban redevelopment face-lift. Brunswick Square, the waterfront Market Square, and the Saint John Trade and Convention Centre, all linked by "pedways," form the heart of a revitalized city center. Fresh seafood, fruit, vegetables, and local crafts are offered at Old City Market (not to be confused with Market Square), in one of Canada's oldest market buildings. This farmers' market has been in operation since 1876.

Half of Saint John was destroyed by fire in 1877, but Loyalist House (1817) survived, and today is a museum. Jewish contributions to the city, which began with a wave of Russian immigrants in the 1890s, are recalled in the Jewish Historical Museum, 29 Wellington Row. Among the Russian immigrants was Louis B. Mayer (1885-1957), founder of MGM.

Prince William Street and the Trinity Royal Heritage area have beautifully restored Victorian architecture. Barbour's General Store opposite City Hall stocks vintage 19th-century goods. Also worth seeing are the Imperial Theatre on King Square South, built in 1913 and restored to its Edwardian opulence, and the New Brunswick Museum (1842), Canada's first museum of natural history, on Market Square.

Moosehead Beer, brewed at 89 Main St. West, offers free samples during scheduled tours.

The city's biggest tourist attraction is the world famous Reversing Falls. This twice daily natural phenomenon occurs when Fundy tides, the highest in the world, try to push their way up the Saint John River.

Oromocto

Across the Saint John River from Maugerville, Oromocto was designed by the Department of

Barbour's General Store and Little Re[d] Schoolhouse (righ[t] are attractive restorations in Sai[nt] John's bustling Market Square (above). King's Square (below) is a garden oasis.

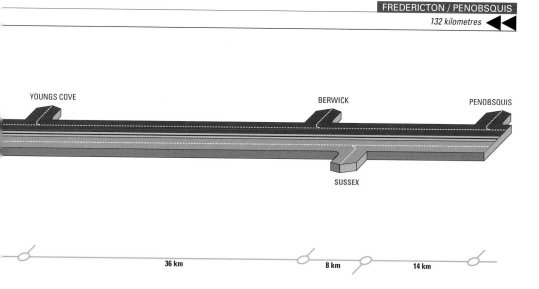

YOUNGS COVE   BERWICK   PENOBSQUIS

SUSSEX

36 km   8 km   14 km

National Defense in the 1950s as a model town for support personnel employed at nearby Camp Gagetown. It takes its name from the Maliseet word for "deep river." For more than a century, a ship-rigging yard that folded in the 1870 had stood on the riverbank here. Oromocto has a replica of Fort Hughes, a blockhouse built by the British during the American Revolution, a first-class military museum, and a marina with free overnight docking. The town hosts an annual Highland Games in June.

Jemseg

Grand Lake—at 109 km², the largest lake in New Brunswick— empties into the Saint John River here. The lake's freshwater beaches are something of a curiosity in a province bounded by salt water. Grand Lake Provincial Park, on the Trans-Canada Highway some 15 km east of Jemseg, has an indoor activity center, fully equipped playground, and supervised pool.

Gagetown

From Jemseg, a scenic road leads to a ferry that crosses the Saint John River to the pine-treed village of Gagetown. This community was supposed to become the provincial capital, but lost out to Freder-

icton. Gagetown was a quiet farming community when the Armed Forces combat training center opened nearby in 1954. (Prince Charles trained to be a helicopter pilot there in 1975.) River traffic there is almost as busy as traffic on the narrow village streets, where dozens of artisans occupy elegant gabled, verandaed homes. A 200-year-old blockhouse houses Loom-crafters, noted designers and weavers of tartans and plaids. The restored Tilley House (1786), birthplace of Sir Samuel Leonard Tilley (1818-1896), a Father of Confederation, is now the Queen's County Museum.

Sussex

In 1992 a national magazine named Sussex one of the 10 best Canadian towns of its size in which to live. Home to the Agricultural Museum of New Brunswick, Sussex hosts the colorful Atlantic Balloon Fiesta and the Antique Car Covered Bridge Tour in September.

Luscious strawberries are among the fruit and vegetable bounty of the Saint John River valley, which is enriched annually by silt from the swollen river.

193

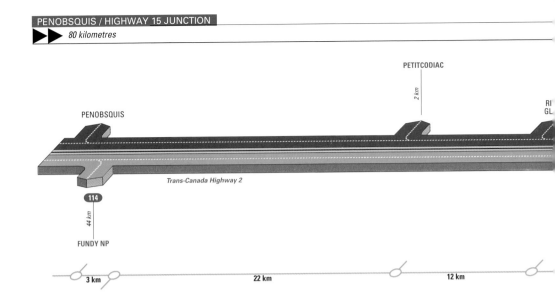

PETITCODIAC

2 km

PENOBSQUIS

RI
GL

Trans-Canada Highway 2

114

44 km

FUNDY NP

3 km   22 km   12 km

**SOUTHERN
NEW
BRUNSWICK**

Campbell Kids and Gerber babies; Shirley Temples, Dionne Quintuplets, Barbara Ann Scotts, Peggy Nesbitts, and just about every doll you can name is living in Delia's Dollhouse in Petitcodiac. Here you will find dolls made of porcelain, celluloid, rubber, plastic, vinyl, and chalk; dolls from around the world; dolls attired for all seasons. Furthermore, visitors, young and old, are encouraged to touch, and hold, the exhibits. Some well-loved (secondhand) and new dolls can be bought in an adjoining shop.

Fundy National Park

Set in the Caledonian Highlands, high above the Bay of Fundy, this park offers a heated saltwater pool, a nine-hole golf course, and tennis courts. Fishing is popular with visitors and the park's three rivers—the Upper Salmon, the Point Wolfe, and the Goose—are stocked with trout and salmon. Licenses are required but are readily available at the Alma headquarters, or any campground kiosk. Hikers can explore dozens of backcountry trails, many of which double as snowshoeing or cross-country skiing paths in winter. More than 180 species of birds inhabit the dense red spruce and balsam forest of the interior, where damp cliff faces sprout unusual plants such as dwarf bilberry, green spleenwort, primitive low selaginella, and mountain club moss. Hastings Hill prospect offers a panoramic view of Chignecto Bay, and there are several vantage points from which you can see the mighty Fundy tides rise and fall.

Petitcodiac

English settlers mistook this village's Mi'Kmaq placename for "Petticoat Jack" (Petitcodiac means "bend in the river"), a name that still surfaces from time to time. East of town on the Trans-Canada is Delia's Dollhouse, an amazing private gallery of more than 4,000 dolls and heirloom quilts that is open to tourists. Artisans at nearby Honey Tree Farm turn out beeswax ornaments, candles, and handcrafted pine furniture.

Magnetic Hill

Tourists have been fascinated by Magnetic Hill since it was first popularized in 1933. A side road at the site appears to be going uphill, when the opposite is true, an illusion attributed to the way the land slopes at this spot. Motorists can check out the illu-

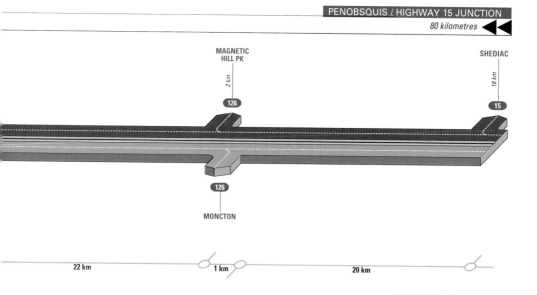

MAGNETIC
HILL PK

2 km

126

SHEDIAC

18 km

15

126

MONCTON

22 km   1 km   20 km

*This Doulton Burslem Romeo
and Juliet teapot in the Lutz
Mountain Heritage Museum at
Magnetic Hill is from the estate
of Muriel Lutz Sikorski, a
descendant of Moncton's first
permanent settler, and the original owner and developer of
Magnetic Hill, where she operated a china shop for 43 years.
Musicians entertain in Moncton's Bore Park (right). On
main street, the park is one of
the best places to view the
twice-daily spectacle of high-
rising Fundy tides forcing a
muddy, riverwide, 20- to 45-cm
high wave, or bore, up the
Petitcodiac River.*

sion by putting their vehicles in
neutral at the bottom of the hill,
then experiencing the sensation of coasting back-
ward up the slope.

Magic Mountain Water
Park nearby features a
zoo, wave pools, giant
and kiddies' water-slides,
mini-train rides, a go-cart
run, and miniature golf. Access
is from Hwy. 126, 2 km north of
the Trans-Canada. Another
2 km along Hwy. 126 will take
you to the Lutz Mountain Heritage Museum in a former Baptist
church. Its genealogical records
include an inventory of tomb-
stones in 92 area cemeteries.

Moncton

Ironically, this "Gateway to Acadia" is named in honor of Robert
Monckton, the British colonel
who supervised the expulsion of
the Acadians in 1755. (When the
town was incorporated in 1855
the clerk of the legislature mis-
spelled the name, and it has been
Moncton ever since.) After the
deportations, German families
from Pennsylvania arrived. Their
settlement flourished, first as a
shipbuilding center, then as an
important railway divisional
point. The city's oldest building,
The Free Meeting House (1821),
has been a center of worship for
many religious denominations
down the years. Moncton Museum next door traces local history
from Moncton's beginnings as
Mi'Kmaq portage point to the
present day. Visitors to the
handsomely restored Thomas
Williams Heritage House at 103
Park Street can glimpse the

life-style of a turn-of-the-century
railway executive's family.
The Capitol Theatre, built as a
vaudeville house in 1922, has
also been refurbished, part of a
$45 million downtown face-lift,
which included construction of a
city hall. An extensive collection
of Acadian artifacts and historical
documents is housed in the
Musée Acadien in the Clément-
Cormier Pavilion of the Univer-
sité de Moncton.

Water from Shepody Bay
pushes up the Petitcodiac River
estuary twice each day at high
tide to create the Tidal Bore that
briefly floods the riverbanks.

Shediac

A giant 14 m, 80 tonne statue of
a crustacean in Rotary Park pro-
claims Shediac's claim to Lobster
Capital of the World. For 50
years, this popular summer
resort has held a week-long lobster festival every July. Shediac
is a Mi'kmaq expression for "running far in," a reference to the
town's location on a deep coastal
indentation. Because of its warm
saltwater beaches, nearby Parlee
Beach Provincial Park is sometimes called "Florida North."

195

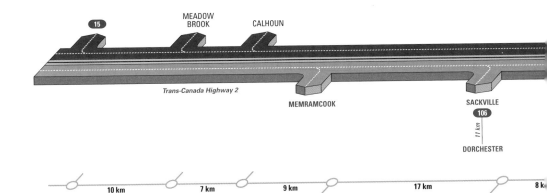

MEADOW BROOK — CALHOUN — 15

Trans-Canada Highway 2

MEMRAMCOOK — SACKVILLE 106 — 11 km — DORCHESTER

10 km — 7 km — 9 km — 17 km — 8 k

SOUTHERN NEW BRUNSWICK

Confederation Bridge, the world's longest multispan bridge over ice-covered water, arcs 13 km over the Northumber-land Strait between Cape Jourimain, N.B., and Borden–Carleton, P.E.I. Opened in 1997, the $840 million, reinforced concrete toll bridge, fulfills an 1873 federal committment to provide year-round transportation between P.E.I. and the mainland.

At the Sackville Water Fowl Park, a five-minute walk from down-town, you can picnic to a songbird serenade or explore the boardwalks, trails, and viewing platforms over-looking salty marshes inhabited by scores of wetland wildlife.

Memramcook

Visitors to the Acadian Odyssey National Historic Site in Monu-ment Lefebvre relive the tragic history of Acadia, a territory that once encompassed most of the Maritime provinces and part of Maine. Ignored for generations by rulers in Quebec and Paris, the colony's inhabitants grew into a distinctive people—con-tented, practical, hospitable, independent, and indifferent to authority. But in the end, they fell victim to the wars of Britain and France and a treaty that said they must choose between exile and an oath of allegiance to the British Crown. And so, between 1755 and 1762, some 10,000 Acadians were rounded up and deported to British colonies to the south. Most never returned. For the few who did, and the 2,500 who escaped the round-ups, the Collège Saint-Joseph (1864) in Memramcook, the first French-language, degree-grant-ing college in the Maritimes, played an empowering role in their renaissance. Fittingly, Monument Lefebvre, named for the college founder, occu-pies part of that former college.

Sackville

A mellow university town, Sackville is home to the campus of Mount Allison, a liberal arts institution founded in 1839 by a local merchant, Charles Freder-ick Allison. It has the distinction of being the first university in the British Empire to grant a degree to a woman—a bachelor of science to Grace Annie Lockhart in 1875—and having the oldest university art gallery in Canada—the 1895 Owens Gallery. Sackville also claims the first Baptist (1763) and Methodist (1781) churches in Canada.

A waterfowl park and board-walk in the downtown core are filled with migrating shorebirds in late July and early August.

Tantramar Marshes

Once the Trans-Canada High-way crosses the Tantramar River just east of Sackville, it cuts past a series of meadows and marshes that are typical of this area. Aca-dian dikes (known as *aboiteaux*) reclaimed the wetlands three centuries ago and the vast mead-owlands that resulted have been dubbed "the world's largest hay field." As dikes fall into disrepair,

To Nova Scotia
(See pages 204-205)

AULAC

PORT ELGIN

CONFEDERATION
BRIDGE

Trans-Canada Highway 16

USÉJOUR NHS

27 km

23 km

the sea reclaims sections of its old tidal ground. Many of these marshy areas are now waterfowl preserves, where wildlife experts hope to encourage the breeding of several species, including marsh hawks and muskrats. With the increasing presence of noisy wild birds, the appropriateness of "Tantramar" is apparent. The word is thought to be a corruption of the Acadian *tintamarre*, meaning "din."

Dorchester

Historic public properties here include the imposing Keillor House Museum, and The Maples, a Victorian mansion once the home of a prominent Acadian legislator, Sir Pierre Armand Landry. They are a legacy of the Loyalists from Connecticut, who founded this town in 1783. Edward Barron Chandler (1800-1880), a Father of Confederation, built the bed-and-breakfast Rocklyn Inn (1831). (In Chandler's day, the Rocklyn welcomed Canada's first prime minister, Sir John A. Macdonald.) Stage coaches made regular weekly stops at the Bell Inn (1811), the oldest stone building in New Brunswick.

Yorkshire-born John Keillor was a wealthy landowner and judge in 1813 when he moved his family from a log cabin into this early Regency stone mansion, complete with nine fireplaces, in Dorchester. Restored in 1967 it is now the Keillor House Museum.

Equally historic, but much less hospitable, is Dorchester Federal Penitentiary, established in 1879 on the outskirts of town

Fort Beauséjour National Historic Site

Shaped like a five-pointed star, Fort Beauséjour was built in 1751 by the French to guard the Chignecto Isthmus. Four years later, after a 14-day skirmish, it fell to the British, who demanded the Acadians pledge allegiance to the Crown. Those who refused were exiled, most of them to Louisiana. In 1776, American revolutionary forces attacked the fort—by then renamed Fort Cumberland—but were repulsed. The fort was reinforced during the War of 1812, and troops were garrisoned there until 1835. Declared a national historic site in 1926, Fort Beauséjour's ruins were restored in the early 1960s.

Confederation Bridge

At Aulac, Trans-Canada travelers can continue to Nova Scotia or veer northeast on Hwy. 16 to Confederation Bridge. The entrance ramp to the bridge is just north of Bayfield.

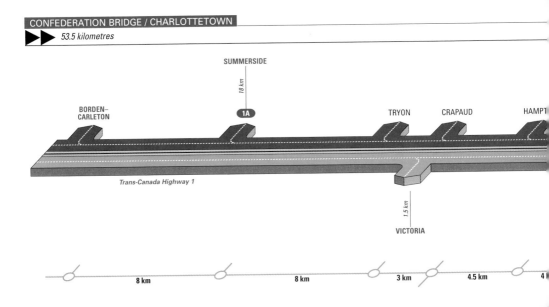

SUMMERSIDE

18 km

BORDEN–
CARLETON

1A

TRYON   CRAPAUD   HAMPT

Trans-Canada Highway 1

1.5 km

VICTORIA

8 km   8 km   3 km   4.5 km   4

**PRINCE
EDWARD
ISLAND**

Borden–Carleton

Long a ferry gateway to Prince Edward Island, Borden–Carleton's reputation as a transportation center has been bolstered by the Confederation Bridge link to the mainland. What were once two communities were amalgamated in 1995 in anticipation of the increased traffic flow. A Gateway Village has visitor and interpretive centers, stores, fast-food outlets, specialty cafes, and a park with a play area. Although the P.E.I. section of the Trans-Canada—from Borden–Carleton to Wood Island— is only 120 km, it is an excellent axis from which to explore many side routes.

Summerside

A major seaport for the island's potato industry, this community was founded in 1790 by Daniel Green, a Quaker Loyalist from Pennsylvania, who called it Green's Shore. In 1839, his son opened a roadside tavern, Summerside House, and when the town was incorporated in 1875, the name stuck. The town was made rich by the turn-of-the-century silver fox fur trade. A number of elegant Victorian houses, known locally as "fox houses," and the International Fox Museum and Hall of Fame are reminders of the fortunes breeders made when a pair of fox pelts could fetch as much as $35,000.

An Armed Forces base, established here in World War II, fell victim to 1990s military downsizing. A police academy now occupies the base. Summerside is

home to the College of Piping and Celtic Performing Arts of Canada and to the Harbour Jubilee Theatre, which features an annual musical revue. Lobster suppers, country music, and harness racing are staples of a Lobster Carni-

val in July. Thunder Boat Racing and mussel feasts are the big draws at the International Hydroplane Regatta in August.

Most of the island's French-speaking population lives in the county west of Summerside. Their Acadian ancestors escaped deportation in 1755 by hiding in the Miscouche swamp. This dark episode in Canadian history is recounted in the Acadian Museum in Miscouche.

Victoria

A placid seaside village, Victoria has a summer repertory theater, a seaport museum, and a hand-dipped chocolate factory.

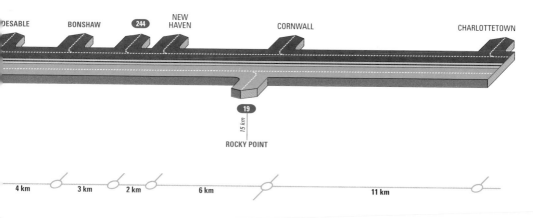

DESABLE BONSHAW **244** NEW HAVEN CORNWALL CHARLOTTETOWN

19
15 km
ROCKY POINT

4 km   3 km   2 km   6 km   11 km

Red soil and sea vistas at DeSable (bottom left), rolling potato fields at Tryon, boats in safe harbor at Victoria, and earthworks (bottom right) at Fort Amherst/Port-LaJoye National Historic Site reveal different faces of Prince Edward Island's peaceful, pastoral charm.

DeSable

🚣 ⛵ 🏊

Preschoolers are admitted free to DeSable's House of International Dolls, which offers guided tours, a gift shop, and a doll factory. National costumes are worn by 1,500 dolls from around the world. Another display features portrait dolls of famous figures.

Bonshaw

🚣 ⛵ 🏊

Bonshaw's Car Life Museum displays vintage automobiles and turn-of-the century farm equipment. Bonshaw (day use only) and Strathgartney provincial parks are pleasant stopovers.

Route 244
[MacArthur Road]

A drive down any of the island's 16 Scenic Heritage Roads is like a pleasant trip into the past. One such road is the stretch of Route 244 that begins some 700 m north of the Trans-Canada Highway, near Strathgartney

Provincial Park. Officially it is Peter's Road, but local people continue to call it MacArthur Road after families who once lived in this area. Canopied by maple, birch, pine, and spruce, the road meanders for some 2 km past apple orchards, pioneer cemeteries, and abandoned farmsteads.

Fort Amherst/Port La Joye National Historic Site, Rocky Point

A British fort's grass-covered earthworks are the only links to a French settlement, Port La Joye, established here in 1720. At first, poor harvests thwarted France's plans for the settlement to grow food for the troops at Louisbourg, in present-day Nova Scotia. Then, in 1745, the British conquered Port La Joye, and rebuilt the fortifications, which they named for Maj.-Gen. Jeffrey Amherst, their North American commander. Visitors can attend audiovisual presentations in the Visitor Centre, where artifacts recovered from the site are displayed, and stroll or picnic on the grounds, which provide a magnificent view of Charlottetown across the harbor.

Mi'Kmaq Indian Village, Rocky Point

This re-creation, just east of Fort Amherst National Historic Site, illustrates early life-styles of the Mi'Kmaq. P.E.I.'s first residents, they maintained communal households, and led a cooperative existence. The museum has birchbark wigwams and vessels, books in Mi'Kmaq ideograms, smokehouses, and a sweat bath.

CHARLOTTETOWN:
THE CITY WHERE CANADA WAS BORN

Often referred to as "the Cradle of Canadian Confederation," Charlottetown seems more like a pristine Victorian community than a political center. Laid out along Hillsborough Bay in 1764 by the British—and named for George III's wife, Charlotte Sophia—the island's principal city is a delightful place to explore on foot. Spick-and-span leafy streets are lined with neat rows of Victorian buildings, and the small-town ambience is soothing.

St. Peter's Cathedral and All Souls Chapel

This red-brick cathedral and adjoining chapel are among architect Robert Harris's finest works. With seating for 250, the French Gothic revival style church is said to be the world's smallest cathedral. Services were first held there in 1869, 20 years before the Victorian Gothic revival style chapel was added. Known for its delicately carved stone arches and rich oak and walnut paneling, the chapel is also noteworthy for its 18 paintings by the architect's brother, Robert, whose best-known work is the *Fathers of Confederation*.

Government House

Tall white birches surround this graceful neoclassic style frame structure, set on a height of land above Charlottetown Harbour. Built in 1834 as the colonial governor's official residence, it is now the provincial lieutenant governor's official residence. The parklike grounds, once known as Fanningbank, are open to the public.

Old Battery Point

↓ To Victoria Park

Beaconsfield

Named for British prime minister Benjamin Disraeli, Earl of Beaconsfield, this imposing 25-room Second French Empire style house near Victoria Park was designed by William C. Harris for shipbuilder, politician, and banker James Peake Jr. Completed in 1877, it had nine decorative fireplaces, central heating, and gaslights in every room. Peake went bankrupt, however, and lost the mansion to his creditors. Over the years, the house was a private residence, a boarding-house, a YWCA, and a nurses' residence. In 1973, it became headquarters for P.E.I.'s Museum and Heritage Foundation, which restored and furnished 11 rooms to the 1877-1915 era. Guided tours are offered year-round. Lectures and theater and music presentations are offered regularly.

FITZROY ST.

ROCHFORD SQUARE

KENT ST.

WEST ST.

ROCHFORD ST.

GRAFTON ST.

POWNAL ST.

RICHMOND ST.

CONNAUGHT SQUARE

SYD

DORCH

KING

WATE

CHARLOTTETOWN BOARDWALK

Charlottetown Yacht Club

Kirk of St. James

Built in 1878 to replace an earlier Presbyterian church on the site, this kirk was designed in early Gothic revival style. The interior is distinguished by a number of stained glass windows. The spire is 45 m high.

Confederation Centre of the Arts

A national memorial to Canada's founding fathers, this art gallery, library, 1,100-seat theater, and "egg crate" roofed memorial hall was paid for by 10 provinces and the federal government. Opened by Queen Elizabeth in 1964, the center's mainstay attraction ever since has been an annual production of the musical *Anne of Green Gables*.

Province House

Built in 1847 to house the colonial parliaments, this Georgian Palladian building is now the meeting place of the provincial legislature. A meeting here in 1864 by the Fathers of Confederation led to the British North America Act that created the Dominion of Canada. As a national memorial, the room where the historic meeting took place—the Confederation Chamber—has been restored to the 1860s.

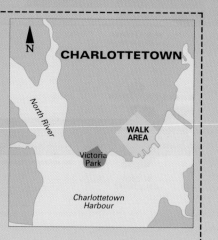

CHARLOTTETOWN

North River

Victoria Park

WALK AREA

Charlottetown Harbour

Trinity United Church

Public Archives

PRINCE ST.

QUEEN ST.

GREAT GEORGE ST.

Great George Street

Often described by urban planners as the finest street in Canada, Great George Street leads from **Confederation Landing Park** to Charlottetown's central square. At the southwest corner of Great George and Richmond streets stands **Victoria Row,** a collection of handsome, brick-fronted shops, restaurants, and offices built in 1884 in the Victorian Italianate and Richardson Romanesque styles.

St. Dunstan's Basilica

Twin 70 m spires make this Roman Catholic cathedral church a major landmark. Among notable features is the exquisite rose window above the main altar. Built in 1907, the third church on this site, it is named for a medieval archbishop of Canterbury. Gutted by fire in 1913, it was reconstructed, like the original, with stone quarried in Wallace, N.S., and New Brunswick's Miramichi region. A prime example of Canadian Gothic Revival architecture, St. Dunstan's is on the east side of Great George Street between Sydney and Dorchester streets. It has been designated a national historic site.

Cruise Ship Wharf

Peake's Wharf

Children's activities, outdoor performers, fresh seafood restaurants, ice-cream parlors, crafts and antiques shops, a convention center, and a public yacht club—all are found at this lively waterfront gathering place named for 19th-century shipbuilder James Peake. Harbor cruises originate from the wharf, or you can walk west along the boardwalk to **Victoria Park** and **Old Battery Point.**

Confederation Landing Park

This harborfront park marks where the Fathers of Confederation landed in 1864. In summer, outdoor vignettes by the Fathers and Mothers of Confederation and many Festival of the Fathers events regale park visitors. In the fall, the Parkdale section of the city becomes the center of Old Home Week events, celebrating with harness racing (culminating in the Gold Cup & Saucer Race), parading bands, and baton twirlers (*above right*).

Old Clock Tower

The city's most distinctive landmark, the Clock Tower on Citadel Hill has been telling Haligonians the time since 1803. Prince Edward, Duke of Kent (1767-1820), father of Queen Victoria and a stickler for punctuality, ordered the clock when he commanded the local garrison. His successors installed the 450-kilo timepiece—an intricate Swiss mechanism of cogs, wheels, pulleys, bells, and pendulum encased in a wrough iron frame—in an ornate, three-tiered, octagonal turret with domed roof. A municipally appointed clock keeper once took care of weekly windups, a task now the responsibility of Parks Canada.

St. Paul's Church

Bishops, governors and generals lie buried beneath this Anglican church, dubbed "the Westminster Abbey of the New World." Built in 1750, it is Halifax's oldest building and Canada's oldest Protestant church.

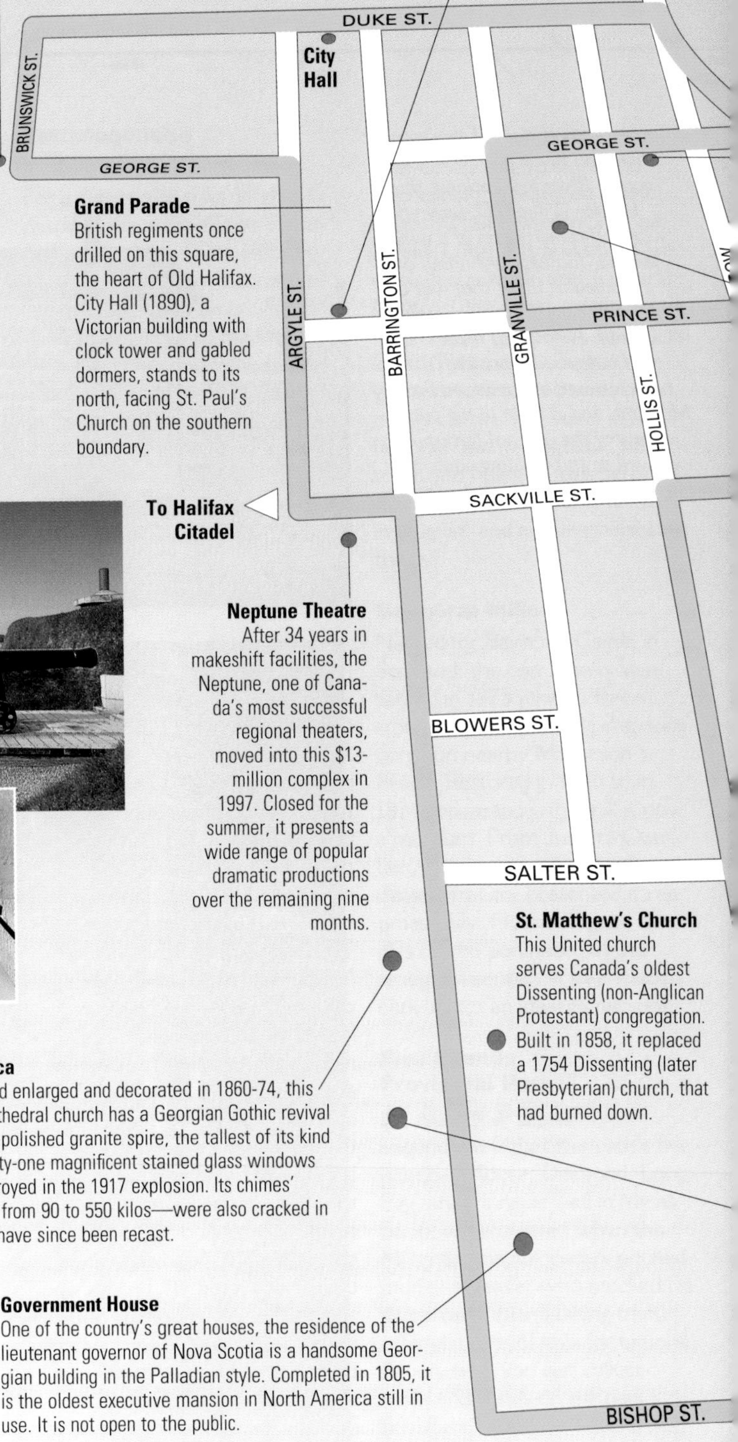

Halifax Citadel National Historic Site

Built by order of the Duke of Wellington (1769-1852), the star-shaped Citadel is the last of four bastions to crown this site overlooking Halifax. Construction, foreseen as a six-year job, began in 1828 and took 28 years to complete. By the time the earthworks were finished, the fortress was obsolete. Today, it is Canada's most visited national historic site. Its ironstone walls and ramparts contain a military museum, a restored powder magazine, garrison cells, and soldiers' barracks.

Grand Parade

British regiments once drilled on this square, the heart of Old Halifax. City Hall (1890), a Victorian building with clock tower and gabled dormers, stands to its north, facing St. Paul's Church on the southern boundary.

To Halifax Citadel

Neptune Theatre

After 34 years in makeshift facilities, the Neptune, one of Canada's most successful regional theaters, moved into this $13-million complex in 1997. Closed for the summer, it presents a wide range of popular dramatic productions over the remaining nine months.

St. Matthew's Church

This United church serves Canada's oldest Dissenting (non-Anglican Protestant) congregation. Built in 1858, it replaced a 1754 Dissenting (later Presbyterian) church, that had burned down.

St. Mary's Basilica

Built in 1820-29 and enlarged and decorated in 1860-74, this Roman Catholic cathedral church has a Georgian Gothic revival facade and a 58 m polished granite spire, the tallest of its kind in the world. Twenty-one magnificent stained glass windows replace those destroyed in the 1917 explosion. Its chimes' bells—they weigh from 90 to 550 kilos—were also cracked in the explosion, but have since been recast.

Government House

One of the country's great houses, the residence of the lieutenant governor of Nova Scotia is a handsome Georgian building in the Palladian style. Completed in 1805, it is the oldest executive mansion in North America still in use. It is not open to the public.

Map labels: DUKE ST., City Hall, BRUNSWICK ST., GEORGE ST., GEORGE ST., ARGYLE ST., BARRINGTON ST., GRANVILLE ST., PRINCE ST., HOLLIS ST., SACKVILLE ST., BLOWERS ST., SALTER ST., BISHOP ST., N

Historic Properties

Restored warehouses and other waterfront buildings, built between 1813 and 1870, have been converted into a shopping arcade of boutiques, craft stores, restaurants, pubs, and a farmers' market. The Nova Scotia College of Art and Design occupies 20 adjoining Properties buildings.

◁ **Ferry to Dartmouth**

Art Gallery of Nova Scotia

Designed in 1868 as a federal office building, this ornate Italianate structure served as a post office and an RCMP headquarters until 1988. The permanent collection includes an outstanding display of regional folk art, and works by Canadian and international artists.

UPPER WATER ST.

Province House

The oldest—and smallest—provincial legislative building in Canada, Province House opened in 1819. During an 1842 visit, Charles Dickens called it "a gem of Georgian architecture." What is now the legislative library was once the Supreme Court of Nova Scotia. There, in 1835, journalist Joseph Howe defended himself against a charge of criminal libel, a milestone in preserving freedom of the press. Headless eagles in the legislative chamber are a reminder of the anti-Americanism prevailing during the War of 1812. An assembly member mistook the birds for eagles and knocked their heads off with his cane.

CSS *Acadia*

HMCS *Sackville*

Maritime Museum of the Atlantic

A showcase of nautical history and marine memorabilia, the museum contains exhibits on the ages of sail and steam, shipwrecks, lifesaving, *Titanic*, the Halifax explosion, and the World War II convoys that sailed in and out of the harbor. Tied up on the adjoining wharf are a hydrographic vessel, CSS *Acadia*, and one of the last convoy escort corvettes, HMCS *Sackville*.

Old Burying Ground

This is Canada's first national historic site cemetery. In use from 1749 to 1844, the first burial here took place the day after Halifax was founded. Its stone Sebastopol Arch is North America's only Crimean War memorial.

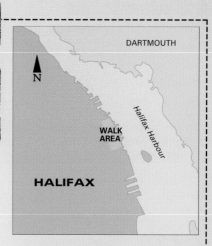

DARTMOUTH

N

WALK AREA

Halifax Harbour

HALIFAX

HALIFAX: SHAPED BY SHIPS AND THE SEA

Blessed with one of the world's largest harbors, this year-round port has had key naval and military roles in international conflicts from its founding in 1749 to the 1940s. Commercial shipping has been another long-standing source of wealth and prestige. Recent redevelopment has revitalized the downtown core, much of it leveled in 1917, when a French munitions ship blew up in the harbor. Restored and rejuvenated, the city remains the Maritimes' main commercial center. This walk explores the business district, whose destiny has been shaped by ships and the sea.

Sailor's Statue
This waterfront memorial beside the Maritime Museum of the Atlantic honors Canadian sailors who served their country in wartime.

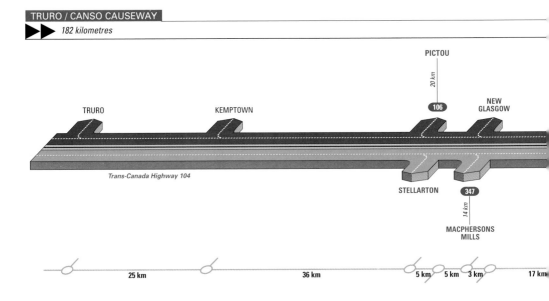

PICTOU

20 km

TRURO   KEMPTOWN   106   NEW GLASGOW

Trans-Canada Highway 104

STELLARTON   347

14 km

MACPHERSONS MILLS

25 km   36 km   5 km 5 km 3 km   17 km

CENTRAL NOVA SCOTIA

At Hector *Heritage Quay (bottom photo) visitors are greeted by the sights and sounds of a 1700s shipyard. Under construction is a replica of* Hector, *the ship that brought the first Scottish immigrants to Nova Scotia. Also in Pictou, you can visit the McCulloch House (below), which is furnished as in the early 1800s.*

Pictou

In 1762, George III granted a group of Philadelphia entrepreneurs, one of them Benjamin Franklin, 350 km² in the Pictou area. Nine years later, *Hector* sailed into harbor carrying Loch Broom Highlanders, Nova Scotia's first Scottish settlers. For the next two centuries, Pictou was a major shipbuilding center. (The last of its shipyards closed in 1983.) *Royal William*, the first steamship to cross the Atlantic (1833), sailed from Pictou Harbour. This and other events from its maritime past are memorialized in the Northumberland Fisheries Museum.

One of Pictou's early residents was Dr. Thomas McCulloch (1776-1843), a Presbyterian minister and proponent of nonsectarian education who founded Pictou Academy (1816) and became first president of Dal-

housie College (1838). His house, a "Scottish domestic" design built of bricks brought from Scotland, is now a museum (see photo left). One exhibit is an original J.J. Audubon *Birds of America* print, a gift to McCulloch from the famous illustrator.

Artifacts and memorabilia pertaining to 200 years of local Presbyterian church history are displayed in the Burning Bush Centre Museum downtown. The Loch Broom Log Church at the edge of town marks the site of the area's first Presbyterian church services (1787).

Pictou sponsors a lobster carnival, the *Hector* Festival, a Celtic celebration, the Pictou North Colchester Exhibition, and a regatta each year.

Stellarton

Samson (1838), Canada's oldest steam locomotive, is one of nine antique railway locomotives among 14,000 exhibits, ranging from simulated mine shafts and factory assembly lines to model railways, in the Nova Scotia Museum of Industry. A showcase of the province's technological history, the museum also contains a Victorian 8 km/h gas driven carriage, and a MacKay Automobile (1912), both manufactured locally. A miners' memorial recalls a 1952 disaster that claimed 19 local lives and the 1992 Westray Mine explosion that killed 26 men.

New Glasgow

A town with steel foundries, machine shops, and clay works, New Glasgow's Scottish and

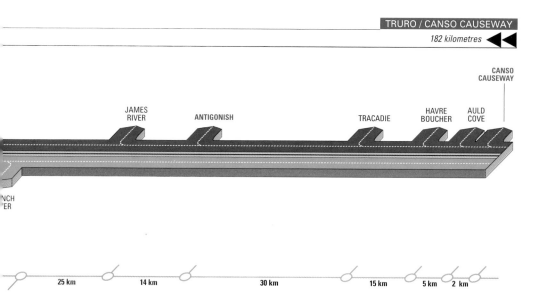

CANSO
CAUSEWAY

JAMES
RIVER — ANTIGONISH — TRACADIE — HAVRE BOUCHER — AULD COVE

NCH
ER

| 25 km | 14 km | 30 km | 15 km | 5 km | 2 km |

industrial heritage dates from the Scots settlers who first mined the Foord Seam, a seam of coal up to 14.7 m thick that ran beneath New Glasgow and Stellarton.

McPhersons Mills Grist Mill and Farm Homestead

This water-powered gristmill, built in 1861, continues to grind oatmeal, wheat, and buckwheat. The original waterwheel was

the Bauer Theatre on campus is host to the plays and musicals of Festival Antigonish.

St. Ninian's Cathedral, built in 1867-74 from locally quarried blue limestone, honors the fifth-century saint who brought Christianity to Scotland. The interior is decorated with frescoes by Quebec artist Ozias Leduc.

Stamp collectors will enjoy a visit to Canada Post's National Philatelic Distribution Centre.

For more than a century, these scenic falls on Sutherlands River near New Glasgow have provided the waterpower for McPhersons gristmill. Now operating merely as a tourist attraction, the mill was once the center of community life and, depending on the season and the water flow, often operated around the clock.

replaced in 1905. Among exhibits is a wheelbarrow with built-in scale for measuring bags of flour. Operated as a museum by the district Women's Institutes, the nearby farmstead is furnished to represent a typical farmhouse of a century ago.

Antigonish

Pride in its Scottish heritage permeates this university town that has hosted North America's oldest continuing Highland games every year since 1861. St. Francis Xavier University has been here since 1853. In July and August,

North America's first Trappist monastery (1852) is on the outskirts of town.

Canso Causeway

Almost 2 km long, the world's deepest causeway (65 m) was built across the Gut of Canso in 1952-55 to link Port Hastings on Cape Breton to Cape Porcupine on mainland Nova Scotia. The job took $20 million and 10 million tonnes of landfill, most of it blasted from a mountain on Cape Porcupine. A drawbridge and moving docks on the Cape Breton allow ships through the S-shaped causeway.

211

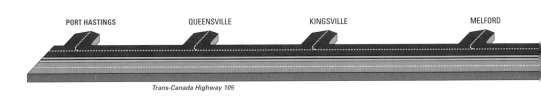

PORT HASTINGS   QUEENSVILLE   KINGSVILLE   MELFORD

Trans-Canada Highway 105

9 km   9 km   12 km   12 kr

CAPE BRETON ISLAND

At Nyanza, fresh water from the Baddeck River empties into the salty waters of Bras d'Or Lake. Like other areas around the mighty lake, Nyanza is a birders' paradise. Great bald eagles, double-crested cormorants, black-backed gulls, herons, ospreys, and yellow and purple finches are just a few of the species that consider this area home.

Port Hastings

At Port Hastings, on the Cape Breton side of the Canso Causeway, the Trans-Canada changes numbers (from 104 to 105) and heads straight north to the scenic shores of Bras d'Or Lake. Both the Ceilidh (*kay lee*) and Fleur-de-lis trails begin at the village of Bras d'Or. The Ceilidh trail (Hwy. 19) follows the west coast through Mabou and Margaree Harbour; the Fleur-de-lis trail (the continuation of Hwy. 104) runs along the east coast from nearby Port Hawkesbury to Fortress Louisbourg.

Area history is the focus of the Port Hastings' Historical Museum and Archives, a remarkable collection put together by a local woman.

Bras d'Or Lake

Many beautiful and secluded anchorages and a fog-free atmosphere make Bras d'Or Lake popular with boaters. The great body of water is really part of the Atlantic Ocean—it was formed when the sea flooded a glacier-depressed valley. Known as the "Great Inland Sea," the lake has a 70 km coastline, barely perceptible tides, is up to 180 m deep, and separates Cape Breton's highlands and lowlands. Salinity levels are about half that of the Atlantic. St. Peter's Canal to the south, and the Great Bras d'Or Channel to the north link lake and ocean.

Whycocomagh

This lovely resort village on the St. Patrick Channel of Bras d'Or Lake was settled by Highland Scots. (Pronounced Why-*cog*-a-mah, the name is a corruption of a Mi'kmaq word for "head-water.") A Mi'kmaq reserve is separated from the village by the River Skye. From the summit of Salt Mountain in Whycocomagh Provincial Park, you have a glorious view of the lake.

212

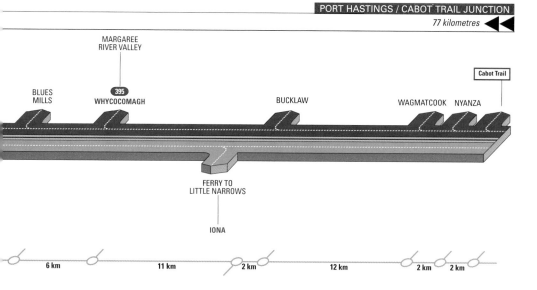

MARGAREE
RIVER VALLEY

BLUES
MILLS

395
WHYCOCOMAGH

BUCKLAW

WAGMATCOOK   NYANZA

Cabot Trail

FERRY TO
LITTLE NARROWS

IONA

| 6 km | 11 km | 2 km | 12 km | 2 km | 2 km |

Lake Ainslie, a popular wind-surfing spot, lies north of Why-cocomagh. Hwy. 395 skirts its eastern shore before heading into the scenic Margaree River valley, a salmon angler's paradise.

Iona

To reach this tiny Washabuck Peninsula community, take Hwy. 223 and the Little Nar-

Built in 1927, St. Andrew's Presby-terian Church in Whycocomagh is typical of many eastern Canada churches in terms of its white clap-board construction, although St. Andrew's two spires set it some-what apart.

rows ferry. After the ferry, you can turn right or left: the road encircles the peninsula. Either way offers a delightful shoreline route to Iona, named by High-land Scots for an island off Scot-land's western coast. Settlers' lives are depicted in the Nova Scotia Highland Village Museum, overlooking Bras d'Or Lake. Costumed guides staff 10 historic structures such as a Hebridean "Taigh Dubh" (Gaelic for "black house"), a log cabin typical of pioneer dwellings in 1830-50, a 1920s one-room school, and a carding mill. Scenic gypsum cliffs enfold nearby Plaster Cove. MacCormack Provincial Park offers shaded picnic areas.

Cabot Trail

Just past Nyanza, the Trans-Canada meets the Cabot Trail. Before continuing to Baddeck, you may decide to turn left at Exit 7 to follow this breathtak-ingly beautiful road that roller-coasts around 300 km of north-ern Cape Breton Island. Named for explorer John Cabot, who reputedly sighted Cape Breton in 1497, the road skirts ocean vis-tas, waterfalls, streams, spectac-ular gorges, forested hills, and rugged headlands. Along the Gulf of St. Lawrence, it hugs clifftops towering some 300 m above the shore.

More than a third of the road passes through Cape Breton Highlands National Park. Visitors have numerous lookoff points to choose from. Those who want to explore deeper into these magnificent highlands can select from some 25 trails—some offer short interpretive hikes; others present more challenging treks to attractions such as Beulach Ban Falls near Big Intervale, or the summit of Franey Mountain.

The park's eastern entrance is at the edge of the Acadian fishing village of Cheticamp; the west-ern gate is at Ingonish Beach. A popular vacation spot, Ingonish Beach is also the site of Keltic Lodge, one of eastern Canada's best-known resorts. A few kilo-metres to the south, you emerge from the park and, if the day is fine, enjoy one of the trail's most splendid views—a sweeping prospect from the top of Cape Smokey. (Travelers can also enter the Cabot Trail at Exit 11 near South Gut St Ann's—see pages 214-215.)

213

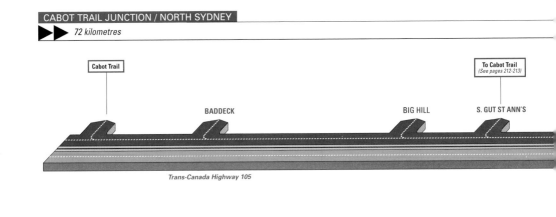

Cabot Trail

To Cabot Trail
(See pages 212-213)

BADDECK

BIG HILL

S. GUT ST ANN'S

Trans-Canada Highway 105

8 km

14 km

6 km

CAPE BRETON ISLAND

As you travel Cape Breton, ever-present lighthouses, such as this one at Baddeck, remind you that you are never far from water, whether it be the surging Atlantic Ocean or the barely tidal Bras d'Or Lake.

Baddeck

This resort community on the shores of Bras d'Or Lake owes its beginnings to Loyalists who fled the United States in 1785 and to an influx of Scottish High-landers who arrived in the 1800s. The town's best-known resident was inventor Alexander Graham Bell (1847-1922). Baddeck made aviation history in 1909, when John Douglas McCurdy (1886-1961) piloted his *Silver Dart* air-craft over Baddeck Bay to com-plete Canada's first manned flight. Cruises from the marina offer lake excursions, and there is a ferry to Kidston Island, popular for picnics and nature hikes.

Alexander Graham Bell National Historic Site, Baddeck

Alexander Graham Bell was so enchanted by Cape Breton, which he first visited in 1885, that Baddeck became his sum-mer residence and the place he spent most of his last 35 years. "I have seen the Canadian and the American Rockies, the Andes, the Alps, and the Highlands of Scotland," he wrote, "but for simple beauty, Cape Breton out-rivals them all." An extensive collection of his inventions, per-sonal papers, and photographs are displayed in the Alexander Graham Bell National His-toric Site at the east end of town. Exhibits include kites, gliders, hydrofoil and helicopter models and his medical vacu-um jacket—an early

iron lung. The site also show-cases the achievements of his wife, Mabel Hubbard Bell (1857-1923), who conducted various horticultural experiments and lobbied for voting rights for women. The Bells are buried on the grounds of *Beinn Bhreagh* (Gaelic for "beautiful moun-tain"), their summer house across the bay. It is private property, not open to visitors.

South Gut St Ann's

If you have ever wanted to learn how to play the bagpipes, do a highland fling, or speak Scots Gaelic, head for this communi-ty's Gaelic College of Celtic Arts and Crafts. The only institution of its kind in North America, the college offers courses in 11 tradi-tional Scottish disciplines and attracts students from all over the world. A walk through its Great Hall of the Clans provides a crash course in Celtic history, and its Craft Centre stocks kilts in hundreds of tartans. (As sub-jects of Queen Elizabeth II, Canadians who are not of Scot-tish descent are entitled to wear the Stuart Tartan.) A seven-day celebration of Celtic culture, the Nova Scotia Gaelic Mod is held on campus in August.

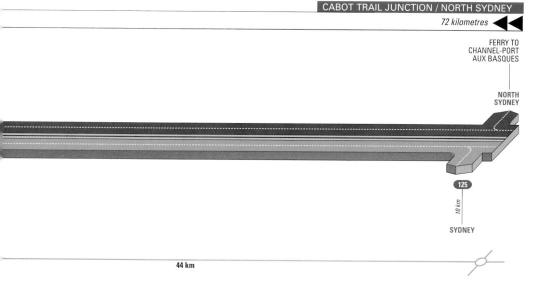

FERRY TO
CHANNEL-PORT
AUX BASQUES

NORTH
SYDNEY

125

10 km

SYDNEY

44 km

North Sydney

A fish-processing center, North Sydney has a worthwhile collection of Victorian frame dwellings with elaborate arches, gables, and verandas. A five-hour, 160 km ferry crossing from here takes you to Channel-Port aux Basques on Newfoundland's west coast, where the Trans-Canada resumes. Another ferry to Newfoundland's Avalon Peninsula makes the 426 km voyage to Argentia in 14 hours (see page 224).

Sydney

Founded by Loyalists, Sydney was the capital of Cape Breton Island from 1784 until 1820, when the island became part of Nova Scotia. Coalfields and iron ore deposits sparked industrial development in the mid-19th century, when the community became known as "The Steel City." With a population of more than 25,000, Sydney is still Nova Scotia's second largest urban region (after Halifax-Dartmouth). Heritage sites include the Jost and Cossit houses, which date from the 1780s, and St. Patrick's Museum, an 1828 church, now a repository of local memorabilia. The Cape Breton Centre for Heritage and Science occupies the nearby Lyceum, a 1904 opera house.

From Sydney, a 23 km jaunt on Hwy. 4 takes you to Glace Bay. At Miners' Memorial Museum there, you can visit Ocean's Deep Colliery, an under-the-ocean mine shaft. The Marconi National Historic Site at nearby Table Head honors Italian inven-

tor Guglielmo Marconi (1874-1937), who built one of the first permanent transatlantic transmitting towers on Cape Breton in 1902. Amateur ham operators can send or receive messages at an onsite radio station.

To visit Louisbourg (say *Lewis*bourg), go 32.5 km south of Sydney on Hwy. 22. The fishing village's train station—once the terminus of the Sydney and Louisbourg Railway, "the world's shortest and most profitable railway"—serves as visitor center for the Fortress of Louisbourg National Historic Site some 1.5 km from town. Some 50 buildings on the site, North America's largest historic reconstruction, re-create about a quarter of the fortified French town there from 1720 to 1760. More than 100 townsfolk in period costume create the impression that you are visiting the fortress in the summer of 1744.

State apartments, the tombs of two colonial governors, a barracks, and a military chapel are housed in the King's Bastion (above), once North America's largest building, and still the largest among several imposing buildings at Fortress of Louisbourg.

In Sydney, N.S., costumed guides welcome visitors to the restored Cossit House, the town's oldest house. The 1787 building was built as a Presbyterian parsonage.

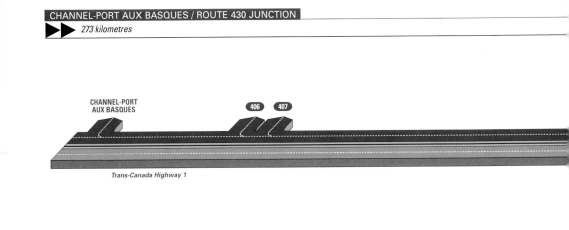

CHANNEL-PORT
AUX BASQUES

406 407

Trans-Canada Highway 1

38 km   4 km   103 km

**WESTERN
NEWFOUNDLAND**

This early navigational instrument, a mint condition Portuguese sea astrolabe dated 1628, has pride of place in the Gulf Museum in picturesque Channel-Port aux Basques (below).

Channel-Port aux Basques

The western terminus of the ferry from North Sydney, N.S., Channel-Port aux Basques was created in 1945 through the amalgamation of five settlements. Its name honors Basque fishermen whose fleets put in here as early as the 16th century. A relic of these days is a priceless 17th-century astrolabe recovered locally in 1981, and displayed in the Gulf Museum. Northwest of town, the Trans-Canada passes Grand Bay West and the J. T. Cheeseman Provincial Park. Both have splendid sandy beaches—something of a rarity in Newfoundland. Farther north, the rugged landscape is dominated by 518 m Table Mountain. Winds hurtling down its flanks and gusting across the highway at 160 km/h can disrupt traffic. As a result, a 16 km stretch of the Trans-Canada is known as Wreck House.

Codroy Valley

Some 35 km north of Channel-Port aux Basques, the Trans-Canada enters the Codroy Valley, a farming area between the Anguille (to the east) and the Long Range mountains (to the west). For a glimpse of this area, take Rte. 407 to St. Andrews and nearby Mummichog Provincial Park. A park lagoon supports mummichog, a small fish found nowhere else in Newfoundland.

Farther north, Rte. 406 will take you to Grand Codroy Provincial Park, which offers superb Atlantic salmon fishing.

Stephenville

From the Trans-Canada, Rte. 490 leads to Stephenville, where an Abitibi-Price paper mill is the main employer. A popular theater festival featuring original works and Broadway hits is a summer highlight. The Port au Port Peninsula east of town is dotted with hamlets such as Lourdes, Grand Jardin, and De Grau that were settled originally by French seafarers. On Port au Port Bay, Piccadilly Head Provincial Park has hiking trails and a sandy, saltwater beach.

Barachois Pond Provincial Park

Newfoundland's largest provincial park, Barachois Pond offers activities ranging from kayaking to mountain biking. One park trail ends with a superb view from the top of Erin Mountain.

Corner Brook

This city boasts one of the largest pulp and paper mills in the world. Visitors can enjoy plays, cabarets, and dinner theater by local and touring professional companies. The story of policing in the province is recounted at the Royal Newfoundland Constabulary Museum. Marble Mountain east of the city is known both for its stony profile of an old man and as Atlantic Canada's largest ski resort.

GROS
MORNE NP

23 km

BARACHOIS POND
PP

CORNER BROOK

PASADENA

DEER
LAKE

430

ENVILLE

11 km   62 km   27 km   23 km   5 km

Glaciers scoured the rocks known as the Tablelands in Gros Morne National Park, a magnificent wilderness of lakes, fjords, mountains, and cliffs. The area's bedrock, soil, and elevation create an atmosphere where diverse plants and animals thrive.

Deer Lake

A busy regional airport is a major contributor to the economic well-being of this transportation and distribution hub. The Roy Whalen Regional Heritage Centre describes bygone days.

Sir Richard Squires Memorial Provincial Park

Travelers following Rte. 430 north from the Trans-Canada to Gros Morne National Park can take Rte. 422 to this park. An angler's paradise, it is renowned for the spectacle of spawning salmon leaping over Big Falls. (See feature, pages 218-219.)

Gros Morne National Park

Set amid the Long Range Mountains, this vast park encompasses mountains, bogs, sand dunes, and mighty fjords. Colliding continents formed the rugged terrain about 450 million years ago, but Ice Age glaciers shaped its present appearance. Just north of Wiltondale, Rte. 430 enters the park's northern sector, skirting 806 m Gros Morne Mountain and Western Brook Pond. Stop at the visitor center for a slide show and displays on the best spots to visit. From Rocky Harbour, just north of the center, you can take cruises to Bonne Bay and Western Brook Pond.

217

Angling for Feisty Atlantic Salmon

HIGHWAY 1 / SIR RICHARD SQUIRES
MEMORIAL PROVINCIAL PARK

LAWRENCE JACKSON *was born in southern Alberta but has lived in Labrador and Newfoundland since 1971. He and his wife moved for a summer job and "loved it too much to leave." He has published articles in most major Canadian magazines, including* Canadian Geographic *and* Reader's Digest.

IF YOU'RE IN THE VICINITY of Deer Lake, visit Sir Richard Squires Memorial Provincial Park. There, if you plonk yourself down by the Humber River's Big Falls, a magnificent Atlantic salmon may leap right into your lap. Some say it has happened— more than once.

All summer long, salmon on their way to the spawning grounds upstream fling themselves over this 4 m waterfall. For hours on end, along its 87 m width, these athletic fish leap again and again. At the height of the run in July and August, 10 to 20 may be spotted in the air at once. Most, however, get to the top using the steps of the fish ladder blasted into the riverbank at the south side of Big Falls. A rock ledge by the falls, accessible by the Viewpoint Trail, is the best spot in the park to see the salmon's progress. Except in times of high water, you may walk right out on the ledge until you are virtually at arm's length of the salmon.

Just downstream from Big Falls lies an angler's paradise. A local guide can row you across the river in one of the park's yellow plywood dories to a choice angling pool near Goosney's Rock or Gulliver's Ledge. The guide will help choose the right fly—maybe a silver-bodied casboon or an orange bug. With a deft hand, good reflexes and a little luck, you may hook a salmon weighing 3 to 4 kg. If you catch one, you'll appreciate why many fly fishermen consider this to be the quintessential angling experience. For one thing, the fish could be airborne half a dozen times before you land it—if you do.

Salmon fishing on the Humber River, already spectacular, seems poised to get better. The stock of adult salmon in the river, estimated at more than 30,000 in 1996, could leap suddenly as the federal government's drastic conservation measures begin to pay off. In 1992, the government, alarmed by a steep decline in cod catches, closed Newfoundland's commercial cod fishery, which had always taken some salmon as an accidental "bycatch." The same year also saw the government shutdown of Newfoundland's commercial salmon fishery. The result of these closures has been a five- or six-fold increase in the number of adult salmon entering the Humber River.

A kind of compound interest is at work here. As more adult salmon return to the river, a "baby boom" occurs when these adult salmon spawn, then spawn again. Because it takes four or five years before the offspring of Newfoundland salmon grow up to spawn themselves, the benefits of the conservation measures take at least that long to appear.

The salmon's life cycle begins when eggs laid in river gravel in summer hatch the following spring. The young salmon will spend three or four years in the river (about half die each year) before heading to sea. But fewer than 10 percent of those that get there will survive. These 2-to-3 kg hardy specimens, known as grilse, will return to the river of their birth the following year.

Unlike the species of Pacific salmon, the Atlantic salmon do not die right after spawning. Most spend a lean winter in the river and return to sea to fatten up, then come back and spawn the next year, and perhaps the year after. Before returning, some salmon may spend two or more years at sea, traveling as far away as western Greenland.

The salmon run on most Newfoundland rivers lasts four to six weeks. But the Humber enjoys an extended migration season, lasting from June to late September. The grilse travel upstream throughout most of the summer. From mid-June to mid-July, there is a run of large salmon, most of which are repeat spawners weighing 10 kg or more. Early August sees another run of large salmon—spawners that have spent two or more years out at sea—but they seem to remain in the Humber's southerly reaches.

At Sir Richard Squires Memorial Provincial Park, the breadth of the river below Big Falls ensures great angling. Despite the volume of water on the Humber—Newfoundland's second longest river—this stretch is wide and shallow enough for anglers in waders to reach many of the best pools without a boat. It can also accommodate several hundred anglers at once, with little crowding. (During the fishing season, anglers are permitted to keep six salmon: three before July 15 and three after. But anglers must release any salmon 63 cm or longer.) Remarkably, this stretch yields about a third of the annual catch on the Humber River, which has more than 120 km of fishable waters.

To reach the park and Big Falls, head north from Deer Lake on Route 430, then take Route 422. Once there, whether you set up camp, stroll the trails to the Humber, or track down a guide, find an excuse to talk with the folk you meet, and you'll be glad you did. You'll discover most of your fellow visitors are Newfoundlanders, notoriously talkative, humorous, and good-natured.

If you're a nonresident who's here for the angling experience of a lifetime, you must buy a license—obtainable from local hardware and sporting goods stores, or service stations—and hire a licensed guide.

Lawrence Jackson

> *"With a deft hand, good reflexes and a little luck, you may hook a salmon weighing 3 or 4 kg."*

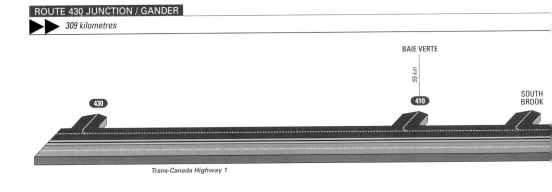

BAIE VERTE

55 km

430

410

SOUTH BROOK

Trans-Canada Highway 1

97 km   34 km

CENTRAL NEWFOUNDLAND

Baie Verte

Lush forest and mineral deposits enrich the Baie Verte Peninsula. Baie Verte, the mining town that doubles as the region's service center, is some 55 km north of the Trans-Canada. There is a Wildlife Interpretation Centre on its outskirts and a Miners Museum built over an abandoned copper mine downtown. A one-time logging camp is now Flatwater Pond Provincial Park.

Buchans

From the logging community of Badger, Rte. 370 takes you 73 km southeast of the Trans-Canada to Buchans, sometimes described as the heart of Newfoundland. Once a booming mining town, Buchans is farther from the sea than any other spot on the island. What remains of its storied past is preserved in the local museum. On Rte. 370, you pass the ruins of a stone corral at Laplanders' Bog near Buchans Junction. It is a relic of a failed experiment by Sir Richard Grenfell, who tried to introduce reindeer to Newfoundland in the 1900s. Grenfell had hoped to domesticate the deer for such tasks as hauling wood.

Grand Falls-Windsor

A plant here is one of the world's major suppliers of newsprint. Exhibits in the Mary March Regional Museum recount 5,000 years of aboriginal history. Mary March (1796-1820) was one of the last of the Beothuks, a people indigenous to Newfoundland, who were exterminated in the early 1800s. Mary's real name was Demasduit, but she was called March because she was captured in that month.

Windsor, just west of Grand Falls, marks the Trans-Canada's halfway point in Newfoundland.

Lewisporte

Near Notre Dame Junction, the "Road to the Isles" (Rte. 340) heads north to this fuel storage and regional supply depot on Notre Dame Bay. From Beothuk arrowheads to royal yacht blueprints, exhibits in the Museum By The Bay celebrate a colorful past. Charter boats take fishermen out in pursuit of giant bluefin tuna. Lewisporte is the

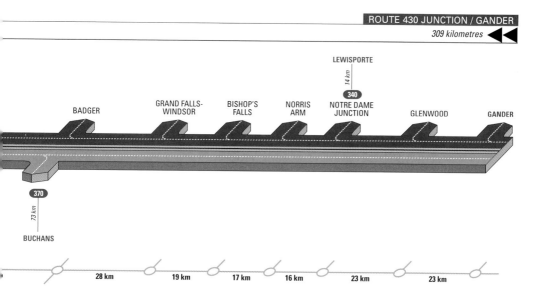

LEWISPORTE

14 km

340

BADGER   GRAND FALLS-WINDSOR   BISHOP'S FALLS   NORRIS ARM   NOTRE DAME JUNCTION   GLENWOOD   GANDER

370

73 km

BUCHANS

28 km   19 km   17 km   16 km   23 km   23 km

Gander's diminished role in international aviation and the loss of island railway service have affected many Newfoundland towns. Gander, however, still attracts many international flights, but trains no longer stop at places such as Badger (below), once an important railway stop. Before the Trans-Canada went through, a bridge on what was then the main road to Grand Falls/Windsor spanned a downtown brook, where this pedestrian walkway now stands.

terminal for ferries heading to Goose Bay, Labrador. (If you intend to take the ferry, book well in advance.) From Lewisporte, Rte. 340 continues on to other picturesque outports. One, Boyd's Cove, some 30 km north of Lewisporte, was a major Beothuk community in 1650-1720. An archaeologic dig and interpretive center chronicles the Beothuks' tragic story.

Some 30 km from Boyd's Cove, you reach the island community of Twillingate. French

fishing fleets came here in the 1600s, but English merchants and fishermen were the first permanent settlers. Museums (the Twillingate Museum in the former Anglican church rectory, the North East Coast Church Heritage Museum, and the Durrell Museum in the Old Church Lads Brigade Lodge) illustrate the community's prosperous, colorful past. There is also a Fishermen's Museum by the causeway leading into town. For the spectacle of icebergs drifting by offshore, drive to Long Point Lighthouse.

Gander

Roadside models of a Hudson bomber and the supersonic *Concorde* are reminders of Gander's importance as a World War II air force base and as a refuelling stop for jet aircraft. At Gander International Airport, an exhibit salutes pioneers of transatlantic flight. A memorial at Gander's North Atlantic Aviation Museum honors members of the Allied air forces. Some 3 km east of Gander is the site of the only Commonwealth war graves cemetery in North America. The nearby Silent Witness Memorial is dedicated to 256 victims of the 101st U.S. Airborne Division who died in a 1985 plane crash.

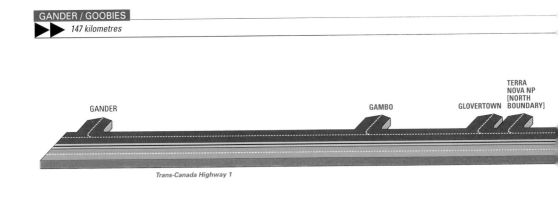

TERRA NOVA NP [NORTH BOUNDARY]

GANDER   GAMBO   GLOVERTOWN

Trans-Canada Highway 1

40 km   16 km   4 km

EASTERN NEWFOUNDLAND

Gambo

This community is proud to be the birthplace of Newfoundland's most famous son, Joey Smallwood (1900-91), who, in 1949, made Newfoundland Canada's 10th province. A bronze statue depicts Smallwood firmly rooted in "The Rock" that is Newfoundland. Joey's Lookout on the Trans-Canada commands a superb vista of the Gambo River valley.

Smallwood's grandfather, David, built Newfoundland's first steam-powered sawmill here in 1862. A nearby provincial park bears his name. It features a working model of a water-powered sawmill, and a ladder that lets spawning salmon bypass a waterfall as they head upstream.

Glovertown

Once a major lumber town, Govertown's sawmills never regained their importance after a 1946 fire destroyed the surrounding forest. Today Glovertown is a service center and gateway to Terra Nova National Park.

Terra Nova National Park

The Trans-Canada cuts through this park, which at first glance seems to contain only a boreal forest studded with black spruce, balsam, and fir. But first impressions can be deceptive. Naturalists point out that Terra Nova's most distinctive feature is that much of it is under water: roughly 15 percent is bogs and fens, and 30 percent consists of fjords—Newman and Clode sounds, and the southwest arm of Alexander Bay. Terra Nova is a sanctuary for more than 65 animal and some 350 plant species, including rare bog orchids. Whales can be seen offshore in spring and summer.

Roughly 8 km from the park's northern boundary, a road turns east to Saltons Wharf, site of the Marine Interpretation Centre. A few kilometres farther south, another road leads to the Newman Sound area, which has a visitor center, campground, lookouts, and other attractions. Another visitor center is located at Port Blandford, just beyond the park's southern boundary.

On Newfoundland roads, unrivaled beauty unfolds at every turn—sometimes gentle panoramas, such as this view of Gambo (above) or sharp-edged brilliance such as this vista of the southwest arm of Alexander Bay, seen from a Malady Head Trail lookout in Terra Nova National Park.

222

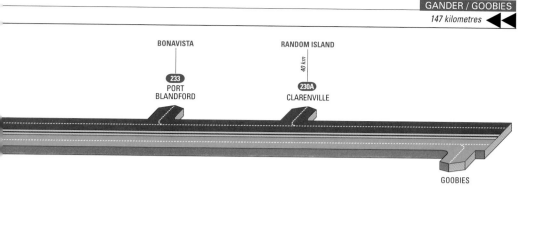

BONAVISTA   RANDOM ISLAND

40 km

233
PORT
BLANDFORD

230A
CLARENVILLE

GOOBIES

40 km   19 km   28 km

Bonavista

Legend says John Cabot (1450-99) sailed into the bay in 1497 and exclaimed *"O Buona Vista,"* (O happy sight). For more than four centuries, Bonavista Peninsula was Newfoundland's cod fishing center, a preeminence that ended with the collapse of the cod supply in 1992.

Just east of Port Blandford, Rte. 233 links up with Rte. 235, which will take you to the tip of the peninsula and the community of Bonavista. Exhibits in a Church Street museum tell of bygone days in this fishing community, one of the oldest in the province. The century-old dwelling house and several outbuildings of the downtown Mockbeggar Property have been restored to the 1940s. Antique furnishings illustrate Newfoundlanders' traditional lifestyles. The nearby Ryan Premises National Historic Site honors James Ryan, (1841-1917) who built up a prosperous fishing enterprise here in the late 1800s. Now restored, his compound includes the proprietor's house, retail and fish stores, a salt shed, and employees' quarters. Other interesting buildings are the Memorial United Church, described as "the largest wooden church in Atlantic Canada," and the 1814 Bridge House, one of Newfoundland's oldest buildings.

A statue of John Cabot stands north of town at the very tip of the peninsula. Nearby is the 1841 Cape Bonavista Lighthouse. Now a provincial historic site, this square-shaped structure has been restored to the 1870s.

Trinity

En route to Bonavista, you can turn off on Rte. 230 to Trinity, once a pirate haunt, now a pleasant fishing village and lively tourist town. Highlights include the Lester-Garland Premises (dating from the early 1800s), the Hiscock House (restored to 1910), the Newfoundland Railway Museum, and The Green Family Forge, a blacksmith museum.

Random Island

At 388 km², this heavily forested and well-logged island is Newfoundland's second largest. A causeway bridges the narrow channel separating it from the mainland. Take Rte. 230 and 231 to Petley on Smith Sound, where *Lois Elaine II* starts a round-trip to Ireland's Eye Island. (According to legend, if you visit this remote island and look to the horizon, you will see Ireland.) The boat trip passes abandoned outports, offering a poignant glimpse of the kind of communities that once thrived along Newfoundland's shores.

Sheds filled with logs and mounds of tarpaulin-covered logs are commonplace in picturesque Hickman's Harbour. For two centuries, logging has been a way of life in this community on Random Island, reputedly the last stronghold of Newfoundland's extinct Beothuk.

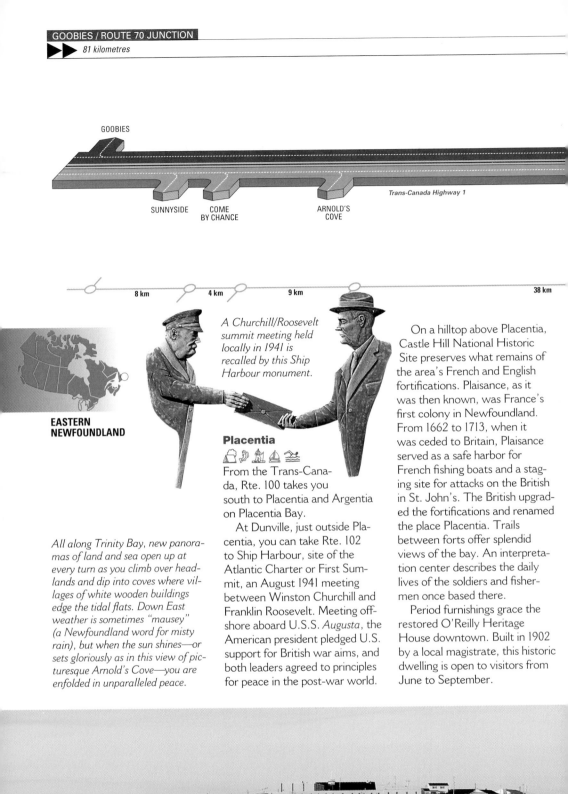

GOOBIES

SUNNYSIDE   COME
            BY CHANCE

ARNOLD'S
COVE

Trans-Canada Highway 1

8 km   4 km   9 km   38 km

**EASTERN
NEWFOUNDLAND**

*A Churchill/Roosevelt
summit meeting held
locally in 1941 is
recalled by this Ship
Harbour monument.*

Placentia

From the Trans-Cana-
da, Rte. 100 takes you
south to Placentia and Argentia
on Placentia Bay.

At Dunville, just outside Placentia, you can take Rte. 102
to Ship Harbour, site of the
Atlantic Charter or First Summit, an August 1941 meeting
between Winston Churchill and
Franklin Roosevelt. Meeting offshore aboard U.S.S. *Augusta*, the
American president pledged U.S.
support for British war aims, and
both leaders agreed to principles
for peace in the post-war world.

*All along Trinity Bay, new panora-
mas of land and sea open up at
every turn as you climb over headlands and dip into coves where villages of white wooden buildings
edge the tidal flats. Down East
weather is sometimes "mausey"
(a Newfoundland word for misty
rain), but when the sun shines—or
sets gloriously as in this view of picturesque Arnold's Cove—you are
enfolded in unparalleled peace.*

On a hilltop above Placentia,
Castle Hill National Historic
Site preserves what remains of
the area's French and English
fortifications. Plaisance, as it
was then known, was France's
first colony in Newfoundland.
From 1662 to 1713, when it
was ceded to Britain, Plaisance
served as a safe harbor for
French fishing boats and a staging site for attacks on the British
in St. John's. The British upgrad-
ed the fortifications and renamed
the place Placentia. Trails
between forts offer splendid
views of the bay. An interpretation center describes the daily
lives of the soldiers and fishermen once based there.

Period furnishings grace the
restored O'Reilly Heritage
House downtown. Built in 1902
by a local magistrate, this historic
dwelling is open to visitors from
June to September.

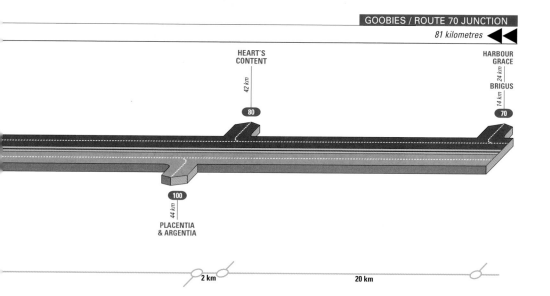

HEART'S CONTENT
42 km
80

HARBOUR GRACE
24 km
BRIGUS
14 km
70

100
44 km
PLACENTIA & ARGENTIA

2 km   20 km

Argentia

Canada's foggiest place, Argentia experiences some 200 fog-bound days a year. Once known as Little Placentia, the community was renamed in the 1880s to mark the opening of a local silver mine—*Argentum* is Latin for "silver". A U.S. naval and air base operated here between 1940 and 1975. Today, Argentia is a terminus for the ferry service to North Sydney, N.S.

Heart's Content

Opinions differ on whether Heart's Content, one of Newfoundland's oldest fishing villages, was named for a ship or for its hold on the heart. Contented settlers get full credit for naming nearby Heart's Delight and Heart's Desire. From the Trans-Canada, Rte. 80 leads north along Trinity Bay to all three picturesque communities.

The first Atlantic telegraph cable (laid by the *Great Eastern* steamship in 1866) terminated at Heart's Content. The original cable relay station is now a museum, restored to 1873.

Brigus

Once a noted seal hunt center, Brigus was also the home of Arctic explorer Robert Abram Bartlett (1875-1946). Commander of some 20 expeditions to the north, Bartlett captained the ship that took Admiral Peary's party to the Arctic on its 1909 trek to the North Pole. Bartlett's house, Hawthorne Cottage—one of the few remaining examples of a picturesque local architectural style

known as *cottage orné*—is a national historic site. Brigus also has a "walled" river. No one knows when or who built the walls but most likely it was settlers seeking a repository for stones cleared from the land and hoping to keep the river from overflowing its banks.

Harbour Grace

Three substantial churches here are among indications that Harbour Grace was once a prosperous town. Immaculate Conception Roman Catholic Church had cathedral status until 1983, when the bishop's see was moved to Grand Falls. A memorial in Harbour Grace United Church honors Rev. Laurence Coughlan, who started North America's first Wesleyan Mission here in 1765, thus introducing Methodism to North America. Newfoundland's oldest stone church, St. Paul's Anglican was built in 1835 as a garrison chapel.

Pirate Peter Easton headquartered locally in the 1600s. A customs house, built on the site of his fort, is now the Conception Bay Museum. Plaques commemorate aviation pioneers Wiley Post (1899-1935) and Amelia Earhart (1897-1937). In the 1930s, both aviators launched solo flights from Harbour Grace, site of North America's first civilian airport (1927).

Multicolored fishnets spill over the dock at Harbour Grace in western Conception Bay. In its early days, this community prospered from seal and cod fisheries, becoming for a time the second largest city in Newfoundland.

225

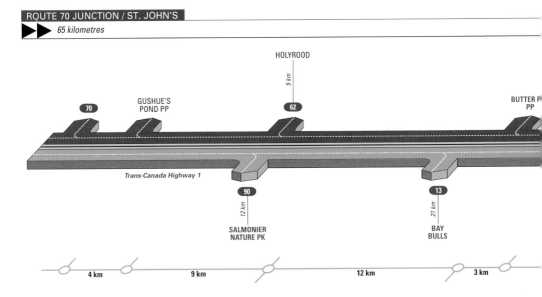

**WEST OF
ST. JOHN'S**

Salmonier Nature Park

A 2 km trail through woods and wetlands passes enclosures where wildlife native to Newfoundland and Labrador lives in simulated natural habitats. The park rehabilitates injured wildlife, and many enclosed birds and animals are orphaned or permanently injured. Naturalists are at hand to answer questions and present interpretive programs.

Holyrood

🌊 ⛵ ⚓ 🌊 ❄

A summer resort and a favorite with sailing enthusiasts, Holyrood is some 5 km along Rte. 62. Founded by Irish settlers in the late 1700s, the community is clearly identifiable from land, sea, and air because of a huge illuminated cross on George Cove Mountain.

Bay Bulls

⛺ 🛶 🌊 ⚓

This place-name, which may be derived from the bull-bird, a dovekie that nests here, was in common usage as far back as 1592. English fishermen began wintering here in 1635. Over the next 160 years, Dutch and French forces periodically attacked and burned the semi-permanent colony. Permanent settlement began in 1800 with Irish immigrants.

Relics of Bay Bulls stormy past include four old cannons, used as gateposts at the local Roman Catholic church. The church has topped the symbols of war with bronze statues of Saints Patrick, Paul, Joseph, and Theresa.

In Witless Bay Ecological Reserve offshore, three islands are havens for vast numbers of petrels, gannets, murres, gulls, and other seabirds. North America's largest puffin colony lives on Gull Island. Charter boats take visitors around the islands during the nesting season (mid-June to early July).

Butter Pot Provincial Park

One of the highlights of this park, just off the Trans-Canada, is the lookoff at the top of 305 m Butter Top Hill. It offers a superb view of Conception Bay.

C.A. Pippy Park, St. John's

From the Kenmount interchange, you can take Freshwater Road to downtown St. John's (see pages 228-229) or continue on Prince Philip Drive, which provides access to Pippy Park, Memorial University, the Arts and Culture Centre, and the Confederation Building.

Spacious Pippy Park has picnic and play areas, hiking and ski trails, 9-hole, 18-hole, and miniature golf courses, and is still roomy enough for fishing and bird-watching. It is named for

Flowers and plants of different heights, textures, and colors make pleasing displays in a variety of garden settings at the botanical garden on Memorial University campus.

Sailboats line the marina at Holyrood, a popular spot with sailors, who can count on gorgeous scenery and brisk Conception Bay breezes.

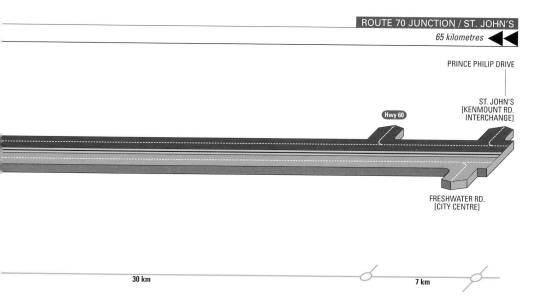

PRINCE PHILIP DRIVE

Hwy 60

ST. JOHN'S
[KENMOUNT RD.
INTERCHANGE]

FRESHWATER RD.
[CITY CENTRE]

30 km   7 km

Chesley Alwyn Pippy (1894-1971), who gave Memorial University the money to expand its campus, which now includes the park. The university's botanical gardens and a museum of transport history are in the park.

Memorial University of Newfoundland, St. John's

Founded in 1925, this institution of higher learning was opened as a memorial dedicated to Newfoundland servicemen who had lost their lives during the First World War. The university was originally a college and assumed its present status in 1949. The departments of ocean studies, earth sciences and folklore enjoy international reputations.

Arts and Culture Centre, St. John's

This center houses the Art Gallery of Newfoundland and Labrador, three libraries, and a 1,000-seat performing arts theater, which is the home of the Newfoundland Symphony Orchestra.

Confederation Building, St. John's

On a hill overlooking St. John's, this 12-story building houses the province's House of Assembly on its ground floor. Busts of once powerful politicians, such as Francis Little (1824-79), John Kent (1835-93) and Bowker Terrington Carter (1819-1900), adorn a hall of fame in the main floor lobby. A mural by Newfoundland artist Harold Goodridge is an allegorical portrait of the province's history.

227

ST. JOHN'S:
A STORIED, SEAFARING CITY

Fog-dampened and brine-scented, this busy port is one of North America's oldest cities. Legend says John Cabot sailed into the harbor on June 24, 1497, Feast of St. John the Baptist—hence, the city's name. When Sir Humphrey Gilbert arrived in 1583 to claim Newfoundland for Elizabeth I, he found no fewer than 36 ships doing business with merchants on the waterfront. The same ground, now called Water Street, is still St. John's commercial heart. This harborside walk takes you along Water Street—said to be the oldest street on the continent—past the vividly painted frame dwellings and storied sites that make this city such a beguiling spot.

Basilica Cathedral of St. John the Baptist
Twin 42 m tall spires on this Roman Catholic church dominate the skyline. Irish missionary Bishop Michael Fleming, who had the Romanesque style church built, died shortly after its completion in 1850, and is buried in the crypt. Noted for its statuary and ornate ceiling, the church was made a basilica in 1955, and declared a national historic site in 1984.

Anglican Cathedral of St. John the Baptist
The work of renowned British church architect Sir Gilbert Scott, designer of London's Albert Memorial, this Anglican cathedral is considered one of the finest examples of ecclesiastical Gothic Revival architecture in North America. Completed in 1885, the church was destroyed in the great fire of 1892, then rebuilt inside the original bluestone walls. Although the reconstruction followed Scott's original plan, a central tower in his design has still to be added. The cathedral is a national historic site.

CHURCH HILL

CATHEDRAL ST.

HENRY ST.

DU

GEORGE ST.

BISHOP'S COVE

BATES HILL

WATER ST.

City Hall
According to a sign in front of this municipal building, "Canada begins right here." The location marks Mile 0 of the Trans-Canada Highway (if you're traveling westward). Built in 1970 into the side of a hill and designed to reflect the province's rugged landscape, City Hall's four floors are filled with historic memorabilia. One plaque honors Terry Fox who began his 1980 Marathon of Hope cross-country walk from the building. There are statues of John Cabot and Sir Humphrey Gilbert, a propellor from the Alcock and Brown aircraft that made the first nonstop Atlantic flight, and a banner presented to the city in 1984 by Pope John Paul II.

Murray Premises
This block of nine restored warehouses and fish packing plants, built in 1847 and gentrified in the 1970s, contains shops and offices. One end building has a mural honoring those who rebuilt the city following each of three great fires that ravaged St. John's.

Newfoundland Museum
Displays here encompass 9,000 years of Newfoundland and Labrador history. Exhibits illustrate the lifestyles of Inuit, Beothuk, and Mi'kmaq peoples, as well as early seafarers and settlers. The museum also contains natural history collections.

Government House

This viceregal residence, built in 1831 for Governor Thomas Cochrane, was to have been patterned on Admiralty House in Plymouth, England. But Cochrane interfered with the design, and the red sandstone mansion cost four times more than budgeted, an extravagance that cost him the governorship. Ceiling frescoes are the work of an artist doing time for forgery who got day parole to complete the painting. The red sandstone building was declared a provincial historic site in 1977. The grounds are open to the public daily. Group tours of the house are by appointment only.

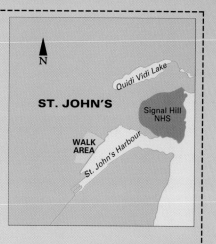

N

ST. JOHN'S

Quidi Vidi Lake

Signal Hill NHS

WALK AREA

St. John's Harbour

Commissariat House

This late Georgian style building was used as military offices from 1821 until British forces withdrew in 1870. Later it served as a rectory for St. Thomas' Anglican Church *(right)* and as a children's hospital. Restored to the 1830s, it is open to the public in summer.

St. Thomas' Anglican Church

Newfoundland's oldest church, black-wooden St. Thomas' was dedicated as a garrison church in 1836. Because it was outside the main areas of destruction, it survived several major fires that swept the city in the 1800s. The black tower is original, but the nave has been enlarged a number of times.

MILITARY ROAD

FLAVIN ST.

KINGS ROAD

COLONIAL ST.

BANNERMAN ST.

COCHRANE ST.

ST.

PRESCOTT

HOLLOWAY ST.

To Quidi Vidi Lake

Quidi Vidi Lake is the site of St. John's Regatta, North America's oldest sporting event, which has been held on this lake every year since 1826. A battery on the hills overlooking the village of Quidi Vidi was built by the French in 1762 and rebuilt by the British in 1811. Guides in Royal Artillery uniforms man the battery from mid-June to mid-October, when it is open to the public.

To Signal Hill National Historic Site

Signal Hill has been St. John's most visible landmark since 1704 when the first signal tower was built for ships sailing into harbor. Fortifications were installed during the Napoleonic War. Cabot Tower was built at the summit in 1897 to commemorate the 400th anniversary of Cabot's arrival in Newfoundland.

War Memorial

Unveiled in 1924, the 8 m granite memorial to Newfoundland's war dead is topped by bronze figures representing Liberty, the Merchant Marine, the Army, the Navy and the Forestry Corps.

St. John's Harbour

Pri

Co
bac
a hi
el, a
Yel
Mu
Col
10,(
loca
artis
silve
and
ings
wes
mus
con
the
way
deve
wate
way
Spec
Firel
of ea

Por

A fis
the !
boas
cann
a livi
toric
has b
lage
can e
proc
work
loft,

Terr

Spor
ation
which
riverb

TRANS-CANADA YELLOWHEAD HIGHWAY

Totem Poles in a Legendary "Land of Plenty"

YELLOWHEAD HWY 16 / THE HAZELTON REGION

CHERYL COULL *is the founding editor of* Beautiful British Columbia Travel Guide. *She has written* A Traveller's Guide to Aboriginal B.C., *published by* Whitecap Books *and* Beautiful British Columbia Magazine.

THE GITKSAN, LIKE ALL NORTHWEST Coast native peoples, are consummate creators of totem poles. "Gitksan" means "people of the 'Ksan, the river of mists." These are the people of the river now known as the Skeena. Their traditional territories begin with the river's first trickles in the Gunanoot Mountains, north of Kispiox, and extend to its middle reaches at the community of Kitselas, on the Yellowhead Highway, just east of Terrace. Within this region lies the highest concentration of totem poles in Canada. The Yellowhead provides access to some of the finest totem poles situated in ancient Gitksan villages (Gitwangak, Kitwancool, Kitseguecla, and Kispiox, as you travel eastward) and at 'Ksan Village, near the community of Hazelton, which lies in the shadow of the mountain Stii Kyo Din (also known as Rocher Déboulé).

At the village of Gitwangak, "the people of the place of rabbits," 12 sculptures look toward the century-old Anglican church. North of Gitwangak on Hwy. 37, Kitwancool (also known as Gitanyow) is home of the "awesome warrior people." Their poles stand adjacent to a carving shed where artists repair old poles, create new ones, and welcome questions. Sometimes, a hereditary chief is present to explain the poles' significance to visitors. At Kitseguecla (Gitsegukla), east of Gitwangak, the magnificent cedar poles of the "people of Segukla mountain" are visible on the south side of the Yellowhead Highway. At 'Ksan, near Hazelton, a reconstructed "model village" showcases Gitksan culture. Here, poles stand in front of a single row of traditional-style plank houses—much as they would have in the old villages a century ago.

It is the immensity of the poles that first strikes us—columns of graying cedar, broad, heavy, and 9 or 10 times the height of a human. We are quickly drawn in by the perfection of the tiniest detail: rhomboid eyes that look right through us, perfectly formed hands, tongues, beaks, fins protruding. The grain of the wood, as it weathers and cracks, pulls us closer still, to something inside ourselves: the aging faces of Grizzly Bear Woman, Weeping Woman, or Mosquito remind us of the transitory nature of all things.

Each totem is carved from the trunk of a Western redcedar tree. Each is adorned with a complexity of images set one above the other, containing as much information as a book—although a totem pole is much more difficult to read. Some of the images are crests that will be known only by those who are familiar with the Gitksan clans—the Fireweed, Wolf, Eagle, and Frog/Raven. Some images may be known only to the carver, or to the family that commissioned the pole (often to commemorate an event—a marriage, a death, the passing on of a hereditary name). Other totems may be understood only by those whose elders have passed on the ancestral legends of supernatural encounters, epic journeys, floods, and famines.

One of these legends tells of a time before the Flood, when some say the ocean—and not the Skeena River—lapped the shores of this region, and it describes a kind of Eden called Tam Lax Aamid that existed then. This was a metropolis so populous that, if everyone shouted up at the sky, geese passing overhead would become confused and tired; so vast that, where the exhausted birds fell, was still Tam Lax Aamid.

North of the Yellowhead Highway and past the village of Gitwangak and

"It is the immensity of the poles that first strikes us... 9 or 10 times the height of a human."

the Kitwanga fortress, a gravel road runs eastward to a little-known stop-of-interest sign that marks the reputed site of Tam Lax Aamid. Although archaeologists have searched and found no tangible evidence of the "Land of Plenty" here, Gitksan histories say this was the site of Tam Lax Aamid.

The legend of the end of Tam Lax Aamid is contained in one of the most evocative of all the Gitksan totem poles, at Kispiox, north of Hazelton. Set up in 1973, the pole was carved by Gitksan artists Earl Muldoe, Walter Harris, and Vic Mowatt. At the top of the totem, the figure of the One Horned Goat ensures that the Gitksan people remember what happened to Tam Lax Aamid—and what happens to all who forget their place in the world around them.

According to legend, the people of Tam Lax Aamid fell deaf to the lessons of their ancestors. Amid abundance, the people of this legendary city took to hunting for sport, killing mountain goats for trophies, wasting their meat. One day, the One Horned Goat, a supernatural being in disguise, lured the people—even high-ranking chiefs—up to the rocky face of Stii Kyo Din for a feast. There, he massacred all but the commoner who had earlier saved a young goat tormented by the cruel antics of children. This cautionary tale has been powerfully etched into the figure of the One Horned Goat with each cut of the blade made by its Gitksan creators.

Cheryl Coull

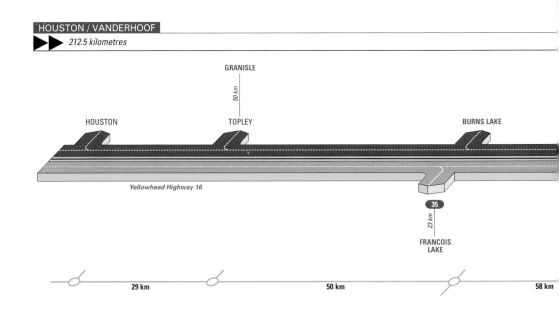

GRANISLE

50 km

HOUSTON   TOPLEY   BURNS LAKE

Yellowhead Highway 16

35

23 km

FRANCOIS
LAKE

29 km   50 km   58 km

**NORTH
CENTRAL
BRITISH
COLUMBIA**

Granisle

Perched on a hillside overlooking Lake Babine, Granisle was a copper-mining base from 1965 until its two open-pit mines packed up in 1992. It has now become the outdoor recreation center for the region. Granisle boasts year-round fishing and also offers mining tours, boating, and an extensive network of hiking trails.

Babine Lake

An anglers' paradise, Lake Babine is British Columbia's largest natural lake (117 km long). Best catches are rainbow trout and char—some specimens weigh as much as 14 kg. A major salmon spawning area, there is a plentiful supply of sockeye every fall.

Burns Lake

There are at least 18 major fishing lakes within a 100 km radius of Burns Lake. Set in the scenic, lake-strewn high country between the Fraser and Skeena watersheds, the village bills itself as the "Heart of the Lakes District." While fishing and boating are paramount pursuits, other popular activities include cross-country skiing and snowmobiling in winter, hiking and horseback riding in summer. A walking tour of local heritage sites and a self-guided tour of the Babine-Augier forest offer a leisurely change of pace. Visitors to the Lakes District Museum will discover the community's colorful past. Originally a tent town, Burns Lake was founded in 1914 by Barney Mulvaney, packer, trapper, and

later magistrate. One museum exhibit is a cabin known as "The Bucket of Blood," a gambling den once operated by Mulvaney.

Francois Lake

Thousands of white and amber agates and rare opals are there for the picking at Eagle Creek Opal Deposits off Hwy. 35 south. Maps of the site are available at the Hwy. 16 information center. There are camping and picnic sites, but be prepared for a long hike to the collection area.

Continue south on Hwy. 35 to reach some of B.C.'s best fishing lakes. Some of the largest char and rainbow trout ever landed in the province came from Francois, Ootsa, and other smaller lakes in this area.

At Francois Lake, you can take a free 20-minute ferry ride to Southbank. From there, the road leads to Ootsa Lake, the northern border of Tweedsmuir Provincial Park. Along the way, inviting byways branch off to Uncha and Takysie lakes.

Vanderhoof

This Nechako Valley community is the geographic center of British Columbia. It is named for Herbert Vanderhoof, a Chicago publicity agent who mounted a campaign to attract settlers to western Canada. Forestry and ranching are the local mainstays. Logging roads provide easy access to lakeside resorts. Thousands of migrating Canada geese make spring and fall stopovers at the Vanderhoof Bird Sanctuary. Restored 1920s buildings are fea-

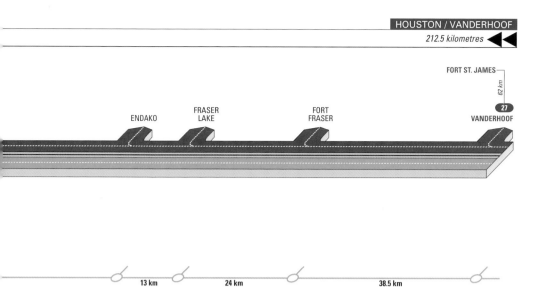

FORT ST. JAMES
62 km
FORT ST. JAMES

FRASER
LAKE
ENDAKO

FORT
FRASER

27
VANDERHOOF

13 km   24 km   38.5 km

tured at the Vanderhoof Heritage Village Museum, where oldtime fixtures, such as the OK Cafe, come to life each summer.

Fort St. James

A pioneer feeling prevails in this Stuart Lake village (known to the residents as The Fort), one of the oldest continuously occupied communities west of the Rockies. The spirit of fur trader-explorer Simon Fraser, who established a post here in 1806, lives on at Fort St. James National Historic Site. Restored to the 1890s, it boasts Canada's largest collection of fur trade structures still standing on their original location. Some 3 km from the fort site, there is another reminder of the past—Our Lady of Good Hope Catholic Church. Built in 1873, it is one of B.C.'s oldest churches.

During the 1930s and 1940s, Fort St. James was a busy base for bush pilots. In Cottonwood Park, a one-third scale model of a Junker floatplane pays tribute to these pioneer aviators. Today, Fort St. James remains a jumping-off point for fly-in adventure in northern B.C.

Fur trade days come alive at remote Fort St. James, where original buildings, period furnishings, and costumed staff re-create daily life as it was in the 1890s. A fur warehouse is filled with real furs (inset), trade goods hang from the rafters and fill shelves in the store/post office (below), a fish cache is stocked with smoked salmon, and fields are fenced and gardens worked as in the old days.

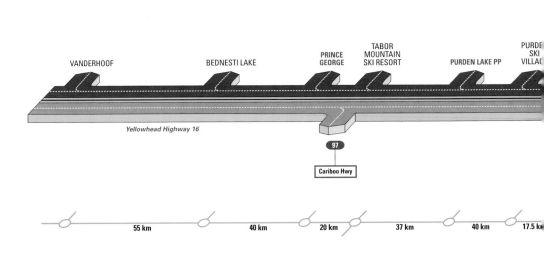

VANDERHOOF	BEDNESTI LAKE	PRINCE GEORGE	TABOR MOUNTAIN SKI RESORT	PURDEN LAKE PP	PURDE SKI VILLAC

Yellowhead Highway 16

97
Cariboo Hwy

55 km	40 km	20 km	37 km	40 km	17.5 k

NORTH CENTRAL BRITISH COLUMBIA

A pelt display in the Fraser–Fort George Regional Museum is topped by these heads of a black bear and three types of timber wolf.

Prince George

🏕️ 🛶 🎣 ⚓ 🏛️ ❄️

A vibrant, modern city in the province's forested interior, Prince George is British Columbia's fastest growing community. Situated where the Fraser and Nechako rivers meet, its economy is based on a thriving forest-products industry. A replica of the fort where Simon Fraser wintered in 1807-08 can be seen in Fort George Park. The actual site of explorer's trading post is marked by the Fraser–Fort George Regional Museum, which tells the area's natural and cultural history. Other museum attractions include hands-on science exhibits, a mini-theater, and a hall of history. Several historic buildings, among them a 1910 one-room schoolhouse and an old-time railway station, complete with a working miniature steam engine and six coaches, occupy the museum grounds.

Magnificent old-growth cottonwood trees line the riverbanks in Cottonwood Island Nature Park, one of more than 120 parks within the city. This peaceful retreat has canoe and boat launches, and a fish hatchery that raises salmon in the spring,

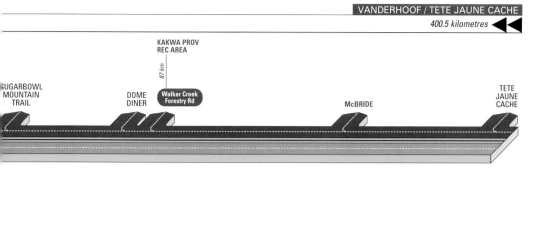

KAKWA PROV
REC AREA

87 km

SUGARBOWL
MOUNTAIN
TRAIL

DOME
DINER

Walker Creek
Forestry Rd

McBRIDE

TETE
JAUNE
CACHE

| 45.5 km | 10 km | 76.5 km | 59 km |

Overlooking Prince George from its lofty setting on Cranbrook Hill, the University of Northern British Columbia, Canada's newest university (1994), specializes in First Nations, northern and environmental studies, and distance education programs (for off-site students).

trout in the summer. Adjacent to the park is every rail buff's dream: the Prince George Regional Railway and Forest Industry Museum's collection of vintage rolling stock and logging and sawmilling equipment. Highlights include a 1914 Grand Trunk railway station and a restored first-class passenger coach with a polished brass and oak lounge. Downtown Connaught Park offers elaborately manicured gardens and panoramic views of the city and surrounding mountains. On Cranbrook Hill, an escarpment west of the city, you will find Forests for the World, where you can learn about reforestation techniques and plant seedlings, part of the park's "Leave your roots in Prince George" program. Other attractions include a spectacular lookout, extensive trails, and Shane Lake, home to wildfowl and several families of beaver.

Purden Lake Provincial Park

This forested park has campsites, extensive lakeside trails, one sandy beach area for swimmers and another for boaters and water-skiers, and a log picnic shelter complete with a wooden stove. Travelers might want to gas up at the nearby Purden Lake Resort, as there is no other gas station until McBride

Kakwa Provincial Recreation Area

This Rocky Mountain getaway offers spectacular alpine scenery, fossils and cave formations, and

opportunities for viewing wildlife—grizzlies and black bears, mountain goats, bighorn sheep, wolverines, moose, wolves, and caribou. Weather permitting (traffic may be restricted by bridge washouts and high water levels), you can get there via the Walker Creek Forestry Road. This is strictly a side trip for the adventurous who enjoy roughing it in the wild.

McBride

From Purden Lake to the picturesque market town of McBride is a scenic but lonely stretch of highway. There are a few small communities, but services are few. Nestled in the lush Robson Valley, surrounded by the Cariboo and Rocky mountains, McBride is a truly welcome sight. Once a railway boomtown, the community is now a service center for the region's farms and ranches. Resorts here offer cabins in pristine wilderness areas. Backcountry adventures from canoeing and kayaking to heli-skiing and snowmobiling are all just minutes away from town.

McBride also has an artisan community, with local shops displaying quality handmade goods: lace and fabrics, claw and antler jewelry, and woolens from valley sheep. Local attractions include Horseshoe Lake (with a wheelchair-accessible bird-viewing platform) and Koeneman Regional Park on the outskirts of town. Named for the homesteading family whose hand-built log house still stands here, the park features an original Grand Trunk Pacific Railway station.

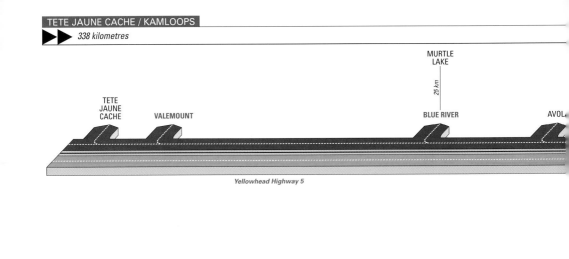

Yellowhead Highway 5

21 km   88 km   39 km

**CENTRAL
B.C. INTERIOR**

*Under a rainbow's arc and with
a muffled roar, the Murtle River
plunges 137 m over Helmcken Falls
in Wells Gray Provincial Park. The
most famous wonder in this awesome wilderness, Helmcken is 2.5
times higher than Niagara Falls.*

Valemount

Once a logging camp, this village,
in the folds of the Cariboos, the
Monashees, and the Rockies, is
now a popular all-season base for
outdoor enthusiasts. Activities
range from heli-skiing, skiing, and
snowmobiling to hiking, rafting,
canoeing, golfing, and horseback
riding. From observation towers
overlooking wetlands at the
Robert W. Starratt Wildlife
Sanctuary, visitors can see and
hear songbirds and waterfowl.
From mid-August to mid-September, the George Hicks
Regional Park offers close-ups of
chinook salmon nearing the end
of the 1,280 km upstream run.

Blue River

This logging and tourist center is
an increasingly popular base for
heli-skiers to the Monashee and
Caribou mountains. Eleanor
Lake offers cross-country skiing
and ice fishing in winter, and
swimming, hiking, and fishing in
summer. From Blue River, a
25 km gravel road followed by
a 1.5 km portage, leads to Murtle
Lake in Wells Gray Provincial
Park. All motorized craft are prohibited from Murtle Lake, a
turquoise oasis and a favorite
with canoeists. (The lengthy
portage is designed to discourage
anyone who might be tempted to
carry in a small outboard motor.)

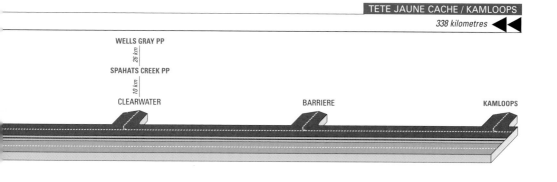

WELLS GRAY PP

26 km

SPAHATS CREEK PP

10 km

CLEARWATER　　　　　　　　　　BARRIERE　　　　　　　　　　KAMLOOPS

68 km　　　　　　　59 km　　　　　　　63 km

Spahats Creek Provincial Park

Clearwater is the gateway to Spahats Creek and Wells Gray provincial parks. From that community's travel information center, a 10 km drive on the Clearwater Valley Road takes you to the Spahats Creek parking lot. An observation deck near the entrance offers a breathtaking overview of the 150 m deep canyon Spahats Creek has carved through an ancient lava flow. Where the canyon ends, Spahats Creek Falls tumbles some 70 m. Another lookout at the park's north end offers a magnificent view of the Clearwater River valley.

Helmcken Falls Lodge

From Spahats Creek Provincial Park, another 24 km along the Clearwater Valley Road takes you to Helmcken Falls Lodge. This rustic log hostelry some 2 km from Wells Gray Provincial Park entrance boasts a homey atmosphere and incredibly beautiful surroundings. It also offers guiding and outfitting programs—horseback riding, hiking, canoeing, white water rafting, wilderness camping, and sightseeing—geared to a variety of activity levels.

Wells Gray Provincial Park

This untamed wilderness in the Cariboo Mountains is one of British Columbia's most spectacular parks. From bloom-filled alpine meadows in the south to snowcapped peaks and glaciers to the north, it encompasses an extraordinary diversity of scenery and wildlife. Nestling in the peaks are pristine lakes and waterways, extinct volcanoes and lava beds, and more than 100 icy mineral springs. Among the most striking features are a dozen breathtaking waterfalls, two of the largest within a short walk of the parking lot: Dawson Falls, known as "Little Niagara," is an 18 m cascade that fans out a full 91 m across the Murtle River; Helmcken Falls (*left*) is a few kilometres downstream. A hiking trail along the canyon rim offers views of this 50-story-high drop. Wildlife abounds. Among the larger animals are mule deer, caribou, moose, mountain goats, grizzlies and black bears.

Secwepemc Museum and Heritage Park, Kamloops

For a glimpse of the cultural history of the Shuswap Nation, visit this site, located east of the Kamloops Pow-Wow grounds on Kamloops Indian Reserve. Housed in a former Indian residential school, the museum displays birchbark and dugout canoes, a mat lodge, and photographs and artifacts relating to Native hunting, fishing, clothing, games, and food. Park trails lead to a 2,000-year-old winter village site containing reconstructions of winter pit houses and the tule mat lodge, smokehouse, salmon fishing station, and hunting lean-to that were part of summer life. Park programs include craft exhibitions and song, dance, and theater performances. (For more details about the City of Kamloops, see page 53.)

243

Yellowhead Highway 16

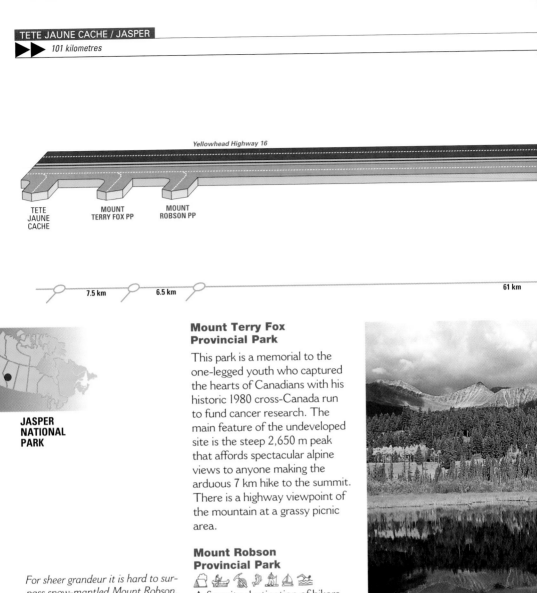

| TETE JAUNE CACHE | MOUNT TERRY FOX PP | MOUNT ROBSON PP |

7.5 km   6.5 km   61 km

JASPER NATIONAL PARK

Mount Terry Fox Provincial Park

This park is a memorial to the one-legged youth who captured the hearts of Canadians with his historic 1980 cross-Canada run to fund cancer research. The main feature of the undeveloped site is the steep 2,650 m peak that affords spectacular alpine views to anyone making the arduous 7 km hike to the summit. There is a highway viewpoint of the mountain at a grassy picnic area.

Mount Robson Provincial Park

For sheer grandeur it is hard to surpass snow-mantled Mount Robson, at 3,954 m the highest peak in the Canadian Rockies. Hiking trails from the Yellowhead Highway take you through the Valley of a Thousand Falls to the north flank of this "Monarch of the Rockies."

A favorite destination of hikers and mountain climbers, this is one of the province's oldest and largest parks. Its southwest corner is the birthplace of the 1,370 km Fraser, British Columbia's longest river. If you like waterfalls, you will love the Berg Lake Trail through the Valley of a Thousand Falls. More than 15 glaciers border the trail, which ends at Berg Lake, which is dotted with ice slabs broken from the Berg Glacier.

Yellowhead Pass

At an elevation of 1,131 m, the Yellowhead Pass straddles the Continental Divide between British Columbia and Alberta, separating B.C.'s Mount Robson from Jasper National parks. Its name is said to derive from Pierre Bostonais, a 19th-century blond Iroquois trapper, nicknamed *Tête Jaune*. A guide for the Hudson's Bay Company, *Tête Jaune* led fur-trading expeditions through the pass and is thought to have

cached his furs near the present-day Tête Jaune Cache. The pass itself came into regular use with the opening of the Grand Trunk Pacific Railway early this century. Today, both the Canadian National Railway and Yellowhead Highway traverse the pass. A hiker's paradise, it has extensive trails, good campsites, and spectacular viewpoints.

Jasper National Park

Canada's largest Rocky Mountain park, this 10,878 km^2 reserve is a showcase of emerald-green lakes, broad U-shaped valleys, shimmering glaciers, evergreen forests, and towering mountain peaks. Its unparalleled beauty

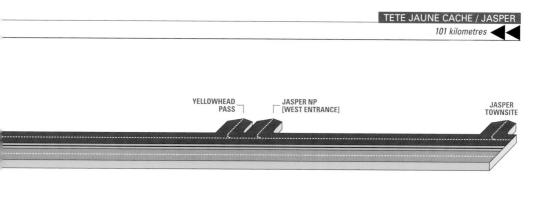

YELLOWHEAD PASS   JASPER NP [WEST ENTRANCE]   JASPER TOWNSITE

2 km   24 km

Pyramid Lake acts as a reflecting pool for autumn tints and snow-capped Pyramid Mountain. Some 7 km from Jasper townsite, this sparkling, glacial lake is a mecca for sailors, canoeists, and windsurfers.

This Packard pump organ is among treasured exhibits in the Jasper-Yellowhead Museum and Archives.

Jasper visitors, the Columbia Icefield, where Snocoaches take visitors out onto a 350 m deep, 325 km² crevassed remnant of the Ice Age, is a high point. Hotel, dining and other facilities are available for those wishing to glimpse the glacier at daybreak. Getting there from Jasper townsite involves a 103 km drive on the Icefields Parkway, past attractions such as Mount Edith Cavell's hanging glacier and Athabasca and Sunwapta falls.

Jasper Townsite

A bustling visitors' mecca, at the junction of the Yellowhead Highway and Icefields Parkway, this picturesque spot offers five-star shopping, dining, and accommodations. Pick up *Jasper... A Walk in the Past* from the Information Centre and take in the townsite's historic sites. One of the world's most scenic and challenging golf courses is on the grounds of the deluxe Jasper Park Lodge. Also on lodge property, Lac Beauvert offers a scenic 3.5 km lakeside stroll. Local human history, from early Native peoples, through the fur trade years, to the arrival of the railway, is the focus of the Jasper–Yellowhead Museum and Archives. One exhibit, the pump organ (*left*), departed Nebraska by train in 1902 but arrived locally by wagon and mule team. On the lower level of Whistlers Inn, the Den Wildlife Museum is crammed with 130 wildlife specimens mounted in cases depicting natural habitats. Just 6 km from the townsite, Lakes Annette and Edith offer great picnic sites, sandy beaches, and hiking trails.

attracts more than 2 million visitors each year. Indians and fur traders, geologists and railway surveyors, naturalists and prospectors are part of its history. A cairn near the townsite marks where the park's namesake, North West Company clerk Jasper Hawes, set up a trading post on the Athabasca River in 1813.

Wildlife is the main attraction in present-day Jasper, a sanctuary for bighorn sheep, elk, deer, moose, and black bear that wander near roads and campsites. Less conspicuous are grizzly bears that roam the back country, and mountain goats that vie with golden eagles for space on the highest ledges. For many

245

JASPER TOWNSITE

Yellowhead Highway 16

Maligne Lake Rd

21 km

MEDICINE L
& MALIGNE L

2 km

46 km

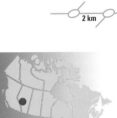

**JASPER
NATIONAL
PARK / WEST
CENTRAL
ALBERTA**

Maligne Canyon, Jasper National Park

From the Yellowhead Highway, the Maligne Lake Road takes you to this site, one of the most spectacular gorges in the Canadian Rockies. Carved by the churning Maligne River, the canyon's limestone walls plunge to depths of more than 50 m. Self-guiding trails and footbridges provide heart-stopping views.

Medicine Lake, Jasper National Park

Some 30 km farther along the Maligne Lake Road is the mysterious "disappearing" Medicine Lake. Fed by melting ice and snow, the lake level rises dramatically in summer. In fall and winter, its waters escape through subterranean limestone channels, reemerging at spots such as Lac Beauvert in Jasper townsite.

Maligne Lake, Jasper National Park

The largest lake (22 km long and 97 m deep) in Jasper National Park, Maligne Lake is also the world's second largest glacier-fed lake. Set amid snow-mantled peaks, pine forests, and alpine meadows, it is famed for its stunning scenery. Guided fishing, trail riding (to a 2,100 m lookout), and rowboat rentals are available at the lake's concession area. Especially popular is a 90-minute cruise to one of the most photographed spots in the Rockies, tiny pine-studded Spirit Island.

Miette Hot Springs, Jasper National Park

After a long day exploring the great outdoors, there's nothing like a soothing soak in mineral-rich water. Miette Hot Springs (see facing page), the hottest mineral springs in the Canadian Rockies, features two outdoor bathing pools, one deep, the

A few kilometres from Jasper Townsite, the Maligne River plunges into mighty Maligne Canyon.

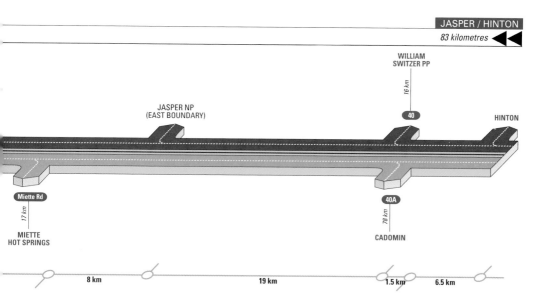

WILLIAM
SWITZER PP

16 km

JASPER NP
(EAST BOUNDARY)

40

HINTON

Miette Rd

17 km

78 km

40A

MIETTE
HOT SPRINGS

CADOMIN

8 km   19 km   1.5 km   6.5 km

other shallow. Fed by hot sulfur springwaters, these pools are chlorinated and cooled to about 40°C. Interpretive displays lead past ruins of the old pool site to the source of the springs.

William A. Switzer Provincial Park

A hot spot for wilderness adventure, this year-round outdoor recreation site is worth a 30-minute detour on Hwy. 40 north of the Yellowhead. Occupying a broad valley of lodgepole pine, spruce, and aspen forest in the Rocky Mountain foothills, it offers everything from hiking, biking, and bird-watching to canoeing and cross-country skiing. Trout, whitefish and pike are plentiful in its numerous streams and five interconnected lakes. These waterways attract wildlife ranging from muskrat and beaver to osprey and bald eagles. Grizzlies, black bears, wolves, cougar, moose, and elk all make their home in the park. Canoes, kayaks, fishing gear, and camping equipment can be rented at Blue Lake Adventure Lodge, which also offers outdoor recreation and wilderness survival training.

Cadomin

Officially a ghost town but with a general store and cafe still in business, Cadomin is the lone survivor of a chain of railway-linked mining towns known as the "Coal Branch." An hour's hike up a steep hill takes you to Cadomin Cave, which has an elaborate system of caverns linked by 3 km of passageways.

Hinton

This "Gateway to the Rockies" lies in the picturesque Athabasca River valley. Encircled by lush forests, lakes, and trout streams, Hinton boasts an extensive system of paved and graveled trails, including a 20 km restored section of an early pack trail that provides scenic views of the surrounding valley and mountains. A base for outdoor enthusiasts—anglers, hunters, kayakers, and mountaineers—Hinton is also one of Alberta's foremost forestry centers. Visitors can tour Weldwood of Canada's pulp mill, the Hi-Atha Sawmill, and the Alberta Forest Service Museum at the Environmental Training Centre. Displays there tell the early history of Alberta's forest ranger service. Fortech Adventures offers tours of the old-growth forests and hoodoos of the foothills, where wildlife sightings are almost a certainty.

A scenic mountain valley sprinkled with hiking trails and picnic sites is the superb setting for the Miette Hot Springs, one of Jasper National Park's "must see" sites. Piping hot water from three natural mountain springs is cooled to a comfortable 40°C bathing temperature in these outdoor pools. One pool is specially adapted for wheelchair-bound bathers.

247

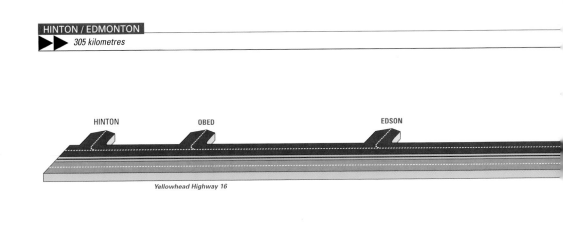

HINTON   OBED   EDSON

Yellowhead Highway 16

30 km   55 km   82 km

**WEST CENTRAL
EDMONTON**

At the West Edmonton Mall, the world's largest indoor shopping and entertainment complex, visitors can stroll along European-style streets, shop for everything from fashions to furniture in more than 800 stores, swim, skate, golf, or gamble, watch a movie or a dolphin show, or even try bungee jumping.

Obed

This tiny community is noteworthy for having the highest elevation along the Yellowhead (more than 1,160 m). It is also the starting point for several popular summer coal mine tours of the area. Offered by Luscar Ltd., the tours show visitors the various processes of open pit mining.

Edson

Midway between Jasper and Edmonton, Edson hosts Canada's largest slo-pitch tournament. This variation of softball, played on a 21-diamond ballpark, attracts more than 250 competing teams each July.

You can step back into Edson's pioneer past at the Red Brick Arts Centre and Museum, housed in a refurbished 1913 school, or at the Galloway Station Museum, which tells about the transportation, lumber and coal mining industries that built the area.

Wabamun Lake Provincial Park

This park encompasses an abundance of flora and fauna—from tiny bog orchids to an immense bull moose—and a 20 km long lake, stocked with pike, perch, and whitefish. Visitors can canoe on Moonlight Bay (delightful at sunset), or hike through the rolling landscape, armed with one of the self-guided activity kits dispensed at the permit office.

Some 20 km east of Wabamun Lake, Hwy. 16A splits off from Hwy. 16. To visit Stony Plain, follow Hwy. 16 and turn south on Rd. 779, or take Hwy. 16A. From Stony Plain, turn north on 779 to return to 16.

At Stony Plain's Multicultural Heritage Centre, housed in a 1925 high school, you can sample Ukrainian dishes in a homesteader's kitchen, visit a re-created settler's cabin, or browse through a craft shop. Stony Plain's past is also celebrated in 15 murals decorating exterior walls throughout the town.

West Edmonton Mall

Even the most jaded shopper will be impressed by the immensity of this mall. Sprawling over an area big enough to accommodate 104 football fields, the complex claims to have the largest enclosed shopping center and the largest indoor amusement park in the world. It also boasts world records for the largest indoor, triple-loop roller coaster, largest wave pool, and largest indoor lake, a 122 m long, 6 m deep artificial reservoir regularly patrolled by four 36 tonne submarines.

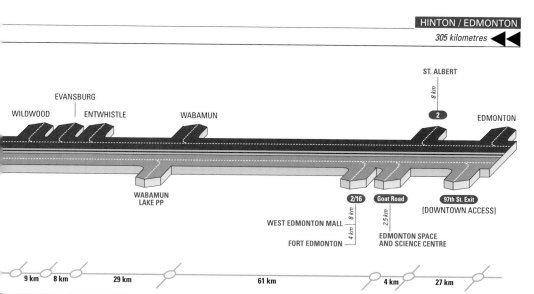

ST. ALBERT

8 km

WILDWOOD | EVANSBURG | ENTWHISTLE | WABAMUN | 2 | EDMONTON

WABAMUN LAKE PP

2/16 | Goat Road | 97th St. Exit [DOWNTOWN ACCESS]

WEST EDMONTON MALL | 8 km

4 km | 2.5 km

FORT EDMONTON | EDMONTON SPACE AND SCIENCE CENTRE

9 km | 8 km | 29 km | 61 km | 4 km | 27 km

Fort Edmonton Park

Costumed guides and 70 turn-of-the-century buildings re-create Edmonton's early days here at the junction of Fox and Whitemud drives. Canada's largest historical park, Fort Edmonton features an 1846 fur trading post; an 1885 settlement; and streetscapes from 1905 (when Edmonton became Alberta's capital) and 1920.

St. Albert

On the Sturgeon River, next to Edmonton's northern suburbs, this rapidly growing city was born in 1861 with the arrival of an Oblate priest, Rev. Albert Lacombe. His log chapel, now a museum and provincial historic site, exhibits his books (written in Cree and Blackfoot) and the snowshoes he wore on treks to remote Indian camps. Vital-Justin Grandin, another tireless Oblate missionary and the area's first bishop, is commemorated at the Vital Grandin Centre, a restored church, grotto, crypt, and bishop's residence. Built originally as a Grey Nuns convent, the residence is a striking example of Quebec gable-roof convent architecture. World-renowned architect Douglas Cardinal designed St. Albert Place, a red-brick curvilinear cultural center that houses the Heritage Museum, a 500-seat performing arts theater, a library, and an arts and crafts center.

Edmonton Space and Science Center

This center's ultramodern jagged design hints at the wonders within. Major drawing cards are the music laser light shows at the Margaret Zeidler Star Theater, and the "you-are-there" sensation of audiences viewing images on the four-story-high IMAX theater screen. At the Challenger Centre, visitors can experience a simulated voyage into outer space. Games, models, and demonstrations in several Discovery Galleries explore scientific phenomena.

Five galleries of interactive games and models enthrall visitors to Edmonton Space and Science Center.

EDMONTON: A CAPITAL THAT OIL BUILT

Edmonton's soaring skyline and lush parklands dominate the bluffs over-looking the winding North Saskatchewan River. Founded in 1795 as a Hudson's Bay Company post and later named Fort Edmonton, the settlement acquired capital status in 1905. It grew as a service center to the North—first as jumping-off point for the Klondike Gold Rush of 1897-98, then in the 1930s as an aviation center for bush planes and, finally, in the 1940s as a construction base for the Alaska Highway. The 1947 discovery of oil at Leduc, south of Edmonton, sparked the city's modern development. Since the oil boom of the 1970s, there have been impressive additions to its stock of public buildings in the city's downtown core, particularly around Sir Winston Churchill Square. But, here and there amid the hubbub of the city, business blocks and dwellings of early eras evoke its quieter Prairie past.

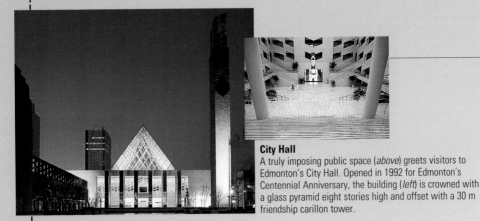

City Hall
A truly imposing public space (*above*) greets visitors to Edmonton's City Hall. Opened in 1992 for Edmonton's Centennial Anniversary, the building (*left*) is crowned with a glass pyramid eight stories high and offset with a 30 m friendship carillon tower.

McKay Avenue School
Built in 1905, this school was used by the Alberta legislators who met in the third-floor assembly hall during 1906-07. The school (located at 10425 99 Avenue) was closed in 1982 and then converted into the Edmonton Public Schools Archives and Museum. In the schoolyard is an 1881 public school, the first built outside the walls of Fort Edmonton.

Salvation Army Citadel
This interesting castlelike structure was built for the Salvation Army in the 1920s. It became the first home of the Citadel Theatre in 1965 and now is given over to various uses.

Masonic Temple
The exterior of this handsome structure, built in 1931 for the Masons, is profusely adorned with Gothic tracery.

McDougall United Church
Constructed in the Italianate style in 1909 as a Methodist church, the building can accommodate a congregation of 2,500.

Gariepy House
This dwelling, built in 1902 by wealthy merchant Joseph Gariepy, is a survivor from the day when Edmonton was a small Prairie town.

To Alberta Legislature Building & the High Level Bridge

MACDONALD DRIVE

100 AVE.

104 ST.

102 ST.

101 ST.

N

Alberta Legislature
Built in the Beaux-Arts style and topped by an eye-catching 16-story vaulted terra-cotta dome, the legislature rises on the site of Fort Edmonton. Completed in 1912, this imposing structure of imported marble and sandstone is attractively situated in a park that has pools, monuments, and fountains. Free tours of the building are available from the Legislative Interpretive Center.

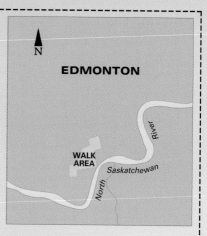

EDMONTON

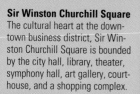

Sir Winston Churchill Square
The cultural heart at the downtown business district, Sir Winston Churchill Square is bounded by the city hall, library, theater, symphony hall, art gallery, courthouse, and a shopping complex.

Edmonton Art Gallery
Opened in 1969, the gallery presents permanent and changing exhibits. The collection includes some examples of Canadian art since 1800, but its main focus is on modern Canadian works.

Law Courts Building
Edmonton's courthouse resembles an upside-down concrete wedding cake. Opened in the early 1980s, the building was designed by Edmonton-based architect Junichi Hashimoto.

To Grant MacEwan Community College
The $100 million architecturally striking city center campus was designed by three architectural firms and built in 1983 on what used to be the CN railyards. 35,000 students are enrolled.

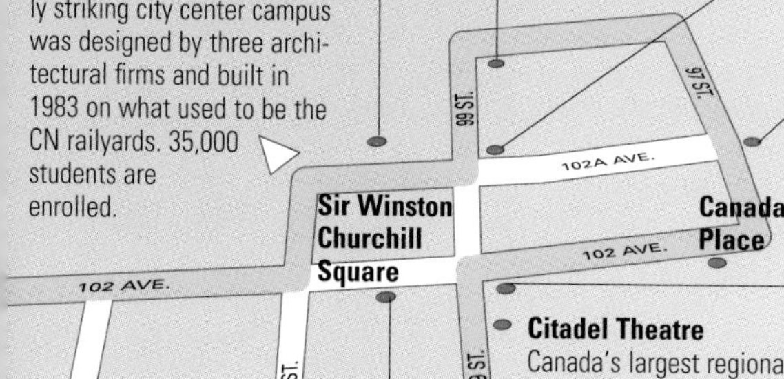

China Gate
A gift to Edmonton from Harbin, China, the portal to Chinatown is 23 m wide, 12 m high and features two hand-carved lions of quartz.

Winspear Centre for Music
Home to the Edmonton Symphony, the 1,900-seat concert hall which opened in 1997 is named for philanthropist Dr. Francis Winspear (1903-97).

Citadel Theatre
Canada's largest regional theater complex has five stages and attracts more than 150,000 theatergoers each year. The complex's atrium contains a garden and waterfalls.

Convention Centre
Stepped into the bank of the North Saskatchewan River, the $82 million convention center opened in 1983 and contains 48,000 m² of exhibition space on three levels. The Canadian Country Music Hall of Honour is on one level.

Stan Milner Public Library
With more than 1.3 million visitors a year, Edmonton's public library is one of the busiest in the country. Its catalogue contains more than 1.4 million titles. The library is named for the city councillor who spearheaded its construction as a Canadian centennial project in 1967.

To the Low Level Bridge & the Muttart Conservatory

Hotel Macdonald
A grand railway hotel with a commanding river view, "The Mac" opened in 1915 and has been restored to its original Edwardian elegance.

Map labels: 99 ST., 99 ST., 96 ST., 102A AVE., 102 AVE., 102 AVE., RICE HOWARD WAY, JASPER AVE., 100 ST., 100 ST., Sir Winston Churchill Square, Canada Place

North Saskatchewan River

North Saskatchewan River

North Saskatchewan

Muttart Conservatory
You can walk across the Low Level Bridge from downtown Edmonton to the Muttart Conservatory. Various ecological climates are re-created in three glass pyramids that house exotic, tropical, temperate, and arid vegetation. A fourth pyramid contains a floral garden, where a young couple (*left*) chose to hold their wedding.

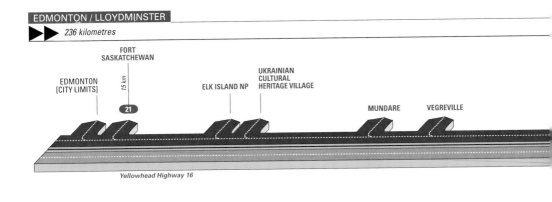

FORT
SASKATCHEWAN

EDMONTON
[CITY LIMITS]   *15 km*   ELK ISLAND NP   UKRAINIAN
CULTURAL
HERITAGE VILLAGE   MUNDARE   VEGREVILLE

21

Yellowhead Highway 16

4 km   27 km   3.5 km   30.5 km   15 km   49 km

**EAST CENTRAL
ALBERTA**

Fort Saskatchewan

🏛⛵❄

A small downtown park over-looking the North Saskatchewan River is the setting for the Fort Saskatchewan Museum and Historic Site. Amid its collection of restored turn-of-the-century homes, school, blacksmith shop, church, vintage cars, and farm equipment is Alberta's first courthouse (1909). Its exhibits tell the town's history from 1875, when the North West Mounted Police established a post here. The community that grew up next to the Mountie fort is one of Alberta's oldest settlements.

Elk Island National Park

🏕🚲🎣🏛⛵🏊❄

This relatively small national park (194 km²) is Canada's only fenced-in national park and the first federal wildlife reserve for large mammals. Established to protect a small elk herd, it continues to be a refuge for elk and species such as wood bison (North America's largest native mammal), the smaller plains bison, and trumpeter swans. In all, it shelters some 44 species of mammals and more than 240 species of birds. Set off from the surrounding flat farmland by low rolling hills, the park is strewn with meadows and wetlands. Camping and recreational areas adjoin Astotin and other lakes.

Ukrainian Cultural Heritage Village

Step into this open-air museum to discover the lifestyles and traditions of Ukrainian immigrants. Thirty buildings—stores, churches, wooden houses, thatched barns, community hall, school, and railway station—most transported from original sites in neighboring communities, are furnished as in 1892-1930. Costumed staff tend homes, livestock, fields, and gardens as in pioneer days. Visitors can see bread baked in clay ovens, learn how early grain elevators worked, and ride in horse-drawn wagons. (See also pages 254-255.)

A variety of trails let visitors explore Elk Island National Park and view its wildlife. Its most noticeable mammals are two different subspecies of bison. Wood bison are found in an area south of Hwy. 16, and the smaller plains bison (below) to the north, or, in summer, in a special display paddock just off the parkway.

Visitors from around the world marvel at the geometric detail on this giant pysanka in a Vegreville park. Such Easter egg artistry was among traditions of immigrants like those depicted in the Ukrainian Cultural Heritage Village sculpture (above).

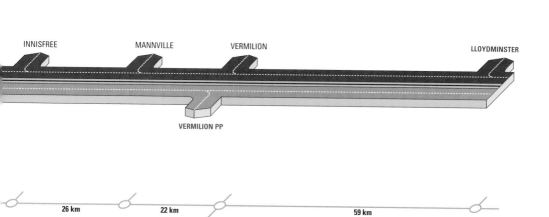

INNISFREE	MANNVILLE	VERMILION		LLOYDMINSTER

VERMILION PP

26 km   22 km   59 km

displays, an international egg decorating match, and Canada's largest youth dance competition.

Vermilion Provincial Park

Car-weary youngsters can burn up some energy at a lakeside playground in this scenic park. Marshes and oxbow lakes are visible from trails crisscrossing its rolling hills and aspen parkland. (Discovery packs are available to aid in wildlife observation.) Trails are groomed for cross-country skiing in winter, when a restored CN railway station serves as a warm-up shelter.

Lloydminster

In this city—the only one in Canada to straddle two provinces—the main north-south street (50th Ave.) is the Alberta-Saskatchewan border. Along its length, four 30 m tall monuments portray themes that characterize the area: agriculture, oil, Native peoples, and the Barr colonists, who founded the city in 1903. An Anglican church group, the colonists were led by Rev. Isaac Barr, who is commemorated by the Barr Colony Heritage Cultural Centre. More than 10,000 of the colonists' belongings (from farm implements to furnishings) are in the center's Richard Larsen Museum. The center also contains some 254 paintings by Count Berthold von Imhoff, a local artist renowned for his huge religious canvases and striking portraits, and hundreds of wildlife mounted in dioramas that simulate their natural habitats.

Mundare

Ukrainian culture and history are everywhere in this community. The highlight is Basilian Fathers Museum, a Main Street complex committed to preserving the heritage of early settlers. A repository of Ukrainian religious and folk art, the museum has an extensive collection of paintings, textiles, photographs, Easter eggs, embroidery, church vestments, and a collection of rare 16th- and 17th-century liturgical books.

Vegreville

This is the home of the world's largest Easter egg (*left*). The 9.4 m tall, gold, silver and bronze *pysanka*, weighing 2,270 kg, was built by the community in 1974-75 to mark the RCMP's centenary in Alberta. The egg's colors, stars, windmills, and wolves' teeth symbolize the immigrants' faith, the prosperity they found, and the protection accorded them by the Mounties.

A three-day Pysanka Festival in early July showcases Ukrainian arts and culture. The largest such festival in Western Canada, it features ethnic cuisine, folk art

Silver Domes on the Prairie Skyline

BARB & RON KROLL *are an award-winning photojournalism team. They have been published widely in books and travel guides. Among their credits are articles written for* Harrowsmith, Maclean's, *and* Time, *and for newspapers such as the* Globe & Mail *and the* Vancouver Sun.

AS WE DRIVE EAST FROM EDMONTON along the Yellowhead Highway, we reach a spot only 30 km from the city's hubbub—and yet it seems a world away. On the south side of the road, a swath of pasture parts the forest to reveal a thatched-roof building and a silver-domed church. Enchanted by the view, we turn off the highway to enter the Ukrainian Cultural Heritage Village.

During the 1890s, the Canadian government attracted immigrants to the Prairie Provinces with offers of 65 hectares of land for 10 dollars. Settlers arrived from Galicia and Bukovyna in the Western Ukraine, hoping to escape political oppression and find a better life. By 1930, roughly a quarter million Ukrainians had established thriving farms and communities across the Prairies.

One of the main areas of Ukrainian settlement was east-central Alberta, stretching from Fort Saskatchewan to Vermilion. Today, more than 30 historic buildings from different parts of this region have been moved to the 135-hectare Ukrainian Cultural Heritage Village. In rural and town settings reminiscent of the 1890-1930 period, the village's costumed guides reenact the lives of the settlers and recount for visitors like ourselves the immigrants' dreams, joys and hardships.

Our walking tour begins at the village's reception centre, where a poignant statue sums up the fortitude of Ukrainians newly arrived in Canada. A woman with a scarf wrapped around her head and an embroidered apron over her dress clasps an infant to her chest. Her husband wears work boots, pants and tunic, and a sheepskin vest. One hand clutches a leather bag of possessions, the other tenderly rests on his young daughter's shoulder.

In the village's rural section, we meet our first costumed guide, Kaska, who plays the role of a new immigrant. She is working in a potato field on land belonging to her husband. She puts down her hoe and invites us into her temporary dwelling, called a *burdei*. The sod-roofed dugout, set about a metre deep in the ground, shelters a small bed, a wooden table and a trunk filled with clothing, tools, religious icons and other possessions that she and her husband brought from the old country. In broken English, Kaska explains that, while she toils alone, her husband is far away, working in a coal mine to raise money for a more substantial dwelling.

Just across the road, Xenia has already moved into the kind of home that Kaska dreams of—a log cottage cemented together with clay, sand, straw, and water. The cottage has been built in the traditional Ukrainian style, with the windows and doors facing south, to cope with the harsh Prairie climate, the direct sunlight, and the prevailing winds. Although the cottage's two main rooms are cramped, the dwelling is almost luxurious in comparison with Kaska's *burdei*. As Xenia bakes bread in a clay oven, she tells how she picked mushrooms in the forest this morning, then made a hot borscht soup for lunch. (The thought of Xenia's cooking prompts us to stop at a nearby food kiosk for steaming bowls of this delicious beet-and-cream soup.)

The sound of wood being chopped leads us next to Annie, who puts down her ax and wipes her brow. Annie explains that her uncle has paid her way to Canada. In return, she now helps him by cooking and cleaning, and feeding the animals in the barn.

Afterward we continue along a dirt road to a clay-plastered log house, where Gregory greets us. His hands are hardened from tilling the fields all day, and he complains about the task of clearing the rocks and roots cluttering his land. But Gregory brightens as he tells us about his recent marriage and shows us the red-and-black embroidered blouse worn by his wife at their wedding.

Strolling into the village's townsite, we note how life eventually improved for the settlers. The townsite, typical of most communities in east-central Alberta, sits by the rail line. We recall that, as the railways spread their tracks across the Prairie Provinces, it became easier to ship grain to distant markets. Prior to the First World War, grain production and prices rose dramatically, and farmers' crops fetched handsome profits.

This prosperity encouraged local folk to buy all sorts of exciting newfangled items, all brought in by train. Still displayed in town are an icebox, purchased from Eaton's by the Canadian National Railway stationmaster, and a Smith-Corona typewriter, acquired by the proprietor of Wostok's Hardware. Shiny black cars (the latest 1925 models) may also be seen on the village's dusty rural roads, overtaking horse-drawn hay wagons traveling at a leisurely clip-clop.

> "...a poignant statue sums up the fortitude of the Ukrainians newly arrived in Canada."

Our walk through the Ukrainian Cultural Heritage Village ends at the silver-domed St. Vladimir's Ukrainian Greek Orthodox Church, situated beside a flaxen field of grain. In the quiet interior, we gaze admiringly at the frescoed ceiling and the gold-painted wooden chandelier, which can be lowered by rope to light the candles. These splendors remind us that, after the first Ukrainian settlers put up their first dwellings, they built their churches, initiallly simple log structures. Eventually, as their lives improved materially, the settlers replaced these simple structures with the imposing churches whose gleaming domes still crown the Prairie skyline.

For a rewarding visit to the Ukrainian Cultural Heritage Village, plan to spend at least a few hours there. Open from late May to early October, the village offers a farmer's market at weekends, as well as special events throughout the year.

Barb & Ron Kroll

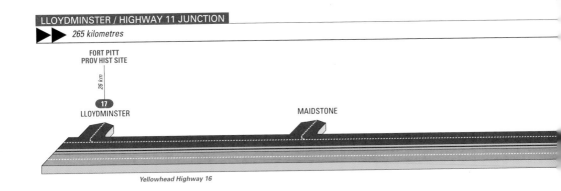

FORT PITT
PROV HIST SITE

26 km

17
LLOYDMINSTER

MAIDSTONE

Yellowhead Highway 16

55 km

80.5 km

**NORTHWEST
SASKATCHEWAN**

*Saskatchewan's longest bridge
spans the North Saskatchewan
River between Battleford, one of
the province's oldest communities,
and its sister city, North Battleford.
At Fort Battleford Historic Park
(top photo), staff in period costume
reenact the days when the NWMP
(forerunners of the RCMP) brought
law and order to the West.*

Fort Pitt
Provincial Historic Site

Interpretive panels at this North
Saskatchewn River site describe
Fort Pitt's fur-trading years and
its role in the Northwest Rebellion. It was sacked In 1885 by Big
Bear's war chief, Wandering
Spirit, who took 50 civilian pris-
oners and put the defending
North West Mounted Police to
flight. Rebuilt in 1886, the fort
never regained its former glory
and closed in 1890. A replica of
the HBC factor's log house and a
memorial cemetery remain.

Cut Knife

Many streets here are named for
prominent figures from the 1885
Northwest Rebellion. The
world's largest tomahawk (its
9 m long fir handle supports a
massive reinforced fiberglass
blade) dominates Tomahawk
Park. Indian and pioneer artifacts
collected by an area pioneer can
be seen in 11 refurbished buildings
in the Clayton McLain Memorial
Museum in the park. Included
are a tiny log house, a country
church, and a train station com-

plete with an operating railway
handcar. At Poundmaker Cree
Nation north of town, an open
teepee on a lonely hill marks the
grave of Poundmaker, a revered
leader of the 1880s. Visitors to
the reserve's Chief Poundmaker
Historical Centre and Teepee
Village can explore Cree history
and cultural displays ranging from
beaded-jewelry making to open-
fire buffalo roasts.

Battleford

Capital of the Northwest Territories from 1876 to 1882, Battleford's prized historic buildings
include Government House
(1878), a post office (1911) and
the town hall (1912). Items
assembled by one of Battleford's
pioneers are featured in the Fred
Light Museum, which has a comprehensive collection of firearms,

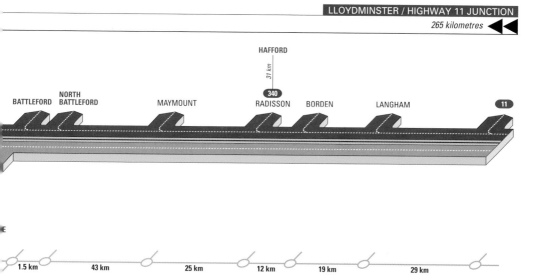

military uniforms, and turn-of-the-century objects, such as shaving mugs, coal oil lamps, and mustache cups. Fort Battleford National Historic Site honors the North West Mounted Police's role in developing the West. Four original buildings—officers' quarters, the commanding officer's residence, a guardhouse, and a stable for such horses, all furnished as in 1885—stand within a reconstructed stockade.

North Battleford

This community came into being in 1905 when the CNR followed the north rather than the south bank of the North Saskatchewan, thus bypassing Battleford which had long expected the railway to come through. A major outfitting site for recreation on nearby rivers and lakes, North Battleford town is noted for its art gallery dedicated to internationally acclaimed Cree artist Allen Sapp. Its permanent collection contains 120 of Sapp's depictions of life on the nearby Red Pheasant Reserve. Agriculture on the prairies is the focus of the Western Development Museum Heritage Farm and Village, a collection of 1920s farmhouses, churches, businesses, a railway station, and grain elevator. In summer, cows, horses, and chickens occupy its barn and fields, which are tilled with vintage farm machinery.

Hafford

A detour north along Hwy. 340 leads to this farming community known for its rich Ukrainian heritage. Hafford is also a convenient jumping-off point for many nearby lakes and regional parks. One of the most popular destinations is a federal bird sanctuary at Redberry Lake, 10 km east of town. The lake's salty waters and saline marshes nourish plants, insects, small fish, and amphibians that feed hundreds of migratory bird species. American white pelicans breed on islands in the lake and rare piping plovers nest on its open beaches. Visitors can golf, follow a self-guiding nature trail, swim, sail or canoe the lake. A bird-watching boat tour past the island pelican colonies can be arranged at the information center, which contains dioramas on local wildlife and birdlife, and presentations on the lake's ecosystem. Screens at the center show images being recorded by video cameras hidden on the nesting colonies and panning other wildlife-frequented areas.

Young Native dancers drink in the spectacle of sound and color surrounding them at a powwow near North Battleford, Sask.

257

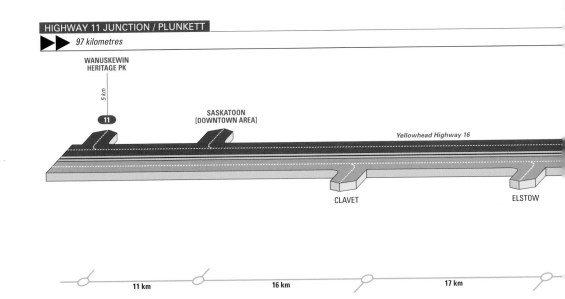

WANUSKEWIN HERITAGE PK
5 km
11
SASKATOON [DOWNTOWN AREA]
Yellowhead Highway 16
CLAVET
ELSTOW

11 km   16 km   17 km

CENTRAL SASKATCHEWAN

Many of Saskatoon's most prominent buildings overlook the South Saskatchewan River, which dissects the city. Landmarks and parklands on either side are linked by promenades and trails. This riverfront clock tower near the castlelike Bessborough Delta Hotel was erected to commemorate the 1989 Canada Games.

Wanuskewin Heritage Park

More than 6,000 years of Northern Plains history are evoked by fascinating hands-on and computer-activated exhibits in the visitor center of this park north of Saskatoon. (Take Hwy. 11 to Warman Road, which provides access to the park.) Teepee rings from ancient encampments and a 1,500-year-old medicine wheel are among the finds unearthed by archaeologists at the park's 19 prehistoric sites. Trails to ongoing digs pass bison jumps (where hunters stampeded buffalo over a cliff) and reconstructed encampments. Park staff demonstrate traditional skills, such as raising a teepee, tanning a hide, and baking bannocks (flat cakes) over an open fire. Aboriginal dancing, singing, and storytelling are featured at an outdoor amphitheater. Works of native artists and artisans are sold at the gift shop. (See also pages 260-261.)

Saskatoon

Saskatchewan's largest city has come a long way from its temperance colony roots. A vibrant, cosmopolitan hub of commerce and industry, its businesses include many high-tech and mining companies. Home to the University of Saskatchewan and world-class museums and art galleries, to trendy coffeehouses and craft shops, and to year-round festivals and recreational events, the city also exudes the lively ambience of a college town.

Meewasin Valley Centre, Saskatoon

For an entertaining overview of the area's history, flora, and fauna, stop by this center's exhibits. The center is also the starting point of a 19 km valley trail that takes you to panoramic lookouts, as it winds through scenic city parks and picnic areas along both sides of the South Saskatchewan River.

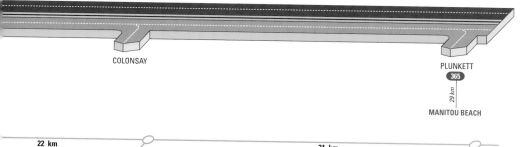

COLONSAY

PLUNKETT
365
29 km
MANITOU BEACH

22 km

31 km

Western Development Museum, Saskatoon

You can experience Saskatoon's boomtown years at the Western Development Museum's re-creation of a 1910 prairie town. More than 30 old-time shops and businesses stocked with early settlement goods line its main street. Agricultural and trans-portation galleries display vintage farm equipment and restored antique automobiles, wagons, and buggies.

Ukrainian Museum of Canada, and Ukraina Museum, Saskatoon

Beginning with turn-of-the-century mass immigration to escape religious persecution, the Ukrai-nian Museum of Canada docu-ments the rich history and cultur-al heritage of Ukrainians in this country. Exhibits include one of the finest textile collections in North America, regional folk costumes, ceramics, wood carv-ings, and beautifully decorated *pysankee* (Easter eggs). Ukrai-nian civilization from prehistory to emigration is the focus of the Ukraina Museum, which houses costumed dolls, religious articles, and pioneer and musical instru-ments. Art and iconography in the adjacent East Byzantine-style cathedral may be viewed upon request.

University of Saskatchewan, Saskatoon

Gothic-style gray-stone buildings set amid treed grounds make this one of Canada's most beautiful campuses. Its museums cover such diverse fields as antiquities, biology, and the natural sciences.

A replica of John G. Diefenba-ker's office and cabinet room and a wealth of memorabilia and archives relating to Canada's 13th prime minister are housed in the Diefenbaker Canada Cen-tre. History on a smaller scale is brought to life in the one-room Little Stone School, Saskatoon's first school and oldest public building. Constructed in 1887 of local granite boulders, its furnish-ings include a pump organ and writing slates.

Mendel Art Gallery and Civic Conservatory, Saskatoon

For a tranquil break, take in the seasonal floral displays set amid the conservatory's tropical trees. Traveling exhibits by local, national, and international artists augment the gallery's more than 3,500 artworks. Among its per-manent collection are 13 Group of Seven paintings, donated by the gallery's original benefactor, Fred S. Mendel.

Manitou Beach

A detour south at Plunkett leads to this resort community on shallow, spring-fed, saline Little Manitou Lake. Dubbed "Lake of Good Spirit" by early Plains Indi-ans, it became a chic vacation spot (the "Karlsbad of Canada") in the 1930s and 1940s. Today, the Manitou Springs Mineral Spa, an hotel/spa complex and one of Saskatchewan's major tourist attractions, offers guests three pools of heated mineral water pumped in from Little Manitou Lake, massage therapy, reflexology, and a fitness center.

The supposed curative power of its waters, which are three times saltier than seawater, has long attracted visitors to Little Manitou Lake in central Saskatchewan.

259

Listening to the Heart of the Land

YELLOWHEAD HIGHWAY 16 / WANUSKEWIN HERITAGE PARK

LOUISE BERNICE HALFE, *also known as Sky Dancer, has been published in many anthologies. Her first book of poetry,* Bear Bones & Feathers, *won the Milton Acorn Award. A second book,* Blue Marrow, *is published by McClelland and Stewart.*

I'VE WALKED THE TRAILS OF WANUSKEWIN many times, lifting my Reebok moccasins in a slow, deliberate step, imitating my Cree ancestors whose shadows move among the hills and trees of Opimihaw Valley. On this visit, I ask the staff interpreters to treat me as if my arrival were my first journey. They take turns and walk with me through this heritage park, explaining the substance and sustenance of this place.

On the grounds, outside the entrance of the interpretive center, I am led down a funnel of stone cairns that mark the lane used by Indians to drive buffalo over the cliffs into the valley below. At the center's entrance, Lloyd Pinay's sculpture depicts stampeding buffalo rising from the earth, goaded onward to the fatal plunge by two Indians, a warrior and a woman. In my mind's eye, ghostly figures of Indians, shrouded in hides, press their ears against the rocks, their bellies quivering as they prepare for the roundup. I imagine myself one of those brave women braced there, heart pounding, taking my chance at being trampled on by the herd. Yet I know that, after the first skinning of the kill, we will celebrate in prayer, feast, and dance.

A staff interpreter leads me into the atrium of the center, where the white-dressed statue of a shaman lifts a buffalo skull in prayer. Here, and at the center's exhibit of buffalo bones, I hear the great thunder of bison becoming dying snorts mingled with the delighted cries of hunters, knives raised to their gods. This is Wanuskewin where the bones live. Where legends say that the buffalo rose from the rocks. The stone, the heart and ribs of the buffalo. Today, archaeologists dig the remains of buffalo hunts among the stones of the Opimihaw Valley.

For thousands of years, the Northern Plains Indians came here to hunt and camp. Here, in the mid-1970s, Mike Vitkowski, the then owner of the valley site, and the University of Saskatchewan archaeologist Dr. Ernie Walker, first discovered its cache of buffalo bones and other treasures. In

1982, Vitkowski turned down offers from developers and sold the land to the city of Saskatoon. The park, opened in 1992 and now run by the Wanuskewin Heritage Park Corporation, centers around 19 internationally recognized archaeological sites (dating back 6,000 years and more), concentrated in an area of one square kilometre. Walking trails lead to these places—encampments and buffalo jumps—which explain the nomadic life of the Northern Plains Indians.

From the visitors' centre, I follow a trail into the valley, where Opimihaw Creek meanders to the South Saskatchewan River. I've stood on the bridge, watched the amorous dance of muskrats and seen beavers rippling the water, their heads surveying. In this valley, the rocks are graced in orange-mustard lichen; the goldfinches, meadowlarks, and orioles thrill in throat-bursting songs. I have spent hours here, listening and feeling the heart of the land, listening to its Native tongue.

Out in the fields of Wanuskewin's tall prairie grass, where the 1,500-year-old medicine wheel and excavated teepee rings lie, I envision the past. I hear the village drum resonate the Morning Song. The wails of a hungry toddler are hushed by a mother as she stirs a clay pot of buffalo and arrowroot stew. Outside, the father bends his knee and breaks twigs and branches needed for the fire. He makes tallow, smokes meat, and starts the strenuous labor of tanning hides. The women sew a teepee covering, using a bone awl to slip sinew through tough, smoke-blond hides. I'm drawn back to the present at a teepee raising, a tradition still thriving at Wanuskewin. I watch as lodge poles —long honored, stripped of bark and dried—are laid out on the ground. A young man ties the three poles of the tripod together at the crown with a strip of rawhide. With his peers, he raises the poles, and the rawhide strip hangs down in the center. (For the Cree, the doorway is accommodated to the East and each subsequent pole is laid out in a spiral within the heart of the tripod. The crown's rawhide strip must hang in the tripod's center, for it symbolizes the umbilical cord that binds together the community.) Once the last pole is up, the men unfold the sewn hides until they cover all the ribs. A child is hoisted and laces the bone pegs where the folds meet.

> 66 *This is Wanuskewin where the bones live. Where legends say that the buffalo rose from the rocks.* 99

Inside, workers space out the poles—and the teepee fills like an expanding lung. Once the hide is taut, they peg the outside hems to the earth. The outer flaps, held by feathered poles, are adjusted to allow smoke to rise or to close out the rain. The home is then smudged with sweet grass.

At my journey's end, I realize Wanuskewin's essence lies in its activities: teepee raising, dance, storytelling, pottery making, and other traditions. An overnight stay at the teepee village may enrich the experience of this place. Here, under a full moon, visitors are invited to gaze at the stars before turning in for a peaceful slumber in a teepee.

Wanuskewin is embosomed in the Opimihaw Valley north of Saskatoon, off Hwy. 11. An encircled "Dancing Buffalo" sign leads travelers from Hwy. 16. Seekers should pack in their bundles the medicines of honor, love, and respect for the land and its ancestors. Go softly. The flute of the land is already in your bones; you need only to stop and listen. All my relations.

Louise 6 halfe

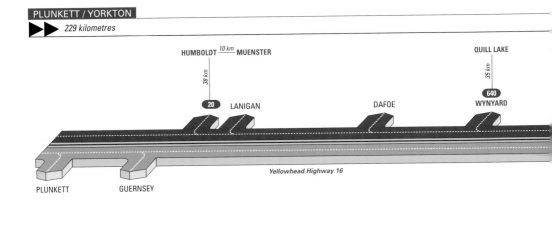

HUMBOLDT _10 km_ MUENSTER   QUILL LAKE

38 km   35 km

20   LANIGAN   DAFOE   **640**
                              WYNYARD

Yellowhead Highway 16

PLUNKETT   GUERNSEY

19 km   3 km   8 km   34 km   24 km   25 k

CENTRAL SASKATCHEWAN

Humboldt

Named for a German scientist, this large town has cultivated a German flavor highlighted by colorful festivals and folk art, half-timbered buildings, and a tourist *willkommen* center. Humboldt is also the "mustard capital of the world" and a major flour exporter. Local art, history, and wildlife exhibits dominate the Humboldt and District Museum and Gallery. Displays of 1885-1970 lifestyles include a railway station, a prairie homestead, an old-style chapel, and a Red River cart.

Muenster

A 10 km drive east of Muenster takes you to this village, where the outstanding attraction is St. Peter's Benedictine Abbey. Visitors can roam the spacious grounds, taking in SS. Peter and Paul Abbey Church, a farm, orchard, cemetery, greenhouse, and printing press. Twin-towered St. Peter's Cathedral across the road is famous for 80 life-size portraits of saints gracing its walls and ceilings. They were painted in 1919 by Count Berthold von Imhoff, the renowned Saskatchewan artist whose murals and canvases enhance churches across North America.

Wynyard

A popular stopping-off point for bird-watchers and hunters, Wynyard, site of major poultry-processing and hatchery plants, includes Chicken Chariot Races in its annual community carnival. Several of the nine local churches have magnificent stained glass

windows and ornate interiors. An 1891 wedding dress and the town's first X-ray machine are among antiques exhibited in the Frank Cameron Museum.

Quill Lake

A bird-watcher's and photographer's paradise, Big, Middle and Little Quill lakes lie between Dafoe and Wynyard just north of Hwy. 16. Information on viewing sites and local history and folklore is available at an interpretive center in the village of Quill Lake, some 35 km north on Rd. 640. Quill Lakes Nature Tours, also based in the village, uses all-terrain vehicles for guided tours. The shallow, saline, waterfowl-teeming lakes are a staging area for thousands of migrating ducks, geese, and sandhill cranes. Rare and endangered birds are among some 34 species of shorebirds inhabiting the surrounding mud-flats and marshes. Middle Quill Lake supports a colony of 400 white pelicans.

Eighty life-size figures of saints in the sanctuary of St. Peter's Cathedral at Muenster are the work of Berthold von Imhoff. Painted in 1919 as a gift to the first abbot of nearby St. Peter's Abbey and College (above), the master artist painted faces of the abbey's monks onto many of his sainted subjects.

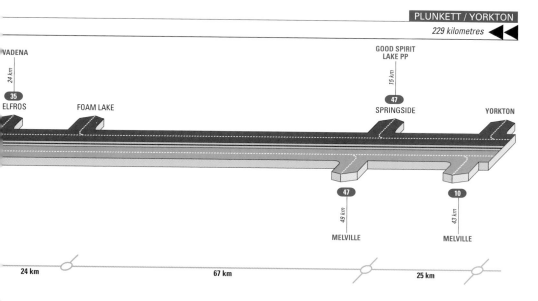

WADENA

24 km

35
ELFROS

FOAM LAKE

GOOD SPIRIT
LAKE PP

15 km

47
SPRINGSIDE

YORKTON

47

49 km

MELVILLE

10

43 km

MELVILLE

24 km   67 km   25 km

Wadena

Scenic lakeshore hiking trails, marshland boardwalks, an observation tower, and interpretive signs guarantee pleasant exploration of the Wadena Wildlife Wetlands, an international shorebird reserve and bird-watching hotspot at the eastern edge of Little Quill Lake. The Wadena and District Museum and Gallery displays its collection in various pioneer settings, such as an original farmstead, a one-room schoolhouse, and a refurbished train station and caboose.

Good Spirit Lake Provincial Park

Shifting dunes, sandy beaches with warm, shallow weed-free water, and a full range of recreational activities from tennis to fishing make this park a popular holiday spot. Stretching more than 3.5 km along the shoreline, the dunes are the habitat for birds such as spotted sandpipers and killdeers.

Melville

The railway is the major employer in this city, named for a railway president when founded in 1907-08, and now a major rail crossroads. Featured attractions in a railway museum in a restored Grand Trunk Pacific station are a CN steam engine and old-style caboose, and a Grand Trunk Pacific flatcar. Artifacts relating to the Lutheran Church in Canada, and facets of Melville's first 25 years, can be seen in a heritage museum at the Luther Academy Building. It features a chapel, some 800 German-language books, a music room, and more than 80 black-and-white photos.

Yorkton

You will pass three-brick-thick Doukhobor homes and a bungaloid-style house (the upper-half story is concealed to make it look like a bungalow) on a self-guided heritage walking tour designed to reflect Yorkton's ethnic diversity. For more background, explore the Western Development Museum, where room-size exhibits—a Ukrainian kitchen, an American parlor, a Swedish bedroom, and so on—tell the story of more than 50 ethnic immigrant groups.

Take time to view the inside dome of St. Mary's Ukrainian Catholic Church, where artist Stephen Meusch reproduced the

brilliant indigo, orange, and dull red hues of Saskatchewan sunsets in his magnificent depiction of the Virgin Mary's coronation.

At Yorkton's Western Development Museum, steam and gas engines hiss and chug to life at such popular events as the Threshermen's Show and Seniors' Festival.

See more of Saskatchewan's pioneer past at Parkland Heritage Centre, 10 km to the southeast.

263

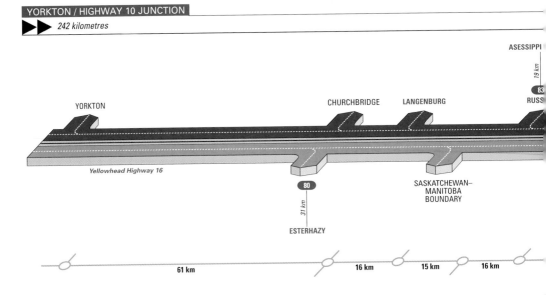

ASESSIPPI

19 km

83

RUSS

YORKTON   CHURCHBRIDGE   LANGENBURG

Yellowhead Highway 16

80

31 km

ESTERHAZY

SASKATCHEWAN–
MANITOBA
BOUNDARY

61 km   16 km   15 km   16 km

**EAST-CENTRAL
SASKATCHEWAN/
WEST-CENTRAL
MANITOBA**

Esterhazy

Billing itself the "Salt of the Earth," Esterhazy straddles huge deposits of potassium-rich potash, which is exported world-wide for plant fertilization. Mining began in the 1950s and you can tour one of two mines now operating. Theme rooms at a community museum include a country store, an old-fashioned doctor's office, and a 1910 living room and kitchen. Esterhazy's multiethnic roots (English, Czech, German, Hungarian, and Swedish) are reflected in the churches scattered throughout the community. The town is named for a Hungarian aristocrat who settled 35 Hungarian families here in 1886. Their story is told at the Kaposvar Historic Site Museum, which features a 1906 stone church, a pioneer home-stead complete with barn, milk house, and smokehouse.

Langenburg

Gopherville, a frontier village and amusement park, is one of this community's chief attractions. Shuttle trains take visitors to craft and Santa Claus stores, a land of miniatures, a 44-passenger bicycle, the "world's highest swing," and an 18-hole miniature golf course. For something more down-to-earth, tour the local Wheat Pool grain elevator, where guides explain how a vertical conveyer belt elevates grain from an unloading area at the bottom to a distribution system at the top, and describe the process of buying and selling grain in bulk.

Russell

As you head into Manitoba, it is evident that you are in a banner land for prime beef and grain. One of Russell's major attractions is Boulton Manor (1894), home of Maj. Charles Arkoll Boulton, who founded the community and organized the Boulton Scouts to help quell the 1885 Northwest Rebellion.

Asessippi Provincial Park

This park sits at the southern tip of Lake of the Prairies, one of the best walleye lakes in Manitoba. Created through 1960s dam building, the 64 km long lake is also stocked with northern pike and perch. Hiking trails let you explore the park's aspen forests and mixed-grass prairie meadows.

Riding Mountain National Park

Perched on a plateau of the Manitoba escarpment, Riding Mountain rises almost 500 m above the prairie landscape. Its blend of northern boreal forest,

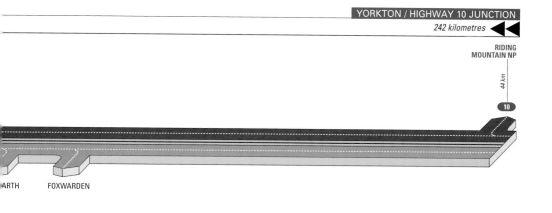

ARTH   FOXWARDEN

19 km   96 km

Asessippi Beach on Lake of the Prairies (top) *has swimming and boat rental facilities. Visitors to Riding Mountain National Park* (lower photo) *will find bicycles, boats, and horses for hire, golf, tennis, picnic sites, and hiking trails alive with bird song and wild creatures.*

wildflower meadow, shallow kettle ponds, and a beaver dam; the Burls and Bittersweet Trail (2.2 km) is named for the tree warts (burls) and climbing vine (bittersweet or "tree strangler") found in this unusual pocket of eastern hardwood forest. From a floating boardwalk and a small viewing blind, you can explore the watery world of the Ominnik Marsh.

Wasagaming, Riding Mountain National Park

This quaint townsite and visitor center at the park's southern entrance was built in the 1930s to resemble a wilderness resort. Today it has a range of hotel, motel, and cottage accommodations, restaurants ranging from fast-food to fine dining, an art gallery, museum, cinema and theater, and facilities for golf, tennis, lawn bowling, and arts and crafts courses. The log-and-stone visitor information center has exhibits on the natural and human history of the area and organizes interpretive programs, such as nature walks, campfires, and evening lectures. Located on the south shore of spring-fed Clear Lake, Wasagaming has a superb beach, excellent fishing, and boat-launching ramps. It is the starting point for Anishinabe Camp and Cultural Tours, which showcase native traditions through powwows and interpretive programs ranging from outdoor survival skills to bead and quill work. On these tours, you can stay overnight in a teepee, participate in traditional daybreak ceremonies, and visit nearby First Nations communities.

western grasslands, and eastern mixed deciduous woods is home to more species of wildlife than any other spot in Manitoba. In addition to a small herd of free-roaming bison in a fenced enclosure near Lake Audy, there are 60 kinds of mammals, more than 260 species of birds (including white pelicans and great gray owls), 500 plant varieties, and 68 kinds of butterfly.

An extensive trail system lets you explore on bike, foot, or horseback. Two self-guiding loop trails are especially popular: the Arrowhead (3.4 km) leads past a

265

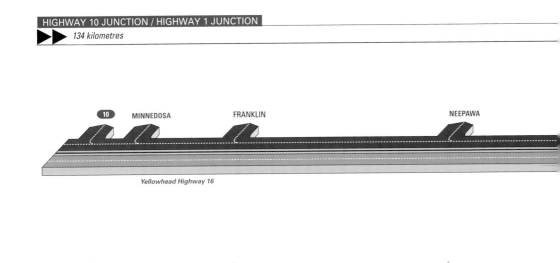

10   MINNEDOSA   FRANKLIN   NEEPAWA

Yellowhead Highway 16

6 km   13 km   28 km   37 k

**WEST-CENTRAL
MANITOBA**

*Thousands of remnants and
reminders of Neepawa's past—
everything from sports paraphernalia and photos of local sporting
heroes to military gear dating to
the Riel Rebellion, and from richly
embroidered Ukrainian costumes
to a turn-of-the-century post office
(with a mannequin postmistress
behind the wicket) and medical hall
(a pharmacy)—fill Beautiful Plains
Museum, which is housed in a
building that also figured prominently in town history, a former
CNR station.*

Minnedosa

Surrounded by grain and livestock farms, this scenic valley
town is a lively tourist center
with an artificial lake and campground, a nine-hole golf course,
restaurants, and a country museum. An hour-long walking tour
takes you to historic sites marking its beginnings as a trading
post, serving fur traders and
homesteaders, to its days as a
bustling railway community.
Along the way, you can follow
sections of the Oxbow Nature
Trail, which winds along elevat-
ed board walkways through
waterfowl-rich marsh. For more
bird-watching, visit Manitoba
Habitat Heritage Corporation's
extensive preserves, which contain some of the richest duck
breeding grounds in the world.

Neepawa

This community (the name is
derived from a Cree term for
"plenty") has time and again
been voted Manitoba's "most
beautiful town." Nestled in rich
agricultural land known as the
"Beautiful Plains," it is a thriving
service center for surrounding
grain and livestock farms.

Homesteading began in the
1870s and the arrival of the railway in 1883 sparked the town's
growth. Several impressive buildings from those years are now
preserved as heritage sites. A
self-guided walking tour leads to
the majestic Knox Presbyterian
Church (1891), a fine example of
Romanesque Revival church
architecture. Beautiful Plains
County Court Building (1884) is
the oldest operating courthouse

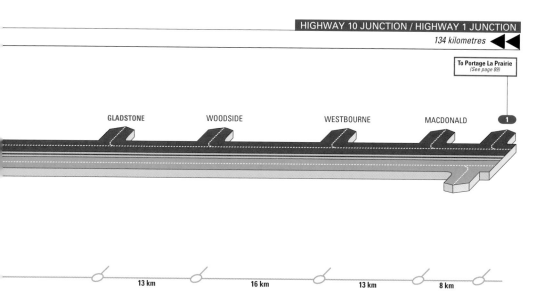

To Portage La Prairie
(See page 89)

GLADSTONE   WOODSIDE   WESTBOURNE   MACDONALD   1

13 km   16 km   13 km   8 km

on the Prairies and the second oldest public building in Manitoba. The one-time CNR station houses the Beautiful Plains Museum, a showcase of Neepawa's pioneer days. Its three stories are brimming with donated artifacts—everything from washtubs and irons to farm and carpentry tools—that reflect pioneer life. Thematic rooms include a chapel with pump organ, wooden pews, and silver sacrament trays, and a turn-of-the-century general store with an old-fashioned glass counter and an assortment of goods, ranging from bolts of cloth to barrels of cheese.

Neepawa inspired the fictional town of Manawaka, the backdrop for *The Stone Angel, A Jest of God, The Diviners,* and other Margaret Laurence novels. No tour of town would be complete without visiting the acclaimed novelist's girlhood home (*see below and photo right*), a mecca for scholars and writers from around the world.

Margaret Laurence Home, Neepawa

Now a provincial heritage site, this imposing brick house was built in 1893 by the author's grandfather. Nine-year-old Margaret Wemyss, as Laurence then was, lived there from 1935 to 1944. It was this house more than any other, she wrote, "I carry with me." It was there that the 14-year-old Margaret resolved to be a writer. Restored as a museum and cultural center, it now houses artifacts and memorabilia ranging from original furniture and honorary degrees (she

received 14) to her eyeglasses and portable, green typewriter. Following her death at Lakefield, Ont., in 1987, she was buried in Neepawa's Riverside Cemetery, not far from the stone angel she immortalized.

Gladstone

At the heart of a mixed farming district, Gladstone is a service center for neighboring communities. Area history is showcased at a museum housed in a former CNR station. Among displays are a pioneer kitchen, dining and sitting rooms, store, and church. Uniformed mannequins and displays of medals and berets bring its Legion Room to life. The town's nine-hole golf course is in scenic William's Park, which stretches along the north bank of Whitemud River. Picnic facilities, a heated pool, and a riverside campground lie adjacent to baseball diamonds and a tennis court.

Apart from memorabilia of one of Canada's most acclaimed writers, the Margaret Laurence Home in Neepawa contains an art gallery, research area, and meeting room, and is a popular spot for book launchings, writers' workshops, and Elderhostel educational programs.

267

CROWSNEST
HIGHWAY

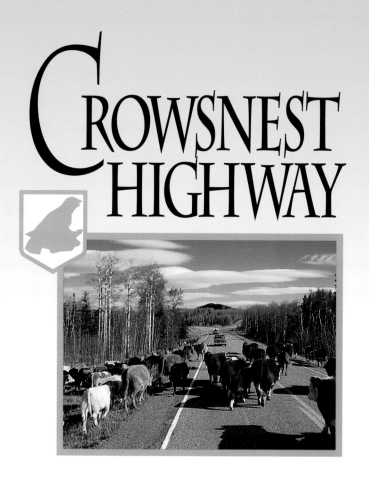

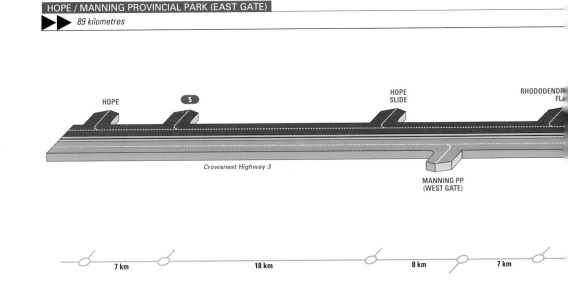

HOPE

5

HOPE SLIDE

RHODODENDR
FL

Crowsnest Highway 3

MANNING PP
(WEST GATE)

7 km   18 km   8 km   7 km

**SOUTHWESTERN
BRITISH
COLUMBIA**

*From July to mid-August the
subalpine meadows in Manning
Provincial Park appear resplendent
in mountain flowers. The 5 km
wide, multihued floral carpet
stretches 24 km from Blackwall
Peak to Three Brothers Mountain.*

Hope

This community is the western
terminus of the Crowsnest Highway (Hwy. 3), which stretches
eastward to Medicine Hat, Alta.,
linking enroute major towns of
the lower B.C. mainland. (For
the detailed entry on Hope, see
page 45.)

Coquihalla Highway
(Hwy. 5)

Beginning just east of Hope, this
four- to six-lane toll highway is a
quick route to Merritt and Kamloops. (For details on both communities, see pages 52-53.)
Although the Coquihalla Highway has no restaurants or gas
stations, it is well maintained and
patrolled. Travelers looking for
scenic viewpoints and a variety
of services will be better off taking the Trans-Canada (Hwy. 1)
through the Fraser Canyon.

Hope Slide Viewpoint

If you pull off the Crowsnest
Highway (Hwy. 3) some 16 km
east of Hope, you will see the
remnants of a devastating 1965
landslide. One January morning,
triggered by a minor earthquake,
the entire side of Johnson Peak,
a 1 km wide swath, hurtled into
the valley at speeds of more than
160 km/h. When the landslide
stopped, four people, the road,
and an adjacent lake lay buried
under 46,000,000 m³ of earth,
rock and snow. It took 21 days to
build a temporary road through
the disaster site. From the lookout, you can see the remaining
half of the mountain.

Manning Provincial Park

From its starting point in Hope,
the Crowsnest Highway
(Hwy. 3) climbs steadily through
the rugged forest-clad Cascade

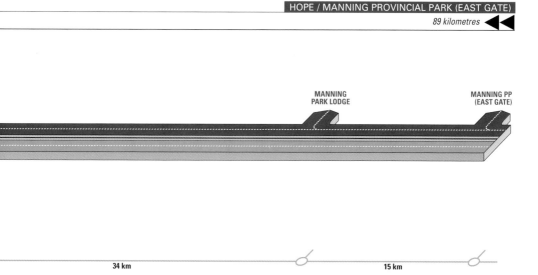

MANNING
PARK LODGE

MANNING PP
(EAST GATE)

34 km   15 km

Mountains to 1,346 m high Allison Pass in Manning Provincial Park. Within the park are wetlands, dryland stands of pine and alpine larch, subalpine meadows, crystal lakes, and two major white water rivers, the Skagit and the Similkameen. Although mule deer, muskrat, and coyote are plentiful, chief among residents are black bears and hoary marmots. Signs throughout the park mark the best spots to see hoary marmots and hear these rodents' piercing whistles.

Rhododendron Flats, Manning Provincial Park

A kilometre-long trail near Manning Provincial Park's west gate leads to Rhododendron Flats, one of the few B.C. sites where the bright red flowers grow wild. Visitors are forbidden to pick the rhododendrons, which reach their peak about mid-June.

Manning Park Lodge, Manning Provincial Park

At the heart of the park, the luxurious, 40-room lodge is the centerpiece of a resort area containing cabins, chalets, The Last Resort (a group complex that can sleep 40 to 50 people), restaurants, lounges, and a country store. It is also a great jumping-off point for several park attractions. From July through September, visitors can follow a paved road north of the lodge to Cascade Lookout, which offers a superb mountain view. From the lookout, a 6 km gravel road leads to Blackwell Peak alpine meadows, where yellow snow lilies, towhead babies and Indian hellebores bloom in abundance during the frost-free season—July and August. The nearby Alpine Naturalist Hut is the starting point for a 1 km long self-guiding

nature trail (the Paintbrush Trail) and the 21 km Heather Trail across the park's flowering mountain meadows.

West of Manning Park Lodge, a horse corral offers hourly, daily, and multiday rides on a network of scenic horse trails. From the corral, a 5 km paved road leads to Lightning Lake, ideal for swimming, canoeing, and fishing. Just off this road, a trail climbs through the wilderness to the top of 2,408 m Frosty Mountain, the highest point in the park.

About 1 km east of the lodge, the park headquarters offers guided walks through valley and alpine meadows. (The self-guiding 500 m Beaver Pond, east of the center, is ideal for bird-watching in May and June.) Summer programs include evening talks, slide shows, and children's games and activities.

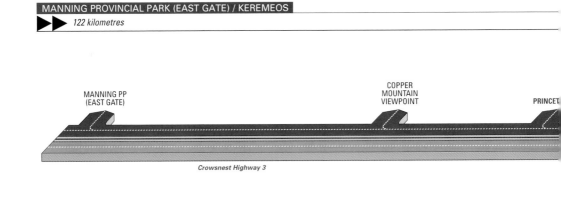

MANNING PP
(EAST GATE)

COPPER
MOUNTAIN
VIEWPOINT

PRINCET

Crowsnest Highway 3

35 km

19 km

SOUTHWESTERN
BRITISH
COLUMBIA

Princeton

Ranching country surrounds this town situated at the junction of the Tulameen and Similkameen rivers. Its location in the foothills of the Cascade Mountains makes it an ideal base for hiking, mountain biking, horseback riding, and other wilderness recreations. In addition to its own secluded beaches, it provides access to 48 lakes, which make for great swimming, boating, and fishing.

A center for gold mining in the late 1800s, it is surrounded by ghost towns and abandoned mines. You can explore old townsites once famous for gold rushes and coal deposits and try your hand at gold panning or rock hounding. Mining memorabilia, as well as pioneer artifacts, cram the Princeton Museum and Archives. On display in the adjacent Coach House is the Welby Stagecoach, the only public transport hereabouts before it was retired in 1909.

Hedley

This charming Similkameen Valley community has witnessed boom and bust since an 1898 gold bonanza at nearby Nickel Plate Mountain. As the valuable ore poured out of Nickel Plate and Mascot mines, a 3 km aerial tramway was built to link both to a processing mill in burgeoning Hedley. (Tramway ruins and a jumble of wooden bunkhouses can still be seen on a 1,200 m cliff overlooking town.) By the early 1900s, there were lively saloons, fashionable stores, five hotels, and a population of some

For more than 50 years mining drove the economy of Hedley, B.C. By the time the mines closed in 1955, the Mascot (right) and Nickel Plate mines had yielded $47 million in gold, silver, and copper.

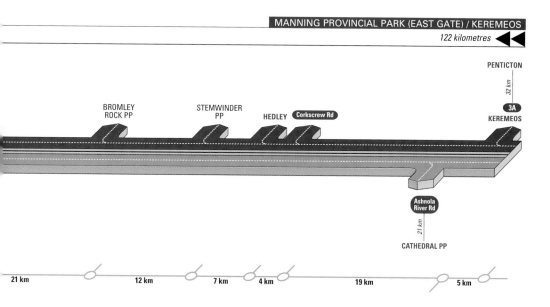

PENTICTON

32 km

3A
KEREMEOS

BROMLEY
ROCK PP

STEMWINDER
PP

HEDLEY

Corkscrew Rd

Ashnola
River Rd

21 km

CATHEDRAL PP

| 21 km | 12 km | 7 km | 4 km | 19 km | 5 km |

5,000—10 times what it is today. Photographs of Hedley's mining and social history, and a delightful garden of drought-resistant plants, are featured at Heritage House Museum. Corkscrew Road east of town leads to Mascot Mine. Only the toughest vehicles can navigate the steep, rugged, 13 km trip. Check locally before setting out.

Cathedral Provincial Park

Ashnola River Road takes you south from the Crowsnest (Hwy. 3) to a parking lot outside this remote, mountainous park. To reach the core area, you can hike one of three trails (they range from 16 to 28 km) to Quiniscoe Lake, or hire an "alpine taxi" from privately owned Cathedral Lakes Resort for the hour-long jeep ride. Either way, you may glimpse mountain goats, California bighorn sheep, and mule deer. Park headquarters and three campgrounds are at Quiniscoe Lake. From there, a 50 km network of hiking trails take in the park's scenic wonders, including unusual rock formations with fanciful names such as Devil's Woodpile, Stone City, and Macabre Tower. Quiniscoe and other park lakes abound with rainbow and cutthroat trout.

Keremeos

Mountains rising to 2,400 m surround this town at the widest section of the Similkameen River valley. Blessed with fertile soil, a mild sunny climate, and an efficient irrigation system, the area's orchards, ranches, and vineyards have British Columbia's longest growing season. With produce ranging from apples and apricots to peaches and plums offered at some 40 outdoor stands, Keremeos dubs itself the "Fruit Stand Capital of Canada."

Police uniforms and pioneer artifacts adorn a former jailhouse and provincial police office restored as the South Similkameen Museum. At The Grist Mill & Garden, original machinery from 1877, reassembled and reconstructed, drives the province's only fully operational water-powered flour mill.

Penticton

This city's name comes from a Salish word for "a place to live forever." With 2,000 hours of sunshine a year, climate is high among nature's favorable attributes. The area's orchards and fruit fields thrive, and bountiful vineyards have nurtured a winemaking industry (see pages 274-275). Nature has a starring role even in man-made attractions, such as a massive sundial known as the Skaha Solar Timepiece, and the solar heated Art Gallery of the South Okanagan. Rubber rafting is popular on the 6 km river channel linking Okanagan and Skaha lakes, both popular recreation sites. At Okanagan Lake Beach, you can tour S.S. *Sicamous*, a stern-wheeler that plied the lake in 1914-35. Displays at the R.N. Atkinson Museum and Archives range from native and pioneer artifacts to military memorabilia and a vast taxidermy collection.

Goodies fresh-baked with the mill's own flour are served in a tearoom at The Grist Mill & Garden in Keremeos, B.C., a living museum of agricultural history. Surrounding the mill are heritage gardens of vegetable and flower varieties cultivated locally more than 100 years ago, heirloom apple orchards, and historic wheatfields.

A Tasting Tour of Okanagan's Winning Wines

CROWSNEST HIGHWAY 18 / PENTICTON

JURGEN GOTHE *hosts the CBC FM radio program* DiscDrive *and writes about his two passions—food and drink—as columnist for the* Vancouver Sun, Vancouver Lifestyles *magazine, and* Air Canada's in-flight magazine, enRoute.

BRITISH COLUMBIANS TAKE A WAYWARD pleasure in navigating tiny, twisty roads through Okanagan's lakeshore vineyard country to find a semisecret cellar door and cart away a case of fine wine.

All wineries in the Okanagan Valley produce at least one outstanding wine. The biggest choice and the best bets yet are Okanagan's white wines, including, just a few years ago, the best Chardonnay in the world. The Mission Hill winery won the Avery's Trophy in 1994 for its Grand Reserve Barrel Select Chardonnay.

German-style white wines—ehrenfelser, kerner, and the like—are also in the forefront, as are French country varieties: Pinot blanc and Alsatian-style Gewurztraminer. Riesling can reach a level of high art in the Okanagan. Auxerrois and chasselas can be exquisite. The long-held opinion that the valley cannot make red wines of quality is fading. Wineries such as the Cedar Creek, the Kettle Valley, the Sumac Ridge, and the Quails' Gate, are busy proving themselves with each new vintage and each new medal won at competitions.

All found, British Columbia's wine industry is just over a century and a half old, starting in 1860 when the first grape vines were planted in the Okanagan south of what is now Kelowna, near Okanagan Mission, by a missionary named Father Pandosy. The wine was for religious use and daily table consumption. In 1932, Calona founded a winery in the valley—the first commercial enterprise for grape processing in the Okanagan.

Today, except for large commercial operations, all Okanagan wineries have their own vineyards. They must grow most of their own grapes to qualify for an estate license. Smaller operations—the farmgate wineries—must grow one hundred percent their grapes in order to sell their product directly to the public at the "farm's gate."

In many Okanagan Valley wineries, the setting is hardly elaborate. There's just a door leading into a dark room full of wine barrels. Tasting rooms tend to be small, cozy, and crowded come the height of summer. Some wineries welcome only the call-ahead visitor who arranges to visit at an appointed time. In many small operations, time spent tasting wines with visitors, pleasant though it may be for both parties, is time away from vital work. If you're a drop-in visitor, focus on the large wineries.

Wineries want visitors to get a good sampling of what is produced, but they also want buyers, so be prepared to taste the wines currently on sale. The best way to taste is according to a theme. Go for favorites. Nothing is worse than a gulp of Riesling here, a splash of merlot there. If you are fond of Pinot Blanc, make a day of it.

> "*Wineries…are busy proving themselves with each new vintage and each new prize won…*"

You'll get a stem glass and a small amount of wine in it. Don't expect a big pour. The idea is to look and taste. Look for color and clarity by holding the glass up to the light. Then, take a sniff. Professional tasters put more emphasis on aroma. Now, swirl the wine to aerate it, then take a sip. Swish the wine around in your mouth to awaken all the taste buds. Now, spit, if you want to, or swallow. Why does a taster spit? To avoid the effects of all that alcohol. If you taste 30 or 40 wines in a morning, you will consume the better part of a bottle before day's end.

You can design your own wine tour of the Okanagan Valley. Just follow the grape cluster on Hwy. 97's roadside signs—an indication that you're on the Okanagan's "wine road." Penticton is a good base to start from. On Canada Day 1997, the British Columbia Wine Country Visitors Center opened at Penticton's Trade and Convention Center. It stocks wines of all three styles: farmgate, estate, and major wineries. The annual Okanagan Wine Festival, held here in early autumn, includes wine tastings, judgings, and wine-food pairing events. It's an industry- and valley-wide event that attracts visitors from across North America.

From Penticton, head north to Summerland, Peachland, Westbank, and Kelowna, all major wine towns. On the outskirts of Westbank, stop in at Quails' Gate and Mission Hill. Kelowna's fledgling Wine Museum, housed in a reconfigured 1917 fruit-packing plant, hosts Sunday afternoon wine tastings and other events. Just south of Kelowna, visit St. Hubertus, a charming family operation; or Cedar Creek, with its award-winning red wines; or Summerhill, the dedicated-to-bubbly winery that ages its products inside a pyramid.

At the southeastern end of Okanagan Lake, Naramata has the biggest concentration of outstanding farmgate wineries in the valley. Lang, Nichol, and Kettle Valley are among the must-stops.

The south Okanagan is home to Hawthorne Mountain, Vincor, Blue Mountain, tiny Stag's Hollow, and the family-operated Wild Goose. Around Oliver and Osoyoos, a few more wineries make a stand: Tinhorn Creek and Gehringer Bros., Hester Creek and the new Inniskillin Okanagan, and the uncompromising Domaine Combret. The sights and tastes on the wine road never end. Best of all, they will be all new, all over again, with next year's vintage.

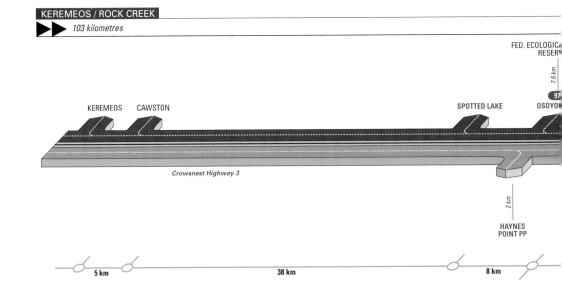

FED. ECOLOGIC
RESERV

7.5 km

97

KEREMEOS   CAWSTON   SPOTTED LAKE   OSOYO

Crowsnest Highway 3

2 km

HAYNES
POINT PP

5 km   38 km   8 km

Spotted Lake

Two lakes are visible on the south side of the highway just west of Osoyoos, and some 43 km east of Keremeos. The one nearest the road, Spotted Lake, contains extraordinary high concentrations of minerals such as magnesium, calcium, and sodium sulfates, and traces of silver and titanium among others. When summer heat reduces the water to shallow mud pools, the crystallized minerals appear as "salt plates." Now on private property, Spotted Lake was once a favorite bathing ground of local Indians who credited it with curative properties. They called it Kliluk (Medicine Lake) because soaking in its mud and waters eased their arthritic aches and battle wounds.

SOUTHWESTERN
BRITISH
COLUMBIA

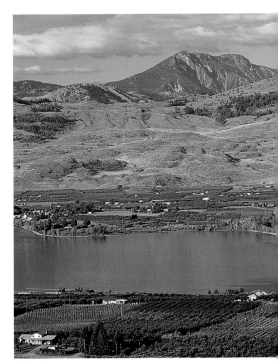

Osoyoos

On a lake of the same name, said to be Canada's warmest fresh-water body of water, Osoyoos claims the country's warmest year-round temperatures. Twenty years ago, the townspeople decided to capitalize on the Mediterranean-like climate by adding white stucco, red tile, and wrought iron to its buildings, and proclaiming the town "the Spanish capital of Canada." You can tour an operational Dutch windmill and a community museum chockablock with native, pioneer, and wartime artifacts, a large butterfly collection, a moonshine still, and an 1891 log school. Once an arid landscape, irrigation has transformed the Osoyoos

Evaporation at Spotted Lake reveals white-rimmed mineral clusters known as "salt plates." This curiosity is caused by high concentrations of 11 minerals and traces of several others.

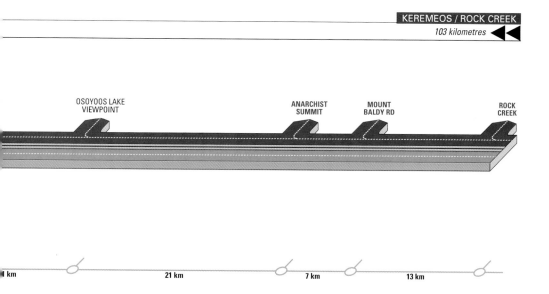

OSOYOOS LAKE VIEWPOINT   ANARCHIST SUMMIT   MOUNT BALDY RD   ROCK CREEK

km   21 km   7 km   13 km

Some people claim that Haynes Point Provincial Park (top photo) is Canada's most popular park. One section consists of a sand spit stretching three-quarters of the way across Osoyoos Lake. Camp Mckinney (lower photo), a ghost town on Mount Baldy Road, is the only reminder that one of British Columbia's richest gold mines operated in the area in 1887-1903.

region into fruit-laden orchards and vineyards. The only remaining dry patch is the Federal Ecological Reserve off Rd. 22, some 7.5 km north of town. This "pocket desert" contains diverse flora and fauna, from antelope bush and prickly pear cactus to pygmy horned toads and burrowing owls.

Haynes Point Provincial Park

This delightful park south of Osoyoos is known for its fine beaches, warm waters, and lakefront campgrounds, some on a sandspit stretching way out into Osoyoos Lake. Boating, fishing (for rainbow trout and bass), and picnicking are all popular pastimes. Haynes Point is home to some exotic wildlife, such as spadefoot toads, burrowing owls, and desert night snakes. Its rich bird life ranges from turkey vultures to Canada's tiniest bird, the calliope hummingbird.

Anarchist Summit

You will exchange a mild valley climate for snowy heights, and navigate some hair-raising switchbacks, as you ascend from 277 m at Osoyoos to 1,233 m at Anarchist Summit. The mountain is said to be named for an early rancher with radical political views. It offers sweeping views of the surrounding region.

Mount Baldy Road

This road takes you north of the highway to the Camp Mckinney ghost town, site of one of British Columbia's richest pioneer

mines, and to the Mount Baldy ski area. You turn onto Mount Baldy Road at Rock Creek Canyon Bridge (between Bridesville and Rock Creek) for an 11.5 km trip to Camp Mckinney. There, between 1887 and 1903, mines yielded 80,000 ounces of gold, and prospectors still scour the area in search of the mother lode. Mount Baldy ski area is 7 km beyond Camp Mckinney.

This general area, known locally as the Gold Canyon Highlands, has numerous bed-and-breakfast establishments and a host of tourist attractions. Canyon Creek Ranch, south of the highway at Canyon Bridge, offers canyon tours on which you follow a stretch of the Dewdney Trail, a road built in the 1860s to connect the goldfields to the B.C. coast. In July, the ranch also hosts an annual cowboy campfire, complete with guest speakers, cowboy poetry, and western music.

Rock Creek

This Kettle River hamlet lies between the fertile Okanagan–Similkameen region and the rocky Kootenay peaks. Gold, discovered here in 1857, drew some 5,000 hopefuls, but local copper mines proved more profitable in the end. The boom times are remembered at the 1893 Rock Creek Hotel, where guests eat in the Gold Pan Restaurant. Rock Creek's community fall fair draws crowds from across the lower B.C. mainland for livestock judging, logging sports, carnival rides, and other events.

277

ROCK   MIDWAY   BOUNDARY   GREENWOOD   GRA
CREEK   CREEK PP   FOR

Crowsnest Highway 3

| 19 km | 8.5 km | 7.5 km | 40 km | 21 k |

**SOUTH-CENTRAL
BRITISH
COLUMBIA**

Midway

This small sawmilling town was the midpoint of the Dewdney Trail, a 1.2 m wide path blazed between Hope and the Kootenay goldfields in 1865. The restored turn-of-the-century Kettle Valley Railway Station is now a museum honoring the builders of the Kettle Valley Railway (KVR). An engineering marvel in use from 1916 to 1959, the KVR spanned 18 trestle bridges to link southern B.C. towns from Vancouver to the West Kootenays. Adjoining the station, the Kettle River Museum tells the history of local miners and cattle ranchers, through exhibits from the 1890s, such as a schoolhouse, mining recording office and trapper and prospector's cabin.

Greenwood

This community of some 900 souls bills itself "The Smallest City in Canada." Incorporated in 1897, at the height of a mining boom, it soon had 3,000 residents, 16 hotels, 15 general stores, and three banks. When mining collapsed after World War I, Greenwood became a virtual ghost town, only to be revived in World War II as an internment camp for Japanese

Canadians. Forestry and tourism drive Greenwood's economy today, but mementos of its various pasts remain. A 40 m smelter stack in Lotzkar Memorial Park recalls its mining boom years, as do several restored heritage buildings. Included are the turn-of-the-century post office—with a clock that still chimes the hours—and the grand 1902 courthouse (now city hall), with its second-story stained glass skylights and windows depicting Canada's first seven provinces. Greenwood Museum contains old-time mining and logging equipment, and facts about the tragic incarceration here of 1,200 Canadians of Japanese ancestry.

Grand Forks

At the junction of the Granby and Kettle rivers, this valley town enjoyed a copper mining boom in the 1890s. Many fine Victorian

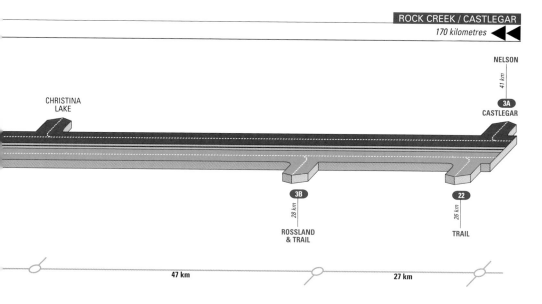

ROCK CREEK / CASTLEGAR
170 kilometres ◄◄

NELSON
41 km

CHRISTINA
LAKE

3A
CASTLEGAR

3B
28 km

ROSSLAND
& TRAIL

22
26 km

TRAIL

47 km

27 km

Nelson prides itself on a streetcar named "Desire" (below) and an imposing City Hall (left), Greenwood on its restoration of buildings such as the lovely turn-of-the-century Greenwood Inn (bottom left).

homes from that era have been restored. Doukhobors—a Russian religious sect—established communal farms here in the early 1900s. A communal farmhouse can be seen at Mountainview Doukhobor Museum. Doukhobor relics also figure among 10,000 artifacts in the Boundary Museum. North of town, a scenic 17 km road leads to old mining camps and Granby Valley towns.

Rossland

Gold mining began here in the 1890s and in 1900-1916 Rossland produced 50 percent of British Columbia's gold. Mining artifacts and mineral samples are displayed at the Rossland Gold Mine and Museum Complex, and visitors can tour Le Roi Mine, the only hard-rock gold mine in Canada open to the public. The B.C. Firefighters Museum contains old-time fire fighting apparatus. Rossland also offers first-class skiing on nearby Red Mountain. Olympic skiing champion Nancy Greene (1968) was raised here and Rossland Museum exhibits her many trophies.

Castlegar

The Columbia and Kootenay rivers meet in Castlegar, which also marks the junction of highways 3, 3A, and 22. A perfect base for mountain hiking and biking, the city provides access to the fish-rich, 400 km Arrow Lakes Waterway, that links Revelstoke to Grand Coulee Dam in Washington State. Doukhobor Village Museum has a reconstructed Doukhobor village con-

taining communal homes, sauna, and a smithy. The tomb of Peter Verigin (1859-1924), an early Doukhobor leader, is nearby. A suspension bridge gives access to Zuckerberg Island Heritage Park, site of Kootenai Indian burial pits and a restored onion-domed chapel. The chapel was built by a teacher who is buried here and for whom the park is named.

Nelson

This community boasts more than 350 heritage buildings—one of the largest such concentrations in Canada. Walking and driving tours pass the Victorian style Courthouse and City Hall (*see above*), the Art Deco Capitol Theatre, and other architectural treasures. Nelson Museum provides a glimpse into the city's past. The Chamber of Mines Museum recalls the Silver King and other mines that spurred Nelson's growth in the 1890s.

Trail

A 120 m smokestack near this "Silver City of the Kootenays" marks the site of the world's largest zinc, lead, and silver smelting and refining complex. Retired employees conduct free guided tours. A stroll through town reveals many elegant turn-of-the-century homes. Colorful dwellings and lush gardens and vineyards of Italian immigrants grace some steep hillside streets. Exhibits at the Sports Hall of Memories and the City Museum honor local heroes such as Olympic skiing gold medalist Kerrin Lee-Gartner (1992).

279

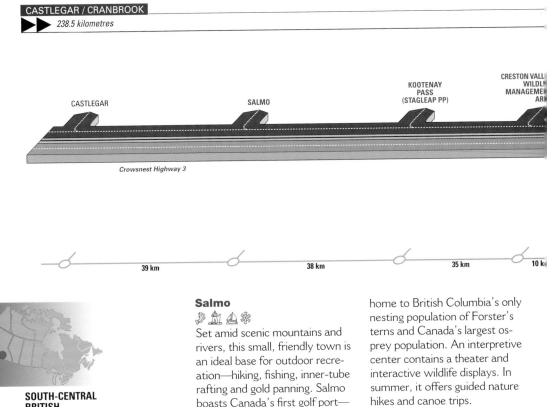

CASTLEGAR SALMO KOOTENAY PASS (STAGLEAP PP) CRESTON VALL WILDL MANAGEMEI AR

Crowsnest Highway 3

39 km   38 km   35 km   10 k

SOUTH-CENTRAL BRITISH COLUMBIA

Residents of Salmo, B.C., claim this telephone booth outside a local motel is world's oldest. Seeing as it is carved into a 465-year-old tree trunk, their claim may be hard to beat.

Salmo

Set amid scenic mountains and rivers, this small, friendly town is an ideal base for outdoor recreation—hiking, fishing, inner-tube rafting and gold panning. Salmo boasts Canada's first golf port—a combined airstrip and nine-hole golf course—and the world's oldest telephone booth, carved into a tree trunk. Other attractions include hand-cut stone wall murals, created by students from the local school of masonry.

Kootenay Pass

On its way through Kootenay Pass, this thrilling stretch of Hwy. 3 (called "The Skyway" or sometimes "Mile High Pass") becomes Canada's highest paved road. It is at its highest (1,774 m) at Stagleap Provincial Park. At Summit Creek Campground (east of the park, beside the wildlife centre described below), you can cross Summit Creek on a swinging footbridge and take a short hike on the 1860s Dewdney Trail.

Creston Valley Wildlife Management Area

Through this lush and lovely valley between the Selkirk and Purcell mountains, the Kootenay River flows up from the United States into Kootenay Lake. A wetland conservation area occupies up to one-quarter of the valley. A major stopover for migrating waterfowl, the preserve is a refuge for more than 250 species of birds ranging from tundra swans to bald eagles. It is home to British Columbia's only nesting population of Forster's terns and Canada's largest osprey population. An interpretive center contains a theater and interactive wildlife displays. In summer, it offers guided nature hikes and canoe trips.

Creston

Creston overlooks a valley of orchards, dairy farms, and alfalfa fields. The nearby mountains offer many recreation opportunities—canoeing, fishing, horseback riding, and hand gliding. The sprawling, stone Creston and District Museum was constructed over 15 years by a local stonemason. Within "talking mannequins" sing and tell about local history. One museum curiosity is a sturgeon-nosed Kutenai canoe, with bow and stern pointing downward.

Yahk

This logging and sawmilling community is said to be named for a Kutenai Indian word for "bend in the river." It lies in British Columbia's only time-change-free area: when the rest of the province is observing daylight saving time, communities along Hwy. 3 from Creston to Yahk stay on Mountain Standard Time.

In the early 1900s, Yahk was a major railway depot operating 18 lumber camps and a mill that produced railway ties. Although prosperity and population declined during the 1930s, remnants of past glory can be seen in the old hotels on the main street.

CRESTON   YAHK   MOYIE

Crowsnest Highway 3/95

95

CRANBROOK

44.5 km   4 km   33 km   35 km

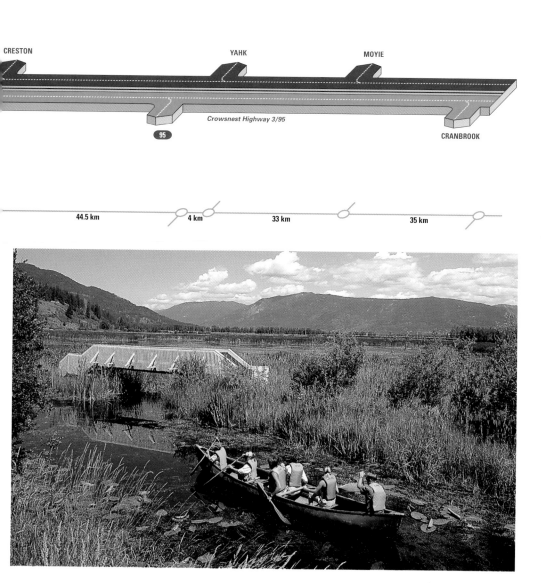

At Creston Valley Wildlife Management Area, visitors learn about the area's bird, mammal, and plant species on naturalist-led hikes and canoe trips through valley marshes.

Inlaid black walnut and Honduran mahogany paneling create a luxurious background in restored dining cars at the Canadian Museum of Rail Travel in Cranbrook.

Moyie

This hillside village sprang up in 1893 after a Kutenai Indian named Pierre discovered high-grade galena ore near Moyie Lake. He showed the site to an oblate missionary, Father Coccola, and a miner, James Cronin, and all three staked claims. Pierre and Father Coccola later sold their claims to Cronin, who started St. Eugene Mine, one of B.C.'s richest lead-silver mines. With his share, Father Coccola built St. Peter's Church, recently restored, and the St. Eugene Mission (see page 282).

Cranbrook

Cranbrook lies at the western edge of the Rocky Mountain Trench, a broad valley framed by the Rocky and Purcell mountain ranges. Creatures of the mountains are displayed life-size in natural settings in Cranbrook Wildlife Museum.

The city's role as a divisional railway point is highlighted at the Canadian Museum of Rail Travel. Among elaborately restored exhibits are nine original cars from the CPR Trans-Canada Ltd. Introduced in 1929 on the Vancouver-Montreal run, this train functioned as a luxury hotel-on-wheels. Dining, sleeping, and solarium lounge cars feature exquisite wood paneling, brass light fixtures, and plush and leather upholstery. Also on view is the largest public collection of CPR china, silver and glassware. A baggage car converted into an exhibition gallery displays an operating model railway.

281

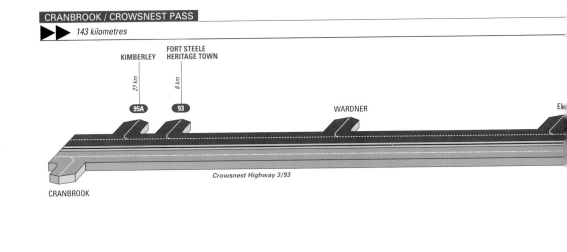

KIMBERLEY
FORT STEELE
HERITAGE TOWN

27 km   8 km

95A   93

WARDNER   E▸

Crowsnest Highway 3/93

CRANBROOK

4 km   6 km   23.5 km   30 km

SOUTHEASTERN BRITISH COLUMBIA

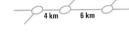

St. Eugene Mission

On the mission grounds, just off Hwy. 95A, on St. Mary's Indian Reserve near Kimberley, an 1897 restored church with stained glass windows, scalloped louvers, and blind windows is regarded as B.C.'s finest Gothic-style mission church. It was built by an Oblate priest when he sold his claim in one of B.C.'s richest lead-silver mines. One of Western Canada's largest hotel chains is transforming the mission's residential industrial school (1912-70)—once the largest building in interior British Columbia—into a 124-room luxury resort. Scheduled to open in spring '98, it will have an aquatic center, 18-hole championship golf course, casino, and Native interpretive center.

Kimberley

Canada's highest city sits some 1,120 m above sea level on the slopes of the Sullivan and North Star mountains. The old Sullivan mine—the world's largest producer of silver, lead, and zinc—has long been the source of Kimberley's wealth. More recently, it has become a major outdoor recreation center. Kimberley Ski and Summer Resort offers world-class skiing, go-carts, bumper boats, mountain-bike rentals, and an exhilarating water-slide. Summer chair lifts provide superb views of the surrounding mountains, meadows, and valley.

Gingerbread facades and brightly painted shutters have helped make Kimberley the "Bavarian City of the Rockies." In the platzl, or main square, you can explore shops and cafes, enjoy band concerts, maybe even shake hands with Happy Hans, the jovial Julyfest mascot and real-life representation of Hans (*left*) who occupies the world's largest operating cuckoo clock. Above the public library, Kimberley Heritage Museum features hockey and skiing items, heritage furniture, and mining exhibits. A forested footpath leads from the platzl to beautifully landscaped Cominco Gardens.

For a look at local mining operations, hop aboard Bavarian City Mining Railway's mine train. In open cars, visitors make a 2.5 km ride to the Sullivan mine. Highlights enroute are a 61 m long timber trestle, a haunted schoolhouse, and viewpoints of the city and the surrounding mountains.

Fort Steele Heritage Town

At the junction of the Kootenay and St. Mary's rivers, this community, originally called Galbraith's Ferry, was renamed for Sam Steele of the North West Mounted Police. Settler-Native disputes were rampant in 1887, when a 75-man force led by Steele built a fort and barracks here, quickly defusing tensions in the region.

When silver-lead ore was discovered nearby in 1892, miners flocked to the site by stagecoach and riverboat. The community continued to prosper until 1898, when it was bypassed by the

Boutiques and outdoor cafes serving strudels and schnitzels line Kimberley's Platzl, a bricked pedestrian mall at the heart of British Columbia's highest city. A yodeling, life-size Happy Hans (top) emerges hourly atop a giant cuckoo clock.

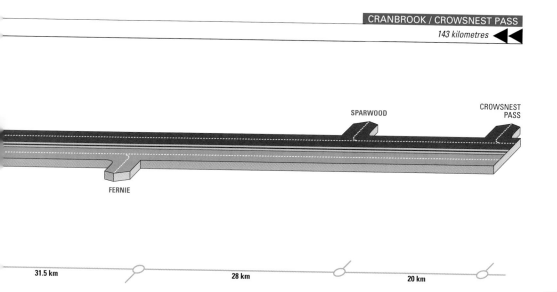

CROWSNEST PASS

SPARWOOD

FERNIE

31.5 km   28 km   20 km

CPR. All but abandoned in 1961, it was revived as a "living history" town. Today it boasts more than 60 restored or reconstructed buildings—hotels, theaters, churches, smithy, jail, dentist's office, and other structures. Staff in 1890s costumes perform street dramas, and demonstrate arts such as wheel making, horse-shoeing, baking, and quilting. You can sample old-fashioned sweets at Mrs. Sprague's Confectionery, buy bread fresh from the City Bakery's wood-fired brick oven, shop at Kershaw's General Store, and enjoy music-hall fare at the Wild Horse Theatre. The foot-weary can explore by horse-drawn wagon, steam train, or stagecoach.

Fernie

This scenic Elk Valley coal town is known for a legendary curse put on prospector William Fernie in the 1890s for jilting an Indian maiden. Fires, floods and famine followed until 1964 when a chieftain lifted the curse in a peace-pipe ceremony. Even so, many claim the maiden's shadow can still be seen riding across nearby Mount Hosmer at sundown.

Fernie's distinctive brick-and-stone heritage buildings include a château-style courthouse built after a 1908 fire leveled the town. One of the few surviving structures was a 1905 Roman Catholic Church rectory that now houses the Fernie and District Historical Museum.

Sparwood

Using the world's largest mining equipment, Westar mining complex produces 5 million tonnes of coal here annually. The mining operation—the largest strip mine in Canada— is open for public tours. Downtown murals tell the region's coal-mining story.

A vast population of elk, as well as deer and bighorn sheep, inhabit the surrounding valley. Hikers and mountain bikers frequently spot wildlife along forestry trails and powerline roads. Elk River and its tributaries are ideal for white water rafting, and offer some of the best cutthroat and rainbow trout fishing in British Columbia.

For present-day visitors, Fort Steele shows how teams of Clydesdale horses arrived in the 1890s with wagonloads of supplies. At that time, major coal, silver, and lead discoveries had produced a thriving center of trade and transportation. People and supplies came and went regularly by stage and riverboat.

Hiking Through Meadows at Alpine Heights

CROWSNEST HIGHWAY / KIMBERLEY

VIVIEN BOWERS *is also the author of "Artillery Fire Keeps Rogers Pass Traffic on the Move" (pp. 60-61).*

MOST TRAVELERS VIEW British Columbia's awesome mountains from below. But let me take you up a thousand metres or so to the alpine world, and you'll be truly impressed. As far as the eye can see, in every direction, is a sea of mountains.

The setting is Kimberley, at 1,097 m elevation on the eastern slopes of the Purcell Mountains. The uplifting, fracturing, and erosion that formed this chain of mountains also created favorable conditions for mineralization, particularly silver-lead-zinc, which explains Kimberley's mining roots. The Purcells form the western flank of a wide, U-shaped valley known as the Rocky Mountain Trench. Looking across the Trench, you see the Rocky Mountains forming the eastern wall.

From about mid-July to mid-August, the alpine meadows here explode into life and glorious color. The plants have only a few short weeks of alpine summer during which they must flower, seed, and store food for the future. In addition to the short growing season, plants must cope with cold, drying winds. You'll have to get down on your knees for a good look at their survival tricks. Many of the plants lie low to the ground, out of the wind, and their stems or leaves are coated with wooly hairs to reduce evaporation and protect against frost.

In the higher elevation, where water is scarce, some plants store water in their leathery, succulent leaves. The plants struggle each year to grow a few millimetres and to set a few seeds. Some years they don't make any headway at all. The springy heather plants you are kneeling on may be a hundred years old. Damaged vegetation takes years to recover, so walk softly and try to stay on established paths.

The first wave of flowers brings perennials that start blooming before the last patches of snow have melted. The energy stored in their bulbs and tuberous roots gives them a head start (as well as providing nutritious munching for grizzly bears)

Yellow glacier lilies, avalanche lilies, spring beauty, and western anemone are the first blooms to appear. The second wave of flowers provides a greater array of species and color—red Indian paintbrush, blue lupines, yellow arnica, avens and ragwort, white valerian, purple daisies and asters.

The western anemone gives an example of how these plants survive in such difficult conditions. The cream-colored flowers lie low to the ground, cup-shaped to trap the heat. But later in summer, their stems shoot up 20 to 30 cm and they produce a distinctive mop head that sways above the height of the surrounding blooms. Exposed to the wind, the long-tasseled anemone seeds are blown far afield.

Many of these meadows are in the subalpine zone, where they share the landscape with coniferous trees. True "alpine" refers to the area above tree line, where there's not enough frost-free time for a tree to harden the new summer growth before winter returns. In winter, winds blast off the protective snow coating and draw water out of exposed needles. The trees, with their roots still frozen in the rocky soil, can't replace this water. But you'll see that some trees have adapted to alpine conditions by growing in stunted mats close to the ground, called krummholz. Incredibly gnarled and wind-blasted, this krummholz survives the winter under an insulating blanket of snow.

Ready to go and see all this for yourself? One of the more accessible meadow areas nearby is at Lakit Lookout, northeast of Fort Steele. The lookout is an old forest fire watchtower built on an alpine ridge. The trail from the parking area is steep, but well maintained and only 2 km long. To reach it, leave Hwy. 93 north of Fort Steele and turn east on the Fort Steele/Wardner Road. Turn left onto Wildhorse Road, then turn left again onto the road to the lookout.

Visitors able to tackle longer, more difficult hikes will enjoy the Forest Service trails in Top of the World Provincial Park, northeast of Kimberley. Hiking in St. Mary Alpine Provincial Park, northwest of Kimberley, is for experienced backpackers and route finders only, as there are no marked trails.

On hikes, keep your eyes and ears open for other forms of alpine life. Around rocky talus slopes, listen for the high-pitched whistle of the little pika, a short-eared relative of the rabbit family. Pikas gather grasses and spread them on the rocks to dry before carrying them underground to store for the winter. Hoary marmots, the size of beavers, can be seen trundling across the meadows and disappearing behind rocks.

You may catch a glimpse of a hummingbird as it hones in on the bright red and orange leaves of the Indian paintbrush. The long, tubular flowers that hide at the leaves' base are just the right shape for the hummingbird's bill. Later in the summer, the Clark's nutcracker—a cousin of the jay—will be ripping open white-bark pine cones, carrying seeds to store in his caches for the winter ahead, and unknowingly helping the pine tree disperse its seeds.

The East Kootenays are also famous for big game, so watch for mountain goats, bighorn sheep, migrating elk or deer, and bears. You may even see where grizzlies have been digging up the surface vegetation with long claws to expose the roots of glacier lily or spring beauty.

> "The springy heather plants you are kneeling on may be a hundred years old."

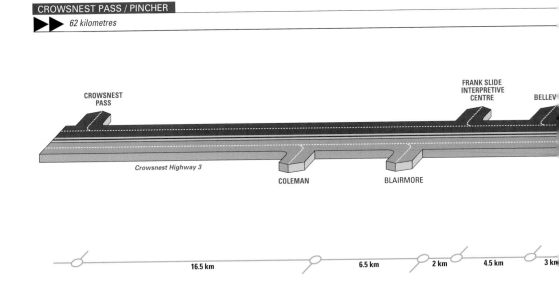

CROWSNEST PASS

FRANK SLIDE INTERPRETIVE CENTRE

BELLEV

Crowsnest Highway 3

COLEMAN

BLAIRMORE

16.5 km   6.5 km   2 km   4.5 km   3 km

SOUTHWESTERN ALBERTA

In Waterton Lakes' townsite, the seven-storied, gabled Prince of Wales Hotel (right), built to withstand the fiercest gales, overlooks a chain of lakes stretching to the horizon. Several townsite businesses offer wide-ranging, first-class tourist services from guided cruises and excursions to 18-hole golfing, to convention and conference facilities.

Riding trails around spectacularly beautiful Crowsnest Pass—one of the few Alberta Rocky Mountain communities where you can own land—cater to all ages and skill levels. Alpine hiking, trout fishing, and high-country snowmobiling are also popular in the area.

Crowsnest Pass

The Crowsnest Highway (Hwy. 3) takes its name from this 1,357 m Rocky Mountain pass between southern B.C. and Alberta. For centuries, Kutenai Indians from what is now British Columbia made their way across the pass to buffalo-hunting grounds in the Alberta foothills.

After the Canadian Pacific Railway arrived in this region in 1898, a string of five mining communities—Coleman, Blairmore, Frank, Hillcrest, and Bellevue—sprang up to supply coal for steam trains. The five amalgamated in 1979 as the Municipality of Crowsnest Pass.

Coleman

Mining apparel and equipment, a wedding-dress collection, and musical, military, and sports displays in the Crowsnest Museum depict local history from 1899 to 1950. Other exhibits include a wildlife diorama and models of mine rescues and Coleman's Main Street (ca. 1920).

Frank Slide Interpretive Centre

A 1.5 km trail here winds through 3 km² of debris, the remains of a terrible April morning in 1903, when 82 million tonnes of Turtle Mountain limestone crashed down on the sleeping town of Frank. Within two minutes, part of the town was buried and 70 townspeople were dead. Photographs, artifacts, and a multimedia presentation at the interpretive center describe the massive landslide, as well as the history of the Crowsnest Pass.

Bellevue

You can don a hard hat and a miner's lamp for a tour of a restored underground mine. The West Canadian Collieries operated here from 1903 to 1961, when Canada's locomotives switched to diesel fuel. More than 300 m of original mine tunnel have been retimbered and secured. Guides demonstrate mining techniques and describe the miner's way of life.

Leitch Collieries

Now a provincial historic site, Leitch Collieries, the only fully Canadian owned mine in the Crowsnest Pass, operated here from 1907 to 1915. The roofless stone ruins of its surface building are open to the public. Interpretive trails pass the remains of the mine manager's residence, powerhouse, washery and coke ovens. Displays, "listening posts," and guided tours explain the early mining and coal extraction process known as coking.

Pincher Creek

Nestled between the Rocky Mountains and the Prairies, this community, the largest in the southern Alberta foothills, is known for its thermal drafts. Not surprisingly it is a favorite venue of wind-powered sports enthusiasts—soarers, kite flyers, windsurfers, and hang gliders. Canada's largest wind-power project also operates here, converting Chinook winds into electricity. Visitors can tour commercial wind farms.

Area residents' saddles, tools, photo albums, and records are

LEITCH
COLLIERIES

PINCHER

LUNDBRECK FALLS
REC AREA

16
5 km

PINCHER CREEK

46 km

WATERTON LAKES NP

10.5 km   19 km

among 7,000 items at the Pincher Creek and District Museum & Kootenai Brown Historical Park. Its 12 historic buildings include the log cabin of trader John George "Kootenai" Brown, first superintendent of Waterton Lakes National Park.

Other popular local attractions include Heritage Acres Museum's antique farm implements and the Lebel Mansion (1910), formerly a hospital, now an art gallery and community center.

Waterton Lakes National Park

In 1932, this stunningly beautiful park joined up with Montana's adjacent Glacier National Park to become the world's first international peace park. A U.N.-designated world heritage biosphere site, Waterton embraces lofty mountain ranges, rolling grasslands, sculpted glacial valleys, and a chain of lakes. More than 800 wildflower species are found

there. Prairie antelope, coyote, mountain goat, bighorn sheep, black and grizzly bear are plentiful. Waterton Valley is a migratory waterfowl route. Scenic drives, backcountry hikes and horseback rides, canoeing, and board sailing are just a few of the recreational possibilities. Popular outings are the international boat cruise on Upper Waterton Lake and the 15 km Red Rock Parkway drive through Blakiston Valley to striking Red Rock Canyon.

BROCKET

Crowsnest Highway 3

PINCHER

14 km

**SOUTHWESTERN
ALBERTA**

Head-Smashed-In
Buffalo Jump

During more than 6,000 years of buffalo hunts, Plains Indians killed their quarry by driving them over cliffs at hundreds of jump sites across the Prairies. This national historic site and a UNESCO World Heritage Site, one of the oldest, largest, and best preserved jumps, is west of Route 2; the turnoff is about 7 km north of the Crowsnest Highway. According to legend, the name dates from a kill during which a hunter's skull was crushed.

Head-Smashed-In re-creates the gathering basin, where hunters herded the bison; drive lanes, marked by stone cairns, along which the bison were driven; and the kill site, the high cliff over which the stampeding animals plunged. Skeletal remains and stone tools lie almost 10 m deep at the base of the cliff. Butchering and processing of the carcasses took place at an adjoining campsite.

A five-level interpretive center, built into the cliff side, documents the buffalo hunting culture and presents a reenactment of the hunt. Exhibits describe the prairie ecology, the lifestyle of the Plains Indians, the tactics of the jump, and how traditional hunting methods declined.

Claresholm

Once a NATO training center, Claresholm continues to be a hub of ultralight aircraft activity, and regularly hosts national and international soaring and parachuting championships. In an area renowned for horse breeding and raising high-quality cattle, Claresholm serves as a base for hiking and fishing in the nearby Porcupine Hills. Horse shows, indoor rodeos, and other equestrian events occur weekly at the local Agriplex. The National Appaloosa Horse Club of Canada Museum displays photos and prints of this famous spotted horse breed, along with saddles, clothing, and weapons of riders of yesteryear. Claresholm's first

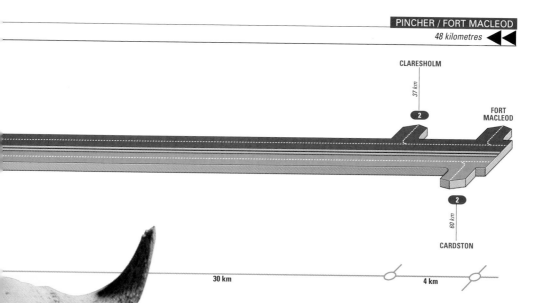

CLARESHOLM
37 km

2

FORT MACLEOD

2

60 km

CARDSTON

30 km   4 km

A buffalo skull, central to many Plains Indians' ceremonies, overlooks Head-Smashed-In Buffalo Jump, where bison were herded over a precipice to their deaths. The kill yielded not only food, but clothing and sleeping robes (from hides), thread and bow backing (from sinew), tools and utensils (from bone and horn), and transport (ribs made fine sled runners).

schoolhouse (1902) and a pioneer log cabin (1903) stand on the grounds of the sandstone Claresholm Museum. Through a a fascinating collection, housed in a former CPR station, the museum recaptures diverse lifestyles of farmers, ranchers, Indians, and Mounties in the early 1900s.

Fort Macleod

This agricultural community was born in 1874, when the North West Mounted Police (NWMP) set up a fort on a nearby island in the Oldman River. A replica of the fort, complete with wooden palisade and guard tower, now lies at the edge of town. The Fort Museum contains original and reconstructed buildings that include a chapel, dispensary, blacksmith shop, and horse stables. Displays range from NWMP weapons and uniforms to a large Indian beadwork collection. In summer, students on horseback, dressed in old NWMP uniforms, perform a musical ride four times daily.

The downtown core has been designated a provincial historic district. Among more than 30 heritage buildings are brick and sandstone structures from the early 1900s. Especially interesting is the restored Empress

Theatre (1912), Alberta's oldest operating theater. Once the site of vaudeville roadhouse and silent movie presentations, it now hosts first-run movies, and community and professional theater productions.

Cardston

A farming and ranching community, Cardston is the site of Canada's first Mormon settlement. Charles Ora Card led 10 Utah families here in 1887. His log cabin, now a provincial historic site, is open to the public. The imposing white-granite Alberta Temple—Canada's only Mormon temple—is the town's outstanding landmark. Visitors can tour the grounds and visit the information center, but the temple itself is not open to visitors. Cardston's sandstone Court House Museum (1907), a provincial historic site, retains the original judge's bench, witness stand, and jail cells.

One of North America's largest and finest collections of horse-drawn vehicles can be seen at the Remington–Alberta Carriage Centre. With more than 200 vehicles on hand, the center alternately showcases selections from its royal coaches, elegant velvet-lined carriages, winter sleighs, and fire engines. Visitors can ride in a carriage, see horses being groomed and harnessed in stables and tack rooms, and visit the restoration shops, where craftsmen are reconstructing carriages. Interactive displays and videos also help to whisk you back to the horse-and-buggy era.

289

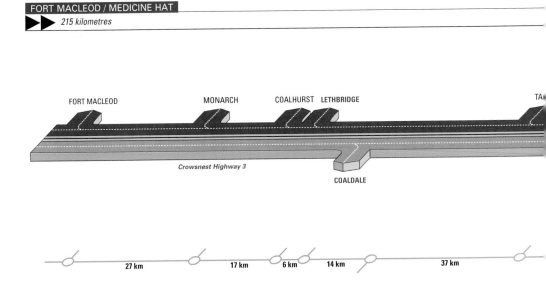

FORT MACLEOD   MONARCH   COALHURST LETHBRIDGE   TA

Crowsnest Highway 3   COALDALE

27 km   17 km   6 km   14 km   37 km

**SOUTHERN
ALBERTA**

Lethbridge

Alberta's third largest city serves as the commercial and service center for an area whose economy is based on livestock, grain, sugar beets, gas, and oil. Set beside the Oldman River, it relies on irrigation to counterbalance its semiarid climate and nourish 70 parks and green areas that provide 60 km of walking, jogging, and biking trails. Henderson Lake is popular for fishing and canoeing. The surrounding park has the Nikka Yuko Japanese Garden (*see below*), a golf course, campground, tennis courts, bowling greens, a swimming pool, and a rose garden. High Level Bridge, a prominent city landmark, is one of the world's highest (96 m) and longest (more than 1.6 km) steel viaduct railway bridges. Visitors may tour the architecturally pleasing University of Lethbridge, designed by Vancouver architect Arthur Erickson. The university's Performing Arts Centre features top performing artists, and its art gallery is open year-round.

Indian Battle Park, Lethbridge

In this park, in 1870, Cree and Blackfoot warriors fought the last intertribal battle in North America. At the park's Fort Whoop-Up Interpretive Centre, a replica of the most notorious whisky post of the late 1800s is among exhibits describing how American traders gave Canada's Native peoples liquor and rifles in return for furs and buffalo robes. Because forts like Whoop-Up abused Indians and threatened

the new Confederation's sovereignty—the forts operated under American flags—the North West Mounted Police was created in 1874.

The park's Coal Banks Interpretive Site traces Lethbridge's origins as a coal-mining center.

Also popular is the Lethbridge Nature Reserve. Guided nature tours, seasonal hands-on displays, and interpretive programs at its Helen Schuler Coulee Centre introduce visitors to Oldman River valley wildlife, plants, and landforms. Visitors may also follow self-guided trails through arid coulees and lush floodplains.

Sir Alexander Galt Museum, Lethbridge

More than 100 years of local history are featured in this museum dedicated to a man who financed one of the first local mining operations. Housed in a former hospital, its four galleries of exhibits focus on coal mining and dry farming themes. A glass-walled viewing gallery provides a panoramic view of the city.

Nikka Yuko Japanese Garden, Lethbridge

This peaceful oasis in Henderson Lake Park blends ancient Oriental designs with a prairie setting. Five traditional Japanese gardens, graced with ornamental trees and shrubs, rock, sand, streams, and ponds are linked by meandering paths and footbridges. Rare cypress wood from Taiwan is featured. The pavilion, tea ceremony room, shelter, bridges, and gates were built in Japan by artisans who reassembled them here.

Traditional Japanese garden design inspired the different settings—a dry garden, mountain and waterfall, streams, ponds and islands, and a flat prairie garden—at Nikka Yuko Japanese Garden. Kimono-clad hostesses explain the symbolism, and encourage visitors to discover the garden's tranquillity at their own pace.

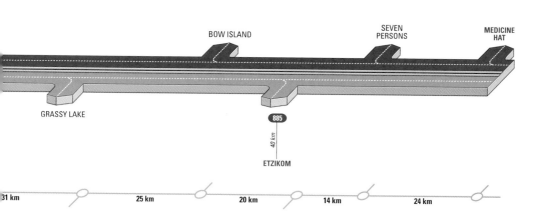

SEVEN
PERSONS

BOW ISLAND

MEDICINE
HAT

GRASSY LAKE

885

40 km

ETZIKOM

31 km   25 km   20 km   14 km   24 km

breeding program for threatened and endangered species, for return to their native habitats. On a self-guiding nature walk, visitors can view the breeding and rehabilitative areas, hold a specially trained bird, see rare species such as a burrowing owl—the world's only under-ground owl—and watch hawks and falcons take to the air during daily flying shows.

Etzikom

Hundreds of pioneer antiques and artifacts are housed at the Etzikom Museum and Canadian National Historic Windpower Centre. Fully furnished displays re-create an old-time general store, hotel/rooming house, school, blacksmith and barber shops, post office, and a 1900s home, complete with parlor, bedroom, and kitchen. Player pianos and other instruments of yesteryear are displayed in a music room. A great variety of windmills and a special interpretive center relate the history of wind power in Canada.

Medicine Hat

This Alberta city is the eastern terminus of the Crows-nest Highway (Hwy. 3) and the junction with the Trans-Canada Highway. For more details about Medicine Hat, see page 74.

Coaldale

Extensive irrigation here has created lakes and reservoirs, some of which have been a boon for water sports enthusiasts. At one such reservoir, Stafford Lake, a day-use park area that is a mecca for swimmers and boaters, wind-surfers have chalked up world speed records. However, Coaldale's chief claim to fame is the Alberta Birds of Prey Centre, the only breeding and rehabilitation facility of its kind in Western Canada. Injured and orphaned eagles, falcons, hawks, and owls are treated and released to the wild. There is also a captive

291

Highways
401, 20 & 40

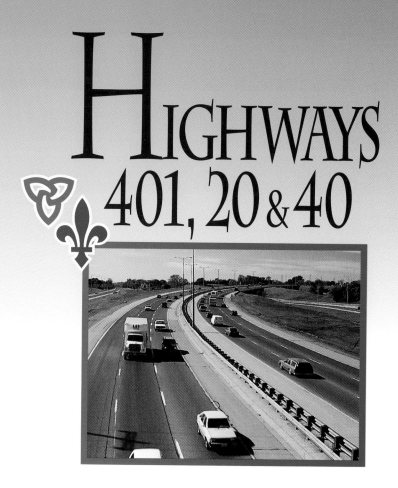

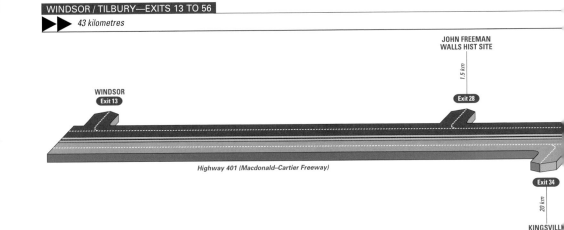

JOHN FREEMAN
WALLS HIST SITE

1.5 km

WINDSOR
Exit 13

Exit 28

Highway 401 (Macdonald–Cartier Freeway)

Exit 34

20 km

KINGSVILLE

15 km   6 km

SOUTHWESTERN
ONTARIO

Point Pelee, with more species of plants, birds, mammals, and other fauna than anywhere else in Canada, jealously guards the safety of all, including its marine reptiles. Many examples of the park's rare and fascinating wildlife can be seen from a 1.5 km circular boardwalk that crisscrosses the sea of cattails clothing its marshlands— roughly two-thirds of the park. The remaining uplands are cloaked in dunes and forests that contain many tree species usually found farther south.

Windsor

🚴 ⛵ ⛴ 🏊

Canada's automotive capital and southernmost city, Windsor is the busiest entry point on the Canada–U.S. border. A tunnel under the Detroit River and the 2.8 km Ambassador Bridge (the world's longest international suspension bridge) link the city to neighboring Detroit. Hwy. 401 (the Macdonald–Cartier Freeway)—which spans southern Ontario to the Quebec border— begins at the city limits.

Windsor's abundant parkland and riverside gardens offer relaxing strolls and spectacular views. At riverside in Coventry Gardens, the Peace Fountain— North America's largest floating fountain—is a dazzling show of water jets and colored lights.

A community museum is housed in the François Bâby House, a Georgian-style dwelling used as American headquarters in the War of 1812. In December 1838, the last battle in Upper Canada's 1837-38 Rebellion was fought on the grounds.

A butler's pantry with silver sinks is among fascinating features in the 36-room Tudor-Jacobean Willistead Manor. Thousands attend Art in the Park, a craft exhibit held each spring on the grounds, and the Willistead Classic and Antique Car Show in August.

Visitors can see whisky in the making at the Canadian Club Distillery, founded in 1858 by Hiram Walker, or purchase fresh produce and flowers at the city market, which operates Tuesday to Saturday. Seven days a week, crafters and artisans demon-

strate their skills and showcase their work at the Crafters Marketplace.

Lunch, brunch, dinner, and sightseeing cruises are offered by *The Pride of Windsor*–MV *Stella Borealis*, which departs daily from Dieppe Gardens downtown.

John Freeman Walls Historic Site

Just north of Hwy. 401, this site honors a fugitive slave who settled here in 1846, and whose cabin can still be seen. An hour-long guided tour tells the story of the Underground Railroad (see pages 296-297).

Kingsville

🎣 🏛 ⛴ 🏊

A bird sanctuary established here by naturalist Jack Miner (1865-1944) has become a stopover for some 30,000 migrating wild geese and ducks. The best viewing times are late October and late March. There is a heated pond where visitors can feed ducks, geese, and swans, and a museum, that traces the Atlantic and Mississippi flyways.

Other local attractions include Pelee Island Winery, which has wine tastings and tours, and the cactus and exotic plant displays at Colasanti's Tropical Gardens.

Leamington

🎣 🏛 🏊

Exit 48 (Hwy. 77) takes you to Leamington, which dispenses tourist information from a tomatolike

TURTLE
CROSSING

LIEU DE PASSAG
DES TORTUES

TILBURY
Exit 56

COMBER

Exit 48

24 km

LEAMINGTON

6 km

POINT PELEE NP

14 km

8 km

building and bills itself "Canada's Tomato Capital" (because of a local ketchup plant). Visitors can tour area greenhouses. Leamington has become an important diving center because of numerous Great Lakes' wrecks offshore in Lake Erie. A Marine Heritage Interpretive Centre features interactive displays and treasures from 15 of 50 identified wreck sites. Local dive shops and charter operators offer lessons and equipment rentals, as well as diver and non-diver excursions.

Point Pelee National Park

Just southwest of Leamington, this day-use park covers an arrow-shaped sandspit jutting 17 km into Lake Erie. Canada's southernmost point, it embraces marsh, forest, fields, and beach. Various trails reveal its different faces. The Woodland Trail leads through wooded swamp, dryland forest, and an abandoned orchard; the DeLaurier Trail combines the park's natural features with a glimpse of its past— a partially restored 1840s homestead and derelict man-made canals. Tilden's Woods and the Tip trails are popular with birdwatchers, who come in the thousands in spring and fall to observe the flow of migrating ducks, geese, and swans. More than 350 bird species, many rare and endangered, have been recorded. The park is noted for its songbirds, especially wood warblers. Shrubs at the park's tip are often covered by Monarch butterflies during their fall migration. The visitor center has fascinating flora and fauna exhibits.

295

Journey's End on a "Railroad" to Freedom

HIGHWAY 401 / SOUTHWESTERN ONTARIO

Don Gillmor *is a contributing editor for* Saturday Night *magazine. He also writes frequently for* Toronto Life *and other national magazines, as well as the* Globe & Mail.

From the beginning of the 19th century up until 1865, when the American Civil War ended, thousands of escaped slaves made their way to Canada. They traveled along the celebrated Underground Railroad—an escape network of hidden "stations" maintained by volunteer "conductors"—and crossed the Detroit River near Windsor, settling in the communities of southwestern Ontario: Windsor, Amherstburg, North Buxton, Chatham, and Dresden. They traveled by night, guided by the North Star, moving through the forests and swamps, away from main roads. Canada was seen as the Promised Land, as "Canaan."

Canada was surprisingly cold, and prejudice still existed, but it offered the runaways freedom and the opportunity to become landowners. Six museums have been set up to celebrate their bravery and fortitude. Independently conceived and operated, the six share an alliance as part of the African-Canadian Heritage tour, contained in a triangle of southern Ontario extending 70 km out of Windsor. The tour is marked along Hwy. 401 where signs display the North Star.

The first site is the Sandwich First Baptist Church, located in a suburb of Windsor. It is the oldest black church in Canada, constructed with logs in 1841, then rebuilt 10 years later with bricks made by former slaves, using clay from the banks of the Detroit River. Behind the pulpit, there is an escape route. The carpet is peeled back and two sheets of plywood are removed to reveal stairs leading to an earthen basement. When slave hunters came for escaped slaves, the runaways went down the stairs, out the windows and disappeared into the nearby woods.

In Amherstburg, 24 km south of Windsor, the North American Black Historical Museum and Cultural Center is located near the point on the Detroit River where many slaves crossed. The museum was conceived in 1964 by the late Melvin

"Mac" Simpson who was inspired to raise awareness of the black experience. Inside is a bust of Harriet Tubman (1821-1913), a former slave who guided hundreds of refugees to freedom. (The background photograph shows Tubman at the extreme left.) Among the mementos, a copy of a 19th-century handbill reads: "TO BE SOLD on board the Ship Bance-Island, on Tuesday the 6th of May next, at Ashley-Ferry; a choice cargo of about 250 fine healthy NEGROES just arrived from the Windward and Rice Coast."

Some 25 km east of Windsor is the John Freeman Walls Historic Site and Underground Railroad Museum. The site is marked by an explanatory plaque: "In 1846 John Freeman Walls, a fugitive slave from North Carolina, built this log cabin on land purchased from the Refugee Home Society." The tiny log cabin where Walls lived with his family of nine has been carefully restored. Outside, visitors are encouraged to ring the large red "freedom bell."

Other museum buildings are located on the grounds. A chronology details the conditions in ships crossing the Atlantic, the hardships of slavery, the route of the Underground Railroad, and the modern civil rights struggle. In the Rosa Parks Peace Chapel, a cross is made of bricks taken from the demolished Lorraine Motel in Memphis where U.S. civil rights leader Martin Luther King was assassinated on April 4, 1968.

The next stop is the town of North Buxton and the Raleigh Township Centennial Museum. It commemorates the model community that was established in 1849 by the Reverend William King, an Irish Presbyterian who had spoken out against slavery—then found himself in the awkward position of inheriting 14 slaves. He freed them and brought them north to become the first occupants of his new community, where they owned the land they worked. The Raleigh Township Centennial Museum has King's bed, dresser, and diaries, as well as evidence of the settlers' tidy, labor-intensive lives.

North of Hwy. 401, Chatham has its own First Baptist church. Built in 1851, it was razed in 1958 and rebuilt on the same foundation. Here, the white American abolitionist John Brown held a meeting on May 10, 1858, to plan a revolution. He wanted to found an independent, slave-free republic in the United States, and drilled his troop in Chatham's Tecumseh Park. Black recruits practiced maneuvers where the Kiwanis Music Shell now stands.

Brown's raid on the federal armory at Harper's Ferry, Virginia, on October 1859, ended in disaster and he was captured, convicted of treason, and hanged. Two years later Union soldiers adopted him as a martyr in the U.S. Civil War, and he became the subject of a popular song: "John Brown's body lies a-mouldering in the grave . . . His truth goes marching on."

Travelers can reach the sixth site on this tour, Uncle Tom's Cabin Historic Site, by heading east from Thamesville for 20 km on Hwy. 21. The centerpiece of the site is the dwelling of the Reverend Josiah Henson (1789-1881), whose early life as a slave inspired Harriet Beecher Stowe's novel *Uncle Tom's Cabin* (1851). Like the other destinations on this African-Canadian Heritage tour, the site illuminates a dramatic chapter of our history.

"They traveled by night, guided by the North Star, moving through the forests and swamps..."

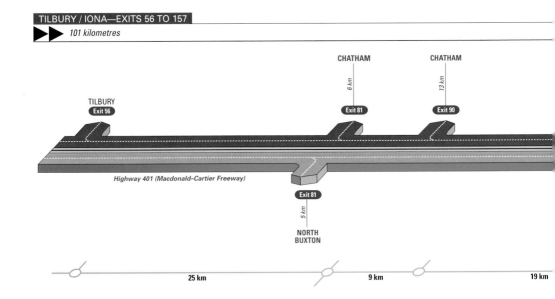

CHATHAM
6 km
CHATHAM
13 km

TILBURY
Exit 56
Exit 81
Exit 90

Highway 401 (Macdonald–Cartier Freeway)

Exit 81
5 km
NORTH
BUXTON

25 km — 9 km — 19 km

**SOUTHWESTERN
ONTARIO**

Ridge House, built in Ridgetown in 1874 by a local tradesman and a typical home of the day, was restored in 1975. It is open to the public daily in summer, weekends in the fall. Christmas programs at Ridge House are a local highlight.

North Buxton

Raleigh Township Centennial Museum celebrates the history of slaves who found refuge here in 1848. The community was founded by William King, an Irish-born Presbyterian minister, and 14 freed slaves, who cleared the fields and built homes here. King, an abolitionist, inherited the slaves in his father-in-law's will. When he freed them in Ohio, he offered them a chance to build a settlement here. Museum exhibits include King's journal and personal belongings. (See also pages 296-297.)

Chatham

⚓ 🏊

A military settlement of the late 1700s, Chatham was a refuge for escaped slaves in the years preceding the U.S. Civil War. An enduring symbol of the times is First Baptist Church, founded by the refugees in 1851. A plaque recalls that American abolitionist John Brown met here with anti-slavery supporters just before the 1858 raid on Harper's Ferry, Virginia. (After the raid, Brown was captured, tried, and hanged.)

Brown's possessions are displayed at the Chatham–Kent Museum, which describes Chatham's role as a terminal on the Underground Railroad (see pages 296-297). Among War of 1812 exhibits are the powder horn and war club of Tecumseh (1763-1813), the Shawnee chief who died in an 1813 battle with American invaders at nearby Moraviantown (*see* Thamesville).

Chatham's Railroad Museum, in a restored 1955 baggage car, has curiosities such as tie-tongs,

waybills, and a caboose chair. Downtown Tecumseh Park is the site of band concerts and special events, such as Highland Games, Waterfront Weekends (a series of musical events), and the multi-cultural Festival of Nations.

Thamesville

Some 7 km east on Hwy. 2, the Fairfield Museum and Avenue of Peace marks the site of a 1792 village founded by Moravian missionaries. Fairfield was a haven for Delaware Indian converts to Christianity who fled here from the United States to escape religious persecution. During the War of 1812, American invaders destroyed the village, which was reestablished across the Thames River in 1815 as New Fairfield.

A tree-lined pathway—the Avenue of Peace—follows Fairfield's original main street. A monument and plaques commemorate the first settlers and peaceful Canada–U.S. relations down the years. Across the river you can see New Fairfield Church, which was built in 1848.

Ridgetown

This tree-lined community set amid rich agricultural country bills itself the "Friendliest Town in Ontario." Ridge House and Gallery, a restored 1875 dwelling, contains a parlor, kitchen, dining room, and bedrooms decorated with Victorian furnishings and objects. Gallery folk art exhibits are changed every six weeks. Visitors can tour the Ridgetown College of Agricultural Technology. Youngsters will enjoy Romoe Restorick's Buffalo Head Ranch, at the edge of town.

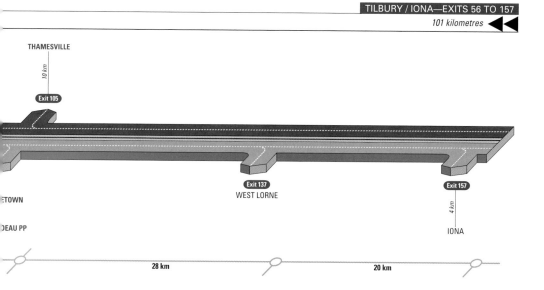

THAMESVILLE

10 km

Exit 105

ETOWN

DEAU PP

Exit 137
WEST LORNE

Exit 157

4 km

IONA

28 km   20 km

Rondeau Provincial Park

Ontario's second oldest park, this triangular peninsula jutting into Lake Erie embraces dunes, marshes, and the province's largest remnant of Carolinian forest. A mild climate and plentiful rainfall nurture the lofty, flowering tulip trees, shagbark hickory, black walnut, sassafras, and sycamore that flourish here enmeshed in Virginia creepers and wild grape vines.

Marshes along warm, shallow Rondeau Bay abound in exotic plants and wildlife—swamp rose mallows, yellow pond lilies, and such rare reptiles as spiny soft-shell turtles and fox snakes.

With some 334 recorded bird species (about 80 percent of Ontario's total bird species),

Rondeau is a bird-watcher's heaven. This is Canada's main breeding ground for Acadian fly-catchers and prothonotary warblers. Bald eagles nest in the trees near the marshes. An array of migrating ducks and geese make a stopover in the park.

Various trails enable visitors to explore the diverse habitats. The Spicewood Trail leads through the dense Carolinian forest, and the Black Oak Trail through oak and pine. One of the best bike paths is the 15 km Marsh Trail, and the 12 km of sandy beach-front makes for great strolls. You can also sail, windsurf, swim on Rondeau Bay, or take part in one of the visitor services programs of guided hikes, bird-watching workshops, sand-castle contests, and coyote howls.

Rondeau Provincial Park might be summed up as a birding hot spot with exotic plants and wildlife, extensive marshlands, a Carolinian forest, and 8 km of beach bordering warm, shallow Rondeau Bay.

299

Highway 401 (Macdonald–Cartier Freeway)

Exit 157

4 km

IONA

Exit 177

12 km

ST. THOMAS

20 km

SOUTHWESTERN
ONTARIO

the GUY
LOMBARDO
MUSEUM

A museum in Springbank Park honors the London-born bandleader who died in 1977. Displays include photographs, song sheets, posters, and other memorabilia of his career.

St. Thomas

Founded in 1813, this city is named for Sir Thomas Talbot (1771-1853), who opened up this region and ruled it with an iron fist for some 50 years. Many of his personal effects can be seen in the Elgin County Pioneer Museum. Housed in an 1848 doctor's house, the museum also contains many of the home's original furnishings, 19th-century medical equipment, and pioneer tools and utensils.

Just across from the museum, a life-size statue honors Jumbo, a Barnum & Bailey Circus African elephant killed here in 1885 by a Grand Trunk Railway locomotive. Jumbo (said to be the largest and heaviest elephant ever in captivity) was the circus' star attraction for 20 years.

The old Michigan Central Railroad Shops are home to Elgin County Railway Museum. Exhibits include a 1910 CPR handcar, a 1939 Pullman sleeping car, and CNR locomotive 5700—a high-speed steam-powered engine. Canadians at war is the focus of Elgin Military Museum, which displays local memorabilia from the War of 1812 onward.

St. Thomas is known for its beautiful parkland, notably Waterworks and Pinafore (named for a Gilbert and Sullivan operetta) parks. Old St. Thomas Church (1824), the Courthouse (1853), and the imposing Town Hall (1899) are fine examples of Victorian architecture.

An old-fashioned train runs from St. Thomas to Port Stanley, a popular vacation spot and fishing village on Lake Erie. En route, there is a stop at Union, where passengers can inspect the one-room railway station, said to be North America's smallest.

London

In 1792 Col. John Graves Simcoe founded this prosperous commercial and industrial center he hoped would become the capital of Upper Canada. His hopes were dashed when York (Toronto) got the honor, but the city thrived anyhow, becoming a leader in education and medicine, and developing a lively cultural scene. Patients from around the world attend the ground-breaking neurological unit of University Hospital (London is home to the University of Western Ontario). Local arts organizations include a symphony orchestra, numerous art galleries and museums, and community and professional theater companies—the latter perform in the restored turn-of-the-century Grand Theatre. Springbank, the largest of many parks, contains Storybook Gardens,

The beauty and tranquillity of a 19th-century-style garden surround Eldon House (1834), once the center of social life in London, Ont. It had been home to four generations of the Harris family, who donated it to the city in 1960, together with its elegant furnishings, and priceless and exotic treasures. Tours, offered year-round, are especially popular at Christmas, when the mansion is festooned with Victorian and Edwardian decorations.

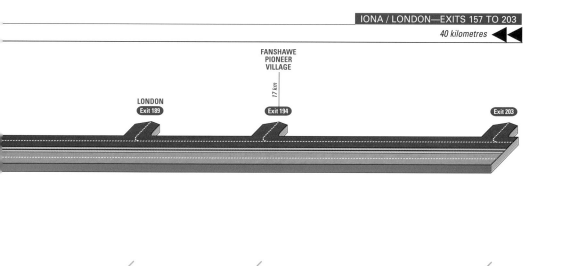

FANSHAWE
PIONEER
VILLAGE

17 km

LONDON
Exit 189

Exit 194

Exit 203

6 km   5 km   9 km

which features nursery rhyme characters, a minitrain, and petting zoo, Playworld, a large play area, and the Guy Lombardo Museum (*see left*). From Storybook Landing, visitors can board *London Princess* for a 45-minute cruise on the Thames River to downtown.

Banting Museum, London

Insulin codiscoverer Sir Frederick Banting (1891-1941) lived and practiced medicine here in 1920-21. Period furnishings and accessories re-create his bedroom, office, and adjoining apothecary. One room resembles a battlefield operating room like those where Banting served during World War I. Other displays tell the story of insulin and describe the roles of Banting's associates— Drs. C. H. Best, J.J.R. Macleod, and J. B. Collip.

Eldon House, London

Original furnishings and curiosities such as African hunting trophies decorate London's oldest residence. A re-created Victorian garden is the scene of an old-fashioned garden party in June. Traditional afternoon teas are served in summer.

Royal Canadian Regiment Museum, London

Housed in Wolseley Hall (1886) at Canadian Forces headquarters, the museum tells the story of this infantry regiment, which dates from 1883. Displays of weapons, uniforms, and memorabilia trace regimental history from the Riel Rebellion to United Nations peacekeeping operations.

London Museum of Archaelogy, London

With more than 40,000 items, this museum traces 11,000 years of Indian habitation in southwestern Ontario. Exhibits depict five periods of development, ranging from nomadic beginnings to settled village life. A 500-year-old Iroquoian village of 2,000 inhabitants has been partially reconstructed at nearby Lawson Prehistoric Indian Village.

London Regional Children's Museum, London

Here in Canada's first children's museum, hands-on exhibits invite exploration of the past, present, and future. Youngsters can dig for fossils, blast off into outer space, crawl into a life-size igloo, and visit a bat-occupied cave.

Fanshawe Pioneer Village, London

More than 25 restored and reconstructed buildings have been assembled here to re-create a late 1800s rural settlement. Included are log houses and barns, a church, a sawmill, a fire hall, and the Labatt Pioneer Brewery.

At Fanshawe Pioneer Village—a collection of 19th-century buildings near London, Ont.—costumed interpreters demonstrate black-smithing, weaving, baking, and other skills related to farm husbandry in bygone years.

301

Exit 203

Highway 401 (Macdonald–Cartier Freeway)

15 km

**SOUTHWESTERN
ONTARIO**

*Set amid velvety parkland on the
Avon River, Stratford's Shakespearean Festival Theatre draws
close to half a million theatergoers
between May and mid-November
each year. They know they will see
top-flight artists perform classic and
contemporary plays, operettas, and
concerts in the 2,262-seat semi-
circular festival theater (below),
where the audience sits on three
sides of an open stage, and in the
traditional proscenium-stage Avon
Theatre, and the informal theater-
in-the-round setting of The Tom
Patterson Theatre.*

Ingersoll

Canada's cheese export trade
began in this town in 1865 after
local cheesemakers exhibited a
3,330 kg cheese at the State Fair
in Saratoga, N.Y., and later at
numerous shows throughout
Britain. At tour's end, a 136 kg
slice was brought home for local
consumption. Descriptions of the
promotion and other Ingersoll
highlights, as well as facts about
the cheesemaking process, fill the
Ingersoll Cheese Factory Museum and Sports Hall of Fame.
The five-building Centennial
Park complex has an agricultural
museum, a blacksmith shop, a
local history museum, and photographs and memorabilia about
local sports heroes, and the 10 m
Miss Canada IV mahogany
speedboat that set an official
world speed record in the 1940s.

Salford

Cheesemaking in southwestern
Ontario got its start here in
1836, when the Ranney family
acquired land and stocked it with
100 cows. Today, the Village
Cheese Mill sells more than 50
kinds of cheese (including 12 different cheddars). Exhibits at the
on-site Salford Heritage Museum tell about the local cheese
industry and native-born evange-
list Aimee Semple McPherson
(1890-1944).

Tillsonburg

Visitors can tour
Annandale House
Museum, construct-
ed in the early 1880s
by Edwin Tillson

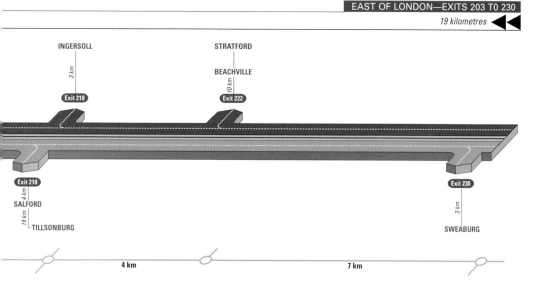

INGERSOLL
3 km
Exit 218

STRATFORD
BEACHVILLE
10 km
Exit 222

Exit 218
4 km
SALFORD
19 km
TILLSONBURG

Exit 230
3 km
SWEABURG

4 km   7 km

with white brick from his own yard and wood paneling from his factories. Built in the highly ornamental "aesthetic" style then popular, it featured stained glass windows, painted ceilings, central heating, hot and cold running water, and gas lighting. Restored to its former glory, the mansion is open to the public year-round.

Local crafts and artworks are sold in The Great Western Railway Station (1887), which also houses a farmers' market on summer Saturdays. Theatre Tillsonburg shows can be seen at the Otter Valley Playhouse.

Beachville

Hwy. 6 takes you north to County Road 9, where you will find some of Canada's largest lime quarries. According to a letter in the Beachville District

Museum, the first recorded baseball game in North America was played in the village in June 1838—one whole year before the legendary Abner Doubleday game at Cooperstown, N.Y. The letter (to *Sporting Life* magazine) by a local physician gives details of the Beachville game, played with four bases, called "byes." Other museum exhibits, some dating back to 1789, include a one-man threshing machine and re-creations of a summer kitchen, schoolroom, and general store.

Stratford

Hwy. 6 continues north to Stratford, home of Canada's acclaimed theater festival. From May to October, a dozen or so plays, ranging from Shakespearean to contemporary and even

musical productions, are performed on three different stages. Theatergoers can take backstage tours, visit the costume warehouse, and check out Gallery Stratford's display of festival costumes together with the sketches from which they were designed.

Sweaburg

At Jakeman's Maple Farm, a family business dating since 1876, 8,000 tapped maples yield some of Ontario's finest syrup. Maple syrup and candies, jams and relishes are sold in the Sweaburg General Store and Post Office (1855). A museum displays century-old syrup-making equipment and a pancake house operates from March to May.

► ► *40 kilometres*

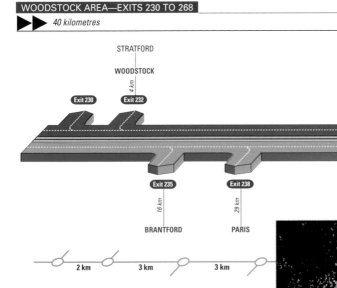

STRATFORD

WOODSTOCK

4 km

Exit 230   Exit 232

Highway 401 (Macdonald–Cartier Freeway)

Exit 235   Exit 238

16 km   *29 km*

BRANTFORD   PARIS

2 km   3 km   3 km

**SOUTH-
CENTRAL
ONTARIO**

Woodstock

Set amid farms, orchards, and conservation areas, and regarded as Canada's dairy capital, industrial Woodstock salutes its dairying business with a statue of Springbank Snow Countess—a local cow that set the world's record (4,110 kg) for lifetime butterfat production. The bounty of neighboring farms is offered at a 100-year-old farmers' market, held in the local fairgrounds each Saturday morning. Harness racing takes place at the local raceway on Tuesdays from June to September.

Woodstock glories in a rich architectural heritage. A local history museum is housed in the restored majestic yellow-brick Old Town Hall (1853), a national historic site. The ground floor council chamber, restored to 1879, contains its original portraits and furniture, including a grand horseshoe-shaped table. A second-floor grand hall, which has served as lecture hall, opera house, and courthouse, and is noted for its intricately wallpapered ceiling, has been restored to 1889. Other well-preserved historic sites include the 1854 Italianate-style jail, notable for its 2½-story octagonal tower; the 1876 Registry Office (also in the Italianate style); the 1899 Fire Hall, from which a bell once rang out for fires, curfews, and lost children; the 1901 Post Office, notable for its four-clock corner tower; the 1904 stone and brick Armouries; and the 1892 County Courthouse, which has monkey heads hidden in the capitals crowning its two entrance pillars.

A 1,000-year-old stone cross, a gift of Queen Marie of Romania, marks where legendary "Klondike" Joe Boyle, native son and an adventurer of the Yukon Gold Rush and World War I, lies in the local Presbyterian Cemetary. South of Hwy. 401, the Ross Butler Studio-Agricultural Art Gallery has paintings and sculptures ranging from Percheron stallions to Ayrshire cows by Ontario's premier farm artist.

Brantford

This vibrant city is named for Mohawk chief Joseph Brant (1742-1807), who led the Six Nations here in 1784 after British allegiance during the American Revolution cost them their lands in upstate New York. Six

Magnicent Victorian houses on Woodstock's oldest street, tree-lined Vansittart Avenue, are a legacy of the United Empire Loyalists and the Scottish and British immigrants who built this Ontario town in the early 1800s.

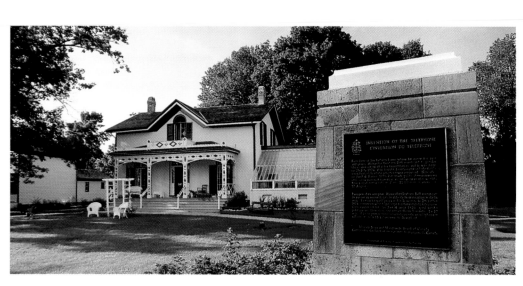

Scottish-born Alexander Graham Bell grew up in this spacious two-story house overlooking the Grand River at Brantford. In 1874, he was vacationing from Boston, where he worked as a speech therapist, when he conceived the idea that became the basis of the telephone. Two years later the first "long-distance" phone call was made from Brant-ford to nearby Paris. Restored and furnished with Bell family furniture, paintings, china, silver, and books, and staffed by costumed guides, this national historic site is now open to the public.

Nations' heritage is the focus of the Woodland Cultural Centre, built in 1831 as a Native boarding school, and now a museum, art gallery, resource center, and gift shop featuring Native crafts.

With 19th-century storefronts, rooms in period settings, and a collection of Brantford pottery, the Brant County Museum traces local history from Native settlement to World War II. A collection of military vehicles and a "Women at War" exhibit are among the Canadian Military Heritage Museum's recounting of Canada's wartime roles from the 1700s to the present.

Brantford's best-known historic site is the Bell Homestead, the 1870-81 family home of Alexander Graham Bell, inventor of the telephone. Next door, Henderson Home—from 1877 to 1880, Canada's first telephone business office—illustrates the history of the telephone industry with displays of antique and modern equipment.

Lithographs, etchings, drawings and other works by some of Canada's finest printmakers and photographers can be seen in the Glenhyrst Art Gallery. In an 11-room mansion in landscaped grounds overlooking the Grand River, the gallery has the country's largest collection of paintings—Brant County portraits and landscapes—by the 19th-century Whale family, father Robert Reginald, sons John Claude and Robert Heard, and nephew John Hicks.

Paris

Set amid rolling wooded hills, at the forks of the Grand and Nith rivers, Paris is named for local gypsum deposits used by pioneer Hiram "King" Capron to make plaster of paris. Some houses and churches in and around town are fine examples of the cobble-stone architecture of the 1830s, when stones from riverbanks and fields were used as a veneer on a building's front wall.

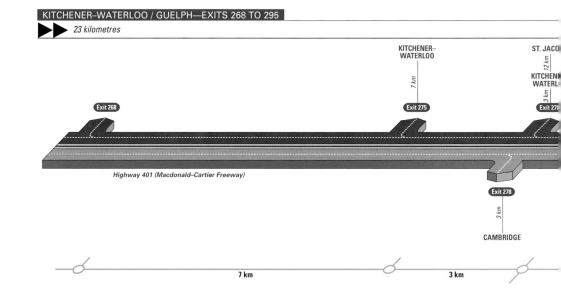

KITCHENER–
WATERLOO

7 km

ST. JACO

12 km

KITCHENE
WATERL

3 km

Exit 268

Exit 275

Exit 27

Highway 401 (Macdonald–Cartier Freeway)

Exit 278

3 km

CAMBRIDGE

7 km   3 km

**SOUTH-
CENTRAL
ONTARIO**

Kitchener–Waterloo

These industrial twin cities share first-class museums, art galleries, and other attractions. The area's German heritage finds expression in Oktoberfest, North American's largest Bavarian festival. German food is part of the bounty at both the Kitchener and Waterloo farmers' markets.

In Kitchener, the Joseph Schneider Haus, home of one of the Mennonites from Pennsylvania who settled here in the 1800s, has been restored to the 1850s. A modern wing features Germanic folk and decorative art; seasonal events range from sheepshearing demonstrations to quilting bees.

Doon Heritage Crossroads re-creates a 1914 rural village adapting to automobiles and electricity. This living museum consists of more than 20 buildings and two farms, complete with livestock and heritage gardens. Doon was also the home of Homer Watson (1855-1936), Canada's first internationally renowned landscape artist. His paintings and a frieze he painted on his studio wall can be seen at his home, alongside his palette, easel, and paint box. Works of contemporary Canadian artists hang in other rooms.

Games from ancient Egypt are among some 5,000 items at a Museum and Archive of Games at the University of Waterloo. Other campus museums include the Museum of Visual Science and Optometry, which has eyeglasses dating back to 1700, and the Biology-Earth Sciences Museum, which displays

dinosaur skeletons and mineral and crystal collections. On the north campus, the Brubacher House is furnished in the style of a Mennonite home of 1850-90.

Woodside National Historic Site, Kitchener

Amid well-treed grounds, this 10-room boyhood home of William Lyon Mackenzie King, Canada's 10th prime minister, re-creates the lifestyle of an upper-middle-class Victorian family. Among original family possessions are relics of King's rebel grandfather, William Lyon Mackenzie.

St. Jacobs

Mennonites who came here from Pennsylvania after the American Revolution settled this region. Their descendants still ride about in horse-drawn buggies. Photographs, films, and recordings at The Meeting Place describe their history, lifestyle and beliefs. A 19th-century shoe factory houses the Maple Syrup Museum of Ontario, which traces maple syrup production from aboriginal and pioneer methods to present-day techniques.

▶

Known as the city of stone, for the many 1800s churches and industrial and public buildings built of local limestone, downtown Cambridge stands stonily solid on the Grand River banks.

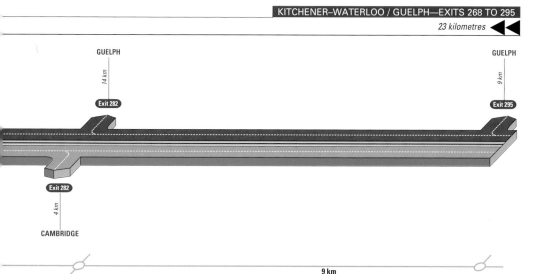

GUELPH

14 km

Exit 282

GUELPH

9 km

Exit 295

Exit 282

4 km

CAMBRIDGE

9 km

Cambridge

🏠 📖 🏛 ⚓ 🏊 ❄

In the roads around St. Jacobs and Kitchener–Waterloo, Old-Order Mennonites in horse-drawn buggies are an everyday sight.

This community, which grew around a thriving textile industry, is said to have more designated historical buildings than any other city of its size in Canada. Many of these limestone structures line the Grand River, along which you can admire the architectural legacy on a variety of walking and driving tours. Cambridge is noted for its array of factory outlets ranging from shoes and shirts to towels and table linens. The Library and Gallery's permanent collection of modern fiber art is worth a visit.

Guelph

🏠 📖 🏛 ⚓ 🏊

Like Cambridge, Guelph also glories in its rich architectural heritage. Walking tours lead past century-old limestone buildings: the Renaissance Revival-style City Hall and the twin-towered Church of Our Lady Immaculate. Guelph Civic Museum, in a 19th-century limestone structure, traces the city's growth from its founding in 1827 by Scottish novelist John Galt to the present. A restored mid-19th-century cottage is the birthplace of John McCrae (1872-1918), the physician and soldier who wrote *In Flanders Fields*.

Contemporary Canadian work is featured at the Macdonald Stewart Art Centre, which occupies a renovated turn-of-the-century school. More than 500 Inuit drawings, textiles, and rare print stones are among its 3,000-piece collection.

Nature lovers can explore the University of Guelph's Arboretum, which has more than 2,100 kinds of trees and shrubs. Some 4 km south of Guelph, the Kortright Waterfowl Park shelters more than 90 different species. An observation tower overlooks the park, and there are interpretive displays and nature trails.

When 400 members of the Timber Framers Guild of North America met in Guelph in 1992, they built this 37 m long, lattice-covered footbridge for the city. Based on an 1800s design, the footbridge is a key link on the city's 18 km Royal Recreation Trail.

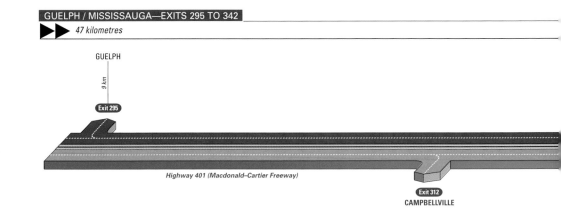

GUELPH

9 km

Exit 295

Highway 401 (Macdonald–Cartier Freeway)

Exit 312
CAMPBELLVILLE

17 km   8 km

**WEST OF
TORONTO**

▶ *Ontario farm-
steads inspired
the designers of
Mississauga's
multipurpose
Civic Center, in
which the office
tower is said to
reflect a farm-
stead, the
facade, a barn,
the council
chamber (in
which a domed
ceiling depicts
an evening sky),
a silo, and the
clock tower, a
windmill. Inside
are a three-
story granite-
and-marble
Great Hall,
which has
served as loca-
tion for several
major movies,
an art gallery,
and a sports
hall of fame.
Surrounding
Civic Square
contains gar-
dens, a sculp-
ture court, a
reflecting pool
that doubles as
a skating rink,
and an
amphitheater.*

Campbellville

A hamlet within the larger community of Milton, Campbellville
has some fine 19th-century brick-
and-clapboard buildings housing
antique, craft, and specialty
shops. Mountsberg Conservation
Area, a popular bird-watching
spot to the west, can be reached
via Rd. 9. Mountsberg also offers
a maple-sugar bush, a demonstration farm, hiking trails, and a
raptor center with facilities for
treating injured birds of prey.

Just east of Campbellville,
Hwy. 401 cuts through the Niagara Escarpment, a limestone
ridge extending across southern
Ontario from the Niagara Peninsula to the tip of the Bruce Peninsula. A nature center at Crawford Lake Conservation Area
describes the escarpment's botanical, geological, and zoological
features. Interpretive stations at
a 500-year-old, reconstructed
Iroquois village tell of the culture
of the people who hunted and
fished there thousands of years
ago. At Crawford Lake, the
Bruce Trail (see pages 310-311)
crosses the escarpment on its
way north to Rattlesnake Point
and Kelso conservation areas.

Milton

This town is an ideal base for exploring some of the parks, trails,
and historic sites on the Niagara
Escarpment. Just west of Milton, Kelso Conservation Area, a
great spot for boating, fishing,
and swimming, contains the Halton Region Museum. Thousands
of artifacts in its Exhibits Building
offer a window on 12,000 years

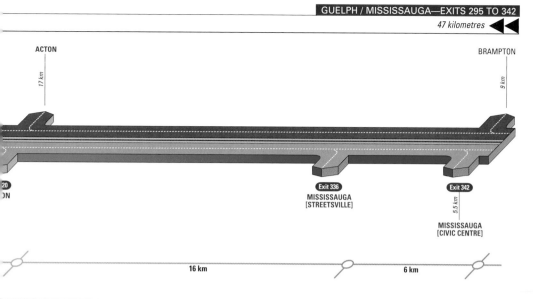

ACTON
17 km

BRAMPTON
9 km

20
ON

Exit 336
MISSISSAUGA
[STREETSVILLE]

Exit 342
5.5 km

MISSISSAUGA
[CIVIC CENTRE]

16 km   6 km

of local history. Its five pioneer buildings—a restored 1860s barn, a blacksmith's shop, carriage house, craft building, and log cabin—depict area life from the early 1800s to the 1940s. (For more about Kelso Conservation Area, see pages 310-311.)

Rattlesnake Point Conservation Area, south of Milton, attracts hikers and climbers. In the park, a 90 m high ledge offers panoramic views of the region.

Sixteen Mile Creek tumbles over the escarpment at Hilton Falls Conservation Area, north of Hwy. 401. Beaver meadows, limestone potholes, wildlife-rich wetlands, the endangered West Virginia white butterfly, and the ruins of Edward Hilton's 1835 mill are some of the attractions in this sprawling reserve.

Acton

Leather tanning became big business here in the mid-1800s. The tannery built employee housing and sports facilities, and ran a cooperative store and an outdoor arena. An historic walking tour passes The Olde Hide House, once a warehouse and now a leather goods outlet. Built in 1899 with half a million bricks and huge wooden beams, it was used until 1933 to store hides that were shipped in by rail and destined for the tannery.

At nearby Rockwood, the Halton County Radial Railway Museum contains a collection of inter-urban (known as radial in Ontario) and work cars, and vintage streetcars. Visitors can take 20-minute rides in these electrically operated vehicles, all of

them used or built in Ontario, and restored on site. The 1912 Rockwood station is also on site.

Mississauga [Streetsville]

One of Canada's fastest growing cities, Mississauga has absorbed Streetsville, Port Credit, and other long-established villages. From Exit 336, the Mississauga Road follows the Credit River south through Streetsville to Port Credit and Lake Ontario. Streetsville, where some 30 buildings from the 1800s evoke small-town Ontario, calls itself "the village in the city." Buildings on a heritage tour include the two-story clapboard Montreal House (1821), Streetsville's oldest site, the brick-and-stone Timothy Street House (1825), home of the millowner for whom the village is named, John McMaster's Store (1850), the multiple-gabled Robinson-Bray House (1885), Franklin House (1885), a former hotel, and The Graydon Block (1891).

Mississauga [Civic Centre]

Striking contemporary architecture and a roster of performing and visual arts and community events give a vibrancy to the Civic Centre (accessible from Exit 342 via Hurontario Street South and Burnhamthorpe Road). The adjoining Living Arts Centre houses theaters, studios, exhibition areas, and a concert hall that promises to be an exciting venue for opera, ballet, symphony and choral music lovers.

Trekking Through a World-class Wilderness

HIGHWAY 401 / KELSO CONSERVATION AREA

DAN SCHNEIDER *is a naturalist with the Grand River Conservation Authority in Guelph, Ontario. He is a frequent contributor to* Canadian Geographic, Nature Canada, *and* Canadian Wildlife.

AT DAWN, AS THE MIST SOFTENS THE LANDSCAPE, I start my hike along a stretch of the Bruce Trail in Kelso Conservation Area, just west of Milton. At this point, the 776 km trail has already covered nearly 200 km from its southernmost point in Queenston on the Niagara River. Just north of the conservation area, the Bruce sneaks under Hwy. 401 before winding its way to its terminus at Tobermory, a small community at the tip of the Bruce Peninsula. This trail—Canada's oldest long-distance pathway—attracts 1.3 million visitors a year. I am one of them.

The Bruce follows the Niagara Escarpment—a lofty spine of rock outcrops and cliff faces rising above the gentle landscape of southern Ontario. Although the escarpment is more or less geologically uniform everywhere, it offers a diversity of fascinating attractions.

In my hiking experience, I've sipped wine from vineyards sheltered by the escarpment in the Niagara Peninsula. I've also searched out delicate wild orchids on the Bruce Peninsula and explored deep grottoes along the brilliant blue waters of Georgian Bay. Along the way, I've marveled at the trail's abundance of ferns and mosses, liverworts and spleenworts, plants from an era when dinosaurs trundled over the escarpment's rock.

Trekking the entire length of the Bruce Trail is a challenge, even for backpackers. But, like many hikers, I prefer to tackle the trail in manageable sections, such as my choice for today's hike—the short stretch that runs through Kelso Conservation Area (accessible by Exit 320 from Hwy. 401). Here, I follow the trail up Glen Eden ski hill and delight in the clifftop view, which overlooks Kelso dam and lake. In the distance, I can see the escarpment marching northward to the Bruce Peninsula. Behind me lies the deep forest, where the calls of birds echo through the trees.

The Bruce links the escarpment's woodlands, creating a vital natural corridor in an increasingly urban and intensively cultivated area of Canada. In the 19th century, the early settlers avoided this rocky, unprofitable strip and unknowingly preserved its natural beauty for future generations.

Today, the escarpment shelters over 300 species of birds, 53 types of mammals, 35 species of reptiles and amphibians, and more than 90 kinds of fish. But what makes the escarpment truly impressive is the geology, which determines which species will survive here. One of the best spots to see the escarpment's geological magnificence is at Kelso Conversation Area.

In 1990, the United Nations recognized the Niagara Escarpment's unique ecological environment and proclaimed it a UNESCO World Biosphere Reserve. This designation places the escarpment in a world-class category with the Florida Everglades, the Serengeti Plain in northern Tanzania, and Ecuador's Galapagos Islands.

As I hike through Kelso, I realize that the rock beneath my feet dates back 440 million years. At that time, a vast area of south-central Canada was bathed in a warm, shallow sea. Sediment eroded from the surrounding Canadian Shield and washed into the sea, forming an immense delta. Plankton and marine shells were also deposited here. Over millions of years, these deposits hardened into rock, and the shells became the limestone-embedded fossils visible today.

About 300 million years ago, tectonic forces created an 800 km wide depression, somewhat like an immense dish within the sea. The rim of this "dish" is the Niagara Escarpment, eroded by ice and water to its present shape. Dolomite is the secret of the escarpment's longevity, protecting its top from erosion while the softer limestone cliff face continues to crumble away.

On today's hike, I notice a rock fissure created by erosion. This is a crevice cave, formed when a section of the cliff cracked away and left behind debris topped by large rocks. I crawl into the cave, clamber over boulders, and with one tight squeeze, return to the surface—exhilarated by my underground exploration.

Nearby trees, mostly cedars, survive by clinging to the cliff's fissures. Twisted and gnarled, they defy old age and the elements to reach remarkable ages. Some of the cedars here may be almost 1,000 years old—among the oldest trees in Canada.

As my hike draws to an end, I spot a turkey vulture soaring, riding updrafts created by the cliff face. All along the escarpment, the vultures nest safely in crevices. The Halton Region Conservation Authority, which runs Kelso Conservation Area and other escarpment parks, has adopted the turkey vulture as its emblem.

The Bruce Trail is a remarkable achievement. Two-thirds of the trail lies on private property, surviving through the generosity of landowners. But an even more ambitious footpath—the Trans-Canada Trail—is scheduled for completion by July 1, 2000. It will link sections of existing trails, such as the Bruce, to new pathways. Once completed, it will stretch a total of 15,000 km from St. John's to Victoria, and north from Calgary through the Yukon to the Arctic community of Tuktoyaktuk on the Beaufort Sea. It will be the longest continuous trail of its kind in the world.

> *" ... settlers avoided this rocky, unprofitable strip and unknowingly preserved its natural beauty... "*

BRAMPTON

9 km

KLEINBURG

3 km

WILD WATER KINGDOM

5 km

Exit 348

Highway 401 (Macdonald–Cartier Freeway)

Exit 342

5.5 km

MISSISSAUGA

6 km   11 km

GREATER
TORONTO

A limestone polar bear by Cape Dorset sculptor Pauta graces the entrance to the McMichael Canadian Art Collection at Kleinberg, Ont. Begun as a hobby by Robert and Signe McMichael, the collection, donated to the province of Ontario in the 1960s, has now grown to some 5,000 paintings and other works of art.

Brampton

A revamped 19th-century county jail, reincarnated as Peel Heritage Complex, houses an art gallery, a museum and archives (located in the adjacent registry office), and is a major local attraction. Museum displays illustrate the history of the region from prehistoric times, including a history of the old jail. One intriguing exhibit is a cell furnished with various restraints and locking devices. Blacksmith, shoemaker, and general store displays describe 1800s life in the area. The art gallery has a permanent collection and also presents special exhibitions by local artists. An animal farm and formal gardens at Chinguacousy Park (Bramlea Road and Hwy. 7) are also worth a visit.

Wild Water Kingdom

Canada's largest outdoor water park offers a vast wave-action pool, inner tube rides, seven-story speed slides, river rides, and a children's water play area. Dryland activities include bank shot bastkeball, batting cages, and miniature golf. (To get to this popular attraction from Hwy. 427, drive 2 km west on Finch Avenue.)

312

CANADA'S WONDERLAND

10 km

BLACK CREEK PIONEER VILLAGE

7 km

Exit 359

Exit 367

To Downtown Toronto

8 km

Kleinburg

One of Canada's largest collections of works by the Group of Seven and its famed forerunner Tom Thomson is housed at the McMichael Canadian Art Collection, a stone-and-timber gallery overlooking the Humber River valley. In 1965, Robert and Signe McMichael, who began the collection, donated the property and its 194-painting treasure to Ontario. Now a major international gallery, the McMichael boasts displays of First Nations and Inuit art and sculpture, and the largest display anywhere of 20th-century Canadian art. A small cemetery on the grounds contains the graves of five members of the Group of Seven.

Eaton Beauties, bisque dolls, and a ventriloquist's dummy are among 165 prized antique and character dolls at Kleinburg's Doll Museum.

In the nearby valley, Kortright Centre for Conservation has a wetland boardwalk and 10 km of walking and cross-country ski trails. Interpretive center exhibits and demonstrations are designed to inform visitors about conserving energy, forests, land, water, and wildlife. Programs are conducted at a sawmill, beehouse, maple syrup shack, bird-box building, and on wildflower walks.

Black Creek Pioneer Village

Pre-1867 rural Ontario has been re-created in this heritage village. Its heart is a homestead of five log buildings, fashioned in 1816 by Daniel Strong, who came here from Pennsylvania. Assembled in the vicinity are 40 restored buildings, relocated from other area sites. Two outstanding exhibits are the 1844 Burwick House, which is furnished with 1800s antiques, tapestries, and rugs, and the huge cantilevered Daziel Barn Museum (1809), which boasts Canada's largest collection of 19th-century toys. Other highlights are the four-story, stone Robin's Mill, and picturesque Halfway House, a former inn with a two-tiered veranda. Costumed staff perform traditional crafts, such as weaving, spinning, quilting, and cooking on open hearths.

Paramount Canada's Wonderland

Often described as a Canadian Disneyland, this huge fun park offers more than 160 razzle-dazzle attractions—exhibits, games, animals, shows, and rides. It features a man-made mountain with a waterfall, different theme areas, such as "Hanna Barbera Land" and the "Medieval Faire," and live shows. Top attractions include Splash Works, a humongous water park; Day of Thunder racing simulator ride; Skycoaster, a 15-story free-fall plunge; and nine roller coasters, each with its own special thrill.

Avenue Road, Toronto

Take Exit 367 to Avenue Road [Hwy. 11A], which provides a route to Toronto's downtown. For a walking tour of this area, see pages 314-315.

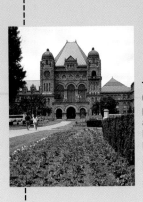

To Queen's Park
Ontario's MLAs debate provincial legislation in a bulky red-sandstone Romanesque Revival building that dominates parkland established in Queen Victoria's honor one and a half centuries ago.

Nathan Phillips Square
This downtown square is named for the 1960s mayor who championed the landmark **City Hall** (*above*), a twin-towered "clamshell" designed by Finnish architect Viljo Revell. A reflecting pool in front becomes a skating rink in winter. The **Old City Hall,** an 1899 Romanesque red-sandstone building with a distinctive clock tower, now a municipal courthouse, borders the square's east side; **Osgoode Hall,** home of the provincial law courts, is to the west. Also in the square are a Henry Moore sculpture, "Three Way Piece Number 2," dubbed *The Archer,* and a Peace Garden.

Campbell House
An 1825 model of Toronto, when it was still called York, is among period furnishings in this elegant Georgian house built in 1822 for Chief Justice Sir William Campbell (1758-1834). Dining and drawing rooms, kitchen, and master bedroom are open to the public. One of Toronto's oldest houses, it was saved from demolition by The Advocates Society, a group of trial lawyers, who raised funds to move it six blocks from its original site and have it restored.

Entertainment District, King St. West
A 1907 beaux arts gem of chandeliers, carved woods, frescoes, and Italian marble, the **Royal Alexandra Theatre** (the "Royal Alex") was taken over in the 1960s by discount sales magnate Honest Ed Mirvisch, who restored it to its original glory and presents a mix of Broadway shows and top-notch Toronto productions. Nearby is the **Princess of Wales Theatre,** opened in 1993 by the late Lady Diana. A concert hall and permanent home for the Toronto Symphony, the Arthur Erickson-designed, mirrored glass **Roy Thomson Hall** is named for newspaper magnate Lord Thomson of Fleet.

Financial District
Five of Canada's largest banks are headquartered in skyscrapers along King and Bay streets. A stone's throw from each other are I.M. Pei's 57-story **Commerce Court**; the Bank of Montreal's, Edward Durell Stone-designed, 72-story, white-marble **First Canadian Place**; Mies van der Rohe's classic 56-story, black-towered **Toronto-Dominion Centre**; **Scotia Plaza's** 68-story, red-tinted trapezoid tower; and the 26-story, twin-towered, gold-mirrored **Royal Bank Plaza.** The **Toronto Stock Exchange**, also in the business district, is one of the largest in North America.

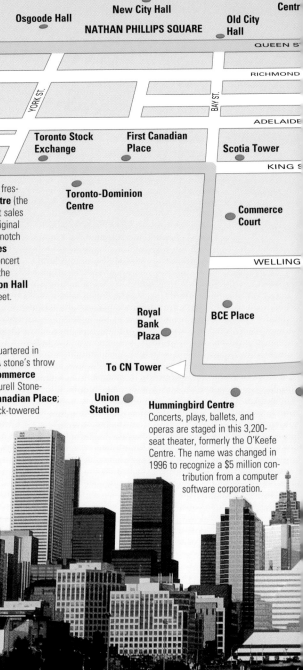

Hummingbird Centre
Concerts, plays, ballets, and operas are staged in this 3,200-seat theater, formerly the O'Keefe Centre. The name was changed in 1996 to recognize a $5 million contribution from a computer software corporation.

Map labels:
Eaton Centre
New City Hall
Osgoode Hall
NATHAN PHILLIPS SQUARE
Old City Hall
QUEEN ST
RICHMOND
UNIVERSITY ST.
YORK ST.
BAY ST.
ADELAIDE
Toronto Stock Exchange
First Canadian Place
Scotia Tower
KING S
Toronto-Dominion Centre
Commerce Court
WELLING
Royal Bank Plaza
BCE Place
To CN Tower
Union Station

TORONTO: CITY ON THE GO

Sleek, rich, and cosmopolitan, our biggest city mirrors Canada's vitality. Up to the early 1900s, it was something of a backwater, dull, conservative, puritanical—and variously known as Muddy York, Hogtown, and Toronto the Good. Primness gave way to purpose and excitement with post-World War II immigration, and the neighborhood restorations, and business, cultural, and entertainment enterprises the city fostered. When late 1900s political uncertainty blunted Montreal's competitive edge, Toronto became Canada's corporate capital.

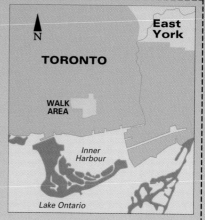

TORONTO

East York

WALK AREA

Inner Harbour

Lake Ontario

Mackenzie House

Friends bought this two-story, stone house for cash-strapped William Lyon Mackenzie (1795-1861), Toronto's first mayor, fiery newspaper publisher, and leader of the 1837 revolt against British rule in Upper Canada. A printshop in the house, which is open to the public and furnished as in his time, turns out copies of his rebel-rousing "Colonial Advocate."

Elgin, Winter Garden, and Pantages theaters

When the two-tiered Elgin and Winter Garden vaudeville houses opened in 1914, they were the most opulent in the country. The downstairs Elgin was swathed in gold leaf and red plush velvet; the upstairs Winter Garden, the world's first "atmospheric" theater, had trellised walls and a ceiling of real foliage. A movie theater occupied the building after vaudeville died. Restored and re-opened in 1989, both theaters are now maintained by the Ontario Heritage Foundation. Up the street is the equally magnificent Pantages Theatre (1920), which also began as a vaudeville house. In 1989, Cineplex Odeon spent $18 million redesigning, rebuilding, and restoring the fluted columns, domed ceilings, and crystal chandeliers.

St. Lawrence Market

This district, where markets have been held since 1803, was the site of Toronto's first City Hall (1845-99). Converted into a public market in 1904, the building has undergone extensive alterations. Historic photographs and other archival materials are showcased in the former council chambers.

St. Lawrence Centre for the Arts

Home to the Canadian Stage Company, the center's two theaters host plays, classical music concerts, dance performances, and film screenings. It often serves as a venue for public forums on topics of local concern.

CN Tower

Like an exclamation mark on the city skyline, the world's tallest freestanding structure soars 553.33 m above Toronto. Elevators to a revolving restaurant on the 351 m level, and to indoor and outdoor observation decks, travel 6 m per second. On a clear day you can see Niagara Falls, 160 km away.

Skydome

One of the world's largest amphitheaters, this home of the Toronto Blue Jays boasts 60,000 seats under a retractable roof. Its electronic scoreboard is the world's largest.

St. James Cathedral

Flatiron Building

FRONT ST.

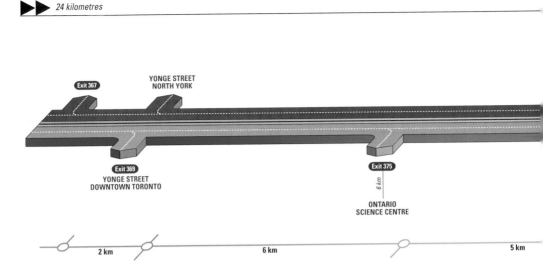

Exit 367

YONGE STREET
NORTH YORK

Exit 369
YONGE STREET
DOWNTOWN TORONTO

Exit 375

6 km

ONTARIO
SCIENCE CENTRE

2 km   6 km   5 km

**GREATER
TORONTO**

Yonge Street [Hwy. 11]

Toronto's east-west divider, this thoroughfare stretches 1,886 km from Lake Ontario to Rainy River near the Manitoba border, thus earning the distinction of being the world's longest street. Lt.-Gov. John Graves Simcoe began the Toronto–Lake Simcoe stretch in 1796 and named the road after then British Minister of War, Sir George Yonge.

North York

In the early nineties, imposing public buildings, slick office towers, and condominiums transformed a 4 km stretch of strip malls that had previously occupied Yonge Street just north of Exit 369 on Hwy. 401. The centerpiece of this redevelopment is the North York City Centre, where major points of interest include City Hall, Douglas Snow Aquatic Centre, and Mel Lastman Square, site of year-round arts events, carnivals, concerts, and celebrations of all kinds.

Within easy reach of the Civic Centre are Gibson House (see facing page) and the restored and relocated Dempsey Brothers Store at 250 Beecroft Road, which houses the North York Archives.

Garth Drabinsky's acclaimed production of *Show Boat* premiered at the opening of the Ford Centre for the Performing Arts in October 1993. It has since served as a base of his productions of *Sunset Boulevard* and *Ragtime*. This center also houses a recital hall, a studio theater, and an art gallery.

Challenging trails weave over gullies and pinnacles, and parklands provide attractive recreation areas at the foot of the weather-scoured Scarborough Bluffs. Looming 90 m above Lake Ontario, the bluffs were formed when receding glaciers dumped boulders, clay, and sand onto what had been the vast sandy delta of a mighty preglacial river.

316

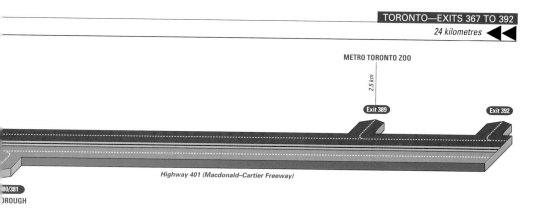

METRO TORONTO ZOO

2.5 km

Exit 389

Exit 392

Highway 401 (Macdonald–Cartier Freeway)

80/381
ЈROUGH

8 km

3 km

Gibson House, North York

This red-brick Georgian-style dwelling at 5172 Yonge Street evokes 1850s life on the Gibson family farm. It was built in 1851 by surveyor David Gibson, one of the 1837 rebels, who lived here with his wife Eliza and their seven children. Guides in period dress show visitors around, and demonstrate 1800s crafts and cooking skills. Special seasonal events take place throughout the year.

Ontario Science Centre

As many as 1 million people a year visit this center, which has been described as "a vast playground of science." Designed by Vancouver-born architect Raymond Moriyama and built into the side of a Don River ravine, it consists of a series of concrete and glass structures connected by enclosed escalators. Technological developments are traced through some 650 interactive displays, organized by theme—the Living Earth, Space Technology, the Information Highway, and Body Science.

Scarborough

South of Hwy. 401, exits 380 (Brimley Road) and 381 (Mc-Cowan Road) give access to the Scarborough Civic Centre, another Raymond Moriyama landmark (see above). Daily tours are available. The adjacent Albert Campbell Square offers concerts in summer, and ice-skating in winter.

Head south on Brimley Road (at the west side of the Civic Centre) to get to Scarborough Historical Museum in Thomas Memorial Park. Four restored late-19th-century buildings are showcased: the Kennedy Display House, the Hough Carriage Works, the McCowan Log House, and the Cornell House.

Bluffers Park, some 4 km farther south on Brimley Road, offers the best views of Metro Toronto's most prominent natural feature, the 16 km stretch of jagged bluffs along the Scarborough lakeshore.

Metro Toronto Zoo

Rolling Rouge River valley countryside is the setting for the Metro Toronto Zoo, one of the largest in the world. Science Centre architect Raymond Moriyama also designed the zoo, which contains some 4,000 animals—representing 400 species. Eight glass-roofed pavilions re-create diverse habitats for denizens with climatic backgrounds ranging from arctic to equatorial. Endangered and rare animals include Siberian tigers, snow leopards, Malayan tapir, pygmy hippopotamuses, and the Liberian mongoose. There is black-light area for observing nocturnal creatures, and an underviewing area for studying aquatic animals, such as beavers, polar bears, and seals. Visitors can ride a Monorail or Zoomobile, or follow color-coded trails.

Flamingos are among the more popular—and photogenic—birds at Metro Toronto Zoo, which also boasts such large species as emus, ostriches, laughing kookaburras, and brush turkeys.

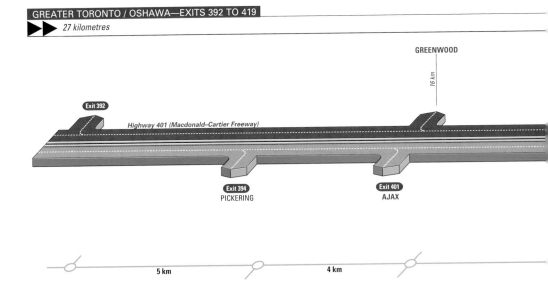

GREENWOOD

16 km

Exit 392

Highway 401 (Macdonald–Cartier Freeway)

Exit 394
PICKERING

Exit 401
AJAX

5 km   4 km

**EAST OF
TORONTO**

Ajax

This town, a thriving center of light industry and a bedroom community for Metro Toronto, developed around a munitions factory set up by the federal government in 1941. It was named for HMS *Ajax*, the British warship that cornered the German pocket battleship *Graf Spee* in the harbor at Montevideo, Uruguay, in 1939. *Ajax*'s bell and anchor are now part of the town hall, and streets are named for the warship's crew. The modest dwellings built in the 1940s to house munitions plant workers still stand virtually unchanged.

Ajax residents are diligently preserving their architectural heritage and have listed some 200 buildings of significant aesthetic or historical interest. Pickering Village, a 19th-century Quaker settlement north of Hwy. 401, retains much of its original architecture now transformed into shops and restaurants. Two "must-see" sites are The Quaker Meeting House and The Village Store.

Pickering Museum Village, Greenwood

This historical re-creation on the banks of Duffin's Creek north of Ajax evokes mid-1800s-to-early-1900s life in Durham Region. Among 13 restored structures in this fully functioning settlers' village are a blacksmith's shop, a church, and a hotel. Old-time gas and steam engines on site include tractors, threshers, and sawmill machines. Demonstrations of spinning and other pioneer skills are popular with visitors.

Whitby

Named for a seaside community in England, Whitby has its share of fine 19th-century buildings. Many can be seen on walking tours of the downtown and Old Port Whitby. The Station Gallery, in what was formerly Whitby's train station, is regarded as one of Ontario's finest public art galleries.

Cullen Gardens and Miniature Village (to the north of town, via Hwy.12) present seasonal floral displays. The mini-village showcases more than 250 historic and modern Ontario structures, built to 1:12 their actual scale. Hundreds of tiny figures fly kites, fight fires, chop wood, and ride a

This Faith, Hope and Charity *fountain is typical of the exquisite sculptures complementing the formal landscaping at Parkwood, Oshawa home of automobile tycoon R.S. McLaughlin. Priceless antiques furnish every room in the 55-room mansion.*

318

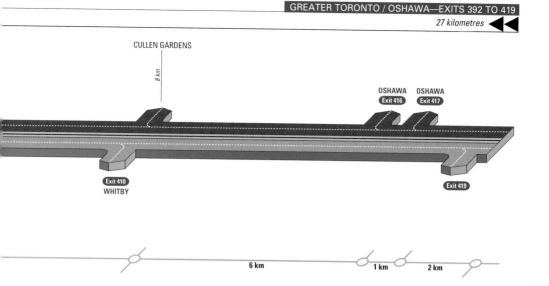

CULLEN GARDENS

8 km

OSHAWA
Exit 416

OSHAWA
Exit 417

Exit 410
WHITBY

Exit 419

6 km

1 km

2 km

fall fair merry-go-round in this small world. Its Cottage Country section re-creates provincial campgrounds and well-known vacation spots such as Mukoka's famed resorts. Just outside Cullen Gardens, animated mannequins bring the 1850s to life in the restored Lynde House, built in 1812 by a local sheriff. Costumed guides are on hand to describe the history of the house and the region.

Cullen Gardens is west of Hwy. 12; Family Kartways, a theme park featuring a midway, water-slide, mini-golf, and what is said to be the world's longest Gokart track lies to the east. You can watch professional race drivers go through their paces, or you can rent a cart and take a spin yourself.

Oshawa Aeronautical, Military and Industrial Museum

To reach this museum, take Exit 416 and head north on Park Road to Oshawa Airport. Exhibits include uniforms and military vehicles ranging from Sherman tanks and antitank guns to armored ambulances and Oshawa-built army trucks. Displays also trace the Ontario Regiment's wartime role.

Oshawa

🏠 🎣 ⛵ 🏊 ❄

This major industrial center is the birthplace of Canada's automobile industry. Here in 1908, Col. Robert Samuel McLaughlin (1871-1972) began making Buick car bodies in the family-owned plant that had previously produced horse carriages. Within a

decade, the McLaughlin firm had become part of General Motors of Canada, which today employs more than a third of the city's work force. Colonel McLaughlin's Parkwood Estate (270 Simcoe St. North), a 55-room Greek Revival mansion, filled with art, antiques, tapestries, and surrounded by gardens adorned with fountains, pools, and statuary, is open to the public.

Works of contemporary Canadian artists are regularly shown at the Robert McLaughlin Art Gallery in the Civic Centre. A gift to Oshawa by Ewart McLaughlin, the colonel's son, the gallery's permanent collection includes many paintings by the Group of Seven and Painters Eleven (a 1950s group of Canadian abstract artists).

At Oshawa's Canadian Automotive Museum (99 Simcoe St. South), more than 70 historic cars trace automobile development from the early 1900s. Highlights include a handcrafted Rolls Royce, and rarities such as an amphibious car and Canada's only steam-driven car.

Life before the automobile is depicted in three 19th-century restored homes at Oshawa Sydenham Museum (1450 Simcoe Street South) in Lakeview Park. Henry House (1849), a stone cottage with landscaped gardens, portrays life and customs in 1850-90. Pioneer life and Oshawa's early history is the focus of exhibits in the yellow-brick Robinson House (1846). Guy House (1835), typical of frame farm homes of the time, houses museum offices, a gift shop, and community archives.

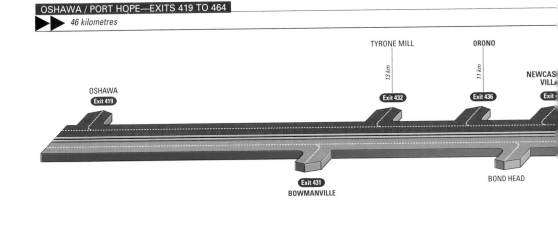

TYRONE MILL   ORONO

13 km   *11 km*

NEWCAS
VILL

OSHAWA
Exit 419

Exit 432   **Exit 436**   **Exit**

Exit 431
BOWMANVILLE

BOND HEAD

12 km   1 km   4 km   4 km

**EAST OF
TORONTO**

Bowmanville

A 19th-century mill town, this lakeshore community offers a welcoming harbor for boaters. Bygone times are the theme of the Bowmanville Museum, housed in a Provincial Italianate-style 1860s dwelling. Visitors can wander through 10 rooms with Victorian appointments and a gallery of 2,000 dolls and toys, many of them antiques. Among the furnishings is a piano manufactured locally by the Dominion Organ and Piano Company, which once shipped products to customers around the world.

You can get to Bowmanville Zoo—the oldest operating facility of its kind in Canada—by taking Liberty Street north of Hwy. 401. A scenic parkland with more than 300 lions, tigers, monkeys, and other animals, the zoo was set up in 1919 as a marketing ploy to introduce families to Cream of Barley cereal. Animal shows are given daily, and elephant and camel rides are available.

Continue on Liberty Street to reach the 1846 Tyrone Mill—restored as a working sawmill and cider press. Century-old methods are used to produce the cider, cheese, baked goods, jams, and handicrafts sold on site.

Orono

At Orono's Jungle Cat World, snow leopards rub whiskers with cougars, lynx, and bobcats. The spacious enclosures also house lions, tigers, and wolves. Deer and donkeys roam free, ready to be fed and petted by visitors.

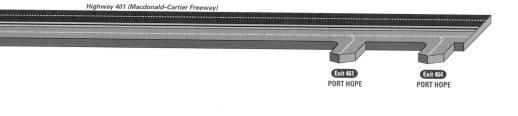

Highway 401 (Macdonald–Cartier Freeway)

Exit 461
PORT HOPE

Exit 464
PORT HOPE

21 km   4 km

Port Hope delights visitors with its impressive concentration of well-preserved 19th-century dwellings. Building styles embrace the simplicity of single-storey "Ontario cottages" (above), the charming decorative trim of Victorian verandas (middle), and the imposing mansard roofs and lofty towers of opulent mansions (below).

Newcastle Village

A blend of modern housing and fine 19th-century homes, Newcastle Village encompasses the quaint harbor community of Bond Head and the picturesque Port of Newcastle Marina. Red brick King Street buildings once housed foundries of the farm equipment manufacturing Masseys, whose members included Governor General Vincent Massey (1887-1967) and acclaimed actor Raymond Massey (1896-1983). A gracious cobblestone dwelling at 285 Mill Street was once the Massey family home.

Port Hope

Originally a fur-trading post, this town on the Ganaraska River was settled by Loyalists. By the mid-1800s, it had become a prosperous industrial and railway center, and a rich legacy of Victorian buildings remains from those years. More than 90 public buildings, churches, and homes are designated heritage sites. Film and television producers in search of Victorian streetscapes often look to Walton Street, where many handsome commercial buildings date from the 1840 to 1870 era.

Outstanding public buildings include the Port Hope Customs House (1840s), the Bank of Upper Canada (1857), the Town Hall (1851), notable for its domed clock tower and grand Palladian windows, and the Capitol Theatre (1930), now a performing arts center, but originally a movie house where decor and lighting evoked evening in a medieval castle garden.

Some of the finest dwellings can be seen just by walking down King and Dorset streets. Architectural gems on King Street include Canada House (1822), the oldest house in town, and the Little Bluestone and the Bluestone (both 1834). Named for the blue-tinted plaster coating their porous stone, both homes were built as wedding gifts for members of Port Hope's founding Smith family. A Georgian-style dwelling with an Ionic columned porch and other Greek Revival details, the Bluestone is one of Ontario's premier historic houses. King Street is the site of St. Mark's Church (1822), the oldest church in Port Hope and one of the earliest surviving frame churches in Ontario. (Governor General Vincent Massey is buried here.) Also near King Street is the Octagon, one of several eight-sided houses built locally in the mid-1880s. On Dorset Street West are Wimbourne, a Regency cottage of the early 1850s, The Cone (1847), a board-and-batten dwelling with Gothic details, Hillcrest (1874) and Homewood mansions (1904).

The Canadian Fire Fighter's Museum tells the story of fire fighting in Canada from 1830 to 1955. Helmets and turnout gear, old-time extinguishers and alarms (including a working box alarm system), and breathing machines and rescue devices are some of the items on display. On the grounds are 15 restored fire fighting vehicles, representing the hand-drawn, horse-drawn and motorized periods.

321

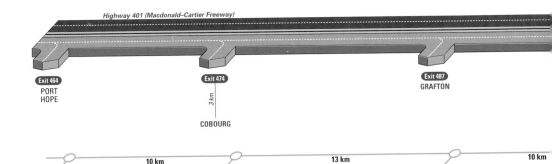

Highway 401 (Macdonald–Cartier Freeway)

Exit 464 — PORT HOPE

Exit 474 — 3 km — COBOURG

Exit 487 — GRAFTON

10 km   13 km   10 km

SOUTHEASTERN ONTARIO

Cobourg

This lakeshore community boasts a splendid waterfront walkway and avenues of stately summer dwellings, many built by wealthy visitors in the late 1800s. Mid-19th-century prosperity as a major lake port also endowed Cobourg with some outstanding public buildings. Most notable is Victoria Hall, a Palladian-style edifice with soaring clock tower and an imposing portico with four Corinthian columns. Its interior includes the council chamber, a concert hall, an "Old Bailey-"style courtroom (one of Canada's few remaining "deep-well" courtrooms), and the Art Gallery of Northumberland, which contains some 4,000 works ranging from European paintings to Inuit artifacts.

On a humbler scale is the 1833 cottage that was the birthplace of stage and screen star Marie Dressler (1869-1934). Amid Dressler House's collection of gowns, photos, recordings, and other memorabilia is a wax tableau of a scene from *Min and Bill*, the 1931 movie for which Dressler won an Oscar.

Grafton

Amid this community's wealth of heritage buildings, the showpiece is the Barnum House Museum, said to be one of the finest examples of neoclassical architecture in Ontario. Built in 1819 by Col. Eliakim Barnum, an entrepreneur from Vermont, it has been fully restored to reflect a well-to-do, 19th-century gentleman's dwelling. Grafton House has lovely period details, such as the original

Grafton's Barnum House consists of a central building flanked by wings. Frontal pilasters linked by elliptical arches grace the facade of this dwelling, which is a fine example of neoclassical style.

paint colors and wallpapers. Furnishings and memorabilia of early settlers are also displayed, while an interpretive gallery features rotating displays spanning the 1820 to 1890 era.

Colborne

A lakeside town set amid apple orchards, Colborne's most imposing feature is the world's largest apple—a four-story structure (10.6 m high, 11.6 m wide) that encloses a lookout and audiovisual displays on the local apple industry. More than 650,000 people a year visit The Big Apple, the main build-

The Big Apple

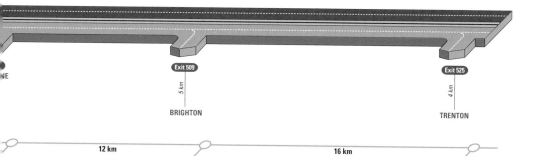

Exit 509
5 km
BRIGHTON

Exit 525
4 km
TRENTON

12 km   16 km

Some 650,000 visitors a year, including some 4,000 bus tours, drop into The Big Apple, a restaurant and theme park complex off Hwy. 401 at Colborne, Ont. In addition to extensive restaurant and bakery facilities, The Big Apple has mini-golf, a petting zoo, playground, and gift shop, and is planning an "apple train" for 1998 on which riders will get facts about apples while enjoying the picturesque countryside.

ing of a family-run restaurant and theme park complex. Crowds are seldom absent from an observation window, through which you can see pastry makers at work in a pie factory. On busy days, the restaurants may serve as many as 3,000 pieces of apple pie from the factory, plus scores of muffins, tarts, cakes, and sandwiches. At the petting zoo, or on a nature walk, you may cross paths with ducks, geese, miniature goats, or llamas. Brian McFarlane's Hockey Museum features action photos, films and videos. Other attractions include miniature golf, a children's playground, and a gift shop offering apple-themed items.

Brighton

At Proctor Conservation Area, a well-groomed trail leads to a lookout with a spectacular view of Lake Ontario. Its centerpiece is elegant Proctor House, built by a wealthy shipping merchant in 1867, restored a century later by Brighton, and now open to the public as a museum, and a site for weddings and other special celebrations. The interior of this hilltop Italianate-style mansion reflects the era from 1840 to 1880.

Some 9 km south of Brighton, Presqu'ile Provincial Park occupies a sand-and-limestone peninsula jutting into Lake Ontario. (*Presqu'île* is French for "almost an island.") A swimmers' paradise, the park is renowned for

its wide sandy beach and its warm, shallow waters. It is also noted for the variety of its landscapes—sand dunes, forests, and even abandoned farmlands. Its wetlands (rated as the most important in Ontario) provide a sanctuary for shorebirds and waterfowl, including nesting colonies of gulls, herons, terns, and cormorants. Birders come here year-round in hopes of spotting some of the more than 310 species recorded in the park. Great bird-watching is assured during the spring and fall migratory seasons.

Trenton

A magnet for vacationers, this city is an access point to the Bay of Quinte, where sailing, swimming, and fishing are top recreations. Its downtown core, where the Trent River flows into the bay, can be reached from Exit 525.

Trenton is also the eastern terminal of the Trent-Severn Waterway, which links the Bay of Quinte with Port Severn on Georgian Bay. (See pages 164-165.) Just across the Trent River, Exit 526 leads to Lock Two, where you can watch pleasure craft sailing by in summer.

East of the Trent, the RCAF Memorial Museum, located on Canada's largest military air base, is open to the public free of charge. It consists of an indoor memorial center and gallery of paintings, photographs, and other memorabilia of the force's history, and an outdoor Airpark featuring an extensive collection of vintage and modern aircraft.

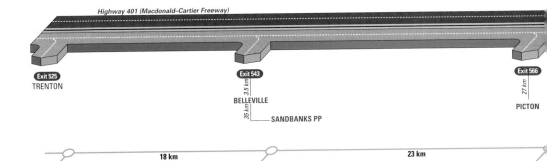

Highway 401 (Macdonald–Cartier Freeway)

Exit 525
TRENTON

Exit 543
BELLEVILLE
3.5 km
35 km
SANDBANKS PP

Exit 566
27 km
PICTON

18 km   23 km

SOUTHEASTERN ONTARIO

Belleville

This picturesque city lies at the mouth of the Moira River on the Bay of Quinte. Once a lumbering and shipping center, and now the business hub of the Quinte area, it is known for its popular harbor, waterfront trails, and superb fishing. Self-proclaimed "sport fishing capital of Ontario," it boasts some of the best bass fishing and walleye ice fishing in North America.

Restored historic dwellings lining its leafy streets reflect Belleville's 19th-century prosperity. Lofty Glanmore House is now the Hastings County Museum. Built in 1883 for a wealthy financier, this Italianate-style mansion features a mansard roof and decorative windows, and a lavish interior that includes an ornate frescoed ceiling and a sweeping suspended staircase. Period rooms typical of well-to-do, turn-of-the-century life are graced by antique furniture and European oil paintings in enormous gilded frames. The museum also contains one of the best collections of lighting devices (apparatus spanning 2,500 years) in North America.

Sandbanks Provincial Park

Hwy. 62 heads south through Prince Edward County to aptly named Sandbanks Provincial Park. This popular park's West Lake sector has the world's largest freshwater sand dune system, and a smaller, more stable dune area surrounds its East Lake. As a result, Sandbanks boasts two of Ontario's largest

and most gorgeous beaches. Up to the mid-1800s, grass and scrubby trees had contained the dunes, in ridges 12 to 25 m high, along swaths of Lake Ontario shoreline. Then farmers began grazing their livestock amid the dunes, and sand that had formerly been anchored by grass mats began to drift inland, burying forests, farms, roads, and even buildings. By the 1920s, local farmers were fighting back, planting trees and barrier fences.

Grand beaches, golden dunes, and sparkling waters that are perfect for boating, canoeing, sailing, sailboarding, swimming, and windsurfing draw visitors by the thousand to Sandbanks Provincial Park.

Exit 579	Exit 611
NAPANEE	KINGSTON

13 km   32 km

now the Prince Edward County Museum, the imposing Georgian-style Macaulay House (1830), which is furnished in the style of the 1850s and staffed by costumed guides, a small cemetery and Victorian gardens.

Canada's first prime minister, Sir John A. Macdonald, argued cases in Picton's 1834 Greek Revival stone courthouse. A jail behind the courthouse displays a double-oak gallows from 1884.

East of Picton, Lake on the Mountain, a tiny lake fed by underground streams, is perched on a limestone cliff 60 m above the Bay of Quinte. Boardwalk exhibits in the adjoining park recount facts and folklore of the lake, long a local curiosity because of its unusual setting. A great spot for strolling or picnicking, the park offers panoramic views of the Bay of Quinte.

Napanee

Loyalists who settled here in 1786 used the Napanee River's falls to power their grist and lumber mills. Millowner and Justice of the Peace Allan Macpherson built a white frame Georgian-style mansion in 1826 that is now open to visitors. The "Laird of Napanee" also owned a distillery, a general store, and a newspaper, and often entertained Sir John A. Macdonald. Sir John made his last political speech from the local Town Hall balcony in 1891. Picton's 1864 courthouse and county jail now house the Lennox and Addington County Museum and Archives. Its collection of maps, dioramas, and domestic, farm, and industrial artifacts retell local history.

Eventually a 1960s government reforestation program stemmed the advance. By then the area had become a recreational mecca, with tourist hotels, summer cottages, and parkland. Park staff offer slide and film shows, campfire evenings, and guided walks over boardwalks and trails. The self-guiding Cedar Sands Trail winds through juniper heaths and cedar forests in the East Lake sector to a platform overlooking the Outlet River.

Picton

Accessible by Hwy. 49, this town is the recreational, commercial and administrative hub of Prince Edward County (Quinte's Island), which juts into Lake Ontario. Picton's Victorian stone-and-brick dwellings and Edwardian-era commercial buildings recall its 19th-century prosperity as a lake port. Macaulay Heritage Park encompasses St. Mary Magdalene Church (1825),

325

A Touch of Beauty by the Roadside

HIIGHWAY 401 / TRENTON TO BELLEVILLE

ORLAND FRENCH *has been a frequent contributor to* Cottage Life *and other magazines, and writes a weekly newspaper column. He also teaches journalism at Loyalist College in Belleville, Ontario.*

AS YOU DRIVE ALONG THE QUINTE WILD-FLOWER HIGHWAY—the 18 km stretch of Hwy. 401 from Trenton to Belleville—you may be surprised by the pink, blue, and pale yellow wildflowers brightening the gentle greenness of the roadside. These flowers, set in carefully arranged roadside sites, are the result of an intriguing collaboration between local private firms and volunteers, and the Ontario Ministry of Transportation (MTO).

The Quinte Wildflower Project—part of the MTO's Adopt-A-Highway Program—belies the concerns of Catharine Parr Traill. In 1868, the noted Canadian writer and botanist predicted that the natural beauty of Canada's wilderness was "destined to be swept away, as the onward march of civilization clears away the primeval forest, reclaims the swamps and bogs, and turns the waste places into fruitful field."

The "onward march of civilization" slashed the 4-lane Hwy. 401 across southern Ontario and right through parts of Traill's "primeval forest." A regular commuter on this superhighway during the mid-1990s, Belleville businessman William Schyven appreciated its convenience. But, as he drove to a job in Toronto, Schyven began to think his weekly trip might be more pleasant if the roadside were abloom with flowers.

So Schyven contacted the MTO's Kingston office and said he wanted to plant wildflowers along the 401's Trenton–Belleville stretch. The ministry staff, throughly familiar with the Adopt-A-Highway elsewhere in the province, embraced Schyven's idea—and the wildflower project was born.

Schyven raised money from local sponsors to cover the project's costs and rallied the support of local volunteers. A chemical company donated the herbicide used to prepare the ground (wildflowers will not "take" unless all other competing growth is killed off), a farm equipment dealer offered the use of a tractor, and other companies kicked in with cash. A farmer loaned a Rototiller; kids in church groups turned out to weed the roadside plots.

The MTO's contribution involved planning and preparing the roadside sites, and providing the assistance of experts. It continues to supply the wildflower mixtures, developed for easy maintenance and hardy enough to survive the hostile roadside environment. The mixtures consist of native and nonnative species: blue flax, yarrow, dame's rocket, black-eyed Susan, spike-blazing star, and gray-stemmed goldenrod. Botanists are reluctant to identify which species are strictly native to the region. Some species originated elsewhere—for example, the new england aster and the wild lupine, which grows in parts of Newfoundland. Other species may have been brought here more than 200 years ago by the United Empire Loyalists who settled locally after the American Revolution.

The Quinte Wildflower Project—the largest of its kind in Ontario—was inaugurated in the spring of 1996. The initial roadside plantings covered 4 ha, and the goal is to cultivate more than 20 ha. The project continues a North American trend to beautify highways begun in the 1960s. Ladybird Johnson, wife of U.S. President Lyndon Johnson, prevailed upon her husband to introduce legislation to improve the appearance of U.S. roadways. The first Adopt-A-Highway programs were intended to remove the signs and litter that disfigured the roadside landscape. Since the U.S. National Environmental Act of 1969, other pieces of legislation have broadened these programs in the United States.

In Canada, enormous amounts of time and money were being spent to mow and clip roadside grasses right from the gravel shoulder back to the right-of-way fence. Weeds and wildflowers alike were sprayed with herbicides to kill them off. Roadsides were as green and bland as a well-kept lawn. Eventually, the high cost of roadside maintenance forced provincial governments to abandon their mowing machines. Since the mid-1980s, Ontario has turned to volunteers and private sponsors for landscaping projects along highways. (This recalls a time when the early settlers in Ontario were sometimes compelled to do roadwork at least a few days a year as a form of taxation.)

The organizers of the Quinte Wildflower Project have learned that, while you can assist nature, you cannot always control it. Some wildflowers fail after showing early success, while others refuse to stay where they were planted. Care must be taken to avoid species, however attractive, that invade neighboring fields. The appealing oxeye daisy causes havoc in strawberry beds. Queen Anne's lace (wild carrot) grows quite well on its own and displays a delicate white lacy flower. But farmers detest it and consider it a noxious weed. Blue flax and dame's rocket are planted in isolated roadside spots where they can be effectively corralled by paved access lanes.

Late spring and summer are the best times to enjoy the roadside displays on the Quinte Wildflower Highway. If you decide to stop and smell the flowers, pull off at an interchange, where you are bound to find some of the best plantings.

"The ministry staff…embraced Schyven's idea—and the Quinte Wildflower Project was born."

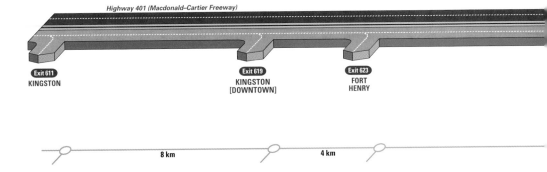

SOUTHEASTERN ONTARIO

Kingston

Since its founding in 1673, Kingston has undergone many reincarnations: it has been an Indian settlement, a French fort, a British citadel, and, briefly, Canada's capital (1841-43). From Hwy. 401, Exit 619 offers the quickest access to the downtown. Dominating the heart of this thriving city at the junction of Lake Ontario, the Rideau Canal, and the Thousand Islands stretch of the St. Lawrence is City Hall. This Tuscan Revival-style limestone edifice was planned to become Canada's parliament building, but while construction was under way, the government of the day—the legislative assembly—moved from Kingston to Montreal. Hour-long tours of the city's historic sites, museums, and galleries begin in a park across from City Hall.

On the waterfront, the Marine Museum of the Great Lakes has exhibits about shipbuilding, shipwrecks, and the natural history of the lakes, as well as models and diagrams of freighters, naval vessels, and recreational boats that plied these great bodies of water. In a restored 1849 waterworks nearby, the Pump House Steam Museum features the world's largest collection of steam engines. A Martello tower on the Macdonald Park waterfront, a survivor of 1840s coastal defenses, is now the Murney Tower Museum.

Bellevue House (1840) was the residence of Sir John A. Macdonald, Canada's first prime minister. Now a national historic site, this Italianate villa, restored and furnished in period style, portrays Macdonald's early life and career as a lawyer and politician. Thematic exhibitions from its

The Marine Museum of the Great Lakes at Kingston tells a proud story of sailing the inland seas. Visitors can tour the icebreaker Alexander Henry, *where officers' cabins are kept "shipshape and Bristol fashion" (spare and spotless) for a bed-and-breakfast clientele.*

Exit 648
GANANOQUE

27 km

At Kingston's Fort Henry, fife music floats on the air, just as it might have done when British garrisons occupied this post-War of 1812 bastion.

10,000-work collection are featured at the Agnes Etherington Art Centre at Queen's University. Some 150 years of prison life is the focus of the Correctional Service of Canada Museum on Kingston Penitentiary grounds. Hundreds of hockey players, coaches, and referees from amateur and professional leagues throughout North America are enshrined in a photographic gallery at the International Ice Hockey Hall of Fame.

Exit 623 from Hwy. 401 takes you to Kingston Mills Lock Station, a restored military blockhouse built to protect the southern entrance to the Rideau Canal. Exhibits depict the history of the canal, which links Kingston and Ottawa (see also page 135).

Fort Henry, Kingston

Once the largest military establishment in Canada, Fort Henry was built in the 1830s to guard the Rideau Canal and the local naval base whose ships protected settlements along Lake Ontario. Restored a century later, its mighty limestone walls enclose cells, kitchens, barracks and officers' quarters, furnished and equipped to reflect garrison life of the 1860s. Its museum rooms contain Canada's finest

collection of military artifacts, including artillery, uniforms, and other regalia. Daily, in summer, the Fort Henry Guard, a precision-trained, university-student corps, stages a stirring military drill on the parade grounds. Nearby Fort Frederick Tower (1846) houses the Royal Military College of Canada Museum. Exhibits include regimental plate and one of the best small arms collections in North America. The museum also chronicles the history of the college, which was established in 1876.

Gananoque

This resort town calls itself the "Gateway to the Thousand Islands." Local triple-decker vessels offer 1½- to 3-hour cruises through this scenic waterway. Except for the last trip of the day, the three-hour cruise stops at Boldt Castle on Heart Island, N.Y. Built by U.S. hotelier George C. Boldt for his wife, the turreted, six-story, 120-room castle, abandoned at her death in 1904, is being meticulously restored by the Thousand Island Bridge Authority.

Gananoque (pronounced Gan-an-*ock*-way) began in the 1780s as a Loyalist settlement. The neoclassic Town Hall (1831) was built as a home for his bride by John Macdonald, whose family helped develop the town. Gananoque Historic Museum occupies the former Victoria Hotel (1863). Displays include 19th-century furnishing, antique dolls, duck decoys, military uniforms, and 1800s deeds and documents.

▶▶ *84 kilometres*

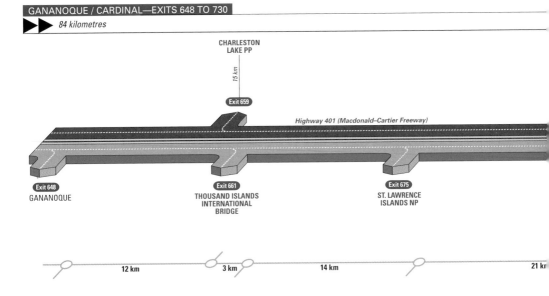

CHARLESTON
LAKE PP

15 km

Exit 659

Highway 401 (Macdonald–Cartier Freeway)

Exit 648
GANANOQUE

Exit 661
THOUSAND ISLANDS
INTERNATIONAL
BRIDGE

Exit 675
ST. LAWRENCE
ISLANDS NP

12 km   3 km   14 km   21 kr

**SOUTHEASTERN
ONTARIO**

Charleston Lake
Provincial Park

Island-studded Charleston Lake
is renowned for its ample supply
of bass and lake trout. The
park's diverse terrain—rocky
outcrops, gently rolling hills,
sandy beaches—supports a fascinating array of creatures. Woodlands shelter deer, foxes, raccoons, porcupines, and flying
squirrels; the wetlands are home
to beavers, muskrats, turtles, and
frogs. An excellent trail system
includes the Quiddity Trail,
which follows woods and wetlands to an observation tower
overlooking Charleston Lake,
and the Sandstone Island Trail,
which leads to a prehistoric
campsite of aboriginal hunters

*Rising to 45 m above
the Saint Lawrence
River, the Thousand
Islands International
Bridge, which links
Ontario to New York
State, offers spectacu-
lar views of the island-
studded river and its
host of secluded
summer getaways.*

and gatherers. The park has children's programs, guided hikes,
campfire gatherings, and a special
stargazing evening in August.

Thousand Islands
International Bridge

Hwy. 137 leads to this Ontario–
New York State link, opened by
Prime Minister Mackenzie King
and President Franklin Roosevelt
in 1938. Hill Island, accessible
from the midpoint of the bridge,
is Canadian territory and site of
the 120 m Thousand Islands Sky-
deck. Elevators take you to three
observation levels; from the top-
most, on clear days, you can see
up to 65 km.

Rockport

On the Thousand Islands Parkway (4 km east of Hwy. 137
on the way to the international
bridge), this village is a departure
point for cruises to Millionaires'
Row, a series of privately owned
islands with palatial summer
dwellings. The tour's oddest
sight is the world's shortest international bridge, a 10 m span linking a cottage on a Canadian
island to an American islet containing the Canadian's flagpole.

St. Lawrence Islands
National Park

Mallorytown Landing, south
from Exit 675, is the headquarters and jumping-off point for
this, our smallest national park. A
boater's paradise, it encompasses
21 islands or parts of islands.
Most are wooded, with poetic
names such as Camelot,
Endymion, and Mermaid, and

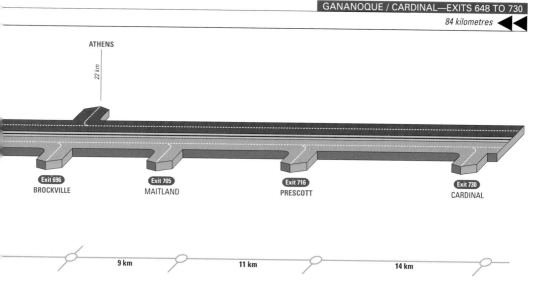

ATHENS

22 km

| Exit 696 | Exit 705 | Exit 716 | Exit 730 |
| BROCKVILLE | MAITLAND | PRESCOTT | CARDINAL |

9 km   11 km   14 km

have docks, walking trails, and primitive campsites.

St. Lawrence Islands supports flora and fauna usually found farther south. Plant species include black oak, mayapple, and shaggymane, and Canada's only deerberry. The park's symbol is another rarity—the scraggy Pitch Pine. Some creatures, such as the harmless, tree-climbing black rat snake, are unique to this region.

At Mallorytown Landing, you will find a supervised beach and playground for children, a campground, nature trails, picnic and boating facilities. Visitor center displays describe the park's natural history and the settlement of the Thousand Islands.

Brockville

One of the first Loyalist settlements in Upper Canada, this city is named for War of 1812 hero, Gen. Isaac Brock. Loyalists arrived here in 1784, and their history is enshrined at the Brockville Museum, an 1840 graystone building overlooking the St. Lawrence River. One prized exhibit is a restored St. Lawrence skiff. King Street is lined with many fine buildings and dwellings from the Victorian era. Fulford Place, once visited by prime ministers and royalty, is now open to the public. This 35-room stone mansion was built in the early 1900s by George Fulford, who made a fortune in patent medicines. A cobblestoned street links King to Courthouse Green and the County Courthouse (1842), one of Ontario's oldest public buildings.

Athens

Settled by Loyalists in the 1780s, this village takes pride in its 19th-century civic buildings, business blocks, and houses. Under a decade-long ongoing project, professional artists have painted 12 bold, exterior, giant murals of small-town life in bygone days throughout the village.

Prescott

Fort Wellington National Historic Site is Prescott's outstanding landmark. Built by the British in the War of 1812, the fort was rebuilt during the Rebellion of 1838-39. Earthen ramparts from 1813 surround three later structures that include officers' quarters and a three-story stone blockhouse. Furnishings and summer military drills by costumed guides re-create the 1840s, when the Royal Canadian Rifle Regiment was stationed here. At July Loyalist Days, Fort Wellington hosts Canada's largest annual military pageant.

When folk from Athens, Ont., tell you they're painting their town, you can take them at their word. Since 1985, they have been commissioning professional artists to work their magic on civic and commercial buildings in the village. The result to date: a dozen giant outdoor murals of rural life in the 1800s, and a major tourist attraction.

331

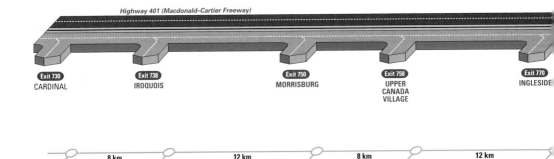

Highway 401 (Macdonald–Cartier Freeway)

Exit 730	Exit 738	Exit 750	Exit 758	Exit 770
CARDINAL	IROQUOIS	MORRISBURG	UPPER CANADA VILLAGE	INGLESIDE

8 km   12 km   8 km   12 km

SOUTHEASTERN ONTARIO

Iroquois

Seven towns hereabouts were inundated by rising river levels during the construction of the St. Lawrence Seaway in 1958. While six were totally lost or partially moved, all of Iroquois was relocated a kilometre north of its original site. Carman House (1820), one of three buildings to escape the upheaval, is now a craft shop and museum. Its pioneer kitchen contains a beehive oven, a wide, deep cooking fireplace, and a stone sink set in a windowsill.

The Seaway Lock Lookout is ideal for viewing oceangoing vessels pass through the only deepwater locks on the Canadian side of the seaway.

Morrisburg

Only a third of Morrisburg was moved to high ground during the seaway construction. A riverside park occupies part of the old downtown, which was razed. Houses and churches untouched by the flooding and still on their original sites can be seen on a walking tour of town.

Upper Canada Village

This showpiece of mid-19th century rural Ontario contains some 40 pioneer buildings: dwellings, churches, and shops. Some were moved here from sites flooded during construction of the seaway, others are reconstructions. Interiors have been meticulously re-created, right down to paint colors, wallpapers, and fabrics. There are two working farms, a cheese factory, an 1860 general store, an 1835 tavern, a school, a blacksmith's shop, and saw, flour, and woolen mills. Staff in period costume demonstrate bygone skills. Crysler Hall has films and displays of village history. A Children's Activity Centre introduces youngsters to crafts and games of pioneer times.

Upper Canada Village can be explored by horse-drawn wagon, canal boat, or on a miniature wood-burning train. The latter passes Crysler Farm Battlefield Monument to British and Canadian troops who defeated a much larger U.S. force here during the War of 1812.

Just east of the village, the Upper Canada Migratory Bird Sanctuary is a haven for more than 200 bird species. Some 8 km of trails wind through wetlands and woodlands; an interpretive center offers nature programs. An observation tower is located beside a feeding station for migrating ducks and geese.

Ontario's past lives on at Upper Canada Village, where ox- and horse-drawn vehicles, and dozens of restored stores, houses, taverns, and mills—all staffed by guides dressed as their Loyalist forebears—mirror pioneer lifestyles.

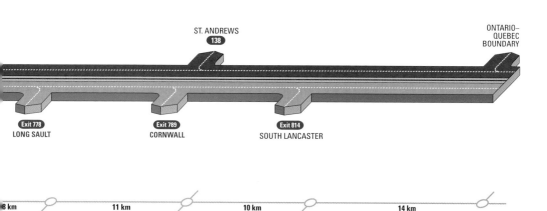

ST. ANDREWS
138

ONTARIO–
QUEBEC
BOUNDARY

Exit 778
LONG SAULT

Exit 789
CORNWALL

Exit 814
SOUTH LANCASTER

8 km   11 km   10 km   14 km

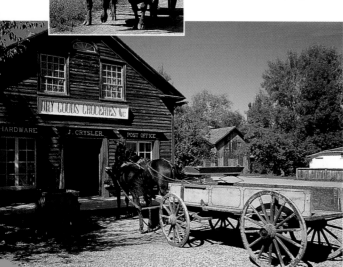

Ingleside

This is one of two towns (the other is Long Sault) set up to accommodate inhabitants of villages flooded by the St. Lawrence Seaway. Ingleside is the western gateway to scenic Long Sault Parkway, an 11 km series of causeways and bridges linking 11 islets that were pre-flood hilltops.

Long Sault

Riverside towns and farms sacrificed for the St. Lawrence Seaway are remembered in Lost Villages Museum, housed in an 1840 log cabin in nearby Ault Park. Mock-ups of stores, churches, schools, and train stations re-create the pre-seaway face of the region. Slides and photos convey the impact of relocation on local people.

Cornwall

By the late 1800s, textile and paper mills in this Loyalist bastion were attracting French-speaking Quebeckers, whose descendants now form roughly half the local population. Local history is the focus of exhibits in the United Counties Museum, originally a limestone farmhouse, built in 1840 by Loyalist William Wood. Another museum, the restored Inverarden Regency Cottage Museum, is a fine example of 1800s Regency architecture. Built in 1816 for his retirement by Nor'Wester John Macdonald, the cottage features many period antiques including some original furnishings.

Hwy. 138 north takes you to St. Andrews West, site of one of Ontario's oldest stone structures—an old church (1801), now a parish hall, built by Gaelic-speaking Highland settlers—St. Andrews Church (1860), a Gothic building with a bell tower and lofty spire, and Quinn's Inn (1865), a stagecoach stopover, now a dining room and pub.

Hwy. 138 south leads to Cornwall Island and the Seaway International Bridge to New York State. Singers, dancers, and speakers, whose presentations at conferences, schools, and universities celebrate their aboriginal heritage, are based at the island's Native North American Travelling College. A museum on the grounds has exhibits on Cree, Ojibway, and Iroquois lifestyles and government systems, and a re-created Indian Village features traditional dwellings of various Native groups.

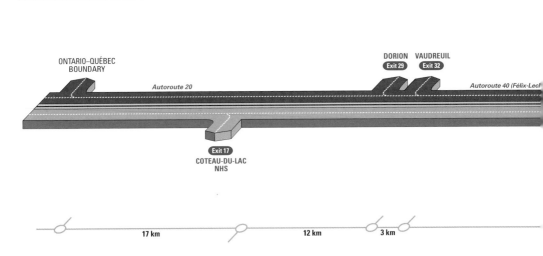

ONTARIO–QUÉBEC
BOUNDARY

DORION   VAUDREUIL
Exit 29   Exit 32

Autoroute 20

Autoroute 40 (Félix-Lecl

Exit 17
COTEAU-DU-LAC
NHS

17 km   12 km   3 km

**IN AND
AROUND
MONTREAL**

Autoroutes 20 and 40

At the Ontario–Quebec boundary, Hwy. 401 becomes Autoroute 20, which takes you to Vaudreuil-Dorion. There, a 3 km stretch of 540 links up with Autoroute 40 (Félix-Leclerc), which crosses to the island of Montreal, and continues along the north shore of the St. Lawrence to the bridge over the Montmorency River, east of Quebec City.

Coteau-du-Lac National Historic Site

Traces of a canal built by the French in 1750 to bypass St. Lawrence River rapids, and its replacement, North America's first lock canal, built 30 years later by British authorities, can still be seen here. Some 300 m long, the now dry lock canal raised ships 2.7 m. Up to the 1850s, it was a vital passageway for military and commercial shipping between Montreal and Kingston. Earthworks, mounted cannon, trenches where the British kept watch on the St. Lawrence, and a reconstructed octagonal blockhouse now housing military memorabilia are part of British fortifications built between 1781 and 1814. A reception center has models of the fortifications and displays about navigation on the St. Lawrence.

Coteau-du-Lac is named for a small hill (*coteau*), where the community built its first church. Now the church is a visitors' centre.

Vaudreuil-Dorion

For details about this community, see pages 170-171.

Montreal

Autoroute 40, also known as the Métropolitaine, cuts across the northern districts of Montreal, providing acess to the Botanical Gardens and Olympic Park. Autoroute 15 (Décarie Expressway) leads to the downtown. (For a walking tour, see pages 172-173.)

Montreal Botanical Gardens

Among the largest and finest in the world, these gardens were founded in 1931 by renowned botanist Frère Marie-Victorin (1885-1934). Today they encom-

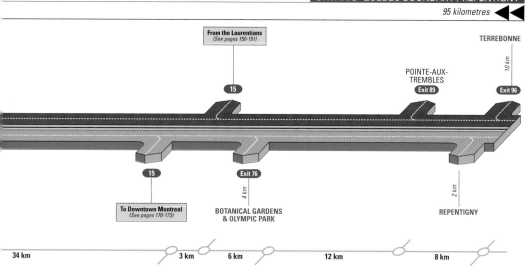

From the Laurentians
(See pages 150-151)

TERREBONNE

POINTE-AUX-
TREMBLES

Exit 89

Exit 96

15

10 km

15

Exit 76

To Downtown Montreal
(See pages 170-173)

4 km

BOTANICAL GARDENS
& OLYMPIC PARK

2 km

REPENTIGNY

34 km   3 km   6 km   12 km   8 km

At Montreal's Botanical Gardens, the Olympic Stadium forms a back-drop for the exquisite Meng Hu Yuan or Dream Lake Garden, the largest Chinese garden outside China. Garden pavilions were designed in China by artisans who came here to ensure their proper assembly.

and a venue for special events, can hold up to 80,000. A cable car takes visitors to the top of 190 m high Olympic Park Tower, the highest inclined tower in the world. The view is spectacular.

A life sciences museum known as the Biodôme occupies the Vélodrome, site of Olympic cycling events. In simulated trop-ical, polar, maritime, and Lau-rentian climates, 5,000 plants and 4,000 small animals live in their appropriate ecosystem.

Repentigny

At the junction of the St. Law-rence and L'Assomption rivers, this town is named for a sei-gniory set up here in 1647. A Louis XV high altar, designed in 1761 by Louis-Philippe Liebert, is among treasures in the restored Église de la Purification, which dates from 1723. Its two towers and facade date from 1850.

A striking contrast is provided by the modern design of Notre-Dame-des-Champs Church (1963), the creation of Quebec architect Roger D'Astous.

Terrebonne

Île des Moulins, in the old town, is the picturesque setting for four 19th-century buildings: a bakery (1803), a sawmill (1846), and a seigneurial office and flour mill (both 1850). An interpretation center in the seigneurial office displays memorabilia of the Mas-son family, who ran the mills from the 1830s to the 1880s. This island on Rivière des Mille Îles is ideal for picnics or a river-side stroll to the nearby rapids.

pass 26,000 plant species, 30 outdoor gardens, 10 exhibition greenhouses, and noted Japan-ese and Chinese gardens. A bug-shaped Insectarium houses some 250,000 insects from around the world.

Olympic Park

Site of the 1976 Olympic Games, the park's centerpiece is Olympic Stadium, the innovative creation of French architect Roger Tailli-bert. Built at great expense and amid much controversy, "The Big O," as it is called locally, home to the Montreal Expos

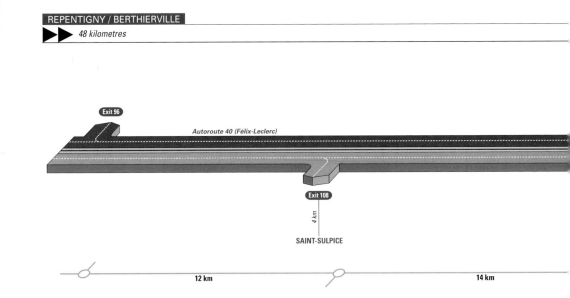

Exit 96

Autoroute 40 (Félix-Leclerc)

Exit 108

4 km

SAINT-SULPICE

12 km   14 km

**EAST OF
MONTREAL**

Saint-Sulpice

The fieldstone Saint-Sulpice Church—the third church on the site—dates from 1832. Victor Bourgeau redid the church in Gothic Revival style in 1873. Its tabernacle and high altar have survived from the second church: they were carved in 1750 by Francois-Noël Levasseur. Other interesting features include a baptismal font carved from a tree trunk, and a wooden chapel dating from 1830.

Joliette

Barthélemy Joliette, who opened up this region and founded the town in 1823, named it L'Industrie for the progress and prosperity it represented. After his death, the townspeople renamed the thriving community for its founder. Nowadays, symphony orchestras, opera singers, and choirs from around the world come to Joliette in July and August for the prestigious Festival international de Lanaudière. Major performances take place in the festival's 2,000-seat outdoor amphitheater, where surrounding grassy slopes can accommodate another 8,000 people. More inti-

mate recitals are scheduled in area churches and schools.

Joliette also boasts one of Quebec's most renowned art museums. An impressive collection of religious art dating back to the Middles Ages and a broad selection of Canadian art are among some 5,000 works in the Musée d'Art de Joliette. Major works include paintings by Jean-Paul Riopelle and Emily Carr and works by English sculptor Henry Moore. Other intriguing items include gold-crafted objets d'art and about 1,000 rare books.

Lanoraie

The restored Hetu and Hervieux houses are local examples of Quebec fieldstone construction of the early 1800s. The community was named for Monsieur de la Noraye, a French army officer, who owned a seigneury here in the early 1700s.

Berthierville

This picturesque St. Lawrence River community is the hometown of legendary racing-car champion Gilles Villeneuve. Personal memorabilia, trophies, and racing cars at the Musée Gilles

Music lovers from across Quebec converge on Joliette in July and August for concerts of classical and popular music presented as part of the Festival international de Lanaudière. While some events take place in local schools and church halls, open-air concerts are presented in this vast 2,000-seat amphitheater.

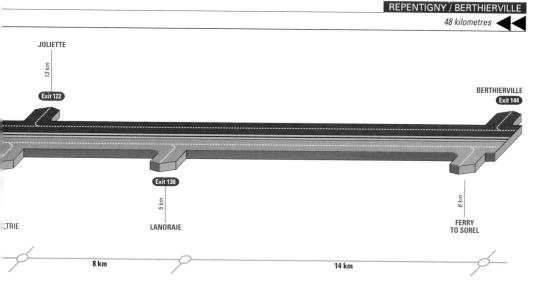

JOLIETTE

13 km

Exit 122

BERTHIERVILLE
Exit 144

Exit 130

5 km

6 km

_TRIE

LANORAIE

FERRY
TO SOREL

8 km

14 km

Villeneuve trace the career of much loved Formula 1 driver, killed at age 32 during qualifying trails for the 1982 Belgian Grand Prix. Also included are films, photos, and interactive displays such as a Ferrari Formula 1 driving simulator.

The Cuthbert Chapel is Quebec's oldest Protestant church. Built in 1786 by British officer James Cuthbert in memory of his wife, the building is now a cultural and visitor center. In summer, it comes alive with guided tours, historical and cultural exhibits, and entertainment.

Sorel

On the St. Lawrence River at the mouth of the Richelieu, Sorel is a year-round port, industrial and shipbuilding center, and commercial hub for the Richelieu Valley. To get there, take Hwy. 158—which crosses the Sorel Islands—to the ferry across the St. Lawrence. A stone monument on the east side of Richelieu marks where Fort Richelieu was built by the French in 1642. No trace of the fort nor of its successor, Fort Saurel, remains. (The community, named in 1672 for French army officer Pierre de Saurel, was renamed William-Henry by the British in 1787, but reverted to a variation of the original name in 1845.) In the early 1780s, Sir Frederick Haldimand, the British governor of Quebec, laid out Sorel's present checkerboard street plan. Haldimand also built the white-stucco Maison des Gouverneurs, long a summer residence for Canada's governors general and now a conference center and exhibition hall. German-born Baron von Riedesel and his family, who occupied the house in 1781, adorned their Christmas tree with lights. This was the first lit Christmas tree in North America, an event commemorated by a sculpted Christmas tree in front of the mansion.

Carré Royal (Royal Square), a magnificent downtown park laid out in 1791, is said to be landscaped to mirror the Union Jack. The parc du Regard sur le fleuve offers a fine view of the St. Lawrence River.

The restored Hervieux house at Lanoraie is a fine example of the solid fieldstone houses with steep gable roofs, dormers, and multi-paned casement windows that were typical of the 1- and 1½-story homes prevalent in early Quebec.

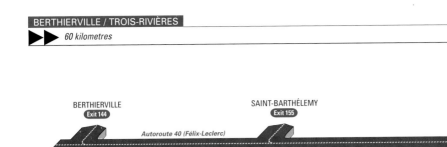

BERTHIERVILLE
Exit 144

SAINT-BARTHÉLEMY
Exit 155

Autoroute 40 (Félix-Leclerc)

11 km   25 km

**NORTH SHORE,
ST. LAWRENCE
RIVER**

While much of Trois- Rivières was leveled by a disastrous fire in 1908, a few buildings from the Old Town, such as the Maison des vins and the adjoining Monastère des Ursulines (below), survived.

Shawinigan

Just before Trois-Rivières, Hwy. 40 merges with a 3 km stretch of the north-south Autoroute 55, also called the Autoroute Transquébécoise. Travelers who wish to visit Shawinigan can head north on 55 at the point of juncture. Now best-known for its famous native son, Prime Minister Jean Chrétien, the city's earlier claim to fame was as a producer of hydroelectric power. In 1899, Shawinigan Water & Power first harnessed Shawinigan Falls on the St. Maurice River and began serving customers over a wide area, including Montreal. The availability of cheap power attracted aluminum, chemical, and other industries to Shawinigan, sparking rapid development. Exhibits, dioramas, and artifacts at Shawinigan's Centre d'interprétation de l'industrie describe the industrial and technological achievements

that followed here and throughout Quebec.

A 100 m observation tower offers views of the spectacular Shawinigan Falls. Visitors can tour the local aluminum plant, and the 1911 Italian-Renaissance style Power Station 2 and its 1932 Art Deco addition.

Some 30 km north of Shawinigan, a tract of the Laurentians' rugged grandeur is preserved in La Mauricie National Park. To experience this wilderness, head north on Hwy. 351, which links up with a 60 km parkway bisecting the park's southern sector.

Trois-Rivières

This city takes its name from three channels of the St. Maurice River that flow into the St. Lawrence. Beginning as a fur trade fort in 1634, the city is now an industrial center and hub of the province's pulp and paper manufacture. At the waterfront Parc Portuaire, photos, scale models, and videos detail all facets of the industry, from lumbering to recycling techniques. From May through September, visitors can embark from this park on cruises of the St. Maurice and St. Lawrence rivers.

Rue des Ursulines in the old city is named for the community's first religious congregation of cloistered nuns who came here in 1697 and established a hospital and a school for girls. This street, the only one to survive a terrible 1908 fire, is lined with buildings from the New France era. Silverware, books, paintings, liturgical garments, and needlework are displayed in a museum at the

SHAWINIGAN

36 km

55

Exit 180
YAMACHICHE

Exit 199
TROIS-RIVIÈRES

18 km

6 km

Ursuline Monastery. The Maison Hertel-de-la-Fresnière next door is an architectural gem of the 1820s. Across the street, St. James Anglican Church occupies a 1742 convent, the only convent of the Récollet order still standing in Quebec. Farther along, the 18th-century Manoir de Tonnancour (rebuilt in 1974) now houses an art gallery.

Another survivor of the 1908 fire, the Manoir Boucher-de-Niverville (1668), 168 Rue Bonaventure, has antique furniture and dioramas of local history. Trois-Rivières' links with fur traders and missionaries are also evoked at the Pierre Boucher Museum, housed at 858 Rue Laviolette, in the imposing Séminaire Saint-Joseph (1929). A collection of arms and 19th- and 20th-century military uniforms and medals are displayed at the Musée Militaire du 12e Régiment Blindé (the Armoury Museum), 574 Rue Saint-François-Xavier.

The Musée des arts et traditions populaires du Québec, 200 Rue Laviolette, focuses on 8,000 years of arts and crafts—textiles, tools, toys, furniture, and artifacts from prehistoric times to the recent past. Across the street, a renovated 1822, 20-cell jail depicts prison life.

Les Forges du Saint-Maurice, Trois-Rivières

From downtown Trois-Rivières, Rue des Forges takes you 13 km northward to this national historic site, birthplace of Canada's iron and steel industry. Cannons for the king and stoves for his subjects were the main products when the ironworks—the first in

Canada—began in 1730. Within a decade, it was busily turning out pots and pans, tools, and plowshares. Pathways guide you to ruins where casters, foundry workers, blacksmiths lived, to sites of forges, and to a 12 m high chimney. The Grande Maison, home of the foreman or ironmaster, was rebuilt in the 1970s in the style of the original 1737 dwelling. It has a model of the 1845 community and offers film and slide shows of the work done here. Other displays describe iron and cast-iron manufacturing in the 18th and 19th centuries.

Anchors, cannons, horseshoes, pots, plowshares, stoves, and tools were all mass-produced at Les Forges du Saint-Maurice near Trois-Rivières, New France's most important industry in the 1700s. Today's visitors can see various ruins as well as reconstructions of the blast furnace and the ironmaster's house, once the centerpiece of the workers' community.

339

Autoroute 40 (Félix-Leclerc)

Exit 199	Exit 203	Exit 220	Exit 229	Exit 236
TROIS-RIVIÈRES	CAP-DE-LA-MADELEINE	CHAMPLAIN	BATISCAN	SAINTE-ANNE-DE-LA-PÉRA

3 km   *4 km*

4 km   17 km   9 km   10 km

NORTH SHORE, ST. LAWRENCE RIVER

▶

Since 1659, a wooden chapel at Cap-de-la-Madeleine has honored the Virgin Mary. In 1714, the stone chapel (foreground) was erected on the site, and it contains what many claim to be a miraculous statue of the virgin. Behind the chapel stands the 2,000-seat, octagonal Basilica of Our Lady of the Rosary.

Cap-de-la-Madeleine

Known as "le Cap," this industrial city and popular pilgrimage destination at the mouth of the St. Maurice River began as a seigneury and Jesuit mission.

Visitors come from around the world to pray at the Shrine of Our Lady of the Cape. Canada's national shrine to the Virgin Mary here is third in importance (after St. Joseph's Oratory in Montreal, and Ste-Anne-de-Beaupré) among places of pilgrimage in Quebec.

Devotion here began in 1888, when three parishioners claimed they saw the eyes of the statue of the Virgin become momentarily animated. The statue is now housed in a 1717 stone chapel, that is said to have the oldest belfries in Canada.

The shrine contains a riverside garden with Stations of the Cross, a service center for pilgrims, and Our Lady of the Rosary Basilica. Built in 1955-64, this 2,000-seat edifice boasts an imposing 78 m conical tower, 350 stained glass windows and a mighty 75-stop organ. Also on the grounds, the Bridge of the Rosaries commemorates a St. Lawrence River ice bridge that, during exceptionally mild weather, held up until parishioners had transported stones for the parish church across the river in 1879.

Champlain

Champlain's treasures include steep-roofed stone houses, pastel-painted wooden dwellings with wraparound verandas, and Notre-Dame-de-la-Visitation

Church. Built in 1879 to replace a 1710 church, this Neo-Roman building contains a 300-year-old painting of the Immaculate Conception and a gilt-trimmed sanctuary lamp carved in maple that was used in the 1710 church.

Batiscan

This village's architectural highlight is the Vieux Presbytère (Old Presbytery), once the manor of Jesuit priests who were Batiscan's first seigneurs. It was built in 1816 with stones from the original presbytery of 1696. A handsome rectangular structure, it features triple chimneys, dormer windows, and flared eaves. Now a museum, it exhibits more than 1,000 antiques of different styles

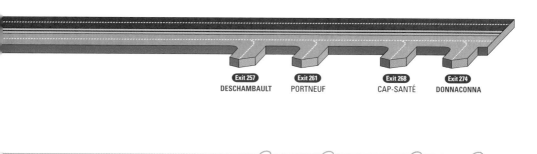

| Exit 257 | Exit 261 | Exit 268 | Exit 274 |
| DESCHAMBAULT | PORTNEUF | CAP-SANTÉ | DONNACONNA |

| 25 km | 5 km | 7 km | 5 km |

and periods, ranging from a 17th-century four-poster bed to a 19th century English-style piano.

Sainte-Anne-de-la-Pérade

One of the most popular ice-fishing spots in the province, this farming village sits midway between Trois-Rivières and Quebec City. In January and February—tommycod season—hundreds of multicolored plywood cabins, equipped with electricity and stoves, spring up on the frozen St. Anne River. Winter carnival events enliven the occasion with singing, dancing, and prizes for the longest fish, best decorated cabin, and best ice sculpture.

Sainte-Anne-de-la-Pérade Church (1869), a Gothic-Revival edifice with twin bell towers, is modeled after Montreal's Notre-Dame Basilica. Paintings and handicrafts are exhibited on summer weekends at the Manoir

Madeleine-de-Verchères, which is noted for its ornamental and medicinal gardens. The manor is named after a Quebecker who, at age 14, defended her father's fort against an Iroquois attack. She married the seigneur of La Pérade, and lived in the seignorial manor from 1706 to 1747. Her son built the present manor about 1772.

Deschambault

At least a third of the dwellings here are a hundred years old. One of the finest, the late-18th-century Maison Deschambault, houses an inn and a restaurant. Two massive steeples and a hipped roof crown Saint-Joseph Church (1841). Among several works of art inside are six wooden statues that adorn the chancel and pulpit. A small 1815 presbytery behind the church now serves as a cultural center and offers fine views of the St. Lawrence River. An exhibition and tourist information center, and a crafts school occupy the 1802 Chevrotière Mill.

Donnaconna

A *passe migratoire* (migration channel), the main attraction here, was built to ease the journey of Atlantic salmon along the Jacques Cartier River. Constructed when the original migratory route was obstructed by dam construction and logging, it is an ideal spot for viewing the salmon swimming upstream, especially in July. The site has an interpretation center and picnic tables, and controlled fishing is permitted on the river.

During the two-month tommycod festival each winter, an enchanting miniature village blooms on the Sainte Anne River here at Sainte-Anne-de-la-Pérade. Ice fishers from across the province converge on the town, where they set up hundreds of brightly painted cabins on the frozen waters.

Where Old Stone Dwellings Evoke Early Days

AUTOROUTE 40 / CHAMPLAIN TO CAP-ROUGE

ANDRÉ ROBITAILLE *is a writer, architect, and urban planner who teaches at Laval University. He has been involved in the restoration of Quebec City's Place Royale. This translation from French is by* ALAN HUSTAK.

ON THE WAY TO QUEBEC CITY, the busy Hwy. 40 parallels the less hectic Hwy. 138, which follows the route of the *Chemin du Roi* (the King's Road). From Hwy. 40, you can take side roads to this old royal road and explore the architectural gems of riverside villages—Champlain, Batiscan, Deschambault and others—that evoke Quebec's early days.

Until the completion of the King's Road in the 1730s, the St. Lawrence was the only transportation route linking the seigneuries along the north shore. The seigneurs—persons of rank granted vast domains by the French crown—parceled out lots to individual tenant farmers, known as habitants, in return for an annual charge. The lots stretched back from the St. Lawrence in deep, narrow strips. As well, they were angled northeast to southwest, perpendicular to the river's edge to take advantage of the sunlight and to give protection against the prevailing winds. The habitants built their dwellings in the middle of the lot, with cultivated fields front and back. North of the house, the forest was a source of wood for fuel and timber for building. Here, too, the habitants hunted wildlife, and tapped the maple trees for syrup.

The habitants adapted the building techniques of their native France to the new conditions—the excessive cold, the frozen ground, and the different materials. The walls of the earliest dwellings were built with posts driven vertically into the ground or, later, supported on stone sills or foundations above ground level. Fieldstones or other materials were used to fill the spaces between the posts. Eventually, the habitants developed the *pièce-sur-pièce* technique: squared logs were laid horizontally and dovetailed at the corners.

As the habitant prospered, he replaced his small wooden dwelling with a larger, more comfortable stone house. The barn, the cowshed, the stable, and the creamery were all separate buildings, a wise precaution taken in case of fire.

Inside the habitant's house, a fireplace dominated a large open space. Beside the fireplace were the oven and a stove where stews and soups were kept warm over an open fire. In the corner of the kitchen area was a cold-storage pantry with a small windowlike opening for ventilation; and, in the center of this area, a hand pump for drawing water from a basement well. There was also a stone sink with a drainage spout on the exterior wall. A steep ladder led to the grain storage bin in the attic, and a trapdoor opened to the basement. These arrangements ensured the self-sufficiency of the habitant and his family through the long winter.

In the early days, the exterior of the habitant's house had haphazard openings, square peepholes for windows, and narrow doors. But all the basic architectural elements—the stone foundation, the rectangular plan, and the unroofed front veranda—appeared early on. The chimney was situated at the northeast corner or, if the dwelling had been enlarged, in the center of the building. In time, the habitant moved the sleeping quarters into the attic, where dormer windows were added. Initially, the basement was a crawl space but, as it was deepened for storage, the overall height of the house was raised. The steeply pitched roof, covered with horizontal planks or, later, cedar shingles, was eventually extended over the veranda. This traditional style of domestic architecture, well established by the end of the French regime, remained in favor into the mid-1800s.

With the arrival of the King's Road, the village sprouted in the center of the seigneury. Important buildings went up in stages: first an inn, then a general store, followed by an apothecary and a lawyer's office. A church with its presbytery and cemetery dominated the public square; a school or convent was added at a later stage. At one end of town stood the seigneurial manor and its small administrative office, and a flour mill (wind- or water-driven). Sometimes the mill was used for sawing wood or other purposes.

Along Hwy. 138, villages preserve examples of New France's dwellings and town layouts. At Cap-Santé, there is a beautiful church (1755) with its grand presbytery next door (1849). What is probably the most beautifully proportioned town square is at Deschambault. Here, too, you'll find a magnificent church (1833), a community hall, a convent, and a park with a spectacular view of the river. The 1815 presbytery with its remarkable roof has been painstakingly restored and converted into a museum. Nearby is the stagecoach station, the 1802 La Chevrotière mill (now a museum), and the first mill (1766), which is surrounded by the manor, the blacksmith's shop, and other historic structures.

Other roadside reminders of bygone days include: the Maison Quézel (1750) at Saint-Augustin; the Manoir Larue (1834) and the small Fiset House (1801) at Neuville; the Solard House (1759) at Portneuf; and the Delisle House (1648) at Deschambault, which Comte de Frontenac, governor of New France in the late 1600s, converted into a storehouse for his troops in 1672. At Grondines, situated between Sainte-Anne-de-la-Pérade and Deschambault, the beautifully proportioned, almost classic, presbytery built in 1842 marks more or less the last example of the traditional architecture of New France.

> *This traditional style ... remained in favor into the mid-1800s...*

André Robitaille

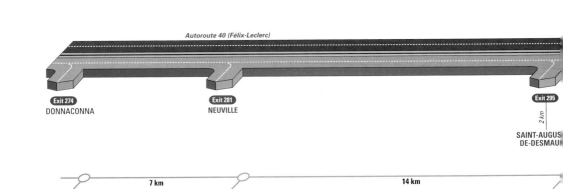

Autoroute 40 (Félix-Leclerc)

| Exit 274 | Exit 281 | Exit 295 |
| DONNACONNA | NEUVILLE | SAINT-AUGUS DE-DESMAU |

2 km

7 km   14 km

AROUND QUEBEC CITY

Neuville

Houses here are set into the hillside at various elevations, thus ensuring their occupants an unspoilt view of the St. Lawrence. Local limestone has been used for major buildings throughout Quebec since the time of New France. Rue des Érables has many fine examples of buildings constructed with local stone: the Maisons Larue (at 306, 624 and 681), Maison Angers (at 715), and Sainte-Anne Chapel (666). Another landmark on this street is Saint-François-de-Sales Church, which dates from 1696, and has a high altar by François Baillargé (1759-1830) and paintings by Antoine Plamondon (1804-95). One of its greatest treasures is a richly ornamented wooden canopy known as a *baldaquin* created in 1695 for the episcopal palace in Quebec City. In 1717, the bishop gave it to Neuville in exchange for wheat to feed his starving flock.

Saint-Augustin

Saint-Augustin-de-Desmaures Church, an early 1800s building, contains works by famed Quebec artists and craftsmen: paintings by Antoine Plamondon (1804-96), gold objects by

François Ranvoyzé (1739-1819), and two carved angels by Louis Jobin (1845-1928).

Cap-Rouge

A plaque here commemorates Jacques Cartier's 1541 attempt to set up the first French colony in Canada. His frail forts were no match for the harsh winter and few of his crew survived. Those who did returned to France the following spring.

L'Ancienne-Lorette

In 1673, Jesuit Father Chaumonot and 200 Huron Indians established a mission here, modeled on a pilgrimage site in Loreto, Italy. A plaque on Ancienne-Lorette Church, built in the early 1900s, identifies the site of the original mission. (You can get there by taking Exit 306, then heading north on Hwy. 540.) The mission moved to Loretteville (see facing page) in 1697.

A replica of La Grande Hermine, *Jacques Cartier's flagship on his 1535-36 expedition, and an aboriginal longhouse are among attractions at Cartier-Brébeuf National Historic Site in Quebec. Cartier and his men wintered beside the St. Charles River, where the park now stands. In Stadacona, a Native village a short distance from his ice-encrusted huts and ships, some 600 Iroquois lived in longhouses such as this reconstruction. When scurvy struck the Frenchmen, claiming 25 lives, the Indians taught them how to combat the disease with a brew made from the bark and leaves of eastern white cedar trees.*

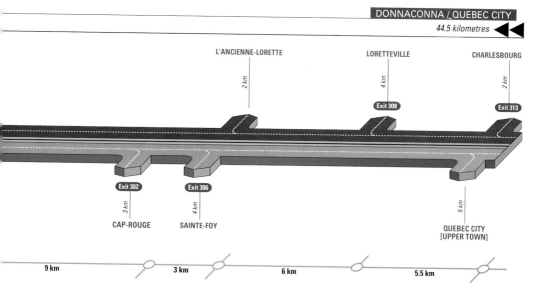

L'ANCIENNE-LORETTE   *2 km*

LORETTEVILLE   *4 km*   Exit 308

CHARLESBOURG   *2 km*   Exit 313

Exit 302   *3 km*   CAP-ROUGE

Exit 306   *4 km*   SAINTE-FOY

5 km   QUEBEC CITY [UPPER TOWN]

9 km   3 km   6 km   5.5 km

Sainte-Foy

From Exit 306, you can go south on Hwy. 540 to Sainte-Foy, home to Laval University. Founded in 1852, this is the oldest French-language institution of higher learning in North America. The Louis-Jacques-Casault Pavilion houses the university's art collections. Exhibitions and concerts are presented in the Maison Hamel-Bruneau.

Six of the Canadian martyr saints inhabited a mission established in 1637 in what is now the affluent Sillery district. Artifacts unearthed at the site are in a museum at the Maison des Jésuites (1700). In the 1760s, writer Frances Brooke and her military chaplain husband lived in the Jesuit House, where she set *The History of Emily Montague* (1769), the first Canadian novel.

Crocodiles, lizards, snakes, and piranhas are among the more exotic of 1,700 fish and amphibians, representing more than 300 species, in the Aquarium du Québec. From the aquarium, you overlook both the 548 m Quebec and the 668 m Pierre-Laporte bridges. One of North America's longest cantilever bridges, the Quebec Bridge collapsed twice—in 1907 and 1916—before it finally spanned the St. Lawrence in 1918.

Loretteville

Once called Jeune-Lorette (to distinguish it from Ancienne-Lorette), this community is accessible via Exit 308 and Hwy. 371 north. On the Wendake reserve, across the Saint-Charles River, exhibits in the Maison Aroüanne tell the story

This handsome cat is among 600 wild creatures, representing some 125 species, in the Jardin zoologique de Québec at Orsainville, north of Charlesbourg.

of this Huron settlement since 1697. Notre-Dame-de-Lorette Chapel (1862), on the site of a 1730 chapel, also has a small museum. Other attractions include the Parc de la Falaise and its Kabir Kouba Falls and, just north of Wendake, the replica of a traditional Huron village.

Charlesbourg

From Exit 313, Hwy. 151 North (Autoroute Laurentienne) leads to Charlesbourg. Streets here radiate from the Trait-Carré, a square dominated by the Palladian-style, Thomas Baillargé-designed Saint-Charles-Borromée Church (1826)—a layout dating back to the town's 1659 Jesuit founders. An interpretive center in the restored 1740 Moulin des Jésuites offers walking tours that pass such historic buildings as the 18th-century Maison Ephraim-Bédard (which houses the local historical society) and the 1846 Maison Pierre-Lefebvre, now an art gallery.

At Orsainville, some 5 km north of Charlesbourg, the Jardin zoologique de Québec shelters some 600 animals and birds.

Quebec City

From Exit 313, Hwy. 175 South leads to the Saint-Jean, Kent, and Saint-Louis gates of Quebec City's Upper Town. (For a walking tour of this area, see pages 346-347.) Before crossing the Saint-Charles River, Hwy. 175 passes Cartier Brébeuf National Historic Site, 175 Rue L'Espinay East. Its centerpiece is a replica of Jacques Cartier's *La Grande Hermine* (see facing page).

QUEBEC: STORIED CITY ON A CAPE

Founded in 1608 by Samuel de Champlain, Quebec is one of North America's most beguiling cities. The only walled city on the continent, it crowns Cape Diamond, a strategic cliff above a narrowing of the St. Lawrence River. Almost since its founding, it has been divided into an Upper Town, where political and religious institutions are located, and a residential and commercial Lower Town. Much of the city's historic ambience has been preserved. Undefaced by high rises, the downtown core, which has been inhabited continuously for some 400 years, looks much the way it did during the French regime. It is not just history that defines the city, however, but rather the atmosphere that emanates from its architecture, its narrow winding streets, its hidden courtyards, and a unprepossessing grandeur that flows from the past and inhabits the present. So unique is Quebec's urban character that the United Nations designated the city a World Heritage Site, putting it in such distinguished company as Cairo, Damascus, Florence, Havana, and Tunis.

The Citadel and National Battlefields Park

Often called "The Gibraltar of North America," the star-shaped Citadel (*above*) was built by the British in the 1820s on the site of French fortifications. It contains a regimental museum and a summer residence for Canada's governor general. The Promenade des Gouverneurs follows the Citadel's outer walls to National Battlefields Park, which contains the Plains of Abraham. Granite tablets there trace events of Sept. 13, 1759, when British and French forces fought for control of North America in the most decisive battle in Canadian history. An interpretive center in the basement of an old city jail, now part of the park's Musée du Québec, describes the battle which lasted less than 20 minutes, and cost the lives of Wolfe and Montcalm, the opposing commanding generals.

Parc de l'Esplanade

This park is one of the main sites of the city's famous winter carnival. For 10 days in late February each year, the city erupts with winter sports, parades, music, dances, and other kinds of revelry, including a canoe race across the St. Lawrence River. Throughout the festivities, streets are alive with lights and decorations, and parks are adorned with fanciful ice statues. Presiding over all is the figure of a giant snowman, Bonhomme Carnaval (*above*).

Parc de l'Esplana

PORTE SAINT-LOUIS

To National Battlefields Park

RUE SAINT

CÔTE DE LA CITADELLE

RU

Fortifications of Quebec

Visitors can stroll along promenades skirting sections of the ramparts encircling Quebec City. Built between 1713 and 1812 and reinforced in the 1870s, the 5 km long walls are 6 m high in places and 17 m wide at their thickest point. Four gates pierce the fortifications: St. Louis, Kent, Prescott, and St. Jean. The gates no longer control access but serve as bridges for pedestrians on the fortifications walkway.

Ursuline Monastery

Founded as a school for girls in 1639 by Marie Guyart de l'Incarnation, the convent, twice damaged by fire, is still contained behind the original walls. The votive lamp in the chapel has never been extinguished since it was first lit in 1717. Montcalm is buried in a crypt beneath the altar; his skull is displayed in the convent's museum. Other exhibits include gilded liturgical paintings, engravings, ornaments, embroidery, and beadwork.

Augustinian Museum and Convent

Founded as a hospital by Augustinian nuns, who arrived from France in 1639, the museum displays 17th- and 18th-century medical instruments, as well as paintings, silverware, and embroidery.

QUEBEC

WALK AREA

St. Lawrence River

Lévis

Artillery Park

French garrison buildings constructed here in 1712 continued to be used for military purposes until 1964. Visitors to this national historic site can explore richly furnished officers' quarters and the underground vaults of the Dauphine Redoubt.

Seminary Museum

The history of the French in North America is the theme of this museum, said to be the oldest in Quebec. Housed in a former Laval University students' residence, the museum also displays religious paintings, gold objects, silverware, and scientific instruments. In summer, there are guided tours of the seminary chapel and buildings.

PORTE VT-JEAN

RUE SAINT-JEAN

RUE CHARLEVOIX

CÔTE DU PALAIS

RUE DAUPHINE

RUE SAINTE-ANGLE

RUE SAINT-STANISLAS

RUE COOK

RUE SAINTE-ANNE

RUE CHAUVEAU

CÔTE DE LA FABRIQUE

SAINTE-URSULE

RUE SAINTE-ANNE

Hôtel de ville

RUE STE-FAMILLE

Notre-Dame Cathedral

Champlain's tomb is in the crypt of this cathedral, but no one knows the exact spot. Churches have stood on the site since 1632: the present cathedral is the oldest parish church in Canada. Although Notre-Dame dates from the late 1700s—it replaced a cathedral destroyed by the British during the siege of 1759—its ornate baroque interior was restored in 1922. Its episcopal throne was a gift from Louis XIV.

RUE DONNACONA

RUE DES JARDINS

Fort Museum

Lower Town

A steep flight of steps, appropriately known as the Breakneck Stairs, leads to Quebec's oldest district, site of Champlain's original settlement. More than 80 heritage buildings around Place Royale have been restored, including the oldest, the 1684 Hazeur House. Unlike most restorations, Lower Town is a lively neighborhood, where refurbished buildings are used as apartments, restaurants, and boutiques.

RUE DU TRESOR

RUE DU FORT

Maison Kent

Maison Maillou

Built about 1736, this restored dwelling now houses the Quebec City Chamber of Commerce. Nearby **Maison Kent** dates from the 1830s.

To Place Royale

Château Frontenac

Terrasse Dufferin

Château Frontenac Hotel

Balanced on a cliff above Lower Town, this 660-room hotel has dominated the city skyline since it opened in 1893. It stands where the former French governors' residence, the Château St. Louis, used to be. Adjoining the Château Frontenac, **Dufferin Terrace** commands a panoramic view of the St. Lawrence River. A boardwalk, the Promenade des Gouverneurs, extends from the terrace along the summit of Cape Diamond to National Battlefields Park.

Fleuve Saint-Laurent

St. Lawrence River

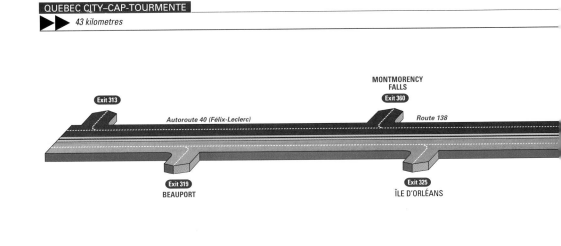

Exit 313

MONTMORENCY FALLS
Exit 360

Autoroute 40 (Félix-Leclerc)

Route 138

Exit 319
BEAUPORT

Exit 325
ÎLE D'ORLÉANS

5 km   7 km   3 km

**EAST OF
QUEBEC CITY**

Beauport

Now part of Quebec City, this community was first settled in 1634. Its Bourg-du-Fargy district contains fine heritage buildings. One of the oldest, Maison Bellanger-Girardin (1735), is notable for winterizing devices such as thick doors and small windows. It houses the Centre d'Exposition de la Société d'Art et d'Histoire de Beauport.

Montmorency Falls

A lookout on the Montmorency River at the crest of "Quebec's Niagara" offers a grand view of this thundering 83 m cascade. Roughly 35,000 litres of water flow over the falls every second, an amount that just about quadruples during the spring runoff. Although not as wide as Niagara, the Montmorency Falls are one and a half times higher. In winter, the water freezes into a huge ice cone known as the *pain de sucre*, or sugar loaf.

At Montmorency Falls, visitors can view the 30-story cataract from a cable car, a cross-falls bridge, two-level platforms, panoramic stairways, a hillside esplanade, and the restaurant and lounges of the historic Manoir Montmorency.

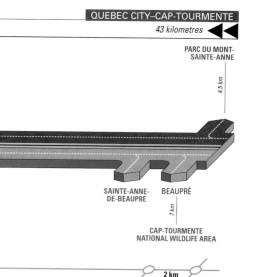

PARC DU MONT-
SAINTE-ANNE

4.5 km

SAINTE-ANNE-   BEAUPRÉ
DE-BEAUPRÉ

7 km

CAP-TOURMENTE
NATIONAL WILDLIFE AREA

26 km   2 km

To explore Île d'Orléans is to savor history. Although centuries of isolation ended in 1935, when a bridge finally linked island and mainland, islanders still proudly cling to the traditions and rich architectural heritage of New France.

A manor house, a hospital, and a monastery formerly occupied the site of Manoir Montmorency, a hotel with superb views of the falls, the St. Lawrence River, and Île d'Orléans. In its manor house days, it hosted famous visitors and residents: Queen Victoria's father (Edward, Duke of Kent) and his mistress spent three summers here during the 1790s. As a result, the dwelling was long known as Kent House.

Île d'Orléans

At Montmorency, a bridge from Hwy. 40 leads south to this island in the St. Lawrence River. Jacques Cartier first called this spot the Island of Bacchus (for the Greek god of wine) after he found wild grapes growing here, but later renamed it for the Duc d'Orléans. Because many fine heritage properties survive on the island, the entire region has been designated an historic site.

Hwy. 368—the 70 km *Chemin Royal*—encircles the island,

linking six historic villages rich in centuries-old churches and homes. To the west, within easy reach of the bridge, Sainte-Pétronille boasts the island's oldest dwelling, the Maison Gordeau de Beaulieu (1648), still in De Beaulieu hands. A church dating from 1716, the oldest in Quebec, can be seen in Saint-Pierre, east of the bridge. Poet Félix Leclerc (1914-88) is buried in the churchyard.

Sainte-Anne-de-Beaupré

A famous shrine to Quebec's patron saint has drawn pilgrims here since the mid-1600s. More than 1.5 million visitors a year flock to the town's granite, twin-spired, 2,000-seat basilica. Among its treasures are a beautiful stained glass rose window, exquisite frescoes, art deco chapels, and an oak statue of Saint Anne atop a marble pedestal. The grounds contain a memorial chapel, erected in 1878 on the foundation of the first chapel on the site, and the Scala

Santa (1871), a three-story building housing a chapel and a replica of the 28 steps Jesus ascended in Pontius Pilate's court. In summer, torchlight processions are held on the Chemin de la Croix (Stations of the Cross) hillside. A domed cyclorama depicting Jerusalem as it would have looked in Christ's day and a waxwork reconstruction of Saint Anne's life are contained in an historical building.

Parc du Mont-Sainte-Anne

This year-round park has hiking trails, cycling paths, 40 downhill ski runs, and 181 km of cross-country ski trails. An 800 m cable car climbs to the top of Mont St. Anne, which offers magnificent views of the region.

Cap-Tourmente National Wildlife Area

During April and October, as many as 300,000 snow geese, migrating between breeding grounds on Baffin Island and winter refuges in New Jersey, Virginia, and North Carolina, touch down here. Open year-round, the reserve has observation points from which you can see the geese wheeling through the sky in spectacular formations. At low tide, they can be seen feasting on bulrushes that cover the St. Lawrence River mud flats. From mid-April to late October, an interpretive center offers audiovisual shows and guided tours. Naturalists are on hand to give information on the geese and 250 other bird and 45 mammal species here.

349

NORTHERN HIGHWAYS

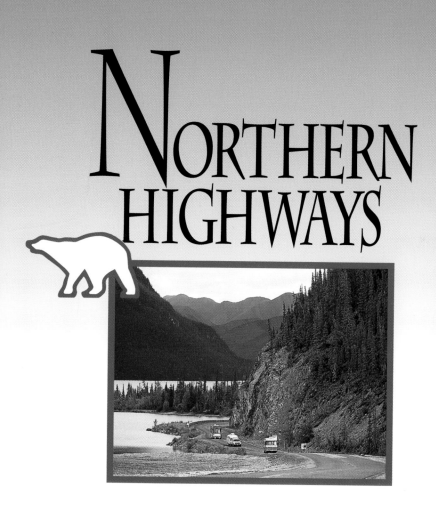

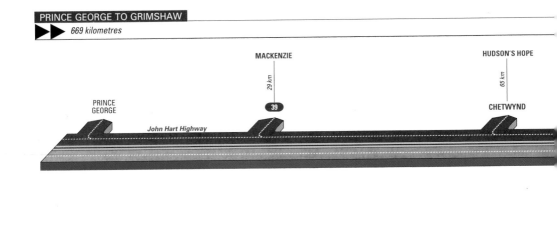

MACKENZIE

HUDSON'S HOPE

29 km

65 km

PRINCE
GEORGE

39

CHETWYND

John Hart Highway

112 km

152 km

97 k

**NORTHEASTERN
BRITISH
COLUMBIA/
NORTHWESTERN
ALBERTA**

*It took five years to fill the 2 km
long, 183 m high W.A.C. Bennett
Dam in the Peace River valley, west
of Hudson's Hope, B.C. One of the
largest earthfill structures in the
world, it was built on Williston
Lake in the 1960s with rocks and
debris from a glacial moraine. Visitors can take an underground bus
tour of the powerhouse.*

John Hart Highway

Named for a 1940s premier of
British Columbia, this northern
extension of Hwy. 97 runs from
Prince George to the Alberta
border. (For details about Prince
George, see pages 240-241.) The
Hart links up with the Alaska
Highway at Dawson Creek, and
with Alberta's Hwy. 2 at the
provincial boundary. Hwy. 2
links up with the Mackenzie at
Grimshaw.

Mackenzie

Hwy. 39 takes you north to this
town named for explorer Alexander Mackenzie, who camped here
on his 1793 trail-blazing journey to
the Pacific Coast. Mackenzie
came into being in 1965 when
pulp, paper, and saw mills began
operating in the area. A popular
fishing spot, it is at the south end
of Williston Lake, which is
stocked each year with 50,000

rainbow trout. Canada's largest
man-made reservoir (1,773 km^2),
Williston was created in the
1960s by diverting waters from
the Finlay and Parsnip rivers,
source of the Peace River, into a
section of the Rocky Mountain
Trench. (The Peace now flows
from the east arm of the lake.)
Logging roads around town lead
to other backcountry fishing
spots, as well as to camping and
hunting destinations. Nearby
Morfee Lake has good swimming, boating, and waterskiing.

Chetwynd

Calling itself the "Chain Saw
Capital of the World," this
forestry, mining, and farm center
has embellished its streets and
businesses with wooden sculptures of local wildlife—all created
by B.C. artists. Trapping and
farming implements, and a railway caboose are among exhibits
in the Little Prairie Heritage
Museum.

Hudson's Hope

One of B.C.'s oldest settlements, Hudson's Hope dates
back to 1805, when explorer
Simon Fraser founded a trading
post here. Fraser arrived via the
Peace River; today's traveler can
follow Hwy. 29. A community
museum has fossils, prehistoric
stone tools, and trapping and
coal-mining artifacts. Outdoor
exhibits include a log church, a
trapper's cabin, and a replica of
a Hudson's Bay trading post.

A visitor center at the Peace
River Dam some 3 km south of
town has exhibits on the hydro-

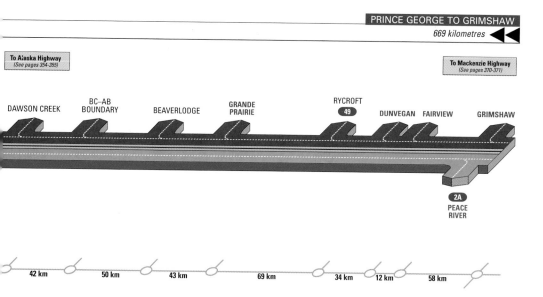

To Alaska Highway
(See pages 354-355)

To Mackenzie Highway
(See pages 370-371)

DAWSON CREEK   BC–AB BOUNDARY   BEAVERLODGE   GRANDE PRAIRIE   RYCROFT 49   DUNVEGAN   FAIRVIEW   GRIMSHAW

2A PEACE RIVER

42 km   50 km   43 km   69 km   34 km   12 km   58 km

electric project and the area's natural and human history. Displays include life-size models of duck-billed dinosaurs, and casts of dinosaur footprints taken from local bedrock.

Photographs and artifacts at the W.A.C. Bennett Dam, some 22 km west of town, describe the geology of the region and how the dam was built. Interactive exhibits explain how power is generated and transmitted.

Dawson Creek
For details, see pages 354-355.

Grande Prairie
This community is the business and transportation center of Peace River country. Extensive parkland around a man-made reservoir offers hiking, swimming, and golf. A walking tour takes in the downtown murals that depict this area's natural and pioneer history. Fossils, dinosaur bones, and aboriginal and pioneer artifacts can be seen in the Pioneer Museum, which also contains a one-room school, country store, homesteader's cabin, and church.

Dunvegan
The community preserves three historic structures: the Factor's House (1877-78), once part of the Hudson's Bay trading post here; the chapel of St. Charles Mission, the first Roman Catholic church in northern Alberta (1885); and the mission's rectory (1889). The Anglican mission site has also been restored and furnished. Guided walks and special

programs describe the history of the site.

Fairview
Known as the "Heart of the Peace," Fairview is the hub of a district known for its fine grain, oilseed, fruit, and vegetable crops. A community museum housed in a onetime RCMP barracks depicts early 20th-century pioneer life in this area. Exhibits include an old trading post and schoolroom, a post office, and hospital equipment.

Grimshaw
For details, see pages 370-371.

Peace River
A 3.5 m statue honors Henry Fuller "Twelve-Foot" Davis, a prospector of legendary generosity who died here in 1900. His tombstone at the nearby junction of the Peace and Smoky rivers states that "he was every man's friend and never locked his cabin door." Other points of interest include a restored 1916 Northern Alberta Railway Station and the Centennial Museum. The latter has a model of Fort Fork, built nearby on the Peace by Alexander Mackenzie on his 1792-93 journey to the Pacific. Its fireplace was reconstructed with stones from the original site.

St. Charles Church and rectory, built in the 1880s of hand-hewn timbers, are among several restored historic buildings at Dunvegan, once a major fur, provision, and mission post of the Peace River district.

DAWSON CREEK   FORT ST. JOHN   Alaska Highway (Hwy. 97)   FO NEL

73 km   387 km   28 k

NORTHERN BRITISH COLUMBIA/ YUKON TERRITORY

Dawson Creek

This lively spot is the southern terminus of the Alaska Highway, which extends 2,400 km northwest to Fairbanks, Alaska. Now the main artery for anyone driving to Alaska or Yukon, the rugged road was built in 1942 as a supply route to U.S. military in Alaska. Nestled on the edge of rolling farmland, Dawson Creek is also an important grain shipping center, with interests in forestry, oil, and natural gas. A renovated railway station houses a tourist information center and a museum containing pioneer artifacts, natural history, wildlife displays, and Alaska Highway memorabilia. Local arts and crafts are showcased in the annex of a grain elevator next door. Two churches, a log schoolhouse, a blacksmith shop, a store, and other pioneer buildings in the Wright Pioneer Village offer a glimpse of Dawson Creek before the highway builders arrived. An extensive collection of farm equipment is also displayed.

More than 30,000 Alaska Highway travelers pass through Dawson Creek each year. The route's starting "0" Milepost and Mile "0" cairn are in the center of town.

Fort St. John

Billed as B.C.'s energy capital, this community, founded in 1794 as a fur-trading outpost, is also one of the oldest non-Native settlements on the B.C. mainland. A four-season recreational destination, it caters to activities ranging from canoeing and horseback riding to skiing and snowmobiling. A 42 m oil derrick outside the Fort St. John–North Peace Museum pays tribute to the local petroleum industry. Inside, some 6,000 artifacts depict city history from trading post days to the development of the local oilpatch.

Fort Nelson

Although settlement here at the junction of the Nelson, Prophet, and Muskwa rivers dates back to an 1805 fur-trading post, real growth began with the construction of the Alaska Highway. Recreational facilities include an indoor aquatic center and the most northerly green grass golf course in British Columbia. Nearby mountains, lakes, and rivers are a mecca for fly-in fishers and hunters. Pioneer artifacts and vintage vehicles are displayed in a local museum. As

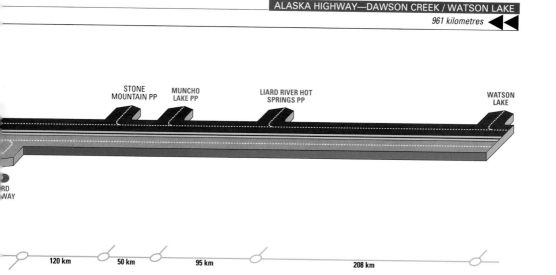

STONE MOUNTAIN PP   MUNCHO LAKE PP   LIARD RIVER HOT SPRINGS PP   WATSON LAKE

120 km   50 km   95 km   208 km

part of a summer-long Welcome Visitors program, residents demonstrate traditional crafts and give talks on local customs.

Liard Highway

This 400 km gravel road links Fort Nelson with the Mackenzie Highway, joining up with it just south of Fort Simpson, NWT.

Muncho Lake Provincial Park

Arctic grayling and Dolly Varden abound in this park's 12 km long, jade green Muncho (Big) Lake, which skirts the highway. Loons, grebes, mergansers, and other migratory birds feed along its swampy shores. Stone sheep, moose, and mountain caribou can be seen at mineral licks and roadside salt deposits.

Liard River Hot Springs Provincial Park

For details, see pages 356-357.

Watson Lake, Yukon

A transportation and distribution center for miners and loggers, Watson Lake in Yukon is also a major stopover for Alaska Highway travelers. In 1942, homesick GI's building the legendary highway erected signposts showing distances and directions to their hometowns. The deed caught on and now thousands of signs and license plates from around the world form a Sign Post Forest. Dioramas and audiovisual presentations at an interpretive center describe the engineering feats it took to build the highway.

In Muncho Lake Provincial Park, wrinkled Folded Mountain is one of several peaks showing the awesome effects of tectonic folding and faulting.

355

A Hot Spot on the Alaska Highway

ALASKA HIGHWAY / LIARD HOT SPRINGS PROVINCIAL PARK

ROSEMARY NEERING *is a frequent writer and editor for* Beautiful British Columbia *magazine. She has written several travel books, including* Down The Road: Journeys through Small-Town British Columbia, *which won her a B.C. Book Prize for nonfiction.*

SOME 750 KM UP THE ALASKA HIGHWAY, at 56 degrees north latitude, lies Liard Hot Springs, where weary travelers loll in two crystal-clear, hot-water pools whose temperatures range from 38° to 49°C. The springs, set in a provincial park, provide an oasis just where you appreciate it most after driving through the landscape of northern British Columbia.

The Kaska-Dene native people, who have wandered these lands for centuries, undoubtedly found and reveled in the warm waters that gush forth from the earth just north of the Liard River. Hudson's Bay Company factor Robert Campbell, who held sway at Fort Liard far to the north in the 1830s, took note of the springs in his diaries.

In the 1920s, a homesteader variously recorded as Tom or John Smith lived there with his daughter, and word spread of an almost tropical paradise. The springs, incidentally, brought him no luck: trying to go out to civilization along the Liard River he took the wrong channel and was swept away, though his daughter somehow survived.

The arrival of Alaska Highway construction crews in 1942 really put Liard Hot Springs on the map. It isn't hard to imagine the delight these men felt when—slicing a military "highway" from Dawson Creek to Alaska—they discovered clear, clean hot-water pools in the inhospitable north. They dubbed the place Theresa Hot Springs and built a rough boardwalk and bathing floats at what is now known as Alpha Pool. In the depths of the winter, the soldiers vied to have their photographs taken swimming through the hot pools, with ice and snow all around.

At war's end, the military left, and civilians began driving the highway in the late 1940s. Since then, hundred of thousands of travelers have braved the road, now vastly improved from the mud, gravel, and potholes that made it famous.

Just south of the hot springs, the Liard River curls across the northern end of the Rocky Mountains, cutting through the Rabbit Plateau and the southern reaches of the Yukon Plain. It is a region of folded and faulted sedimentary rock, thrust upwards and jumbled aeons ago and now overlain by glacial drift. Some of these faulted layers are permeable limestone. Surface water percolates through this porous rock and travels deep underground. There it is heated, though scientists have not determined precisely how: perhaps by hot gases, perhaps by subterranean volcanic action, perhaps by chemical reactions that give off heat. It is then forced back to the surface, spilling out at Liard Hot Springs.

At the top end of Alpha Pool, almost 3,000 litres of 49°C water gush from the ground every minute. Because the flow is so great and the pool bottom pea gravel, the waters of the 20 m long pool are clear and welcoming. This has the hottest water, and few visitors remain submerged for long—they emerge, lobster-red. A further five-minute walk away along the boardwalk lies Beta Pool, smaller, cooler, mud-bottomed and a little murkier, but also less frequented.

Winter is a special time here. As the temperature drops toward 45°C below, the locals come to visit, free from the tourists who crowd the springs in warmer weather. Hoar frost coats the trees and bushes that surround the pools, and steam rises in the chill northern air. The joy is in the contrast from deep freeze to sauna.

Humans are not the only creatures who find Liard Hot Springs hospitable. The warmth of the water raises the overall temperature some 2°C, creating a micro-climate where vegetation grows lusher and greener than in the surrounding area—and

provides a reliable food supply for animals. Moose are often visible in the marshes, green tendrils of marsh plants dripping from their long muzzles. Late in August, black bears descend from the hills to gorge on red highbush cranberries that rarely grow in such profusion this far north. From spring through fall, gulls, geese, ducks, owls, kingfishers, and many other birds pass through or nest near the springs.

Some of the 80 plant species that grow here flourish beyond what is considered their normal range. Bladderwort floats in tangled masses in the marshes, the tiny bladders opening to devour unwary water insects. Wild sarsaparilla, monkey flowers, and rare grasses thrive. Even violets bloom earlier in this area than those not many kilometres away. And cow parsnip goes crazy, reaching a metre and a half in height.

In one spot between Alpha and Beta pools, the calcium-laden water that emerges from underground drips over a near-vertical surface, and calcium crystallizes out as a soft, porous rock known as tufa. Plants root on the rock, forming a lush mat of vegetation constantly moistened by the warm water. They may not rival Babylon's, but these Hanging Gardens are another unique aspect of this site.

At Liard Hot Springs Provincial Park, 20 of the 53 campsites can be reserved; the rest are first-come, first-served. Although the campsites are almost always full from June through September, travelers arriving by noon usually find a spot. Limited private-lodge accommodation is also available at Liard River.

> "The arrival of Alaska Highway construction crews…put Liard Hot Springs on the map."

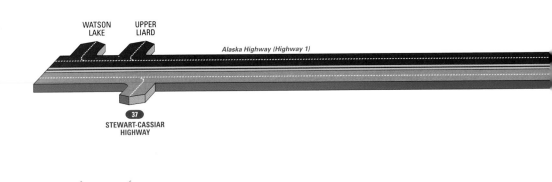

WATSON LAKE   UPPER LIARD

Alaska Highway (Highway 1)

37
STEWART-CASSIAR HIGHWAY

21 km   10 km   239 km

YUKON TERRITORY

This 1 km² area north of Carcross—what remains of a glacial lake bottom—is said to be the world's smallest desert. Because strong winds from nearby Lake Bennett keep its sands in perpetual motion, vegetation other than kinnikinnick and lodgepole pine has failed to put down lasting roots.

Stewart-Cassiar Highway

This highway (Hwy. 37) links the Yellowhead and Alaska highways, beginning near Kitwanga, B.C., and joining the Alaska near Watson Lake, Yukon.

Teslin

The Nisutlin Bay Bridge crosses an arm of Teslin Lake at this Tlingit village, an Alaska Highway service center. A museum named for Native leader George Johnston has a replica of his trading post and photographs taken by him before his people's traditional way of life was disrupted by construction of the Alaska Highway. Tlingit artifacts displayed include ceremonial robes and a rare gambling mat.

Carcross

From the Alaska Highway, you can take Hwy. 8 to Carcross, passing through Tagish, which has take-out food, campgrounds, a marina, and fishing and boating

guides. The Matthew Watson General Store—in business in Carcross since 1898—boasts old-time furnishings, such as gunsmithing tools and World War II army rations. It sells souvenirs, snacks, and Yukon-sized ice-cream cones. Carcross Desert (*see photo below*) and Frontierland/Museum of Yukon Natural History—a giant heritage park—are a few kilometres north of town. Visitors can see many of Yukon's elusive wildlife (some live, others mounted in dioramas), explore Yukon history, and hike to a lookout on Lake Bennett and historic Carcross.

Whitehorse

Set in a mountain valley, on a narrow shelf of land by the Yukon River, this city takes its name from a local rapids said to resemble the mane of a white horse. Now a busy commercial center and territorial capital, Whitehorse was born when thousands of prospectors streamed through during the 1898 Klondike gold rush.

A plethora of museums document every aspect of Yukon's colorful past. Moose-skin boats, snowshoes, dogsleds, stagecoaches, a full-size replica of *Queen of the Yukon* (sister ship to Charles Lindberg's *Spirit of St. Louis*), and other early forms of northern transport fill the Yukon Transportation Museum, located near the airport. A restored DC-3 on airport property is said to be the world's largest weather vane. Permanently mounted, the craft pivots in such a way that it always points into the wind.

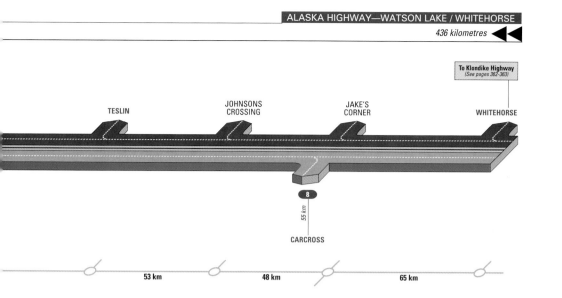

To Klondike Highway
(See pages 362-363)

TESLIN   JOHNSONS CROSSING   JAKE'S CORNER   WHITEHORSE

8

55 km

CARCROSS

53 km   48 km   65 km

Stern-wheelers, the legendary White Pass & Yukon Railway, Native transportation, early aviation, and events surrounding construction of the Alaska Highway are depicted on this 18 m mural by local artists adorning the entrance to the Yukon Transportation Museum in Whitehorse.

SS Klondike II *rests at dry dock in downtown Whitehorse, where this statue of a malamute honors the pack animals that accompanied prospectors on summer forays.*

A fascinating collection at the Yukon Beringia Interpretive Centre includes fossil remains of wooly mammoths, scimitar cats, giant steppe bison, giant beaver, ancient horses, giant short-faced bears, and American lions. The center focuses on Yukon's early inhabitants and on Beringia, the ice bridge between Alaska and Siberia, which disappeared when glaciers receded some 11,000 years ago.

Yukon's natural and cultural heritage is also celebrated through a diverse collection at the MacBride Museum. A 1900 Anglican church, one of Whitehorse's oldest structures, is now the Old Log Church Museum. Its exhibits focus on Anglican missionaries in the north.

A national historic site, the SS *Klondike II,* restored to the 1930s, is permanently retired on the Yukon River. Built in 1937, it replaced *Klondike I,* which struck a reef the previous year. Both vessels were notably larger than other stern-wheelers that plied the river from the 1860s into the 1950s.

A 424-seat theater and a gallery devoted to the work of professional Yukon artists are contained in the Yukon Arts Centre. Major traveling national and international exhibits are regularly showcased.

Paths in Yukon Gardens pass rock gardens, wild and domestic flowerbeds, hardy vegetable patches, and an herbal garden.

The Yukon Historical and Museums Association sponsors 45-minute walking tours of Whitehorse's historic sites. MV *Schwatka,* docked 3 km southeast of town, offers 2-hour cruises on the Yukon River.

359

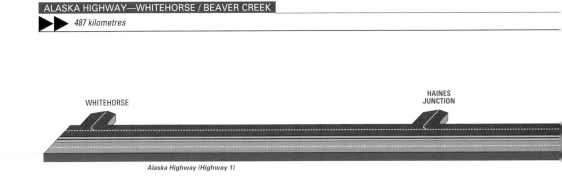

WHITEHORSE

HAINES
JUNCTION

Alaska Highway (Highway 1)

158 km

108 km

**YUKON
TERRITORY**

Haines Junction

The Alaska Highway links up here with the Haines Highway (Yukon Hwy. 3), which runs south to Haines, Alaska. Local recreational possibilities include mountaineering, trail riding, river rafting, and flightseeing (by fix-winged aircraft or helicopter). Kluane (pronounced kloo-*wa*-nee) National Park Reserve is headquartered in the village. Visitors on overnight hikes or camping expeditions must register there. Interpretive exhibits and slide presentations let them preview the park's wonders, and the visitors' center provides information on guided programs, campfire activities, and hiking trails.

Kluane National Park

The Alaska Highway skirts the eastern edges of this magnificent preserve of high mountains, vast icefields, and lush valleys. Road and park touch only at Haines Junction and the south end of scenic Kluane Lake. From the highway, travelers see the Kluane Range, where peaks average 2,500 m. Deeper in the park, in the Icefield Range—the mightiest of the St. Elias Mountains—as many as 20 peaks soar more than 5,000 m. Among them is 5,959 m Mount Logan, Canada's highest mountain. Glaciers, some 10 km wide and 100 km long, surge through the valleys from icefields—the largest outside the polar regions—covering half the park. Kluane, together with contiguous parks in Alaska and British Columbia, is a UNESCO World Heritage Site.

Travelers wanting to glimpse the park's rich birdlife can explore a section of the Dezadeash River wetlands on a 4.8 km loop trail that begins at the Haines Junction day-use area. Dall sheep, Kluane's most abundant large mammal, can be spotted from the Sheep Moun-

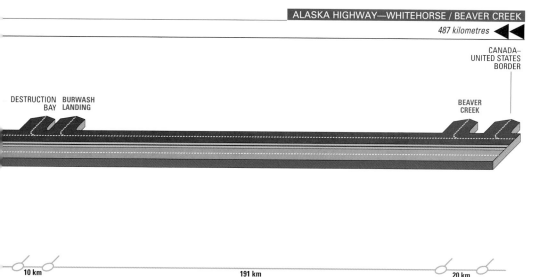

CANADA–
UNITED STATES
BORDER

DESTRUCTION BURWASH
BAY LANDING

BEAVER
CREEK

10 km   191 km   20 km

Thousands of snow-capped peaks, including Canada's highest mountains, characterize Kluane National Park, where range after range of enormous mountains are separated by wide, wildlife-rich, forested valleys, clear mountain lakes, and vast icefields from which hundreds of glaciers snake down the mountainsides and across the valley floors.

tain Interpretive Centre at the south end of Kluane Lake, some 105 km to the north. Just north of Sheep Mountain, the Soldier Summit Trail leads to where the Alaska Highway was officially opened in 1942.

Burwash Landing

This tiny village was born in 1903-04, when gold was discovered in streams running into Kluane Lake. Originally called Jacquot Post for brothers Louis and Jean Jacquot, whose trading posts supplied the miners, it was renamed in the 1940s for mining engineer and Arctic explorer Maj. Lachlan Taylor Burwash, who had just died. Today, the community offers camping, boat rentals, fishing trips, and flight-seeing to Kluane National Park. Kluane Museum of Natural History exhibits mounted wildlife (some in dioramas), handmade Native crafts and costumes, and a mineral and fossil collection containing such rarities as 18,000-year-old hairy mammoth tusks. An 8 m high gold pan

beside the museum is said to be the world's largest. Our Lady of the Holy Rosary, founded here in 1944 by the Oblates, was the first mission and school north of Whitehorse. The school and living quarters have been restored as a museum.

Beaver Creek

A visitors' center wildflower display greets arrivals here in Canada's westernmost community, a hamlet of some 125 souls. (The next stop before the Alaska–Yukon border is the Canadian Customs post some 10 km farther north.) It was in Beaver Creek that two Alaska Highway construction crews working from opposite directions—south from Alaska, north from Whitehorse—met on Oct. 20, 1942, thus connecting the highway. Professional entertainers, singing servers, and colorful highway lore are the stuff of Rendezvous Dinner Theatre, a May-to-September family-style presentation at a local inn. Up to 320 can be seated for the 2½-hour show.

WHITEHORSE   CARMAC

Klondike Highway (Highway 2)

167 km   23.5 ▶

**YUKON
TERRITORY**

Klondike Highway (Hwy. 2)

These pages describe the Whitehorse to Dawson City stretch
of this highway, a paved road
that runs south from Whitehorse
to Skagway, Alaska, passing
through Carcross (see page 358).

Carmacks

This Yukon River village is
named for George Washington
Carmack, who found coal here
and set up a trading post in 1893.
Three years later, Carmack
became even more famous when
he and two others discovered the
Bonanza Creek gold that started
the Klondike gold rush.

A 1903 roadhouse, one of the
largest on the Overland Trail
that linked Whitehorse to Dawson City, has been restored.

Hiking trails abound locally.
The 1.6 km Coal Mine Lake Trail
from the Yukon River bridge
leads to a popular fishing and
swimming spot. Five local rockhounding trails—rich in geodes,
agates, and other minerals—also
double as hiking trails. From the
visitors' center, the Interpretive
River Front Boardwalk extends
2 km to a riverside park.

The Five Finger Rapids
Recreation Site (*see photo above*)
some 23 km north of Carmacks
is named for sandstone channels
on the Yukon River. In Klondike
gold rush days, riverboat skippers
had to winch their vessels past
the rapids when traveling to and
from the goldfields. Today, a
closed-cabin boat takes visitors
from Carmacks to the recreation
site, where an interpretive observation platform overlooks the
swirling rapids.

Pelly Crossing

"Our pumps never close" is the
motto of a garage in this village
halfway between Whitehorse
and Dawson City. Home to the
Selkirk Indian Band, it is located
where the highway crosses the
Pelly River. Local facilities
include a campground, trading
post, and store.

Stewart Crossing

Built in 1886 as a trading post to
supply local gold miners, Stewart Crossing later became the
site of a roadhouse on the Overland Trail. Today, its facilities
include a lodge, a campground,
RV parks, and a visitors' center.
The village marks the intersection of the Klondike Highway
and the Silver Trail (Hwy. 11),
which goes eastward to Mayo,
and the old silver-mining region
of Elsa and Keno. (See following
entries.)

Mayo

This community dates to the
early 1900s when it was a center
for river steamers docking with
supplies for local mining operations and departing with the
area's silver-lead ore. Riverboat
traffic and Mayo's business
declined after Hwy. 11 opened in
1949. Today, the village's chief
attraction is the Binet House
Interpretive Centre, which has
exhibits on the Silver Trail. Historical photos, medical artifacts,
and local flora and fauna are displayed. A geology display
includes a 3-D relief map pin-
pointing area mineral deposits.

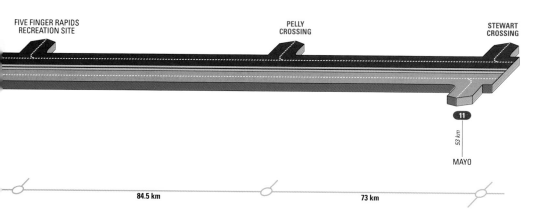

FIVE FINGER RAPIDS
RECREATION SITE

PELLY
CROSSING

STEWART
CROSSING

11

53 km

MAYO

84.5 km   73 km

Unlike the seething currents at a narrowing of the river a short distance away, serenity prevails where this section of the Yukon River flows through the Five Finger Rapids Recreation Site.

Elsa

A community sprang up here in 1919, when silver was discovered at Keno Hill. Ore extracted from underground shafts was milled locally, then shipped to Whitehorse. For a time, the local United Keno Hill Mines operation was North America's richest and longest continuously operating silver mine. But the town was "mothballed" in 1989, when silver prices fell and the mine closed. The tiny hamlet now survives as a service center to the area's few remaining miners.

Keno City

Fewer than 50 people now live in this hamlet marking the end of the Silver Trail. However, its glory days, and the story of gold and silver mining in the Yukon, live on at the Keno City Mining Museum, fittingly housed in a 1920s dance hall. Exhibits also include blacksmithing tools, early mining equipment, and a wide selection of photos by local photographers.

Keno City lies amid magnificent scenery. For a panorama of nearby McQuesten Valley, take Signpost Road to the top of Keno Hill. You can also explore byways of old by following any of the Keno City hiking trails, which wind through historic mining areas, picturesque valleys, and pretty alpine meadows.

363

STEWART
CROSSING

Klondike Highway (Highway 2)

11

140 km

YUKON
TERRITORY

Left to right are these Dawson buildings, all restored to their former splendor. The Palace Grand Theatre (1899) still mounts Gaslight Fol-lies, a high-kicking variety show popular in gold rush days. A miner's cabin, a smithy, old newspapers and diaries, silent films, and vintage photos are among gold rush relics in Dawson City Museum, housed in the former Territorial Administration Building (1901). Mail is still processed at the Post Office (1901), and visitors can explore the painstakingly restored, lavishly furnished Commissioner's Residence (1902), where local and foreign dignitaries were equally welcome.

Bear Creek

Some 65 buildings just off the highway south of Dawson City were once a corporate mining headquarters and the administrative and repair center for huge dredges that worked the gold-fields. Highlights of guided summer tours are a large machine shop, and the Gold Room where ore was cleaned, melted, and poured into bars for shipping.

Bonanza Creek Road

This road takes you to two national historic sites closely linked to gold mining's heyday. Some 12 km from the turnoff,

eight-story-high Dredge No. 4 covers an area almost as big as a football field. The largest dredge of its kind in North America, it was one of two dozen behe-moths used to recover gold from the creekbeds of the Klondike River valley. Introduced in the early 1900s by the large mining concern that bought out individ-ual miners, they operated into the mid-1960s. Their legacy— vast tailing piles—is a prominent feature of the local landscape.

Some 2 km farther south, a plaque marks Discovery Claim, where, in August 1896, brothers-in-law George Washington Car-

mack, "Skookum Jim" and "Tag-ish Charley" discovered gold in a tributary of the Klondike River. News of the Bonanza Creek dis-covery reached the outside world the next year, setting off the Klondike gold rush. Today, you can pan for gold, picnic, and visit a souvenir/snack shop at the spot. (For more about gold pan-ning on Bonanza Creek, see pages 366-367.)

Dawson City

After the Bonanza Creek discov-ery (see above), the tiny settle-ment at the junction of the

DEMPSTER
HIGHWAY
5

BEAR
CREEK

DAWSON
CITY

BONANZA
CREEK ROAD

25 km   9 km   4 km

POST OFFICE

Yukon and Klondike rivers became the hot spot for more than 30,000 gold seekers from around the world. Those who struck it rich spent their wealth, often with reckless abandon, in the splendid hotels, theaters, dance halls, and stores that sprang up overnight amid the tents and shacks in this new "Paris of the North." By 1898, Dawson City was the capital of the newly formed Yukon Territory. But as gold deposits became depleted or less accessible, the city's fortunes declined. It failed to share in the Yukon's growth after World War II, and lost its capital status to Whitehorse in 1953.

Today, its legendary past attracts visitors by the thousand. A visitors' center presents slide shows and films about the old days. It also offers walking tours along wooden sidewalks that pass restored buildings of the gold rush era. Some notable survivors are Diamond Tooth Gertie's Gambling Hall, an old-time saloon, now a legalized casino where profits go to the town's restoration efforts; the 1900 Harrington's Store, which houses a photographic exhibit, *Dawson as They Saw It*; and a 1902 clapboard Anglican church.

Authors' Avenue salutes poet Robert Service (1874-1958) and novelist Jack London (1876-1916). Visitors can attend readings of *Songs of a Sourdough, The Shooting of Dan McGrew,* and other Service rhymes in the log dwelling where the poet lived in 1909-1912, while employed by a local bank. The Jack London Interpretive Centre describes the novelist's 1897 Yukon sojourn, which inspired *The Call of the Wild* and *White Fang.*

On June 21, Midnight Dome, some 8 km north of the city, is a favorite spot for watching the midnight sun dip briefly behind the Ogilvie Mountains. From the dome's summit one has sweeping views of the city, the mountains, and the valleys of the Yukon and Klondike rivers. You can also enjoy spectacular views from the Top of the World Highway. From Dawson City, a ferry takes travelers across the Yukon River to this summer-only gravel road to the Yukon–Alaska border. Along its 109 km length, you are surrounded by magnificent mountain scenery.

With Pan and Shovel in the Klondike

KLONDIKE HIGHWAY / DAWSON CITY

LARRY PYNN *is also the author of* "Rope-Tethered Rafters Defy the Roiling Fraser Rapids" *(pp. 48-49).*

ALMOST A CENTURY AFTER HIS FATHER established a claim on Hunker Creek in 1903, in the wake of Yukon's famous Klondike gold rush, 78-year-old John Gould is still searching for this precious metal in the Klondike River valley.

Yukon-born Gould hardly fits the popular image of the grizzled miner squatting on a riverbank, plucking gold nuggets from a pan (as shown in the background photograph on these pages). This method, used by pioneer gold prospectors in the Klondike a century ago, is the most primitive kind of placer mining. These days Gould works his family's dozen placer claims along Hunker Creek. He uses heavy industrial equipment—large enough to pump through perhaps 500 yd^3 of gravel an hour—to sift out the heavy gold particles from lighter waste materials.

Gold is the prized resource of the Klondike area—a 2,000 km^2 area of west-central Yukon. Because the region escaped the last Ice Age, the gold deposits on the ground were never scraped away by glaciers, but remained undisturbed—a magnet for all sorts of mining operations throughout the 20th century.

In the early days, individual miners found sluicing a better method of recovering gold than panning. They shoveled muck, gravel, and rock fragments into sluice boxes—long sloping troughs—and then poured water into the boxes to wash away waste. Riffles or bars at the bottom of the boxes retained the concentrate containing gold particles. When large mining companies entered the business, they brought in a wide range of heavy machinery: large hoses to wash away the overburden of topsoil, giant dredges with bucket wheels to scoop up tonnes of gravel, and, eventually, million-dollar bulldozers and backhoes.

After more than a century's relentless toil by miners and machines, Yukon gold finds are decreasing. But this has not deterred today's visitors who come here, inspired by the legend of the 1897-98 gold rush. To commemorate this historic event, Dawson City hosts the yearly Yukon Goldpanning Championships on July 1 Canada Day. Every half dozen years it also sponsors the World Goldpanning Championships, most recently in 1996, attracting 300 competitors from more than 20 countries as far away as Italy, Japan, France, Finland, Scotland, and Australia. Each competitor receives a bucket filled with sand and gravel and a predetermined number of gold flakes. The first person to pan out all the gold flakes and cap them in a vial is declared the winner. At the 1996 world championships, a competitor from the Czech Republic won with a time of 2 minutes 17 seconds.

Visitors to Dawson City who want to try their hand at gold panning will find several sites open from mid-May to mid-September. One such site is the Guggieville RV Park, the largest of four private gold-panning operations in the Klondike area, which is located just five minutes from Dawson City. Each visitor is taught to use boxes, which make it easier to recover gold particles. The charge of this attraction covers a vial in which to store your gold.

Guggieville's owner Brenda Caley admits that she gets gravels from nearby placer mines and regularly "salts" the boxes with gold flakes, just enough to ensure that every visitor walks away with some precious particles.

Visitors with gold fever can also strike out on their own. You can rent a shovel and pan from Guggieville RV Park and head for the Klondike Visitors Association Claim No. 6 on Bonanza Creek, where there is no charge for panning. This site is located km upstream from the spot where George Carmark, Skookum Jim and Tagish Charley struck gold on Aug. 17, 1896, sparking off the Klondike gold rush.

Gold Bottom Mine Tours also offers a tour of a placer mine and the chance to pan for gold either in troughs or from a pile of pay dirt beside the creek.

In their enthusiasm to relive the gold rush, visitors may sometimes show up unannounced with shovel and pan on a seemingly unoccupied stretch of Klondike riverbank. It is important to remember that all creek beds are claimed, and panning is strictly forbidden without permission from the owner. If asked, some owners may give their consent, but others refuse on the grounds that it is too dangerous to have visitors wandering around heavy gold-mining machinery.

> **"** *The first person to pan out all the gold flakes and cap them in a vial is declared the winner.* **"**

Panning for gold takes practice, but the basic principles are straightforward. Fill your pan with gravel, put it into the water, and stir it up until you have a slurry—a watery mixture of mud and insoluble materials. Then wash the slurry, tipping the pan slightly away from you into the water and lifting it out to flush some of the dirt off the top. Do that a few times, then rake your fingers through the pan, picking out the rocks. And shake the pan to ensure that the heavy gold particles work their way to the bottom.

Placer mining has changed over the past century; so, too, has its most basic equipment, the pan. Beside the large, circular metal pan of yesteryear, there are now models in a variety of sizes. Some are made of plastic or have a square design. Traditionalists insist that there is no substitute for the old-style 16-inch iron pan.

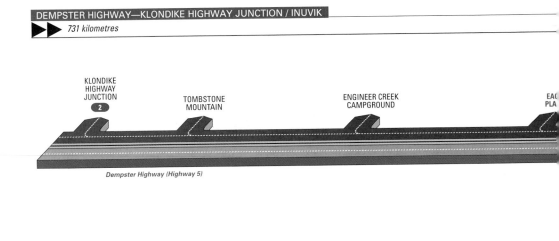

KLONDIKE
HIGHWAY
JUNCTION
2
TOMBSTONE
MOUNTAIN
ENGINEER CREEK
CAMPGROUND
EA(
PLA

Dempster Highway (Highway 5)

75 km   119 km   178 km   30 k

YUKON/
NORTHWEST
TERRITORIES

Dempster Highway

North America's most northerly highway and the only one to cross the Arctic Circle, the Dempster runs north from Dawson City, Yukon, to Inuvik, N.W.T. A hard-packed gravel road, it follows routes once used by Mounties on sled-dog patrols. Its name honors one of them, Insp. W.J.D. Dempster, who searched for, and found, the Lost Patrol (see Fort McPherson).

Tombstone Campground

About here, the sparse stands of poplar and spruce give way to tundra and the soaring magnificence of the Ogilvie Mountains. Roughly 2.5 km north of the campground, wedge-shaped, 2,192 m Tombstone Mountain—long an orientation point for Mountie patrols and other travelers—comes into view.

Eagle Plains

At the midpoint of the Dempster, Eagle Plains has one of only three vehicle service centers on the entire highway. Set between the Ogilvie and Richardson mountains, it also boasts a hotel and an RV campground. A tablet some 5 km north of the village describes the 1932, month-long manhunt for Albert Johnson, the "Mad Trapper."

Arctic Circle

An interpretive display north of Eagle Plains marks where the highway crosses the Arctic Circle. Above this latitude, the sun never sets during midsummer; in midwinter, it never rises. For

years, Yukoner Harry Waldron, self-styled "Keeper of the Arctic Circle," summered here. Nattily tuxedoed, he sat in a rocking chair beside the highway, drinking champagne and swapping stories—and hospitality—with any travelers who happened by.

Fort McPherson

On a plateau above the Peel River, this is the largest Gwich'in (Dene) village in the Northwest Territories. A thriving tent-and-canvas shop produces high-quality briefcases, bags, and backpacks. Leatherwork, beading, and other crafts are available through the local Band Office. A walking tour passes the graves of the Lost Patrol—four Mounties who never returned from patrol in the winter of 1910-11. Their mysterious disappearance was solved when their frozen bodies were found near here by Mountie W.J.D. Dempster—at that time, a young corporal.

Arctic Red River

Traditional Gwich'in ways prevail in this village, which

This exhibit on the Dempster Highway, a short drive north of Eagle Plains, marks the spot where the Arctic Circle—latitude 66°33' north—intersects the highway.

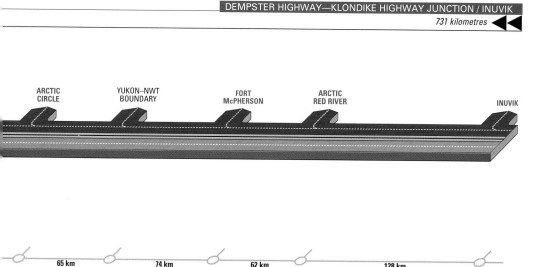

ARCTIC CIRCLE | YUKON–NWT BOUNDARY | FORT McPHERSON | ARCTIC RED RIVER | INUVIK

65 km | 74 km | 62 km | 128 km

developed in the 1860s around a Hudson's Bay Company post and a Roman Catholic mission. Northbound visitors see the mission spire as they head toward the Mackenzie River ferry.

Inuvik

In this northern community virtually all the buildings are set on piles driven into the permafrost. Heat, water, and sewer pipes—protected by aluminum conduits called utilidors—are also aboveground. The visitors' center is modeled on an Inuvialuit sod house.

In 1954 the federal government built Inuvik on the eastern channel of the Mackenzie River: it needed a new western arctic administrative center to replace Aklavik where flooding was an ongoing threat. Popular activities include river tours, fishing expeditions, and sled-dog rides. From here, visitors can fly to Aklavik and Tuktoyaktuk.

Aklavik

Founded in 1912 as a Hudson's Bay Company post, Aklavik was a federal government town until the 1950s. When government offices moved to Inuvik, the Inuvialuit and Gwich'in locals refused to relocate, preferring to carry on in their traditional way. Attractions of "the town that wouldn't die" include the original HBC post, a museum, and some restored log cabins.

Tuktoyaktuk

This Beaufort Sea community has long been an Inuit whale-hunting site. Since the 1970s, Tuktoyaktuk (Inuktituk for "looks like cariboo") has also been a hotspot for offshore oil exploration. Walking trails (with interpretive signs) describe Inuvialuit culture. Pingos are prominent features of the local landscape. Volcano-shaped hills, with solid ice cores, pingos are created by upwardly expanding permafrost. Tuktoyaktuk claims the world's largest concentration of these hills—more than 1,400.

Igloo-shaped Our Lady of Victory Church in Inuvik is built of plywood and painted white to resemble ice.

369

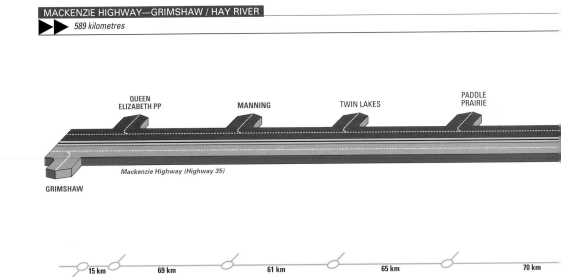

QUEEN
ELIZABETH PP   MANNING   TWIN LAKES   PADDLE
PRAIRIE

Mackenzie Highway (Highway 35)

GRIMSHAW

15 km   69 km   61 km   65 km   70 km

**NORTHERN
ALBERTA/
NORTHWEST
TERRITORIES**

Mackenzie Highway

Several roads make up this route system named for explorer Alexander Mackenzie (1764-1820). The paved stretch from Grimshaw, Alta., to Hay River, N.W.T., continues by gravel road to Wrigley, N.W.T., about two-thirds of the way to the eventual terminus, Tuktoyaktuk, on the Beaufort Sea (see page 369).

Grimshaw

Mackenzie Highway information is available at the local tourist center: a monument on Hwy. 35 marks the highway's Mile 0. This mixed farming community was once known as "the Grain Capital of the British Empire." A lake stocked with rainbow trout is among attractions in a wilderness park some 3 km east of town.

Queen Elizabeth Provincial Park

Swimming, boating, sailing, and waterskiing are attractions in this park alongside Lac Cardinal. There are also campgrounds, playgrounds, hiking trails, and a pond-side viewing platform, where you can observe some of the park's 115 bird species. A Pioneer Village and Museum has working saw-and-shingle mills, old farm machinery, two furnished pioneer homes, and the region's 1919 municipal office.

Manning

The Charles Plavin Homestead (1918), one of northern Alberta's oldest farms and a provincial historic site, can be found at North Star, south of town. Forests around this picturesque community have so many moose that the area is called the "land of the mighty moose." Local attractions include a snake pit and a bird sanctuary on a private farm outside town. The restored Old Hospital Gallery and Museum welcomes summer visitors.

High Level

This last sizable community before the Alberta–N.W.T. border is named for a height of land separating the northward flowing Hay River from the eastbound Peace River. From High Level, the highway parallels the Hay. Alberta's largest sawmill and the world's northernmost grain elevators can be seen here. The Mackenzie Crossroads Museum and Visitors Centre dispenses local history and travel information. Those who detour via Hwy. 58 to Fort Vermilion— "where Alberta began"—can explore a village that dates back to 1778.

60th Parallel

Information comes with free coffee at the 60th Parallel Campground and Visitor Information Centre on the Alberta–N.W.T. boundary. The center also marks the changeover from Alberta's Hwy. 35 to N.W.T.'s Hwy. 1. A campground is nearby.

Twin Falls Gorge Territorial Park

A path from the highway, which cuts through this park, leads to a viewpoint overlooking 33 m high

TWIN FALLS
GORGE PK

HIGH
LEVEL

STEEN
RIVER

60TH PARALLEL

ENTERPRISE

HAY
RIVER

Mackenzie Highway (Highway 1)

RT
MILION

142 km   49 km   72 km   11 km   35 km

Alexandra Falls. An hour's walk along a steep gorge noted for its 400-million-year-old, fossil-rich, limestone and sandstone formations takes you to Louise Falls, which plunges 15 m in three steps. A series of rapids makes an attractive backdrop to the Escarpment Creek picnic site.

Enterprise

Visit the local gas station, restaurant, and crafts store and you've been to every business in town. At Enterprise, the Mackenzie Highway turns west, providing access to the Yellowknife Highway (see pages 372-373). Travelers who decide to detour via Hwy. 2 to Hay River will pass through the Territory's premier market gardening country. Enriched by Hay River floods, soils hereabouts yield bountiful fruit and vegetable crops that thrive in the area's long summer days.

Hay River

A scenic, modern town, this Great Slave Lake port and commercial fishing headquarters is renowned for its world-class sports fishing. At the Hay River Reserve (off Hwy. 5), the Dene Cultural Institute sells footwear with tufted moose-hide designs, beaded items, leather goods, and other Native crafts. Hay River is also the gateway to Wood Buffalo National Park, some 280 km to the east via Hwy. 5.

Ringed by trembling aspen, jack pine, spruce, and birch, the Hay River thunders over a limestone ledge to form spectacular 33 m high Alexandra Falls in Twin Falls Gorge Park.

371

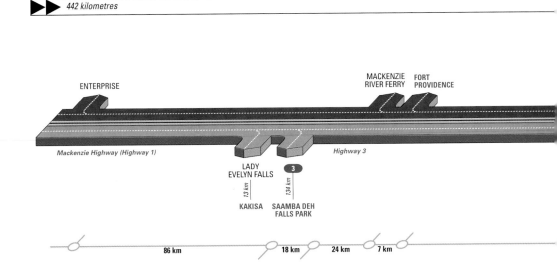

ENTERPRISE

MACKENZIE RIVER FERRY

FORT PROVIDENCE

Mackenzie Highway (Highway 1)

Highway 3

LADY EVELYN FALLS

3

13 km

134 km

KAKISA   SAAMBA DEH FALLS PARK

86 km   18 km   24 km   7 km

NORTHWEST TERRITORIES

Kakisa

Picturesque falls have made the road between Enterprise and the Hwy. 3 junction known as the "Waterfalls Route." Lady Evelyn Falls, where the Kakisa River drops some 15 m in a limestone gorge, enhances a side trip to Kakisa. A nature trail leads to the falls in a park which offers great camping, picnicking, swimming, hiking, fossil hunting, and seasonal fishing for grayling and pickerel. Most houses in Kakisa, a Dene (Slavey) community, are built of logs. Local women are renowned for their exquisite tufted moose-hair and porcupine-quill apparel and crafts.

Saamba Deh Falls Territorial Park

The Trout River rushes through a narrow gorge here to create the dramatic Saamba Deh (Whittaker) Falls, then cascades over Coral Falls a little farther upstream. Trails give access to both waterfalls. Other facilities include picnic sites and a campground in an old spruce forest.

Fort Providence

If bound for Fort Providence or Yellowknife, you must turn north on Hwy. 3 (the Yellowknife Highway), then take a ferry across the Mackenzie River. (Hwy. 1 continues on to Wrigley, farther downstream.) Folk in Fort Providence, a Dene (Slavey) community, still follow their traditional hunting and fishing way of life. River cruises are available in the town, which has motels, a restaurant, a craft shop, and a campground. North of town, Hwy. 3 skirts the vast Mackenzie Bison Sanctuary, a refuge for some 1,700 wood bison—the world's largest free-

Artifacts, photos, and other exhibits at the outstanding Prince of Wales Northern Heritage Centre in Yellowknife trace northern life from prehistory to exploration. Dioramas depict the culture and lifestyles of the Northwest Territories' first peoples, Inuit and Dene.

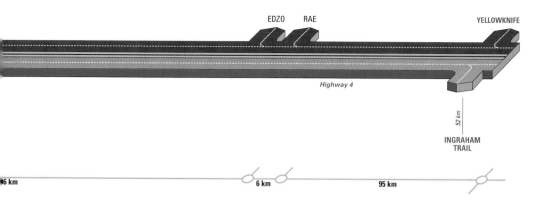

EDZO   RAE   YELLOWKNIFE

Highway 4

52 km

INGRAHAM
TRAIL

6 km   6 km   95 km

Much as it did when Willy "Wiley Road" Wiley and "Smoky" Stout opened for business in 1937, Yellowknife's frontier Wild Cat Cafe serves wild game and fish dishes to a summer clientele of prospectors, miners, pilots, locals, and visitors from around the world. The porch, a 1939 addition, was Yellowknife's first ice-cream parlor.

roaming herd. Grazing bison are sometimes seen from the road. Canadian Shield landscape—rocky outcrops crowned by stunted spruce and birch—begins north of Edzo and Rae. Often called Rae/Edzo, these traditional Dene (Dogrib) communities are at either end of a bridge spanning the North Arm of Great Slave Lake.

Yellowknife

Capital of the Northwest Territories, Yellowknife's name is derived from a Dene tribe skilled in manufacturing copper tools. Although Native peoples hunted in this area for thousands of years, there was no permanent settlement until gold was discovered in 1934. Old Town, a colorful maze of gold rush structures, occupies a strip of land jutting into Yellowknife Bay. To its south sits the bustling New

Town of government offices and business blocks. At the tip of Latham Island in Old Town, the Ndilo Cultural Village offers interpretive programs and demonstrations of traditional Dene (Dogrib) skills. For panoramic views of the town and lake, stop by another Old Town landmark, the Bush Pilot's Monument to northern aviators.

The Prince of Wales Northern Heritage Centre offers fascinating insights into the North's natural history and peoples. One gallery is devoted to northern aviation. A prized exhibit is one of the earliest planes used in the North—the Fox Moth of Wardair founder Max Ward. Other highlights include a giant stuffed polar bear, a moose-skin boat, and a fine collection of Inuit art.

A kennel and veterinary clinic at the Eskimo Dog Research Foundation has more than 100 *kingmik*, rare Inuit dogs.

Ingraham Trail (Hwy. 4)

This partially paved road, named for pioneer innkeeper Vic Ingraham, extends 70 km east from Yellowknife to Tibbett Lake. Built originally to give access to central N.W.T.'s mineral resources, the trail cuts through popular cottage and recreation country, giving access to numerous rivers and lakes ideal for canoeing and fishing (trout, pike, and pickerel). Along the road, there are seven boat-launching sites, two campgrounds, several lakeside beaches, and short hiking trails. (The Yellowknife Highway meets the Ingraham Trail on Yellowknife's outskirts.)

373

FAIRS AND FESTIVALS

A selection of major popular events held every year across the country at some of the places described in *Canada Coast to Coast*.

ABBOTSFORD, B.C.

INTERNATIONAL AIRSHOW

ABBOTSFORD INTERNATIONAL AIRPORT
SECOND WEEKEND OF AUGUST

North America's leading air show set in the panoramic splendor of B.C.'s Fraser Valley. Three-day event features ground displays of military, civilian and vintage aircraft, along with a variety of acts—from wing-walkers to the aerial acrobatics of the world-famous Canadian Forces Snowbirds.

AGASSIZ, B.C.

FALL FAIR AND CORN FESTIVAL

MID-SEPTEMBER

The "Corn Capital of B.C." hosts a small-town country fair complete with midway, field crops exhibits, an old-time tractor-pulling contest, and a cornhusking competition.

AMHERST, N.S.

ANTIQUE MECHANICAL FAIR

CUMBERLAND COUNTY MUSEUM
MID-AUGUST

Antique automobiles are the focus of this fair, where antique gas engines, steam engines, and flat-belt machinery are also sold.

ANTIGONISH, N.S.

HIGHLAND GAMES

MID-JULY

Highland dance, bagpipe competitions, and heavyweight sporting events, such as the caber toss, are the highlights at Antigonish, home of the oldest continuous highland games outside of Scotland.

ATIKOKAN, ONT.

SPORTS DAYS

EARLY AUGUST

Ten-day sports festival for the entire family. Events include bike races and a scavenger hunt for children, tennis, basketball, and roller-blade hockey tournaments for teens, watercross, raft and canoe races for adults, and darts, horseshoes, and lawn bowling for seniors.

AUSTIN, MAN.

MANITOBA THRESHERMEN'S REUNION AND STAMPEDE

MANITOBA AGRICULTURAL MUSEUM
LAST WEEK OF JULY

Four-day heritage festival demonstrates early farming practices with horse, steam- and gas-powered machinery. Threshing, plowing, and sawmill displays are complemented by a vintage parade, a fashion show, and home-craft displays.

BADDECK, N.S.

CENTRE BRAS D'OR FESTIVAL OF THE ARTS

JULY/SEPTEMBER

This summer-long festival of music and theater features the East Coast's finest musicians, songwriters, and playwrights. Folk, country and Maritime classics, including French-Acadian and Cape Breton Celtic music, take center stage.

BALA, ONT.

CRANBERRY FESTIVAL

WEEKEND AFTER THANKSGIVING

Learn about the cranberry in a festival atmosphere during the peak of the harvest season. Sample the many and varied foods made from cranberries.

BANFF, ALTA.

BANFF FESTIVAL OF THE ARTS

THE BANFF CENTRE
JUNE/AUGUST

This popular summer festival showcases nearly 1,000 emerging artists from around the world who put on a dazzling array of performances—from jazz and chamber music to opera and ballet.

WINTER FESTIVAL

LATE JANUARY/EARLY FEBRUARY

A tradition in Banff since 1917, this winter celebration features the Mountain Madness Relay Race, Torchlight Parade and Town Party. Other highlights include ice castles, silent auctions, and casinos.

BATTLEFORD, SASK.

SASKATCHEWAN HANDCRAFT FESTIVAL

JULY

One of Saskatchewan's largest handcraft exhibitions showcases the innovative, diverse crafts of the province's most highly skilled artisans. Excellent examples of quality handcrafts include pottery, woodworking, and weaving.

BELLEVILLE, ONT.

WATERFRONT FESTIVAL AND FOLKLORAMA

JULY

A grand opening parade and fireworks extravaganza launch a weekend filled with summertime fun. Featured attractions include international cuisine and entertainment at Ethnic Village, the International Drum Corps competition featuring the best bands in North America, and Children's Village, replete with face painting, trick bike riders, and carnival thrills.

BLIND RIVER, ONT.

COMMUNITY DAYS

SECOND WEEKEND OF JULY

A summer festival for families that celebrates the town's lumber heritage and its present status as a major summer cottage and camping area. Lumbering skills, such as log-rolling and canoe tipping, are featured, plus a traditional parade, midway, and old-time fiddling contest.

BRANDON, MAN.

ROYAL MANITOBA WINTER FAIR

KEYSTONE CENTRE
LATE MARCH

Western Canada's largest spring agricultural show offers everything from livestock exhibits and commercial displays to children's entertainment and world-class equestrian events.

BRIGHTON, ONT.
APPLEFEST
LATE SEPTEMBER
This four-day tribute to the annual apple harvest combines a country fair and street bazaar, complete with marching bands, carnival rides, craft shows, and outdoor bake sales.

BROCKVILLE, ONT.
RIVERFEST
LATE JUNE/EARLY JULY
This celebration of life on the banks of the mighty St. Lawrence River is a 10-day extravaganza of fireworks, a festive parade, canoe races, and open-air concerts featuring world-class entertainers.

CALGARY, ALTA.
COWBOY FESTIVAL
EARLY FEBRUARY
Genuine cowhands read poetry and demonstrate roping, branding, and other skills. Other highlights include Western Art and Gear Exhibits, Cowboy Concerts, and an old West Film Fest.

INTERNATIONAL CHILDREN'S FESTIVAL
MAY
Six magical days of engaging theater, exquisite puppetry, and original music from Canada and around the world in over 130 main stage performances.

INTERNATIONAL JAZZ FESTIVAL
JUNE/JULY
A 10-day celebration of jazz, blues, and world-beat music featuring local, national, and international artists at concerts, workshops, club dates, and free outdoor events.

INTERNATIONAL NATIVE ARTS FESTIVAL
AUGUST
Native artists, dancers, and musicians gather from across North and South America to share their culture and heritage in performances and workshops.

THE CALGARY STAMPEDE
MID-JULY
Billed as the "Greatest Outdoor Show on Earth," this 10-day wild West extravaganza has everything from chuckwagon races and livestock shows to glittering parades and lively street dances. A major highlight is the Half Million Dollar Rodeo, which attracts the world's top professional cowboys with the richest purse in the history of the sport.

WINTER FESTIVAL
FEBRUARY
A legacy from Calgary's hosting of the 1988 Winter Olympics, this dynamic 10-day festival celebrates winter through a host of seasonal sports and entertainment. Main attractions include dogsledding, snow boarding, and the Winter Village.

CANMORE, ALTA.
HERITAGE DAY FOLK FESTIVAL
CENTENNIAL PARK
FIRST WEEKEND IN AUGUST
Alberta's longest running folk festival presents some of the finest traditional and contemporary folk music in North America. Other highlights include an arts-and-crafts fair and a children's area that features everything from clowns and jugglers to horse rides.

CAP-DE-LA-MADELEINE, QUE.
STREET ENTERTAINERS' FESTIVAL
EARLY AUGUST
Young and old alike will marvel at the magicians, jugglers, tightrope walkers, and mime artists at this Quebec festival.

CARLETON PLACE, ONT.
HARVEST FESTIVAL AND SCARECROW DISPLAY
LATE SEPTEMBER/OCTOBER
Fall is ushered in with pumpkin decorating and horse-drawn trolley rides, a pie-baking contest and chili cook-off, and a two-week downtown display of more than 70 scarecrows.

MISSISSIPPI RIVER DAYS SPORTSFEST
MID-JULY
This sports festival is enlivened races and parades, a street dance and triathlon, and skateboarding, tai-chi, and kayak polo demonstrations. A classic car show and historical encampment round out the weekend's festivities.

CARMACKS, YK.
GOLD DAYS
EARLY JULY
The Klondike Gold Rush of the late 1890s is celebrated with a barbecue, dance, and reenactment of events surrounding the first shipment of gold out of the Klondike.

CHARLOTTETOWN, P.E.I.
FESTIVAL OF LIGHTS
CONFEDERATION LANDING PARK
LATE JUNE TO JULY 1
Canada's four-day birthday is launched by a vaudeville show, parade, and official light-up of the park. Festivities continue with international dance performances, children's concerts, and evening pubs, and wind up with a spectacular laser-and-fireworks display shot from a barge in the harbor.

FESTIVAL OF THE FATHERS
CONFEDERATION LANDING PARK
LATE AUGUST
The "Birthplace of Confederation" celebrates the historic 1864 conference that gave birth to Canada. Observe the meetings and social activities of this historic event, brought to life by the Confederation Players. Or take part in a range of traditional festivities—from an old-fashioned family picnic to the Ten Tavern Tour.

OLD HOME WEEK PROVINCIAL EXHIBITION
CHARLOTTETOWN DRIVING PARK
MID-AUGUST
The fastest horses and best drivers in Eastern Canada take part in 10 days of harness racing that culminates in the renowned $20,000 Gold Cup and Saucer Race. The agricultural industry is also celebrated with livestock and light horse shows, handicraft and baking displays, and a midway.

P.E.I. FALL HARVEST WINE FEST
SEPTEMBER
This prestigious two-day wine extravaganza features wines from around the world. Learn about vintage products, both old and new, through educational seminars and wine tastings.

THE CHARLOTTETOWN FESTIVAL
CONFEDERATION CENTRE OF THE ARTS
LATE JUNE/EARLY SEPTEMBER

Canada's largest festival of musical theater showcases original Canadian productions, including the perennial favorite *Anne of Green Gables*. Lively cabaret-style musicals and children's theater are also featured.

CHATHAM, ONT.
FESTIVAL OF NATIONS
TECUMSEH PARK
LATE JUNE/EARLY JULY

Five-day celebration of Canada's multicultural heritage features ethnic food, cultural entertainment, and a grand Canada Day parade adorned with colorful costumes.

CHEMAINUS, B.C.
CHEMAINUS DAZE
WATERWHEEL PARK AND OLD TOWN
LATE JUNE/EARLY JULY

Pancake/hamburger cookout, parade, and children's activities take place against a backdrop of colorful public murals.

CHILLIWACK, B.C.
COUNTRY LIVING DAYS
MAY

This agricultural community celebrates its heritage with the annual Country Living Days—a month-long event featuring horse races, plays, concerts, a parade, and displays of local arts and crafts.

CLINTON, B.C.
CLINTON ANNUAL BALL
CLINTON MEMORIAL HALL
LATE MAY

B.C.'s oldest annual event dates back to 1867. Ball Week—the week between the ball and annual rodeo—features period costumes, an Old Timer's Tea, fox hunts, and dancing demonstrations.

COBALT, ONT.
MINERS' FESTIVAL
AUGUST CIVIC HOLIDAY WEEKEND

Local and regional miners compete in Jack-Leg Drilling, Hand Mucking and Machine Mucking contests at this community festival. Other traditional activities include dances, parades, children's games, and a wagon ride through town.

COBOURG, ONT.
WATERFRONT FESTIVAL
VICTORIA PARK
JULY 1 WEEKEND

Internationally acclaimed artists display and sell their works under giant colorful tents along the waterfront at one of the largest outdoor arts-and-crafts shows in Canada. Canada Day is celebrated with a parade, live band shell entertainment, and a spectacular waterfront fireworks display.

COCHRANE, ONT.
"CHIMO" WINTER CARNIVAL
LAKE COMMANDO
FEBRUARY

The highlight of this major town attraction is the famous Polar Bear Dip, in which brave "dippers" warm up in a sauna and then plunge into a large ice hole carved into Lake Commando.

CORNER BROOK, NFLD.
WINTER CARNIVAL
FEBRUARY

This carnival of snowy fun boasts more than 100 activities centered around Marble Mountain. Enjoy some of the best skiing in Atlantic Canada, along with horse races, snow sculptures and a spectacular ice show.

CORNWALL, ONT.
AWESOME AUGUST FESTIVAL
AUGUST

Late-summer fun with hot-air balloon rides, a downtown Cornfest featuring live entertainment, and *Arts in the Park*, a waterfront showcase for theater, music, and art.

JUMP INTO JULY FESTIVAL
LATE JUNE/EARLY JULY

Get a "jump" on summer with exciting pro and amateur canoe races, Canada Day festivities, and Worldfest/Festimonde's multicultural celebration with international entertainment.

CRANBROOK, B.C.
SAM STEELE DAYS
THIRD WEEKEND OF JUNE

This action-packed celebration honors Sam Steele, who established the first North West Mounted Police post west of the Rockies in 1887. Logger sports, arm wrestling championships, and a tug-of-war tournament are offset by more unusual contests such as the outhouse race and bartenders competition.

DAWSON CITY, YK.
DISCOVERY DAYS
THIRD WEEKEND OF AUGUST

Dawson commemorates the Klondike Gold Rush with three days of festivities, including a parade, demolition derby, horticultural show, and poker tournament. Pancake breakfasts and salmon barbecues, along with canoe and raft races, are also on the menu.

MUSIC FESTIVAL
CONFEDERATION LANDING PARK
THIIRD WEEKEND OF JULY

Annual outdoor music festival features entertainers from across Canada and the United States. A wide variety of contemporary music is complemented by a craft table exhibition, salmon barbecue, workshops, and all-night dancing.

THAW-DI-GRAW SPRING CARNIVAL
THIRD WEEKEND OF MARCH

Dawson celebrates the arrival of spring with a multitude of family events, including toboggan races, a scavenger hunt, and lip sync contests. Among the more offbeat attractions are snowshoe baseball, a blindfolded snow machine race, and snowshoe can-can dancers.

DEER LAKE, NFLD.
HUMBER VALLEY STRAWBERRY FESTIVAL
LATE JULY/ EARLY AUGUST

Home of the world's sweetest strawberries, Humber Valley pays tribute to the luscious fruit with Strawberry Square Dancers, the province's largest shortcake, and recipes galore.

DORCHESTER, N.B.
SHIRETOWN DAYS FESTIVAL
LAST WEEK OF JUNE

This community festival has something for everyone—from motorcycle and fire truck rides for children to a village dunk tank and mock jail for local "lawbreakers."

DRUMMONDVILLE, QUE.

WORLD FOLKLORE FESTIVAL
JULY

Folk dance troupes from 20 countries perform in the largest event of its kind in North America. Traditional crafts demonstrations, featuring Quebec and international artisans, round out the colorful spectacle.

EDMONTON, ALTA.

CANADIAN FINALS RODEO AND FARMFAIR
MID-NOVEMBER

The best riders and ropers compete to determine the Canadian all-around Cowboy in the final rodeo on the Canadian Pro Rodeo Circuit. Canada's biggest "money rodeo" is held concurrently with Farmfair, one of the country's top international livestock exhibits.

DREAMSPEAKERS
LATE MAY

First Nations artists and performers from across the globe congregate at this Native arts and film festival to share their cultures through displays, performances, and traditional foods.

FOLK MUSIC FESTIVAL
GALLAGHER PARK
EARLY AUGUST

One of the top folk festivals in North America is a four-day celebration of music from around the world. More than 60 acts—from traditional folk and bluegrass music to Gospel and world-beat—take center stage in a natural river valley amphitheater.

HERITAGE FESTIVAL
HAWRELAK PARK
EARLY AUGUST

The largest three-day multicultural festival in the world boasts over 50 outdoor ethnic pavilions featuring continuous singing and dancing, arts-and-crafts displays and demonstrations, and traditional apparel and cuisine.

INTERNATIONAL STREET PERFORMERS FESTIVAL
JULY

The world's best street performers—from mimes and minstrels to clowns and acrobats—bring the city's parks and streets to life in over 100 impromptu performances.

KLONDIKE DAYS
JULY

Relive the vibrant gold rush era of the 1890s with pancake breakfasts and gold panning at this world-famous 10-day event. Highlights include the World Championship Sourdough Raft Race, the King of the Klondike Competition, Canada's oldest casino, and a festive parade.

PLANET OF THE FRINGE
OLD STRATHCONA AREA
MID-AUGUST

The largest and most exciting alternative theater festival in North America features innovative interpretations of old and new plays, dance, music, mime, street entertainment, and theater in the park.

THE WORKS: A VISUAL ARTS CELEBRATION
LATE JUNE/EARLY JULY

The only visual arts festival in North America brings together Canadian artists and artisans with exhibitions of original crafts and fine art in downtown foyers, parks, and art galleries.

EDMUNDSTON, N.B.

LA FOIRE BRAYONNE
LATE JULY/EARLY AUGUST

The biggest francophone festival east of Quebec is a vibrant celebration of the rich heritage of the region, whose French-speaking inhabitants call themselves Brayon. Choose from an array of cultural and recreational activities, including major outdoor stage shows, sporting events, and massive picnics featuring typical Brayonne fare.

ELLIOT LAKE, ONT.

URANIUM FESTIVAL
LATE JUNE/JULY

Week-long festival boasts a multitude of special events—from a colorful parade and gigantic fireworks display to the main event consisting of a drilling and ore-mucking competition.

FREDERICTON, N.B.

FREDERICTON EXHIBITION
EARLY SEPTEMBER

This fall fair and exhibition boasts a major draft horse show and the largest flower display in the province, along with harness racing, livestock shows, and agricultural displays.

HARVEST JAZZ AND BLUES FESTIVAL
MID-SEPTEMBER

Jazz galas in the city's concert halls combine with free open-air concerts and late-night jam sessions in downtown bars as jazz, blues, and Dixieland entertainers from across North America let loose.

MACTAQUAC CRAFT FESTIVAL
MACTAQUAC PROVINCIAL PARK
LATE AUGUST

Two-day outdoor craft festival features everything from pewter and porcelain to stained glass and stoneware. A children's craft area, musical entertainment, and concessions are also featured.

NEW BRUNSWICK HIGHLAND GAMES AND SCOTTISH FESTIVAL
OLD GOVERNMENT HOUSE GROUNDS
JULY

An entertaining weekend of Scottish culture features highland dancing, piping and drumming competitions. Celtic entertainment, genealogy tents, and clan booths are other festival features.

STORYFEST
FEBRUARY

This mid-winter celebration combines storytelling performances, workshops for adults and children, and a special evening gala featuring master raconteurs.

FORT FRANCES, ONT.

FUN IN THE SUN FESTIVAL
LATE JUNE TO JULY 1

Children's festival features a bathtub derby, a dinosaur egg hunt, sandcastle building, and a breathtaking display of skydiving. Ends in a fanfare of fireworks on July 1.

FORT LANGLEY, B.C.

FUR BRIGADE DAYS
EARLY AUGUST

Re-creation of the annual arrival of the fur brigade at the fort. A variety of period encampments, along with demonstrations, a parade, games, and entertainment.

GANANOQUE, ONT.

FESTIVAL OF THE ISLANDS
AUGUST

One of the largest summer festivals in eastern Ontario brings 10 days of family fun to the Thousand Islands. Choose from a wide array of activities, including waterfront concerts, sporting events, island shore breakfasts and historical reenactments.

GANDER, NFLD.

INTERNATIONAL FLIGHT AND HOT-AIR BALLOON FESTIVAL
LATE JULY/EARLY AUGUST

Fun-filled family events—from parades to pet shows, folk music to fireworks—commemorate Gander's aviation history and cultural heritage. The crowning glory is the international balloon festival's Special Night Glow that lights up the balloons like colossal light bulbs.

GRAND FALLS, N.B.

POTATO FESTIVAL
JULY 1 WEEKEND

Friendly celebration in the land of the spud offers everything from folksingers and family picnics to a grand gala and closing parade.

GRAND FALLS-WINDSOR, NFLD.

EXPLOITS VALLEY SALMON FESTIVAL
MID-JULY

Newfoundland's largest festival and premier entertainment event celebrates the mighty Atlantic salmon with everything from a salmon derby and antique car show to a major concert featuring big-ticket performers.

GUELPH, ONT.

SPRING FESTIVAL
LATE APRIL/MAY

This renowned performing arts celebration presents diverse programs of chamber, classical, jazz, and world music, as well as a Family Sunday Series and 30 free community concerts.

HAINES JUNCTION, YK.

ALSEK MUSIC FESTIVAL
SECOND WEEKEND OF JUNE

An annual outdoor music festival showcases northern talent under a big tent on the banks of the Dezadeash River. Also includes workshops, children's events, and handicraft and food booths.

HALIFAX, N.S.

ATLANTIC WINTER FAIR
EARLY OCTOBER

The largest agricultural fair in Atlantic Canada comes complete with horse and cattle shows, a large midway and craft competition, and various musical, comedy, and circus acts.

DU MAURIER ATLANTIC JAZZ FESTIVAL
MID-JULY

A nine-day festival of live jazz featuring performers from around the world in intimate settings from workshops and clinics to concerts and clubs. Also free outdoor stages on the waterfront..

INTERNATIONAL BUSKER FESTIVAL
AUGUST

This famous 10-day street performers festival features the top buskers from Canada, the U.S., Britain, and Australia. Local and international bands are also showcased.

NOVA SCOTIA INTERNATIONAL AIR SHOW
SHEARWATER AIRPORT
EARLY SEPTEMBER

Atlantic Canada's largest outdoor two-day spectator event boasts a ground display of over 100 military and civilian aircraft, high-tech aerospace industry exhibits, and a spectacular 2½-hour air show.

NOVA SCOTIA INTERNATIONAL TATTOO
HALIFAX METRO CENTRE
EARLY JULY

Two-hour spectacular features over 2,000 Canadian and international military and civilian performers, including marching bands, singers, dancers, and acrobats.

HARRISON HOT SPRINGS, B.C.

FESTIVAL OF THE ARTS
JULY

Nine-day celebration of world music, dance, theater, and visual arts, with the focus on African and Latin American performers. Special events include the Festival Dance in a hotel ballroom and the popular Children's Day.

WORLD CHAMPIONSHIP SAND SCULPTURE COMPETITION
HARRISON LAKE BEACH
EARLY SEPTEMBER

Individual and team carvers from around the world shape fantastic castles, cottages, and creatures into the largest sand sculptures ever produced.

HAZELTON, B.C.

PIONEER DAY
SECOND SATURDAY OF AUGUST

Old-fashioned celebration of town's pioneer history offers a wide range of activities from outhouse races to logger sports.

HOLYROOD, NFLD.

SQUID JIGGIN' FESTIVAL
LATE JULY/EARLY AUGUST

This fun family festival celebrates the unpredictable arrival of an unusual ocean delicacy. Highlights include a beach party with a popular band and fireworks, and a yacht sailing race in which fishermen gather their harvest of squid.

HOPE, B.C.

BRIGADE DAYS
SECOND WEEKEND IN SEPTEMBER

A tribute to the fur "brigadiers" who settled the area. Activities range from children's games and riverside fireworks to a demolition derby and logging sports.

HUMBOLDT, SASK.

SOMMERFEST
LAST WEEKEND OF JUNE

This three-day German festival has everything from folk art, ethnic foods, and yodeling to a Bierfest under the big top and a 10 km Volksmarsch (folkwalk) to a nearby community.

INGERSOLL, ONT.

THRESHING DAYS
LATE AUGUST

The good old days come to life at this community event with pioneer displays, antique cars and tractors, log sawing and nail pounding contests, and grain threshing and plowing demonstrations.

INUVIK, N.W.T.

DELTA DAZE
THANKSGIVING WEEKEND

This traditional fall event includes the Delta Prince and Princess competition, "honey bucket" races, the Gold Bar Raffle Barbecue, and midnight dancing.

GREAT NORTHERN ARTS FESTIVAL
THIRD WEEK OF JULY
More than 60 Northern artists gather north of the Arctic Circle to participate in a variety of exhibitions, workshops, and demonstrations at the N.W.T.'s premier cultural event. More than 1,000 works of art are for sale, ranging from original art cards to exquisite soapstone carvings.

MIDNIGHT MADNESS
MID-JUNE
Northern games and foods are features of this event, which celebrates the arrival of the summer solstice, 24 hours of daylight.

SUNRISE FESTIVAL
EARLY JANUARY
Inuvik welcomes the sun's return after the 24-hour darkness of winter with dancing and skating parties, bonfires, and a breathtaking fireworks display.

JASPER, ALTA.
JASPER HERITAGE FOLK FESTIVAL
CENTENNIAL PARK
EARLY AUGUST (BIENNIAL EVENT)
An unparalleled mountain backdrop provides the setting for an eclectic range of high-caliber folk music, including roots, bluegrass, country, and ethnic. Of special interest are the community group booths and an aboriginal village.

JASPER IN JANUARY
JANUARY
This three-weekend-long winter festival has everything from skiing, skating, and canyon-crawling to a chili cookoff and snow-sculpting contest.

JOLIETTE, QUE.
FESTIVAL INTERNATIONAL DE LANAUDIÈRE
LATE JUNE / AUGUST
The greatest names in classical music perform at Joliette's huge 2,000-seat open-air amphitheater and in the region's most beautiful churches.

KAMLOOPS, B.C.
POW WOW DAYS
CHIEF LOUIS CENTRE
MID-AUGUST
"The Biggest Little Pow Wow in the West" attracts Native dancers and performers from as far away as New Mexico. Intertribal dance and drumming competitions are featured alongside Native arts and crafts, and a Princess Pageant.

KENORA, ONT.
LAKE OF THE WOODS INTERNATIONAL SAILING REGATTA
LATE JULY
This international seven-day race on the Lake of the Woods is the largest inland sailing regatta in North America. For less competitive sailors, there's also a week devoted to cruising through this lake's waterways.

KIMBERLEY, B.C.
JULYFEST
THIRD WEEKEND OF JULY
The "Bavarian City of the Rockies" celebrates summer with platzl entertainment, a Family Fun Fair, and a sports festival featuring boccie, soccer, and a soapbox derby.

WINTERFEST
SECOND WEEKEND OF FEBRUARY
The Bavarian theme continues into winter with platzl hockey and entertainment, kid and mutt races, a torchlight parade, and the Friendship Wall (made out of ice).

KINGS LANDING, N.B.
AGRICULTURAL FAIR
LATE AUGUST
A true "Loyalist" agricultural fair awaits at Kings Landing, where staff in 19th-century costumes busy themselves selling produce and livestock at this restored Saint John River valley village.

KINGSTON, ONT.
BUSKERS RENDEZVOUS
JULY
Third largest festival of its kind in Canada brings together more than 100 street performers (including musicians, magicians, jugglers, and mimes) from around the world.

CELTIC FESTIVAL
FORT HENRY
EARLY SEPTEMBER
Enjoy pipe bands at this lively celebration of Celtic food, music, dance, and traditions. A Celtic marketplace and a children's crafts area are also part of this event.

CHILI FESTIVAL
CONFEDERATION PARK
EARLY OCTOBER
More than 50 restaurants compete in a chili-tasting contest complete with celebrity judges. Prizes are awarded for best Tex-Mex, Vegetarian and Family Recipe, as well as Most Original and People's Choice.

KINGSVILLE, ONT.
MIGRATION FESTIVAL
THIRD WEEKEND OF OCTOBER
Kingsville celebrates the annual return of Canada geese to Jack Miner's Bird Sanctuary with a sportsmen's show, arts-and-crafts exhibits, winery tours, and international bird carvings.

KISPIOX, B.C.
KISPIOX VALLEY RODEO
FIRST WEEKEND OF JUNE
Cowboys and cowgirls come from all over North America to compete in "the biggest little rodeo in the Northwest." Crafts, foods, and dances with live country music are all part of the action.

KITCHENER-WATERLOO, ONT.
OKTOBERFEST
SECOND WEEK OF OCTOBER
Eat, drink, and be merry at festival halls throughout the twin cities during the world's second largest Bavarian festival (after Munich's, in Germany). The famous Thanksgiving Day Parade kicks off more than 45 family, sporting, and cultural events—from the Miss Oktoberfest Pageant to the Great Barrel Race.

LADYSMITH, B.C.
FESTIVAL OF LIGHTS
LAST THURSDAY IN NOVEMBER THROUGH DECEMBER
Breathtaking Christmas light displays in the "Christmas Light-Up Capital of Vancouver Island." Outdoor turn-on ceremony features a light-up parade, community spaghetti dinner, fireworks extravaganza, and Santa's Corner.

LATCHFORD, ONT.
HERITAGE LOGGING DAYS
JULY
Town's logging heritage is celebrated with related activities, including a horse log-skidding contest, pulp toss, and chain saw competition.

LEAMINGTON, ONT.

TOMATO FESTIVAL
SEACLIFFE PARK
THIRD WEEK OF AUGUST

The "Tomato Capital of Canada" honors its chief produce with an array of family fun—from a beauty pageant and tomato stomp to the battle of the bands and a classic cruiser car show.

LETHBRIDGE, ALTA.

INTERNATIONAL AIR SHOW
THIRD WEEKEND OF AUGUST

One of the largest air shows in Western Canada draws top-notch civilian and military aviators from around the world. Also featured is a varied display of aircraft from old biplanes to high-tech jet fighters.

WHOOP-UP DAYS
EXHIBITION GROUNDS
SECOND WEEKEND OF AUGUST

Lively summer fair draws its name from the notorious 19th-century trading post. A full slate of events includes pancake breakfasts, grandstand entertainment, logging competitions, and a professional rodeo with chuckwagon races.

LONDON, ONT.

NEW LONDON ARTS FESTIVAL
LATE SEPTEMBER

Downtown London comes alive with a wide spectrum of art forms—everything from concerts, films, and theater to over a dozen visual art displays, buskers, and even sidewalk chalk painting.

ROYAL CANADIAN BIG BAND MUSIC FESTIVAL
LATE JUNE/EARLY JULY

Enjoy the favorites of the big band era, along with ballroom dance demonstrations and fine arts and crafts, at this popular festival, held in honor of London-born bandleader Guy Lombardo.

WESTERN FAIR
WESTERN FAIRGROUNDS
SEPTEMBER

One of Canada's largest and oldest fairs, this 130-year-old institution has everything from carnival rides and circus animals to farm exhibitions and food booths.

LLOYDMINSTER, ALTA.

COLONIAL DAYS
EXHIBITION GROUNDS
SECOND WEEK OF JULY

This major Prairie exposition and fair comes complete with a parade, midway, and casino, as well as agricultural and home arts exhibits.

MANITOULIN ISLAND, ONT.

WIKWEMIKONG POW-WOW
WIKWEMIKONG UNCEDED INDIAN RESERVE
FIRST WEEKEND OF AUGUST

Elaborately costumed First Nations dancers, drummers, and singers compete for prizes at one of the largest and longest running pow-wows in North America. A wide variety of Native cuisine and colorful crafts are also on display.

MAPLE CREEK, B.C.

RANCH RODEO
EARLY JULY

Teams of ranchers compete in typical ranching events such as penning cattle, horse catching, doctoring, and wild-cow milking.

MARATHON, ONT.

NEYS NOSTALGIA DAYS
NEYS PROVINCIAL PARK
SECOND WEEKEND OF AUGUST

"Spirits" from the past gather round the campfire to tell tales of the railway and the fur trade and to reenact the logging games and dances favored by early explorers and voyageurs.

MASSEY, ONT.

FALL FAIR
LATE AUGUST

One of the largest agricultural fairs in Ontario comes complete with midway, games of chance, old-time stage shows, motocross races, and heavy horse pulls.

MAYO, YK.

WINTER CARNIVAL
THIRD WEEK OF MARCH

This winter family festival features individual and team events for kids and adults—from tea boiling and egg tossing to nail pounding and moose calling.

MEDICINE HAT, ALTA.

STAMPEDE
LATE JULY/EARLY AUGUST

Large fair with a small town atmosphere captures the spirit of southern Alberta. Attractions include Canada's second largest Pro Rodeo and top name country and western singers.

MERRITT, B.C.

NICOLA VALLEY RODEO AND FALL FAIR
LABOUR DAY WEEKEND

Nationally sanctioned rodeo events, a pancake breakfast, community dance, and old-time fiddling contests reflect daily life in the heart of cowboy country.

MILTON, ONT.

ONTARIO RENAISSANCE FESTIVAL
JULY/AUGUST

A mock King Henry VIII and his royal court preside over this country fair set in a 16th-century Tudor village, replete with theatrical performers, artisans, food purveyors, and period amusement—from authentic jousting matches to human chess games.

MINNEDOSA, MAN.

COUNTRY FUN FEST
SECOND WEEK OF JULY

Country fun for everyone—from the kids' trout derby and mini folk festival to the agricultural fair and farmers' market.

MISSION, B.C.

FOLK MUSIC FESTIVAL
FRASER RIVER HERITAGE PARK
LATE JULY

One of the premier festivals on the folk music circuit featuring recent immigrants to Canada performing a wide spectrum of music—from Celtic fiddling to flamenco guitar. Also offers an import market, ethnic food, and workshops.

MONCTON, N.B.

MONCTON JAZZ AND BLUES FESTIVAL
LATE JUNE/EARLY JULY

Week-long jazz and blues festival features a host of national and international musicians, supported by local and regional artists, at a combination of indoor and outdoor concerts, club acts and a grand finale concert.

VICTORIA PARK ARTS AND CRAFTS FAIR
VICTORIA PARK
AUGUST

Artisans from across the Maritime provinces showcase their work in a beautiful park setting at the largest outdoor sale of top-quality arts and crafts in the Maritimes.

MONTMAGNY, QUE.
SNOW GOOSE FESTIVAL
OCTOBER
Celebrates the annual arrival of nearly 300,000 snow geese with goose watching and interpretation, parades, painting exhibits, and tastings of goose-based dishes.

WORLD ACCORDION JAMBOREE
ECONOMUSÉ DE L'ACCORDÉON
SEPTEMBER
This important four-day event draws accordionists from around the world to a unique accordion museum housed in a magnificent ancestral home. Concerts, workshops, and an impressively diverse assortment of instruments are on the program.

MONTREAL, QUE.
BENSON & HEDGES INTERNATIONAL FIREWORKS COMPETITION
LA RONDE
JUNE/JULY
The most prestigious pyrotechnics competition in the world features fireworks masters from round the world. Enjoy a ticketed up-close view with access to the amusement park or take in the spectacle for free from various vantage points across the water.

INTERNATIONAL FOOD FESTIVAL
ÎLE NOTRE-DAME
AUGUST
Feast on exotic fare from the four corners of the earth at this immense open-air food festival seasoned with ethnic entertainment. Food samples —from Arctic salmon to Salvadorian yucca—are available on a pay-per-plate basis.

JAZZ FESTIVAL
PLACE DES ARTS AREA
LATE JUNE/EARLY JULY
One of the world's top jazz festivals is unique in combining top-dollar talent with free-for-all entertainment. Each year, some 1.5 million spectators flock to more than 400 concerts, 300 of which are free in four city blocks closed to traffic.

JUST FOR LAUGHS FESTIVAL
JULY
The world's largest comedy festival is a bilingual affair that features some 650 international comedy acts in over 1,000 performances. Ticketed headliner concerts are complemented by more affordable laughs at the Jacques Cartier Pier in the Old Port, transformed into a comedy park.

THEATRE OF THE AMERICAS FESTIVAL
MAY/JUNE
An impressive and varied program of innovative and avant-garde productions by some of the best theater companies in the world.

WINTER FESTIVAL
PARC DES ÎLES
FEBRUARY
Ten-day winter carnival offers everything from snow castles and giant ice slides to dog-sled races and lively costumed characters. Competitive winter sports, such as ski competitions, round out the outdoor festivities.

WORLD FILM FESTIVAL
PLACE DES ARTS AREA
AUGUST/SEPTEMBER
The largest publicly attended film festival in North America is a glittering showcase for major international film premieres. Some 350,000 film fans are the first on their blocks to see 400 films from more than 60 countries around the world.

MOOSE JAW, SASK.
MOOSE JAW CHAUTAUQUA
AUGUST
Popular in the West during the 1920s and 1930s, the Chautauqua offers old-time entertainment with sing-alongs, comedy skits, and dance hall shows.

SASKATCHEWAN AIR SHOW
EARLY JULY
The largest annual air show on the Prairies features exciting military and civil aerial demonstrations by some of the world's best formation flying teams, including the famous hometown Snowbirds.

NANAIMO, B.C.
MARINE FESTIVAL AND BATHTUB RACE
DOWNTOWN AND WATERFRONT AREA
LATE JULY
Tens of thousands of visitors descend upon Nanaimo to witness the zany World Championship Bathtub Race in which 100 motor-powered bathtubs race across the Strait of Georgia to Vancouver. The four-day Marine Festival also includes a Silly Boat regatta, a jet-ski competitions, a street fair, and fireworks.

VANCOUVER ISLAND EXHIBITION
MID-AUGUST
Old-fashioned country fair complete with livestock competitions, agricultural and crafts exhibits, and open-air stage performances, as well as a horse show and midway.

NEW GLASGOW, N.S.
FESTIVAL OF THE TARTANS
JULY
The flavor of modern Scottish life comes to the fore with mass pipe band displays, a tartan store front competition, and a kilted golf tournament.

NEW WESTMINSTER, B.C.
FRASERFEST
WESTMINSTER QUAY
JULY
This three-day salute to the Fraser River is packed with family-oriented attractions from kite flying and model boat building to the annual Workboat Parade.

HYACK FESTIVAL
MAY
The history of New Westminster comes alive with the ancient Anvil Battery 21 gun salute to Queen Victoria and the May Day Celebration, the oldest event of its kind in the Commonwealth. Another highlight is the largest parade in B.C., featuring outstanding marching bands from the United States.

NORTH BAY, ONT.
HERITAGE FESTIVAL AND AIR SHOW
FIRST WEEKEND OF AUGUST
Four-day family-oriented festival features a midway, headliner entertainment, and children's activities. Special attraction is the breathtaking two-day air show with civilian and military solo and precision team aerobatic performances.

ORILLIA, ONT.

LAUGH WITH LEACOCK FESTIVAL OF HUMOUR
STEPHEN LEACOCK MUSEUM
LATE JULY/EARLY AUGUST

This fun-filled tribute to Canada's foremost humorist, Stephen Leacock, who once summered in Orillia, features musical entertainment, English teas, a popular reading series with some of Canada's foremost authors, and Leacock plays performed by an eclectic cast of characters.

PERCH FESTIVAL
APRIL/MAY

Canada's largest registered fishing derby is a fun family event with adult and children's categories for prizes.

ORWELL CORNER, P.E.I.

WEDNESDAY CEILIDHS
ORWELL COMMUNITY HALL
JUNE/SEPTEMBER

Prince Edward Island's best fiddlers, pipers, and dancers provide traditional, toe-tapping entertainment under the glow of kerosene lamps at traditional Scottish gathering called ceilidhs (pronounced *kaylees*). Homemade fudge, strawberries and ice cream are available during the intermission.

OTTAWA, ONT.

BLUESFEST
MAJOR'S HILL PARK
EARLY JULY

Canada's largest blues festival features international blues acts in an idyllic outdoor setting bordered by the Ottawa River.

CANADA DAY CELEBRATION
JULY 1

Held in honor of Canada's "birthday," this all-day party comes complete with marching bands, pealing bells, thundering jets, and star entertainers. Culminates in spectacular fireworks over Parliament Hill.

CANADIAN TULIP FESTIVAL
MID-MAY

A spectacular display of springtime tulips provides the centerpiece for a wide variety of cultural, floral, and horticultural activities. The world's largest tulip festival is a legacy of a gift from the Queen of the Netherlands for the refuge Canada granted the Dutch royal family during the Second World War.

CENTRAL CANADA EXHIBITION
LANSDOWNE PARK
MID-AUGUST

This large-scale country fair has everything from craft shows and agricultural exhibits to more than 60 rides, and live entertainment.

CHILDREN'S FESTIVAL
CANADIAN MUSEUM OF NATURE
EARLY JUNE

A carousel of magical performances in mime, dance, music, and theater is complemented by a museum full of dinosaurs, birds, and bats.

FOLK FESTIVAL
BRITTANIA PARK
AUGUST

The rich folk tradition of the Ottawa Valley is celebrated with top Canadian performers, interactive workshops, and a Family Area complete with storytelling and crafts.

FRANCO-ONTARIAN FESTIVAL
JUNE

Franco-Ontarian performers are showcased in this lively celebration of francophone culture, arts, music, and comedy.

INTERNATIONAL JAZZ FESTIVAL
IN AND AROUND CONFEDERATION PARK
LATE JULY

A kaleidoscope of jazz styles are represented at this popular and affordable jazz festival. More than 400 jazz musicians from across Canada and around the world perform at indoor and outdoor venues within walking distance of each other.

WINTERLUDE
FIRST THREE WEEKENDS OF FEBRUARY

This major North American winter carnival centers around the world's longest skating rink—the Rideau Canal. Highlights include speed and figure skating competitions, sleigh rides, snow sculptures, parades, and fireworks.

OXFORD, N.S.

CUMBERLAND COUNTY EXHIBITION & BLUEBERRY FESTIVAL
LATE AUGUST

Feast on traditional treats in the "blueberry capital of the world." Blueberry baking and pie-eating contests are complemented by a midway, a street parade, and livestock and agricultural exhibits.

PARRY SOUND, ONT.

FESTIVAL OF THE SOUND
JULY/AUGUST

World-renowned classical and jazz musicians are featured in evening and brunch concerts on the shores of Georgian Bay. Also offered are afternoon tea talks and musical cruises among the Thirty Thousand Islands.

PENTICTON, B.C.

PEACH FESTIVAL
EARLY AUGUST

Five-day family festival features over 30 events, including summer wine tasting, a sand-castle competition, and the B.C. Square Dance Jamboree.

PERTH, ONT.

FESTIVAL OF THE MAPLES
LAST SATURDAY OF APRIL

Grand finale of a regional two-month maple festival in the "Maple Syrup Capital of Ontario." This popular event features the finest assortment of maple products, fiddling, square dancing, and maple syrup competitions.

PERTH FAIR
LABOUR DAY WEEKEND

This traditional agricultural fair runs the gamut from field crop and giant vegetable exhibits to a kickoff parade and grandstand entertainment. A perennial children's favorite is the Fantasy Farm with farm animals, rabbits, and poultry on display.

PERTH-ANDOVER, N.B.

WABANAKI MUSIC FESTIVAL
LATE AUGUST/EARLY SEPTEMBER

This showcase of aboriginal talent in drama, music, dance, fine art, and crafts aims to create a greater understanding between cultures.

PETERBOROUGH, ONT.

FESTIVAL OF TREES
PETERBOROUGH MEMORIAL CENTRE
NOVEMBER

Victorian Village features more than 200 decorated Christmas trees, refreshments, and live entertainment. Games and amusement are also on hand at the Children's Magic Castle and the Country Fair.

SUMMER FESTIVAL OF LIGHTS
CRARY PARK ON LITTLE LAKE
JUNE/AUGUST

Series of outdoor shows features top-name musical, dance, and theatrical entertainment. Performances are followed by a musically choreographed, illuminated boat spectacle, capped with precision-timed fireworks.

PICTOU, N.S.

HECTOR FESTIVAL
AUGUST

Five-day tribute to the town's Scottish heritage features Celtic and Scottish musicians, a pictorial display of early Pictou, rug-hooking demonstrations, and a reenactment of the landing of the ship *Hector* in 1773.

LOBSTER CARNIVAL
EARLY JULY

Enjoy a plate of fresh boiled lobster and drawn butter, followed by a harborside lobster boat race. Other highlights include lobster trap-hauling contests, scallop-shucking competitions, and massed pipe-band concerts.

PINCHER CREEK, ALTA.

COWBOY POETRY GATHERING
COMMUNITY HALL
SECOND WEEKEND OF JUNE

Cowboys from near and far come together to share their reflections on the ranching way of life with cowboy poetry, Western art and music, and an open-air cowboy church service.

PLACENTIA, NFLD.

FESTIVAL OF FLAGS
JULY

Month-long festival salutes the importance of Placentia in world military history with a regatta, music festivals, garden parties, sports, games, and international cuisine.

PLESSISVILLE, QUE.

MAPLE FESTIVAL
LATE APRIL/EARLY MAY

Spring fair attracts thousands of taffy fans with sugaring-off parties, maple products competitions, cooking demonstrations, and musical entertainment.

PORTAGE LA PRAIRIE, MAN.

CANADA'S NATIONAL STRAWBERRY FESTIVAL
MID-JULY

One of central Manitoba's premier festivals, this strawberry extravaganza takes place in the "Strawberry

Capital of Canada." Features main-stage musical entertainment, accompanied by fresh strawberries and strawberry desserts.

PRINCE GEORGE, B.C.

CANADIAN NORTHERN CHILDREN'S FESTIVAL
LATE MAY

Clowns, musicians, and colorful characters draw thousands of families to one of the largest events in the North for four days of theater, puppetry, face painting, and juggling.

MARDI GRAS OF WINTER
FEBRUARY

This madcap mid-winter festival for the whole family boasts more than 100 events, from bed races to a zany parade decked out in crazy costumes.

PRESCOTT, ONT.

LOYALIST DAYS
FORT WELLINGTON
THIRD WEEKEND OF JULY

This 10-day celebration of the town's founding by the United Empire Loyalists features Canada's largest military pageant, complete with large-scale mock battles and demonstrations of pioneer skills.

PUGWASH, N.S.

GATHERING OF THE CLANS
EARLY JULY

A Gaelic welcome is extended at this five-day Scottish heritage celebration complete with highland dancing and piping competitions, heavyweight games, lobster dinners, and midway rides.

QUEBEC CITY, QUE.

CARNAVAL DE QUÉBEC
FEBRUARY

This popular 17-day celebration of winter, with the 2 metre tall snowman Bonhomme as master of ceremonies, is a showcase for Quebec art, culture, entertainment, and winter sports. Highlights include the provincial dogsled racing championship, snow sculpture contests, canoe races over the partially frozen St. Lawrence, and a glittering night parade.

DU MAURIER QUEBEC SUMMER FESTIVAL
JULY

Ten-day celebration of Quebec's cultural heritage is the largest French-language street and stage arts festival in North America. Streets and parks in the heart of the Old City overflow with 400 free shows featuring singers, dancers, acrobats, and magicians from 20 countries.

EXPO-QUÉBEC (AGRICULTURAL EXHIBITION)
EXPOSITION PARK
AUGUST

Quebec's largest agricultural exhibition has everything from a miniature farm and fun fair to hockey and harness racing.

LES NUITS BLEUES INTERNATIONALES DE JAZZ
LATE JUNE

This popular musical and cultural celebration presents a wide range of musical styles in auditoriums, bars, and restaurants, as well as on outdoor stages and under the big top.

RED LAKE, ONT.

NORSEMAN FLOAT PLANE FESTIVAL
LATE JULY

Community floatplane festival honoring the Noorduyn Noresman airplane, the first Canadian-designed bush plane. Highlights include a flypast parade of historic, single-engined Norsemen, and street activities, such as float pumping contests and model floatplane flying.

REGINA, SASK.

BUFFALO DAYS EXHIBITION
LATE JULY/EARLY AUGUST

The "Old West" comes to life with locals dressed up in western attire, homecraft displays, livestock exhibits, midway rides and agricultural shows. Also features a casino, a parade, and Canada's largest outdoor picnic in Wascana Park.

CANADIAN WESTERN AGRIBITION
LAST WEEK OF NOVEMBER

Livestock producers from around the world check out cattle, sheep, horses, and swine at Canada's premier agriculture and trade show. Other highlights include one of Canada's largest indoor professional rodeos and the Western Lifestyles Showcase featuring food and fashion.

FOLK FESTIVAL
THIRD WEEKEND OF JUNE

Folk musicians from across Canada perform blues, country, and homestyle music at Saskatchewan's premier folk festival. The mainly outdoor family event includes evening concerts, afternoon workshops, and children's entertainment.

INTERNATIONAL CHILDREN'S FESTIVAL
WASCANA CENTRE
JUNE

Magical family entertainment for the "young at art." Artists and performers from around the world present music and drama, storytelling and puppetry, along with arts activities suited for young audiences.

KINSMEN BIG VALLEY JAMBOREE
THIRD WEEKEND OF JULY

One of Canada's top country music events is renowned for its world-class lineup of country music stars on a giant outdoor stage in the scenic Qu'Appelle River valley.

MOSAIC—FESTIVAL OF CULTURES
FIRST WEEK OF JUNE

Visitors present passports to enter 24 pavilions featuring the crafts of skilled artisans, folk dancing, lively music, and food from around the world.

SASKATCHEWAN INDIAN FEDERATED COLLEGE POW WOW
EARLY APRIL

Dancers from across North America perform at one of Canada's largest indoor pow wows. Native crafts and traditional foods can also be purchased.

RUSSEL, MAN.

BEEF AND BARLEY FESTIVAL
THANKSGIVING WEEKEND

Russel celebrates its agricultural base with a beef supper and dance,

curling bonspiel, demolition derby, and bull chip throwing contest.

SACKVILLE, N.B.

ATLANTIC WATERFOWL CELEBRATION
SACKVILLE WATERFOWL PARK
SECOND WEEKEND OF AUGUST

Nationally acclaimed festival is timed to coincide with the peak of the season for waterfowl and shorebird activity. The only festival of its kind in Canada celebrates conservation of the wetland habitat with guided nature walks, educational workshops, a wildlife art exhibit, and photography contest.

ST. ANN'S, N.S.

HIGHLAND GATHERING
THE GAELIC COLLEGE OF CELTIC ARTS AND CRAFTS
EARLY AUGUST

This week-long Scottish cultural celebration at the only Gaelic college in North America is an international gathering of the clans, complete with ceilidhs, genealogy workshops, and two days of Highland Games.

SAINT JOHN, N.B.

FESTIVAL BY THE SEA
MID-AUGUST

Spectacular national performing arts festival spotlights Canadian music, dance, and culture. The 10-day cultural extravaganza showcases 300 entertainers representing the myriad of cultures that make up Canada.

GRAND OLE ATLANTIC NATIONAL EXHIBITION
LAST WEEK OF AUGUST

The largest exhibition in the Maritimes combines stage shows, midway rides, and harness racing with local arts-and-crafts displays, and horticultural and livestock exhibits.

LOYALIST DAYS' HERITAGE CELEBRATION
SECOND WEEK OF JULY

The city celebrates its heritage with tricorn hats and colorful costumes, parades, ceremonies, and special events, including a reenactment of the landing of the United Empire Loyalists.

ST. JOHN'S, NFLD.

FIRST LIGHT CELEBRATIONS
DECEMBER 31

A festival of entertainment, music, and dancing draws people from far and wide to be the first in North America to ring in the New Year as the ships in port blow their horns and whistles to a breathtaking display of fireworks.

GEORGE STREET FESTIVAL
EARLY AUGUST

A pub-lined party street hosts five nights of live entertainment with some of Newfoundland's and Canada's top acts.

NEWFOUNDLAND AND LABRADOR FOLK FESTIVAL
BANNERMAN PARK
FIRST WEEKEND OF AUGUST

The cream of Newfoundland and Labrador folk musicians, dancers, and storytellers gather for the biggest folk festival of the year. This three-day open-air extravaganza boasts more than 200 performers, a feast of traditional foods, and a special stage just for kids.

ROYAL ST. JOHN'S REGATTA
QUIDI VIDI LAKE
FIRST WEDNESDAY OF AUGUST

Stores and businesses close in St. John's as everyone gathers at the shore of Quidi Vidi to play games of chance, listen to music, and watch North America's oldest continuous sporting event, dating back to 1826.

SIGNAL HILL TATTOO
MID-JULY/MID-AUGUST

Dressed in traditional red tunics, cadets reenact British military drills performed by the Royal Newfoundland Companies garrisoned at Signal Hill in the 1860s.

SOUND SYMPOSIUM
JULY (BIENNIAL EVENT)

Artists and musicians from around the world gather to explore the relationship of sound to their art forms in this nine-day celebration of sound. Concerts, workshops, and visual art exhibitions run the gamut from homemade instruments to computer-activated works.

ST. THOMAS, ONT.

IRON HORSE FESTIVAL
LATE AUGUST

This community-based tribute to St. Thomas's railway heritage comes complete with train rides and railway vendors, food booths, and displays of railway rolling stock.

ST-HYACINTHE, QUE.

AGRICULTURAL FAIR
JULY

Quebec's most important agricultural show boasts a wide range of attractions, including animal judging, a tractor pull, casino, rides, and shows.

FESTIVAL RÉTRO DE SAINT-HYACINTHE
AUGUST

A back-to-the-'60s weekend with best retro band performances, an exhibition of cars and guitars from the rock 'n roll era, and twist, limbo, and hula hoop competitions.

SAINT-JEAN-PORT-JOLI, QUE.

INTERNATIONAL SCULPTURE FESTIVAL
LATE JUNE

The capital of traditional Quebec wood sculpture hosts well-known local, regional, and international artists. Ten days of lively activities feature exhibits and demonstrations against the backdrop of an international live wood-sculpting event.

SAINTE-ANNE-DE-LA-PÉRADE, QUE.

TOMCOD CARNIVAL
LATE DECEMBER/MID-FEBRUARY

Thousands of fishermen converge on the Sainte-Anne River to celebrate the annual tomcod fishing season at one of Quebec's most popular ice-fishing spots. Ice sculptures, singing and dancing, and prizes for the best catch and most colorful fishing cabin make for a festive occasion.

SASKATOON, SASK.

FOLKFEST
AUGUST

Hop on a free Folkfest bus to visit up to 25 international pavilions for a sampling of the food, song, dance, and cultural displays that represent the city's colorful heritage.

INTERNATIONAL FRINGE FESTIVAL
BROADWAY AREA
EARLY AUGUST

Over 50 theatrical troupes from around the world present everything from high-wire acts and improvisational comedy to original plays and novel approaches to classic and contemporary dramas.

NORTHERN SASKATCHEWAN'S INTERNATIONAL CHILDREN'S FESTIVAL KIWANIS PARK
EARLY JUNE

World-class performing arts for children of all ages are presented in a beautiful riverside park. Presentations of music, dance, theater, and puppetry are complemented by activity tents with face painting and cooperative games.

PION-ERA
WESTERN DEVELOPMENT MUSEUM
LATE JULY

Experience the pioneer skills and talents of yesteryear at 1910 Boomtown. Two-day show brings history to life with antique machinery, horse and wagon rides, an old-fashioned hymn sing, and demonstrations galore—from threshing and hay baling to quilting and butter churning.

SASKATOON EXHIBITION
PRAIRIELAND EXHIBITION CENTER
MID-JULY

Saskatoon's largest single event, the century-old summer fair features grandstand shows, a major midway, harness racing, Kidsville, and the Emerald Casino.

SASKTEL SASKATCHEWAN JAZZ FESTIVAL
LATE JUNE/EARLY JULY

Over 500 jazz and blues musicians from around the world perform in a variety of venues—from riverside parks and nightclubs to ballrooms and shopping malls. Photography exhibits, workshops, and seminars complement the main concert series and free outdoor performances.

SHAKESPEARE ON THE SASKATCHEWAN FESTIVAL
JULY/AUGUST

This internationally acclaimed festival is renowned for its entertaining and contemporary approach to Shakespeare, including classics and musicals, in an informal tent setting on a scenic riverbank.

SUNDOG HANDCRAFT FAIRE
SASKATCHEWAN PLACE
EARLY DECEMBER

Western Canada's finest artists and artisans come to Saskatchewan's premier festival of handcrafts to display their wares and demonstrate their skills.

SAULT STE. MARIE, ONT.

ALGOMA FALL FESTIVAL
SEPTEMBER/OCTOBER

Sixteen-day showcase of the visual and performing arts with Canadian and international artists from all disciplines, including music, theater, and dance. Festival of the Arts spotlights talented local artists and artisans.

ONTARIO WINTER CARNIVAL BON SOO
LATE JANUARY/EARLY FEBRUARY

One of Canada's largest winter carnivals offers over 100 outdoor and indoor events and activities. Ten days of festivities kick off with a spectacular fireworks display on the waterfront and wind up with a polar bear dip. A featured attraction is a winter playground sculpted entirely of snow.

SHEDIAC, N.B.

LOBSTER FESTIVAL
JULY

The self-proclaimed "Lobster capital of the world" holds a week-long festival in honor of the succulent deep-sea delicacy. Festivities include a lobster-eating contest, lobster suppers, outdoor stage shows, and a giant parade.

SIOUX LOOKOUT, ONT.

BLUEBERRY FESTIVAL
EARLY AUGUST

This popular 10-day community celebration is held at the height of the blueberry season. Tuck into the luscious blue berries at a pancake breakfast or old-fashioned picnic, or take in the triathlon, music festival, or ladies auction.

SMITHERS, B.C.

BULKLEY VALLEY EXHIBITION
LAST WEEKEND IN AUGUST

One of the largest agricultural exhibitions in the province hosts the B.C. Championship Draft Horse Pull and Light Horse Show. Livestock judging, 4-H shows, and home-baked goodies make for a real country fair.

STEINBACH, MAN.

PIONEER DAYS

MENNONITE HERITAGE VILLAGE
LATE JULY/EARLY AUGUST

This celebration of pioneer life features the largest parade in southeastern Manitoba, along with horse shows, youth bands, and a variety of interpretive demonstrations—from quilting and butter churning to threshing and log cutting.

STELLARTON, N.S.

HOMECOMING FESTIVAL

JULY/AUGUST

Old-fashioned fun—from horse and buggy rides to an old-time fiddling contest—is the order of the day at this community festival. Dances and a variety of social gatherings and sporting events round out the week's festivities.

STEPHENVILLE, NFLD.

THEATRE FESTIVAL

MID-JULY/EARLY AUGUST

This established professional theatre festival explores the region's four major founding cultures: British, Canadian, American, and French. Theatrical delights range from popular classics to rollicking cabaret in various venues, including Newfoundland's largest wooden church.

STRATFORD, ONT.

THEATRE FESTIVAL

MAY/NOVEMBER

Theatre lovers from around the world flock to this lovely city on the Avon River to enjoy North America's largest repertory theatre festival. Shakespeare, classical, and modern plays are presented on three stages, the largest being the Festival Theatre with its innovative thrust stage.

SUDBURY, ONT.

CANADIAN GARLIC FESTIVAL

AUGUST

This festival pays tribute to the humble bulb with savory foods, entertainment by ethnic choirs and dancers, and children's activities, such as the Great Garlic Hunt.

NORTHERN LIGHTS FESTIVAL

JULY

Canada's longest running bilingual and multicultural outdoor arts festival offers more than 100 concerts, an Arts Village, an international food fair, and crafts demonstrations.

SNOWFLAKE FESTIVAL

LAKE RAMSEY AND SCIENCE NORTH
FEBRUARY

Winter celebration features indoor and outdoor fun for the entire family—from science and craft workshops to horse-drawn sleigh and dogsled rides.

SUSSEX, N.B.

ATLANTIC BALLOON FIESTA

SEPTEMBER

This high-flying event draws hot-air balloons and their pilots from across Canada and the U.S. Highlights include hot-air balloon launches, parachute demonstrations, and helicopter rides.

SWIFT CURRENT, SASK.

FRONTIER DAYS REGIONAL FAIR AND RODEO

LATE JUNE

Annual exhibition conjures up the frontier west with everything from horse and cattle shows to cowboy poetry and world-class grandstand entertainment.

WESTERN CANADIAN AMATEUR OLDE TYME FIDDLING CHAMPIONSHIP

EARLY OCTOBER

Enjoy toe-tapping fun at this two-day competition, which attracts 750 fiddlers from across Western Canada, Yukon, and the United States.

SYDNEY, N.S.

ACTION WEEK

FIRST WEEK OF AUGUST

Sydney celebrates its heritage with a colorful nine-day festival of music, sports, and special events—from street dances and parades to a heritage tea and guided walk of the harbor.

TATAMAGOUCHE, N.S.

OKTOBERFEST

NORTH SHORE RECREATION CENTRE
LAST WEEKEND OF SEPTEMBER

The biggest Oktoberfest east of Kitchener, Ont., is decked out with beer gardens, dances, German foods, and alpine store displays.

THUNDER BAY, ONT.

GREAT CANADIAN RENDEZ-VOUS FESTIVAL

OLD FORT WILLIAM
JULY

One of the largest living history sites in North America hosts this 10-day tribute to the fur-trading days of the early 1800s. A spirited reenactment of the annual arrival of the fur brigades comes complete with a marketplace atmosphere and unique competitions such as ax throwing and voyageur wrestling.

OJIBWA KEESHIGUN

OLD FORT WILLIAM
LATE AUGUST

Old Fort William comes alive as it celebrates Native life during the historic days of the fur trade with craft shows, demonstrations, such as skinning and tanning hides, and performances of Native dances and songs.

TEMAGAMI, ONT.

GREY OWL'S WILDERNESS FESTIVAL

JULY 1 WEEKEND

Take part in the white-bear challenge—swim, run, paddle, and portage—or the moose-calling contest in this wilderness tribute to the conservationist and writer Grey Owl.

TORONTO, ONT.

BENSON & HEDGES SYMPHONY OF FIRE

ONTARIO PLACE
MID-JUNE/EARLY JULY

The world's largest offshore international fireworks competition lights up the skies above Lake Ontario with the spectacular fireworks of five competing countries (Canada, Spain, Italy, France, and China).

CANADIAN ABORIGINAL FESTIVAL

SKYDOME
LATE NOVEMBER

This celebration of Native heritage and culture features striking performances by over 1,000 First Nations dancers, drummers, and singers from across North America. Literary readings and theater are also on the program, along with traditional foods, crafts, and an arts show.

CANADIAN NATIONAL EXHIBITION
EXHIBITION PLACE
MID-AUGUST THROUGH LABOUR DAY

One of Canada's most popular annual attractions has everything from food exhibits and equestrian events to grandstand performances by top musical stars. A featured attraction is the dazzling Canadian International Air Show starring Canada's own Snowbirds.

CARIBANA
LATE JULY/EARLY AUGUST

Sway to the sounds of reggae, calypso, soca, and steel bands at this dynamic celebration of Caribbean music, art, and culture. Festivities include a children's carnival, ferry cruises, and the festival highlight—a 12-hour-long parade extravaganza ablaze with exuberant floats and dancers in elaborate costumes.

DU MAURIER JAZZ FESTIVAL
LATE JUNE

Some 1,800 top Canadian and international musicians cover the jazz spectrum at free daily outdoor concerts, nightclubs, and other venues.

INTERNATIONAL FESTIVAL OF AUTHORS
HARBOURFRONT
LATE OCTOBER

Writers from around the globe give public readings, sign books and mingle with the audience at the largest literary festival of its kind in the world.

INTERNATIONAL FILM FESTIVAL
SEPTEMBER

The biggest names in the film industry rub elbows with cinephiles for 10 days of premieres, galas, and marathon movie watching. Ranked among the top four film festivals in the world, this star-studded event features over 250 films from 70 countries.

METRO INTERNATIONAL CARAVAN
JUNE

The great cultural capitals of the world are represented at 50 pavilions across Toronto. Feast on exotic gourmet foods, shop for treasures, and be entertained by an array of cultural events and displays at North America's largest international festival.

ROYAL AGRICULTURAL WINTER FAIR
NOVEMBER

The largest indoor agricultural fair in the world features the famous International Royal Horse Show, the highlight of Canada's equestrian season, and the Winter Garden Show. Over 10,000 animals and agricultural products are also on display.

TORONTO FRINGE FESTIVAL
EARLY JULY

Eighty Canadian and international theater companies move into the Annex neighborhood with 500 performances of unique and innovative theater.

TROIS-RIVIÈRES, QUE.
AGRICULTURAL EXHIBITION
JULY

This country fair and exhibition has something for everyone—from livestock exhibitions and equestrian events to a casino and circus.

INTERNATIONAL POETRY FESTIVAL
OCTOBER

Poetry takes center stage among more than 200 activities, from public readings and concerts to films and exhibitions.

INTERNATIONAL VOCAL ARTS FESTIVAL
LATE JUNE

For six days, the downtown streets and parks are alive with the sound of sacred, popular, ethnic, and traditional songs, as well as opera and choral music.

TRURO, N.S.
NOVA SCOTIA PROVINCIAL EXHIBITION
AUGUST

Nova Scotia's premier agricultural fair features a major 4-H show, a midway, harness racing, a heavy horse pull and strong man's competition.

TWILLINGATE, NFLD.
FISH, FUN AND FOLK FESTIVAL
LATE JULY

One of the province's longest running and most popular events offers traditional Newfoundland folk music and fish dinners against a backdrop of spectacular icebergs.

TUKTOYAKTUK, N.W.T.
BELUGA JAMBOREE
SECOND WEEKEND OF APRIL

One of several spring jamborees celebrated by Beaufort-Delta communities on the shores of the Arctic Ocean. Among the variety of traditional and modern activities are snowmobile races, harpoon throwing and drum dancing.

VANCOUVER, B.C.
BARD ON THE BEACH SHAKESPEARE FESTIVAL
VANIER PARK
JUNE TO AUGUST

A summer fixture renowned for its high-performance standards, elaborate staging under an open-ended tent, and stunning backdrop of the city skyline, sea, and mountains. Special events include "Symphony and Shakespeare" and "Bard B-Q & Fireworks."

CANADA DAY CELEBRATIONS
JULY 1

The biggest celebration of Canada's birthday west of Ottawa with 12 hours worth of multicultural entertainment capped off by a spectacular fireworks finale.

CANADIAN INTERNATIONAL DRAGON BOAT FESTIVAL
LATE JUNE

It's a fierce race to the finish as rowers paddle their Chinese dragon boats across False Creek to the beat of pounding drums. Surrounding the two days of races are nonstop entertainment, an international food fair, and arts-and-crafts displays.

DU MAURIER INTERNATIONAL JAZZ FESTIVAL
LAST TWO WEEKS OF JUNE

Vancouver's biggest and most exciting music festival features cutting-edge jazz from around the world. A highlight is the free two-day New Orleans style street festival in historic Gastown.

FOLK MUSIC FESTIVAL
JERICHO BEACH PARK
MID-JULY

The summer's definitive West Coast event is a showcase for traditional and contemporary folk music in a scenic waterfront setting.

INTERNATIONAL CHILDREN'S FESTIVAL
VANIER PARK
MID-LATE MAY

This innovative festival, designed for kids aged 3 to 14, incorporates theater, music, dance, storytelling, and puppetry. Roaming performers and activity tents add to the fun.

INTERNATIONAL WRITERS FESTIVAL
GRANVILLE ISLAND
LATE OCTOBER

One of North America's premiere literary events features B.C., Canadian, and international writers of the highest caliber—from poets and novelists to mystery, sci-fi and nonfiction authors.

PACIFIC NATIONAL EXHIBITION
LATE AUGUST THROUGH LABOR DAY

The largest agricultural fair in B.C. has everything from rodeos, smash-car derbies and livestock shows to concerts, carnival games, and pony rides.

POWELL STREET FESTIVAL
OPPENHEIMER PARK
FIRST WEEKEND OF AUGUST

Celebration of Asian-Canadian art, culture, and heritage. Includes food booths and performances, a craft fair, and historical displays.

STORYTELLING FESTIVAL
MID-JUNE

This three-day event brings together local and international storytellers in a workshop and open-stage setting. Music and family-oriented stages are also on hand.

VICTORIA, B.C.

A VICTORIA CHRISTMAS
MID-NOVEMBER/EARLY JANUARY

The Christmas spirit shines bright with festivities galore—from wreath making and caroling to horse-drawn carriage rides and the Festival of the Trees.

CLASSIC BOAT FESTIVAL
INNER HARBOUR
LATE AUGUST/EARLY SEPTEMBER

Spectacular display of maritime heritage showcases some 100 wooden sail and power vessels from the Pacific Coast and beyond. Three-day festival includes rowing competitions, entertainment, and a colorful steamboat parade.

FIRST PEOPLES FESTIVAL
IN AND AROUND
ROYAL BRITISH COLUMBIA MUSEUM
EARLY AUGUST

Canada's largest aboriginal arts and cultural event with over 150 First Nations artists, musicians, storytellers, and dancers from across North and South America. Featured attractions include an artists' market, a children's craft corner, and traditional dance performances.

MOSS STREET PAINT-IN
MID-JULY

Free, annual festival of the visual arts in which more than 100 well-known and emerging artists work at "stations" along Moss Street using a wide variety of media and styles.

SYMPHONY SPLASH
INNER HARBOUR
EARLY AUGUST

Seated on board a barge moored in mid-harbor, members of the Victoria Symphony blend orchestral classics with popular favorites. Victoria's most popular summer event.

VICTORIA, P.E.I.

VICTORIA PLAYHOUSE SUMMER FESTIVAL
LATE JUNE/LATE AUGUST

Professional repertory productions and musical concerts are presented in a charming heritage theater. The Monday night concert series features traditional, folk and country music.

VICTORIAVILLE, QUE.

INTERNATIONAL FESTIVAL OF MODERN MUSIC
MID-MAY

Anything goes—jazz, rock, electric, acoustic—at the best avant-garde music festival in North America. More than 120 musicians from around the world stretch the limits of improvised, contemporary music.

VIRDEN, MAN.

INDOOR RODEO & WILD WEST DAZE
LATE AUGUST

Activity-filled weekend is packed with western rodeo performances, mer-

chant displays and musical entertainment. A demolition derby, horseshoe tournament, and parade are also featured.

WADENA, SASK.

SHOREBIRDS AND FRIENDS FESTIVAL
WADENA WILDLIFE WETLANDS
LATE MAY

Celebrate the spring arrival of 150,000 shorebirds to the Quill lakes with guided bird-watching and tours of critical wildlife habitat. On-site displays feature wildlife artists, photographers and carvers, and conservation organizations.

WATROUS, SASK.

MANITOU COUNTRY MUSIC JAMBOREE
THIRD WEEKEND OF JUNE

This top country music event attracts more than 5,000 fans with its outdoor afternoon concerts, evening cabaret, and beer garden.

WATSON LAKE, YK.

DISCOVERY DAYS
MID-AUGUST

This celebration of the Klondike Gold Rush has fun-filled activities for everyone, from a casino and pool party to a mini-triathlon and rubber duck race.

WATSON LAKE RODEO
FIRST WEEKEND OF JULY

Two-day amateur rodeo attracts international competitors of all ages for 12 rodeo events, including bull riding and bareback riding.

WHITE RIVER, ONT.

WINNIE'S HOMETOWN FESTIVAL
THIRD WEEKEND OF AUGUST

Fun-filled celebration of the hometown bear, Winnie-the-Pooh, features a parade, trade fair and bear competition, as well as heritage displays and demonstrations on teddy-bear making.

WHITEHORSE, YK.

FROSTBITE MUSIC FESTIVAL
SECOND WEEKEND OF FEBRUARY

Canada's only winter music festival features contemporary and world music performed by artists from across Canada.

KLONDYKE HARVEST FAIR
FOURTH WEEKEND OF AUGUST

This agricultural exhibition and fair is a cornucopia of produce and livestock, crafts, and midway rides. Sheep-shearing, ax-throwing and pie-eating contests add to the fun.

YUKON INTERNATIONAL FESTIVAL OF STORYTELLING
THIRD WEEKEND OF JUNE

Storytellers, drummers, and dancers from around the circumpolar region gather to celebrate the North's rich storytelling tradition. Ancient Indian and Inuit narratives, as well as those of other cultures, are brought to life through mime, music, and words.

YUKON SOURDOUGH RENDEZ-VOUS
THIRD WEEKEND OF FEBRUARY

The pioneer days of 1898 are re-created at the Yukon's largest winter carnival, complete with turn-of-the-century entertainment. A full slate of attractions range from flour-pack carrying and chain-saw chucking to can-can girls and casinos.

WINDSOR, ONT.
INTERNATIONAL FREEDOM FESTIVAL
LATE JUNE/EARLY JULY

This two-week celebration of the peace and freedom enjoyed by the U.S. and Canada encompasses the national holidays of both countries. More than 100 special events include tugboat races, sports tournaments, parades, dances, and a Gospel festival, all capped off with a spectacular riverfront fireworks display.

WINNIPEG, MAN.
FOLKLORAMA
FIRST TWO WEEKS OF AUGUST

The world's largest multicultural event serves up a jubilant feast of international tastes and traditions. Each year, half a million visitors flock to more than 40 international pavilions to sample exotic cuisine, authentic handicrafts, and colorful entertainment.

INTERNATIONAL CHILDREN'S FESTIVAL
THE FORKS
EARLY JUNE

World-class performing artists entertain youngsters with six days of dance, mime, music, puppetry, and vaudeville. Roving performers and creative hands-on activities add to the fun.

JAZZ WINNIPEG FESTIVAL
JUNE

Canada's only thematic jazz festival highlights some of the hottest local, national, and international jazz artists on free outdoor stages and in concerts and workshops.

RED RIVER EXHIBITION
RED RIVER EXHIBITION PARK
JUNE

Known locally as "The Ex," this major fair boasts a wide variety of family attractions, including free entertainment and the largest midway in Manitoba. Commercial and creative exhibits round out the province's largest 10-day exhibition.

SCOTTISH HERITAGE FESTIVAL
RED RIVER EXHIBITION PARK
JUNE

A cultural celebration in true Gaelic style with highland dancing, piping and drumming competitions, heritage workshops, and a Celtic parade and pageant.

WOODSTOCK, ONT.
WOOD SHOW
WOODSTOCK FAIRGROUNDS
EARLY OCTOBER

North America's premier show of its kind hosts the Upper Canada Woodworking Championship. It also serves as a showcase for woodcrafts and woodworking equipment.

YELLOWKNIFE, N.W.T.
CARIBOU CARNIVAL
LATE MARCH

This northern capital's biggest festival celebrates spring with a wide range of outdoor fun, including the Ice-sculpting Contest, the Caribou Capers Variety Show, and the Waiter/Waitress Relay races. A featured attraction is the three-day, 240 km Canadian Championship Dog Derby, which draws mushers from across North America.

FESTIVAL OF THE MIDNIGHT SUN
JULY

Week-long showcase of northern art and culture celebrates the mosaic of talents in the Northwest Territories

from caribou hair tufting to theater improvisation.

FOLK ON THE ROCKS
MID-JULY

Staged along the sand-rock shoreline of Long Lake, this outdoor summer highlight features Inuit and Dene performers and folk artists from across the Northwest Territories, southern Canada and the U.S. Arts-and-crafts displays, as well as workshops for artists and a children's stage, are also on hand.

RAVEN MAD DAZE
JUNE

Yellowknifers take to the streets for the official kickoff to summer on the longest night of the year. Festivities under the midnight sun include street dances, late-night bargain shopping, and children's games and activities.

YORKTON, SASK.
SHORT FILM AND VIDEO FESTIVAL
LATE MAY/EARLY JUNE

North America's longest running short film and video festival brings together an eclectic collection of Canada's best productions for competition and free public viewing. Cinerama, the annual street festival with local ethnic food booths and dance groups, adds to the festive spirit.

THRESHERMEN'S SHOW AND SENIORS' FESTIVAL
WESTERN DEVELOPMENT MUSEUM
LATE JULY/EARLY AUGUST

Try your hand at stooking, grain bag tying or bucksawing at this celebration of bygone times. Working vintage farm equipment and demonstrations of pioneer and homemaking skills are rounded out by variety entertainment, including old-time songs and square dancing.

YORKTON EXHIBITION
EARLY JULY

This century-old industrial and agricultural exhibition features livestock shows, grandstand entertainment, chuckwagon and chariot races, and midway rides.

INDEX

Page numbers in *italics* refer to photographs. Index abbreviations: Gdns. (Gardens), Hist. (Historic), Interprov. (Interprovincial), Is. (Island), Mus. (Museum), NHS (National Historic Site), NP (National Park), Pk. (Park), PP (Provincial Park), and Prov. (Provincial).

399

Film work: Tri-Graphics Litho Services Ltd.
Printing: Transcontinental Printing Inc. Division Drummondville
Binding: Transcontinental Inc. Division Metropole Litho
Paper: Westvaco